ALSO BY WALTER ISAACSON

The Innovators: How a Group of Hackers, Geniuses, and Geeks Created the Digital Revolution

Steve Jobs

American Sketches

Einstein: His Life and Universe

A Benjamin Franklin Reader

Benjamin Franklin: An American Life

Kissinger: A Biography

The Wise Men: Six Friends and the World They Made
(with Evan Thomas)

Pro and Con

LEONARDO DA VINCI

WALTER ISAACSON

Simon & Schuster
NEW YORK LONDON TORONTO SYDNEY NEW DELHI

Simon & Schuster
1230 Avenue of the Americas
New York, NY 10020

First Simon & Schuster hardcover edition October 2017

Interior design by Paul Dippolito

Manufactured in the United States of America

13 15 17 19 20 18 16 14 12

Library of Congress Cataloging-in-Publication Data
Title: Leonardo da Vinci / Walter Isaacson.
Description: New York : Simon & Schuster, 2017. |
Includes bibliographical references and index.
Identifiers: LCCN 2017020817 (print) | LCCN 2017021625 (ebook) |
ISBN 9781501139178 (ebook) | ISBN 9781501139154 (hardback) |
ISBN 9781501139161 (trade paperback)
Subjects: LCSH: Leonardo, da Vinci, 1452-1519. |
Artists--Italy--Biography. | Scientists--Italy--Biography. | Gifted persons--Italy--Biography. |
BISAC:
BIOGRAPHY & AUTOBIOGRAPHY / Artists, Architects, Photographers. |
BIOGRAPHY & AUTOBIOGRAPHY / Science & Technology. | BIOGRAPHY &
AUTOBIOGRAPHY / Historical.
Classification: LCC N6923.L33 (ebook) | LCC N6923.L33 I827 2017 (print) |
DDC 709.2 [B] --dc23
LC record available at https://lccn.loc.gov/2017020817

ISBN 978-1-5011-3915-4
ISBN 978-1-5011-3917-8 (ebook)

CONTENTS

ACKNOWLEDGMENTS

Marco Cianchi professionally read the manuscript of this book, made many suggestions, helped with translations, and was a guide in Italy. A professor at the Accademia di Belle Arti in Florence, he has degrees in art history from the universities of Florence and Bologna. He is a longtime collaborator with Carlo Pedretti and is the author of many books, including *Le macchine di Leonardo* (Becocci, 1981), *Leonardo, I Dipinti* (Giunti, 1996), and *Leonardo, Anatomia* (Giunti, 1997). He has become a delightful friend.

Juliana Barone of Birkbeck College, University of London, was also a professional reader of much of the manuscript. She wrote her doctoral dissertation on Leonardo at Oxford and is the author of *Leonardo: The Codex Arundel* (British Library, 2008), *Studies of Motion: Drawings by Leonardo from the Codex Atlanticus* (De Agostini, 2011), *The Treatise on Painting* (De Agostini, 2014), and the forthcoming books *Leonardo, Poussin and Rubens* and *Leonardo in Britain*.

Dr. Barone was recommended to me by Martin Kemp, emeritus professor of art history at Oxford University and one of the great Leonardo scholars of our era. Over the past fifty years, he has authored or co-authored seventy-two books and scholarly articles on Leonardo. He graciously spent time with me at Trinity College, Oxford, shared with me his research findings and an early manuscript of his co-authored book *Mona Lisa: The People and the Painting* (Oxford University Press, 2017), and in countless emails offered his opinions on a variety of issues.

Frederick Schroeder, the curator of the Codex Leicester for Bill Gates, and Domenico Laurenza, an author of many books on Leonardo's engineering and inventions, read my sections on the Codex Leicester and provided me with their own updated translations from that work, scheduled for publication in 2018. David Linley took me to Windsor Castle to see the Leonardo drawings there and introduced me to the curator and Leonardo scholar Martin Clayton.

Other Leonardo scholars and curators who read parts of the manuscript, gave me access to collections, provided assistance, or offered ideas include Luke Syson, formerly of the National Gallery in London and now at the Metropolitan Museum of Art in New York City; Vincent Delieuvin and Ina Giscard d'Estaing of the Louvre; David Alan Brown of the National Gallery of Art in Washington, DC; Valeria Poletto of the Gallerie dell'Accademia in Venice; Pietro Marani of the Politecnico di Milano; Alberto Rocca of the Biblioteca Ambrosiana in Milan; and Jacqueline Thalmann of Christ Church, Oxford. I am also grateful to the staffs of the Villa I Tatti in Florence, the Dumbarton Oaks Library in Washington, DC, and the Harvard Fine Arts Library. Getty Images, led by Dawn Airey, adopted this book as a special project; the team overseeing the acquisition of images included David Savage, Eric Rachlis, Scott Rosen, and Jill Braaten. At the Aspen Institute, my deep thanks go to Pat Zindulka, Leah Bitounis, Eric Motley, Chloe Tabah, and other indulgent colleagues.

I also want to thank Filippo Dal Corno, an Aspen Italia Board Member and Milan's Councilor for Culture, who arranged a private tour of the Leonardo exhibition at Palazzo Reale with its renowned curator Pietro Marani, as well as the other delightful colleagues at Aspen Italia who helped me get access to Leonardo resources in Florence, Venice, and Milan.

All of my books for more than three decades have been published by Simon & Schuster, and that is because the team there is extraordinarily talented: Alice Mayhew, Carolyn Reidy, Jonathan Karp, Stuart Roberts (who shepherded this book and its illustrations), Richard Rhorer, Stephen Bedford, Jackie Seow, Kristen Lemire, Judith Hoover, Julia Prosser, Lisa Erwin, Jonathan Evans, and Paul Dippolito. During my entire writing career, Amanda Urban has been my agent, adviser, wise counselor, and friend. Strobe Talbott, my colleague from when I joined *Time* in 1979, has read the drafts of every one of my books, beginning with *The Wise Men*, made incisive comments, and offered encouragement; as we enter the dessert course of our careers, I savor the procession of memories that began when we were in our salad days.

As usual, my greatest gratitude goes to my wife, Cathy, and our daughter, Betsy, who are wise, smart, supportive, and very loving. Thank you.

MAIN CHARACTERS

Cesare Borgia (c. 1475–1507). Italian warrior, illegitimate son of Pope Alexander VI, subject of Machiavelli's *The Prince*, Leonardo employer.

Donato Bramante (1444–1514). Architect, friend of Leonardo in Milan, worked on Milan Cathedral, Pavia Cathedral, and St. Peter's in the Vatican.

Caterina Lippi (c. 1436–1493). Orphaned peasant girl from near Vinci, mother of Leonardo; later married Antonio di Piero del Vaccha, known as Accattabriga.

Charles d'Amboise (1473–1511). French governor of Milan from 1503 to 1511, Leonardo patron.

Beatrice d'Este (1475–1497). From Italy's most venerable family, married Ludovico Sforza.

Isabella d'Este (1474–1539). Beatrice's sister, the Marchesa of Mantua, tried to get Leonardo to paint her portrait.

Francesco di Giorgio (1439–1501). Artist-engineer-architect who worked with Leonardo on Milan's cathedral tower, traveled with him to Pavia, translated Vitruvius, and drew a version of Vitruvian man.

Francis I (1494–1547). King of France from 1515, last patron of Leonardo.

Pope Leo X, Giovanni de' Medici (1475–1521). Son of Lorenzo de' Medici, elected pope in 1513.

Louis XII (1462–1515). King of France from 1498, conquered Milan in 1499.

Niccolò Machiavelli (1469–1527). Florentine diplomat and writer, became envoy to Cesare Borgia and friend of Leonardo in 1502.

Giuliano de' Medici (1479–1516). Son of Lorenzo, brother of Pope Leo X, Leonardo's patron in Rome.

Lorenzo "the Magnificent" de' Medici (1449–1492). Banker, art patron, and de facto ruler of Florence from 1469 until his death.

Francesco Melzi (c. 1493–c. 1568). From a noble Milan family, joined Leonardo's household in 1507 and became a surrogate son and heir.

Michelangelo Buonarroti (1475–1564). Florentine sculptor and rival of Leonardo.

Luca Pacioli (1447–1517). Italian mathematician, friar, and friend of Leonardo.

Piero da Vinci (1427–1504). Florentine notary, father of Leonardo, did not marry Leonardo's mother, subsequently had eleven other children with four wives.

Andrea Salai, born Gian Giacomo Caprotti da Oreno (1480–1524). Entered Leonardo's household at age ten and was dubbed Salai, meaning "Little Devil."

Ludovico Sforza (1452–1508). De facto ruler of Milan from 1481, Duke of Milan from 1494 until his ouster by the French in 1499, patron of Leonardo.

Andrea del Verrocchio (c. 1435–1488). Florentine sculptor, goldsmith, and artist in whose workshop Leonardo trained and worked from 1466 to 1477.

CURRENCY IN ITALY IN 1500

The ducat was the gold coin of Venice. The florin was the gold coin of Florence. Both contained 3.5 grams (0.12 ounces) of gold, which would make them worth about $138 in 2017. One ducat or florin was worth approximately 7 lire or 120 soldi, which were silver coins.

NOTE REGARDING THE COVER

The cover is a detail of an oil painting in Florence's Uffizi Gallery that was once thought to be a self-portrait painted by Leonardo. Based on recent X-ray analysis, it is now considered to be a portrait of Leonardo by an unknown artist done in the 1600s. It is based on, or is the basis for, a similar portrait rediscovered in Italy in 2008, called the Lucan portrait of Leonardo da Vinci. It has been copied many times. A watercolor-on-ivory version painted in the 1770s by Giuseppe Macpherson is in the British Royal Collection and in 2017 was in the show "Portrait of the Artist" in the Queen's Gallery of Buckingham Palace.

PRIMARY PERIODS OF LEONARDO'S LIFE

Vinci
1452–1464

Florence
1464–1482

Milan
1482–1499

Florence
1500–1506

Milan
1506–1513

Rome
1513–1516

France
1516–1519

1452

Born on April 15

c.1473

Becomes a member of the painters' guild; first known drawing is a landscape

c.1475

Collaborated with Verrocchio on the *Baptism of Christ*

c.1478

Portrait of Ginevra de' Benci, daughter of a wealthy Florentine banker

End 100 Years' War; fall of Constantinople

Michelangelo is born

Ludovico Sforza becomes ruler of Milan; Magellan is born

Gutenberg prints the Bible

Machiavelli is born; Lorenzo de' Medici takes power

Copernicus is born

Johannes de Spira starts publishing house in Venice

Raphael is born

c.1468

Becomes an apprentice in Verrocchio's studio in Florence

c.1472

The *Annunciation*: youthful experiment with perspective is flawed, but heralds brilliance

1481

The *Adoration of the Magi* commissioned

1482

Moves to Milan and begins keeping notebooks

science life world art

1493

Lady with an Ermine; clay model for the horse monument is put on display in Milan

1496

Does the drawings for Pacioli's *De divina proportione*

1498

First attempt at a flying machine

1489

Studies anatomy & rchitecture

Dias of Portugal rounds the southern tip of Africa

Christopher Columbus sails to the New World; Lorenzo de' Medici dies; Rodrigo Borgia becomes Pope Alexander VI

Vasco da Gama finds a sea route to India; Louis XII becomes King of France; Savonarola's Bonfire of the Vanities; France conquers Milan

Süleyman I, of the Ottoman Empire, is born; Ludovico officially becomes Duke

Savonarola deposes the Medici in Florence; King Charles VIII of France invades Italy

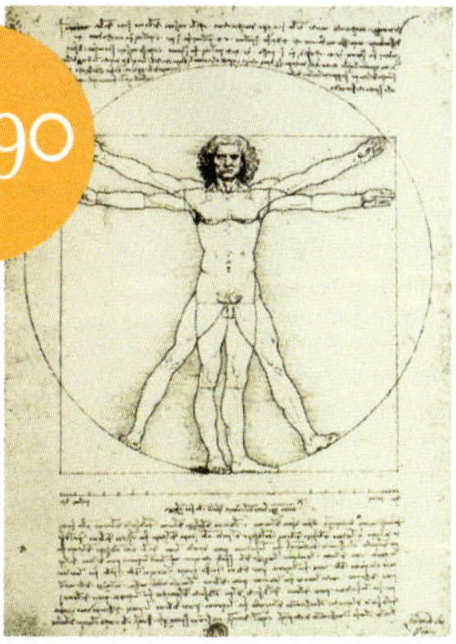

c.1490

Vitruvian Man; Feast of Paradise is presented for the wedding feast of the duke's nephew; Salai comes to live with Leonardo

1483

Commissioned, along with the de Predis brothers, to paint *Virgin of the Rocks*

1495

Begins *The Last Supper* in the refectory in the convent of Santa Maria delle Grazie

1499

Leaves Milan

1503

Returns to Florence, begins painting the *Mona Lisa* and works on it for the rest of his life

1505

Studies the flight of birds; second unsuccessful attempt to fly; struggles to paint the *Battle of Anghiari*, a major commission in Florence that is eventually abandoned, unfinished.

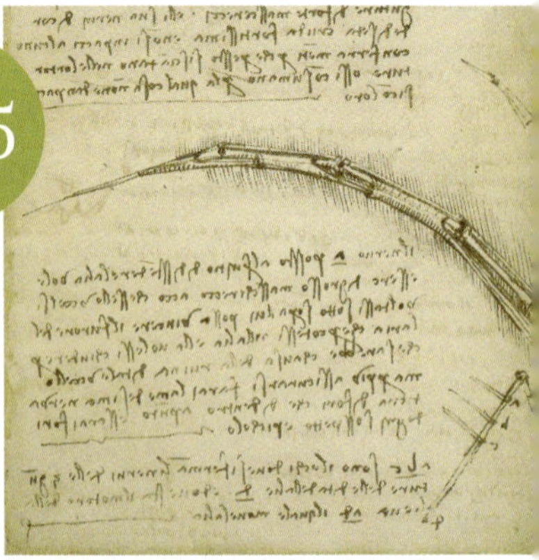

Michelangelo's statue of David; young Raphael comes to Florence to study with Leonardo and Michelangelo

Leonardo's friend, Amerigo Vespucci, publishes his account of sailing to the New World

The architect Donato Bramante is hired by the pope to rebuild St. Peter's church in Rome

1502

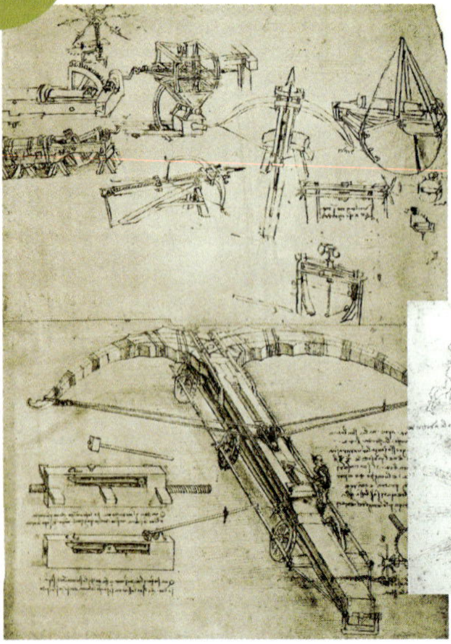

Begins to work for Cesare Borgia as military engineer

1506

Returns to Milan, where he remains, on and off, for seven years

1507

Painter and engineer to Louis XII

1513

c.1508

Divides his time between Milan and Florence; studies of waterworks; designs the Trivulzio monument; second *Virgin of the Rocks*

Moves to Rome; the iconic Turin drawing, a possible self-portrait done in the preceding years, often defines our image of Leonardo

Michelangelo finishes painting the Sistine Chapel; erardus Mercator, who produces the first map of the world, is born; Medici return to power in Florence

Andreas Vesalius, who publishes the first accurate book on human anatomy, is born in Brussels

Martin Luther launches Protestant Reformation

King Henry VIII becomes king of England

Vasari is born

Giovanni de' Medici becomes Pope Leo X

Francis I becomes king of France

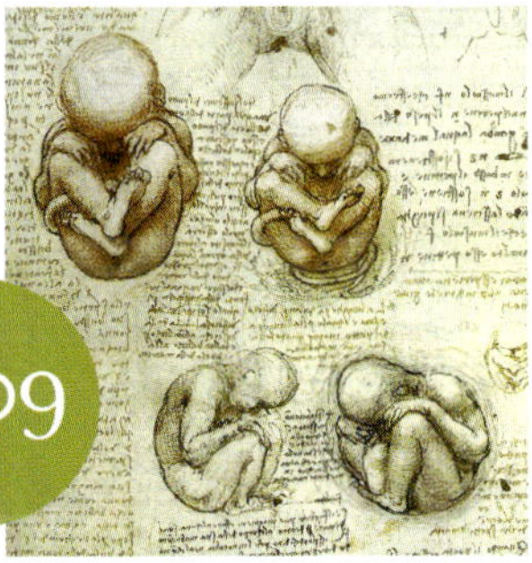

1509

1516

Moves to Amboise as a guest of Francis I

1514

Pursues his studies of anatomy and continues with hydraulics

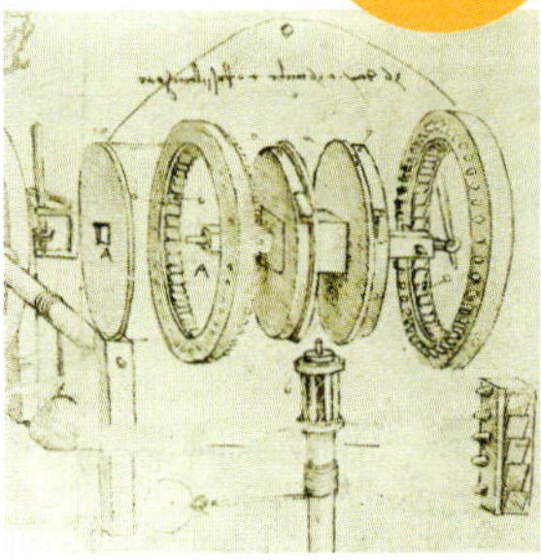

Visits Parma and Florence; Plans to drain the Pontine Marshes

dies on May 2

1519

LEONARDO
DA VINCI

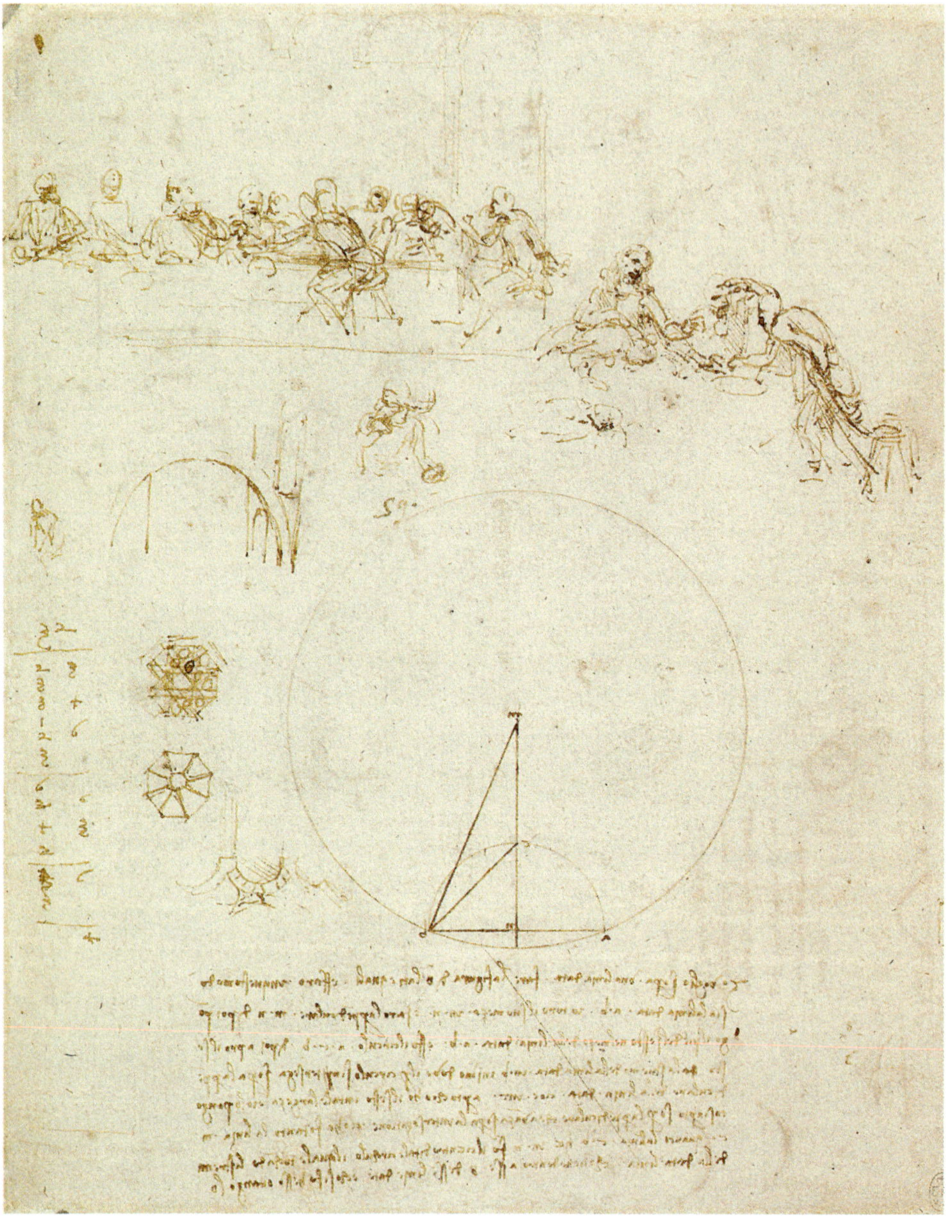

From Leonardo's notebooks c. 1495: a sketch for *The Last Supper*, geometric studies for squaring a circle, octagonal church designs, and a passage in his mirror-script writing.

INTRODUCTION

I Can Also Paint

Around the time that he reached the unnerving milestone of turning thirty, Leonardo da Vinci wrote a letter to the ruler of Milan listing the reasons he should be given a job. He had been moderately successful as a painter in Florence, but he had trouble finishing his commissions and was searching for new horizons. In the first ten paragraphs, he touted his engineering skills, including his ability to design bridges, waterways, cannons, armored vehicles, and public buildings. Only in the eleventh paragraph, at the end, did he add that he was also an artist. "Likewise in painting, I can do everything possible," he wrote.[1]

Yes, he could. He would go on to create the two most famous paintings in history, *The Last Supper* and the *Mona Lisa*. But in his own mind, he was just as much a man of science and engineering. With a passion that was both playful and obsessive, he pursued innovative studies of anatomy, fossils, birds, the heart, flying machines, optics, botany, geology, water flows, and weaponry. Thus he became the archetype of the Renaissance Man, an inspiration to all who believe that the "infinite works of nature," as he put it, are woven together in a unity filled with marvelous patterns.[2] His ability to combine art and science, made iconic by his drawing of a perfectly proportioned man spread-eagle inside a circle and square, known as *Vitruvian Man*, made him history's most creative genius.

His scientific explorations informed his art. He peeled flesh off the faces of cadavers, delineated the muscles that move the lips, and then painted the world's most memorable smile. He studied human skulls, made layered drawings of the bones and teeth, and conveyed the skeletal agony of *Saint Jerome in the Wilderness*. He explored the mathematics of optics, showed how light rays strike the retina, and produced magical illusions of changing visual perspectives in *The Last Supper*.

By connecting his studies of light and optics to his art, he mastered the use of shading and perspective to model objects on a two-dimensional surface so they look three-dimensional. This ability to "make a flat surface display a body as if modeled and separated from this plane," Leonardo said, was "the first intention of the painter."[3] Largely due to his work, dimensionality became the supreme innovation of Renaissance art.

As he aged, he pursued his scientific inquiries not just to serve his art but out of a joyful instinct to fathom the profound beauties of creation. When he groped for a theory of why the sky appears blue, it was not simply to inform his paintings. His curiosity was pure, personal, and delightfully obsessive.

But even when he was engaged in blue-sky thinking, his science was not a separate endeavor from his art. Together they served his driving passion, which was nothing less than knowing everything there was to know about the world, including how we fit into it. He had a reverence for the wholeness of nature and a feel for the harmony of its patterns, which he saw replicated in phenomena large and small. In his notebooks he would record curls of hair, eddies of water, and whirls of air, along with some stabs at the math that might underlie such spirals. While at Windsor Castle looking at the swirling power of the "Deluge drawings" that he made near the end of his life, I asked the curator, Martin Clayton, whether he thought Leonardo had done them as works of art or of science. Even as I spoke, I realized it was a dumb question. "I do not think that Leonardo would have made that distinction," he replied.

I embarked on this book because Leonardo da Vinci is the ultimate example of the main theme of my previous biographies: how the ability to make connections across disciplines—arts and sciences, humanities and technology—is a key to innovation, imagination, and genius. Benjamin Franklin, a previous subject of mine, was a Leonardo of his era: with no formal education, he taught himself to become an imaginative polymath who was Enlightenment America's best scientist, inventor, diplomat, writer, and business strategist. He proved by flying a kite that lightning is electricity, and he invented a rod to tame it. He devised bifocal glasses, enchanting musical instruments, clean-burning stoves, charts of the Gulf Stream, and America's unique style of homespun humor. Albert Einstein, when he was stymied in his pursuit of his theory of relativity, would pull out his violin and play Mozart, which helped him reconnect with the harmonies of the cosmos. Ada Lovelace, whom I profiled in a book on innovators, combined the poetic sensibility of her father, Lord Byron, with her mother's love of the beauty of math to envision a general-purpose computer. And Steve Jobs climaxed his product launches with an image of street signs showing the intersection of the liberal arts and technology. Leonardo was his hero. "He saw beauty in both art and engineering," Jobs said, "and his ability to combine them was what made him a genius."[4]

Yes, he was a genius: wildly imaginative, passionately curious, and creative across multiple disciplines. But we should be wary of that word. Slapping the "genius" label on Leonardo oddly minimizes him by making it seem as if he were touched by lightning. His early biographer, Giorgio Vasari, a sixteenth-century artist, made this mistake: "Sometimes, in supernatural fashion, a single person is marvelously endowed by heaven with beauty, grace, and talent in such abundance that his every act is divine and everything he does clearly comes from God rather than from human art."[5] In fact, Leonardo's genius was a human one, wrought by his own will and ambition. It did not come from being the divine recipient, like Newton or Einstein, of a mind with so much processing power that we mere mortals cannot fathom it. Leonardo had almost no schooling and could barely read Latin or do long division. His genius was of the type we can understand, even take lessons from. It was based on skills we can aspire to improve in ourselves, such as curiosity and intense observation. He had an imagination so excitable that it flirted with the edges of fantasy, which is also something we can try to preserve in ourselves and indulge in our children.

Leonardo's fantasies pervaded everything he touched: his theatrical productions, plans to divert rivers, designs for ideal cities, schemes for flying machines, and almost every aspect of his art as well as engineering. His letter to the ruler of Milan is an example, since his military engineering skills then existed mainly in his mind. His initial role at the court was not building weapons but conjuring up festivals and pageants. Even at the height of his career, most of his fighting and flying contraptions were more visionary than practical.

At first I thought that his susceptibility to fantasia was a failing, revealing a lack of discipline and diligence that was related to his propensity to abandon artworks and treatises unfinished. To some extent, that is true. Vision without execution is hallucination. But I also came to believe that his ability to blur the line between reality and fantasy, just like his sfumato techniques for blurring the lines of a painting, was a key to his creativity. Skill without imagination is barren. Leonardo knew how to marry observation and imagination, which made him history's consummate innovator.

My starting point for this book was not Leonardo's art masterpieces but his notebooks. His mind, I think, is best revealed in the more than 7,200 pages of his notes and scribbles that, miraculously, survive to this day. Paper turns out to be a superb information-storage technology, still readable after five hundred years, which our own tweets likely won't be.

Fortunately, Leonardo could not afford to waste paper, so he crammed every inch of his pages with miscellaneous drawings and looking-glass jottings that seem random but provide intimations of his mental leaps. Scribbled alongside each other, with rhyme if not reason, are math calculations, sketches of his devilish young boyfriend, birds, flying machines, theater props, eddies of water, blood valves, grotesque heads, angels, siphons, plant stems, sawed-apart skulls, tips for painters, notes on the eye and optics, weapons of war, fables, riddles, and studies for paintings. The cross-disciplinary brilliance whirls across every page, providing a delightful display of a mind dancing with nature. His notebooks are the greatest record of curiosity ever created, a wondrous guide to the person whom the eminent art historian Kenneth Clark called "the most relentlessly curious man in history."[6]

My favorite gems in his notebooks are his to-do lists, which sparkle with his curiosity. One of them, dating from the 1490s in Milan, is that day's list of things he wants to learn. "The measurement of Milan and its suburbs," is the first entry. This has a practical purpose, as revealed by an item later in the list: "Draw Milan." Others show him relentlessly seeking out people whose brains he could pick: "Get the master of arithmetic to show you how to square a triangle. . . . Ask Giannino the Bombardier about how the tower of Ferrara is walled. . . . Ask Benedetto Protinari by what means they walk on ice in Flanders. . . . Get a master of hydraulics to tell you how to repair a lock, canal and mill in the Lombard manner. . . . Get the measurement of the sun promised me by Maestro Giovanni Francese, the Frenchman."[7] He is insatiable.

Over and over again, year after year, Leonardo lists things he must do and learn. Some involve the type of close observation most of us rarely pause to do. "Observe the goose's foot: if it were always open or always closed the creature would not be able to make any kind of movement." Others involve why-is-the-sky-blue questions about phenomena so commonplace that we rarely pause to wonder about them. "Why is the fish in the water swifter than the bird in the air when it ought to be the contrary since the water is heavier and thicker than the air?"[8]

Best of all are the questions that seem completely random. "Describe the tongue of the woodpecker," he instructs himself.[9] Who on earth would decide one day, for no apparent reason, that he wanted to know what the tongue of a woodpecker looks like? How would you even find out? It's not information Leonardo needed to paint a picture or even to understand the flight of birds. But there it is, and, as we shall see, there are fascinating things to learn about the tongue of the woodpecker. The reason he wanted to know was because he was Leonardo: curious, passionate, and always filled with wonder.

Oddest of all, there is this entry: "Go every Saturday to the hot bath where you will see naked men."[10] We can imagine Leonardo wanting to do that, for reasons both anatomical and aesthetic. But did he really need to remind himself to do it? The next item on the list is "Inflate the lungs of a pig and observe whether they increase in width and in length, or only in width." As the *New Yorker* art critic Adam Gopnik once wrote, "Leonardo remains weird, matchlessly weird, and nothing to be done about it."[11]

To wrestle with these issues, I decided to write a book that used these notebooks as its foundation. I started by making pilgrimages to see the originals in Milan, Florence, Paris, Seattle, Madrid, London, and Windsor Castle. That followed Leonardo's injunction to begin any investigation by going to the source: "He who can go to the fountain does not go to the water-jar."[12] I also immersed myself in the little-tapped trove of academic articles and doctoral dissertations on Leonardo, each of which represents years of diligent work on very specific topics. In the past few decades, especially since the rediscovery of his Codices Madrid in 1965, there have been great advances in the analysis and interpretation of his writings. Likewise, modern technology has revealed new information about his painting and techniques.

After immersing myself in Leonardo, I did the best I could to be more observant of phenomena that I used to ignore, making a special effort to notice things the way he did. When I saw sunlight hitting drapes, I pushed myself to pause and look at the way the shadows caressed the folds. I tried to see how light that was reflected from one object subtly colored the shadows of another object. I noticed how the glint of a lustrous spot on a shiny surface moved when I tilted my head. When I looked at a distant tree and a near one, I tried to visualize the lines of perspective. When I saw an eddy of water, I compared it to a ringlet of hair. When I couldn't understand a math concept, I did the best I was able to visualize it. When I saw people at a supper, I studied the relationship of their motions to their emotions. When I saw the hint of a smile come across someone's lips, I tried to fathom her inner mysteries.

No, I did not come anywhere close to being Leonardo, mastering his insights, or mustering a modicum of his talents. I did not get a millimeter closer to being able to design a glider, invent a new way to draw maps, or paint the *Mona Lisa.* I had to push myself to be truly curious about the tongue of the woodpecker. But I did learn from Leonardo how a desire to marvel about the world that we encounter each day can make each moment of our lives richer.

There are three major early accounts of Leonardo by writers who were almost contemporaries. The painter Giorgio Vasari, born in 1511 (eight years before Leonardo died), wrote the first real art history book, *Lives of the Most Eminent Painters, Sculptors, and Architects,* in 1550 and came out with a revised version in 1568 that included corrections based on further interviews with people who knew Leonardo, including his pupil Francesco Melzi.[13] A Florentine chauvinist, Vasari gave Leonardo and especially Michelangelo the most fulsome treatments for creating what he dubbed, for the first time in print, a "renaissance" in art.[14] As Huckleberry Finn said of Mark Twain, there were things that Vasari stretched, but he told the truth, mainly. The remainder is a mix of gossip, embellishments, inventions, and unintentional errors. The problem is knowing which picturesque anecdotes—such as Leonardo's teacher throwing down his own brush in awe of his pupil—fall into which category.

An anonymous manuscript written in the 1540s, known as the "Anonimo Gaddiano" after the family that once owned it, contains colorful details about Leonardo and other Florentines. Once again, some of the assertions, such as that Leonardo lived and worked with Lorenzo de' Medici, may be embellished, but it provides colorful details that ring true, such as that Leonardo liked to wear rose-colored tunics that reached only to his knee even though others wore long garments.[15]

A third early source is by Gian Paolo Lomazzo, a painter who became a writer when he went blind. He wrote an unpublished manuscript called *Dreams and Arguments* in about 1560 and then published a voluminous treatise on art in 1584. He was the student of a painter who had known Leonardo, and he interviewed Leonardo's pupil Melzi, so he had access to some firsthand stories. Lomazzo is especially revealing about Leonardo's sexual proclivities. In addition, there are shorter accounts contained in writings by two Leonardo contemporaries, Antonio Billi, a Florentine merchant, and Paolo Giovio, an Italian physician and historian.

Many of these early accounts mention Leonardo's looks and personality. He is described as a man of eye-catching beauty and grace. He had flowing golden curls, a muscular build, remarkable physical strength, and an elegance of bearing when he was walking through town in his colorful garb or riding on a horse. "Beautiful in person and aspect, Leonardo was well-proportioned and graceful," according to the Anonimo. In addition, he was a charming conversationalist and a lover of nature, renowned for being sweet and gentle to both people and animals.

There is less agreement about certain specifics. In the course of my research I discovered that many facts about Leonardo's life, from the site of his birth to the scene at his death, have been the subject of debate, mythology, and mystery. I try to give my best assessment and then describe the controversies and counterarguments in the notes.

I also discovered, at first to my consternation and then to my pleasure, that Leonardo was not always a giant. He made mistakes. He went off on tangents, literally, pursuing math problems that became time-sucking diversions. Notoriously, he left many of his paintings unfinished, most notably the *Adoration of the Magi*, *Saint Jerome in the Wilderness*, and the *Battle of Anghiari*. As a result, there exist now at most fifteen paintings fully or mainly attributable to him.[16]

Although generally considered by his contemporaries to be friendly and gentle, Leonardo was at times dark and troubled. His notebooks and drawings are a window into his fevered, imaginative, manic, and sometimes elated mind. Had he been a student at the outset of the twenty-first century, he may have been put on a pharmaceutical regimen to alleviate his mood swings and attention-deficit disorder. One need not subscribe to the artist-as-troubled-genius trope to believe we are fortunate that Leonardo was left to his own devices to slay his demons while conjuring up his dragons.

In one of the quirky riddles in his notebooks is this clue: "Huge figures will appear in human shape, and the nearer you get to them, the more their immense size will diminish." The answer: "The shadow cast by a man at night with a light."[17] Although the same may be said of Leonardo, I believe he is, in fact, not diminished by being discovered to be human. Both his shadow and his reality deserve to loom large. His lapses and oddities allow us to relate to him, to feel that we might emulate him, and to appreciate his moments of triumph even more.

The fifteenth century of Leonardo and Columbus and Gutenberg was a time of invention, exploration, and the spread of knowledge by new technologies. In short, it was a time like our own. That is why we have much to learn from Leonardo. His ability to combine art, science, technology, the humanities, and imagination remains an enduring recipe for creativity. So, too, was his ease at being a bit of a misfit: illegitimate, gay, vegetarian, left-handed, easily distracted, and at times heretical. Florence flourished in the fifteenth century because it was comfortable with such people. Above all, Leonardo's relentless curiosity and experimentation should remind us of the importance of instilling, in both ourselves and our children, not just received knowledge but a willingness to question it—to be imaginative and, like talented misfits and rebels in any era, to think different.

The town of Vinci and the church where Leonardo was baptized.

CHAPTER 1

Childhood

Vinci, 1452–1464

DA VINCI

Leonardo da Vinci had the good luck to be born out of wedlock. Otherwise, he would have been expected to become a notary, like the firstborn legitimate sons in his family stretching back at least five generations.

His family roots can be traced to the early 1300s, when his great-great-great-grandfather, Michele, practiced as a notary in the Tuscan hill town of Vinci, about seventeen miles west of Florence.* With the rise of Italy's mercantile economy, notaries played an important role drawing up commercial contracts, land sales, wills, and other legal documents in Latin, often garnishing them with historical references and literary flourishes.

* Leonardo da Vinci is sometimes incorrectly called "da Vinci," as if that were his last name rather than a descriptor meaning "from Vinci." However, the usage is not as egregious as some purists proclaim. During Leonardo's lifetime, Italians increasingly began to regularize and register the use of hereditary surnames, and many of these, such as Genovese and DiCaprio, derived from family hometowns. Both Leonardo and his father, Piero, frequently appended "da Vinci" to their names. When Leonardo moved to Milan, his friend the court poet Bernardo Bellincioni referred to him in writing as "Leonardo Vinci, the Florentine."

Because Michele was a notary, he was entitled to the honorific "Ser" and thus became known as Ser Michele da Vinci. His son and grandson were even more successful notaries, the latter becoming a chancellor of Florence. The next in line, Antonio, was an anomaly. He used the honorific Ser and married the daughter of a notary, but he seems to have lacked the da Vinci ambition. He mostly spent his life living off the proceeds from family lands, tilled by sharecroppers, that produced a modest amount of wine, olive oil, and wheat.

Antonio's son Piero made up for the lassitude by ambitiously pursuing success in Pistoia and Pisa, and then by about 1451, when he was twenty-five, establishing himself in Florence. A contract he notarized that year gave his work address as "at the Palazzo del Podestà," the magistrates' building (now the Bargello Museum) facing the Palazzo della Signoria, the seat of government. He became a notary for many of the city's monasteries and religious orders, the town's Jewish community, and on at least one occasion the Medici family.[1]

On one of his visits back to Vinci, Piero had a relationship with an unmarried local peasant girl, and in the spring of 1452 they had a son. Exercising his little-used notarial handwriting, the boy's grandfather Antonio recorded the birth on the bottom of the last page of a notebook that had belonged to his own grandfather. "1452: There was born to me a grandson, the son of Ser Piero my son, on the 15th day of April, a Saturday, at the third hour of the night [about 10 p.m.]. He bears the name Leonardo."[2]

Leonardo's mother was not considered worth mentioning in Antonio's birth notation nor in any other birth or baptism record. From a tax document five years later, we learn only her first name, Caterina. Her identity was long a mystery to modern scholars. She was thought to be in her mid-twenties, and some researchers speculated that she was an Arab slave, or perhaps a Chinese slave.[3]

In fact, she was an orphaned and impoverished sixteen-year-old from the Vinci area named Caterina Lippi. Proving that there are still things to be rediscovered about Leonardo, the art historian Martin Kemp of Oxford and the archival researcher Giuseppe Pallanti of Florence produced evidence in 2017 documenting her background.[4]

Born in 1436 to a poor farmer, Caterina was orphaned when she was fourteen. She and her infant brother moved in with their grandmother, who died a year later, in 1451. Left to fend for herself and her brother, Caterina had a relationship in July of that year with Piero da Vinci, then twenty-four, who was prominent and prosperous.

There was little likelihood they would marry. Although described by one earlier biographer as "of good blood,"[5] Caterina was of a different social class, and Piero was probably already betrothed to his future wife, an appropriate match: a sixteen-year-old named Albiera who was the daughter of a prominent Florentine shoemaker. He and Albiera were wed within eight months of Leonardo's birth. The marriage, socially and professionally advantageous to both sides, had likely been arranged, and the dowry contracted, before Leonardo was born.

Keeping things tidy and convenient, shortly after Leonardo was born Piero helped to set up a marriage for Caterina to a local farmer and kiln worker who had ties to the da Vinci family. Named Antonio di Piero del Vacca, he was called Accattabriga, which means "Troublemaker," though fortunately he does not seem to have been one.

Leonardo's paternal grandparents and his father had a family house with a small garden right next to the walls of the castle in the heart of the village of Vinci. That is where Leonardo may have been born, though there are reasons to think not. It might not have been convenient or appropriate to have a pregnant and then breast-feeding peasant woman living in the crowded da Vinci family home, especially as Ser Piero was negotiating a dowry from the prominent family whose daughter he was planning to marry.

Instead, according to legend and the local tourist industry, Leonardo's birthplace may have been a gray stone tenant cottage next to a farmhouse two miles up the road from Vinci in the adjacent hamlet of Anchiano, which is now the site of a small Leonardo museum. Some of this property had been owned since 1412 by the family of Piero di Malvolto, a close friend of the da Vincis. He was the godfather of Piero da Vinci and, in 1452, would be a godfather of Piero's newborn son, Leonardo—which would have made sense if Leonardo had been born on his property. The families were very close. Leonardo's grandfather Antonio had served as a witness to a contract involving some parts of Piero di Malvolto's property. The notes describing the exchange say that Antonio was at a nearby house playing backgammon when he was asked to come over for that task. Piero da Vinci would buy some of the property in the 1480s.

At the time of Leonardo's birth, Piero di Malvolto's seventy-year-old widowed mother lived on the property. So here in the hamlet of Anchiano, an easy two-mile walk from the village of Vinci, living alone in a farmhouse that had a run-down cottage next door, was a widow who was a trusted friend to at least two generations of the da Vinci family. Her dilapidated cottage (for tax purposes the family claimed it as uninhabitable) may have been the ideal place to shelter Caterina while she was pregnant, as per local lore.[6]

Leonardo was born on a Saturday, and the following day he was baptized by the local priest at the parish church of Vinci. The baptismal font is still there. Despite the circumstances of his birth, it was a large and public event. There were ten godparents giving witness, including Piero di Malvolto, far more than the average at the church, and the guests included prominent local gentry. A week later, Piero da Vinci left Caterina and their infant son behind and returned to Florence, where that Monday he was in his office notarizing papers for clients.[7]

Leonardo left us no comment on the circumstances of his birth, but there is one tantalizing allusion in his notebooks to the favors that nature bestows upon a love child. "The man who has intercourse aggressively and uneasily will produce children who are irritable and untrustworthy," he wrote, "but if the intercourse is done with great love and desire on both sides, the child will be of great intellect, witty, lively, and lovable."[8] One assumes, or at least hopes, that he considered himself in the latter category.

He split his childhood between two homes. Caterina and Accattabriga settled on a small farm on the outskirts of Vinci, and they remained friendly with Piero da Vinci. Twenty years later, Accattabriga was working in a kiln that was rented by Piero, and they served as witnesses for each other on a few contracts and deeds over the years. In the years following Leonardo's birth, Caterina and Accattabriga had four girls and a boy. Piero and Albiera, however, remained childless. In fact, until Leonardo was twenty-four, his father had no other children. (Piero would make up for it during his third and fourth marriages, having at least eleven children.)

With his father living mainly in Florence and his mother nurturing a growing family of her own, Leonardo by age five was primarily living in the da Vinci family home with his leisure-loving grandfather Antonio and his wife. In the 1457 tax census, Antonio listed the dependents residing with him, including his grandson: "Leonardo, son of the said Ser Piero, *non legittimo*, born of him and of Caterina, who is now the woman of Achattabriga."

Also living in the household was Piero's youngest brother, Francesco, who was only fifteen years older than his nephew Leonardo. Francesco inherited a love of country leisure and was described in a tax document by his own father, in a pot-calling-the-kettle way, as "one who hangs around the villa and does nothing."[9] He became Leonardo's beloved uncle and at times surrogate father. In the first edition of his biography, Vasari makes the telling mistake, later corrected, of identifying Piero as Leonardo's uncle.

"A GOLDEN AGE FOR BASTARDS"

As Leonardo's well-attended baptism attests, being born out of wedlock was not a cause for public shame. The nineteenth-century cultural historian Jacob Burckhardt went so far as to label Renaissance Italy "a golden age for bastards."[10] Especially among the ruling and aristocratic classes, being illegitimate was no hindrance. Pius II, who was the pope when Leonardo was born, wrote about visiting Ferrara, where his welcoming party included seven princes from the ruling Este family, among them the reigning duke, all born out of wedlock. "It is an extraordinary thing about that family," Pius wrote, "that no legitimate heir has ever inherited the principate; the sons of their mistresses have been so much more fortunate than those of their wives."[11] (Pius himself fathered at least two illegitimate children.) Pope Alexander VI, also during Leonardo's lifetime, had multiple mistresses and illegitimate children, one of whom was Cesare Borgia, who became a cardinal, commander of the papal armies, an employer of Leonardo, and the subject of Machiavelli's *The Prince*.

For members of the middle classes, however, illegitimacy was not as readily accepted. Protective of their new status, merchants and professionals formed guilds that enforced moral strictures. Although some of the guilds accepted the illegitimate sons of their members, that was not the case with the Arte dei Giuduci e Notai, the venerable (founded in 1197) guild of judges and notaries to which Leonardo's father belonged. "The notary was a certified witness and scribe," Thomas Kuehn wrote in *Illegitimacy in Renaissance Florence*. "His trustworthiness had to be above reproach. He had to be someone fully in the mainstream of society."[12]

These strictures had an upside. Illegitimacy freed some imaginative and free-spirited young men to be creative at a time when creativity was increasingly rewarded. Among the poets, artists, and artisans born out of wedlock were Petrarch, Boccaccio, Lorenzo Ghiberti, Filippo Lippi, his son Filippino, Leon Battista Alberti, and of course Leonardo.

Being born out of wedlock was more complex than merely being an outsider. It created an ambiguity of status. "The problem with bastards was that they were part of the family, but not totally," wrote Kuehn. That helped some be, or forced them to be, more adventurous and improvisational. Leonardo was a member of a middle-class family but separate from it. Like so many writers and artists, he grew up feeling a part of the world but also detached. This limbo extended to inheritance: a combination of conflicting laws and contradictory court precedents left it unclear whether a son born out of wedlock could be an heir, as Leonardo was to find out in legal battles with his half-brothers many years later. "Management of such ambiguities was one of the hallmarks of life in a Renaissance city-state," explained Kuehn. "It was related to the more celebrated creativity of a city like Florence in the arts and humanism."[13]

Because Florence's guild of notaries barred those who were *non legittimo*, Leonardo was able to benefit from the note-taking instincts that were ingrained in his family heritage while being free to pursue his own creative passions. This was fortunate. He would have made a poor notary: he got bored and distracted too easily, especially when a project became routine rather than creative.[14]

DISCIPLE OF EXPERIENCE

Another upside for Leonardo of being born out of wedlock was that he was not sent to one of the "Latin schools" that taught the classics and humanities to well-groomed aspiring professionals and merchants of the early Renaissance.[15] Other than a little training in commercial math at what was known as an "abacus school," Leonardo was mainly self-taught. He often seemed defensive about being an "unlettered man," as he dubbed himself with some irony. But he also took pride that his lack of formal schooling led him to be a disciple of experience and experiment. "Leonardo da Vinci, disscepolo della sperientia,"[16] he once signed himself. This freethinking attitude saved him from being an acolyte of traditional thinking. In his notebooks he unleashed a blast at what he called the pompous fools who would disparage him for this:

> I am fully aware that my not being a man of letters may cause certain presumptuous people to think that they may with reason blame me, alleging that I am a man without learning. Foolish folk! . . . They strut about puffed up and pompous, decked out and adorned not with their own labors, but by those of others. . . . They will say that because I have no book learning I cannot properly express what I desire to describe—but they do not know that my subjects require experience rather than the words of others.[17]

Thus was Leonardo spared from being trained to accept dusty Scholasticism or the medieval dogmas that had accumulated in the centuries since the decline of classical science and original thinking. His lack of reverence for authority and his willingness to challenge received wisdom would lead him to craft an empirical approach for understanding nature that foreshadowed the scientific method developed more than a century later by Bacon and Galileo. His method was rooted in experiment, curiosity, and the ability to marvel at phenomena that the rest of us rarely pause to ponder after we've outgrown our wonder years.

To that was added an intense desire and ability to observe the wonders of nature. He pushed himself to perceive shapes and shadows with wondrous precision. He was particularly good at apprehending movement, from the motions of a flapping wing to the emotions flickering across a face. On this foundation he built experiments, some conducted in his mind, others with drawings, and a few with physical objects. "First I shall do some experiments before I proceed further," he announced, "because my intention is to consult experience first and then with reasoning show why such experience is bound to operate in such a way."[18]

It was a good time for a child with such ambitions and talents to be born. In 1452 Johannes Gutenberg had just opened his publishing house, and soon others were using his moveable-type press to print books that would empower unschooled but brilliant people like Leonardo. Italy was beginning a rare forty-year period during which it was not wracked by wars among its city-states. Literacy, numeracy, and income were rising dramatically as power shifted from titled landowners to urban merchants and bankers, who benefited from advances in law, accounting, credit, and insurance. The Ottoman Turks were about to capture Constantinople, unleashing on Italy a migration of fleeing scholars with bundles of manuscripts containing the ancient wisdom of Euclid, Ptolemy, Plato, and Aristotle. Born within about a year of Leonardo were Christopher Columbus and Amerigo Vespucci, who would lead an era of exploration. And Florence, with its booming merchant class of status-seeking patrons, had become the cradle of Renaissance art and humanism.

CHILDHOOD MEMORIES

The most vivid memory Leonardo had of his infancy was one he recorded fifty years later, when he was studying the flight of birds. He was writing about a hawk-like bird called a kite, which has a forked tail and elegant long wings that allow it to soar and glide. Observing it with his typical acuity, Leonardo perceived precisely how it opened its wings and then spread and lowered its tail when it landed.[19] This aroused a memory from when he was a baby: "Writing about the kite seems to be my destiny since among the first recollections of my infancy, it seemed to me that, as I was in my cradle, a kite came to me and opened my mouth with its tail and struck me several times with its tail inside my lips."[20] Like much of what came from Leonardo's mind, there was probably some fantasy and fabulism in the brew. It is hard to imagine a bird actually landing in a cradle and prying open a baby's mouth with its tail, and Leonardo appears to acknowledge this by using the phrase "it seemed to me," as if it were perhaps partly a dream.

All of this—a childhood with two mothers, an often absent father, and a dreamlike oral encounter with a flapping tail—would provide great fodder for a Freudian analyst. And it did—from Freud himself. In 1910 Freud used the kite tale as the foundation for a short book, *Leonardo da Vinci and a Memory of His Childhood*.[21]

Freud got off to a stumbling start by using a poor German translation of Leonardo's note that mistakenly called the bird a vulture rather than a kite. This sent him into a long tangential explanation about the symbolism of vultures in ancient Egypt and the etymological relationship of the words for *vulture* and *mother*, all of which was irrelevant and, Freud later admitted, embarrassing.[22] Leaving aside the bird mix-up, the main thrust of Freud's analysis was that the word for *tail* in many languages, including Italian (*coda*), is slang for "penis" and that Leonardo's memory was related to his homosexuality. "The situation contained in the fantasy, that a vulture opened the mouth of the child and forcefully belabored it with its tail, corresponds to the idea of fellatio," Freud wrote. Leonardo's repressed desires, he speculated, were channeled into his feverish creativity, but he left many works unfinished because he was inhibited.

These interpretations have prompted some devastating critiques, most famously by art historian Meyer Schapiro,[23] and they seem, at least to me, to reveal more about Freud than about Leonardo. Biographers should be cautious about psychoanalyzing someone who lived five centuries earlier. Leonardo's dreamlike memory may have simply reflected his lifelong interest in the flight of birds, which is how he framed it. And it does not take a Freud to understand that sexual drives can be sublimated into ambition and other passions. Leonardo said so himself. "Intellectual passion drives out sensuality," he wrote in one of his notebooks.[24]

A better source for insight into Leonardo's formative character and motivations is another personal memory he recorded, this one about hiking near Florence. The recollection involved chancing upon a dark cave and pondering whether he should enter. "Having wandered some distance among gloomy rocks, I came to the mouth of a great cavern, in front of which I stood some time, astonished," he recalled. "Bending back and forth, I tried to see whether I could discover anything inside, but the darkness within prevented that. Suddenly there arose in me two contrary emotions, fear and desire—fear of the threatening dark cave, desire to see whether there were any marvelous thing within."[25]

Desire won. His unstoppable curiosity triumphed, and Leonardo went into the cave. There he discovered, embedded in the wall, a fossil whale. "Oh mighty and once-living instrument of nature," he wrote, "your vast strength was to no avail."[26] Some scholars have assumed that he was describing a fantasy hike or riffing on some verses by Seneca. But his notebook page and those surrounding it are filled with descriptions of layers of fossil shells, and many fossilized whale bones have in fact been discovered in Tuscany.[27]

The whale fossil triggered a dark vision of what would be, throughout his life, one of his deepest forebodings, that of an apocalyptic deluge. On the next side of the sheet he described at length the furious power once held by the long-dead whale: "You lashed with swift, branching fins and forked tail, creating in the sea sudden tempests that buffeted and submerged ships." Then he turned philosophical. "Oh time, swift despoiler of all things, how many kings, how many nations hast thou undone, and how many changes of states and of circumstances have happened since this wondrous fish perished."

By this point Leonardo's fears were about a realm far different from whatever dangers might be lurking inside the cave. Instead they were driven by an existential dread in the face of the destructive powers of nature. He began scribbling rapidly, using a silverpoint on a red-tinted page, describing an apocalypse that begins with water and ends with fire. "The rivers will be deprived of their waters, the earth will no longer put forth her greenery; the fields will no more be decked with waving corn; all the animals, finding no fresh grass for pasture, will die," he wrote. "In this way the fertile and fruitful earth will be forced to end with the element of fire; and then its surface will be left burnt up to cinder and this will be the end of all earthly nature."[28]

The dark cave that Leonardo's curiosity compelled him to enter offered up both scientific discoveries and imaginative fantasies, strands that would be interwoven throughout his life. He would weather storms, literally and psychologically, and he would encounter dark recesses of the earth and soul. But his curiosity about nature would always impel him to explore more. Both his fascinations and his forebodings would be expressed in his art, beginning with his depiction of Saint Jerome agonizing near the mouth of a cave and culminating in his drawings and writings about an apocalyptic deluge.

Florence in the 1480s, the cathedral with Brunelleschi's dome in the center and the Palazzo della Signoria, the seat of government, to its right.

CHAPTER 2

Apprentice

THE MOVE

Until he was twelve, Leonardo had a life in Vinci that, despite the complexities of being part of an extended family, was quite settled. He lived primarily with his grandparents and his idle uncle Francesco in the family house in the heart of Vinci. His father and stepmother were listed as living there when Leonardo was five, but after that their primary residence was in Florence. Leonardo's mother and her husband lived with their growing brood of children, along with Accattabriga's parents and his brother's family, in a farmhouse an easy walk from town.

But in 1464 this world was disrupted. His stepmother, Albiera, died in childbirth, along with what would have been her first child. Leonardo's grandfather Antonio, the head of the Vinci household, also had recently died. So just as Leonardo was reaching the age when he needed to prepare for a trade, his father, living alone and probably lonely, brought him to Florence.[1]

Leonardo rarely wrote in his notebooks about his own emotions, so it is hard to know what he felt about the move. But the fables he recorded sometimes give a glimpse of his sentiments. One described the sad odyssey of a stone perched on a hill surrounded by colorful flowers and a grove of trees—in other words, a place like Vinci. Looking at the crowd of stones along the road below, it decided it wanted to join them. "What am I doing here among these plants?" the stone asked. "I want to live in the company of my fellow stones." So it rolled down to the others. "After a while," Leonardo recounted, "it found itself in continual distress from the wheels of the carts, the iron hoofs of horses, and the feet of the passers-by. One rolled it over, another trod upon it. Sometimes the stone raised itself up a little as it lay covered with mud or the dung of some animal, but it was in vain that it looked up at the spot whence it had come as a place of solitude and tranquil peace." Leonardo drew a moral: "This is what happens to those who leave a life of solitary contemplation and choose to come to dwell in cities among people full of infinite evil."[2]

His notebooks have many other maxims praising the countryside and solitude. "Leave your family and friends and go over the mountains and valleys into the country," he instructed aspiring painters. "While you are alone you are entirely your own master."[3] These paeans to country living are romantic and, for those who cherish the image of lonely genius, quite appealing. But they are infused with fantasy. Leonardo would spend almost all of his career in Florence, Milan, and Rome, crowded centers of creativity and commerce, usually surrounded by students, companions, and patrons. He rarely retreated alone to the countryside for an extended period of solitude. Like many artists, he was stimulated by being with people of diverse interests and (willing to contradict himself in his notebooks) declared, "Drawing in company is much better than alone."[4] The impulses of his grandfather and uncle, who both practiced the quiet country life, were imprinted in Leonardo's imagination but not practiced in his life.

During his early years in Florence, Leonardo lived with his father, who arranged for him to get a rudimentary education and would soon help him get a good apprenticeship and commissions. But there is one significant thing that Ser Piero did not do, which would have been easy enough for a well-connected notary: go through the legal process of having his son legitimated. This could be accomplished by the father and child appearing before a local official known as a "count palatine," usually a dignitary who had been granted power to act on such matters, and presenting a petition as the child knelt.[5] Piero's decision not to do this for Leonardo is particularly surprising, since he then had no other children of his own.

Perhaps one reason that Piero did not legitimate Leonardo was that he hoped to have as his heir a son who would follow family tradition and become a notary, and it was already clear, by the time Leonardo turned twelve, that he was not so inclined. According to Vasari, Piero noticed that his son "never ceased drawing and sculpting, pursuits which suited his fancy more than any other." In addition, the notary guild had a rule, which may have been difficult to circumvent, that denied membership even to out-of-wedlock sons who had been legitimated. So Piero apparently saw no reason to go through the process. By not legitimating Leonardo, he could hope to have another son who would be his heir as a notary. A year later Piero married the daughter of another prominent Florence notary, but it would only be after his third marriage, in 1475 to a woman six years younger than Leonardo, that he would produce a legitimate heir who indeed became a notary.

FLORENCE

There was no place then, and few places ever, that offered a more stimulating environment for creativity than Florence in the 1400s. Its economy, once dominated by unskilled wool-spinners, had flourished by becoming one that, like our own time, interwove art, technology, and commerce. It featured artisans working with silk makers and merchants to create fabrics that were works of art. In 1472 there were eighty-four wood-carvers, eighty-three silk workers, thirty master painters, and forty-four goldsmiths and jewelry craftsmen working in Florence. It was also a center of banking; the florin, noted for its gold purity, was the dominant standard currency in all of Europe, and the adoption of double-entry bookkeeping that recorded debits and credits permitted commerce to flourish. Its leading thinkers embraced a Renaissance humanism that put its faith in the dignity of the individual and in the aspiration to find happiness on this earth through knowledge. Fully a third of Florence's population was literate, the highest rate in Europe. By embracing trade, it became a center of finance and a cauldron of ideas.

"Beautiful Florence has all seven of the fundamental things a city requires for perfection," the essayist Benedetto Dei wrote in 1472, when Leonardo was living there. "First of all, it enjoys complete liberty; second, it has a large, rich, and elegantly dressed population; third, it has a river with clear, pure water, and mills within its walls; fourth, it rules over castles, towns, lands and people; fifth, it has a university, and both Greek and accounting are taught; sixth, it has masters in every art; seventh, it has banks and business agents all over the world."[6] Each one of those assets was valuable for a city, just as they are today: not only the "liberty" and "pure water," but also that the population was "elegantly dressed" and that the university was renowned for teaching accounting as well as Greek.

The city's cathedral was the most beautiful in Italy. In the 1430s it had been crowned with the world's largest dome, built by the architect Filippo Brunelleschi, which was a triumph of both art and engineering, and linking those two disciplines was a key to Florence's creativity. Many of the city's artists were also architects, and its fabric industry had been built by combining technology, design, chemistry, and commerce.

This mixing of ideas from different disciplines became the norm as people of diverse talents intermingled. Silk makers worked with goldbeaters to create enchanted fashions. Architects and artists developed the science of perspective. Wood-carvers worked with architects to adorn the city's 108 churches. Shops became studios. Merchants became financiers. Artisans became artists.[7]

When Leonardo arrived, Florence's population was 40,000, which is about what it had been for a century but down from the 100,000 or so who lived there in 1300, before the Black Death and subsequent waves of plague. There were at least a hundred families that could be considered very wealthy, plus some five thousand guild members, shopkeepers, and merchants who were part of a prosperous middle class. Because most of them were new to wealth, they had to establish and assert their status. They did so by commissioning distinctive works of art, buying luxurious clothes of silk and gold, building palatial mansions (thirty went up between 1450 and 1470), and becoming patrons of literature, poetry, and humanist philosophy. Consumption was conspicuous but tasteful. By the time Leonardo arrived, Florence had more wood-carvers than butchers. The city itself had become a work of art. "There is no place more beautiful in all the world," the poet Ugolino Verino wrote.[8]

Unlike some city-states elsewhere in Italy, Florence was not ruled by hereditary royalty. More than a century before Leonardo arrived, the most prosperous merchants and guild leaders crafted a republic whose elected delegates met at the Palazzo della Signoria, now known as the Palazzo Vecchio. "The people were kept amused every day by shows, festivals, and novelties," the fifteenth-century Florentine historian Francesco Guicciardini wrote. "They were well fed from the provisions with which the city abounded. Industry of every sort flourished. Talented and able men were maintained, and a welcome and a position secured to all teachers of literature, art, and every liberal pursuit."[9]

The republic was not, however, democratic or egalitarian. In fact, it was barely a republic. Exercising power from behind its façade was the Medici family, the phenomenally wealthy bankers who dominated Florentine politics and culture during the fifteenth century without holding office or hereditary title. (In the following century they became hereditary dukes, and lesser family members became popes.)

After Cosimo de' Medici took over the family bank in the 1430s, it became the largest in Europe. By managing the fortunes of the continent's wealthy families, the Medici made themselves the wealthiest of them all. They were innovators in bookkeeping, including the use of debit-and-credit accounting that became one of the great spurs to progress during the Renaissance. By means of payoffs and plotting, Cosimo became the de facto ruler of Florence, and his patronage made it the cradle of Renaissance art and humanism.

A collector of ancient manuscripts who had been schooled in Greek and Roman literature, Cosimo supported the rebirth of interest in antiquity that was at the core of Renaissance humanism. He founded and funded Florence's first public library and the influential but informal Platonic Academy, where scholars and public intellectuals discussed the classics. In art, he was a patron of Fra Angelico, Filippo Lippi, and Donatello. Cosimo died in 1464, just as Leonardo arrived in Florence from Vinci. He was succeeded by his son and then, five years later, his famous grandson, Lorenzo de' Medici, aptly dubbed Lorenzo the Magnificent.

Lorenzo had been tutored in humanist literature and philosophy under the watchful eye of his mother, an accomplished poet, and he patronized the Platonic Academy, launched by his grandfather. He was also an accomplished sportsman, distinguishing himself in jousting, hunting, falconry, and breeding horses. All of this made him a better poet and patron than he was a banker; he took more delight in using wealth than in making it. During his twenty-three-year reign, he would sponsor innovative artists, including Botticelli and Michelangelo, as well as patronize the workshops of Andrea del Verrocchio, Domenico Ghirlandaio, and Antonio del Pollaiuolo, which were producing paintings and sculptures to adorn the booming city.

Lorenzo de' Medici's patronage of the arts, autocratic rule, and ability to maintain a peaceful balance of power with rival city-states helped to make Florence a cradle of art and commerce during Leonardo's early career there. He also kept his citizenry amused with dazzling public spectacles and grandly produced entertainments, ranging from Passion Plays to pre-Lenten carnivals. The work done for these pageants was ephemeral, but it was lucrative and stimulated the creative imagination of many of the artists involved, most notably young Leonardo.

Florence's festive culture was spiced by the ability to inspire those with creative minds to combine ideas from disparate disciplines. In narrow streets, cloth dyers worked next to goldbeaters next to lens crafters, and during their breaks they went to the piazza to engage in animated discussions. At the Pollaiuolo workshop, anatomy was being studied so that the young sculptors and painters could better understand the human form. Artists learned the science of perspective and how angles of light produce shadows and the perception of depth. The culture rewarded, above all, those who mastered and mixed different disciplines.

BRUNELLESCHI AND ALBERTI

The legacy of two such polymaths had a formative influence on Leonardo. The first was Filippo Brunelleschi (1377–1446), the designer of the cathedral dome. Like Leonardo, he was the son of a notary. Desiring a more creative life, he trained to become a goldsmith. Fortunately for his wide-ranging interests, goldsmiths were lumped together with other artisans as members of the guild of silk weavers and merchants, which also included sculptors. Brunelleschi's interests soon embraced architecture as well, and he traveled to Rome to study classical ruins with his friend Donatello, another young Florentine goldsmith, who later achieved fame as a sculptor. They measured the Pantheon dome, studied other great buildings, and read the works of ancient Romans, most notably Vitruvius's paean to classical proportions, *De Architectura*. Thus they became embodiments of the multidisciplinary interests and rebirth of classical knowledge that shaped the early Renaissance.

To build his cathedral dome—a self-supporting structure of close to four million bricks that is still the largest masonry dome in the world—Brunelleschi had to develop sophisticated mathematical modeling techniques and invent an array of hoists and other engineering tools. In an example of the diverse forces that were animating creativity in Florence, some of these hoists were then used to stage Lorenzo de' Medici's magnificent theatrics involving flying characters and moving scenery.[10]

Brunelleschi also rediscovered and greatly advanced the classical concepts of visual perspective, which had been missing in the art of the Middle Ages. In an experiment that foreshadowed the work of Leonardo, he painted a panel that depicted the view of the Florence Baptistery across the plaza from the cathedral. After drilling a small hole in the panel, he put the back of it up to his eye while he faced the Baptistery. Then he took a mirror and held it at arm's length, reflecting back on the painting. As he moved the mirror in and out of his line of sight, he would compare the reflection of his painting to the real Baptistery. The essence of realistic painting, he thought, was to render a three-dimensional view onto a two-dimensional surface. After accomplishing this trick on a painted panel, Brunelleschi showed how parallel lines seemed to converge in the distance toward a vanishing point. His formulation of linear perspective transformed art and also influenced the science of optics, the craft of architecture, and the uses of Euclidean geometry.[11]

Brunelleschi's successor as a theorist of linear perspective was another of the towering Renaissance polymaths, Leon Battista Alberti (1404–1472), who refined many of Brunelleschi's experiments and extended his discoveries about perspective. An artist, architect, engineer, and writer, Alberti was like Leonardo in many ways: both were illegitimate sons of prosperous fathers, athletic and good-looking, never-married, and fascinated by everything from math to art. One difference is that Alberti's illegitimacy did not prevent him from being given a classical education. His father helped him get a dispensation from the Church laws barring illegitimate children from taking holy orders or holding ecclesiastical offices, and he studied law at Bologna, was ordained as a priest, and became a writer for the pope. During his early thirties, Alberti wrote his masterpiece analyzing painting and perspective, *On Painting*, the Italian edition of which was dedicated to Brunelleschi.

Alberti had an engineer's instinct for collaboration and, like Leonardo, was "a lover of friendship" and "open-hearted," according to the scholar Anthony Grafton. He also honed the skills of courtiership. Interested in every art and technology, he would grill people from all walks of life, from cobblers to university scholars, to learn their secrets. In other words, he was much like Leonardo, except in one respect: Leonardo was not strongly motivated by the goal of furthering human knowledge by openly disseminating and publishing his findings; Alberti, on the other hand, was dedicated to sharing his work, gathering a community of intellectual colleagues who could build on each other's discoveries, and promoting open discussion and publication as a way to advance the accumulation of learning. A maestro of collaborative practices, he believed, according to Grafton, in "discourse in the public sphere."

When Leonardo was a teenager in Florence, Alberti was in his sixties and spending much of his time in Rome, so it is unlikely they spent time together. Alberti was a major influence nonetheless. Leonardo studied his treatises and consciously tried to emulate both his writing and his demeanor. Alberti had established himself as "an avatar of grace in every word or movement," a style that very much appealed to Leonardo. "One must apply the greatest artistry in three things," Alberti wrote, "walking in the city, riding a horse, and speaking, for in each of these one must try to please everyone."[12] Leonardo mastered all three.

Alberti's *On Painting* expanded on Brunelleschi's analysis of perspective by using geometry to calculate how perspective lines from distant objects should be captured on a two-dimensional pane. He also suggested that painters hang a veil made of thin thread between themselves and the objects they are painting, then record where each element falls on the veil. His new methods improved not only painting but endeavors ranging from mapmaking to stage designs. By applying mathematics to art, Alberti elevated the painter's status and advanced the argument that the visual arts deserve a standing equal to that of other humanist fields, a cause that Leonardo would later champion.[13]

EDUCATION

Leonardo's only formal learning was at an abacus school, an elementary academy that emphasized the math skills useful in commerce. It did not teach how to formulate abstract theories; the focus was on practical cases. One skill that was emphasized was how to draw analogies between cases, a method that Leonardo would use repeatedly in his later science. Analogies and spotting patterns became for him a rudimentary method of theorizing.

His enthusiastic early biographer Vasari wrote, with what seems to be typical exaggeration, "In arithmetic, during the few months that he studied it, he made so much progress, that, by continually suggesting doubts and difficulties to the master who was teaching him, he would very often bewilder him." Vasari also noted that Leonardo was interested in so many things that he got easily distracted. He turned out to be good in geometry, but he never mastered the use of equations or the rudimentary algebra that existed at the time. Nor did he learn Latin. In his thirties he would still be trying to remedy this deficiency by drawing up lists of Latin words, painstakingly writing out awkward translations, and wrestling with grammar rules.[14]

A left-hander, Leonardo wrote from right to left on a page, the opposite direction of the words on this and other normal pages, and drew each letter facing backward. "They are not to be read save with a mirror," as Vasari described these pages. Some have speculated that he adopted this script as a code to keep his writings secret, but that is not true; it can be read, with or without a mirror. He wrote that way because when using his left hand he could glide leftward across the page without smudging the ink. The practice was not completely uncommon. When his friend the mathematician Luca Pacioli described Leonardo's mirror writing, he made the point that some other left-handers wrote likewise. A popular fifteenth-century calligraphy book even shows left-handed readers the best way to do *lettera mancina*, or mirror script.[15]

Being left-handed also affected Leonardo's method of drawing. As with his writing, he drew from right to left so as not to smudge the lines with his hand.[16] Most artists draw hatching strokes that slope upward to the right, like this: ////. But Leonardo's hatching was distinctive because his lines started on the lower right and moved upward to the left, like this: \\\\. Today this style has an added advantage: the left-handed hatching in a drawing is evidence that it was made by Leonardo.

When viewed in a mirror, Leonardo's writing is somewhat similar to that of his father, indicating that Piero probably helped Leonardo learn to write. However, many of his numerical calculations are written in conventional fashion, showing that the abacus school probably did not indulge his use of mirror script for math.[17] Being left-handed was not a major handicap, but it was considered a bit of an oddity, a trait that conjured up words like *sinister* and *gauche* rather than *dexterous* and *adroit*, and it was one more way in which Leonardo was regarded, and regarded himself, as distinctive.

VERROCCHIO

Around the time Leonardo was fourteen, his father was able to secure for him an apprenticeship with one of his clients, Andrea del Verrocchio, a versatile artist and engineer who ran one of the best workshops in Florence. Vasari wrote, "Piero took some of his drawings and carried them to Andrea del Verrocchio, who was his good friend, and asked if he thought it would be profitable for the boy to study drawing." Piero knew Verrocchio well, and he notarized at least four legal settlements and rental documents for him around this time. But Verrocchio probably gave the boy an apprenticeship on merit, not just as a favor to his father. He was, Vasari reported, "astonished" at the boy's talent.[18]

Verrocchio's workshop, which was nestled in a street near Piero's notarial office, was the perfect place for Leonardo. Verrocchio conducted a rigorous teaching program that involved studying surface anatomy, mechanics, drawing techniques, and the effects of light and shade on material such as draperies.

When Leonardo arrived, Verrocchio's workshop was creating an ornate tomb for the Medici, sculpting a bronze statue of Christ and Saint Thomas, designing banners of white taffeta gilded with flowers of silver and gold for a pageant, curating the Medici's antiques, and generating Madonna paintings for merchants who wanted to display both their wealth and their piety. An inventory of his shop showed that it had a dining table, beds, a globe, and a variety of books in Italian, including translated classical poetry by Petrarch and Ovid as well as humorous short stories by the fourteenth-century popular Florentine writer Franco Sacchetti. The topics of discussion in his shop included math, anatomy, dissection, antiquities, music, and philosophy. "He applied himself to the sciences, and particularly geometry," according to Vasari.[19]

Verrocchio's bottega, like those of his five or six main competitors in Florence, was more like a commercial shop, similar to the shops of the cobblers and jewelers along the street, than a refined art studio. On the ground floor was a store and workroom, open to the street, where the artisans and apprentices mass-produced products from their easels, workbenches, kilns, pottery wheels, and metal grinders. Many of the workers lived and ate together in the quarters upstairs. The paintings and objects were not signed; they were not intended to be works of individual expression. Most were collaborative efforts, including many of the paintings commonly attributed to Verrocchio himself. The goal was to produce a constant flow of marketable art and artifacts rather than nurture creative geniuses yearning to find outlets for their originality.[20]

With their lack of Latin schooling, the artisans in such shops were not considered to be part of the cultural elite. But the status of artists was beginning to change. The rebirth of interest in the ancient Roman classics had revived the writings of Pliny the Elder, who extolled classical artists for representing nature so accurately that their grapes could fool birds. With the help of the writings of Alberti and the development of mathematical perspective, the social and intellectual standing of painters was rising, and a few were becoming sought-after names.

Trained as a goldsmith, Verrocchio left much of the brushwork of painting to others, most notably a crop of young artists that included Lorenzo di Credi. Verrocchio was a kind master; students such as Leonardo often continued to live with and work for him after their apprenticeships were completed, and other young painters, including Sandro Botticelli, became part of his circle.

Verrocchio's collegial nature did have one downside: he was not a tough taskmaster and his workshop was not renowned for delivering commissions on time. Vasari noted that Verrocchio once made preparatory drawings for a battle scene of nude figures and other narrative works of art, "but for some reason, whatever it may have been, they remained unfinished." Verrocchio held on to some paintings for years before completing them. Leonardo would far exceed his master in all things, including in his propensity to get distracted, walk away from projects, and linger over paintings for years.

One of Verrocchio's most captivating sculptures was a four-foot bronze of the young warrior David standing in triumph over the head of Goliath (fig. 1). His smile is tantalizing and a bit mysterious—What exactly is he thinking?—like the ones Leonardo would later

Fig. 1. Verrocchio's *David.*

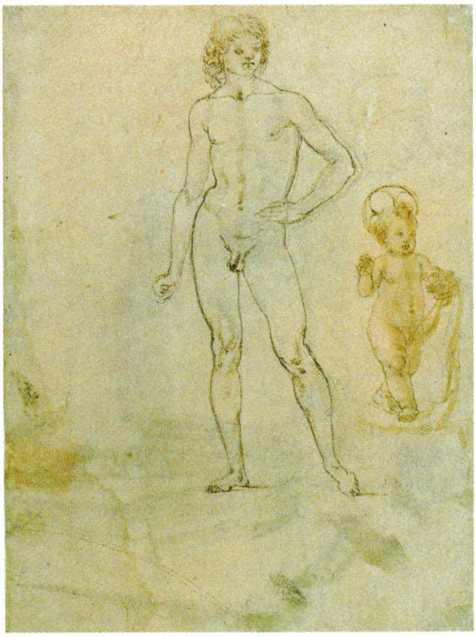

Fig. 3. Drawing possibly of Leonardo modeling for Verrocchio's *David.*

Fig. 2. Presumed self-portrait by Leonardo in the *Adoration of the Magi.*

paint. It quavers between expressing a childlike glory and a dawning realization of future leadership; a cocky smile is caught in the moment of being transformed into resolution. Unlike Michelangelo's iconic marble statue of a muscular David as a man, Verrocchio's David seems to be a slightly effeminate and strikingly pretty boy of about fourteen.

That was the age of Leonardo, newly apprenticed in the studio, when Verrocchio probably began work on the statue.[21] Artists of Verrocchio's era typically blended the classical ideal with more naturalistic features, and it is unlikely that his statues are exact portraits of a particular model. Nevertheless there are reasons to think that Leonardo posed for Verrocchio's *David*.[22] The face is not the usual broad type that Verrocchio had previously favored. He clearly used a new model, and the recently arrived boy in the shop was the obvious candidate, especially because, according to Vasari, young Leonardo had "a beauty of body beyond description, a splendor that rejoiced the most sorrowful souls." Such praises of young Leonardo's loveliness are echoed by his other early biographers. Another piece of evidence: David's face is similar (strong nose and chin, soft cheeks and lips) to that of a young boy Leonardo drew on the edge of the *Adoration of the Magi* that is presumed to be a self-portrait (fig. 2) as well as other supposed likenesses.

So with just a little imagination, we can look at Verrocchio's transfixing statue of the pretty boy David and envision what the young Leonardo looked like when he stood modeling on the ground floor of the studio. In addition, there is a drawing by one of Verrocchio's students that is probably a copy of a study made for the statue. It shows the boy model in exactly the same pose, down to his finger placement on his hip and the little hollow where his neck hits his collarbone, but nude (fig. 3).

Verrocchio's art was sometimes criticized as workmanlike. "The style of his sculpture and painting tended to be hard and crude, since it came from unremitting study rather than any inborn gift," Vasari wrote. But his statue of David is a beautiful gem that influenced the young Leonardo. David's curls and those of the hair and beard of Goliath's head are luxurious spirals of the type that would become a signature feature of Leonardo's art. In addition, Verrocchio's statue (unlike, say, Donatello's version in 1440) displays a care and mastery of anatomical details. For example, the two veins visible in David's right arm are accurately rendered and pop in just the precise way to show that, despite his seeming nonchalance, he is gripping his dagger-like sword very tightly. Likewise, the muscle connecting David's left forearm to his elbow is flexed in a way that comports with the twisting of his hand.

That ability to convey the subtleties of motion in a piece of still art was among Verrocchio's underappreciated talents, one that Leonardo would adopt and then far surpass in his paintings. More than most previous artists, Verrocchio imbued his statues with twists, turns, and flows. In his bronze *Christ and Saint Thomas*, begun while Leonardo was an apprentice, Saint Thomas turns to his left to touch the wound of Jesus, who is twisting to his right as he lifts his arm. The sense of motion turns the statue into a narrative. It conveys not merely a moment but a story, the one told in the Gospel of John, when Thomas doubts the resurrection of Jesus and responds to his injunction "Reach hither thy hand, and thrust it into my side." Kenneth Clark called it "the first instance in the Renaissance of that complicated flow of movement through a composition, achieved by contrasted axes of the figures, which Leonardo made the chief motif of all his constructions."[23] We can also see Verrocchio's love of movement and flow in the hair of Saint Thomas and beard of Jesus, which again feature a sensuous profusion of spiraling curls and tight coils.

Leonardo had studied the use of math for commercial purposes at his abacus school, but from Verrocchio he learned something more profound: the beauty of geometry. After Cosimo de' Medici died, Verrocchio designed a marble-and-bronze slab for his tomb, which was finished in 1467, a year after Leonardo became his apprentice. Instead of religious imagery, the tomb slab featured geometrical patterns dominated by a circle inside a square, as Leonardo would use for his drawing *Vitruvian Man*. Inside the design, Verrocchio and his workshop carved carefully proportioned rectangles and half-circles in colors that were based on harmonic ratios and the Pythagorean musical scale.[24] There was harmony in proportions, Leonardo learned, and math was nature's brushstroke.

Geometry and harmony combined again two years later, when Verrocchio's studio was given a monumental engineering task: mounting a two-ton ball on top of Brunelleschi's dome of Florence's cathedral. It was a triumph of both art and technology. The crowning moment, which was accompanied by trumpet fanfare and hymns of praise, occurred in 1471, when Leonardo was nineteen. The project, which he would still refer to decades later in his notebook, ingrained in him a sense of the interplay between artistry and engineering; he made loving, meticulous drawings of the hoists and gear mechanisms that Verrocchio's studio used, some of which had originally been devised by Brunelleschi.[25]

The construction of the ball, which was made of stone that was clad with eight sheets of copper and then gilded, also kindled in Leonardo a fascination with optics and the geometry of light rays. There were no welding torches at the time, so the triangular sheets of copper had to be soldered together using concave mirrors, about three feet wide, that would concentrate sunlight into a point of intense heat. An understanding of geometry was needed to calculate the precise angle of the rays and grind the curve of the mirrors accordingly. Leonardo became mesmerized—at times obsessed—by what he called "fire mirrors"; over the years he would make almost two hundred drawings in his notebooks that show how to make concave mirrors that will focus light rays from varying angles. Close to forty years later, when working in Rome on huge curved mirrors that might turn the heat of the sun into a weapon, he jotted in his notebook, "Remember how the ball of Santa Maria del Fiore was soldered together in sections?"[26]

Leonardo was also influenced by Verrocchio's primary commercial competitor in Florence, Antonio del Pollaiuolo. Even more than Verrocchio, Pollaiuolo was experimenting with the expression of moving and twisting bodies, and he performed surface dissections of humans to study anatomy. He was, wrote Vasari, "the first master to skin many human bodies in order to investigate the muscles and understand the nude in a more modern way." In his engraving *Battle of the Nudes* and his sculpture and painting *Hercules and Antaeus*, Pollaiuolo depicted warriors contorted in powerful yet realistic ways as they struggle to stab or subdue each other. The anatomy of muscles and nerves informs the grimaces on faces and the twists of limbs.[27]

Leonardo's father came to appreciate, and in one case profit from, his son's fevered imagination and ability to connect art to the wonders of nature. A peasant who worked in Vinci one day made a small shield of wood and asked Piero to take it to Florence and have it painted.

Piero gave the task to Leonardo, who decided to create a terrifying image of a dragon-like monster breathing fire and belching poison. To make it naturalistic, he assembled parts from real lizards, crickets, snakes, butterflies, grasshoppers, and bats. "He labored over it so long that the stench of the dead animals was past bearing, but Leonardo did not notice it, so great was the love that he bore towards art," Vasari wrote. When Piero finally came to get it, he recoiled in shock from what in the dim light appeared at first to be a real monster. Piero decided to keep his son's creation and buy another shield for the peasant. "Later, Ser Piero sold the buckler of Leonardo secretly to some merchants in Florence, for a hundred ducats; and in a short time it came into the hands of the Duke of Milan, having been sold to him by the merchants for three hundred ducats."

The shield, perhaps Leonardo's first recorded piece of art, displayed his lifelong talent for combining fantasy with observation. In the notes for his proposed treatise on painting, he would later write, "If you wish to make an imaginary animal invented by you appear natural, let us say a dragon, take for the head that of a mastiff or hound, for the eyes a cat, and for the ears a porcupine, and for the nose a greyhound, and the brows of a lion, the temple of an old cock, the neck of a terrapin."[28]

DRAPERIES, CHIAROSCURO, AND SFUMATO

One of the exercises in Verrocchio's studio was the drawing of "drapery studies," most done with delicate brushstrokes of black and white washes on linen. According to Vasari, Leonardo "would make clay models of figures, draping them with soft pieces of cloth dipped in plaster, and would then draw them patiently on thin sheets of cambric or linen, in black and white, with the point of the brush." The velvety renderings of the folds and waves of drapery featured deft depictions of light, nuanced gradations of shadow, and the occasional glint of luster (fig. 4).

Some of the drapery drawings from Verrocchio's studio appear to be studies for paintings. Others were probably done just as learning exercises. The drawings have given rise to a vibrant academic industry

Fig. 4. Drapery study from Verrocchio's studio, attributed to Leonardo, c. 1470.

that tries to sort out which were done by Leonardo and which were more likely by Verrocchio, Ghirlandaio, or their coworkers.[29] The fact that the attributions are difficult to resolve is evidence of the collegial nature of Verrocchio's bottega.

For Leonardo, the drapery studies helped foster one of the key components of his artistic genius: the ability to deploy light and shade in ways that would better produce the illusion of three-dimensional volume on a two-dimensional surface. They also helped him hone his ability to observe how light subtly caresses an object, causing a glistening of luster, a sharpened contrast on a fold, or a hint of reflected glow creeping into the heart of a shadow. "The first intention of the painter," Leonardo later wrote, "is to make a flat surface display a body as if modeled and separated from this plane, and he who surpasses others in this skill deserves most praise. This accomplishment, with which the science of painting is crowned, arises from light and shade, or we may say chiaroscuro."[30] That statement could stand as his artistic manifesto, or at least a key element of it.

Chiaroscuro, from the Italian for "light/dark," is the use of contrasts of light and shadow as a modeling technique for achieving the illusion of plasticity and three-dimensional volume in a two-dimensional drawing or painting. Leonardo's version of the technique involved varying the darkness of a color by adding black pigments rather than making it a more saturated or richer hue. In his Benois Madonna, for example, he painted the Virgin Mary's blue dress in shades ranging from almost white to almost black.

When mastering drapery drawings in Verrocchio's studio, Leonardo also pioneered sfumato, the technique of blurring contours and edges. It is a way for artists to render objects as they appear to our eye rather than with sharp contours. This advance caused Vasari to proclaim Leonardo the inventor of the "modern manner" in painting, and the art historian Ernst Gombrich called sfumato "Leonardo's famous invention, the blurred outline and mellowed colors that allow one form to merge with another and always leave something to our imagination."[31]

The term *sfumato* derives from the Italian word for "smoke," or more precisely the dissipation and gradual vanishing of smoke into the air. "Your shadows and lights should be blended without lines or borders in the manner of smoke losing itself in the air," he wrote in a series of maxims for young painters.[32] From the eyes of his angel in the *Baptism of Christ* to the smile of the *Mona Lisa,* the blurred and smoke-veiled edges allow a role for our own imagination. With no sharp lines, enigmatic glances and smiles can flicker mysteriously.

WARRIORS WITH HELMETS

In 1471, around the time the copper ball was placed atop the Duomo, Verrocchio & Co. was involved, as were most of the other artisans of Florence, in the festivities organized by Lorenzo de' Medici for the visit of Galeazzo Maria Sforza, the cruel and authoritarian (and soon-to-be-assassinated) Duke of Milan. Accompanying Galeazzo was his swarthy and charismatic younger brother Ludovico Sforza, who was nineteen, the same age as Leonardo. (It was to him that Leonardo would address his famous job-seeking letter eleven years later.) Verrocchio's shop had two major tasks for the festivities: redecorating the Medici's guest quarters for the visitors and crafting a suit of armor and an ornate helmet as a gift.

The Duke of Milan's cavalcade was dazzling even to Florentines who were used to Medicean public spectacles. It included two thousand horses, six hundred soldiers, a thousand hunting hounds, falcons, falconers, trumpeters, pipers, barbers, dog trainers, musicians, and poets.[33] It's hard not to admire an entourage that travels with its own barbers and poets. Because it was Lent, there were three religious spectacle plays in place of public jousts and tournaments. But the overall atmosphere was far from Lenten. The visit marked the climax of the Medici practice of using public pageants and spectacles to dissipate popular discontent.

To Machiavelli, who wrote a history of Florence in addition to his famous how-to manual for authoritarian princes, the penchant for pageantry was related to a decadence that infected Florence during its period of relative peace, when Leonardo was a young artist there: "The youth having become more dissolute than before, more extravagant in dress, feasting, and other licentiousness, and being without employment, wasted their time and means on gaming and women; their principal study being how to appear splendid in apparel, and attain a crafty shrewdness in discourse. These manners derived additional encouragement from the followers of the duke of Milan, who, with his duchess and the whole ducal court, came to Florence, where he was received with pomp and respect." One church burned to the ground during the festivities, which was considered divine retribution for the fact that, as Machiavelli wrote, "during Lent, when the church commands us to abstain from animal food, the Milanese, without respect for either God or his church, ate of it daily."[34]

Leonardo's most famous early drawing may have been inspired by or related to this visit by the Duke of Milan.[35] It is of a craggy Roman warrior in profile wearing an ornate helmet (fig. 5), and it was derived from a drawing by Verrocchio, whose studio had designed a helmet as one of Florence's gifts to the duke. Intricately drawn with a

Fig. 5. A warrior.

silverpoint stylus on tinted paper, Leonardo's warrior sports a helmet adorned by a frightfully realistic bird wing and the flourishes of curls and spirals that he adored. On the breastplate is a ludicrous but loveable growling lion. The warrior's face is subtly modeled with delicate shadings made by patiently drawn hatch lines, but his jowls and brows and lower lip are exaggerated to the edge of caricature. The hooked nose and jutting jaw create a profile that became a leitmotif in Leonardo's drawings, that of a gruff old warrior, noble but faintly farcical.

The influence of Verrocchio can be clearly seen. From Vasari's *Lives* we know that Verrocchio created sculptured reliefs of "two heads in metal, one representing Alexander the Great in profile, and the other a fanciful portrait of Darius," the ancient Persian king. These are now lost but are known through various copies made at the time. Most notably, in Washington, DC's National Gallery there is a marble relief of a young Alexander the Great, attributed to Verrocchio and his workshop, which features a similar ornate helmet with a winged dragon, a breastplate adorned with a roaring face, and the profusion of curls and fluttering swirls that the master imparted to his apprentice. In his own drawing, Leonardo eliminated a large-jawed animal that Verrocchio had perched atop the helmet, turned the dragon into swirls of plants, and generally made the design less complicated. "What Leonardo's simplifications achieved was to make the beholder's eye focus on the profile heads of the warrior and lion, i.e., on the relationship between the man and the animal," according to Martin Kemp and Juliana Barone.[36]

As with his paired carvings of Darius and Alexander, Verrocchio occasionally juxtaposed a profile of a craggy old warrior with that of a pretty boy, a theme that would become a favorite of Leonardo's, both in his drawings and in random notebook doodles. One example is in Verrocchio's *Beheading of Saint John the Baptist*, a silver relief he did for Florence's Baptistery, where a young warrior and an old one are juxtaposed on the far right. By the time this sculpture was made, starting around 1477, when Leonardo was twenty-five, it is unclear who was influencing whom; the young and old warriors facing each other, as well as an angelic young boy on the far left, have the vibrant movement and emotion-laden facial expressions that make it seem possible Leonardo had a hand in them.[37]

PAGEANTS AND PLAYS

For the artists and engineers in Florence's bottegas, working on the Medici pageants and spectacles was a significant component of their job. For Leonardo it was also a joy. He was already making a name as a colorful dresser, fond of brocade doublets and rose tunics, and as a showman adept at imaginative theatrics. Over the years, both in Florence and especially after he moved to Milan, he spent time devising costumes, theatrical scenery, stage machinery, special effects, floats, banners, and entertainments. His theatrical productions were ephemeral, and they linger only in sketches in his notebooks. They can be dismissed as diversions, but they were also an enjoyable way for him to combine art and engineering, and thus they became a formative influence on his personality.[38]

The artisans who created the sets for theatrical events became masters of the rules of artistic perspective that had been refined in the

1400s. The painted scenery and backdrops had to be unified with the three-dimensional stage settings, props, moving objects, and actors. Reality and illusions were blended. We can see the influence of these plays and pageants on both Leonardo's art and his engineering. He studied how to make the rules of perspective work for different vantage points, loved mixing illusion with reality, and delighted in devising the special effects, costumes, scenery, and theatrical machinery. All of this helps to explain many of the sketches and fantasy writings in his notebooks that scholars sometimes find mystifying.

For example, some of the gears and cranks and mechanisms that Leonardo rendered in his notebooks were, I think, theatrical machinery that he encountered or contrived. Florentine impresarios had created ingenious mechanisms, called *ingegni*, for changing scenery, propelling dazzling props, and turning stages into living paintings. Vasari praises a Florentine carpenter and engineer who climaxed a festival show with a scene of "Christ carried upward from a mountain carved of wood and borne to heaven by a cloud filled with angels."

Likewise, some of the flying contraptions that we find in Leonardo's notebooks were probably for the amusement of theatrical audiences. The Florentine plays often involved characters and props descending from the heavens or being magically suspended in air. Some of Leonardo's flying machines were, as we will see, clearly aimed at real human flight. Others, however, are on notebook pages from the 1480s and seem to have a theatrical purpose. They feature wings with limited range moved by cranks, and they could not possibly have been propelled into the skies by a human pilot. Similar pages include notes on how to project lights onto a scene and drawings of a hook-and-pulley system to raise actors.[39]

Even Leonardo's famous drawing of an aerial screw (fig. 6), often touted as the design for the first helicopter, falls into this category of *ingegni* devised for a theatrical spectacle, I believe. Its spiral mechanism of linen, wire, and cane was, in theory, supposed to turn and bore upward into the air. Leonardo specified certain details, like making sure the linen has "its pores stopped up with starch," but he showed no method for a human to operate it. It is big enough to be amusing but probably not enough to carry a human. In one model,

Fig. 6. A flying machine, probably for the theater.

he specified that the "axis will be made of a fine steel blade, bent by force, and when released it will turn the screw." There were toys at the time that used similar mechanisms. Like some of his mechanical birds, the aerial screw was probably made to transport spectators' imaginations rather than their bodies.[40]

THE ARNO LANDSCAPE

Leonardo enjoyed the collegial and familial atmosphere in Verrocchio's workshop so much that, when his apprenticeship ended in 1472, at the age of twenty, he decided to continue to work and live there. He remained on friendly terms with his father, who lived nearby with his second wife and still had no other children. When Leonardo registered as a member of the Florentine painters' confraternity, the Compagnia di San Luca, he affirmed his relationship by signing himself "Leonardo di Ser Piero da Vinci."

The Compagnia was not a guild but a club-like mutual aid society or fraternity. Other members who registered and paid dues in 1472 included Botticelli, Pietro Perugino, Ghirlandaio, Pollaiuolo, Filippino Lippi, and Verrocchio himself.[41] The Compagnia had been in existence for a century, but it was undergoing a revitalization partly because artists were reacting against Florence's antiquated guild system. Under the old guild structure, they were lumped into the Arte dei Medici e Speziali, which had been founded in 1197 for physicians and pharmacists. By the late 1400s they were eager to assert a more distinctive status for themselves.

Months after becoming a master painter, Leonardo escaped the bustling narrow streets and crammed workshops of Florence and took a trip back to the rolling green hills around Vinci. "I, staying with Antonio, am contented," he scribbled in his notebook in the summer of 1473, when he was twenty-one.[42] His grandfather Antonio had died, so the reference is perhaps to his mother's husband, Antonio Buti (Accattabriga). One can picture him content as he stays with his mother and his large stepfamily in the hills just outside of Vinci; it conjures up his tale of the stone that willed itself to roll down to the crowded road but later yearned to be back up on the quiet hill.

On thc reverse of that notebook page is what may be Leonardo's earliest surviving art drawing, the shimmering start of a career of combining scientific observation with artistic sensibility (fig. 7). In his mirror script he has dated it "day of Holy Mary of the Snows on the 5th August 1473."[43] The drawing is an impressionistic panorama, sketched with quick pen strokes on paper, evoking the rocky hills and verdant valley surrounding the Arno River near Vinci. There are a few familiar landmarks from the area—a conical hill, perhaps a castle—but the aerial view seems to be, typical of Leonardo, a mix of the actual and the imagined, viewed as if by a soaring bird. The glory of being an artist, he realized, was that reality should inform but not constrain. "If the painter wishes to see beauties that would enrapture him, he is master of their production," he wrote. "If he seeks valleys, if he wants to disclose great expanses of countryside from the summits of mountains, and if he subsequently wishes to see the horizon of the sea, he is lord of all of them."[44]

Other artists had drawn landscapes as backdrops, but Leonardo

Fig. 7. Leonardo's Arno Valley landscape, 1473.

was doing something different: depicting nature for its own sake. That makes his Arno Valley drawing a contender for the first such landscape in European art. The geological realism is striking: the craggy rock outcroppings eroded by the river reveal accurately rendered layers of stratified rock, a subject that was to fascinate Leonardo for the rest of his life. So, too, is the near-precision of linear perspective and the way the atmosphere blurs the distant horizon, an optical phenomenon that he would later call "aerial perspective."

Even more arresting is the young artist's ability to convey motion. The leaves of the trees and even their shadows are drawn with quick curved lines that make them seem to tremble in the breeze. The water falling into a pool is made vibrant with flutters of quick strokes. The result is a delightful display of the art of observing movement.

TOBIAS AND THE ANGEL

While working as a master painter in Verrocchio's shop during his late teens and early twenties, Leonardo contributed elements to two paintings: he was responsible for the scampering dog and shiny fish in *Tobias and the Angel* (fig. 8) and for the angel on the far left in the *Baptism of Christ*. These collaborations show what he learned from Verrocchio and how he then surpassed him.

The biblical tale of Tobias, which was popular in late fifteenth-

Fig. 8. *Tobias and the Angel* by Verrocchio with Leonardo.

century Florence, tells of a boy who is sent by his blind father to collect a debt, accompanied by his guardian angel, Raphael. On the journey they catch a fish, the guts of which turn out to have healing powers, including that of restoring the father's sight. Raphael was the patron saint of travelers and of the guild of physicians and apothecaries. The tale of him and Tobias was particularly appealing to the wealthy merchants who had become art patrons in Florence, especially those with traveling sons.[45] Among the Florentines who painted it were Pollaiuolo, Verrocchio, Filippino Lippi, Botticelli, and Francesco Botticini (seven times).

Pollaiuolo's version (fig. 9) was produced in the early 1460s for the church of Orsanmichele. It was well known to Leonardo and Verrocchio, who was sculpting his statue of Christ and Saint Thomas for a niche of that church's wall. In producing his own *Tobias and the Angel* a few years later, Verrocchio engaged in an explicit competition with Pollaiuolo.[46]

The version that came out of Verrocchio's shop includes the exact same elements as Pollaiuolo's: Tobias and the angel walking hand in hand, a Bolognese terrier scampering alongside, Tobias holding a carp on a stick and strings, and Raphael holding a tin with the fish's guts, all in front of a meandering river landscape with clumps of grass and clusters of trees. And yet it is a fundamentally different painting, in both its impact and detail, in ways that reveal what Leonardo was learning.

One difference is that Pollaiuolo's version is stiff, while Verrocchio's conveys movement. As a sculptor, he had mastered the twists and thrusts that impart dynamism to a body. His Tobias leans in as he strides, his cloak billowing out behind him while tassels and threads flutter. He and Raphael turn to each other naturally. Even the way they hold hands is more dynamic. Whereas Pollaiuolo's faces seem vacuous, the body motions in the Verrocchio version connect to emotional expressions, conveying mental as well as physical movements.

Verrocchio, who was more of a sculptor than a painter, developed a reputation for not being a master at portraying nature. True, there is a good raptor sweeping down in his *Baptism of Christ*, but his way with animals was generally considered "indifferent" and "deficient."[47]

Fig. 9. Antonio del Pollaiuolo's *Tobias and the Angel.*

So it is not surprising that to paint the fish and dog he would turn to his pupil Leonardo, whose eye for nature was proving to be astonishing. Both animals are painted on what was already a finished background landscape; we know this because, as sometimes happened with Leonardo's experimental mixtures, his paint has become somewhat transparent.

The shiny and shimmery scales of the fish show that Leonardo was already mastering the magic of how light strikes an object and dances to our eyes. Each scale is a gem. The sunshine coming from the top left of the picture produces a mix of light and shade and sparkle. Both behind the gill and at the front of the liquidy eye is a spot of luster. Unlike other painters, Leonardo even took care to render the blood dripping from the fish's cut belly.

As for the dog prancing just under Raphael's feet, it has an expression and personality that matches in its charm that of Tobias. In stark contrast to Pollaiuolo's stiff terrier, Leonardo's trots naturally and watches alertly. Most notable are its curls. Their painstaking design and lustrous lighting match that of the curls above Tobias's ear, which (an analysis of the left-handed style shows) were also drawn by Leonardo.[48] Swirling and flowing curls, perfectly lit and coiled, were becoming a Leonardo signature.

In this deeply pleasing and sprightly painting, we can see the power of a master-pupil collaboration. Leonardo was already an extreme observer of nature, and he was perfecting the ability to convey the effects of light on objects. Added to that, he had imbibed from Verrocchio, the master sculptor, the excitement of conveying motion and narrative.

BAPTISM OF CHRIST

The culmination of Leonardo's collaborations with Verrocchio came in the mid-1470s with the completion of the *Baptism of Christ*, which shows John the Baptist pouring water over Jesus while two angels kneeling beside the River Jordan watch (fig. 10). Leonardo painted the radiant, turning angel on the far left of the scene, and Verrocchio was so awed when he beheld it that he "resolved never again to touch a brush"—or at least that's what Vasari tells us. Even allowing for Vasari's penchant to mythologize and trot out clichéd themes, there was probably some truth to the tale. Afterward Verrocchio never completed any new painting on his own.[49] More to the point, a comparison between the parts of the *Baptism of Christ* that Leonardo painted with those done by Verrocchio shows why the older artist would have been ready to defer.

Fig. 10. *Baptism of Christ* by Verrocchio with Leonardo.

An X-ray analysis of the painting confirms that the angel on the left and much of the background landscape and the body of Jesus were painted with multiple thin layers of oil paint, the pigments highly diluted, stroked on with great delicacy and sometimes dabbed and smoothed by fingertips, a style that Leonardo was developing in the 1470s. Oil painting had come to Italy from the Netherlands, and Pollaiuolo's workshop was using it, as was Leonardo. Verrocchio, on the contrary, never embraced the use of oils, and instead continued to use tempera, a mix of water-soluble pigments bound with egg yolks.[50]

The most striking trait of Leonardo's angel is the dynamism of his pose. Shown from slightly behind in a twisted three-quarter profile, his neck turns to the right as his torso twists slightly to the left. "Always set your figures so that the side to which the head turns is not the side to which the breast faces, since nature for our convenience has made us with a neck which bends with ease in many directions," Leonardo wrote in one of his notebooks.[51] As evident in his *Christ and Saint Thomas*, Verrocchio was a master of depicting motion in sculptures, and Leonardo became an expert in its painterly conveyance.

A comparison of the two angels shows how Leonardo was surpassing his master. Verrocchio's angel seems vacant, his face flat, and his only emotion seems to be a sense of wonder that he happens to find himself next to a much more expressive angel. "He seems to look with astonishment at his companion, as at a visitant from another world," Kenneth Clark wrote, "and, in fact, Leonardo's angel belongs to a world of the imagination which Verrocchio's never penetrated."[52]

Like most artists, Verrocchio drew lines to delineate the contours of his angel's head and face and eyes. But in Leonardo's angel, there are no clear edges that delineate the features. The curls dissolve gently into each other and the face, rather than creating a hairline. Look at the shadow underneath the jaw of Verrocchio's angel, done with visible brushstrokes of tempera paint that create a sharp jaw line. Then look at Leonardo's; the shadow is more translucent and blends more smoothly, something that's easier done with oil. The almost imperceptible strokes are fluid, thinly layered, and occasionally smoothed by hand. The contours of the angel's face are soft. There are no perceptible edges.

We can also see this beauty in the body of Jesus. Compare his legs, painted by Leonardo, with those of Verrocchio's John the Baptist. The latter have sharper lines, unlike what a careful observer would see in reality. Leonardo even minutely blurs the curls of Jesus' exposed pubic hair.

This use of sfumato, the smokiness that blurs sharp contours, was by now a hallmark of Leonardo's art. Alberti in his treatise on painting had advised that lines should be drawn to delineate edges, and Verrocchio did just that. Leonardo took care to observe the real world, and he noticed the opposite: when we look at three-dimensional objects, we don't see sharp lines. "Paint so that a smoky finish can be seen, rather than contours and profiles that are distinct and crude," he wrote. "When you paint shadows and their edges, which cannot be perceived except indistinctly, do not make them sharp or clearly defined, otherwise your work will have a wooden appearance."[53] Verrocchio's angel has this wooden appearance. Leonardo's does not.

X-ray analysis shows that Verrocchio, with his lesser feel for nature, had originally begun the background by drawing a few rounded clumps of trees and bushes, more wooden than sylvan. When Leonardo took over, he used oils to paint a richly natural view of a languid but sparkling river flowing through rocky cliffs, echoing his Arno River drawing and foreshadowing the *Mona Lisa*. Other than Verrocchio's pedestrian palm tree, the backdrop displays a magical mix of natural realism and creative fantasia.

The geological striations of the rock (except those on the far right, which someone else must have painted) are carefully rendered, though not with the subtlety that Leonardo would later display. As the scene recedes, it gradually blurs, as our eyes would naturally have it, into a hazy horizon where the blue of the sky whitens into the mists just above the hills. "The edges of the mist will be indistinct against the blue of the sky, and towards the earth it will look almost like dust blown up," Leonardo wrote in one of his notebooks.[54]

In painting the background and foreground, Leonardo created the organizing theme of the picture, which is a narrative united by the meandering river. He portrayed the water's movement with scientific mastery and spiritual profundity, imbuing it with metaphorical power as the lifeblood connecting the macrocosm of the earth and the microcosm in humans. The water flows from the heavens and distant lakes, cuts through rocks to form dramatic cliffs and smooth pebbles, and pours from the cup of the Baptist, as if connecting to the blood of his veins. Finally, it swaddles the feet of Jesus and ripples to the edge of the picture, reaching us and making us feel a part of the flow.

There is an inexorable impetus to the water's flow, and when it is obstructed by the ankles of Jesus it forms swirls and eddies as it proceeds along its course. In these acutely observed vortexes and scientifically accurate ripples, Leonardo delights in what will become his favorite pattern: nature's spirals. The curls flowing down his angel's neck look like cascades of water, as if the river had flowed over his head and transformed into hair.

At the center of the picture is a small waterfall, one of many such depictions Leonardo would produce, in his paintings and notebooks, of water falling into a swirling pool or stream. Sometimes these renderings are scientific, at other times darkly hallucinatory. In this case the falling water seems sprightly; it causes splashes that prance around the eddies like Tobias's puppy.

With the *Baptism of Christ*, Verrocchio went from being Leonardo's teacher to being his collaborator. He had helped Leonardo learn the sculptural elements of painting, especially modeling, and also the way a body twists in motion. But Leonardo, with thin layers of oil both translucent and transcendent, and his ability to observe and imagine, was now taking art to an entirely different level. From the mist on the distant horizons to the shadow under the angel's chin to the water at the feet of Christ, Leonardo was redefining how a painter transforms and transmits what he observes.

THE ANNUNCIATION

In addition to the collaborations he did with Verrocchio in the 1470s, the twentysomething Leonardo produced at least four paintings primarily on his own while working at the studio: an Annunciation, two small devotional paintings of the Madonna and Child, and a pioneering portrait of a Florentine woman, *Ginevra de' Benci*.

Paintings of the Annunciation, which portray the moment when the angel Gabriel surprised the Virgin Mary by telling her that she would become the mother of Christ, were very popular in the Renaissance. Leonardo's version depicts the announcement and reaction as a narrative occurring in a walled garden of a stately country villa as Mary looks up from reading a book (fig. 11). Although ambitious, the painting is so flawed that its attribution to Leonardo has been debated; some experts contend that it was the product of an awkward collaboration with Verrocchio and others in his shop.[55] But a variety of evidence shows that Leonardo was the primary if not sole artist. He made a preparatory drawing of Gabriel's sleeve, and the painting exhibits his trademark style of dabbing the oil paint with his hands. His finger smudges can be seen, on very close inspection, on the Virgin Mary's right hand and on the leaves of the base of the lectern.[56]

Among the problematic elements of the picture is the bulky garden wall, which seems to be viewed from a slightly higher vantage point than the rest of the picture and distracts from the visual connection between the angel's pointing fingers and Mary's raised hand.

Fig. 11. Leonardo's *The Annunciation.*

It has an odd angle at its opening, which makes it look like it is being viewed from the right, and is jarring when compared to the wall of the house. The cloths covering the Virgin's lap have a rigidity, as if Leonardo had worked on his drapery studies a little too fastidiously, and the odd configuration of what I assume is her armchair makes it seem as if she has three knees. Her pose makes her look like a mannequin, an effect that is compounded by the blankness of her expression. The flatly rendered cypress trees are the same size, yet the one on the right, next to the house, seems closer to us and thus should be bigger. A spindly trunk of one of the cypresses seems to sprout from the angel's fingers, and the botanical exactness of the Madonna lily that the angel holds contrasts with a generic treatment of the other plants and grasses that is untypical of Leonardo.[57]

The most discomforting lapse involves the awkward positioning of Mary in relation to the ornate lectern, which was based on a tomb Verrocchio designed for the Medici. The lectern's base is a few feet closer to the viewer than Mary is, which makes it seem that she is too far away for her right arm to reach the book, yet her arm extends across it, appearing oddly elongated. This is clearly the work of a young artist. *The Annunciation* gives us an insight into what type of painter Leonardo would have been had he not gone on to immerse himself in observations of perspective and studies of optics.

On careful examination, however, the picture is not quite as bad as it looks. Leonardo was experimenting with the trick known as anamorphosis, in which some elements of a work may look distorted when viewed straight on but appear accurate when viewed from another angle. Leonardo occasionally made sketches of the technique in his notebooks. At the Uffizi, guides will suggest that you take a few steps to the right of *The Annunciation* and look again. That helps, but only partly. The angel's arm looks a bit less odd, as does the angle of the opening of the garden wall. It gets slightly better if you also squat down and view the painting from slightly lower. Leonardo was trying to create a piece that would look good to someone walking into the church from the right. He was also nudging us to the right so that we see the act of Annunciation more from Mary's vantage.[58] It almost works. His tricks of perspective display a youthful brilliance, but one that has not yet been refined.

The greatest strength of the picture is Leonardo's depiction of the angel Gabriel. He has the androgynous beauty that Leonardo was perfecting, and his birdlike wings (ignoring the lamentable light brown extension added by someone else) grow out of his shoulders with Leonardo's wondrous blend of naturalism and fantasy. Leonardo is able to convey Gabriel in motion: he is leaning forward, as if he has just landed, and the ribbon tied around his sleeve is fluttering back (unlike in the preparatory drawing), while the wind from his arrival stirs the grass and flowers beneath him.

Another glorious feature of *The Annunciation* is Leonardo's tinting of the shadows. As the setting sun shines from the left side of the painting, it casts a pale yellow glow on the top of the garden wall and the lectern. But where the sun's glow is blocked, the resulting shadows pick up the blue hue of the sky. The front of the white lectern has a slight blue tinge, since it is lit mainly by the refracted light of the sky rather than the yellowish direct glow of the setting sun.[59] "Shadows will vary," Leonardo explained in his notebooks. "The side of an object that receives a reflected light from the azure of the air will be tinged with that hue, and this is particularly observable in white objects. That side that receives the light from the sun will partake of that color. This may be particularly observed in the evening, when the sun is setting between the clouds, which it reddens."[60]

Leonardo was helped in his subtle coloring by his growing mastery of oil paint. By using pigments that were highly diluted, he could apply them in thin translucent layers, subtly allowing the shades to evolve with each fine stroke or dabbing from his fingers. This is most notable in the face of the Virgin Mary. Bathed in the glow of the setting sun, it seems to radiate light with an incandescence not found in Gabriel's flesh. She has a luminosity that causes her to stand out from the rest of the painting, despite her vacant expression.[61]

The Annunciation shows Leonardo, still in his early twenties, experimenting with light, perspective, and narratives involving human reactions. In the process, he made some mistakes. But even the mistakes, which came from innovating and experimenting, heralded his genius.

MADONNAS

Small devotional paintings and sculptures of the Madonna with the infant Jesus were a staple of the Verrocchio workshop, turned out with regularity. Leonardo did at least two such paintings, *Madonna of the Carnation* (fig. 12), also known as the Munich Madonna because of its current location, and the Hermitage Museum's *Madonna and Child with Flowers* (fig. 13), known as the Benois Madonna after a collector who once owned it.

The most interesting aspect of both is the squirming, chubby

Fig. 12. *Madonna of the Carnation* (Munich Madonna).

baby Jesus, whose folds of fat give Leonardo the chance to go beyond the drapery studies in using modeling, light, and shadows to convey realistic three-dimensionality. They become an early example of his use of chiaroscuro, the forceful contrasts of light and shade that use black pigments to alter the tone and brightness of pictorial elements rather than relying on the deepening color hues. "For the first time his chiaroscuro creates, throughout a picture, fully three-dimensional forms rivaling the roundness of sculpture," wrote David Alan Brown of Washington's National Gallery.[62]

The realistic depiction of the baby Jesus in each painting is an early example of Leonardo's art being informed by anatomical observation. "In little children, all the joints are slender and the portions between them are thick," he wrote in his notebook. "This happens

Fig. 13. *Madonna and Child with Flowers* (Benois Madonna).

because nothing but the skin covers the joints without any other flesh and has the character of sinew, connecting the bones like a ligature. And the fat fleshiness is laid on between one joint and the next."[63] This contrast is noticeable in both pictures when comparing the wrists of the Madonna with those of the infant Jesus.

In the Munich *Madonna of the Carnation*, the focus of the picture is the reaction of the newborn Jesus to the flower. The actions of his chubby arms and the emotions shown on his face are connected. He sits on a cushion adorned with crystal balls, a symbol used by the Medici family and an indication that they may have commissioned the work. The landscape seen through the windows shows Leonardo's love of combining observation with fantasy; the hazy atmospheric perspective gives a gauze of reality to jagged rocks that are purely imaginary.

The *Madonna and Child with Flowers* in Russia's Hermitage Museum also shows the lively emotions and reactions that Leonardo had learned to capture in a scene, thus turning a moment into a narrative. In this case, the baby Jesus is absorbed by the cross-shaped flower Mary is handing him, as if he is, as Brown says, "a budding botanist."[64] Leonardo had been studying optics, and he depicts Jesus carefully focusing on the flower, as if he were just learning to discern the form of an object from its background. He gently guides his mother's hands into his focus of sight. Mother and child are integrated by a narrative of reactions: that of Jesus to the flower and that of Mary delighting in the curiosity of her son.

The power of the pictures comes from the premonition that both mother and child seem to have of the crucifixion. The carnation, according to one Christian legend, sprang from the tears Mary shed at the crucifixion. In the Hermitage Museum's Benois Madonna, the symbolism is starker; the flower itself is shaped like a cross. But the psychological impact of the pictures is disappointing. Neither one shows much emotion other than curiosity on the face of Jesus and love on the face of Mary. In Leonardo's later variations on the theme, most notably his *Madonna of the Yarnwinder* and then the *Virgin and Child with Saint Anne* and its variations, he would turn the scene into a much more intense drama and emotional narrative.

Leonardo had two squirming baby models to observe when painting these pictures. After two childless marriages, his father married a third time, in 1475, and was promptly blessed with two sons, Antonio in 1476 and Giuliano in 1479. Leonardo's notebooks of the time are filled with drawings and sketches of infants in various active situations: squirming with a mother, poking at a face, trying to grab objects or pieces of fruit, and (especially) grappling in many configurations with a cat. Depictions of the Madonna trying to restrain her restless baby would become an important theme in Leonardo's art.

GINEVRA DE' BENCI

Leonardo's first nonreligious painting is the portrait of a melancholy young woman with a moonlike face glowing against the backdrop of a spiky juniper tree (fig. 14). Although somewhat listless and unengaging on first glance, *Ginevra de' Benci* has wonderful Leonardo touches, such as the lustrous, tightly curled ringlets of hair and unconventional three-quarters pose. More important, the picture presages the *Mona Lisa*. As he had done in Verrocchio's *Baptism of Christ*, Leonardo depicts a meandering river flowing from the misty mountains and seeming to connect to a human body and soul. With her earth-tone dress laced by blue thread, Ginevra is unified with the earth and the river that joins them.

Ginevra de' Benci was the daughter of a prominent Florentine banker whose aristocratic family was allied with the Medici and second only to them in wealth. In early 1474, when she was sixteen, she married Luigi Niccolini, who at thirty-two was a recent widower. His family, which was in the cloth-weaving business, was politically prominent but not as wealthy; he soon became the chief magistrate of the republic, but in a 1480 tax return he declared that he had "more debts than property." The return also said that his wife was ill and had been "in the hands of doctors for a long time," which could account for the unnerving pallor of her complexion in the portrait.

It is likely that Leonardo's father helped him get the commission, probably around the time of Ginevra's 1474 marriage. Piero da

Fig. 14. *Ginevra de' Benci.*

Vinci had served as notary for the Benci family on many occasions, and Leonardo had become friends with Ginevra's older brother, who lent him books and would end up as a temporary custodian of his unfinished *Adoration of the Magi*. But it does not seem that *Ginevra de' Benci* was commissioned as a wedding or betrothal portrait. It shows a three-quarter pose rather than the side profile that was typical of the genre, and she is dressed in a starkly plain brown dress unadorned by jewelry rather than one of the elaborate dresses with luxurious jewels and brocades that was then common for an upper-class wedding painting. Her black shawl is an unlikely adornment for a celebration of a marriage.

In an oddity of Renaissance culture and mores, the picture may not have been commissioned by the Benci family but instead by Bernardo Bembo, who became Venice's ambassador to Florence at the beginning of 1475. He was forty-two at the time and had both a wife and a mistress, but he struck up a proudly public Platonic relationship with Ginevra that made up in effusive adoration what it likely lacked in sexual consummation. This was a type of elevated romance that, at that time, was not only sanctioned but celebrated in poems. "It is with these flames and with such a love that Bembo is on fire and burns, and Ginevra dwells in the midst of his heart," the Florentine Renaissance humanist Cristoforo Landino wrote in a verse extolling their love.[65]

Leonardo painted Bembo's emblem of a laurel and palm wreath on the reverse of the portrait, and it encircles a sprig of juniper, in Italian *ginepro* and thus a reference to Ginevra's name. Woven through the wreath and juniper sprig is a banner proclaiming, "Beauty Adorns Virtue," which attests to her virtuous nature, and an infrared analysis shows Bembo's motto, "Virtue and Honor," had been written beneath it. Suffused with the muted and misty dusk light that Leonardo loved, the painting shows Ginevra looking pale and melancholy. There is a vacant trance-like quality to her, echoed by the dreamlike quality of the distant landscape, that seems to go deeper than merely the physical illness her husband reported.

The portrait, which is more closely focused and sculptural than others of the era, resembles a bust sculpted by Verrocchio, *Lady with Flowers*. The comparison would be even closer except that the bottom portion of Leonardo's painting, perhaps as much as one-third, was at some later date lopped off, which removed what writers from the period described as gracious hands with ivory-white fingers. Fortunately we perhaps can imagine how they looked, since a silverpoint drawing by Leonardo, showing folded hands holding a sprig, which may be related to his painting, exists in the collection at Windsor.[66]

As with the other paintings he did in Verrocchio's shop during the 1470s, Leonardo used thin layers of oil gently blended and blurred, sometimes with his fingers, to create smoky shadows and avoid sharp lines or abrupt transitions. If you stand close enough to the painting at the National Gallery in Washington, DC, you can see his fingerprint just to the right of Ginevra's jaw, where her ringlets of hair blur into the background juniper tree and a distinct little spiky sprig juts out. Another can be found just behind her right shoulder.[67]

The most arresting features of the portrait are Ginevra's eyes. The lids are studiously modeled to appear three-dimensional, but this also makes them feel heavy, adding to her somber demeanor. Her gaze looks distracted and indifferent, as if she's looking through us and seeing nothing. Her right eye seems to wander to the distance. At first her gaze seems diverted and looking down and to her left. But the more you stare at each eye separately, the more each seems to focus back on you.

Also noticeable when staring at her eyes is the shiny liquid quality that Leonardo was able to achieve with his oils. Just to the right of each pupil is a tiny spot of luster, showing the sparkling glint from the sunlight coming from the front left. The same use of luster can be seen on her curls.

This perfect glint of luster—the white sparkle caused by a light hitting a smooth and shiny surface—was another of Leonardo's signature marks. It is a phenomenon we see every day but do not often contemplate closely. Unlike reflected light, which "partakes of the color of the object," Leonardo wrote, a spot of luster "is always white," and it moves when the viewer moves. Look at the lustrous glimmer of the curls of *Ginevra de' Benci*, then imagine walking around her. As Leonardo knew, those spots of luster would shift and "appear in as many different places on the surface as different positions are taken by the eye."[68]

After you interact with *Ginevra de' Benci* long enough, what at first seem like a vacant face and distant stare begin to appear suffused with a haunting tinge of emotion. She seems pensive and ruminating, perhaps about her marriage or the departure of Bembo, or because of some deeper mystery. Her life was sad; she was sickly and remained childless. But she also had an inner intensity. She wrote poetry, one line of which survives: "I ask your forgiveness; I am a mountain tiger."[69]

In painting her, Leonardo created a psychological portrait, one that renders hidden emotions. That would become one of his most important artistic innovations. It set him on a trajectory that would culminate three decades later in the greatest psychological portrait in history, the *Mona Lisa*. The tiny hint of a smile that is visible on the right side of Ginevra's lips would be refined into the most memorable smile ever painted. The water flowing from the distant landscape that seems to connect to the soul of Ginevra would become, in the *Mona Lisa*, the ultimate metaphor of the connection between earthly and human forces. *Ginevra de' Benci* is not the *Mona Lisa*, not even close. But it is recognizably the work of the man who would paint it.

CHAPTER 3

On His Own

L'AMORE MASCULINO

In April 1476, a week before his twenty-fourth birthday, Leonardo was accused of engaging in sodomy with a male prostitute. It happened around the time that his father finally had another child, a legitimate son who would become his heir. The anonymous allegation against Leonardo was placed in a *tamburo*, one of the letter drums designated for receipt of morals charges, and involved a seventeen-year-old named Jacopo Saltarelli, who worked in a nearby goldsmith shop. He "dresses in black," the accuser wrote of Saltarelli, "is party to many wretched affairs, and consents to please those persons who request such wickedness of him." Four young men were accused of engaging his sexual services, among them "Leonardo di Ser Piero da Vinci, who lives with Andrea de Verrocchio."

The Officers of the Night, who policed such charges, launched an investigation and may have imprisoned Leonardo and the others for a day or so. The charges could have led to serious criminal penalties if any witnesses were willing to come forward. Fortunately, one of the other four young men was a member of a prominent family that had married into the Medici clan. The case was dismissed "with the condition that no further accusations are made." But a few weeks later, a new accusation was made, this one written in Latin. It said that the four had engaged in multiple sexual engagements with Saltarelli. Because it too was an anonymous allegation and no witnesses came forth to corroborate it, the charges were once again set aside with the same conditions. That, apparently, was the end of the matter.[1]

Thirty years later, Leonardo wrote a bitter comment in a notebook: "When I made a Christ-child you put me in prison, and now if I show him grown up you will do worse to me." The comment is cryptic. Perhaps Saltarelli had modeled for one of his depictions of a young Jesus. At the time, Leonardo felt abandoned. "As I have told you before, I am without any of my friends," he wrote in a note. On the reverse is this: "If there is no love, what then?"[2]

Leonardo was romantically and sexually attracted to men and, unlike Michelangelo, seemed to be just fine with that. He made no effort either to hide or proclaim it, but it probably contributed to his sense of being unconventional, someone who wasn't geared to be part of a family procession of notaries.

Over the years, he would have many beautiful young men as part of his studio and houschold. Two years after the Saltarelli incidents, on a page with one of his many notebook doodles of an older man and a beautiful boy facing each other in profile, he wrote, "Fioravante di Domenico of Florence is my most beloved friend, as though he were my . . ."[3] The sentence is unfinished, but it leaves the impression that Leonardo had found an emotionally satisfying companion. Shortly after this note, the ruler of Bologna wrote to Lorenzo de' Medici about another young man, who had worked with Leonardo and even adopted his name, Paulo de Leonardo de Vinci da Firenze.* Paulo had been sent away from Florence because of the "wicked life he had led there."[4]

One of Leonardo's earliest male companions was a young musi-

* That type of name change was not uncommon for apprentices. A contemporary of Leonardo, the Florentine painter Piero di Cosimo, for example, took his name from his master, Cosimo Rosselli. Leonardo, tellingly, did not do the same and always used his own father's name as part of his full name, Leonardo di ser Piero da Vinci.

cian in Florence named Atalante Migliorotti, whom he taught to play the lyre. Atalante was thirteen in 1480, and around that time Leonardo drew what he described as "a portrait of Atalante raising his face" as well as a full-length sketch of a nude boy from behind playing the lyre.[5] Two years later, Atalante would accompany him to Milan and eventually go on to a successful music career. He would star in a 1491 opera production in Mantua and then make for that city's ruling family a twelve-stringed lyre of "unusual shape."[6]

Leonardo's most serious longtime companion, who joined Leonardo's household in 1490, was angelic looking but devilish in personality, and thus acquired the nickname Salai, the Little Devil. Vasari described him as "a graceful and beautiful youth with fine curly hair in which Leonardo greatly delighted," and he was the subject of many sexual comments and innuendos, as we shall see.

Leonardo was never known to have had a relationship with a woman, and he occasionally recorded his distaste for the idea of heterosexual copulation. He wrote in one of his notebooks, "The sexual act of coitus and the body parts employed for it are so repulsive that, if it were not for the beauty of the faces and the adornment of the actors and the pent-up impulse, nature would lose the human species."[7]

Homosexuality was not uncommon in the artistic community of Florence or in Verrocchio's circle. Verrocchio himself never married, nor did Botticelli, who was also charged with sodomy. Other artists who were gay included Donatello, Michelangelo, and Benvenuto Cellini (who was twice convicted of sodomy). Indeed, *l'amore masculino*, as Lomazzo quoted Leonardo calling it, was so common in Florence that the word *Florenzer* became slang in Germany for "gay." When Leonardo worked for Verrocchio, a cult of Plato was arising among some Renaissance humanists, and it included an idealized view of erotic love for beautiful boys. Homosexual love was celebrated in both uplifting poems and bawdy songs.

Nevertheless, sodomy was a crime, as Leonardo became painfully aware, and it was sometimes prosecuted. During the seventy years following the creation of the Officers of the Night in 1432, an average of four hundred men per year were accused of sodomy, and about sixty per year were convicted and sentenced to prison, exile, or even death.[8] The Church considered homosexual acts a sin. A 1484 papal bull likened sodomy to "carnal knowledge with demons," and preachers regularly railed against it. Dante, whose *Divine Comedy* was beloved by Leonardo and illustrated by Botticelli, consigned sodomites, along with blasphemers and usurers, to the seventh circle of hell. However, Dante displayed Florence's conflicted feelings about homosexuals by praising in the poem one of the denizens he put into this circle, his own mentor, Brunetto Latini.

Some writers, following Freud's unsubstantiated assertions that Leonardo's "passive homosexual" desires were "sublimated," have speculated that his desires were repressed and channeled into his work. One of his maxims seems to give support to the theory that he believed in controlling his sexual urges: "Whoever does not curb lustful desires puts himself on the level of beasts."[9] But there is no reason to believe that he remained celibate. "Those who wish, in the interest of morality, to reduce Leonardo, that inexhaustible source of creative power, to a neutral or sexless agency, have a strange idea of doing service to his reputation," wrote Kenneth Clark.[10]

On the contrary, in his life and in his notebooks, there is much evidence that he was not ashamed of his sexual desires. Instead he seemed amused by them. In a section of his notebooks called "On the Penis," he described quite humorously how the penis had a mind of its own and acted at times without the will of the man: "The penis sometimes displays an intellect of its own. When a man may desire it to be stimulated, it remains obstinate and goes its own way, sometimes moving on its own without the permission of its owner. Whether he is awake or sleeping, it does what it desires. Often when the man wishes to use it, it desires otherwise, and often it wishes to be used and the man forbids it. Therefore it appears that this creature possesses a life and an intelligence separate from the man." He found it curious that the penis was often a source of shame and that men were shy about discussing it. "Man is wrong to be ashamed of giving it a name or showing it," he added, "always covering and concealing something that deserves to be adorned and displayed with ceremony."[11]

How was this reflected in his art? In his drawings and notebook sketches, he showed a far greater fascination for the male body than the female. His drawings of male nudes tend to be works of tender beauty, many rendered in full length. By contrast, almost all of the women he painted, with the exception of a now lost *Leda and the Swan*, are clothed and shown from the waist up.*

Nevertheless, unlike Michelangelo, Leonardo was a master at painting women. From *Ginevra de' Benci* to the *Mona Lisa*, his portraits of women are deeply sympathetic and psychologically insightful. His *Ginevra* is innovative, at least for Italy, by ushering in a three-quarter view for women's poses rather than the full profile that was standard. This allows viewers to look at the eyes of the woman, which, as Leonardo declared, are "the window of the soul." With *Ginevra* women were no longer presented as passive mannequins but were shown as people with their own thoughts and emotions.[12]

On a deeper level, Leonardo's homosexuality seems to have been manifest in his sense of himself as somewhat different, an outsider who didn't quite fit in. By the time he was thirty, his increasingly successful father was an establishment insider and a legal adviser to the Medici, the top guilds, and churches. He was also an exemplar of traditional masculinity; by then he'd had at least one mistress, three wives, and five children. Leonardo, on the contrary, was essentially an outsider. The birth of his half-siblings reinforced the fact that he was not considered legitimate. As a gay, illegitimate artist twice accused of sodomy, he knew what it was like to be regarded, and to regard yourself, as different. But as with many artists, that turned out to be more an asset than a hindrance.

---

* Another possible exception, in addition to the probable *Leda and the Swan*, may have been a half-nude version of the *Mona Lisa*, which does not survive in his own hand but exists in versions by others in his studio. In his series of anatomical drawings, he drew a woman's anatomy, which has a crude and flawed depiction of female genitalia, looking like a forbidding and dark cave. This was a case of not letting experience be a mistress, or vice versa.

SAINT SEBASTIAN

Around the time of the Saltarelli allegations, Leonardo was working on a devotional portrait of Saint Sebastian, the third-century martyr who was tied to a tree, shot with arrows, and later clubbed to death during the Roman emperor Diocletian's persecution of Christians. According to a list of possessions that Leonardo compiled, he drew eight studies for the work, which he apparently never painted.

The image of Sebastian was considered a protection against the plague, but he was also portrayed with homoerotic undertones by some fifteenth-century Italian artists. Vasari wrote that a Saint Sebastian portrait by Bartolommeo Bandinelli was so erotically charged that "parishioners admitted in the confessional that the beautiful nude prompted unclean thoughts."[13]

The surviving Leonardo drawings of Sebastian fall into that category of being beautiful and somewhat charged. The boyish-looking saint is depicted nude with a hand tied behind him to a tree, his face filled with emotion. In one of the drawings, now in Hamburg, you can see how Leonardo wrestled with the movements and contortions and twists of Sebastian's body, sketching his feet in different positions.[14]

Miraculously, one of his missing Saint Sebastian drawings turned up at the end of 2016, when a retired French doctor brought some old artworks that had been collected by his father to an auction house for appraisal. Thaddée Prate, a director at the auction house, spotted one as a possible Leonardo, an attribution that was confirmed by Carmen Bambach, a curator at New York's Metropolitan Museum of Art. "My eyes jumped out of their sockets," Bambach said. "The attribution is quite incontestable. My heart will always pound when I think about that drawing." The newly discovered drawing shows Sebastian's torso and chest modeled by Leonardo's left-handed hatching, but as in the Hamburg version he was still trying different options for the placement of the saint's legs and feet. "It has so many changes of ideas, so much energy in the way he explores the figure," Bambach said. "It has a furious spontaneity. It's like glancing over his shoulder."[15] In addition to showing us Leonardo energetically exploring ideas on paper, the discovery signifies that, even today, there are things about Leonardo that we can find anew.

ADORATION OF THE MAGI

In the accusations against him, Leonardo was described as still living in Verrocchio's workshop. He was twenty-four, and most former apprentices would have flown their master's nest by then. But Leonardo was not only still living with his teacher but was producing Madonnas so lacking in distinctiveness that it is hard to tell whether they were painted by him or someone else in the workshop.

Perhaps prodded by the Saltarelli affair, Leonardo finally broke away and opened a workshop of his own in 1477. Commercially, it was a failure. During the subsequent five years before he headed off to Milan, he would receive only three known commissions, one of which he never started and the other two he left unfinished. Nevertheless, even two unfinished paintings would be enough to enhance his reputation and influence the practice of art.

Leonardo's first commission, which he received in 1478, was to paint an altarpiece for the chapel in the Palazzo della Signoria. His father served as a notary to the Signoria, Florence's governing council, and was thus in a position to help him get the assignment. Some preparatory drawings Leonardo made indicate that he was planning to paint a scene of the shepherds who came to pay their respects to the infant Jesus in Bethlehem.[16]

There is no evidence that he started on the work. However, some of the sketches were inspirations for a painting that he soon began on a related theme, the *Adoration of the Magi* (fig. 15). It was destined to remain unfinished, but it became the most influential unfinished painting in the history of art and, in the words of Kenneth Clark, "the most revolutionary and anti-classical picture of the fifteenth century."[17] The *Adoration of the Magi* thus encapsulates Leonardo's frustrating genius: a pathbreaking and astonishing display of brilliance that was abandoned once it was conceptualized.

The *Adoration* was commissioned in March 1481, when Leonardo was twenty-nine, by the monastery of San Donato, which was just

Fig. 15. *Adoration of the Magi.*

outside the walls of Florence. Once again his father helped. Piero da Vinci was a notary for the monks and bought his firewood from them. That year he was given two chickens for work he had done, which included negotiating a complex contract for his son to paint the *Adoration* as well as to decorate the face of the monastery's clock.[18]

His father was clearly worried, like the parents of many twenty-somethings over the ages, about his talented child's work habits. The monks were as well. The elaborate contract was designed to force Leonardo, already known for leaving paintings unfinished, to buckle down and produce a completed work. It stipulated that he had to supply from his own pocket "the colors, the gold and all other costs arising." The painting had to be delivered "within thirty months at the most," or Leonardo would be forced to forfeit whatever he had done and get no compensation. Even the payment plan was odd: Leonardo would receive some property near Florence that had been donated to the monastery, have the right to sell it back to the monastery for 300 florins, but would also have to pay a young woman's dowry of 150 florins that had been part of the land bequest.

It was clear within three months that these badly laid plans were going awry. Leonardo was unable to pay the first installment on the dowry, and he thus went into debt to the monastery for it. He also had to borrow money to buy paint. He was paid a bundle of sticks and logs for decorating the monastery's clock, but his account was debited for "one barrel of vermilion wine" that he got on credit.[19] Thus one of history's most creative artists found himself decorating a clock for firewood, borrowing money for paint, and cadging wine.

The scene Leonardo set out to paint in the *Adoration of the Magi* was one of the most popular in Renaissance Florence: the moment when the three wise men, or kings, who have followed a guiding star to Bethlehem, present the newborn Jesus with gifts of gold, frankincense, and myrrh. The Feast of the Epiphany, which commemorates the revelation of the divinity of Jesus Christ and the adoration of him by the Magi, was marked every January in Florence by a day of pageants and reenactments of the procession. The festivities reached a peak in 1468, when Leonardo was a fifteen-year-old apprentice working on such Medici extravaganzas. The entire city became a stage, and the processional included close to seven hundred riders, the young ones each wearing a mask carved with their father's face.[20]

Many others had painted the Adoration scene, most notably Botticelli, who produced at least seven versions. His most famous was done in 1475 for a church near where Leonardo lived. Like most other versions of the scene before Leonardo, Botticelli's were stately affairs, with dignified kings and courtly princes comporting themselves with reverence and decorum.

Botticelli, whose workshop turned out devotional Madonnas at a faster clip than even Verrocchio's, was seven years older than Leonardo and had won far greater patronage from the Medici. He was good at courting such favor. His greatest *Adoration* incorporates portraits of Cosimo de' Medici, his sons Piero and Giovanni, and his grandsons Lorenzo and Giuliano.

Leonardo was often critical of Botticelli, whose version of an Annunciation scene, painted in 1481, was probably what prompted Leonardo to write, "I recently saw an Annunciation in which the angel looked as if she wished to chase Our Lady out of the room with movement of such violence that she might have been a hated enemy; and Our Lady seemed in such despair that she was about to throw herself out of the window."[21] Leonardo later noted, correctly, that Botticelli "makes very dull landscapes" and, lacking a feel for aerial perspective, painted both close and distant trees the same shade of green.[22]

Despite his disdain, Leonardo closely studied Botticelli's versions of the *Adoration of the Magi* and adopted some of his ideas.[23] But then he set out to make one that, unlike Botticelli's, was filled with energy, emotion, agitation, and messiness. His concept, which showed how he was influenced by pageants and public spectacles, was to produce a vortex—that spiral form he loved—centered on the infant Jesus, with a frenzied procession of at least sixty people and animals swirling around and engulfing him. This was supposed to be, after all, a tale of the Epiphany, and Leonardo wanted to convey the full power of the astonishment and awe of the wise men and accompanying throngs as they are seized by the revelation that Jesus is the Christ child, God incarnate.

Leonardo made multiple preparatory drawings, which were sketched with a stylus and then refined with a quill and ink. In them he explores various gestures, body turns, and expressions that convey a wave of emotion meant to ripple through the work. Many of the figures in his preparatory drawings are nude; he had come to believe in Alberti's advice that an artist should build a picture of a human body from the inside out, first conceiving of the skeleton, then the skin, then the clothing.[24]

The most famous preparatory drawing is a sheet that lays out Leonardo's initial conception for the entire picture (fig. 16). On it he plots his perspective lines, following the methods used by Brunelleschi and Alberti. As the scene recedes to the vanishing point, the horizontal lines, which he drew with a ruler, are compressed with incredible precision, far more than necessary for a finished painting.

Combined with this meticulous grid are quick, spectral sketches of twisting and scrambling humans, rearing and frenzied horses, and an ultimate bit of Leonardo fantasia: a resting camel twisting his neck to regard the scene with a wild surmise. Mathematically delineated, precise lines work in concert with frenzied motion and emotion. It is a remarkable combination of optical science and imaginative art, and it shows how he constructed his art on a scaffold of science.[25]

As he completed this preparatory drawing, Leonardo had his assistants assemble a large panel, eight-foot square, out of ten planks of poplar wood. Instead of using the traditional method of pricking

Fig. 16. Preparatory study for the *Adoration of the Magi*.

the preparatory drawing and transferring it to the panel, Leonardo made many modifications to the design and then sketched a new version directly on the panel, which he had treated with a chalky white primer coat. This became his underdrawing.[26]

A technical investigation was done in 2002 for the Uffizi Museum by art analyst Maurizio Seracini, who used high-resolution scans along with ultrasound, ultraviolet, and infrared imaging techniques.[27] The resulting images allow us to appreciate this superb underdrawing and the steps Leonardo took as he created his dramatic scene.

First he put a nail near the center of the panel, right in what became the trunk of the tree, and attached a string so that he could etch perspective lines with a fine stylus onto the white priming coat. Then he drew the architectural background, which included steps leading up to a ruined ancient Roman palace, symbolizing the crumbling of classical paganism. The scientific analysis shows that the underdrawing at one point had sketches of construction workers repairing the ruins in the background.[28] The little scene became a metaphorical expression of the ruined house of David, which Christ would reestablish, and of the rebirth of classical works.

Once he had completed the background, Leonardo began to work on the human figures. By using a fine-tipped black chalk to sketch them lightly, he could revise and retouch them, which allowed him to perfect the gestures until he was satisfied that they conveyed the proper emotions.

We are again lucky that Leonardo described in his notebook the artistic principles that he put into practice, in this case the use of light sketching and revisions to capture mental states. It helps us better appreciate his works as well as the thinking that went into them. "Do not draw the limbs of your figure with hard contours or the same fate will happen to you as has happened to many painters who wished every little stroke of charcoal to be definite," he advised. By drawing fixed lines, these artists create figures that "do not move their limbs in a manner that reflects the motions of their mind." A good painter, he continued, should "decide broadly upon the position of the limbs and attend first to the movement appropriate to the mental attitudes of the creatures in the narrative."[29]

When he was satisfied with his chalk sketches, Leonardo inked them with a thin brush and then filled in the proper shadows with a light blue wash. This was a departure from the brown wash he and other painters traditionally used. Through his study of optics, he knew that a dusty and misty atmosphere gave a blue tint to shadows. Once he had finished this underdrawing on the panel, he covered it with a thin layer of white primer so that it was faintly visible. Then he started, very slowly, to paint.

In the center of his composition for the *Adoration of the Magi*, Leonardo placed the Virgin Mary with a squirming infant Jesus on her lap. His hand reaches out, and from it the narrative swirls in a clockwise spiral. As the viewer's eye moves around this frenzied vortex, the painting becomes not merely a moment but a dramatic narrative. Jesus is accepting a gift from one of the kings, while another of the kings, having already given his gift, is bowing his head to the ground in reverence.

Leonardo rarely featured Mary's husband, Joseph, in his paintings, including those of the Holy Family, and it is not immediately clear in the *Adoration* which if any figure is supposed to be him. But Joseph is in one of Leonardo's preparatory drawings, and it seems to me that he is the similar bald and bearded man behind Mary's shoulder holding the lid and peering into the container of the first gift.[30]

Almost all the characters in the picture, the infant Jesus included, are engaged in motions that are—as they would be in *The Last Supper*—connected to emotions: handing a gift, opening one, bowing to the ground, slapping a forehead in amazement, pointing upward. Leaning on a rock are some younger travelers engaged in animated conversation, while just in front of them an awed onlooker raises his palm to the heavens. We are witnessing the physical and mental response, including amazement and reverence and curiosity, to an epiphany. Only the Virgin seems still, the calm in the vortex.

Portraying the swirl of characters was a daunting task, perhaps too much so. Each had to have a unique pose and set of emotions. As Leonardo later wrote in his notebook, "Do not repeat the same movements in the same figure, be it limbs, hands or fingers, nor should the same pose be repeated in one narrative painting."[31] Among the characters he originally considered were a group of fighters on horseback near the top of the picture. They appear in the preparatory sketch and the underdrawing, where they are modeled with careful shadowing, but Leonardo had trouble integrating them into the swirl. They are partly abandoned in the unfinished painting, though they foreshadow the horses he would later use in his (also unfinished) *Battle of Anghiari*.

The result is a whirlwind of drama and emotion. Not only did Leonardo render each of the reactions of those first beholding the Christ child, but he turned the Epiphany into a swirl in which each character is swept by the others' emotions, and then so is the viewer.

ABANDONED

Leonardo went on to paint the sky in the *Adoration of the Magi* and some highlights of the human figures and parts of the architectural ruins. Then he stopped.

Why? One possible reason is that the task he undertook became overwhelming for a perfectionist. As Vasari explained about Leonardo's unfinished works, he was stymied because his conceptions were "so subtle and so marvelous" that they were impossible to execute faultlessly. "It seemed to him that the hand was not able to attain to the perfection of art in carrying out the things which he imagined." According to Lomazzo, the other early biographer, "he never finished any of the works he began because, so sublime was his idea of art, he saw faults even in the things that to others seemed miracles."[32]

Perfecting the *Adoration of the Magi* must have been especially daunting. There were originally more than sixty characters in his underdrawing. As he went along, he reduced this number by turning some groups of fighters or builders in the background into fewer large-scale characters, but that still left more than thirty to be rendered. He was intent on making sure each one reacted emotionally to the others so that the painting would feel like a coherent narrative and not a random assortment of isolated characters.

Even more complex were the lighting challenges, made all the more difficult by his obsession with optics. On the bottom of a notebook page from around 1480 that shows the mechanisms of the crane that Brunelleschi used to erect Florence's cathedral dome, Leonardo sketched a diagram of how light rays hit the surface of a human eye and are focused inside the eyeball.[33] In painting the *Adoration of the Magi*, he wanted to convey the power of the light that shone down from heaven with the Epiphany and how each rebound of reflected light affected the coloration and gradation of each shadow. "He must have faltered at the thought of how to balance the reflections that bounce from one figure to another and to control the myriad variables of light, shade, and emotions for such a multitude," according to the art historian Francesca Fiorani. "Unlike any other artist, he could not ignore an optical problem."[34]

It was an unnerving set of iterative tasks. All thirty characters had to reflect light and project shade that would influence, and be influenced by, the light and shadows of those around them. They also had to initiate and reflect emotions, which in turn affected, and were affected by, the emotions emanating from those around them.

There was another reason, one even more fundamental, that Leonardo did not complete the painting: he preferred the conception to the execution. As his father and others knew when they drew up the strict contract for his commission, Leonardo at twenty-nine was more easily distracted by the future than he was focused on the present. He was a genius undisciplined by diligence.

He seems to have illustrated this personal trait, consciously or not, in an apparent self-portrait he drew on the far right side of the painting (figs. 2 and 15). A boyish character, pointing toward Jesus but looking away, is in the location often used by Renaissance artists to insert a likeness of themselves. (Botticelli portrays himself in the same location in his *Adoration* of 1475.) The boy's nose and curls and other attributes match the description and other presumed depictions that exist of Leonardo.[35]

This boy is what Alberti referred to as "the commentator," the person who is in a picture but out of it, who is not part of the action but instead connects to the world beyond the frame. His body is facing Jesus, his arm points that way, and his right foot is angled as if he had been moving in that direction. But his head is turned sharply to the left, looking toward something else, as if he had become distracted. He has paused before walking into the action. His eyes are looking far away. He is part of the scene but detached from it, an observer and commentator who is immersed but marginalized. He is, like Leonardo, of this world but apart from it.

Seven months after Leonardo was commissioned to create the painting, his payments ended. He had stopped work. When he departed Florence for Milan shortly thereafter, he left the unfinished painting with his friend Giovanni de' Benci, the brother of Ginevra.

The monks of San Donato subsequently commissioned Botticelli's protégé Filippino Lippi to paint a substitute. The young Lippi had learned from Botticelli the fine art of flattery; as in Botticelli's earlier version, Lippi's *Adoration of the Magi* features likenesses of many members of the Medici family. Leonardo, who lacked that instinct to cater to patrons when painting, had paid no such homage to the Medici in his unfinished *Adoration* or in any of his other works. That was likely one reason Botticelli, Filippino Lippi, and his father, Filippo Lippi, all enjoyed the generous Medici patronage that eluded Leonardo.

In some ways, Filippino Lippi tried to follow Leonardo's original design in the *Adoration* he painted as a substitute. The kings kneel before the Holy Family with their gifts, while a cavalcade of onlookers swirl around. Lippi even includes a portrait of a commentator character on the far right, with the exact pose Leonardo had used. But Lippi's commentator is a calm, older sage, not a dreamy and distracted young man. And even though Lippi tried to give his characters some interesting gestures, there is little of the excitement, energy, passions, or movements of the soul that Leonardo had envisaged.

SAINT JEROME IN THE WILDERNESS

Leonardo's dedication to connecting movements of the body with movements of the soul was manifest in the other great painting he probably began around that time,[36] *Saint Jerome in the Wilderness* (fig. 17). The unfinished work shows Saint Jerome, a fourth-century scholar who translated the Bible into Latin, during his retreat as a hermit in the desert. With an outstretched and twisted arm, he holds a rock that he will beat to his chest in penance; at his feet is the lion that became his companion after he pulled a thorn from its paw. The saint is haggard and emaciated, exuding shame as he seems to implore forgiveness, yet his eyes show his inner strength. The background is filled with Leonardo's signature designs, including a rocky outcropping and a misty landscape.

All of Leonardo's paintings are psychological, and all give vent to his desire to portray emotions, but none more intensely than *Saint Jerome*. The saint's entire body, through its twists and uncomfortable kneeling, conveys passion. The painting also represents Leonardo's first anatomical drawing and—as he fiddled with and revised it over the years—shows the intimate connection between his anatomical and artistic endeavors. He became typically obsessive as he carried forward Alberti's injunction that artists should conceive a body from the inside out. Leonardo wrote, "It is necessary for the painter, in order to be good at arranging the parts of the body in attitudes and gestures which can be represented in the nude, to know the anatomy of the sinews, bones and muscles and tendons."[37]

There is one puzzling detail about the anatomy in *Saint Jerome*, which when unpacked helps us better understand Leonardo's art. He began work on the painting around 1480, yet it seems to accurately reflect the anatomical knowledge that he gleaned later, including from dissections he made in 1510. Most notable is the neck. In Leonardo's early anatomical works and in a drawing he made of Judas around 1495 in preparation for *The Last Supper* (fig. 18), he mistakenly showed the sternocleidomastoid, which goes from the collarbone up the side of the neck, as a single muscle, when in fact it is a pair of muscles. But in his 1510 drawings based on human dissections, which are in the Royal Collection at Windsor, he would get it right (fig. 19).[38] It is somewhat puzzling that his depiction of Saint Jerome, with his neck correctly showing two muscles, includes an anatomical detail that he did not know in the 1480s and discovered only in 1510.[39]

Fig. 17. *Saint Jerome in the Wilderness.*

Fig. 18. Drawing in 1495 with neck muscle incorrect.

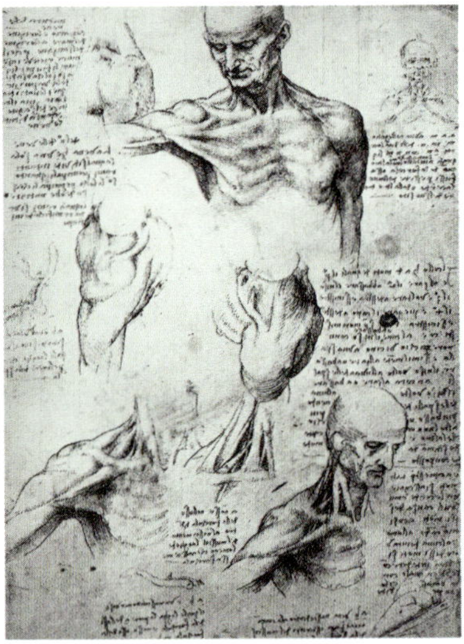

Fig. 19. Anatomy drawing c. 1510 with neck muscle correct.

The curator of drawings at Windsor, Martin Clayton, came up with the most convincing explanation. He posited that the painting was done in two phases, the first around 1480 and the other following the dissection studies he made in 1510. Clayton's theory was supported by infrared analysis, which showed that the dual neck muscles were not part of the original underdrawing and that they were painted with a technique different from the other parts. "Significant parts of the modeling of the *Saint Jerome* were added twenty years after his first outlining of the figure," said Clayton, "and that modeling incorporates the anatomical discoveries that Leonardo made during his dissections of the winter of 1510."[40]

The significance of this goes beyond helping us understand the anatomical aspects of the *Saint Jerome*. It shows that Leonardo's record of unreliability was not simply because he decided to give up on certain paintings. He wanted to perfect them, so he kept hold of many of them for years, making refinements.

Even some of his commissions that were completed, or almost so—*Ginevra de' Benci* and the *Mona Lisa*, for example—were never delivered to clients. Leonardo clung to his favorite works, carried them with him when he moved, and returned to them when he had new ideas. He certainly did that with the *Saint Jerome*, and he may have planned to do the same with the *Adoration of the Magi*, which he entrusted to Ginevra's brother for safekeeping but never sold or gave away. He did not like to let go. That is why he would die with some of his masterpieces still near his bedside. As frustrating as it is to us today, there was a poignant and inspiring aspect to Leonardo's unwillingness to declare a painting done and relinquish it: he knew that there was always more he might learn, new techniques he might master, and further inspirations that might strike him. And he was right.

MOTIONS OF THE MIND

Even unfinished, the *Adoration of the Magi* and *Saint Jerome* show that Leonardo was pioneering a new style that treated narrative paintings and even portraits as psychological expositions. This approach to art was partly informed by his love of pageants, theatrical productions, and court amusements; he knew how actors feign sentiments, and he recognized the tells on the lips and in the eyes of audience members that indicate their reactions. It probably also helped that the Italians, then as now, were expressive in their gestures, which Leonardo loved to capture in his notebooks.

He sought to portray not only *moti corporali*, the motions of the body, but also how they related to what he called "atti e moti mentali," the attitudes and motions of the mind.[41] More important, he was a master at connecting the two. This is most noticeable in his action-packed and gesture-filled narrative works, such as the *Adoration* and *The Last Supper*. But it is also the genius behind his most serene portraits, most notably the *Mona Lisa*.

Portraying the "motions of the mind" was not a new concept. Pliny the Elder complimented the fourth-century BC painter Aristides of Thebes by saying he was "the first to express the mentality, sentiments, character, and passions of a subject."[42] Alberti, in *On Painting*, emphasized the importance of the idea in a clear and crisp sentence: "Movements of the soul are made known by movements of the body."[43]

Leonardo was deeply influenced by Alberti's book, and he repeatedly echoed that injunction in his own notebooks. "The good painter has to paint two principal things, man and the intention of his mind," he wrote. "The first is easy and the second is difficult, because the latter has to be represented through gestures and movements of the limbs."[44] He expanded on this concept in a long passage in his notes for his planned treatise on painting: "The movement which is depicted must be appropriate to the mental state of the figure. The motions and postures of figures should display the true mental state of the originator of these motions, in such a way they can mean nothing else. Movements should announce the motions of the mind."[45]

Leonardo's dedication to portraying the outward manifestations of inner emotions would end up driving not only his art but some of his anatomical studies. He needed to know which nerves emanated from the brain and which from the spinal cord, which muscles they activated, and which facial movements were connected to others. He would even try, when dissecting the brain, to figure out the precise location where the connections were made between sensory perceptions, emotions, and motions. By the end of his career, his pursuit of how the brain and nerves turned emotions into motions became almost obsessive. It was enough to make the *Mona Lisa* smile.

DESPAIR

Leonardo's portrayal of emotions may have been enhanced by the fact that he was wrestling with his own inner turmoil. His inability to finish the *Adoration of the Magi* and *Saint Jerome* may have been caused by, and in turn contributed to, melancholy or depression. His notebooks from around 1480 are filled with expressions of gloom, even anguish. On a page that includes a drawing of a water clock and sundial, he lets loose a lament that touches on the sadness of unfinished work: "We do not lack devices for measuring these miserable days of ours, in which it should be our pleasure that they be not frittered away without leaving behind any memory of ourselves in the mind of men."[46] He began scribbling the same phrase over and over again, every time he needed to try a new pen nib or to fritter away a moment: "Tell me if anything was ever done . . . Tell me . . . Tell me."[47]

And at one point he jotted a cry of anguish: "While I thought that I was learning how to live, I have been learning how to die."[48]

Also in his notebooks from around this time are quotes from others that Leonardo found worth recording. One is from a friend who wrote a very personal poem addressed to him. "Leonardo, why so troubled?" the friend writes.[49] On another page is a quote from someone named Johannes: "There is no perfect gift without great suffering. Our glories and our triumphs pass away."[50] On the same sheet is a transcription from Dante's *Inferno*:

> *"Put off this sloth," the master said, "for shame!*
> *Sitting on feather-pillows, lying reclined*
> *Beneath the blanket is no way to fame—*
> *Fame, without which man's life wastes out of mind,*
> *Leaving on earth no more memorial*
> *Than foam in water or smoke upon the wind."*[51]

While he was despairing about, as he saw it, sitting on feather pillows, lying beneath the blanket, and leaving no legacy more lasting than smoke upon the wind, his rivals were enjoying great success. Botticelli, who was definitely not suffering from an inability to churn out finished work, had become the favored painter of the Medici; he was commissioned by them to do two major works, *Spring* and *Pallas and the Centaur*. In 1478 Botticelli painted a damning public depiction of the conspirators who had assassinated Giuliano de' Medici and wounded his brother Lorenzo. When the final plotter was captured a year later, Leonardo did a careful sketch of his hanging and jotted details in his notebook, as if hoping to do a companion painting (fig. 20). But the Medici gave the commission to someone else. Botticelli was again among the chosen in 1481, when Pope Sixtus IV summoned prominent Florentine and other artists to come to Rome to fresco the walls of the Sistine Chapel; Leonardo was not selected.

As he approached his thirtieth birthday, Leonardo had established his genius but had remarkably little to show for it publicly. His only known artistic accomplishments were some brilliant but peripheral contributions to two Verrocchio paintings, a couple of devotional Madonnas that were hard to distinguish from others being produced in the workshop, a portrait of a young woman that he had not delivered, and two unfinished would-be masterpieces.

"When a man has learned in Florence as much as he can, if he wishes to do more than live from day to day like an animal, and instead desires to become rich, he must take his departure from that place," Vasari wrote. "For Florence treats her craftsmen as time treats its own works, which, when perfected, it destroys and consumes little by little."[52] It was time for Leonardo to move on. The fact that he was feeling consumed and was in a fragile mental state, filled with fantasies and fears, was reflected in his willingness to leave Florence and in a letter he would write to the person he hoped would be his next patron.

Fig. 20. The hanging of Bernardo Baroncelli.

Chapter 4

Milan

CULTURAL DIPLOMAT

In 1482, the year he turned thirty, Leonardo da Vinci left Florence for Milan, where he would end up spending the next seventeen years. Traveling with him was his companion Atalante Migliorotti, now fifteen, the aspiring musician who learned from Leonardo how to play the lyre and became one of the many young men who floated in and out of his retinue over the years.[1] Leonardo estimated in his notebook that the trip was 180 miles long, which was quite accurate; he had devised a type of odometer that measured distance by counting the turns of a vehicle wheel, and he may have experimented with one on the way. It would have taken him and his companions about a week.

With him he carried a *lira da braccio* (lyre for the arm), roughly akin to a fiddle or violin. "He was sent by Lorenzo the Magnificent, along with Atalante Migliorotti, to the Duke of Milan to present him a lyre, since he was unique in playing this instrument," the Anonimo Gaddiano reports. It was made partly of silver, and Leonardo had crafted it in the shape of a horse's skull.

The lyre and Leonardo's services were a diplomatic gift. Lorenzo de' Medici, eager to navigate the swirling rivalries and alliances among the Italian city-states, saw Florence's artistic culture as a source of influence. Botticelli and some of his other favorite artists went to Rome to please the pope, Verrocchio and others to Venice.

Leonardo and Atalante were probably part of a February 1482 diplomatic delegation headed by Bernardo Rucellai, a wealthy banker, arts patron, and philosophy enthusiast who was married to Lorenzo's older sister and had just been made Florence's ambassador to Milan.[2] In his writings, Rucellai introduced the term *balance of power* to describe the continuous conflicts and shifting alliances involving Florence, Milan, other Italian city-states, plus a pride of popes, French kings, and Holy Roman emperors. The competition among the various rulers was not only military but cultural, and Leonardo sought to be useful on both fronts.

Packing almost all of his belongings, Leonardo embarked for Milan with the thought that he might move there indefinitely. The list he made of his possessions sometime after his arrival in Milan seems to encompass most of his work that could be transported. In addition to the drawing of Atalante with his face raised, there were sketches of "many flowers copied from nature . . . some Saint Jeromes . . . designs of furnaces . . . a head of Christ done in pen . . . eight Saint Sebastians . . . many compositions of angels . . . a head in profile with beautiful hair . . . gadgets for ships . . . gadgets for water . . . many necks of old women and heads of old men . . . many complete nudes . . . a Madonna finished . . . another almost finished that is in profile . . . the head of an old man with an enormous chin . . . a narrative of the Passion made in relief" and much more.[3] The inclusion on the list of designs for furnaces and gadgets for ships and for water shows that he was already engaged with engineering as well as art.

Milan, with 125,000 citizens, was three times the size of Florence. More important for Leonardo, it had a ruling court. The Medici in Florence were generous supporters of the arts, but they were bankers who operated behind the scenes. Milan was different. For two hundred years, it had been not a merchant republic but a city-state ruled by militaristic strongmen who crowned themselves hereditary dukes, first the heads of the Visconti family and then the Sforza family. Because their ambitions were grand but their claims to their titles tenuous, their castles were filled with courtiers, artists, performers, musicians, huntmasters, statecrafters, animal trainers, engineers, and any other helpers or ornaments who could burnish their prestige and legitimacy. In other words, Milan's castle provided a perfect environment for Leonardo, who had a fondness for strong leaders, loved the diversity of talent they attracted, and aspired to be on a comfortable retainer.

When Leonardo arrived, Milan was ruled by Ludovico Sforza, who was also thirty. A dark-skinned and burly man nicknamed "Il Moro" (the Moor), he was not actually the Duke of Milan yet, though he exercised the authority and would soon grab the title. His father, Francesco Sforza, one of seven illegitimate sons of a military mercenary, had seized power and made himself duke in 1450, after the Visconti dynasty dissolved. Upon his death, Ludovico's older brother became duke, but he was soon assassinated, leaving the title to his seven-year-old son. Ludovico eased aside the boy's mother as regent, thus effectively taking control of Milan in 1479. He set about beguiling and bullying his hapless nephew, usurping his powers, executing his supporters, and probably poisoning him. He officially invested himself the Duke of Milan in 1494.

Ruthless in a pragmatic way, Ludovico cloaked his calculated cruelty with pretenses of courtesy, culture, and civility. Tutored by the distinguished Renaissance humanist Francesco Filelfo in painting and writing, he sought to legitimize his power and prestige, along with that of Milan, by attracting great scholars and artists to the Sforza court. He had long dreamed of building a massive equestrian monument to his father, partly as a way to enshrine the family's power.

Unlike Florence, Milan was not well-stocked with master artists. That made it more fertile territory for Leonardo. Because he was an aspiring polymath, he also enjoyed that Milan was filled with scholars and intellectuals in a wide variety of fields, partly due to the esteemed university in nearby Pavia, which was officially founded in 1361 but had roots stretching back to 825. It boasted some of Europe's best lawyers, philosophers, medical researchers, and mathematicians.

Ludovico spent profligately on his personal desires: 140,000 ducats to refurbish the rooms of his palace and 16,000 ducats for his hunting hawks, hounds, and horses.* He was stingier with the intellectual and entertainment retainers in his court: his astrologer had an annual stipend of 290 ducats, high-level government officials got 150 ducats, and the artist-architect Donato Bramante, who would become Leonardo's friend, complained of getting only 62 ducats.[4]

THE JOB APPLICATION

It was probably soon after his arrival in Milan that Leonardo drafted the letter to Ludovico described at the beginning of this book. Some historians have supposed that he wrote the letter from Florence, but this seems unlikely. He mentioned the park adjoining Ludovico's castle and the proposed equestrian monument to his father, indications that he had already spent time in Milan and then sent a letter.[5]

Leonardo did not, of course, write it in his usual mirror script. The copy that survives in his notebooks is a draft, marked up with a few changes, that was composed in the conventional left-to-right manner by a scribe or one of his assistants with good penmanship.[6] It reads:

> Most illustrious Lord,
>
> Having now sufficiently studied the inventions of all those who proclaim themselves skilled contrivers of instruments of war, and having found that these instruments are no different than those in common use, I shall be bold enough to offer, with all due respect to the others, my own secrets to your Excellency and to demonstrate them at your convenience.
>
> 1) I have designed extremely light and strong bridges, adapted to be easily carried, and with them you may pursue and at any time flee from the enemy; and others, indestructible by fire and battle, easy to lift and place. Also methods of burning and destroying those of the enemy.
>
> 2) I know how, during a siege, to take the water out of the trenches, and make an infinite variety of bridges, covered ways, ladders, and other machines suitable to such expeditions.

---

* About $19 million worth of gold in 2017.

3) If a place under siege cannot be reduced by bombardment, because of the height of its banks or the strength of its position, I have methods for destroying any fortress even if it is founded upon solid rock.

4) I have kinds of cannons, convenient and easy to carry, that can fling small stones almost resembling a hailstorm; and the smoke of these will cause great terror to the enemy, to his great detriment and confusion.

9) [Leonardo moved up this item in the draft.] And when the fight is at sea, I have many kinds of efficient machines for offense and defense, and vessels that will resist the attack of the largest guns, and powder and fumes.

5) I have ways of making, without noise, underground tunnels and secret winding passages to arrive at a desired point, even if it is necessary to pass underneath trenches or a river.

6) I will make unassailable armored chariots that can penetrate the ranks of the enemy with their artillery, and there is no body of soldiers so great that it could withstand them. And behind these, infantry could follow quite unhurt.

7) In case of need I will make cannons and artillery of beautiful and useful design that are different from those in common use.

8) Where bombardment will not work, I can devise catapults, mangonels, caltrops and other effective machines not in common use.

10) In times of peace I can give perfect satisfaction and be the equal of any other in architecture and the composition of buildings public and private; and in guiding water from one place to another.

Also, I can execute sculpture in marble, bronze and clay. Likewise in painting, I can do everything possible, as well as any other man, whosoever he may be.

Moreover, work could be undertaken on the bronze horse, which will be to the immortal glory and eternal honor of His Lordship, your father, and of the illustrious house of Sforza. And if any of the above-mentioned things seem impossible or impracticable to anyone, I am most readily disposed to demonstrate

> them in your park or in whatsoever place shall please Your Excellency.

Leonardo mentioned none of his paintings. Nor did he refer to the talent that ostensibly caused him to be sent to Milan: an ability to design and play musical instruments. What he mainly pitched was a pretense of military engineering expertise. Partly this was to appeal to Ludovico, whose Sforza dynasty had taken power by force and was faced with the constant threat of a local revolt or French invasion. In addition, Leonardo cast himself as an engineer because he was going through one of his regular bouts of being bored or blocked by the prospect of picking up a brush. As his mood swung between melancholy and exultation, he fantasized and boasted about being an accomplished weapons designer.

These boasts were aspirational. He had never been to a battle nor actually built any of the weapons he described. All he had produced thus far were some elegant sketches of concepts for weapons, many of them more fanciful than practical.

His letter to Ludovico is thus best regarded not as a reliable catalogue of his actual engineering accomplishments but instead as a glimpse into his hopes and ambitions. Nevertheless, his boasts were not completely hollow. Had they been, he would have been easily exposed in a city where weapon design was a deadly serious endeavor. After settling into Milan, he would in fact begin to pursue military engineering earnestly and come up with some innovative concepts for machines, even as he continued to dance around the line between ingenuity and fantasy.[7]

MILITARY ENGINEER

While still living in Florence, Leonardo had sketched a few proposals for clever military devices. One was a mechanism for knocking down the ladders of enemy invaders trying to scale a castle wall (fig. 21).[8] The defenders inside would pull large levers connected to rods that poked through holes in the wall. His drawing includes enlarged details showing how the rods would be attached to the levers plus lively sketches of four soldiers pulling ropes and keeping an eye on the enemy. A related idea was for a propeller-like device that would slash away at those who made it to the top of the castle wall. Gears and shafts turned blades, like those of a helicopter, that would swing just above the wall, chopping down unfortunate soldiers trying to climb over. For when it was time to be on the offense, he designed a rolling armored siege machine that placed a covered bridge over the fortified walls of a castle.[9]

The spread of printing presses helped Leonardo pursue additional military ideas after he arrived in Milan. He borrowed some of his concepts from a book by the thirteenth-century scientist Roger Bacon that had a list of ingenious weapons, including "carts and wagons that could move without animal power; devices used to walk on water and

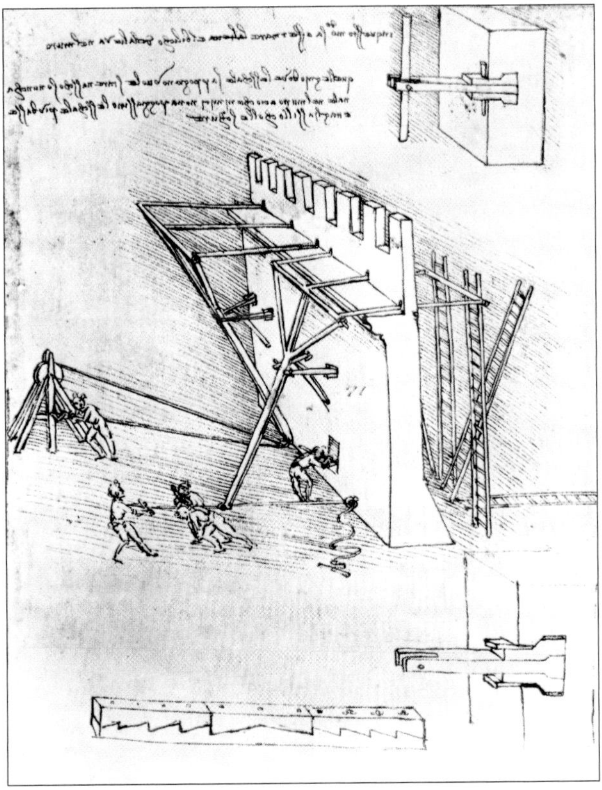

Fig. 21. Machine for pushing away ladders.

to move underneath the water, and contrivances capable of putting man in flight, having a person placed in the center of a mechanical device with artificial wings."[10] Leonardo embellished on all of these ideas. He also studied Roberto Valturio's *On the Military Arts*, a treatise filled with woodcuts of ingenious weapons. It was published in Latin in 1472 and in Italian in 1483, the year after Leonardo arrived in Milan. He bought both versions, annotated them, and struggled to improve his rudimentary Latin by making lists of the terms in the original book alongside their Italian translations.

Valturio's book became a springboard for Leonardo's creativity. For example, Valturio included a drawing of a cart with rotating scythes that was rather tame; each wheel of the clunky cart had only one small, unintimidating blade attached.[11] With his fevered imagination, Leonardo kicked the concept up multiple notches for a fearsome scythed chariot that became one of his most famous—and disconcerting—pieces of military engineering.[12]

Leonardo's drawings of this scythed chariot, which he made soon after he moved to Milan, feature truly frightening whirling blades jutting out from the wheels. It also has a four-bladed spinning shaft that can project in the front or be dragged behind the chariot. He meticulously drew the connection of the gears and cogs to the shafts and wheels, creating artwork so beautiful as to be jarring. The galloping horses and the riders with their billowing capes are dazzling studies of motion, while his hatching strokes create shade and modeling worthy of a museum piece.

One sheet of scythed chariot drawings is especially vivid (fig. 22).[13] On the near side of the moving chariot two bodies lie on the ground, their legs sliced off and the pieces scattered. On the far side he depicts two soldiers just at the moment they are being sliced in half. Here is our gentle and beloved Leonardo, who became a vegetarian because of his fondness for all creatures, wallowing in horrifying depictions of death. It is, perhaps, yet another glimpse of his inner turmoil. Within his dark cave was a demon imagination.

Another of his imagined but unbuilt weapons, which likewise blurs the border between practicality and fantasy, is a giant crossbow (fig. 23) that he drew in Milan around 1485.[14] The proposed machine is huge:

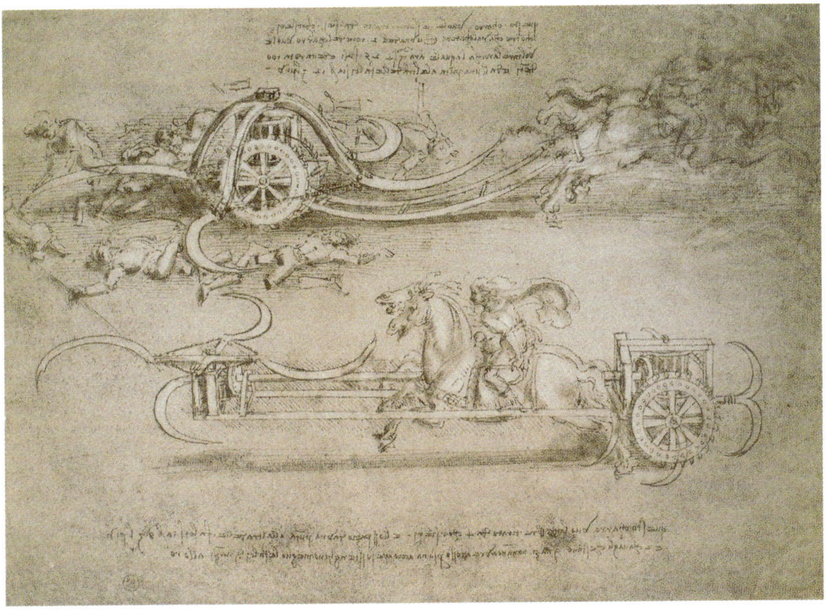

Fig. 22. Scythed chariot.

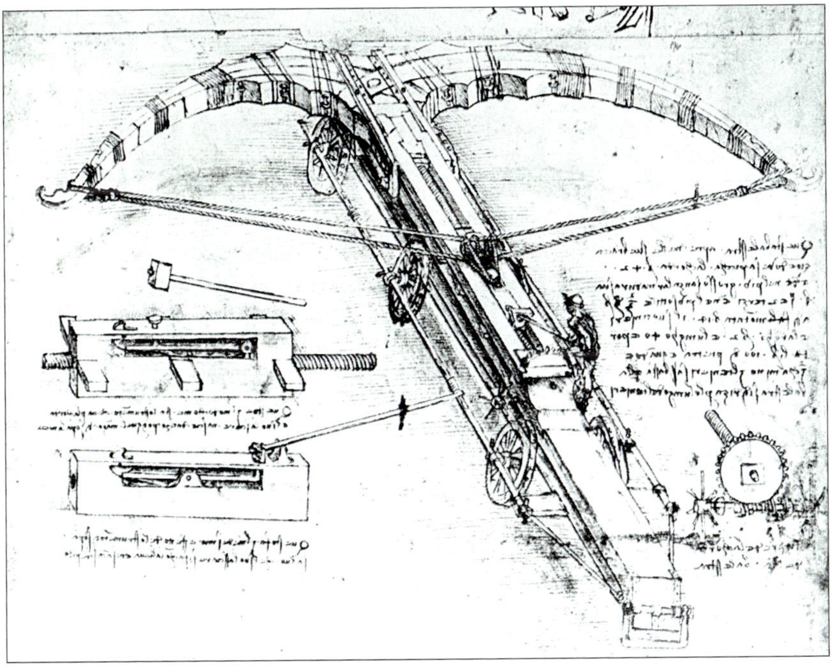

Fig. 23. Giant crossbow.

its armature is eighty feet across, and so is the carriage that would roll it onto the battlefield. To put it in perspective, he shows the weapon dwarfing a soldier who is preparing to unleash the trigger.

Leonardo was a pioneer in propounding laws of proportion: how one quantity, such as force, rises in proportion to another, such as the length of a lever. A super-sized crossbow should, he correctly surmised, be able to hurl projectiles that were bigger or went farther. He tried to figure out the correlation between the distance the bowstring was pulled and the force it exerted on the projectile. At first he thought that a bowstring pulled back twice as far would exert twice the force. But he realized that rate was thrown off by the bending of the bow as the string was pulled. After various calculations, he finally concluded that the force is proportional to the angle of the string at the point where it is pulled back. Pull the string back hard, and it will make (say) a 90-degree angle; pull back even harder, and perhaps you can get the angle down to 45 degrees. A 45-degree angle, he theorized, would deliver twice the force of 90 degrees. That doesn't turn out to be exactly right; Leonardo did not know trigonometry and thus couldn't refine the theory. But in concept he was close. He was learning to use geometric shapes as analogues for nature's forces.

In Leonardo's design, the bow was to be made with interlocking layers of wood, an early example of lamination. That would make it flexible, springy, and less likely to crack. Its string was pulled back by ropes attached to a large gear-and-screw mechanism, which he detailed in a side drawing. Cocked in such a fashion, he wrote, the device should be able to fling "one hundred pounds of stones." Gunpowder was in common use by then, which would seem to make a mechanical crossbow obsolete. However, if the crossbow had worked, it could have been cheaper, easier, and certainly quieter than cannons using gunpowder.

As with the scythed chariot, a question arises: How serious was Leonardo? Was he merely being clever on paper and trying to impress Ludovico? Was the giant crossbow another example of his ingenuity blurring into fantasy? I believe his proposal was serious. He made more than thirty preparatory drawings, and he detailed with precision the gears, worm screws, shafts, triggers, and other mechanisms. Nevertheless, the crossbow should be classified as a work of imagination rather than invention. It was never constructed by Ludovico Sforza. When it was finally built for a television special in 2002, the contemporary engineers were unable to get it to work. During his career, Leonardo would be known for paintings, monuments, and inventions that he conceived but never brought to fruition. The giant crossbow falls into that category.[15]

That was also true, it turned out, for most of the military devices he conceived and drew during the 1480s. "I will make unassailable armored chariots," he promised in his letter to Ludovico. He did in fact design one, at least on paper. His drawing of an armored tank, which looks like a cross between a turtle and a flying saucer, shows metal plates slanted on an angle that would cause it to deflect enemy projectiles. Inside would be eight men, some of them turning cranks to cause the tank to inch ahead, the others firing cannons that project out in all directions. There is one design flaw: a careful look at the crank and gears shows that they would turn the front wheels and the back wheels in opposite directions. Did he draw it that way intentionally so that it could not be easily constructed without his modification? Perhaps. But the issue was moot; the machine was never built.

He had also promised Ludovico, "I will make cannons and artillery of beautiful and useful design that are different from those in common use." One such attempt was a steam cannon, or *architronito*, an idea that Leonardo attributed to Archimedes and that was also in Valturio's book. The concept was that the breach of a cannon would be heated in burning coals until it was super-hot, then a small amount of water would be injected just behind the cannon ball. If the ball was held in place for a second or so, enough steam pressure would build up to fire it a few hundred yards when released.[16] Another proposal he drew was for a machine with many cannons, one with racks of eleven cannons each. While one set of cannons was cooling off and being reloaded, the other sets could be firing. It was the precursor to the machine gun.[17]

Only one of Leonardo's military conceptions is known to have made it off the pages of his notebooks and onto the battlefield, and he arguably deserves priority as its inventor. The wheellock, or wheel lock, which he devised in the 1490s, was a way to create a spark for igniting the gunpowder in a musket or similar hand-carried weapon. When the trigger was pulled, a metal wheel was set spinning by a spring. As it scraped against a stone, it sparked enough heat to ignite the gunpowder. Leonardo used components of some of his previous devices, which included spring-powered wheels. One of the assistants who lived in Leonardo's household at the time was a technician and locksmith named Giulio Tedesco, known as Jules the German, who returned to Germany around 1499 and spread Leonardo's idea there. The wheellock came into use in Italy and Germany around that time and proved to be influential in facilitating both warfare and the personal use of guns.[18]

Leonardo's wondrously imaginative giant crossbows and turtle-like tanks show his ability to let fantasy drive invention. But he had not lashed his imagination to practicality. None of his big machines would be deployed in battle by Ludovico Sforza, who did not face a serious confrontation until the French invaded Milan in 1499, at which time he fled the city. As it turned out, Leonardo would not be involved in military activity until 1502, when he went to work for a more difficult and tyrannical strongman, Cesare Borgia.[19]

The only military project Leonardo actually delivered to Ludovico was a survey of the castle's defenses. He expressed approval of the thickness of the walls, but he warned that the small apertures were directly connected to secret passageways in the castle, which could permit attackers to swarm the castle if breached. While at it, he also noted the proper method for preparing the bath for Ludovico's young new wife: "four parts of cold water to three parts of hot water."[20]

THE IDEAL CITY

Near the end of his job application to Ludovico Sforza, Leonardo touted himself as someone who could "be the equal of any other in architecture and the composition of buildings." But for his first few years in Milan, he had trouble getting any such commissions. So for the time being, he pursued his architectural interests the way he did his military interests: mainly on paper as imaginative visions never to be implemented.

The best example was his set of plans for a utopian city, which was a favorite subject for Italian Renaissance artists and architects. Milan had been ravaged in the early 1480s by three years of the bubonic plague, which killed close to one-third of its inhabitants. With his scientific instincts, Leonardo realized that the plague was spread by unsanitary conditions and that the health of the citizens was related to the health of their city.

He did not focus on marginal improvements in engineering and design. Instead, on multiple pages composed in 1487, he proposed a radical concept, one that combined his artistic sensibilities with his visions as an urban engineer: the creation of entirely new "ideal cities" planned for health and beauty. The population of Milan would be relocated to ten new towns, designed and built from scratch along the river, in order to "disperse its great congregation of people which are packed like goats one behind the other, filling every place with fetid smells and sowing seeds of pestilence and death."[21]

He applied the classic analogy between the microcosm of the human body and the macrocosm of the earth: cities are organisms that breathe and have fluids that circulate and waste that needs to move. He had recently begun studying blood and fluid circulation in the body. Thinking by analogy, he considered what would be the best circulation systems for urban needs, ranging from commerce to waste removal.

The glory of Milan was that it had an ample water supply and a long tradition of channeling the flow of mountain streams and melting snows. Leonardo's idea was to combine the streets and canals into a unified circulation system. The utopian city he envisioned would have two levels: an upper level designed for beauty and pedestrian life, and a level hidden below for canals, commerce, sanitation, and sewage.

"Let only that which is good looking be seen on the upper level of the city," he decreed. The wide streets and arcaded walkways on this level would be reserved for pedestrians and be flanked by beautiful homes and gardens. Unlike the cramped streets of Milan, which Leonardo realized led to the spread of disease, the boulevards in the new town would be at least as wide as the height of the houses. To keep these boulevards clean, they would be sloped to the middle to allow rainwater to drain through central slits into a sewer circulation system below. These were not merely general suggestions; Leonardo got very specific. "Each road must be 20 braccia wide and have ½ braccio slope from the sides towards the middle," he wrote, "and in the middle let there be at every braccio an opening, one braccio long and one finger wide, where the rain water may run off into hollows."*

The lower level, beneath the visible surface, would have canals and roads for deliveries, storage areas, alleys for carts, and a sewerage system to carry away refuse and "fetid substances." Homes would have main entries on the upper level and tradesmen's entrances on the lower level, which would be lit by air shafts and connected to the upper level "at each arch by a winding stair." He specified that these stairs should be spiral, both because he loved that form and because he was a fastidious man. Corners provided a place for men to urinate. "The corners of square ones are always fouled," he wrote. "At the first vault there must be a door entering into public privies." Once again he delved into the details: "The seat of the latrine should be able to swivel like the turnstile in a convent and return to its initial position by the use of a counterweight. The ceiling should have many holes in it so that one can breathe."[22]

As with so many other of Leonardo's visionary designs, he was ahead of what was practical for his time. Ludovico did not adopt his vision of the city, but in this case Leonardo's proposals were sensible as well as brilliant. If even part of his plan had been implemented, it might have transformed the nature of cities, reduced the onslaught of plagues, and changed history.

* A braccio is approximately 2.3 feet.

Chapter 5

Leonardo's Notebooks

THE COLLECTIONS

As the offspring of a long line of notaries, Leonardo da Vinci had an instinct for keeping records. Jotting down observations, lists, ideas, and sketches came naturally. In the early 1480s, shortly after his arrival in Milan, he began his lifelong practice of keeping notebooks on a regular basis. Some of them began as loose sheets the size of a tabloid newspaper. Others were little volumes bound in leather or vellum, the size of a paperback or even smaller, which he carried around to make field notes.

One purpose of these notebooks was to record interesting scenes, especially those involving people and emotions. "As you go about town," he wrote in one of them, "constantly observe, note, and consider the circumstances and behavior of men as they talk and quarrel, or laugh, or come to blows."[1] For that purpose, he kept a small notebook hanging from his belt. According to the poet Giovanni Battista Giraldi, whose father knew Leonardo:

> When Leonardo wished to paint a figure, he first considered what social standing and emotion it was to represent; whether noble or plebeian, joyful or severe, troubled or serene, old or young, irate or quiet, good or evil; and when he had made up his mind, he went

> to places where he knew that people of that kind assembled and observed their faces, their manners, dresses, and gestures; and when he found what fitted his purpose, he noted it in a little book which he was always carrying in his belt.[2]

These little books on his belt, along with the larger sheets in his studio, became repositories for all of his manifold passions and obsessions, many of them sharing a page. As an engineer, he honed his technical skills by drawing mechanisms he encountered or imagined. As an artist, he sketched ideas and made preparatory drawings. As a court impresario, he jotted down designs for costumes, contrivances for moving scenery and stages, fables to be enacted, and witty lines to be performed. Scribbled in the margins were to-do lists, records of expenses, and sketches of people who caught his imagination. Over the years, as his scientific study got more serious, he filled pages with outlines and passages for treatises on topics such as flight, water, anatomy, art, horses, mechanics, and geology. About the only things missing are intimate personal revelations or intimacies. These are not Saint Augustine's *Confessions* but rather the outward-looking enthrallments of a relentlessly curious explorer.

In collecting such a medley of ideas, Leonardo was following a practice that had become popular in Renaissance Italy of keeping a commonplace and sketch book, known as a *zibaldone*. But in their content, Leonardo's were like nothing the world had ever, or has ever, seen. His notebooks have been rightly called "the most astonishing testament to the powers of human observation and imagination ever set down on paper."[3]

The more than 7,200 pages now extant probably represent about one-quarter of what Leonardo actually wrote,[4] but that is a higher percentage after five hundred years than the percentage of Steve Jobs's emails and digital documents from the 1990s that he and I were able to retrieve. Leonardo's notebooks are nothing less than an astonishing windfall that provides the documentary record of applied creativity.

As usual with Leonardo, however, there is an element of mystery involved. He rarely put dates on his pages, and much of their order has been lost. After his death, many of the volumes were disassembled and the interesting pages were sold or reorganized into new codices by various collectors, most notably the sculptor Pompeo Leoni, who was born in 1533.

For example, one of the many repackaged collections is the Codex Atlanticus, now in Milan's Biblioteca Ambrosiana, which consists of 2,238 pages assembled by Leoni from different notebooks Leonardo used from the 1480s to 1518. The Codex Arundel, now in the British Library, contains 570 pages of Leonardo's writings from the same long time span and was assembled by an unknown collector in the seventeenth century. In contrast, the Codex Leicester contains 72 pages, mainly on geology and water studies, that have remained together since Leonardo composed them around 1508 to 1510; it is now owned by Bill Gates. There are twenty-five codices and manuscript collections of notebook pages in Italy, France, England, Spain, and the United States. (See list of Leonardo's Notebooks in Frequently Cited Sources.) Modern scholars, most notably Carlo Pedretti, have tried to determine the order and dates of many of the pages, a task made more difficult because Leonardo sometimes went back to fill in the unused parts of a page or add to an old notebook he had put aside.[5]

Early on, Leonardo primarily recorded ideas that he considered useful to his art and engineering. For example, the early notebook known as Paris Ms. B, begun around 1487, contains drawings of possible submarines, black-sailed stealth ships, and steam-powered cannons, as well as some architectural designs for churches and ideal cities. Later notebooks show Leonardo pursuing curiosity for its own sake, and that in turn evolved into glimmerings of profound scientific inquiry. He became interested not only in how things work but why.[6]

Because good paper was costly, Leonardo tried to use every edge and corner of most pages, cramming as much as possible on each sheet and jumbling together seemingly random items from diverse fields. Often he would go back to a page, months or even years later, to add another thought, just as he would go back to his painting of Saint Jerome, and later his other paintings, to refine his work as he evolved and matured.

The juxtapositions can seem haphazard, and to some extent they are; we watch his mind and pen leap from an insight about mechanics, to a doodle of hair curls and water eddies, to a drawing of a face, to an ingenious contraption, to an anatomical sketch, all accompanied by mirror-script notes and musings. But the joy of these juxtapositions is that they allow us to marvel at the beauty of a universal mind as it wanders exuberantly in free-range fashion over the arts and sciences and, by doing so, senses the connections in our cosmos. We can extract from his pages, as he did from nature's, the patterns that underlie things that at first appear disconnected.

The beauty of a notebook is that it indulges provisional thoughts, half-finished ideas, unpolished sketches, and drafts for treatises not yet refined. That, too, suited Leonardo's leaps of the imagination, in which brilliance was often unfettered by diligence or discipline. He occasionally declared an intent to organize and refine his notebook jottings into published works, but his failure to do so became a companion to his failure to complete artworks. As he did with many of his paintings, he would hang on to the treatises that he was drafting, occasionally make a few new strokes and refinements, but never see them through to being released to the public as complete.

ONE SHEET

One way to appreciate the notebooks is to focus on just one sheet of paper. Let's pick a large one, twelve-by-eighteen inches, that he composed in about 1490, dubbed by Pedretti a "theme sheet" because it encompasses so many of Leonardo's interests.[7] (See fig. 24 to follow along.)

On the center-left is a figure Leonardo loved to draw or doodle: a semiheroic, craggy old man with a long nose and jutting chin. Wearing a toga, he looks both noble and slightly comic. In the list of possessions he had brought to Milan in 1482, Leonardo described one drawing as "the head of an old man with an enormous chin," and we will see variations of this craggy character reappearing often in his notebooks.

Just below the old man are the trunk and branches of a leafless

Fig. 24. A notebook sheet c. 1490.

tree, which blend into his toga and suggest the aorta and arteries of his blood system. Leonardo believed that analogy was a way to appreciate the unity of nature, and among the analogous forms he explored was the branching pattern that could be found in trees, in the arteries of the human body, and in rivers and their tributaries. He studied carefully the rules governing these branching systems, such as how the size of each branch relates to the size of the main trunk, artery, or river. On this notebook sheet, he hints at the similarity of such branching patterns in humans and in plants.

Flowing out of the man's back is a geometrical drawing of a conical shape that contains some equilateral triangles. Leonardo was beginning his long attempt to solve the ancient mathematical challenge of "squaring the circle," constructing a square that has the same area as a given circle using only a compass and straightedge. He was not great at algebra or even arithmetic, but he had a feel for how geometry could be used to transform one shape into another while keeping the area constant. Scattered on the sheet are geometrical drawings with shaded portions that have the same area.

The conical drawing attached to the man's back resembles a hill, and Leonardo has it flow into a sketch of a mountainous landscape. The result is a seamless connection of geometry to nature and a glimpse into Leonardo's art of spatial thinking.

A clear theme emerges as we look at the flow of this part of the drawing from right to left (the direction in which Leonardo drew). The branches of the leafless tree merge into the man's body, then into the conical geometrical pattern, and finally into the mountainous landscape. What Leonardo probably began as four distinct elements ended up woven together in a way that illustrates a fundamental theme in his art and science: the interconnectedness of nature, the unity of its patterns, and the analogy between the workings of the human body and those of the earth.

Just below these elements is something simpler to fathom. It's a quick but energetic sketch of his vision for Ludovico Sforza's horse monument. With just a few strokes, he is able to convey motion and vitality. Farther down are two heavy-looking mechanical devices, unexplained by any notes, perhaps some system for casting the horse. Barely visible at the bottom of the right half of the sheet is a faint little sketch of a walking horse.

Next to the centerfold at the bottom are two leafy stems, which have such precise botanical detail that they seem to have been drawn from direct observation. Vasari wrote that Leonardo studiously drew plants, and his surviving drawings show how sharp his eye was in observing nature. His botanical correctness is evident in his paintings, most notably the Louvre version of the *Virgin of the Rocks*.[8] Continuing his theme of merging patterns in nature and geometry, one of the grass shoots curving from the base of the stems merges into a perfect semicircle drawn with a compass.

On the far right are studies of fluffy cumulus clouds, each with different patterns of light and shading. Below them is a drawing of a column of falling water stirring up turbulence as it plunges into a placid pool; this was a subject that he would still be drawing at the end of his life. And scattered about on the sheet are doodles of other subjects that he would return to often: a bell tower for a church, curls of hair, shimmering branches of foliage, and a lily emerging from swirls of grass.

There is one note on the page that seems disconnected from everything else. It is a recipe for making blond-brown hair dye: "To make hair tawny, take nuts and boil them in lye and immerse the comb in it, then comb the hair and let it dry in the sun." This may have been a notation in preparation for a court pageant. But it is more likely, I think, that the recipe is a rare intimate jotting. Leonardo was deep into his thirties by now. Perhaps he was resisting going gray.

CHAPTER 6

Court Entertainer

PLAYS AND PAGEANTS

Leonardo da Vinci's entrée into the court of Ludovico Sforza came not as an architect or engineer but as a producer of pageants. As a spectacle-loving apprentice in Verrocchio's Florence workshop, he had become enthralled by staging fantasies, a talent that also happened to be much in demand in Sforza's Milan court, which thrived on plays and public entertainments. There were many elements, both artistic and technical, involved in producing such festivities, and all of them appealed to Leonardo: stage designs, costumes, scenery, music, mechanisms, choreography, allegorical allusions, automatons, and gadgets.

From our vantage centuries later, the time and creativity Leonardo applied to such ephemeral affairs seem wasted. There is nothing to show for the dazzling displays except snippets of reports that recount the fleeting moments of splendor. The time he spent could have been more usefully applied, it might seem, to finishing the *Adoration of the Magi* or *Saint Jerome*. But just as today we love halftime shows and Broadway extravaganzas, fireworks displays and choreographed performances, the events staged by the Sforza court were considered vital, and their producers, including Leonardo, were highly valued.

The entertainments were even educational at times, like an ideas festival; there were demonstrations of science, debates over the relative merits of various art forms, and displays of ingenious devices, all of which were a precursor to the public science and edifying discourse that later became popular during the Enlightenment.

By calling on historical and religious imagery, these shows served to legitimize Sforza family rule, which is why Ludovico turned them into an industry. Architects, mechanics, musicians, poets, performers, and military engineers were all engaged in executing them. For Leonardo, who thought of himself as a member of all of these categories, it was the perfect way to earn a role in the Sforza court.

Ludovico's grander pageants served to amuse and distract not only Milan's populace but also his young nephew Gian Galeazzo Sforza, the titular duke until his mysterious death in 1494. Through a combination of feigned solicitousness and intimidation, Ludovico was able to beguile his nephew and induce him to crave his uncle's affection. He encouraged the young man's debauchery, indulged his drinking, and allowed him to preside over the pageants that were performed at court. One festivity Leonardo worked on was the extravaganza that Ludovico orchestrated in 1490 for his nephew's marriage, at age twenty, to Isabella of Aragon, the Princess of Naples.

The centerpiece of the wedding celebration was a performance and feast, filled with sounds and lights and pageantry, of a theatrical extravaganza entitled *The Feast of Paradise*, which climaxed with a stage piece, *The Masque of the Planets*. It had a libretto by one of Ludovico's favorite poets, Bernardo Bellincioni, who later wrote that the scenery was "made with great brilliance and skill by Maestro Leonardo Vinci, the Florentine." Leonardo created panels that depicted inspiring moments of the Sforza family reign, decorated the silk-clad walls of the long hall of the Sforza Castle with symbol-laden foliage, and designed the fanciful costumes.

The play was an allegorical pageant that began with a masked procession in which the players were introduced and then greeted by a Turkish cavalcade. The bride was serenaded by a procession of actors playing ambassadors from Spain, Poland, Hungary, and other exotic lands, and the appearance of each one became a cause for dancing. The music drowned out most of the whirring of the mechanical devices moving the scenery.

At midnight, after much dancing by the players and spectators, the music stopped and the curtain rose on a celestial curved vault that Leonardo had constructed in the shape of a half egg that was gilded with gold on the inside. Torches served as the stars, and in the background the signs of the Zodiac were illuminated. Actors portrayed the seven known planets, turning and revolving in the proper orbits. "You will see great things in honor of Isabella and her virtues," an angel announced. In his notebooks, Leonardo recorded the expenses for "gold and the glue to affix the gold" and twenty-five pounds of wax "to make the stars." It culminated with gods—led by Jupiter and Apollo and followed by the Graces and Virtues—descending from their pedestals to shower verses of praise on the new duchess.[1]

Leonardo's triumph designing *The Masque of the Planets* brought him a modest amount of fame—more than he had received as a painter of unfinished panels and certainly more than he had ever earned as a military engineer. It also delighted him. His notebooks show the interest he took in the mechanism of the automated props and scenery changes. The interplay of fantasy and machinery was something he was born to choreograph.

Another extravaganza was staged the following year, when Ludovico married the politically connected and culturally savvy Beatrice d'Este, a member of one of Italy's most prominent families. A great jousting tournament was planned, and Leonardo arranged the pageant that accompanied it. He recorded in his notebook visiting the site in order to help some of the footmen, who were going to play the role of primitive savages, try on the loincloths he had designed as their costume.

For the pageant, Leonardo again combined his theatrical skills with his love of allegories. "First a wonderful steed appeared, all covered with gold scales which the artist has colored like peacock eyes," Ludovico's secretary recorded. "Hanging from the warrior's golden helmet was a winged serpent, whose tail touched the horse's back." Leonardo described his allegorical intentions in a notebook: "Above the helmet place a half globe, which is to signify our hemisphere. Every ornament belonging to the horse should be of peacock feathers on a gold background, to signify the beauty which comes of the grace bestowed on him who is a good servant."[2] The steed was followed by the horde of cavemen and savages. It was typical of Leonardo's desire to indulge in the scary and exotic; he had an affinity for bizarre demons and dragons.

Leonardo's technical and artistic talents were again combined in January 1496, when he staged one of the most extravagant plays of the era, a five-act comedy titled *La Danae* written by Ludovico's chancellor and court poet, Baldassare Taccone. Leonardo's notes included a list of the actors and their scenes, a drawing of the stage set, and mechanical diagrams of the machinery for changing scenery and creating special effects. His floor plan shows two elevation drawings done in perspective, and he made a sketch of one scene that depicts a god sitting in a flaming niche. The play was filled with special effects and mechanical feats that Leonardo designed: Mercury descended from above using an intricate system of ropes and pulleys; Jupiter was transformed into a rain of gold dust to impregnate Danae; and at one point the sky was lit "by an infinite number of lamps like stars."[3]

His most complex mechanical designs were of the revolving stages for a theatrical scene that he labeled "Pluto's Paradise." A mountain was opened up in halves to display Hades. "When Pluto's paradise is opened, there will be devils who are playing on twelve pots like openings into hell, creating infernal noises," Leonardo wrote. "Here will be Death, the Furies, ashes, many naked children weeping; living fires made of various colors." Then comes a pithy stage direction: "Dances follow."[4] His moveable stages included two semicircular amphitheaters that were initially facing each other and closed into a sphere, and then were swung open and rotated so they would be back to back.

The mechanical elements of the theatrical events interested Leonardo as much as the artistic ones, and he saw them as connected. He delighted in making ingenious contraptions that would fly, descend, and animate in ways that would excite his audiences. Before he had fully begun his writings on the flight of birds, he made a light sketch in his notebook of a mechanical bird, wings outstretched, attached to a guide string, with the caption "A bird for a comedy."[5]

Leonardo's work producing theatrical pageants was enjoyable and remunerative, but it also served a larger purpose. It required him to execute his fantasies. Unlike paintings, performances had real deadlines. They had to be ready when the curtains parted. He could not cling to them and seek to perfect them indefinitely.

Some of the devices that he made, most notably mechanical birds and wings for actors suspended above the stage, spurred him on to more serious scientific studies, including observing birds and envisioning real flying machines. In addition, his love of stage gestures was reflected in his narrative paintings. The time he spent engaged with theatrical amusements stimulated his imagination in both art and engineering.

MUSIC

Leonardo had originally come to the Sforza court partly as a musical envoy bearing his own specially designed version of an instrument that was popular among court entertainers. It was a type of lyre to be held like a fiddle, with five strings meant to be played with a bow and two that were to be plucked. "It had a very bizarre and unusual design that he had made with his own hands," Vasari wrote, "mainly out of silver, in the shape of a horse skull, made so that the harmony might be fuller and more sonorous in tone." Poets used the *lira da braccio* as an accompaniment when they sang their verses, and it was featured in paintings of angels by Raphael and others.

Leonardo knew how to play the lyre "with rare distinction," according to the Anonimo, "and also taught lyre playing to Atalante Migliorotti." His repertoire ranged from the classical love poems of Petrarch to witty lyrics he concocted himself, and he won a contest in Florence with one of his performances. The humanist and physician Paolo Giovio, a near contemporary who met Leonardo in Milan, wrote, "He was a connoisseur and marvelous inventor of all beautiful things, especially in the field of stage performances, and sang masterfully to his own accompaniment on the lyre. When he played the lyre with the bow, he miraculously pleased all princes."[6]

There are no musical compositions in his notebooks. Rather than reading music or composing lyrics, he improvised when performing at the Sforza court. "Since by nature he possessed a lofty and graceful spirit," Vasari explained, "he sang divinely, improvising his own accompaniment on the lyre."

Vasari recounted one special performance that Leonardo gave at the Milan court in 1494, when Ludovico was officially crowned duke after the death of his nephew: "Leonardo, with great fanfare, was brought to the duke to play for him, since the duke had a great liking for the sound of the lyre, and Leonardo brought the instrument which he had built with his own hands. With this, he surpassed all the musicians who came there to play. In addition, he was the best improviser of verses of his time."

Leonardo also dreamed up new instruments as part of his role as a producer of pageants. His notebooks are filled with sketches both innovative and fanciful. As usual, his creativity came from his combinatory imagination. After sketching a few conventional instruments on a page, he concocted one that drew together elements from a variety of different animals to make a dragon-like creature. Another page shows a three-string violin-like instrument that had a goat's skull, a bird's beak, and some feathers, with the strings fastened to teeth carved at one end.[7]

His musical inventions were the product of both his engineering instincts and his fancy for entertainment. He came up with innovative ways to control the vibrations, and thus the pitch and tones, produced by bells, drums, or strings. On one of his notebook pages, for example, he drew a mechanized ringing instrument (fig. 25) composed of a stationary metal bell flanked by two hammers and four dampers on levers that could be operated by keys to touch the bell at different places. Leonardo knew that a bell has different areas that, depending on their shape and thickness, produce different tones. By dampening up to four of these in different combinations, he could turn a bell into a keyboard instrument that played a variety of pitches. "When struck by the hammers, there will be a change of tones like in an organ," he wrote.[8]

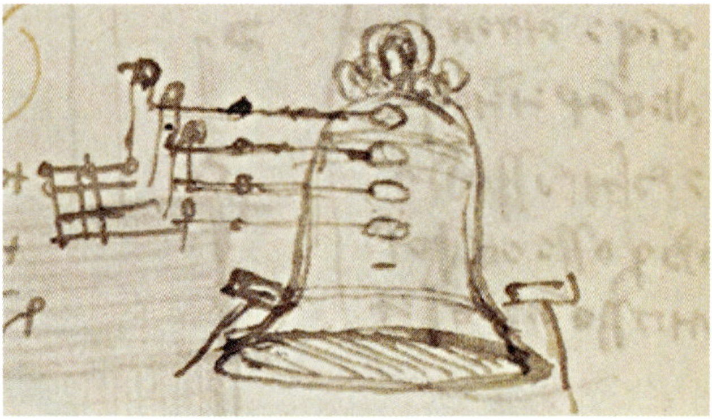

Fig. 25. Keyboard-operated bell.

He likewise tried to create instruments based on drums with different pitches. Some of his sketches involve combining drum skins stretched to various levels of tension. In other cases, he proposed ways to use levers and screws to change the tension of the drum skin while it was being played.[9] He also drew a snare drum with a long cylinder that had holes in its side, like a flute. "Closing of the various holes while beating the skin results in clear pitch differences," he explained.[10] Another method was simpler: he lashed together twelve kettle drums of different sizes and devised a keyboard that allowed each to be hit with a mechanical hammer; the result was a cross between a drum set and a harpsichord.[11]

The most complex of Leonardo's musical instruments, which he drew in many variations on ten different pages of his notebooks, was the *viola organista*, a cross between a violin and an organ.[12] Like a violin, its sound was produced by moving a bow back and forth across some strings, but in this case the bow was moved mechanically. Like an organ, it was played by pressing keys on a keyboard to determine which notes should be produced. In his final and most complex version, a set of wheels turned bowstrings that were looped like the fan belt in a car; pushing a key would cause one of the violin strings to be pressed down onto one of the looping bows, thus producing the desired tone. Multiple strings could be played at once, creating chords. Unlike with a regular bow, the tone produced by the fan belt could be sustained indefinitely. The *viola organista* was a brilliant idea that attempted to combine, in a way that is still not done today, the multitude of notes and chords that a keyboard can produce with the timbre, or tone color, that comes from a stringed instrument.[13]

What started as ways to amuse the Sforza court soon became serious attempts to make better musical instruments. "Leonardo's instruments are not merely diverting devices for performing magic tricks," according to Emanuel Winternitz, a curator of musical instruments at the Metropolitan Museum in New York. "Instead, they are systematic efforts by Leonardo to realize some basic aims."[14] These include new ways to use keyboards, play faster, and increase the range of available tones and sounds. In addition to earning him financial stipends and an entrée at court, his musical pursuits launched him onto more substantive paths: they laid the ground for his work on the science of percussion—how striking an object can produce vibrations, waves, and reverberations—and exploring the analogy between sound waves and water waves.

ALLEGORICAL DRAWINGS

Ludovico Sforza loved complex coats of arms, clever heraldic displays, and family emblems with metaphorical meanings. He owned ornate helmets and shields adorned with personal symbols, and his courtiers created ingenious designs to exalt his virtues, allude to his triumphs, and play with puns on his name. This led to a series of allegorical drawings made by Leonardo that were intended, I think, to be shown at court accompanied by his spoken explanations and tales. Some were designed to justify Ludovico's role as de facto ruler and protector of his feckless nephew. In one, the titular young duke is pictured as a cockerel (the word for cockerel, *galleto*, is a play on the boy's name, Galeazzo) being attacked by a swarm of birds, foxes, and a two-horned fantasy satyr. Protecting him, and serving as representations of Ludovico, are two beautiful virtues, Justice and Prudence. Justice holds a brush and a serpent, which were heraldic symbols of the Sforzas, and Prudence holds a mirror.[15]

Although the allegorical sketches he made while serving Ludovico ostensibly portray the traits of others, a few seem to reveal Leonardo's own inner turmoil. Most notable are the dozen or so drawings depicting Envy. "No sooner is Virtue born than Envy comes into the world to attack it," he wrote on one of them. In his written description of Envy, he seems to have confronted her, in himself and in his competitors: "Envy should be represented with an obscene gesture of the hand towards heaven," he wrote. "Victory and truth are odious to her. Many thunderbolts should proceed from her to signify her evil speaking. Let her be lean and haggard because she is in perpetual torment. Make her heart gnawed by a swelling serpent."[16]

Leonardo portrayed Envy along these lines in several allegorical drawings. He showed her as a wizened hag with sagging breasts on the back of a crawling skeleton accompanied by the explanation "Make her ride upon death, because Envy never dies."[17] Another drawing on the same page portrays her intertwined with Virtue, a serpent springing forth from her tongue, while Virtue tries to stab her in the eyes with an olive branch. Not surprisingly, Ludovico is sometimes depicted as her nemesis. He is shown holding out a pair of eyeglasses to unmask her lies as she cowers away from him. "Il Moro with spectacles, and Envy depicted with False Report," Leonardo captioned the drawing.[18]

THE GROTESQUES

Another set of drawings that Leonardo produced for the amusement of the Sforza court were pen-and-ink caricatures of funny-looking people he dubbed "visi mostruosi" (monstrous faces), which are now commonly called his "grotesques." Most are small, just under the size of a credit card. Satirical in intent, they were, like his allegorical drawings, probably accompaniments to spoken tales, jokes, or performances at the castle. At least two dozen originals survive (fig. 26), and there are many close copies produced by the students in his studio (fig. 27).[19] The grotesques were reproduced or mimicked by later artists, most notably the seventeenth-century Bohemian etcher Wenceslaus Hollar and the nineteenth-century British illustrator John Tenniel, who used them as models for the Ugly Duchess and other characters in *Alice's Adventures in Wonderland*.

With his finely honed ability to see both beauty and ugliness, Leonardo was able to create a satirical combination in his grotesques.

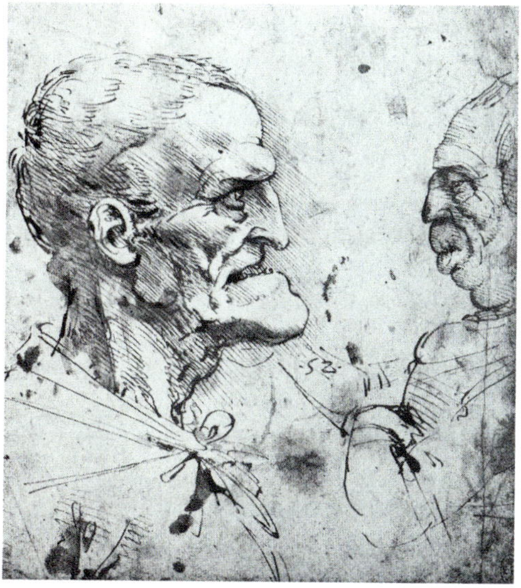

Fig. 26. Leonardo's craggy warrior and a grotesque.

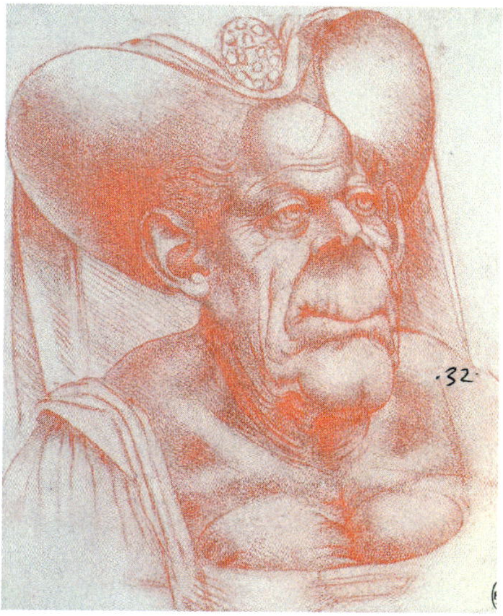

Fig. 27. Copy of a grotesque from Leonardo's studio.

As he wrote in his notes for his treatise on painting, "If the painter wishes to see beauties that charm him, it lies within his power to create them; and if he wishes to see monstrosities that are frightful, buffoonish, or ridiculous, or pitiable, he can be lord thereof."[20]

The grotesques are examples of how Leonardo's observational skills became fodder for his imagination. He would walk the streets with a notebook dangling from his belt, find a group of people with exaggerated features who would make good models, and invite them over for supper. "Sitting close to them," his early biographer Lomazzo recounted, "Leonardo then proceeded to tell the maddest and most ridiculous tales imaginable, making them laugh uproariously. He observed all their gestures very attentively and those ridiculous things they were doing, and impressed them on his mind; and after they had left, he retired to his room and there made a perfect drawing." Lomazzo indicated that part of the purpose was to amuse his patrons at the Sforza court. The drawings "moved those who looked at them to laughter, as if they had been moved by Leonardo's stories at the feast!"[21]

In notes for his treatise on painting, Leonardo recommended to young artists this practice of walking around town, finding people to use as models, and recording the most interesting ones in a portable notebook: "Take a note of them with slight strokes in a little book which you should always carry with you," he wrote. "The positions of the people are so infinite that the memory is incapable of retaining them, which is why you should keep these sketches as your guides."[22]

Sometimes Leonardo used a pen on such face-hunting excursions, and when that was not practical in an outdoor setting he used a stylus. The sharp silverpoint of the stylus made lines on paper that had been coated with ground chicken bones, soot, or other chalky powders, sometimes colored with pulverized minerals. The metal point oxidized this coating, producing silvery gray lines. He also occasionally used chalk, charcoal, or lead. As was his nature, he was constantly experimenting with drawing methods.[23]

These face-finding excursions, along with the sketches that resulted, helped Leonardo in his quest to find ways to relate facial features to inner emotions. At least since the time of Aristotle, who declared, "It is possible to infer character from features,"[24] people had tried to find ways to assess people's innate personality from their head shapes and facial characteristics, a study known as physiognomy. With his empirical mind, Leonardo rejected the scientific validity of this method and dismissed it as akin to astrology and alchemy. "I will not dwell on false physiognomy and palm-reading, because there is no truth in them, and illusions of this kind have no scientific foundation," he insisted.

But even though he did not consider physiognomy a science, he did believe that facial expressions indicate underlying causes. "Characteristics of the face partly reveal the character of men, their vices and temperaments," he wrote. "If the features which separate the cheeks from the lips, or the nostrils from the cavities of the eyes, are strongly pronounced, they belong to cheerful and good-humored men." Those without such distinctive lines are more contemplative, he added, and those "whose facial features stand out in great relief are brutal, bad-tempered, and men of little reason." He went on to associate heavy lines between the eyebrows with bad temper, strong lines on the forehead with regrets, and concluded, "It is possible to discuss many features this way."[25]

He developed a trick for noting these features of a face so that he could draw them later. It involved a shorthand for ten types of nose ("straight, bulbous, hollow . . ."), eleven types of facial shape, and various other characteristics that could be categorized. When he found a person he wished to draw, he would use this shorthand so that he could re-create him or her when he got back to his studio. With the grotesque faces, however, that was not necessary because they were so memorable. "Of grotesque faces I need say nothing, because they are kept in mind without difficulty," he declared.[26]

The most memorable of Leonardo's grotesque drawings is one of five heads that he did around 1494 (fig. 28). The central figure is an

Fig. 28. Five heads.

old man, with the aquiline nose and jutting jaw that Leonardo favored for his typical aging warrior character. He is wearing a wreath of oak leaves and trying to maintain a dignified pose while in fact looking a bit gullible and foolish. The four characters surrounding him are laughing maniacally or smirking.

Leonardo likely drew the scene as part of a facetious tale that he recounted for the amusement of the Sforza court, but no notes survive. That is fortunate, because it allows us to apply our own imagination to the drawing and to Leonardo. Perhaps the man is about to marry the "pug-faced crone" depicted in one of Leonardo's other drawings from the same time, and his friends are showing a mix of derision and compassion. Maybe the drawing is an exaggerated illustration of human traits, such as lunacy and dementia and megalomania.

A more plausible explanation, since this was probably for a performance at court, is that there was a narrative story involved. The man on the right seems to be holding the hand of the wreathed central character, while the man on the left is reaching around his back toward his pocket. Could it be a scene of a man having his palm read and being pickpocketed by gypsies, as Windsor's curator Martin Clayton suggests?[27] Gypsies from the Balkans had spread throughout Europe in the fifteenth century and become such a nuisance in Milan that they were banished by a decree in 1493. In his notebooks, Leonardo mentioned a portrayal of a gypsy in a list of his drawings, and he also recorded spending 6 soldi for a fortune-teller. All of this is speculative, and that is one of the many things that make Leonardo's works, including those with a bit of mystery, so wonderful: his fantasia is infectious.

LITERARY AMUSEMENTS

Another contribution that Leonardo made to life at the Sforza court were little literary amusements, which were also primarily intended to be read aloud or performed. There are at least three hundred of them in his notebooks, in a variety of forms: fables, facetious tales, prophecies, pranks, and riddles. These are scattered in the margins of pages or next to unrelated items, so we know they were not intended to be collections on their own. Instead, they were produced to provide entertainment whenever the occasion warranted.

Oral performances and declamations of riddles and fables were a popular form of amusement at Renaissance courts. Leonardo even included stage directions on some; next to one cryptic prophecy he directed that it should be delivered "in a frenzied or berserk way, as of mental lunacy."[28] He was a clever conversationalist and storyteller, according to Vasari, and that served him well with these slight entertainments that might seem, in retrospect, trivial endeavors. He had not yet been established as one of history's great geniuses, so he was hustling to curry favor at a crowded ducal court.[29]

The fables are pithy moral tales involving animals or objects that take on a personality. They have common themes, most notably the rewards due to virtue and prudence versus the penalties engendered by greed and haste. Although they bear some similarity to Aesop's fables, they are shorter. Most are not particularly clever or even easily comprehensible, at least out of the context of whatever was happening at court that evening. For example, "The mole has very small eyes and it always lives underground; it lives as long as it is in the dark, but when it comes into the light it dies immediately, because it becomes known—and so it is with lies."[30] More than fifty of these fables were jotted in his notebooks during the seventeen years he spent in Milan.

Closely related are the entries in his bestiary, a compendium of short tales of animals and moral lessons based on their traits. Bestiaries were popular among the ancients and in the Middle Ages, and the spread of printing presses meant that many were reprinted in Italy beginning in the 1470s. Leonardo had a copy of the bestiary written by Pliny the Elder and three others by medieval compilers. In contrast to the entries in these collections, Leonardo's tended to be pithy and unadorned with religious trappings. They were probably connected to emblems, heraldic shields, and performances that he created for those in the Sforza circle. "The swan is white without any spot, and it sings sweetly as it dies, its life ending with that song," one of them states. Occasionally Leonardo appended a moral lesson to the entry, such as this: "The oyster, when the moon is full, opens itself wide, and when the crab looks in he throws in a stone or seaweed and the oyster cannot close again, whereby it serves for food to that crab. This is what happens to him who opens his mouth to tell his secret. He becomes the prey of the treacherous hearer."[31]

A third type of literary amusement was one that Leonardo pioneered in the 1490s. He called them "prophecies," and they were often little riddles or trick questions. He was particularly fond of describing some scene of darkness and destruction, in a style that mocked the prophets and doomsayers who hung around the court, then revealing that he was actually referring to something far less apocalyptic. For example, one prophecy begins, "Many people by puffing out a breath with too much haste will thereby lose their sight and soon after all consciousness," but then Leonardo reveals that the description refers to people "blowing out the candlelight when going to bed."

Many of the prophecy-riddles reflect Leonardo's love for animals. "Countless numbers will have their little children taken away and their throats shall be cut," is one prophecy, as if describing a brutal act of war and genocide. But then Leonardo, who had become a vegetarian, reveals that this prophecy refers to the sheep and cows that humans eat. "Winged creatures will support people with their feathers," he wrote in another example, and then revealed that he was not referring to flying machines but "the feathers used to stuff mattresses."[32] As they say in show business, you had to be there.

Leonardo accompanied these literary amusements with pranks and tricks on occasion, such as flash explosions. "Boil ten pounds of brandy to evaporate, but see that the room is completely closed, and throw up some powdered varnish among the fumes," he wrote in his notebook. "Then enter the room suddenly with a lighted torch, and at once it will be set ablaze."[33] Vasari described how Leonardo took a lizard captured by an assistant, pasted on a beard and wings, and kept it in a box to frighten his friends. He also took the intestines of a steer and "made them so fine that they could be compressed into the palm of one hand. Then he would fix one end of them to a pair of bellows lying in another room, and when they were inflated they filled the room in which they were and forced anyone standing there into a corner."[34]

Puns were popular then, and Leonardo often created visual versions of them, such as when he painted a juniper in the portrait of

Ginevra de' Benci. One way he played with puns was by creating for the court cryptograms, pictographs, and rebuses, in which pictures were lined up to create a message that had to be decoded while Leonardo watched. For example, he drew an ear of corn for grain (*grano* in Italian) and a magnetic rock (*calamita*) to make a punning version of the phrase "great calamity" (*gran calimità*). Using both sides of a large notebook sheet, he drew more than 150 of these little puzzles, sketching them quickly, as if he were creating them in front of an audience.[35]

Leonardo's notebooks also contain drafts of fantasy novellas, sometimes in the form of letters describing mysterious lands and adventures. More than a century earlier, the Florentine writer and humanist Giovanni Boccaccio had popularized tales, most notably *The Decameron*, that skated between fantasia and realism. Leonardo did likewise in at least two sustained drafts of long stories.

One of these was probably performed at a farewell party in 1487 for Benedetto Dei, a fellow Florentine who was part of the Sforza court in Milan. It was cast as a letter to Dei, who traveled extensively and spun wondrous (and occasionally embellished) tales. The villain is a black giant, with bloodshot eyes and a "face most horrible," who terrorizes the inhabitants of North Africa. "He lived in the sea and fed on whales, leviathans, and ships," Leonardo wrote. The men of the area swarm all over the giant like ants, but to no avail. "He shook his head and sent the men flying through the air like hail."[36]

The tale is an early example of a theme that Leonardo would return to repeatedly until the end of his life: cataclysmic scenes of destruction and deluge that consume all earthly life. Leonardo's narrator is swallowed by the giant and finds himself swimming in a dark void. The story ends with a lament that describes those nightmarish demons, unleashed from the shadowy cave, that plagued and drove and stymied Leonardo throughout his life. "I do not know what to say or what to do, for everywhere I seem to find myself swimming head downwards through that mighty throat and remaining buried in that huge belly, in the confusion of death."

This dark side of Leonardo's genius is also evident in the other fantasy novella he sketched out while working at the Milan court, which foreshadows the deluge drawings and descriptions he did near the end of his life. This one is composed as a series of letters, written by a prophet and water engineer who is clearly Leonardo himself, to "the Devatdar of Syria, Lieutenant of the Sacred Sultan of Babylon."[37] Once again the narrative involves deluge and destruction:

> First we were assailed by the fury of the winds; and then followed the avalanches from the great mountains of snow which filled up all these valleys and destroyed a great part of our city. And, not content with this, the tempest with a sudden deluge of water has submerged all the lower part of this city. Added to this there came a sudden rain, or rather a ruinous storm full of water, sand, mud, and stones all mingled together with roots, stems, and branches of trees; and every kind of thing came hurtling through the air and descended upon us. Finally there came a great fire—not brought by the wind but carried, it would seem, by thirty thousand devils—completely burnt up and destroyed the country.[38]

The tale shows his fantasies about being a hydraulic engineer. The Syrian storm, Leonardo's narrator recounts, is tamed by building a huge drainage tunnel through the Taurus Mountains.

Some Leonardo scholars have interpreted these writings as a sign that he was suffering bouts of madness. Others have concluded that he actually went to Armenia and had the experience of the deluge he described. I think a more reasonable explanation is that these tales, like many of the odd things Leonardo wrote, were intended for performance at court. But even if merely designed to amuse his patrons, they hint at something deeper, providing a glimpse into the psychological torments swirling in the psyche of the artist playing the entertainer.[39]

CHAPTER 7

Personal Life

OUTSTANDING BEAUTY AND INFINITE GRACE

Leonardo became known in Milan not only for his talents but also for his good looks, muscular build, and gentle personal style. "He was a man of outstanding beauty and infinite grace," Vasari said of him. "He was striking and handsome, and his great presence brought comfort to the most troubled soul."

Even discounting for the effusiveness of sixteenth-century biographers, it is clear that Leonardo was charming and attractive and had many friends. "His disposition was so lovable that he commanded everyone's affection," according to Vasari. "He was so pleasing in conversation that he attracted to himself the hearts of men." Paolo Giovio, a near contemporary who met Leonardo in Milan, similarly remembered his pleasant nature. "He was friendly, precise, and generous, with a radiant, graceful expression," Giovio wrote. "His genius for invention was astounding, and he was the arbiter of all questions relating to beauty and elegance, especially in pageantry."[1] All of this made him a man with many close friends. In the letters and writings of dozens of other prominent intellectuals in Milan and Florence, ranging from the mathematician Luca Pacioli to the architect Donato Bramante and the poet Piattino Piatti, there are references to Leonardo as a valued and beloved companion.

cature showing a large penis with two legs poking toward an object on which "Salai" is scribbled.

In an unpublished "Book of Dreams" written in 1560, Lomazzo, who knew one of Leonardo's students, imagined a dialogue between the ancient Greek sculptor Phidias and Leonardo, who confesses to loving Salai. Phidias asks bluntly whether they had engaged in sex. "Did you perhaps play with him that backside game that Florentines love so much?"

"Many times!" Leonardo merrily responds. "You should know that he was a most beautiful young man, especially at about fifteen," which is perhaps an indication of when their relationship may have become physical.

"Are you not ashamed to say this?" asks Phidias.

Leonardo, or at least Lomazzo's fictionalized version, is not. "Why ashamed? Among men of worth there is scarcely greater cause for pride. . . . Understand that masculine love is solely the product of merit [*virtù*] which joins together men of diverse feelings of friendship so that they may, from a tender age, arrive at manhood as stronger friends."[8]

As soon as he moved in with Leonardo, Salai began earning his nickname. "The second day I had two shirts cut out for him, a pair of hose, and a leather jacket, and when I put aside some money to pay for these things he stole the money," Leonardo recorded. "I could never make him confess, although I was quite certain of it." Nevertheless, he began taking Salai to dinner parties as his companion, which indicates that he was more than a sticky-fingered assistant or student. Two days after he arrived, Leonardo took him to a dinner at the home of the architect Giacomo Andrea da Ferrara, where he proved unmannerly. "[Salai] supped for two and did mischief for four, for he broke three cruets and spilled the wine," Leonardo wrote in his notebook.

Leonardo, who rarely revealed much of a personal nature in his notebooks, mentioned Salai dozens of times, often in tones of exasperation that also betrayed amusement and affection. This included at least five times when he stole things. "On the seventh day of September he stole a stylus worth 22 soldi from Marco, who was staying with me. It was of silver and he took it from his studio, and when

Marco had searched for it a long time he found it hidden in the box of Giacomo." During the wedding pageant for Ludovico Sforza and Beatrice d'Este in 1491, Leonardo noted, "When I was in the house of Messer Galeazzo da San Severino to arrange the festival for his tournament, and certain footmen had undressed to try on some of the costumes of the savages which were to appear at the festival, Giacomo went to the wallet of one of them as it lay on the bed with other clothes and took out whatever money he found there."[9]

As the tales pile up, one can be amused not only by Salai but also by Leonardo for continuing to tolerate and record his transgressions. "Maestro Agostino of Pavia gave me a Turkish hide in order to make a pair of boots, and Giacomo stole it from me within a month and sold it to a cobbler for 20 soldi and with this money, by his own confession, he bought aniseed candy," reads yet another example. The lines of accounting are written in a small, impassive hand, but next to one entry Leonardo's words in the margin are twice as big and scrawled in annoyance: "Thief, liar, obstinate, greedy."

Their bickering would persist over the years. A shopping list that Leonardo dictated to an assistant in 1508 dissolves into "Salai, I want peace, not war. No more wars, I give in."[10] Leonardo nevertheless continued, throughout his life, to indulge Salai and dress him in colorful and dandy clothes, many of them pink, the costs of which (including at least twenty-four pairs of fancy shoes and a pair of stockings so expensive they must have been jeweled) would routinely be recorded in his notebooks.

DRAWINGS OF OLD AND YOUNG MEN

Even before Salai moved in with him, Leonardo began what would be a lifelong pattern of juxtaposing sketches of an androgynous, curly-haired pretty boy facing a craggy older man like the one on the "theme sheet," with a jutting chin and aquiline nose (fig. 24). As he later instructed, "In narrative paintings you should closely intermingle direct opposites, because they offer a great contrast to each other, especially when they are adjacent. Thus, have the ugly one next to the beautiful, the large next to the small, the old next to the young."[11]

The pairing was a motif that he picked up from his mentor Verrocchio, who specialized in virile old warriors and pretty boys, and facing off the two types became a regular feature in his sketchbooks. Kenneth Clark described the combination:

> Most typical of such creations is the bald, clean-shaven man, with formidable frown, nutcracker nose and chin, who appears sometimes in the form of a caricature, more often as an ideal. His strongly accentuated features seem to have typified for Leonardo vigor and resolution, and so he becomes the counterpart of that other profile which came with equal facility from Leonardo's pen—the epicene youth. These are, in fact, the two hieroglyphs of Leonardo's unconscious mind, the two images his hand created when his attention was wandering. . . . Virile and effeminate, they symbolize the two sides of Leonardo's nature.[12]

Leonardo's earliest known pair of such profiles appears on a notebook page from 1478, when he was still in Florence (fig. 29). The old man has a long pointed nose curving down, a sunken upper lip, and an exaggerated jutting chin curving up, forming the nutcracker facial type Leonardo often used. The head of wavy hair hints that Leonardo may be drawing a caricature of his older self. Facing him, rendered

Fig. 29. Nutcracker man and young man, 1478.

in a few simple strokes, is a rather featureless slender boy who gazes up languidly, with a subtle twisting of his neck and bending of his body. The lithe and boyish figure, reminiscent of Verrocchio's statue of David that Leonardo likely modeled for, hints that Leonardo may have, consciously or not, been drawing a reflection of his younger self, juxtaposing his boyish and manly sides. There was also a hint of companionship in these face-offs. It is on this page from 1478 that Leonardo inscribed the words "Fioravante di Domenico of Florence is my most beloved friend, as though he were my . . ."[13]

After Salai moved into his household in 1490, Leonardo's doodles and drawings began to feature a boy who is softer, fleshier, and a bit more sultry. This character, who we can safely assume is Salai, slowly matures over the years. A good example is a version of the craggy jut-jawed man facing a young boy that Leonardo drew in the 1490s (fig. 30). Unlike in his 1478 version, this time the young boy has bounti-

Fig. 30. Old man and probably Salai, 1490s.

ful curls, pouring like a deluge from his head and cascading down his long neck. The eyes are big but more vacant. The chin is fleshy. The full lips are shaped into what may be, on second glance, a *Mona Lisa* smile, though a bit more mischievous. He looks angelic yet also devilish. The older man's arm reaches to the boy's shoulder, but the forearm and the torsos are left partly blank, as if the two bodies are melding. Though not a self-portrait of Leonardo, who was then only in his mid-forties, the older man seems to be a caricature he uses over the years that conveys his own emotions as he faces the prospect of aging.[14]

Throughout his career, Leonardo would repeatedly and lovingly draw Salai. We see him age slowly while remaining, at each stage, soft and sensuous. When Salai is in his early twenties, Leonardo draws him with red chalk and pen, standing in the nude (fig. 31). His lips and chin are still boyish, his hair exuberantly curled, but his body and slightly spread arms have the musculature that we will see in *Vitruvian Man* and some of the anatomical drawings. Another full-length nude drawing, this one from behind, also shows him with arms and legs spread, his body strong with just a hint of fleshiness (fig. 32).

A few years later, around 1510, Leonardo made another chalk drawing of Salai's head in profile, this time facing to our right (fig. 33). It has all of the same features, from the swanlike neck to the fleshy chin and languid eyes, but he is now portrayed as just a touch older, though remembered as still boyish. His top lip is full and thrusting, his lower one soft and receding, forming yet again that hint of a devilish smile.

Even in the last years of his life, Leonardo still seemed to be mesmerized by the Salai image. In one drawing from about 1517, he created a tender sketch of a remembered youthful Salai in profile (fig. 34). His heavy-lidded eyes are still sultry and slightly vacant, his hair is still tightly curled in the way, as Vasari reported, "in which Leonardo greatly delighted."[15]

Leonardo's many drawings of an old and a young man juxtaposed in profile are evoked, in a telling way, in a haunting allegorical draw-

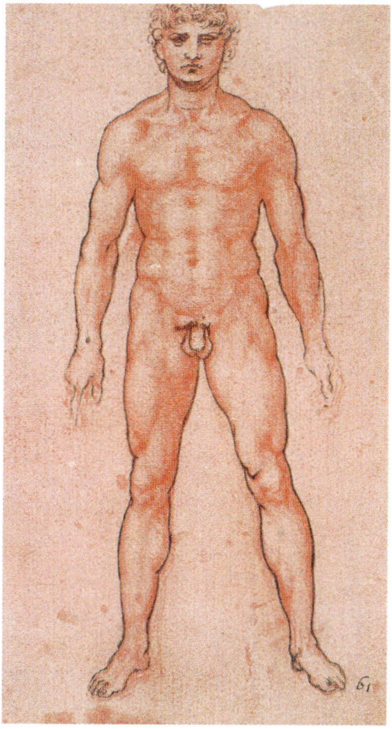

Fig. 31. Salai c. 1504.

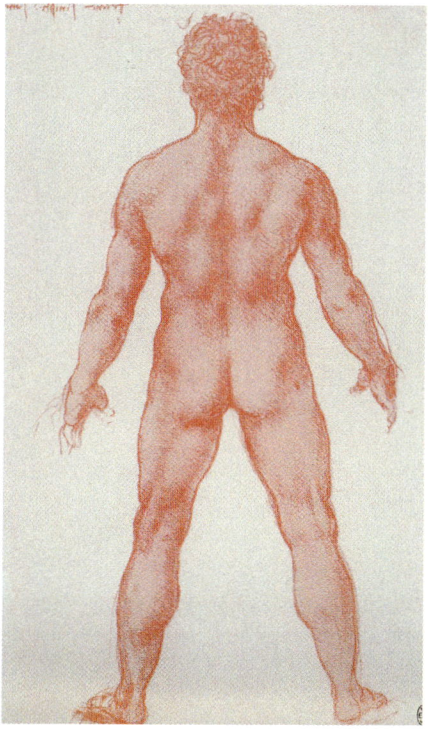

Fig. 32. c. 1504.

Fig. 33. c. 1510.

Fig. 34. c. 1517.

Fig. 35. Allegorical drawing of Pleasure and Pain.

ing that he made of figures representing Pleasure and Pain (fig. 35). The young character depicting Pleasure has some of Salai's looks. He is standing back-to-back and intertwined with the older man, who is the depiction of Pain. Their bodies merge as their arms entangle. "Pleasure and Pain are represented as twins," Leonardo wrote on the drawing, "because there never is one without the other."

As usual with Leonardo's allegorical drawings, there are symbols and puns. Pain stands on mud, while Pleasure stands on gold. Pain is dropping little spiked balls known as *tribolo*, a play on the word *tribolatione*, for "tribulation." Pleasure drops coins and holds a reed. Leonardo explained why the reed evokes the "evil pleasures" that are the source of pain: "Pleasure is here represented with a reed in his right hand which is useless and without strength, and the wounds it inflicts are poisoned. In Tuscany they are used to support beds, to signify that it is here that vain dreams come."

His notion of "vain dreams" appears to include sexual fantasies, and he went on to lament that they can distract a person from getting on with his work. "It is here that much precious time is wasted and many vain pleasures are enjoyed," he wrote of a bed, "both by the mind in imagining impossible things and by the body in partaking of those pleasures that are often the cause of the failing of life." Did this mean that Leonardo believed that some of the vain pleasures he indulged or imagined while in bed were a cause of his own failings? As he warned in his description of the phallic and "useless" reed that Pleasure holds, "If you take Pleasure know that he has behind him one who will deal you Tribulation and Repentance."[16]

Chapter 8

Vitruvian Man

A *TIBURIO* FOR MILAN'S CATHEDRAL

When Milan's authorities in 1487 were seeking ideas for building a lantern tower, known as a *tiburio*, atop their cathedral, Leonardo seized the opportunity to establish his credentials as an architect. That year he had completed his plans for an ideal city, but they had engendered little interest. The competition to design the tiburio was a chance to show that he could do something more practical.

Milan's cathedral (fig. 36) was a century old, but it still did not have the traditional tiburio on the roof at the crossing of the nave and transept. The challenge, which had defeated a few previous architects, was to conform with the building's Gothic style and overcome the structural weakness of its crossing area. At least nine architects entered the 1487 competition, approaching the task in a somewhat collaborative fashion, sharing ideas.[1]

The Italian Renaissance was producing artist-engineer-architects who straddled disciplines, in the tradition of Brunelleschi and Alberti, and the tiburio project gave Leonardo the opportunity to work with two of the best: Donato Bramante and Francesco di Giorgio. They became his close friends, and their collaboration produced some interesting church designs. Far more important, it also led to a set of drawings, based on the writings of an ancient Roman architect, that

Fig. 36. Milan Cathedral, with tiburio.

sought to harmonize the proportions of a human to that of a church, an effort that would culminate with an iconic drawing by Leonardo that came to symbolize the harmonious relationship between man and the universe.

Bramante served as the initial expert judging the tiburio submissions. Eight years older than Leonardo, he was a farmer's son from near Urbino with grand ambitions and appetites. He moved to Milan in the early 1470s to make a name for himself, and he carved out roles that ranged from entertainer to engineer. Like Leonardo, he began his work at the Sforza court by being an impresario of pageants and performances. He also wrote witty verses, offered up clever riddles, and occasionally accompanied his performances by playing a lyre or lute.

Some of Leonardo's allegorical tales and prophecies were complements to Bramante's, and by the late 1480s they were working together on fantasias performed for special occasions and other effusions of the Sforza entertainment industry. Both men displayed dazzling brilliance and effortless charm, despite which they became close friends. In his notebooks Leonardo affectionately called the architect "Donnino," and Bramante dedicated a book of poems about Roman antiquities to Leonardo, calling him a "cordial, dear, and delightful associate."[2]

A few years after he and Leonardo became friends,[3] Bramante painted a fresco that featured two ancient philosophers, Heraclitus and Democritus (fig. 37). Democritus, known to be amused by the human condition, is laughing, while Heraclitus is crying. Round-faced and balding, the former appears to be a self-portrait of Bramante, while the portrait of Heraclitus seems to be based on Leonardo. He has a profusion of flowing, tightly curled hair, rose-colored tunic, prominent eyebrows and chin, and a manuscript book in front of him with the characters in right-to-left mirror script. Thus we can imagine how Leonardo, still clean-shaven, looked in his prime.

Bramante moved on from the role of impresario to being on retainer as an artist-engineer-architect of the Sforza court, thus shaping the role and paving the way for Leonardo. In the mid-1480s, when he and Leonardo were working together, Bramante displayed his combination of art and architecture talents by designing a fake apse, or choir area, behind the altar of Milan's Church of Santa Maria presso San Satiro. Because space was cramped, there was no room for a full apse. Using the knowledge of perspective that was spreading among Renaissance painters, Bramante conjured up a trompe l'œil, a painted optical illusion that made it seem as if the space had more depth.

Within a few years, he and Leonardo would together work on a similar feat of engineering and perspective, when Ludovico Sforza commissioned Bramante to rework the convent of Santa Maria delle Grazie by adding a new dining hall, and Leonardo was hired to paint on its wall a depiction of the Last Supper. Both Bramante and Leonardo favored church designs that were based on strict symmetry. This led them to prefer central temple-like plans that featured overlapping squares, circles, and other regular geometric shapes, as can be seen in many of Leonardo's church sketches (fig. 38).

Fig. 37. Bramante's *Heraclitus and Democritus*, Leonardo on the left.

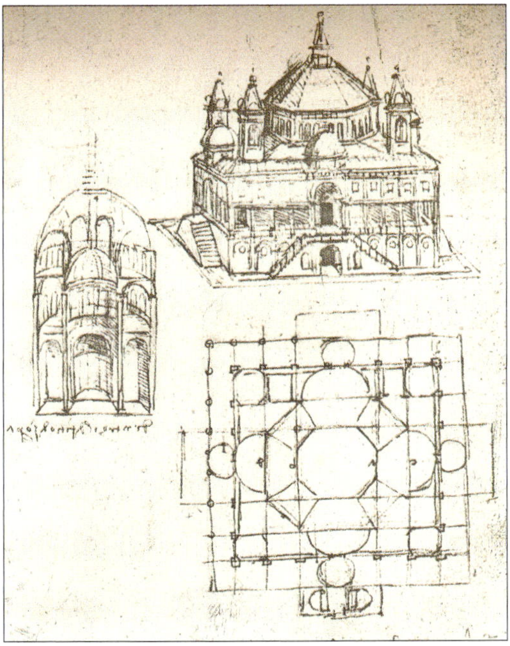

Fig. 38. Church drawings.

Bramante presented his written opinion on the tiburio design ideas in September 1487. One issue was whether the tower should have four sides, which would fit more securely on the support beams of the roof, or eight sides. "I maintain that the square is far stronger and better than the octagon, because it matches the rest of the building far better," he concluded.

Leonardo received six payments in July through September 1487 for his work on the project, which probably included consulting with Bramante as he wrote his opinion. In one of his presentations, Leonardo made a philosophical pitch that drew on the analogy, of which he was so fond, between human bodies and buildings. "Medicines, when properly used, restore health to invalids, and a doctor will make the right use of them if he understands the nature of man," he wrote. "This too is what the sick cathedral needs—it needs a doctor-architect, who understands the nature of the building and the laws on which correct construction is based."[4]

He filled pages of his notebooks with drawings and descriptions of what caused structural weaknesses in buildings, and he was the first to do a systematic study on the origins of fissures in walls. "The cracks that are vertical are caused by the joining of new walls with old ones," he wrote, "for the indentations cannot bear the great weight of the wall added on to them, so it is inevitable that they should break."[5]

To shore up the unsteady parts of the Milan Cathedral, Leonardo devised a system of buttresses to stabilize the area around his proposed tower and, always a believer in experiment, designed a simple test to show how they would work:

> *An Experiment to show that a weight placed on an arch does not discharge itself entirely on its columns; on the contrary, the greater the weight placed on the arches, the less the arch transmits the weight to the columns:* Let a man be placed on a weighing-device in the middle of a well-shaft, then have him push out his hands and feet against the walls of the well. You will find that he weighs much less on the scales. If you put weights on his shoulders you will see for yourselves that the more weight you put on him, the greater will

be the force with which he spreads his arms and legs and presses against the wall, and the less will be his weight on the scales.[6]

With the help of a carpenter's assistant he hired, Leonardo made a wooden model of his design for the tiburio, for which he received a series of payments early in 1488. He did not try to have his tiburio blend in with the cathedral's Gothic design and ornate exterior. Instead, he displayed his inbred fondness for Florence's Duomo; his many sketches for a Tuscan-style cupola seem more inspired by Brunelleschi's dome than the Gothic flying buttresses of Milan's cathedral. His most ingenious proposal was to create a double-shelled dome, like Brunelleschi's. It would be four-sided on the outside, as Bramante had recommended, but on the inside it would be octagonal.[7]

FRANCESCO DI GIORGIO IS CALLED IN

After receiving Bramante's opinion along with proposals from Leonardo and other architects, the Milanese authorities seemed baffled about what to do, so in April 1490 they convened a meeting of all who had been involved. The result was to call in yet another expert, Francesco di Giorgio from Siena.[8]

Thirteen years older than Leonardo, he was another exemplar of an artisan who combined art, engineering, and architecture. He had begun as a painter, moved as a young man to Urbino to work as an architect, returned to Siena to run the underground aqueduct system, and was a sculptor in his spare time. He was also interested in military weaponry and fortifications. In other words, he was the Leonardo of Siena.

Like Leonardo, Francesco kept pocket-size notebooks of design ideas, and in 1475 he began collecting them for a treatise on architecture intended as a successor to the one by Alberti. Written in unpolished Italian rather than Latin, Francesco's was designed as a manual for builders rather than a scholarly work. He tried to ground design in math as well as in art. The range of his ideas was similar to those in Leonardo's notebooks. Spilling across its pages were drawings and discussions of machinery, temple-like churches, weapons, pumps, hoists, urban designs, and fortified castles. In church design, he shared with Leonardo and Bramante a preference for a symmetrical Greek cross interior, in which the central plan has the same length for the nave and transept.

An official cultural diplomacy request was sent from Milan's ducal court to the council of Siena describing the importance of the tiburio project and asking that Francesco be permitted to come work on it. The response was reluctant acquiescence. The Siena councilors insisted that his work in Milan be done quickly, because he had many incomplete projects in Siena. By early June, Francesco was in Milan working on a new model for the tiburio.

A grand meeting was held later that month in the presence of Ludovico Sforza and the deputies of the cathedral. After inspecting three alternatives, they accepted Francesco's recommendations and chose two local architect-engineers who had been part of the competition. The result was an ornate, octagonal Gothic tower (fig. 36). It was very different from Leonardo's more graceful and Florentine approach, and he withdrew from the process.

Leonardo nevertheless remained interested in church design, and he made more than seventy other drawings of beautiful domes and idealized plans for church interiors at the same time that he was studying the transformations of shapes and ways to square a circle. His most interesting church designs featured floor plans that imbedded circles inside squares to form a variety of shapes, with the altar in the center, which were intended to evoke a harmonious relationship between man and the world.[9]

A TRIP WITH FRANCESCO TO PAVIA

While they were working together on the Milan Cathedral's tiburio project in June 1490, Leonardo and Francesco di Giorgio took a trip to the town of Pavia, twenty-five miles away, where a new cathedral was being built (fig. 39). The authorities in Pavia, knowing of the work that Leonardo and Francesco were doing in Milan, had asked Ludovico Sforza to send them as consultants. Ludovico wrote to

Fig. 39. Pavia Cathedral.

his secretary, "The building supervisors of this city's cathedral have requested that we agree to provide them with that Sienese engineer employed by the building supervisors of the cathedral in Milan." He was referring to Francesco, whose name he apparently could not remember. In a postscript, he added that "Master Leonardo of Florence" should also be sent.

Ludovico's secretary replied that Francesco could leave Milan in eight days, after his preliminary report on the tiburio was in hand. "Master Leonardo the Florentine," he added, "is always ready, whenever he is asked." Apparently Leonardo was eager to travel with Francesco. "If you send the Sienese engineer, he will come too," the secretary reported. The expense accounts of the Pavia authorities list a hotel payment on June 21: "Paid to Giovanni Agostino Berneri, host of Il Saracino, in Pavia, for expenses he incurred because of Masters Francesco of Siena and Leonardo of Florence, the engineers with their colleagues, attendants and horses, both of whom were summoned for a consultation about the building."[10]

Their friend and collaborator in Milan, Donato Bramante, had given advice a few years earlier on the design for Pavia's proposed cathedral. In contrast to Milan's cathedral, the resulting plan was decidedly non-Gothic, which made it more to Leonardo's taste. It had a simple façade and a very symmetrical interior design based on the Greek cross layout, with both the nave and the transept having the same length. That produced a balanced and equally proportioned geometric elegance. Like the churches that Bramante designed, most notably Saint Peter's Basilica in the Vatican, as well as the ones that Leonardo sketched in his notebooks, the plan featured circles and squares forming very harmonious and balanced areas.[11]

Francesco was at that time revising the manuscript of his treatise on architecture, and he discussed it with Leonardo as they traveled together. Leonardo would eventually acquire a lavishly illustrated copy. They also discussed another, more venerable book. In the thousand-volume Visconti library in the castle in Pavia there was a beautiful manuscript copy of an architectural treatise by Vitruvius, a Roman military officer and engineer from the first century BC. For years Francesco had been struggling to compile a translation of Vitruvius from Latin into Italian. There were many variations in the manuscript copies made of Vitruvius over the centuries, and he wanted to study the fourteenth-century copy that existed in Pavia. So did Leonardo.[12]

VITRUVIUS

Marcus Vitruvius Pollio, born around 80 BC, served in the Roman army under Caesar and specialized in the design and construction of artillery machines. His duties took him to what are now Spain and France and as far away as North Africa. Vitruvius later became an architect and worked on a temple, no longer in existence, in the town of Fano in Italy. His most important work was literary, the only surviving book on architecture from classical antiquity: *De Architectura*, known today as *The Ten Books on Architecture*.[13]

For many dark centuries, Vitruvius's work had been forgotten, but in the early 1400s it was one of the many pieces of classical writing, including Lucretius's epic poem *On the Nature of Things* and Cicero's orations, that were rediscovered and collected by the pioneering Italian humanist Poggio Bracciolini. At a monastery in Switzerland, Poggio found an eighth-century copy of Vitruvius's opus, and he sent it back to Florence. There it became part of the firmament of rediscovered classical works that birthed the Renaissance. Brunelleschi used it as a reference when he traveled to Rome as a young man to measure and study the ruins of classical buildings, and Alberti quoted it extensively in his treatise on architecture. A Latin edition was published in the late 1480s by one of Italy's new print shops, and Leonardo wrote in a notebook, "Enquire at the stationers about Vitruvius."[14]

What made Vitruvius's work appealing to Leonardo and Francesco was that it gave concrete expression to an analogy that went back to Plato and the ancients, one that had become a defining metaphor of Renaissance humanism: the relationship between the microcosm of man and the macrocosm of the earth.

This analogy was a foundation for the treatise that Francesco was composing. "All the arts and all the world's rules are derived from a well-composed and proportioned human body," he wrote in the foreword to his fifth chapter. "Man, called a little world, contains in himself all the general perfections of the whole world."[15] Leonardo likewise embraced the analogy in both his art and his science. He famously wrote around this time, "The ancients called man a lesser world, and certainly the use of this name is well bestowed, because his body is an analog for the world."[16]

Applying this analogy to the design of temples, Vitruvius decreed that the layout should reflect the proportions of a human body, as if the body were laid out flat on its back upon the geometric forms of the floor plan. "The design of a temple depends on symmetry," he wrote at the outset of his third book. "There must be a precise relation between its components, as in the case of those of a well-shaped man."[17]

Vitruvius described in great detail the proportions of this "well-shaped man" that should inform the design of a temple. The distance from his chin to the top of his forehead should be one-tenth of his whole height, he began, and proceeded with many other such notations. "The length of the foot is one sixth of the height of the body; of the forearm, one fourth; and the breadth of the breast is also one fourth. The other members, too, have their own symmetrical proportions, and it was by employing them that the famous painters and sculptors of antiquity attained to great and endless renown."

Vitruvius's descriptions of human proportions would inspire Leonardo, as part of the anatomy studies he had just begun in 1489, to compile a similar set of measurements. More broadly, Vitruvius's belief that the proportions of man are analogous to those of a well-conceived temple—and to the macrocosm of the world—became central to Leonardo's worldview.

After detailing human proportions, Vitruvius went on to describe, in a memorable visualization, a way to put a man in a circle and square in order to determine the ideal proportion of a church:

> In a temple there ought to be harmony in the symmetrical relations of the different parts to the whole. In the human body, the central point is the navel. If a man is placed flat on his back, with his hands and feet extended, and a compass centered at his navel, his fingers and toes will touch the circumference of a circle thereby described. And just as the human body yields a circular outline, so too a square may be found from it. For if we measure the distance from the soles of the feet to the top of the head, and then apply that measure to the outstretched arms, the breadth will be found to be the same as the height, as in the case of a perfect square.[18]

It was a powerful image. But as far as we know, no one of note had made a serious and precise drawing along these lines in the fifteen centuries since Vitruvius composed his description. Then, around 1490, Leonardo and his friends proceeded to tackle this depiction of man spread-eagle amid a church and the universe.

Francesco produced at least three such drawings that were designed to accompany his treatise and translation of Vitruvius. One of them shows a sweet and dreamy image of a man in a circle and a square (fig. 40). It is a suggestive rather than precise drawing. The circle, square, and body do not attempt to show proportions and are instead rendered casually. Two other drawings that Francesco made (figs. 41 and 42) depict a man more carefully proportioned inside a design of circles and squares in the shape of a church floor plan. None

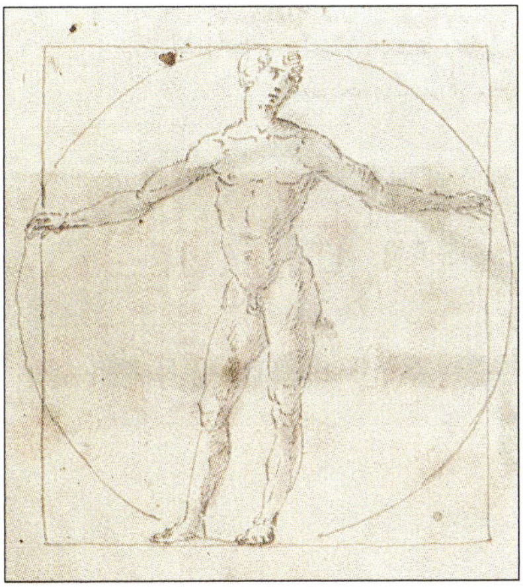

Fig. 40

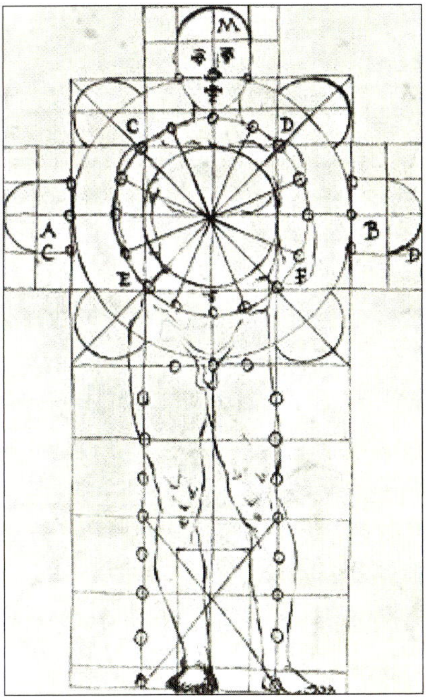

Fig. 41

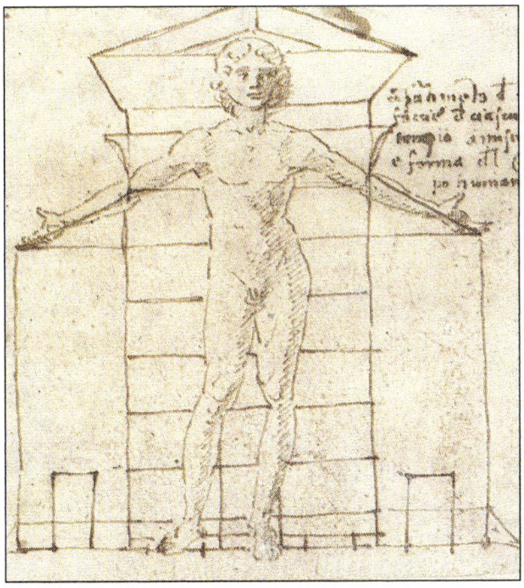

Fig. 42

Francesco di Giorgio's drawings of Vitruvian Man.

of his drawings is a memorable work of art, but they show that Francesco and Leonardo, at the time of their 1490 trip to Pavia, were both enchanted by the image Vitruvius had conceived.

DINNER WITH GIACOMO ANDREA

Around the same time, another dear friend of Leonardo produced a drawing based on Vitruvius's passage. Giacomo Andrea was part of the collaborative circle of architects and engineers gathered by Ludovico at the court of Milan. Luca Pacioli, a mathematician at the court and another close friend of Leonardo, wrote a dedication to an edition of his book *On Divine Proportion* that listed the distinguished members of that court. After hailing Leonardo, Pacioli adds, "There was also Giacomo Andrea da Ferrara, as dear to Leonardo as a brother, a keen student of Vitruvius's works."[19]

We have met Giacomo Andrea before. He was the host of the dinner that Leonardo went to with Salai two days after the ten-year-old scamp had become his assistant, at which Salai "supped for two and did mischief for four," including breaking three cruets and spilling the wine.[20] That dinner happened on July 24, 1490, just four weeks after Leonardo and Francesco returned from their trip to Pavia. It was one of those priceless historical dinners that makes you yearn for a time machine. The conversation, when not being distracted by Salai's antics, was evidently about the manuscript of Vitruvius that Leonardo and Francesco had just seen at the university.

Andrea decided to try his own hand at illustrating Vitruvius's idea, and one can imagine him discussing it over dinner with Leonardo, hoping that Salai didn't spill wine on their sketches. Andrea produced a simple version of a spread-armed man in a circle and a square (fig. 43). Notably, the circle and square are not centered; the circle rises higher than the square, which allows the man's navel to be in the center of the circle and his genitals to be in the center of the square, like Vitruvius had suggested. The man's arms are stretched outward, Christ-like, and his feet are close together.

Andrea would end up being killed and brutally quartered by French troops when they captured Milan nine years later. Shortly

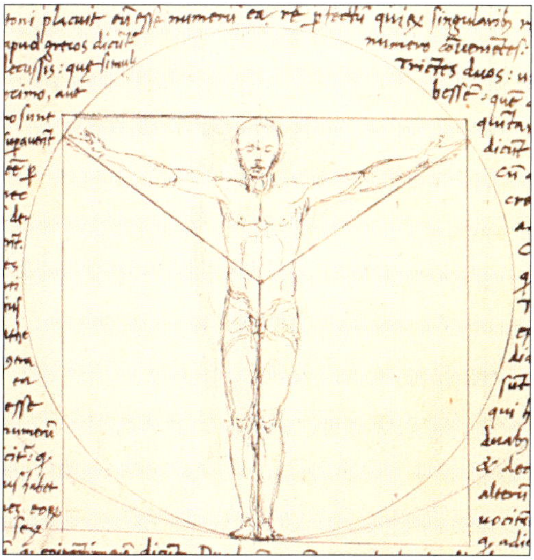

Fig. 43. Giacomo Andrea's drawing of Vitruvian Man.

thereafter, Leonardo would search for and find his manuscript copy of Vitruvius's work. "Messer Vincenzio Aliprando, who lives near the Inn of the Bear, has Giacomo Andrea's Vitruvius," he declared in a notebook entry.[21]

In the 1980s, Andrea's drawing was rediscovered. Architectural historian Claudio Sgarbi found a heavily illustrated manuscript copy of Vitruvius's tome that was languishing in an archive in Ferrara, Italy.[22] He determined that manuscript had been compiled by Andrea. Among its 127 illustrations was Andrea's version of Vitruvian Man.

LEONARDO'S VERSION

There are two key differences that distinguish Leonardo's version of *Vitruvian Man* from those done around the same time by his two friends, Francesco di Giorgio and Giacomo Andrea. In both scientific precision and artistic distinction, Leonardo's is in an entirely different realm (fig. 44).

Rarely on display, because prolonged exposure to light would cause it to fade, it is kept in a locked room on the fourth floor of the Gallerie dell'Accademia in Venice. When a curator brought it out and

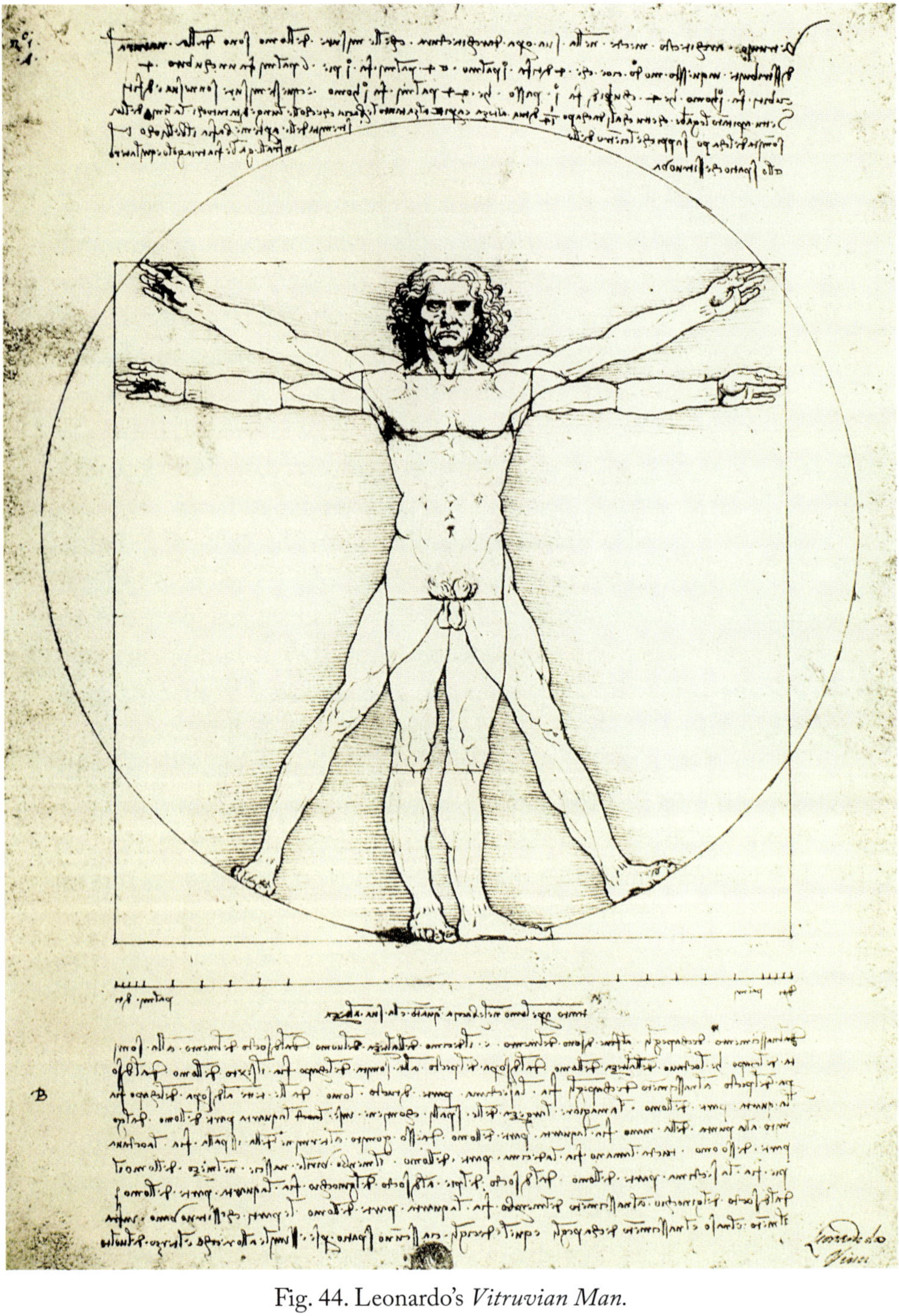

Fig. 44. Leonardo's *Vitruvian Man.*

placed it before me on a table, I was struck by the indentations made by the stylus of Leonardo's metalpoint pen and the twelve pricks made by the point of his compass. I had the eerie and intimate sensation of seeing the hand of the master at work more than five centuries earlier.

Unlike those of his friends, Leonardo's drawing is meticulously done. His lines are not sketchy and tentative. Instead, he dug hard with his stylus, carving the lines confidently into the page as if he were making an etching. He had planned this drawing very carefully and knew precisely what he was doing.

Before he began, he had determined exactly how the circle would rest on the base of the square but extend out higher and wider. Using a compass and a set square, he drew the circle and the square, then allowed the man's feet to rest comfortably on them. As a result, per Vitruvius's description, the man's navel is in the precise center of the circle, and his genitals are at the center of the square.

In one of the notes below the drawing, Leonardo described additional aspects of the positioning: "If you open your legs enough that your head is lowered by one-fourteenth of your height and raise your hands enough that your extended fingers touch the line of the top of your head, know that the center of the extended limbs will be the navel, and the space between the legs will be an equilateral triangle."

Other notes on the page provide more detailed measurements and proportions, which he attributed to Vitruvius:

> Vitruvius, architect, writes in his work on architecture that the measurements of man are distributed in this manner:
>
> The length of the outspread arms is equal to the height of a man.
>
> From the hairline to the bottom of the chin is one-tenth of the height of a man.
>
> From below the chin to the top of the head is one-eighth of the height of a man.
>
> From above the chest to the top of the head is one-sixth of the height of a man.

From above the chest to the hairline is one-seventh of the height of a man.

The maximum width of the shoulders is a quarter of the height of a man.

From the breasts to the top of the head is a quarter of the height of a man.

From the elbow to the tip of the hand is a quarter of the height of a man.

From the elbow to the armpit is one-eighth of the height of a man.

The length of the hand is one-tenth of the height of a man.

The root of the penis [*Il membro virile*] is at half the height of a man.

The foot is one-seventh of the height of a man.

Despite what he stated, instead of accepting what Vitruvius had written, Leonardo relied on his own experience and experiments, as per his creed. Fewer than half of the twenty-two measurements that Leonardo cited are the ones Vitruvius handed down. The rest reflect the studies on anatomy and human proportion that Leonardo had begun recording in his notebooks. For example, Vitruvius puts the height of a man at six times the length of his foot, but Leonardo records it as seven times.[23]

In order to make his drawing an informative work of science, Leonardo could have used a simplified figure of a man. Instead, he used delicate lines and careful shading to create a body of remarkable and unnecessary beauty. With its intense but intimate stare and the curls of hair that Leonardo loved to draw, his masterpiece weaves together the human and the divine.

The man seems to be in motion, vibrant and energetic, just like the four-winged dragonflies that Leonardo studied. Leonardo has made us sense, almost see, one leg and then the other being pushed out and pulled back, the arms flapping as if in flight. There is nothing static except the calm torso, with subtle cross-hatch shadings behind it. Yet despite the sense of motion, there is a natural and comfortable feel to the man. The only slightly awkward positioning is of his left foot, which is twisted outward to provide a measurement guide.

To what extent might *Vitruvian Man* be a self-portrait? Leonardo was thirty-eight when he drew it, about the age of the man in the picture. Contemporary descriptions emphasize his "beautiful curling hair" and "well-proportioned" body. *Vitruvian Man* echoes features seen in many assumed portraits of him, especially Bramante's depiction of Heraclitus (fig. 37), which shows Leonardo still beardless at about that age. Leonardo once warned against falling prey to the axiom "Every painter paints himself," but in a section in his proposed treatise on painting called "How Figures Often Resemble Their Masters," he accepted that it was natural to do so.[24]

The stare of Vitruvian Man is as intense as someone looking in a mirror, perhaps literally. According to Toby Lester, who wrote a book about the drawing, "It's an idealized self-portrait in which Leonardo, stripped down to his essence, takes his own measure, and in doing so embodies a timeless human hope: that we just might have the power of mind to figure out how we fit into the grand scheme of things. Think of the picture as an act of speculation, a kind of metaphysical self-portrait in which Leonardo—as an artist, a natural philosopher, and a stand-in for all of humanity—peers at himself with furrowed brow and tries to grasp the secrets of his own nature."[25]

Leonardo's *Vitruvian Man* embodies a moment when art and science combined to allow mortal minds to probe timeless questions about who we are and how we fit into the grand order of the universe. It also symbolizes an ideal of humanism that celebrates the dignity, value, and rational agency of humans as individuals. Inside the square and the circle we can see the essence of Leonardo da Vinci, and the essence of ourselves, standing naked at the intersection of the earthly and the cosmic.

COLLABORATION AND *VITRUVIAN MAN*

Both the creation of *Vitruvian Man* and the design process for the tiburio of Milan's cathedral have engendered much scholarly dispute over which artists and architects deserve the most credit and should be accorded priority. Some of these discussions ignore the role that collaboration and the sharing of ideas played.

When Leonardo drew his *Vitruvian Man*, he had a lot of interrelated ideas dancing in his imagination. These included the mathematical challenge of squaring the circle, the analogy between the microcosm of man and the macrocosm of earth, the human proportions to be found through anatomical studies, the geometry of squares and circles in church architecture, the transformation of geometric shapes, and a concept combining math and art that was known as "the golden ratio" or "divine proportion."

He developed his thoughts about these topics not just from his own experience and reading; they were formulated also through conversations with friends and colleagues. Conceiving ideas was for Leonardo, as it has been throughout history for most other cross-disciplinary thinkers, a collaborative endeavor. Unlike Michelangelo and some other anguished artists, Leonardo enjoyed being surrounded by friends, companions, students, assistants, fellow courtiers, and thinkers. In his notebooks we find scores of people with whom he wanted to discuss ideas. His closest friendships were intellectual ones.

This process of bouncing around thoughts and jointly formulating ideas was facilitated by hanging around a Renaissance court like the one in Milan. In addition to the troupes of musicians and pageant performers, those on stipend at the Sforza court included architects, engineers, mathematicians, medical researchers, and scientists of various stripes who helped Leonardo with his continuing education and indulged his insatiable curiosity. The court poet Bernardo Bellincioni, who was more accomplished as a sycophant than as a versifier, celebrated the diverse collection that Ludovico curated. "Of artists his court is full," he wrote. "Here like the bee to honey comes every man of learning." He compared Leonardo to the greatest of the ancient Greek painters: "From Florence he has brought here an Apelles."[26]

Ideas are often generated in physical gathering places where people with diverse interests encounter one another serendipitously. That is why Steve Jobs liked his buildings to have a central atrium and why the young Benjamin Franklin founded a club where the most interesting people of Philadelphia would gather every Friday. At the court of Ludovico Sforza, Leonardo found friends who could spark new ideas by rubbing together their diverse passions.

Chapter 9

The Horse Monument

A RESIDENCE AT THE COURT

As he was consulting on the Milan Cathedral in the spring of 1489, Leonardo got the job he had requested at the end of his letter to Ludovico Sforza seven years earlier: designing the proposed monument "to the immortal glory and eternal honor of His Lordship, your father." The plan was for a mammoth equestrian statue. "Prince Ludovico is planning to erect a worthy monument to his father," Florence's ambassador in Milan reported back to Lorenzo de' Medici in July of that year. "In accordance with his orders, Leonardo has been asked to make a model in the form of a large horse ridden by Duke Francesco in full armor."[1]

The commission, along with his service as an impresario and designer of court pageants, finally earned Leonardo an official appointment at court, with a salary and accommodations. He was described as "Leonardo da Vinci, engineer and painter," and listed as one of the four primary ducal engineers. It was the situation he had yearned for.

The job came with rooms for himself and his assistants, plus a studio for making the model for the horse monument, at the Corte Vecchia, the old castle in the center of town next to the cathedral. Once the home of the Visconti dukes, it was a medieval castle, replete with towers and moats, which had recently been renovated. Ludovico preferred the newer, more strongly fortified palace on the west side of town, which became the Sforza Castle, and he used the old palace as a place to house favored courtiers and artists, such as Leonardo.

Leonardo's stipend was generous enough to cover the costs of his retinue, including two assistants and three or four students, at least during those periods when he actually got paid. Ludovico, whose costs for defense were rising, was at times short of funds, and in the late 1490s Leonardo had to send him a plea for overdue payments to cover his costs and those of "the two skilled workmen who are continually in my pay and at my expense."[2] Ludovico eventually made good by giving Leonardo an income-producing vineyard just outside of Milan, which he kept for the rest of his life.

Leonardo's quarters were on two floors facing the smaller of the two courtyards. In one of the larger upstairs rooms, leading out onto a roof, he built one of his attempts at a flying machine. We can imagine what his studio looked like, in reality or at least in Leonardo's imagination, from a description he wrote of an artist at work: "The painter sits in front of his work at perfect ease. He is well dressed and wields a very light brush dipped in delicate color. He adorns himself with the clothes he fancies; his home is clean and filled with delightful pictures, and he is often accompanied by music or by the reading of various beautiful works."

His engineering instincts led him to envision some ingenious conveniences: the windows of the studio should have adjustable blinds so the light could be easily controlled, and the painting easels should be on platforms that could be raised and lowered with pulleys, "so that it would be the painting, not the painter, that would move up and down." He also devised and drew plans for a system to protect his works at night. "You would be able to put your work away and close it, like those chests that can be used as seats when they are closed."[3]

DESIGNING THE MONUMENT

Since his power was not based on long dynastic heritage, Ludovico sought monumental ways to assert his family's glory, and Leonardo's design for an equestrian statue catered to that desire. It was intended to be a bronze horse and rider weighing seventy-five tons, which would have been the biggest one yet made. Verrocchio and Donatello had recently created large equestrian monuments that were twelve or so feet high; Leonardo planned to build one at least twenty-three feet high, three times larger than life.

Although the original purpose was to honor the late Duke Francesco by glorifying him atop a steed, Leonardo focused more on the horse than the rider. In fact, he seemed to lose all interest in the Duke Francesco component, and the monument soon was being referred to, by himself and others, as *il cavallo* (the horse). In preparation, he threw himself into a detailed anatomical study of horses that included making precise measurements and, later, dissections.

Even though it was typical of him, we still should marvel that he would decide that before sculpting a horse he had to dissect one. Once again his compulsion to engage in anatomical investigations for his art eventually led him to pursue the science for its own sake. We can see this process unfold as he worked on the horse: careful measurements and observations are recorded in his notes, which lead to scores of diagrams, charts, sketches, and beautiful drawings in which art and science are interwoven. This eventually leads him into comparative anatomy; in a later set of drawings of human anatomy, he renders the muscles, bones, and tendons of a man's left leg next to those of a dissected back leg of a horse.[4]

Leonardo got so deeply immersed in these studies that he decided to begin an entire treatise on the anatomy of horses. Vasari claimed that it was actually completed, though that seems unlikely. As usual, Leonardo was easily distracted by related topics. While studying horses, he began plotting methods to make cleaner stables; over the years he would devise multiple systems for mangers with mechanisms to replenish feed bins through conduits from an attic and to remove manure using water sluices and inclined floors.[5]

When Leonardo was studying the horses in the royal stables, he became particularly interested in a Sicilian thoroughbred owned by Galeazzo Sanseverino, the Milanese commander who was married

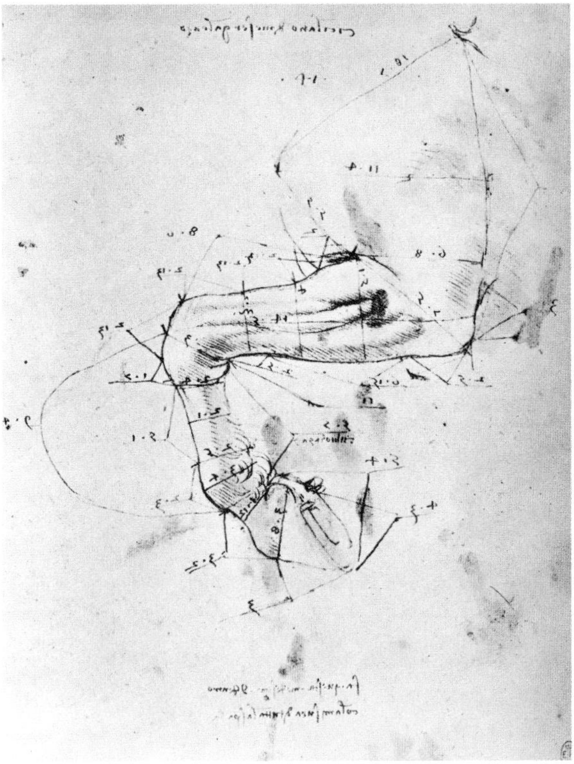

Fig. 45. Leg of horse.

to Ludovico's daughter. He drew it from a variety of angles, and in one detail of its foreleg included twenty-nine precisely diagrammed measurements, from the length of its hoof to the width of its calf in different places (fig. 45). Another drawing, this one using metalpoint and ink on blue prepared paper, is the equestrian version of the *Vitruvian Man*, aesthetically beautiful yet scientifically annotated. In the Royal Collection at Windsor alone, there are more than forty such pieces of his equine anatomical art.[6]

At first Leonardo planned to have the horse rearing on its hind legs, with the left foreleg atop a trampled soldier. In one drawing, he shows the horse's head turning and its muscled legs appearing to move as its tail flutters behind (fig. 46). But even Leonardo was practical enough to realize, eventually, that such a large monument

Fig. 46 Study for the Sforza monument.

so precariously balanced was not a good idea, so he settled for a horse that would be fancifully prancing.

As was often the case, Leonardo's mix of diligence and distraction, focus and delay, made his patrons nervous. The July 1489 report written by Florence's ambassador to Milan mentioned a request from Ludovico that Lorenzo de' Medici "kindly send him one or two Florentine artists who specialize in this kind of work." Apparently Ludovico did not trust Leonardo to complete the task. "Although he has given the commission to Leonardo, it seems that he is not confident that he will succeed," the ambassador explained.

Sensing that he might lose the commission, Leonardo launched a public relations campaign. He enlisted his friend the humanist poet Piattino Piatti to write an epigram for the base of the statue and a poem to celebrate his work on its design. Piatti was not a favorite of the Sforzas, but he had considerable influence with the humanist scholars who formed public opinion around the court. In August 1489, a month after Ludovico solicited suggestions from another sculptor, Piatti sent a letter to his uncle asking him to have "one of your servants deliver as soon as possible the enclosed tetrastich [four-line verse] to Leonardo the Florentine, an excellent sculptor, who requested it some time ago." Piatti told his uncle that he was one of many participants in a public-support campaign: "This task is for me somewhat of an obligation because Leonardo is indeed a good friend of mine. I do not doubt that the same request was made by the same artist to many others, who are probably better qualified than myself to express the same thing." Nevertheless, Piatti persevered in the task. In one poem he wrote of the grandeur of Leonardo's proposed horse: "Art imitating the immortal actions / of the duke, made the horse under the duke a supernatural one." Another of the poems portrayed "Leonardo da Vinci, a most noble sculptor and painter," in humanist terms as an "admirer of the Ancients and their grateful disciple."[7]

Leonardo was successful in hanging on to the commission. "On the 23rd of April 1490, I began this notebook and recommenced the horse," he wrote at the beginning of a new journal.[8]

On his trip to Pavia with Francesco di Giorgio two months later, Leonardo studied one of the few remaining ancient Roman equestrian sculptures. He was struck by how a statue could convey the impression of motion. "The movement is more praiseworthy than anything else," he wrote in his notebook. "The trot almost has the quality of a free horse."[9] He realized that a monument of a horse in a prancing high-stepping walk could be as lively as that of a rearing horse, and it would be far easier to execute. His new design was similar to the monument in Pavia.

Leonardo succeeded in creating a full-size clay model, which was put on display in November 1493 at the celebration for the marriage of Ludovico's niece Bianca Sforza to the future Holy Roman emperor Maximilian I. The mammoth and glorious model occasioned effusions from the court poets. "Neither Greece nor Rome ever saw anything grander," wrote Baldassare Taccone. "See how beautiful this horse is; Leonardo da Vinci alone has created it. Sculptor, fine painter, fine mathematician, so great an intellect rarely does Heaven bestow."[10] Many poets celebrating the colossal scale and beauty of the clay model played on Leonardo's name to herald the Vincian victory over all previous designs, including those of the ancients. They also praised its vitality. Paolo Giovio described it as "vehemently aroused and snorting." The model would, at least for a while, bring Leonardo renown not just as a painter but also as a sculptor and, he hoped, an engineer.[11]

CASTING

Even before he finished the clay model, Leonardo was working on the even greater challenge of casting such a huge monument. With precision and ingenuity, he spent more than two years sketching out plans. "Here a record shall be kept of everything related to the bronze horse, presently under execution," he wrote at the beginning of a new notebook in May 1491.[12]

The traditional way to cast a large monument was in pieces. A separate mold would be made for the head, legs, and torso; the pieces would then be welded together and polished. The result was never perfect, but it was practical. Because Leonardo's monument was so much larger than any ever done, this piecemeal method would seem to be all the more necessary.

Leonardo, however, was dedicated to achieving feats of engineering that would match in beauty and audacity the obsessive perfection he had pursued as an artist. So he decided to cast his huge horse all in one mold. On a captivating page in his notebook, he sketched out many of the mechanisms that would be necessary (fig. 47). His drawings are exuberant and yet detailed, as though a futurist were designing a launch pad for a rocket ship.[13]

Using the clay model he built, Leonardo planned to cast a mold and then coat its inside with a mix of clay and wax. "Dry it in layers," he specified. He would fit the mold around a core made of clay and rubble; the molten bronze would be poured into holes of the mold and displace the wax mixture, then the rubble core would be removed from what would become the hollow inside of the statue. A "little door with hinges" atop the horse, which would eventually be covered by the rider, would serve as a panel through which he could extract the rubble of the core after the bronze had cooled.[14]

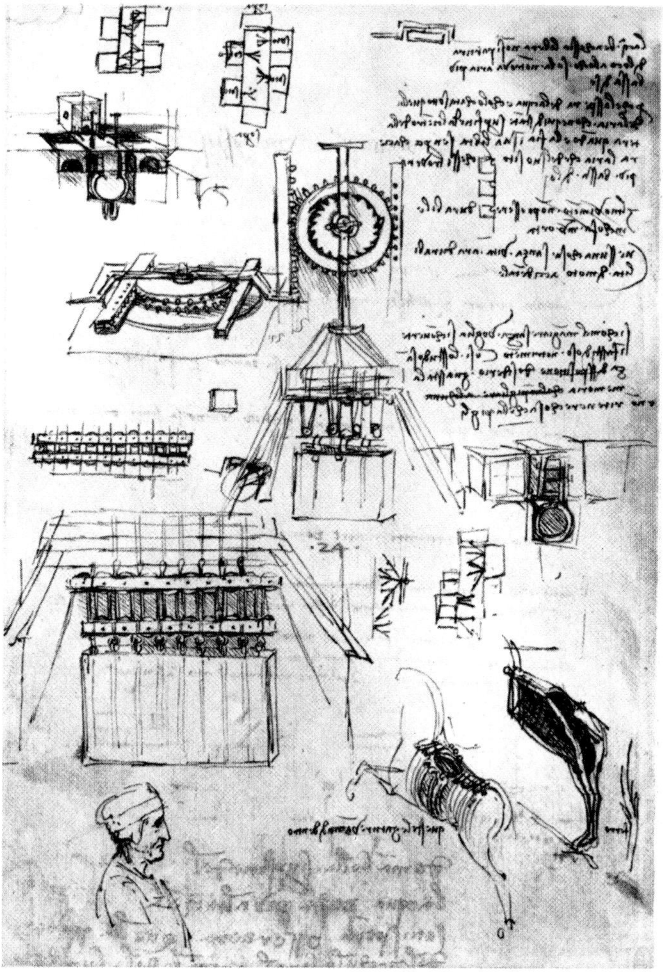

Fig. 47. Plans for casting the monument.

Leonardo then tailored a "casting hood," a lattice iron frame that would be strapped around the outside of the mold like a corset to hold it together and keep it in shape. The hood was not just an ingenious engineering scheme but also a red-chalk piece of art of eerie beauty, with the horse's head gently twisting and latticework elegantly shaded (fig. 48). Crossbars and struts would bolt together the casting hood to the inner core, providing firm support for the entire system. "These are the pieces of the form of the head and neck of the horse with their armatures and irons," he wrote.

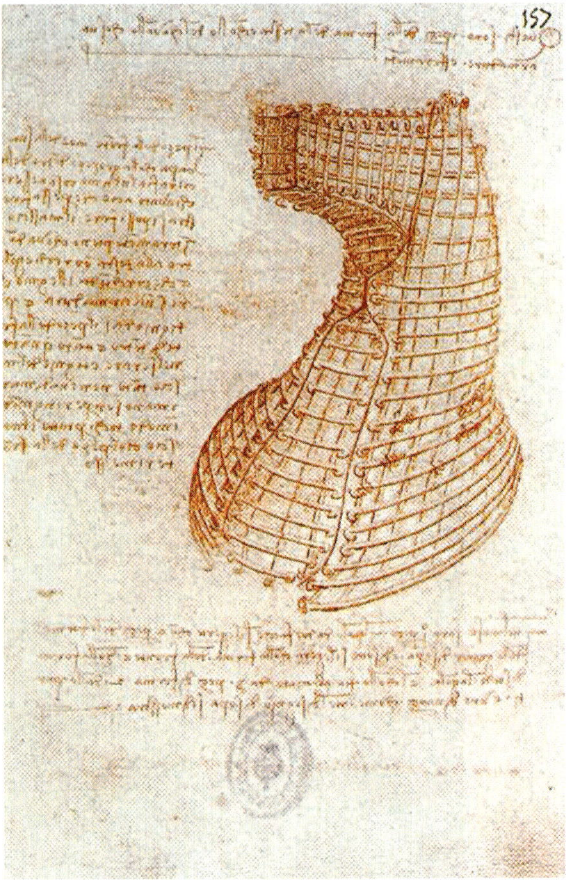

Fig. 48. Casting hood for the monument.

The plan was to pour the molten bronze into the mold through many holes so that it would be distributed evenly. Four furnaces would be arrayed around a pit so that the process could happen quickly and the metal could cool more uniformly. "For the casting, let every man keep his furnace closed with a red-hot iron bar and let the furnaces be opened simultaneously; and let fine iron rods be used to stop any of the holes from becoming blocked by a piece of metal; and let there be four rods kept in reserve at red heat to replace one of the others if they should be broken."

Leonardo experimented with different materials and mixes to get the right components for the casting process. "First of all, test every ingredient and choose the best." For example, he tried out ingredients for the clay-and-rubble mix that formed the inner core. "Try it first," he wrote next to a recipe that included "a mixture of coarse river sand, ash, crushed brick, egg white, and vinegar together with your clay." To keep the mold from being damaged by the damp when it was underground, he concocted many potential coatings. "Let the inside of all the molds be wetted with linseed oil or turpentine, and then take a handful of powdered borax and Greek pitch with distilled alcohol."[15]

At first he considered digging a deep hole and placing the mold in it upside down, with the feet sticking up. The hot metal would be poured into the horse's belly with the steam escaping through holes in the feet. The drawing (fig. 47) shows the hoists, levers, and machinery he planned to use. But by the end of 1493, he had abandoned this approach after realizing that the pit would be so deep that it would hit the water table. Instead, he decided that the mold should be laid sideways in the pit. "I have decided to cast the horse without the tail and on its side," he wrote in December 1493.

Shortly thereafter the project ended. Defense expenditures took precedence over artistic ones. In 1494 the troops of the French king Charles VIII swept through Italy, and the bronze intended for the horse was sent by Ludovico to his father-in-law Ercole d'Este in the town of Ferrara to make three small cannons. In a draft of a letter to Ludovico a few years later, Leonardo seemed dejected but resigned. "Of the horse I will say nothing," he wrote, "for I know the times."[16]

The cannons would end up doing little good, for the French would easily conquer Milan in 1499. And when they did, the French archers used Leonardo's huge clay model for target practice, destroying it. Ercole d'Este, who made the cannons, may have felt bad, because two years later he instructed his agent in Milan to ask the French authorities for the unused mold: "Seeing that there exists in Milan the mold of a horse that Lord Ludovico intended to have cast, made by a certain Messer Leonardo, an excellent master of such things, we believe that if we were granted the use of the mold, it would be a good and desirable thing serving to make our own horse."[17] But his request was never met. Through no fault of his own, Leonardo's horse joined other of his potential masterpieces in the realms of unfulfilled dreams.

CHAPTER 10

Scientist

TEACHING HIMSELF

Leonardo da Vinci liked to boast that, because he was not formally educated, he had to learn from his own experiences instead. It was around 1490 when he wrote his screed about being "a man without letters" and a "disciple of experience," with its swipe against those who would cite ancient wisdom rather than make observations on their own. "Though I have no power to quote from authors as they have," he proclaimed almost proudly, "I shall rely on a far more worthy thing—on experience."[1] Throughout his life, he would repeat this claim to prefer experience over received scholarship. "He who has access to the fountain does not go to the water-jar," he wrote.[2] This made him different from the archetypal Renaissance Man, who embraced the rebirth of wisdom that came from rediscovered works of classical antiquity.

The education that Leonardo was soaking up in Milan, however, began to soften his disdain for handed-down wisdom. We can see a turning point in the early 1490s, when he undertook to teach himself Latin, the language not only of the ancients but also of serious scholars of his era. He copied page after page of Latin words and conjugations from textbooks of his time, including one that was used by Ludovico Sforza's young son. It appears not to have been an enjoyable exercise; in the middle of one notebook page where he copied 130 words, he drew his nutcracker man scowling and grimacing more than usual (fig. 49). Nor did he ever master Latin. For the most part his notebooks are filled with notes and transcriptions from works available in Italian.

In that regard, Leonardo was born at a fortunate moment. In 1452 Johannes Gutenberg began selling Bibles from his new printing press, just when the development of rag processing was making paper more readily available. By the time Leonardo became an apprentice in Florence, Gutenberg's technology had crossed the Alps into Italy. Alberti marveled in 1466 about "the German inventor who has made it pos-

Fig. 49. Trying to learn Latin, with a grimace.

sible, by certain pressings down of characters, to have more than two hundred volumes written out in a hundred days from the original, with the labor of no more than three men." A goldsmith from Gutenberg's hometown of Mainz named Johannes de Spira (or Speyer) moved to Venice and started Italy's first major commercial publishing house in 1469; it printed many of the classics, starting with Cicero's letters and Pliny's encyclopedic *Natural History*, which Leonardo bought. By 1471 there were printing shops also in Milan, Florence, Naples, Bologna, Ferrara, Padua, and Genoa. Venice became the center of Europe's publishing industry, and by the time Leonardo visited in 1500, there were close to a hundred printing houses there, and two million volumes had come off their presses.[3] Leonardo thus was able to become the first major European thinker to acquire a serious knowledge of science without being formally schooled in Latin or Greek.

His notebooks are filled with lists of books he acquired and passages he copied. In the late 1480s he itemized five books he owned: the Pliny, a Latin grammar book, a text on minerals and precious stones, an arithmetic text, and a humorous epic poem, Luigi Pulci's *Morgante*, about the adventures of a knight and the giant he converted to Christianity, which was often performed at the Medici court. By 1492 Leonardo had close to forty volumes. A testament to his universal interests, they included books on military machinery, agriculture, music, surgery, health, Aristotelian science, Arabian physics, palmistry, and the lives of famous philosophers, as well as the poetry of Ovid and Petrarch, the fables of Aesop, some collections of bawdy doggerels and burlesques, and a fourteenth-century operetta from which he drew part of his bestiary. By 1504 he would be able to list seventy more books, including forty works of science, close to fifty of poetry and literature, ten on art and architecture, eight on religion, and three on math.[4]

He also recorded at various times the books that he hoped to borrow or find. "Maestro Stefano Caponi, a physician, lives at the Piscina, and has Euclid," he noted. "The heirs of Maestro Giovanni Ghiringallo have the works of Pelacano." "Vespucci will give me a book of Geometry." And on a to-do list: "An algebra, which the Marliani have, written by their father . . . A book, treating of Milan and its churches, which is to be had at the last stationers on the way to Corduso." Once he discovered the University of Pavia, near Milan, he used it as a resource: "Try to get Vitolone, which is in the library at Pavia and deals with mathematics." On the same to-do list: "A grandson of Gian Angelo's, the painter, has a book on water which was his father's. . . . Get the Friar di Brera to show you *de Ponderibus*." His appetite for soaking up information from books was voracious and wide-ranging.

In addition, he liked to pick people's brains. He was constantly peppering acquaintances with the type of questions we should all learn to pose more often. "Ask Benedetto Portinari how they walk on ice in Flanders," reads one memorable and vivid entry on a to-do list. Over the years there were scores of others: "Ask Maestro Antonio how mortars are positioned on bastions by day or night. . . . Find a master of hydraulics and get him to tell you how to repair a lock, canal and mill in the Lombard manner. . . . Ask Maestro Giovannino how the tower of Ferrara is walled without loopholes."[5]

Thus Leonardo became a disciple of both experience and received wisdom. More important, he came to see that the progress of science came from a dialogue between the two. That in turn helped him realize that knowledge also came from a related dialogue: that between experiment and theory.

CONNECTING EXPERIMENT TO THEORY

Leonardo's devotion to firsthand experience went deeper than just being prickly about his lack of received wisdom. It also caused him, at least early on, to minimize the role of theory. A natural observer and experimenter, he was neither wired nor trained to wrestle with abstract concepts. He preferred to induce from experiments rather than deduce from theoretical principles. "My intention is to consult experience first, and then with reasoning show why such experience is bound to operate in such a way," he wrote. In other words, he would try to look at facts and from them figure out the patterns and natural forces that caused those things to happen. "Although nature begins with the cause and ends with the experience, we must follow the opposite course, namely begin with the experience, and by means of it investigate the cause."[6]

As with so many things, this empirical approach put him ahead of his time. Scholastic theologians of the Middle Ages had fused Aristotle's science with Christianity to create an authorized creed that left little room for skeptical inquiry or experimentation. Even the humanists of the early Renaissance preferred to repeat the wisdom of classical texts rather than test it.

Leonardo broke with this tradition by basing his science primarily on observations, then discerning patterns, and then testing their reliability through more observations and experiments. Dozens of times in his notebook he wrote some variation of the phrase "this can be proved by experiment" and then proceeded to describe a real-world demonstration of his thinking. Foreshadowing what would become the scientific method, he even prescribed how experiments must be repeated and varied to assure their validity: "Before you make a general rule of this case, test it two or three times and observe whether the tests produce the same effects."[7]

He was aided by his ingenuity, which enabled him to devise all sorts of contraptions and clever methods for exploring a phenomenon. For example, when he was studying the human heart around 1510, he came up with the hypothesis that blood swirled into eddies when it was pumped from the heart to the aorta, and that was what caused the valves to close properly; he then devised a glass device that he could use to confirm his theory with an experiment (see chapter 27). Visualization and drawing became an important component of this process. Not comfortable wrestling with theory, he preferred dealing with knowledge that he could observe and draw.

But Leonardo did not remain merely a disciple of experiments. His notebooks show that he evolved. When he began absorbing knowledge from books in the 1490s, it helped him realize the importance of being guided not only by experiential evidence but also by theoretical frameworks. More important, he came to understand that the two approaches were complementary, working hand in hand. "We can see in Leonardo a dramatic attempt to appraise properly the mutual relation of theory to experiment," wrote the twentieth-century physicist Leopold Infeld.[8]

His proposals for the Milan Cathedral tiburio show this evolution.

To understand how to treat an aging cathedral with structural flaws, he wrote, architects need to understand "the nature of weight and the propensities of force." In other words, they need to understand physics theories. But they also need to test theoretical principles against what actually works in practice. "I shall endeavor," he promised the cathedral administrators, "to satisfy you partly with theory and partly with practice, sometimes showing effects from causes, sometimes affirming principles with experiments." He also pledged, despite his early aversion to received wisdom, to "make use, as is convenient, of the authority of the ancient architects." In other words, he was advocating our modern method of combining theory, experiment, and handed-down knowledge—and constantly testing them against each other.[9]

His study of perspective likewise showed him the importance of joining experience with theories. He observed the way objects appear smaller as they get more distant. But he also used geometry to develop rules for the relationship between size and distance. When it came time to describe the laws of perspective in his notebooks, he wrote that he would do so "sometimes by deduction of the effects from the causes, and sometimes arguing the causes from the effects."[10]

He even came to be dismissive of experimenters who relied on practice without any knowledge of the underlying theories. "Those who are in love with practice without theoretical knowledge are like the sailor who goes onto a ship without rudder or compass and who never can be certain whither he is going," he wrote in 1510. "Practice must always be founded on sound theory."[11]

As a result, Leonardo became one of the major Western thinkers, more than a century before Galileo, to pursue in a persistent hands-on fashion the dialogue between experiment and theory that would lead to the modern Scientific Revolution. Aristotle had laid the foundations, in ancient Greece, for the method of partnering inductions and deductions: using observations to formulate general principles, then using these principles to predict outcomes. While Europe was mired in its dark years of medieval superstition, the work of combining theory and experiment was advanced primarily in the Islamic world. Muslim scientists often also worked as scientific instrument makers, which made them experts at measurements and applying theories. The Arab physicist Ibn al-Haytham, known as Alhazen, wrote a seminal text on optics in 1021 that combined observations and experiments to develop a theory of how human vision works, then devised further experiments to test the theory. His ideas and methods became a foundation for the work of Alberti and Leonardo four centuries later. Meanwhile, Aristotle's science was being revived in Europe during the thirteenth century by scholars such as Robert Grosseteste and Roger Bacon. The empirical method used by Bacon emphasized a cycle: observations should lead to a hypothesis, which should then be tested by precise experiments, which would then be used to refine the original hypothesis. Bacon also recorded and reported his experiments in precise detail so that others could independently replicate and verify them.

Leonardo had the eye and temperament and curiosity to become an exemplar of this scientific method. "Galileo, born 112 years after Leonardo, is usually credited with being the first to develop this kind of rigorous empirical approach and is often hailed as the father of modern science," the historian Fritjof Capra wrote. "There can be no doubt that this honor would have been bestowed on Leonardo da Vinci had he published his scientific writings during his lifetime, or had his Notebooks been widely studied soon after his death."[12]

That goes a step too far, I think. Leonardo did not invent the scientific method, nor did Aristotle or Alhazen or Galileo or any Bacon. But his uncanny abilities to engage in the dialogue between experience and theory made him a prime example of how acute observations, fanatic curiosity, experimental testing, a willingness to question dogma, and the ability to discern patterns across disciplines can lead to great leaps in human understanding.

PATTERNS AND ANALOGIES

In lieu of possessing abstract mathematical tools to extract theoretical laws from nature, the way Copernicus and Galileo and Newton later did, Leonardo relied on a more rudimentary method: he was able to see patterns in nature, and he theorized by making analogies. With his keen observational skills across multiple disciplines, he discerned recurring themes. As the philosopher Michel Foucault noted, the "protoscience" of Leonardo's era was based on similarities and analogies.[13]

Because of his intuitive feel for the unity of nature, his mind and eye and pen darted across disciplines, sensing connections. "This constant search for basic, rhyming, organic form meant that when he looked at a heart blossoming into its network of veins he saw, and sketched alongside it, a seed germinating into shoots," Adam Gopnik wrote. "Studying the curls on a beautiful woman's head he thought in terms of the swirling motion of a turbulent flow of water."[14] His drawing of a fetus in a womb hints at the similarity to a seed in a shell.

When he was inventing musical instruments, he made an analogy between how the larynx works and how a glissando recorder could perform similarly. When he was competing to design the tower for Milan's cathedral, he made a connection between architects and doctors that reflected what would become the most fundamental analogy in his art and science: that between our physical world and our human anatomy. When he dissected a limb and drew its muscles and sinews, it led him to also sketch ropes and levers.

We saw an example of this pattern-based analysis on the "theme sheet," where he made the analogy between a branching tree and the arteries in a human, one that he applied also to rivers and their tributaries. "All the branches of a tree at every stage of its height when put together are equal in thickness to the trunk below them," he wrote elsewhere. "All the branches of a river at every stage of its course, if they are of equal rapidity, are equal to the body of the main stream."[15] This conclusion is still known as "da Vinci's rule," and it has proven true in situations where the branches are not very large: the sum of the cross-sectional area of all branches above a branching point is equal to the cross-sectional area of the trunk or the branch immediately below the branching point.[16]

Another analogy he made was comparing the way that light, sound, magnetism, and the percussion reverberations caused by a hammer blow all disseminate in a radiating pattern, often in waves. In one of his notebooks he made a column of small drawings showing how each force field spreads. He even illustrated what happened when each type of wave hits a small hole in the wall; prefiguring the studies done by Dutch physicist Christiaan Huygens almost two centuries later, he showed the diffraction that occurs as the waves go through the aperture.[17] Wave mechanics were for him merely a passing curiosity, but even in this his brilliance is breathtaking.

The connections that Leonardo made across disciplines served as guides for his inquiries. The analogy between water eddies and air turbulence, for example, provided a framework for studying the flight of birds. "To arrive at knowledge of the motions of birds in the air," he wrote, "it is first necessary to acquire knowledge of the winds, which we will prove by the motions of water."[18] But the patterns he discerned were more than just useful study guides. He regarded them as revelations of essential truths, manifestations of the beautiful unity of nature.

CURIOSITY AND OBSERVATION

In addition to his instinct for discerning patterns across disciplines, Leonardo honed two other traits that aided his scientific pursuits: an omnivorous curiosity, which bordered on the fanatical, and an acute power of observation, which was eerily intense. Like much with Leonardo, these were interconnected. Any person who puts "Describe the tongue of the woodpecker" on his to-do list is overendowed with the combination of curiosity and acuity.

His curiosity, like that of Einstein, often was about phenomena that most people over the age of ten no longer puzzle about: Why is the sky blue? How are clouds formed? Why can our eyes see only in a straight line? What is yawning? Einstein said he marveled about questions others found mundane because he was slow in learning to talk as a child. For Leonardo, this talent may have been connected to growing up with a love of nature while not being overly schooled in received wisdom.

Other topics of his curiosity that he listed in his notebooks are more ambitious and require an instinct for observational investigation. "Which nerve causes the eye to move so that the motion of one eye moves the other?" "Describe the beginning of a human when it is in the womb."[19] And along with the woodpecker, he lists "the jaw of the crocodile" and "the placenta of the calf" as things he wants to describe. These inquiries entail a lot of work.[20]

His curiosity was aided by the sharpness of his eye, which focused on things that the rest of us glance over. One night he saw lightning flash behind some buildings, and for that instant they looked smaller, so he launched a series of experiments and controlled observations to verify that objects look smaller when surrounded by light and look larger in the mist or dark.[21] When he looked at things with one eye closed, he noticed that they appeared less round than when seen with both eyes, so he went on to explore the reasons why.[22]

Kenneth Clark referred to Leonardo's "inhumanly sharp eye." It's a nice phrase, but misleading. Leonardo was human. The acuteness of his observational skill was not some superpower he possessed. Instead, it was a product of his own effort. That's important, because it means that we can, if we wish, not just marvel at him but try to learn from him by pushing ourselves to look at things more curiously and intensely.

In his notebook, he described his method—almost like a trick—for closely observing a scene or object: look carefully and separately at each detail. He compared it to looking at the page of a book, which is meaningless when taken in as a whole and instead needs to be looked at word by word. Deep observation must be done in steps: "If you wish to have a sound knowledge of the forms of objects, begin with the details of them, and do not go on to the second step until you have the first well fixed in memory."[23]

Another gambit he recommended for "giving your eye good practice" at observations was to play this game with friends: one person draws a line on a wall, and the others stand a distance away and try to cut a blade of straw to the exact length of the line. "He who has come nearest with his measure to the length of the pattern is the winner."[24]

Leonardo's eye was especially sharp when it came to observing motion. "The dragonfly flies with four wings, and when those in front are raised those behind are lowered," he found. Imagine the effort it took to watch a dragonfly carefully enough to notice this. In his notebook he recorded that the best place to observe dragonflies was by the moat surrounding the Sforza Castle.[25] Let's pause to marvel at Leonardo walking out in the evening, no doubt dandily dressed, standing at the edge of a moat, intensely watching the motions of each of the four wings of a dragonfly.

His keenness at observing motion helped him overcome the difficulty of capturing it in a painting. There is a paradox, which goes back to Zeno in the fifth century BC, involving the apparent contradiction of an object being in motion yet also being at a precise place at a given instant. Leonardo wrestled with the concept of depicting an arrested instant that contains both the past and the future of that moment.

He compared an arrested instant of motion to the concept of a single geometrical point. The point has no length or width. Yet if it moves, it creates a line. "The point has no dimensions; the line is the transit of a point." Using his method of theorizing by analogy, he wrote, "The instant does not have time; and time is made from the movement of the instant."[26]

Guided by this analogy, Leonardo in his art sought to freeze-frame an event while also showing it in motion. "In rivers, the water that you touch is the last of what has passed, and the first of that which comes," he observed. "So with time present." He came back to this theme repeatedly in his notebooks. "Observe the light," he instructed. "Blink your eye and look at it again. That which you see was not there at first, and that which was there is no more."[27]

Leonardo's skill at observing motion was translated by the flicks of his brush into his art. In addition, while working at the Sforza court, he began channeling his fascination with motion into scientific and engineering studies, most notably his investigations into the flight of birds and machines for the flight of man.

CHAPTER 11

Birds and Flight

THEATRICAL FLIGHTS OF FANCY

"Study the anatomy of the wings of a bird together with the breast muscles that move those wings," Leonardo wrote in his notebook. "Do the same for man to show the possibility that man could sustain himself in the air by the flapping of wings."[1]

For more than two decades, beginning around 1490, Leonardo investigated, with an unusual degree of diligence, the flight of birds and the possibility of designing machines that would enable humans to fly. He produced more than five hundred drawings and thirty-five thousand words scattered over a dozen notebooks on these topics. The endeavor wove together his curiosity about nature, his observational skills, and his engineering instincts. It was also an example of his method of using analogy to discover nature's patterns. But in this case the analogy process extended even further: it took him closer than most of his other investigations into the realm of pure theory, including fluid dynamics and the laws of motion.

Leonardo's interest in flying machines began with his work on theatrical pageants. From his early days in Verrocchio's workshop until his final days in France, he threw himself into such spectacles with enthusiasm. His mechanical birds were first used—and last used—as court amusements.[2]

It was at such pageants that he first saw ingenious devices for allowing actors to rise, descend, and float as if they were flying. Brunelleschi, his predecessor as an artist-engineer in Florence, was the "master of effects" at a dazzling production of an *Annunciation* in the 1430s, which was revived using the same machinery in 1471, when Leonardo was nineteen and working in Florence. Suspended from the rafters was a ring holding twelve boys dressed as angels. Contraptions made of large pulleys and hand winches kept everything moving and soaring. Mechanical devices allowed the gilt-winged angels, holding harps and flaming swords, to fly down from heaven and rescue the saved souls, while from below the stage the realm of hell shot forth devils. Gabriel then arrived for the Annunciation. "As the angel ascended amongst the voices of jubilation," one spectator wrote, "he moved his hands up and down, and flapped his wings as if he were truly flying."

Another play performed at the time, *The Ascension*, also featured flying characters. "The sky opened and the Heavenly Father appeared, miraculously suspended in air," according to a report, "and the actor playing Jesus seems to have truly ascended on his own, and without tottering reached a great height." Christ's ascension was accompanied by a group of winged angels, who had been suspended in the make-believe clouds above the stage.[3]

Leonardo's first studies of flight were for such theatrical extravaganzas. One set of drawings that he made just before he left Florence for Milan in 1482 shows bat-like wings, with cranks that would create motion but not actual flight, connected to what appear to be theatrical mechanisms.[4] Another shows a featherless wing connected to gears, pulleys, cranks, and cables: the configuration of the crank and the size of the gears indicate that the whole system is designed for the theater and not for an actual flying machine. But even for his theater designs, he was carefully observing nature. On the back of this sheet he drew a jagged downward line with the caption "This is the manner in which birds descend."[5]

There is one other clue that these drawings from his Florence days were meant for the theater rather than actual flight: in all of the ingenious military devices he says he can build in his job application letter to Ludovico Sforza, there is no boast about being able to make machines for human flight. It was only after he got to Milan that his attention turned from theatrical fantasy to real-world engineering.

BIRD-WATCHING

Here's a test. All of us have looked at birds in flight, but have you ever stopped to look closely enough to see whether a bird moves its wing upward at the same speed as it flaps it down? Leonardo did, and he was able to observe that the answer differs based on species. "There are some birds that move their wings more swiftly when they lower them than when they raise them, and this is the case with doves and such birds," he recorded in a notebook. "There are others which lower their wings more slowly than they raise them, and this is seen with crows and similar birds." And some, such as magpies, raise and lower at the same speed.[6]

Leonardo had a strategy he used to refine his observational skills. He would write down marching orders to himself, determining how he would sequence his observations in a methodical step-by-step way. "First define the motion of the wind and then describe how the birds steer through it with only the simple balancing of the wings and tail," he wrote in one example. "Do this after the description of their anatomy."[7]

He recorded in his notebooks scores of such observations, most of which we find amazing mainly because we never make the effort, in our daily lives, to observe ordinary phenomena so closely. On a trip to the vineyard he had been given by Ludovico in Fiesole, a village just north of Florence, he watched a chukar partridge take flight. "When a bird with a wide wingspan and a short tail wants to take off," he reported, "it will lift its wings with force and turn them to receive the wind beneath them."[8] From observations like that he was able to make a generalization about the relationship between a bird's tail and its wings: "Birds with short tails have very wide wings, which by their width take the place of the tail; and they make considerable use of the helms set on the shoulders when they wish to turn." And later: "When birds are descending near the ground and the head is below the tail, they lower the tail, which is spread wide open, and take short strokes with the wings; consequently, the head is raised above the tail, and the speed is checked so that the bird can alight on the ground without a shock."[9] Ever notice all that?

After twenty years of observing, he decided to compile his notes into a treatise. Much of the work was gathered into an eighteen-folio notebook, now known as the Codex on the Flight of Birds.[10] It begins by exploring the concepts of gravity and density, and it ends by envisioning the launch of a flying machine he had designed and comparing its components with the body parts of a bird. But like much of Leonardo's work, the treatise remained unfinished. He was more interested in nailing concepts than he was in polishing them for publication.

When he was compiling his bird treatise, Leonardo began a section of another notebook with a directive to put them into a broader context. "To explain the science of the flight of birds, it is necessary to explain the science of the winds, which we shall prove by the motion of the waters," he wrote. "The understanding of this science of water will serve as a ladder to arrive at the knowledge of things flying in the air."[11] He not only got the basic principles of fluid dynamics correct, but he was able to turn his insights into rudimentary theories that foreshadowed those of Newton, Galileo, and Bernoulli.

No scientist before Leonardo had methodically shown how birds stay aloft. Most had simply embellished on Aristotle, who mistakenly thought that birds were supported by air the way ships were by water.[12] Leonardo realized that keeping aloft in air requires fundamentally different dynamics than doing so in water, because birds are heavier than air and are thus subject to being pulled down by gravity. The first two folios of his Codex on the Flight of Birds deal with the laws of gravity, which he calls the "attraction of one object to another." The force of gravity, he wrote, acts in the direction of "an imaginary line between the centers of each object."[13] He then described how to calculate the center of gravity of a bird, a pyramid, and other complex shapes.

One important observation he made ended up informing his studies of flight and of the flow of water. "Water cannot be compressed like air," he wrote.[14] In other words, a wing beating down on air will compact the air into a smaller space, and as a result the air pressure underneath the wing will be higher than the pressure of the rarefied air above it. "If the air could not be compressed, the birds would not be able to support themselves upon the air that is struck by their wings."[15] The downward flap of the wing pushes the bird higher and thrusts it forward.

He also realized that the pressure the bird puts on the air is met by an equal and opposite pressure that the air puts on the bird. "See how the wings, striking against the air, sustain the heavy eagle in the thin air on high," he noted, then added, "As much force is exerted by the object against the air as by the air against the object."[16] Two hundred years later, Newton would state a refined version of this as his third law of motion: "To every action there is always opposed an equal reaction."

Leonardo accompanied this concept with a precursor to Galileo's principle of relativity: "The effect of moving air on a stationary object is as great as it is when the object is moving and the air is stationary."[17] In other words, the forces that would act upon a bird flying through air are the same as the forces acting on a bird that is stationary but has air rushing past it (such as a bird in a wind tunnel or one hovering on a windy day over a spot on the ground). He drew an analogy from his studies of water flow, which he had recorded earlier in the same notebook: "The action of a pole drawn through still water resembles that of running water against a stationary pole."[18]

Even more presciently, he had an intimation of what became known, more than two hundred years later, as Bernoulli's principle: when air (or any fluid) flows faster, it exerts less pressure. Leonardo drew a cross section of a bird's wing, which shows that the top is curved more than the underside. (This is also true of airplane wings, which make use of this principle.) The air flowing over the curved top of the wing has farther to travel than the air flowing under the bottom. Therefore, the air on top has to travel faster. The difference in speed means that the air on the top of the wing exerts less pressure than the air on the bottom, thus helping the bird (or airplane) to stay aloft. "The air above birds is thinner than the usual thinness of the other air," he wrote.[19] Leonardo thus realized, before other scientists, that a bird stays aloft not merely because the wings beat downward against the air but also because the wings propel the bird forward and the air lessens in pressure as it rushes over the wing's curved top surface.

FLYING MACHINES

Both his observations on anatomy and his analysis of the physics convinced Leonardo that it was possible to build a winged mechanism that would allow humans to fly. "A bird is an instrument working according to mathematical law, and it is in the capacity of man to reproduce such an instrument," he wrote. "A man with wings large enough and duly attached might learn to overcome the resistance of the air and raise himself upon it."[20]

Combining engineering with physics and anatomy, Leonardo began in the late 1480s to devise contraptions to accomplish this. His first design (fig. 50) looks like a big bowl with four oar-like blades that were to alternate in pairs moving up and down, like the four-winged dragonfly he had studied earlier. To overcome the relative weakness of human breast muscles, this cross between a flying saucer and a health club torture chamber has the operator use his legs to push pedals, his arms to crank a gear-and-pulley mechanism, his head to pump a piston, and his shoulders to pull cables. It is unclear how he would manage to steer the machine.[21]

Seven pages later in the same notebook, Leonardo produced an elegant drawing (fig. 51) of an experiment that used a bat-like wing, its thin bones covered with a membrane of skin rather than feathers, that was similar to those he had drawn for theatrical productions back in Florence. The wing is attached to a thick wooden plank, which, he specified, should weigh 150 pounds, like an average man, and to a lever mechanism that would pump the wing. Leonardo even drew an amusing man in motion, jumping up and down on top of the end of the long lever. A little sketch below shows a clever element: when the

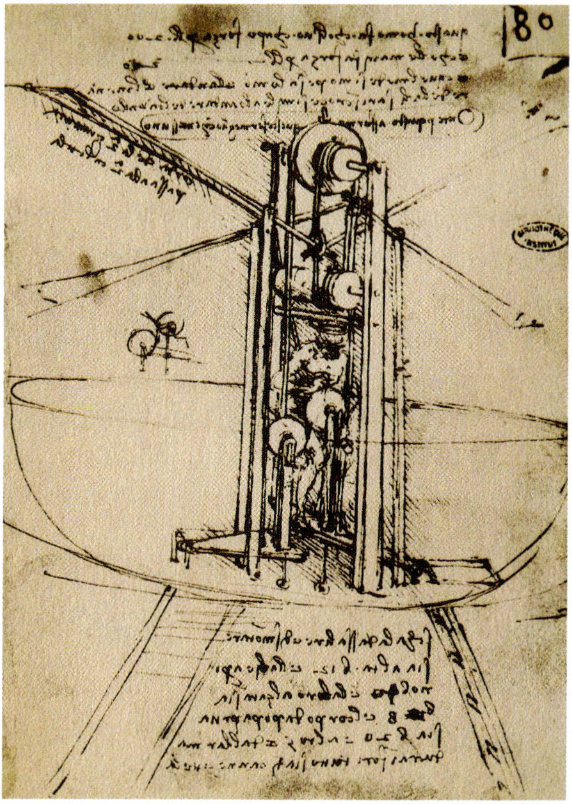

Fig. 50. A human-powered flying machine.

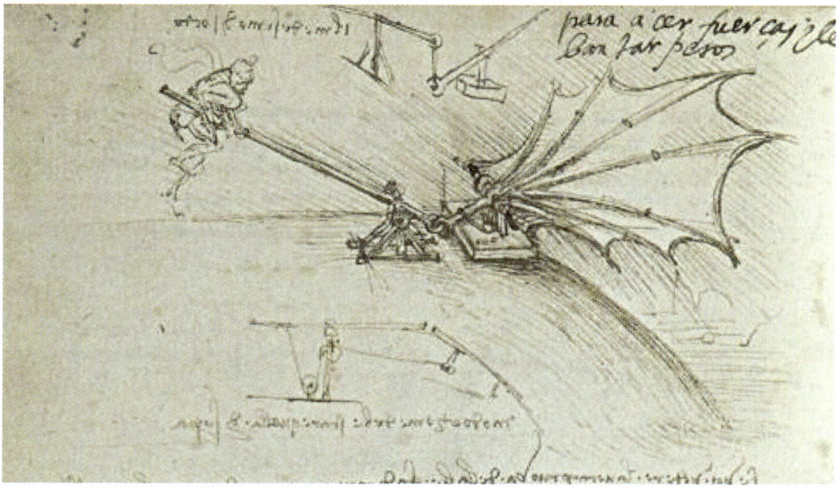

Fig. 51. A wing with hinges.

wing is swinging upward a hinge allows it to point its tips downward and encounter less resistance, then slowly be moved by a spring and pulley back into a rigid position.[22] Later ideas included devising skin flaps in the wings that would be closed on the downswing but fly open on the upswing to minimize air resistance.

At times, Leonardo abandoned the hope of achieving self-propelled flight and designed gliders instead. One of these was shown to be basically workable in a reconstruction done five hundred years later by the ITN television network in Britain.[23] However, for most of his career he remained committed to achieving human-powered flight in birdlike devices with flapping wings. He drew more than a dozen variations, using pedals and levers with the pilot prone or standing, and began referring to his machine as the *uccello*, or bird.

In his spacious accommodations at the Corte Vecchia, Leonardo had what he called "la mia fabrica" (my factory). In addition to being the room where he had worked on the ill-fated horse monument for the Sforzas, it provided space for experimenting with flying machines. At one point he wrote himself a note about how to conduct a flight experiment on the roof without being seen by the workers constructing a tower—the tiburio that he had failed in the competition to design—on the cathedral next door. "Make a large and tall model, and you will have a room on the upper roof," he wrote. "If you stand on the roof at the side of the tower, the men at work upon the tiburio will not see you."[24]

At other times, he envisioned testing a machine over water while wearing a life-preserver. "You will experiment with this machine over a lake and you will wear as a belt a long wineskin, so that if you fall in, you will not drown."[25] And finally, when all of his experiments were nearing an end, he mingled his plans with fantasies. "The large bird will take its first flight from the back of the great Swan," he wrote on the last folio of his Codex on the Flight of Birds, referring to Swan Mountain (Monte Ceceri) near Fiesole, "filling the universe with amazement, filling all writings with its fame, and bringing eternal glory to the nest where it was born."[26]

With beautiful little drawings, Leonardo portrayed the elegance of birds as they twisted, turned, shifted their center of gravity, and maneuvered the winds. He also pioneered the use of vector-like lines and swirls to show invisible currents. But for all the beauty of his art and all the ingenuity of his designs, he was never able to create a human-powered flying machine that could take off on its own. To be fair, it took almost five hundred years before any human did so.

Late in his life, Leonardo sketched a cylinder with two feeble wings, clearly meant as a toy. Look closely, and you can see that it's attached to a wire line. In what may be his last drawing of a mechanical bird, he reverted, in a poignant and slightly sad fashion, to the way he began drawing them thirty years earlier: as dazzling but ephemeral little contraptions for the momentary amusement of audiences at court theatricals and public pageants.[27]

CHAPTER 12

The Mechanical Arts

MACHINES

Leonardo's interest in machinery was linked to his fascination with motion. He saw both machines and humans as apparatuses designed to move, with analogous components such as cords and sinews. As he did with his anatomy drawings of dissected bodies, he drew machines disassembled—using exploded and layered views—to show how motion is transferred from gears and levers to wheels and pulleys, and his cross-disciplinary interests allowed him to connect concepts from anatomy to engineering.

Other Renaissance technologists drew machines, but they did so by presenting them in completed form, without discussing the role and efficiency of each component. Leonardo, on the other hand, was interested in a part-by-part analysis of the transfer of motion. Rendering each of the moving parts—ratchets, springs, gears, levers, axles, and so on—was a method to help him understand their functions and engineering principles. He used drawing as a tool for thinking. He experimented on paper and evaluated concepts by visualizing them.

Take, for example, his drawing, beautifully shaded and in perfect perspective, of a hoist in which a lever can be rocked to ratchet up toothed wheels and lift a heavy load (fig. 52). It shows how an up-and-down cranking motion can be converted into a continuous rotary

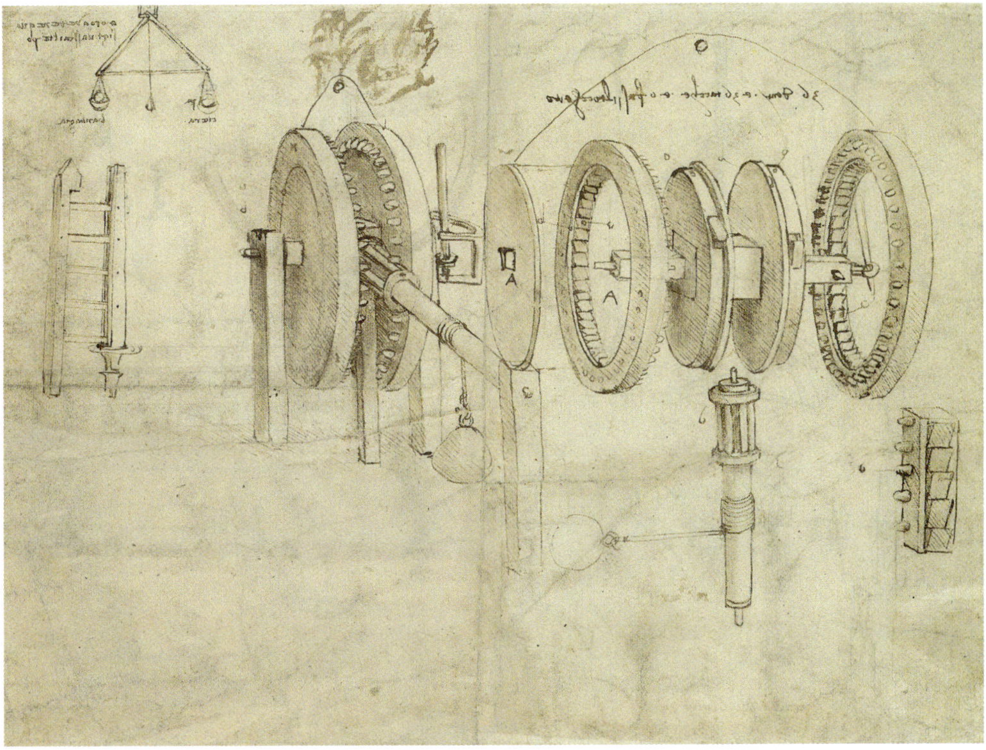

Fig. 52. A hoist with view of components.

motion. The assembled mechanism is on the left side of the page, and to the right is an exploded view of each of the components.[1]

Many of his most beautiful and meticulous drawings explore how to make sure that motion stays at a constant pace, without slowing down, when a coiled spring slowly unwinds. In the beginning, a tightly wound spring transmits a lot of power and causes a mechanism to move quickly, but after a while it has less power and the mechanism slows down. This can be a serious problem for many devices, especially clocks. A major enterprise of the late Renaissance was finding a way to equalize the power of an unwinding spring. Leonardo pioneered the depiction of gears that solve this challenge by using the spiral forms that fascinated him throughout his life. One particularly elegant drawing (fig. 53) shows a spiral gear equalizing the speed of an unwinding barrel spring and transmitting the

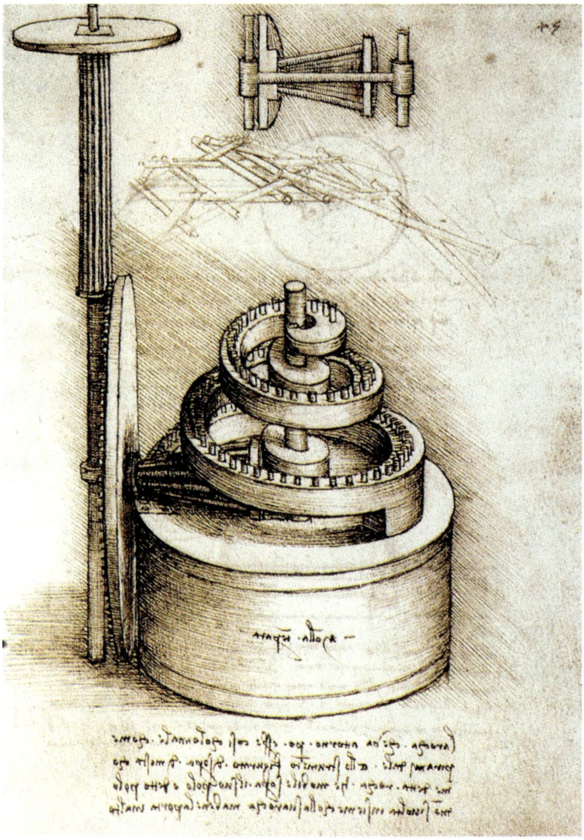

Fig. 53. A spiral gear for equalizing spring power.

constant power to a wheel that pushes a shaft steadily upward.[2] The drawing is one of his most gorgeous works. He used his left-handed hatches to show form and shading, with curved hatchings for the barrel. His mechanical ingenuity is combined with his artistic passion for spirals and curls.

The key purpose of machinery, then as now, is to harness energy and turn it into movements that accomplish useful tasks. For example, Leonardo showed how the energy of humans could be used to pump a treadmill or turn a crank; that power could then be transmitted by gears and pulleys to perform a function. To capture human energy most efficiently, he broke the human body into components; he illustrated how each muscle works, calculated its power, and showed methods for leveraging it. In a notebook from the 1490s, he calculated how much weight a man can lift with his biceps, legs, shoulders, and other muscle groups.[3] "The greatest force a man can apply," he wrote, "will be when he sets his feet on one end of the balance and then leans his shoulders against some stable support. This will raise, at the other end of the balance, a weight equal to his own plus as much weight as he can carry on his shoulders."[4]

These studies were helpful for determining which muscles, if any, would be best at propelling a manned flying machine. But he also applied his findings to other tasks and sources of power. At one point he listed the many practical applications that could come from harnessing the power of the Arno River: "Saw mills, wool-cleaning machines, paper mills, hammers for forges, flour mills, knife grinding and sharpening, burnishing arms, manufacture of gunpowder, the silk spinning power of a hundred women, ribbon weaving, shaping vases made from jasper," and more.[5]

One of the practical applications he explored was using machinery to drive piles in the banks of a river to regulate its flow. His initial concept was to use a drop hammer that was raised by pulleys and ropes. Later he came up with an idea for raising the hammer more efficiently by having men climb a ladder and descend in a stirrup.[6] Likewise, when studying how to harness the power of falling water using a waterwheel, he realized correctly that it would be efficient to have the water fill buckets that would be pulled by gravity down one side of the wheel. He then designed a ratchet system so that the water would be dumped out of each bucket just as it got to the bottom of the turn. In a further modification, he designed a wheel with buckets in the shape of curved scoops.[7]

Leonardo also invented a machine designed to grind needles, which would have been a valuable contribution to the textile industries of Italy. It used human power to revolve a turntable attached to small grinding gears and polishing strips (fig. 54). He thought it might make him rich. "Tomorrow morning on January 2, 1496, I shall try out the broad belt," he wrote in a notebook. He estimated that a hundred such machines could turn out forty thousand needles an hour, each of which could be sold for 5 soldi. With a labored set of

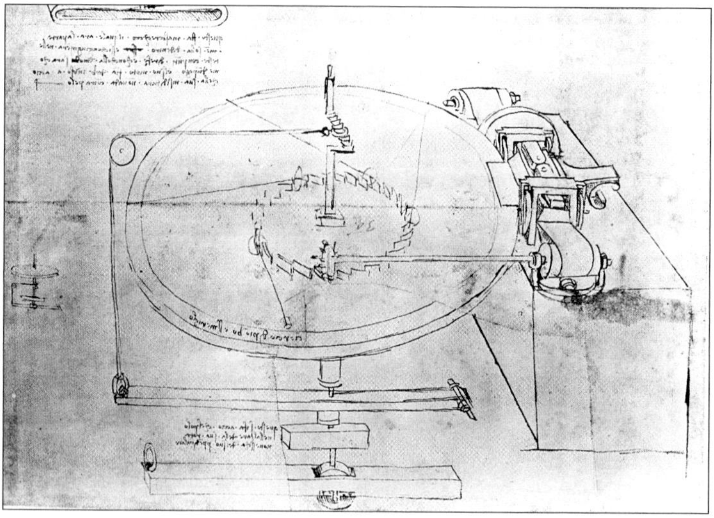

Fig. 54. Needle-grinding machine.

calculations, and a tenfold error in multiplication, he figured that he could reap an annual revenue of 60,000 ducats, the gold equivalent of more than $8 million in 2017. Even allowing for his miscalculation, 6,000 ducats of revenue should have been enticing enough to lure him away from the trade of painting Madonnas and altarpieces. But needless to say, Leonardo never finished executing his plan. Coming up with the conception was enough for him.[8]

PERPETUAL MOTION

Leonardo understood the concept of what he called impetus, which is what happens when a force pushes an object and gives it momentum. "A body in motion desires to maintain its course in the line from which it started," he wrote. "Every movement tends to maintain itself; or, rather, every body in motion continues to move so long as the influence of the force that set it in motion is maintained in it."[9] Leonardo's insights were a precursor to what Newton, two hundred years later, would make his first law of motion: that a body in motion will stay in the same motion unless acted upon by another force.[10]

If you were able to eliminate all forces slowing down an object in motion, then it should be possible, Leonardo thought, for a body to stay in motion forever. So during the 1490s, he used twenty-eight pages of a notebook to explore the possibility of a perpetual-motion machine. He looked for ways to prevent the momentum of an object from draining away, and he studied ways that a system could create or replenish its own impetus. He considered many mechanisms: wheels

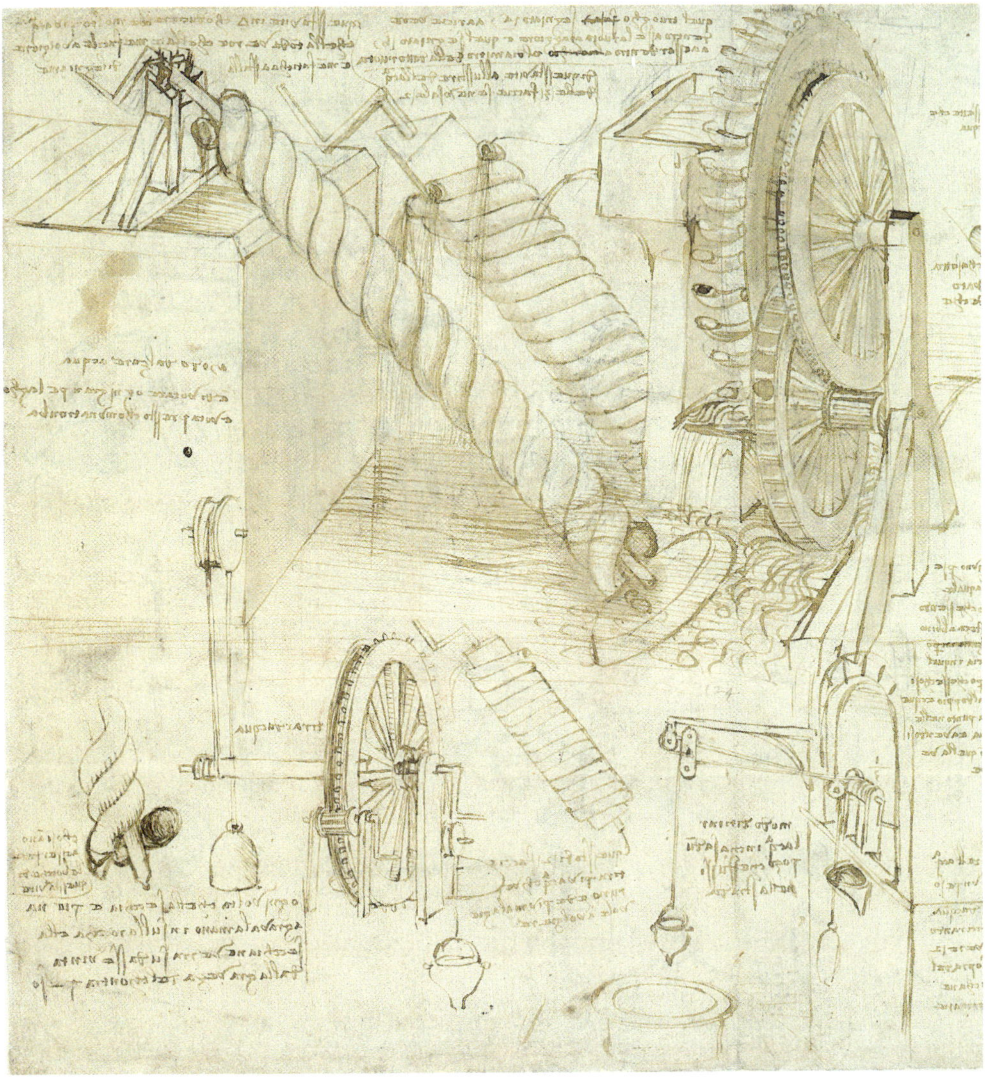

Fig. 55. A perpetual-motion machine using a water screw.

with hammers on hinges that would swing out when their part of the wheel was heading down, ways to hang weights on wheels that would keep them turning, spiral screws that form a double helix, and curved compartments on a wheel with balls that roll to the lowest point when they are heading downward.[11]

He was especially intrigued by the possibility that water devices might be a way to achieve perpetual motion. One such attempt (fig. 55) envisions the use of moving water to turn a coiled tube known as an Archimedes screw, which would carry water upward and then continue turning the screw as it flows downward. Was it possible for the downward flow of water, he asked, to turn the screw with enough power to raise enough water to keep the process going indefinitely? Even though technologists would try ways of accomplishing that trick for the next three centuries, Leonardo concluded, clearly and correctly, that it was impossible. "Descending water will never raise from its resting place an amount of water equal to its weight."[12]

His drawings served as visual thought experiments. By rendering the mechanisms in his notebooks rather than actually constructing them, he could envision how they would work and assess whether they would achieve perpetual motion. He eventually concluded, after looking at many different methods, that none of them would. In reasoning so, he showed that, as we go through life, there is a value in trying to do such tasks as designing a perpetual-motion machine: there are some problems that we will never be able to solve, and it's useful to understand why. "Among the impossible delusions of man is the search for continuous motion, called by some perpetual wheel," he wrote in the introduction to his Codex Madrid I. "Speculators on perpetual motion, how many vain chimeras you have created in this quest!"[13]

FRICTION

What prevents perpetual motion, Leonardo realized, is the inevitable loss of momentum in a system when it rubs against reality. Friction causes energy to be lost and prevents motion from being perpetual. So do air and water resistance, as he knew from his studies of bird flight and fish movement.

Thus he began a methodical study of friction, which resulted in some impressive insights. Through a set of experiments with heavy objects moving down a slope, he discovered the relationship among three determinants of friction: the weight of the object, the smoothness or roughness of the incline's surface, and the steepness of the incline. He was among the first to figure out that the amount of friction is not dependent on the size of the area of contact between the object and the surface. "The friction made by the same weight will be of equal resistance at the beginning of its movement although the contact may be of different breadths and lengths," he wrote. These laws of friction, and in particular the realization that friction is independent of the contact surface area, were an important discovery, but Leonardo never published them. They had to be rediscovered almost two hundred years later by the French scientific instrument maker Guillaume Amontons.[14]

Leonardo then went on to perform experiments to quantify the effects of each factor. To measure the power of an object sliding down an incline, he devised an instrument, now known as a tribometer, that would not be reinvented until the eighteenth century. Using the device, he analyzed what we now call the coefficient of friction, which is the ratio between the force it takes to move one surface over another and the pressure between the surfaces. For a piece of wood sliding against another piece of wood, he calculated this ratio as 0.25, which is about right.

He found that by lubricating the incline, he reduced friction, so he was among the first engineers to include points for the insertion of oil into his mechanical devices. He also devised ways to use ball bearings and roller bearings, techniques that were not commonly used until the late 1800s.[15]

In his Codex Madrid I, which is largely devoted to the design of more efficient machinery, Leonardo drew a new type of screw jack (fig. 56), one of those devices in which a big screw is turned to push upward on a heavy object. These were widely used in the fifteenth century. One drawback is that there is a lot of friction when a heavy load is pressing down. Leonardo's solution, which was likely the first of its kind, was to put some ball bearings between the plate and the

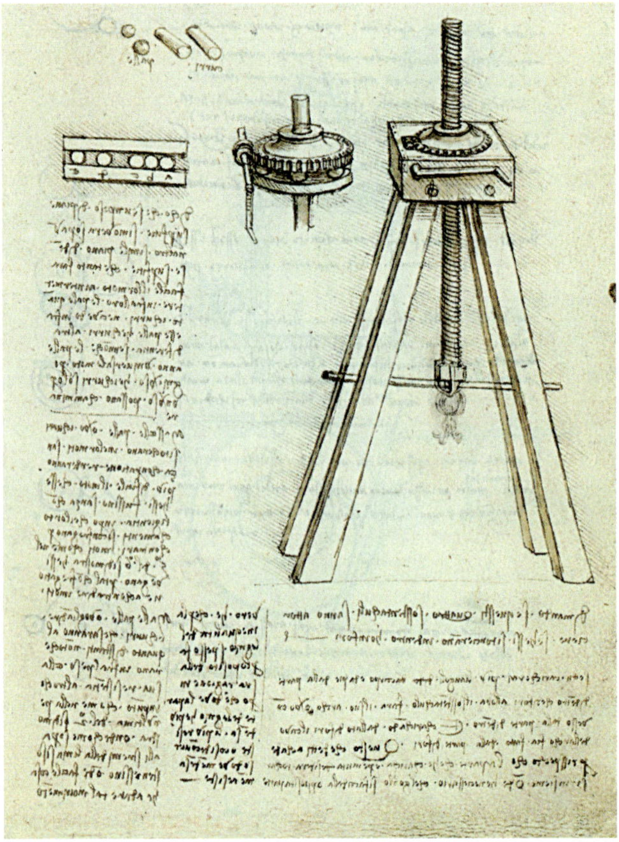

Fig. 56. A screw jack with ball bearings.

gear, which he drew in an exposed view just to the left of the jack. An even closer schematic view is to the left of that. "If a weight of a flat surface moves on a similar surface, its movement will be facilitated by interposing balls or rollers between them," he wrote in the accompanying text. "If the balls or rollers touch each other in their motion, they will make the movement more difficult than if there were no contact between them, because when they touch the friction causes a contrary motion and the movements counteract each other. But if the balls or rollers are kept at a distance from each other . . . it will be easy to generate this movement."[16] Being Leonardo, he then produced many pages of sketched thought experiments in which he varied the size and arrangements of the ball bearings. Three balls are better than four, he determined, because three points define a plane, and thus the three balls will always touch a flat surface, whereas a fourth ball may be out of alignment.

Leonardo was also the first person to record the best mix of metals to produce an alloy that reduces friction. It should be "three parts of copper and seven of tin, melted together," which was similar to the alloy he was using to make mirrors. "Leonardo's formula gives a perfectly working anti-friction composition," wrote Ladislao Reti, the historian of technology who played a role in discovering and publishing the Madrid Codices in 1965. Once again, Leonardo was about three centuries ahead of his time. The first antifriction alloy is usually credited to the American inventor Isaac Babbitt, who patented an alloy containing copper, tin, and antimony in 1839.[17]

Through his work on machinery, Leonardo developed a mechanistic view of the world foreshadowing that of Newton. All movements in the universe—of human limbs and of cogs in machines, of blood in our veins and of water in rivers—operate according to the same laws, he concluded. These laws are analogous; the motions in one realm can be compared to those in another realm, and patterns emerge. "Man is a machine, a bird is a machine, the whole universe is a machine," wrote Marco Cianchi in an analysis of Leonardo's devices.[18] As Leonardo and others led Europe into a new scientific age, he ridiculed astrologers, alchemists, and others who believed in nonmechanistic explanations of cause and effect, and he relegated the idea of religious miracles to the purview of priests.

CHAPTER 13

Math

GEOMETRY

Leonardo increasingly came to realize that mathematics was the key to turning observations into theories. It was the language that nature used to write her laws. "There is no certainty in sciences where mathematics cannot be applied," he declared.[1] He was correct. Using geometry to understand the laws of perspective taught him how math could extract from nature the secrets of its beauty and reveal the beauty of its secrets.

With his visual acuity, Leonardo had a natural feel for geometry, and that branch of math helped him formulate some rules for how nature works. However, his facility with shapes was not matched by one for numbers, so arithmetic did not come naturally. In his notebooks are entries where, for example, he doubles 4,096 to get 8,092, forgetting to carry the 1.[2] As for algebra—that wonderful tool for using numbers and letters to codify nature's laws and variables, bequeathed to later Renaissance scholars by the Arabs and Persians—Leonardo was clueless, which hindered his ability to use equations as brushstrokes for painting the patterns he discerned in nature.

What Leonardo liked about geometry, as opposed to arithmetic, was that geometric shapes are continuous quantities, whereas numbers are discrete digits and thus discontinuous units. "Arithmetic deals with discontinuous quantities, geometry with continuous ones," he wrote.[3] In modern parlance we would say that he was more comfortable with analog tools, including the use of shapes as analogies (yes, that's where the word *analog* comes from), rather than being a digital native. As he wrote, "Arithmetic is a computational science in its calculation, with true and perfect units, but it is of no avail in dealing with continuous quantity."[4]

Geometry also had the advantage of being a visual endeavor. It engaged the eye and the imagination. "When he looked at the way that shells assumed a helical shape," Martin Kemp wrote, "at how leaves and petals originated from stems, and at the reasons why a heart valve worked with perfect economy, geometrical analysis delivered the results he desired."[5]

Not having access to algebra, he instead used geometry to describe the rate of change caused by a variable. For example, he used triangles and pyramids to represent rates of change in the velocity of falling objects, the volume of sounds, and the perspective view of distant objects. "Proportion is not only to be found in number and measure, but also in sounds, weights, times and places and every force that exists," he wrote.[6]

LUCA PACIOLI

One of Leonardo's close friends at Milan's court was Luca Pacioli, a mathematician who developed the first widely published system for double-entry bookkeeping. Like Leonardo, he was born in Tuscany and attended only an abacus school, which provided a trade education in arithmetic but no Latin. He worked as a wandering tutor to boys from wealthy families and then became a Franciscan friar who never moved into a monastery. He wrote a math textbook in Italian, rather than Latin, which was published in Venice in 1494; it thus became part of the explosive spread of learning in vernacular languages triggered by the printing press in the late fifteenth century.

Leonardo bought a copy as soon as it was published, recording the rather high cost (more than twice what he paid for a Bible) in his notebook,[7] and he may have helped recruit Pacioli to become part of the Milan court. The mathematician arrived there in about 1496 and had living quarters along with Leonardo at the Corte Vecchia. They shared a love of geometric shapes. A portrait painted of Pacioli (fig. 57) shows him and a student in front of a table with a protractor, compass, and stylus; a polyhedron of eighteen squares and eight triangles half filled with water dangles from the ceiling.

A lesser-known but important component of Pacioli's work at court involved contributing, alongside Leonardo, to its ephemeral amusements and performances. In a notebook he began just after his arrival, "On the Powers of Numbers," Pacioli compiled riddles, mathematical brain-twisters, magic tricks, and parlor games designed to be presented and solved at court parties. His tricks include how to make an egg walk across a table (it involves wax and strands of hair), how to make a coin go up and down in a glass (vinegar and magnetic powder), and how to make a chicken jump (quicksilver). His parlor

Fig. 57. Luca Pacioli.

games included the first published version of the standard card trick of guessing which card someone has picked from a deck (it involves an accomplice), brain-teasers such as one in which a man has to figure out how to ferry a wolf and a goat and a cabbage across a river, and math games in which a spectator thinks of a number which can then be discovered by asking the result of a few operations performed on it. Particularly appealing to Leonardo were Pacioli's games involving creating circles around triangles and squares using only a ruler and a compass.

Pacioli and Leonardo bonded over their shared fondness for such stimulating amusements and entertainments. Leonardo's name crops up often in Pacioli's notes. After writing the basics of one trick, for instance, Pacioli declares, "Well Leonardo, you can do more of this on your own."[8]

More seriously, Leonardo learned math from Pacioli, a great tutor, who taught him the subtleties and beauties of Euclid's geometry and tried to teach him, with less success, how to multiply squares and square roots. At times when he found a concept difficult to comprehend, Leonardo would copy passages of Pacioli's explanations verbatim into his notebooks.[9]

Leonardo returned the favor by drawing a set of mathematical illustrations, of astonishing artistic beauty and grace, for the book Pacioli began writing upon his arrival in Milan, *On Divine Proportion*, which examines the role of proportions and ratios in architecture, art, anatomy, and math. Given Leonardo's appreciation for the intersection of arts and sciences, he was fascinated by the topic.

Most of Leonardo's drawings for Pacioli's book, which was finished in 1498, are variations of the five shapes known as Platonic solids. These are polyhedrons that have the same number of faces meeting at each vertex: pyramids, cubes, octahedrons (eight faces), dodecahedrons (twelve), and icosahedrons (twenty). He also illustrated more complex shapes, such as a rhombicuboctahedron, which has twenty-six facets, eight of them equilateral triangles that are bordered by squares (fig. 58). He pioneered a new method for making such shapes understandable: instead of drawing them as solids, he made them see-through skeletons, as if constructed of wooden beams.

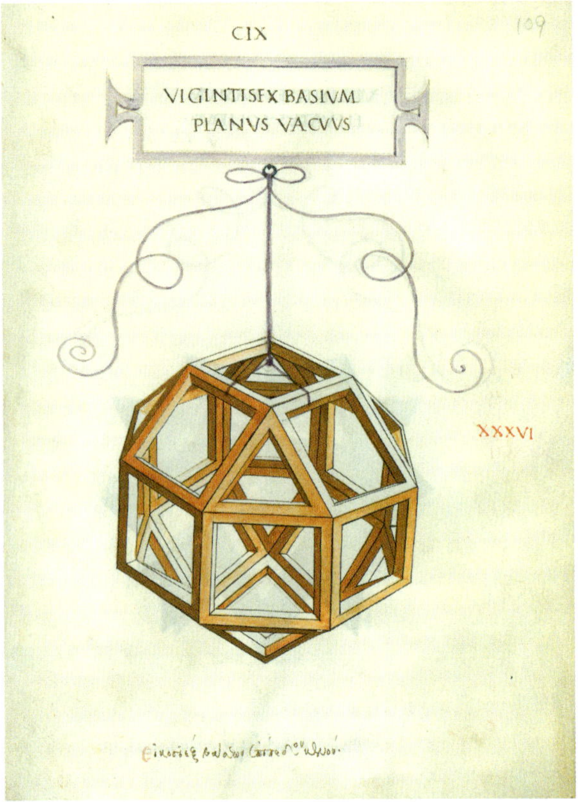

Fig. 58. Leonardo's rhombicuboctahedron
for Pacioli's book.

His sixty illustrations for Pacioli were the only drawings he published during his lifetime.

Part of Leonardo's genius is in the lighting and shading of these illustrations, which make the geometric renderings seem like actual objects dangling before our eyes. The light comes in from an angle, casting shadows both bold and subtle. Each of the object's faces becomes a windowpane. Leonardo's mastery of perspective added to the three-dimensional look. He could envision the shapes in his head as real objects, then convey them on the page. But he probably also used actual wooden models that he hung on a string, like the dangling polyhedron in the portrait of Pacioli. Using both observation and mathematical reasoning, and combining his study of geometric shapes with his inquiries into the flight of birds, Leonardo became the first person to discover the center of gravity of a triangular pyramid (one-quarter of the way up a line from the base to the peak).

In his book, Pacioli gratefully acknowledged that the drawings were "made and formed by the ineffable left hand, so well versed in all the mathematical disciplines, by the prince among mortals today, by the first Florentine, our Leonardo da Vinci, who, in that happy time, together with me, on the same stipends, was in the marvelous city of Milan." Pacioli later called Leonardo the "most worthy of painters, perspectivists, architects and musicians, one endowed with every perfection," and he recalled "that happy time when we were both in the employ of the most illustrious Duke of Milan, Ludovico Maria Sforza Anglo, in the years of Our Lord 1496 to 1499."[10]

Pacioli's book focused on the golden ratio, or divine proportion, an irrational number that expresses a ratio that pops up often in number series, geometry, and art. It is approximately 1.61803398, but (being irrational) has decimals that stretch on randomly forever. The golden ratio occurs when you divide a line into two parts in such a way that the ratio between the whole length and the longer part is equal to the ratio between the longer part and the shorter part. For example, take a line that's 100 inches long and divide it into two parts of 61.8 inches and 38.2 inches. That comes close to the golden ratio, because 100 divided by 61.8 is about the same as 61.8 divided by 38.2; in both cases, it's approximately 1.618.

Euclid wrote about this ratio in around 300 BC, and it has fascinated mathematicians ever since. Pacioli was the first to popularize the name *divine proportion* for it. In his book by that title, he described the way it turns up in studies of geometric solids such as cubes and prisms and polyhedrons. In popular lore, including in Dan Brown's *The Da Vinci Code*, the golden ratio is found throughout Leonardo's art.[11] If so, it is doubtful it was intentional. Although it is possible to draw diagrams of the *Mona Lisa* and *Saint Jerome* asserting this notion, the evidence that Leonardo consciously made use of the precise mathematical ratio is not convincing.

Nevertheless, Leonardo's interest in harmonic ratios was reflected in his intense studies of the ways that ratios and proportions are manifest in anatomy, science, and art. It led him to search for analogies between the proportions of the body, the notes of musical harmonies, and other ratios that underpin the beauty manifest in the works of nature.

TRANSFORMATION OF SHAPES

As an artist, Leonardo was particularly interested in how the shapes of objects transformed when they moved. From his observations on the flow of water, he developed an appreciation for the idea of the conservation of volume: as a quantity of water flows, its shape changes, but its volume remains exactly the same.

Understanding the transformation of volumes was useful for an artist, especially one such as Leonardo, who specialized in portraying bodies in motion. It helped him picture how an object's shape could be distorted or transformed while keeping its volume unchanged. "Of everything that moves," he wrote, "the space which it acquires is as great as that which it leaves."[12] This applies not only to quantities of water, but to a bending arm and twisting torso of a human.

As he became more interested in how geometry could provide analogies for phenomena in nature, Leonardo began to explore more theoretical cases where the conservation of volume held true as one geometric shape morphed into another. An example would be if you took a square and transformed it into a circle with the exact same area. A three-dimensional example would be showing how a sphere could be transformed into a cube with the same volume.

By grappling with these transformations and persistently recording his insights, Leonardo helped to pioneer the field of topology, which looks at how shapes and objects can undergo transformations while keeping some of the same properties. Throughout his notebooks we can see him—sometimes with obsessive focus, at other times distracted and doodling—taking curved shapes and transforming them into rectangular shapes of the same size, or doing the same for pyramids and cones.[13] He could visualize and draw such transformations, and he sometimes replicated them experimentally using soft wax. But he was not good at the math tools of geometry, which involve being able to multiply the squares of numbers, square roots, cubes, and cube roots. "Learn the multiplication of roots from Maestro Luca," he wrote in his notebook, referring to Pacioli. But he never mastered the math and instead spent his career trying to figure out geometrical transformations using drawings rather than equations.[14]

He started collecting his studies on this topic and in 1505 declared his intention to write "a book entitled transformation, namely of one body into another without diminishing or increasing the material."[15] Like his other treatises, it produced brilliant notebook pages but not a published book.

SQUARING THE CIRCLE

One topic related to the conservation of volume that particularly intrigued Leonardo, and would eventually obsess him, came from the ancient Greek mathematician Hippocrates. It involves a lune, a geometric shape that looks like the crescent of a quarter-moon. Hippocrates discovered a delightful mathematical fact: if you create a lune by overlapping a large half-circle with a smaller one, you can construct a right triangle inside the larger half-circle that has the exact same area as the lune. This was the first way discovered to calculate the exact area inside a curved shape, such as a circle or a lune, and to replicate that area in a straight-sided shape, such as a triangle or rectangle.

That fascinated Leonardo. He filled his notebooks with shaded drawings in which he overlapped two half-circles and then created triangles and rectangles that had the same area as the resulting crescents. Year after year, he relentlessly pursued ways to create circular shapes with areas equivalent to triangles and rectangles, as if addicted to the game. Though he never gave the precise dates of any milestones he reached when making a painting, he treated these geometric studies as if each little success was a moment in history worthy of a notarial record. One night he wrote momentously, "Having for a long time searched to square the angle to two equal curves . . . now in the year 1509 on the eve of the Calends of May [April 30] I have found the solution at the 22nd hour on Sunday."[16]

His pursuit of equivalent areas was aesthetic as well as intellectual. After a while, his experimental geometric shapes, such as his curved triangles, became artistic patterns. On one set of pages (fig. 59) he drew 180 diagrams of overlapping circular and straight-sided shapes, each one annotated with how the shaded and unshaded portions relate to each other in area.[17]

As usual, he decided to put together a treatise on the topic—*De Ludo Geometrico*, he called it (On the Game of Geometry)—and it filled page after page of his notebooks. Not surprisingly, it joined his other treatises in never being finished for publication.[18] His choice of the word *ludo* is interesting; it implies a diversion or pastime that is engrossing but like a game. Indeed, the distraction that came from playing with lunes seemed to drive him to lunacy at times. But to him it was an enthralling mind game, one that he believed would get him closer to the secrets of nature's beautiful patterns.

These obsessions led Leonardo to an ancient riddle described by Vitruvius, Euripides, and others. Faced with a plague in the fifth century BC, the citizens of Delos consulted the oracle of Delphi. They were told that the plague would end if they found a mathematical way to precisely double the size of the altar to Apollo, which was shaped as a cube. When they doubled the length of each side, the plague worsened; the Oracle explained that by doing so they had increased the size of the cube eightfold rather than doubling it. (For example, a cube with two-foot sides has eight times the volume of a cube with one-foot sides.) To solve the problem geometrically required multiplying the length of each side by the cube root of 2.

Despite his note to himself to "learn the multiplication of roots from Maestro Luca," Leonardo was never good at square roots, much less cube roots. Even if he had been, however, neither he nor the plague-stricken Greeks had the tools to solve the problem with numerical calculations, because the cube root of 2 is an irrational number. But Leonardo was able to come up with a visual solution. The answer can be found by drawing a cube that is constructed on a plane that cuts diagonally through the original cube, just as a square

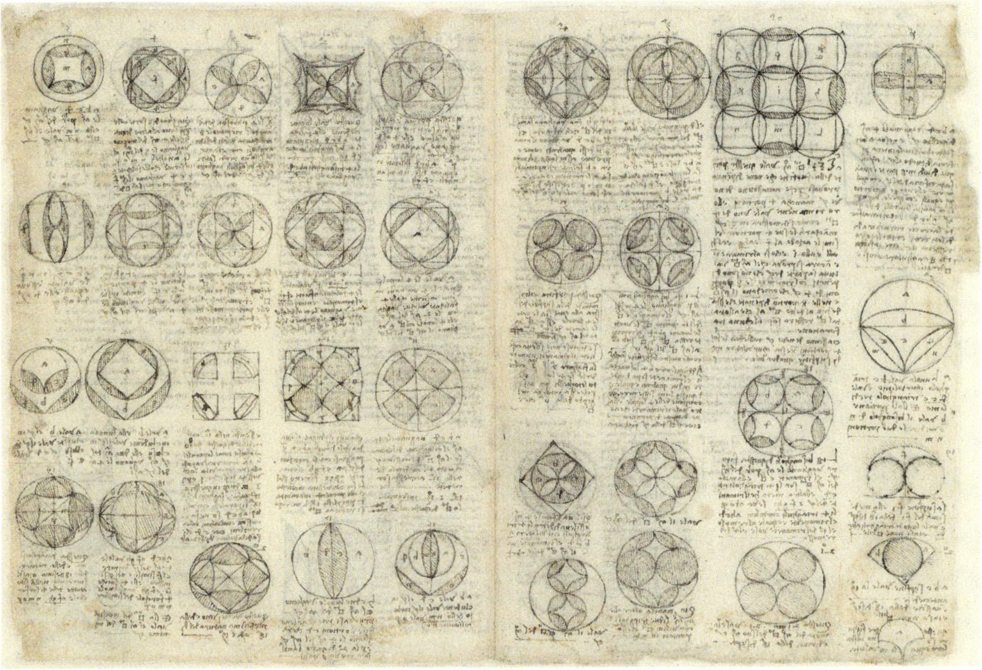

Fig. 59. Finding equivalent geometric areas.

can be doubled in size by constructing a new square on a line cutting it in half diagonally, thus squaring the hypotenuse.[19]

Leonardo also wrestled with a related riddle, the most famous of the ancient math puzzles: squaring the circle. The challenge is to take a circle and, using only a compass and ruler, construct a square that has the exact same area. That quest was what led Hippocrates to work on ways to turn a circular shape into a triangular one with the same volume. For more than a decade, Leonardo became obsessed by the effort.

We now know that a mathematical process for squaring a circle requires use of a transcendental number, in this case π, which cannot be expressed as a fraction and is not the root of any polynomial with rational coefficients.[20] So it's not possible to accomplish with just a compass and ruler. But Leonardo's persistent efforts show the brilliance of his thought process. At one point, exhausted but excited after an all-night effort, he scribbled one of the momentous entries he used for what he thought were mathematical breakthroughs: "On the night of St Andrew [November 30] I reached the end of squaring the circle; and at the end of the light of the candle, of the night, and of the paper on which I was writing, it was completed."[21] But it was a false celebration, and he was soon back at work on different methods.

One approach he took was to calculate the area of a circle experimentally. He sliced a circle into thin triangular wedges and tried to measure the size of each. He also unrolled the circumference to figure out its length. A more sophisticated approach came from his love of lunes. He cut a circle into many rectangles that could be easily measured and then used the methods of Hippocrates to find areas comparable to the remaining curved parts.

Yet another prolonged attempt involved dividing a circle into many sectors, which he then subdivided into triangles and semicircles. He arranged these slices into a rectangle and repeated the process with smaller and smaller slices, approaching the limit of infinitely small triangles. His impulses prefigured those that would lead to the development of calculus, but Leonardo did not have the skills that allowed Leibniz and Newton to devise this mathematical study of change two centuries later.

Throughout his life, Leonardo would remain enchanted by the transformation of shapes. The margins of his notebooks, and sometimes entire pages, would be filled with triangles inside semicircles inside squares inside circles as he played with tricks for turning one geometrical form into another with the same area or volume. He came up with 169 formulas for squaring a circular shape, and on one sheet drew so many examples that it looks like a page from a pattern book. Even the very last notebook page that he is known to have written near the end of his life—a famous one ending with the phrase "the soup is getting cold"—is filled with triangles and rectangles as he tried to calculate comparable areas.

Kenneth Clark once called them "calculations which are of no interest to mathematicians, and of even less interest to the art historian."[22] Yes, but they were interesting to Leonardo. Compulsively so. They may not have led to historic breakthroughs in mathematics, but they were integral to his ability to perceive and portray motion—of bird wings and water, of a squirming baby Jesus and a breast-beating Saint Jerome—like no other artist before him.

CHAPTER 14

The Nature of Man

ANATOMICAL DRAWINGS (FIRST PERIOD, 1487–1493)

As a young painter in Florence, Leonardo studied human anatomy primarily to improve his art. His forerunner as an artist-engineer, Leon Battista Alberti, had written that anatomical study was essential for an artist because properly depicting people and animals requires beginning with an understanding of their insides. "Isolate each bone of the animal, on this add its muscles, then clothe all of it with its flesh," he wrote in *On Painting*, which became a bible for Leonardo. "Before dressing a man we first draw him nude, then we enfold him in draperies. So in painting the nude, we place first his bones and muscles which we then cover with flesh so that it is not difficult to understand where each muscle is beneath."[1]

Leonardo embraced the advice with an enthusiasm that any other artist, or for that matter most anatomists, would have found unimaginable. And in his notebooks he preached the same sermon: "It is necessary for a painter to be a good anatomist, so that he may be able to design the naked parts of the human frame and know the anatomy of the sinews, nerves, bones, and muscles."[2] Following another part of Alberti's creed, Leonardo wanted to know how psychological emotions led to physical motions. As a result, he would also become interested in the way the nervous system works and how optical impressions are processed.

The most basic anatomical knowledge for a painter is the understanding of muscles, and in this Florence's artists were pioneers. Antonio del Pollaiuolo made an influential copperplate engraving of a battle scene of nude men, showing their muscles in more-than-full glory, around 1470, when Leonardo was associated with Verrocchio's nearby workshop. Vasari wrote that Pollaiuolo "dissected many bodies to study their anatomy," though it's likely these were merely surface studies. Leonardo, who probably observed some of these dissections, naturally soon became interested in exploring even more deeply, and he began what would be a lifelong association with Florence's hospital of Santa Maria Nuova.[3]

When he moved to Milan, he discovered that the study of anatomy there was pursued primarily by medical scholars rather than by artists.[4] The city's culture was more intellectual than artistic, and the University of Pavia was a center for medical research. Prominent anatomical scholars were soon tutoring him, lending him books, and then teaching him dissection. Under their influence, he began pursuing anatomy as a scientific as well as an artistic endeavor. But he did not regard these as separate. In anatomy, as in so many of his studies, he saw the art and science as interwoven. Art required a deep understanding of anatomy, which in turn was aided by a profound appreciation for the beauty of nature. As with his study of the flight of birds, Leonardo went from seeking knowledge that could be of practical use and began seeking knowledge for its own sake, out of pure curiosity and joy.

This was evident when he sat down after seven years in Milan with a clean notebook sheet and made a list of the topics he wished to investigate. On top he wrote the date, "on the second of April 1489," which was unusual for him and an indication that he was embarking on an important endeavor. On the left-hand page he drew, with delicate strokes of a pen, two views of a human skull with veins. On the right-hand page, he listed topics to explore:

What nerve is the cause of the eye's movement and makes the movement of one eye move the other?

Of closing the eyelid.

Of raising the eyebrows. . . .

Of parting the lips with teeth clenched.

Of bringing the lips to a point.

Of laughing.

Of expressing wonder.

Set yourself to describe the beginning of man when he is created in the womb and why an infant of eight months does not live.

What sneezing is.

What yawning is.

Epilepsy.

Spasm.

Paralysis. . . .

Fatigue.

Hunger.

Sleep.

Thirst.

Sensuality. . . .

Of the nerve that causes the movement of the thigh.

And from the knee to the foot and from the ankle to the toes.[5]

The list begins with inquiries, such as how eyes move and lips smile, that could be useful for his art. But by the time the list gets to an infant in a womb and the cause of sneezing, it is clear that he's looking for more than information that might help his brush.

That intermingling of artistic and scientific interests is even more evident on another page that he began writing around the same time. With a sweeping scope, ranging from conception to mirth to music, that would have seemed audacious for anyone other than Leonardo, he outlined a treatise on anatomy that he hoped to produce:

> This work should begin with the conception of man, and describe the nature of the womb and how the fetus lives in it, up to what stage it resides there, and in what way it quickens into life and gets food. Also its growth and what interval there is between one stage of growth and another. What forces it out from the body of the mother, and for what reasons it sometimes comes out of the mother's womb before the due time. Then I will describe which parts grow more than the others after the baby is born, and determine the proportions of a child of one year. Then describe the fully grown man and woman, with their proportions, and the nature of their complexions, color, and physiognomy. Then how they are composed of veins, tendons, muscles and bones. Then, in four drawings, represent four universal conditions of men. That is, Mirth, with various acts of laughter, and describe the cause of laughter. Weeping in various aspects with its causes. Fighting, with various acts of killing; flight, fear, ferocity, boldness, murder and everything pertaining to such cases. Then represent Labor, with pulling, thrusting, carrying, stopping, supporting and such like things. Then perspective, concerning the functions and effects of the eye; and of hearing—here I will speak of music—and describe the other senses.[6]

In subsequent notes he described how tissue, veins, muscles, and nerves should be shown from a variety of angles: "Every part will be drawn, using all means of demonstrations, from three different points of view; for when you have seen a limb from the front, with any muscles, sinews, or veins which take their rise from the opposite side, the same limb will be shown to you in a side view or from behind, exactly as if you had that same limb in your hand and were turning it from side to side until you had acquired a full comprehension of all you wished to know."[7] Thus did Leonardo pioneer a new form of anatomical drawing, perhaps better described in his case as anatomical art, that is still in use today.

THE SKULL DRAWINGS

Leonardo's initial anatomy studies of 1489 focused on human skulls. He started with a skull that had been sawed in half, top to bottom (fig. 60). Then the front of the left half was sawed off. His groundbreaking technique of drawing the two halves together made it easy to see how the inner cavities were positioned relative to the face. For example, the frontal sinus, which Leonardo is the first person to correctly depict, is shown to rest just behind the eyebrow.

To appreciate how ingenious this pictorial technique is, cover the right side of the picture with your hand and notice how much less informative the drawing becomes. "The originality of the skull drawings of 1489 is so fundamentally different and superior to all other extant illustrations of the time that they are completely out of character with the age," according to Francis Wells, a surgeon and an expert on the anatomical drawings.[8]

To the left of the face Leonardo drew each of the four types of human teeth, with a note saying that a human typically has thirty-two, including the wisdom teeth. With this, as far as is now known, he became the first person in history to describe fully the human dental elements, including a depiction of the roots that is almost perfect.[9] "The six upper molars have three roots each, of which two roots are on the outer side of the jaw and one on the inner," he wrote, evidence that he had cut through the wall of a sinus to determine the position of the roots. If there were not so much else to remember him for, Leonardo could have been celebrated as a pioneer of dentistry.

In one of the accompanying drawings, Leonardo showed a skull from the left side with a top quarter section and then the entire left side sawed off (fig. 61). What's most striking in the pen-and-ink drawing is its artistic beauty: fine lines, elegant contours, sfumato effects, trademark left-handed cross-hatching, and subtle shadings

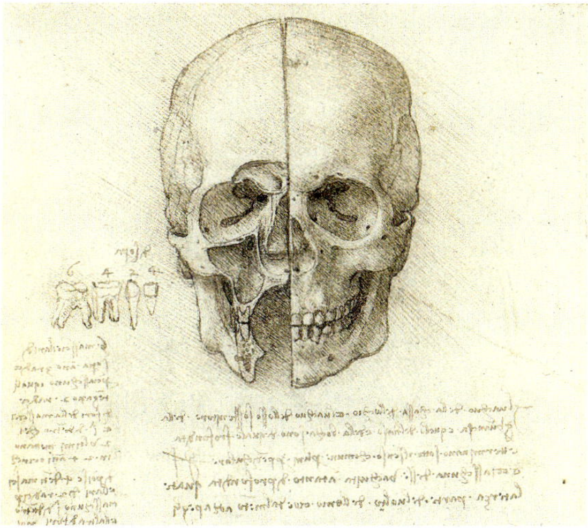

Fig. 60

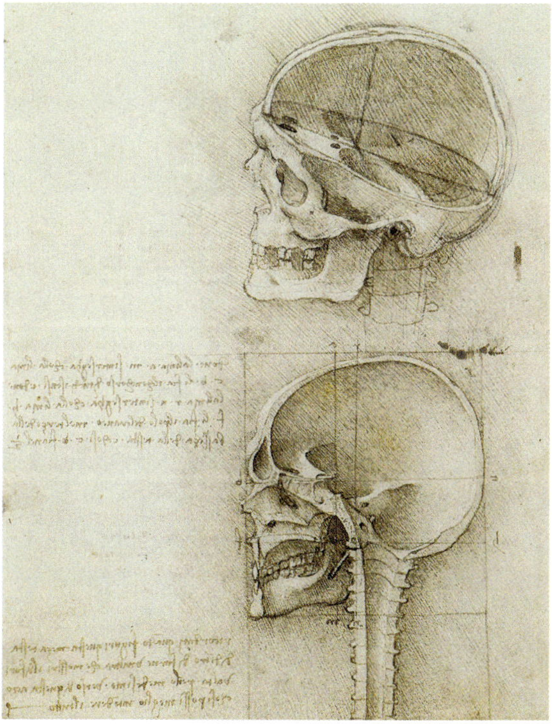

Fig. 61

Skull drawings, 1489.

and shadows adding three-dimensionality. Among Leonardo's many contributions to science was showing how concepts could be developed through drawing. Beginning with the drapery studies done in Verrocchio's studio, Leonardo mastered the art of rendering light hitting rounded and curved objects. Now he was deploying that art to transform, and make beautiful, the study of anatomy.[10]

On this and another of his skull drawings, Leonardo drew a set of axis lines. At their intersection near the center of the brain, he located the cavity that he thought contained the *senso comune*, or confluence of the senses. "The soul seems to reside in the judgment, and the judgment would seem to be seated in that part where all the senses meet; and this is called the *senso comune*," he wrote.[11]

In order to link the movements of the mind to the movements of the body, showing how emotions become motions, Leonardo wanted to locate where that phenomenon occurred. In a series of drawings, he attempted to show how visual observations come in through the eye, are processed, and then are sent to the *senso comune*, where the mind can act on them. The resulting brain signals, he surmised, are transported through the nervous system to the muscles. In most of his drawings, he gave primacy to sight; the other senses did not have a ventricle of their own.[12]

On one drawing from this period showing the bones and nerves of an arm, he drew a faint sketch of the spinal cord and nerves emerging from it. Appended is a note about his experience pithing a frog, the first scientist to record doing what is now a staple of biology classes. "The frog dies instantly when its spinal cord is perforated," he wrote. "And previously it lived without head, without heart or any interior organs, or intestines or skin. Here therefore it appears lies the foundation of movement and life." He repeated the experiment on a dog. His drawings of the nerves and spinal cord are clearly labeled; it was not until 1739 that this pithing experiment would again be illustrated and described correctly.[13]

In the mid-1490s Leonardo put aside his work on anatomy; he would not return to the subject for another decade. Although he was neither fully original nor correct in his description of a *senso comune*, he was right in his general view that the human brain receives visual and other stimuli, processes them into perceptions, then transmits reactions through the nervous system to the muscles. More important, his fascination with the connection between the mind and the body became a key component of his artistic genius: showing how inner emotions are manifest in outward gestures. "In painting, the actions of the figures are, in all cases, expressive of the purpose of their minds," he wrote.[14] As he was finishing his first round of anatomical studies, he was beginning work on what would be the greatest expression in the history of art of that maxim, *The Last Supper*.

STUDIES OF HUMAN PROPORTION

While studying Vitruvius for his work on the Milan and Pavia cathedrals, Leonardo became captivated by the ancient Roman architect's detailed studies of human proportions and measurements. In addition, when he was measuring horses for the Sforza monument, he became interested in how they related to human proportions. Comparative anatomy appealed to his instinct for finding patterns across different subjects. So in 1490 he began measuring and drawing the proportions of the human body.

Using at least a dozen young men as models in his Corte Vecchia studios, he measured each body part from head to toe and produced more than forty drawings and six thousand words. His descriptions included both the average size of body parts and the proportional relationships between different parts. "The space between the mouth and the base of the nose is one-seventh of the face," he wrote. "The space from the mouth to the bottom of the chin is one-fourth of the face and equal to the width of the mouth. The space from the chin to the base of the nose is one-third of the face and equal to the length of the nose and to the forehead." These descriptions and others were accompanied by detailed drawings and diagrams with letters denoting the different measurements (figs. 62 and 63).

Page after page of his notebooks—fifty-one sections in all—are

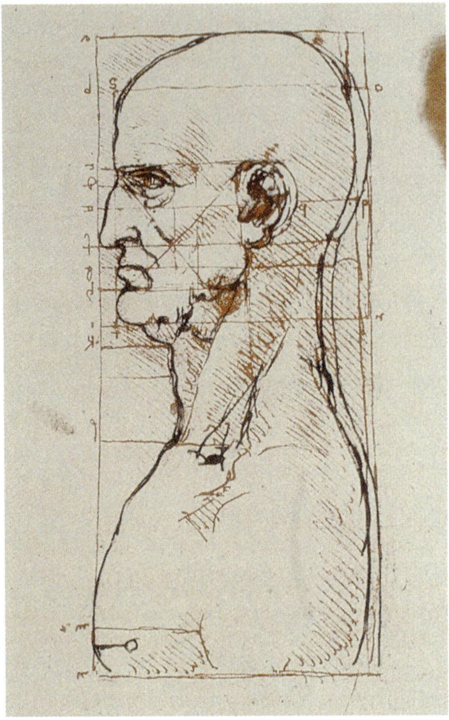

Fig. 62

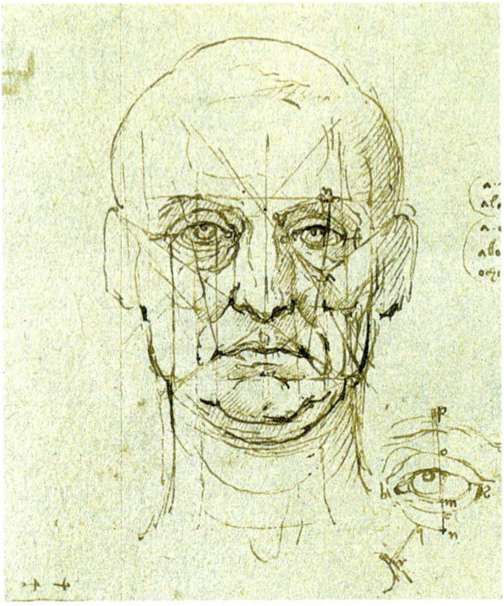

Fig. 63

Proportions of the face.

filled with ever more precise detail. His descriptions were inspired by Vitruvius, but they went far deeper and were based on his own observations. A small sample of his findings:

> The distance from the top of the nose to the bottom of the chin is two-thirds of the face. . . . The width of the face is equal to the space between the mouth and the roots of the hair and is one-twelfth of the whole height. . . . From the top of the ear to the top of the head is equal to the distance from the bottom of the chin to the duct of the eye and also equal to the distance from the angle of the chin to that of the jaw. . . . The hollow of the cheek bone occurs half way between the tip of the nose and the top of the jaw bone. . . . The great toe is the sixth part of the foot, taking the measure in profile. . . . From the joint of one shoulder

> to the other is the length of two faces. . . . From the navel to the genitals is a face's length.[15]

I am tempted to quote him at even greater length because the enormity of his feat, and what it says about his compulsive mind, is evident not in each measurement but in the staggering accumulation of them. He goes on and on, relentlessly. In one entry alone there are at least eighty such calculations or proportions. It becomes both dazzling and dizzying. One tries to imagine him in his studio with measuring string and a handful of compliant assistants dutifully having every body part recorded. Such obsession is a component of genius.

Leonardo was not content merely to measure every aspect of every body part. In addition, he felt compelled to record what occurs when each of these parts moves. What happens to the relative shape of each human feature when a joint moves or a person twists? "Observe how the position of the shoulder changes when the arm moves up and down, inwards and outwards, to the back and to the front, and also in circular movements and any others," he instructs himself in his notebook. "And do the same with reference to the neck, hands and feet and the breast."

We can picture him in his studio, as he made his models move, turn, squat, sit, and lie down. "When the arm is bent, the fleshy part shrinks to two-thirds of its length," he recorded. "When a man kneels down he will diminish by the fourth part of his height. . . . When a heel is raised, the tendon and ankle get closer to each other by a finger's breadth. . . . When a man sits down, the distance from his seat to the top part of his head will be half of his height plus the thickness and length of the testicles."[16]

Plus the thickness and length of the testicles? Once again it is useful to pause and marvel. Why the obsessiveness? Why the need for reams of data? Partly, at least initially, it was to help him paint humans, or horses, in various poses and movements. But there was something grander involved. Leonardo had set for himself the most magnificent of all tasks for the mind of mankind: nothing less than knowing fully the measure of man and how he fits into the cosmos. In his notebook, he proclaimed his intention to fathom what he called "universale misura del huomo," the universal measure of man.[17] It was the quest that defined Leonardo's life, the one that tied together his art and his science.

CHAPTER 15

Virgin of the Rocks

THE COMMISSION

When Leonardo first came to Milan in 1482, he had hopes of working primarily as a military and civil engineer, as he had proposed in his letter to the de facto duke, Ludovico Sforza. That did not happen. Most of his work for the court during the ensuing decade was as a theatrical impresario, then as the sculptor of the unfinished horse monument and a consultant on church designs. Yet his primary talent remained that of a painter, as had been the case in Florence and would be so until his final days.

For his first few years in Milan, before he was given space in the Corte Vecchia, he probably shared a studio with Ambrogio de Predis, one of Ludovico's favorite portrait artists, and his half-brothers, Evangelista and Cristoforo, who was deaf and did not speak. Leonardo later wrote that observing how the deaf communicate was a good way to study the relation between human gestures and thoughts: "Let your figures have actions appropriate to what they are intended to think or say, and these will be well learned by imitating the deaf, who by the motion of their hands, eyes, eyebrows, and the whole body, endeavor to express the sentiments of their mind."[1]

Soon after Leonardo began working with the de Predis brothers, they were jointly given a commission by the Confraternity of the Immaculate Conception, a worship group of rich laymen, to paint altarpieces for the Franciscan church that it used. To Leonardo fell the task of painting the central frame, and his instructions were explicit: it was to feature the Virgin Mary ("her skirt shall be of gold brocade over crimson, in oil, varnished with fine lacquer") and baby Jesus surrounded by "angels done in oil to complete perfection, with the two Prophets." Ignoring these instructions, he decided to paint the Virgin Mary, the baby Jesus, a young John the Baptist, one angel, and no prophets. The scene he chose came from Apocrypha and medieval stories of the Holy Family meeting John on the road to Egypt as they fled Bethlehem after King Herod ordered the Massacre of the Innocents.

Leonardo ended up producing two similar versions of the painting, which became known as the *Virgin of the Rocks*. Reams of scholarship have been produced debating the timing and backstories of these paintings. The most convincing narrative, I believe, is that the first version, done in the 1480s, led to a price dispute with the confraternity and was sold or sent elsewhere; it is now in the Louvre (fig. 64). Leonardo then helped to paint a replacement version, in collaboration with Ambrogio de Predis and his studio, completed sometime around 1508; it is the one now in the National Gallery of London (fig. 65).[2]

The confraternity wanted a painting that would celebrate the Immaculate Conception, a doctrine pushed by the Franciscans asserting that the Virgin Mary was conceived free from all stain of original sin.[3] Some of the iconography in the *Virgin of the Rocks* supports that idea, most notably the setting: a grotto of barren and dramatic rock formations that magically spawns flowering plants and four holy figures. We feel we are looking into the womb of the earth. The figures in front of the cave are bathed in warm light, but the shadowy inside is dark and intimidating. The locale harks back to Leonardo's recollection about coming across the mouth of a mysterious cave while hiking.

The scene is not, however, an obvious evocation of the Immaculate Conception. Even though the Virgin Mary is the central figure, the narrative of the picture centers on John the Baptist, who was the patron saint of Florence and one of Leonardo's favorite subjects. The focus on John is especially true in the first (Louvre) version of the picture, where the angel is dramatically pointing to him, and that may have been one source of the friction between Leonardo and the confraternity.

THE FIRST VERSION (LOUVRE)

Leonardo was a master at storytelling and conveying a sense of dramatic motion, and like many of his paintings, beginning with the *Adoration of the Magi*, the *Virgin of the Rocks* is a narrative. In his first version of the painting, the androgynous curly-haired angel begins the narrative by looking out directly from the scene, catching our eye, smiling enigmatically, and pointing to make us look at the baby Saint John. John in turn is dropping to his knees and clasping his hands in reverence toward the baby Jesus, who returns the gesture with a sign of blessing. The Madonna, her body twisted in motion, glances down at John and grasps his shoulder protectively while hovering her other hand over Jesus. And as our eyes finish a clockwise rotation of the scene, we notice the left hand of the angel holding Jesus as he leans on the rocky precipice over a pond, his hand touching the ledge. Taken in as a whole, it becomes a sequential medley of hand gestures presaging *The Last Supper*.

The angel's pointing finger is the main feature that distinguishes the first version from the second. Thanks to modern technology, we know that Leonardo wrestled with the question of including this gesture. In 2009 technicians at the Louvre deployed an advanced set of infrared imaging techniques on the first version of the *Virgin of the Rocks*, which revealed an underdrawing that Leonardo used to compose the painting. It shows that when he began, he did not plan to have the angel pointing at John. That gesture was added only after most of the background rocks had been painted.[4] Leonardo twice reversed himself, perhaps under pressure from his patrons. The pointing gesture is not in the original underdrawing, is in the first version of the painting, and is not in the second version.

His hesitancy is understandable. The pointing gesture is awkward, and Leonardo seems to have sensed it when he did his second version. The angel's bony finger disrupts, in a jarring way, the connection between the Madonna's hovering hand and the head of her baby. The medley of hands becomes a cacophony of competing gestures.[5]

The narrative flow is rescued by the fluid areas of light, which give the painting a sense of unity. In this masterpiece, Leonardo ushered in a new era of art in which light and shade are juxtaposed in a manner that produces a powerful sense of flow.

In Florence, Leonardo had edged away from using mainly tempera paints and had begun to rely more on oils, as had become the practice in the Netherlands, and in Milan he perfected his use of that medium. The ability to slowly apply thin layer upon layer of translucent color allowed him to create the shadings and gentle blurring of outlines that characterized his chiaroscuro and sfumato techniques. It also allowed him to produce luminous tones. The light would pass through the layers and reflect back from the primer coat, making it seem as if the light was emanating from the figures and objects themselves.[6]

Most artists prior to Leonardo differentiated the brightly lit areas of a painting from the shaded areas by adding more white pigment to their colors. But Leonardo knew that light doesn't merely brighten a color; it also reveals better its true and deep tones. Look at where the sunlight strikes the angel's red cloak and the Madonna's blue gown and golden drapery; the colors are saturated and the tones richer. In his notes for a treatise on painting, Leonardo explained, "Since the quality of color is revealed by means of light, where there is more light will be seen more of the true quality of the illuminated color."[7]

The first version of the *Virgin of the Rocks* is a vivid example of Leonardo's using his knowledge of science to inform his art. Its subject is both the Virgin and the rocks. As Ann Pizzorusso pointed out in her study "Leonardo's Geology," the components of the grotto "are rendered with astounding geological accuracy."[8] Most of the formations are of weathered sandstone, a sedimentary rock. But just above the Virgin's head, and also at the top right of the picture, are jutting hard-edged rock formations, with facets that glimmer in the sun. These are diabase, an intrusive igneous rock formed by the cooling of volcanic lava. Even the vertical cracks caused by the cooling are rendered precisely. So is the seam between the sandstone and igneous formation, running horizontally just above the Virgin's head. This is not merely a case of Leonardo's faithfully rendering a scene he saw in nature. The grotto is clearly a product of his imagination, not an actual place he visited. It took a deep appreciation of geology to conjure up a vision that was both so imaginative and so real.

The plants in the picture are located, as they would be in nature, only in the sandstone regions that have weathered sufficiently to permit roots to take hold, both at the top and the floor of the grotto, but not in the hard igneous rocks. The species chosen are botanically and seasonally correct: he depicted only those that would be found in a moist grotto at the same time of year. Yet within these constraints, he was able to choose plants that conveyed his symbolic and artistic aims. As William Emboden demonstrated in his study *Leonardo da Vinci on Plants and Gardens*, "he introduced them into his paintings for their symbolic language, and yet he was careful to portray them in their proper setting."[9]

For example, a white rose is often used to symbolize the purity of Christ, but it would not have grown in such a grotto; so Leonardo instead paints underneath Christ's raised arm a primrose (*Primula vulgaris*), regarded as a sign of virtue because of its white flowers. Faintly discernible above the Virgin's left hand is a swirl of *Galium verum*. "The plant has long been known as Our Lady's Bedstraw and is traditionally the plant of the manger," Emboden wrote. Joseph used it to make Mary's bed, and its white leaves turned to gold when Jesus was born. Leonardo, who was obsessed with spirals and swirls, sometimes slightly altered plants to suit his artistic tastes. For example, at the lower left of the picture is a yellow flag iris (*Iris pseudacorus*) that is depicted with its sword-like leaves not lined up like a fan but slightly contorted to show a spiral pattern, twisting to reflect the subtle turning motions of Saint John and the Virgin.

By the time this first version of the painting was finished, in 1485, Leonardo and his partners had received payments totaling around

800 lire. But a prolonged dispute began when the painters insisted they had spent more than that on materials, especially the gold gilding, and that the work was worth far more. The confraternity balked, and the painting was probably never installed in their church. Instead, it was either sold to another client, perhaps the French king Louis XII, or paid for by Ludovico Sforza as a wedding gift for his niece Bianca and the future Holy Roman emperor Maximilian I. It eventually made its way into the Louvre.

THE SECOND VERSION (LONDON)

During the 1490s, Leonardo worked with Ambrogio de Predis on a new version of *Virgin of the Rocks* for the Confraternity of the Immaculate Conception, to replace the one that had not been delivered. According to the technical studies reported in 2009, Leonardo began with a far different underdrawing. It featured a kneeling Virgin Mary in a posture of adoration, with one hand across her breast. But then Leonardo changed his mind. He covered the new underdrawing with primer and drew another, one that very closely resembles the first version of *Virgin of the Rocks*, except that (as in the original underdrawing for the first version) the angel is not pointing at John the Baptist.[10] In addition, the angel is not peering out from the picture at the viewer. Instead, his dreamy gaze seems to take in the whole scene.

As a result, the narrative is not as distracting. The Virgin Mary becomes the unchallenged center of attention. Our eyes start on her serene face as she watches John kneel, and her hand hovers protectively over her child, this time not interrupted by the angel's intruding finger. The scene becomes one that features the gestures and emotions of the Virgin rather than the angel or John.

Another subtle difference is that the grotto is more closed and there is less sky above. The light is therefore not as diffused but instead comes in directionally as a beam from the left side of the painting, selectively falling upon and highlighting the four characters. As a result, the modeling, plasticity, and three-dimensionality of the shapes are deeply enhanced. Between the first and second versions, Leonardo had been studying light and optics, and the result is an artistic use of light that was new in the history of art. "In its dynamic qualities of variability and selectivity, in contrast to the static, even universal light of the Louvre version, it is the light of a new era," wrote the art historian John Shearman.[11]

The composition of this second version was clearly the work of Leonardo. The question arises, however, how much of the actual painting, which may have been done over the course of almost fifteen years, was by him and how much was delegated to Ambrogio and the assistants at the studio.

One indication that Leonardo delegated some of the work is that the plants are not as authentic as in the first version. "It's very striking, because they go against everything that Leonardo's always done in terms of his botanical art," according to horticulturalist John Grimshaw. "They're not real flowers. They're odd concoctions, like a half-imagined aquilegia."[12] The same divergences can be found in the geology. "The rocks in the National Gallery painting are synthetic, stilted, grotesque characterizations," Pizzorusso wrote. "The rocks in the foreground are not finely bedded but are roughly weathered and massive, giving the appearance of limestone rather than sandstone. The presence of limestone would be incongruous in this geological setting."[13]

Up until 2010, London's National Gallery had stated that its version was not primarily from Leonardo's hand. But after a thorough cleaning and restoration of the painting, the gallery's then-curator Luke Syson and other experts declared that it was in fact painted mainly by Leonardo. Syson conceded that there are lapses in the accuracy of some of the plants and rocks, but he claimed this reflects a more mature and "metaphysical" way of depicting nature that Leonardo began to pursue in the 1490s: "This is no longer a picture just about devout naturalism. Leonardo combined those ingredients he regarded as essential (sometimes simply the most beautiful) to generate things—plants, landscapes, people—which were even more perfect, more completely themselves, than Nature had made."[14]

Especially when viewed after its recent cleaning, the London version does indeed display hallmarks that appear to be by Leonardo's hand. This is true of the angel, whose characteristic radiant curls seem distinctively his, and whose sheer sleeve caught by the sun rays is rendered with a remarkable translucence that comes from Leonardo's talent for applying thin layers of oil. "No one who has looked at it closely can doubt who was responsible for the mouth and chin, and the characteristic curves of the golden hair," Kenneth Clark wrote of the angel.[15] It is also true of the Virgin's head, which like that of the angel suggests the use of Leonardo's characteristic finger blending of paint. "All these effects lie definitively outside Ambrogio's range, or that of any other known pupil," according to Martin Kemp.[16]

This second version of the painting, like the first, was caught up in contractual disputes with the confraternity, and the prolonged negotiation offers further evidence that Leonardo was personally involved in finishing the painting. It was still deemed incomplete by the time he left Milan in 1499, and in 1506 there was another tussle over whether a final payment was due. Leonardo ended up coming back to put finishing touches on the painting. Only then was it finally deemed complete, after which he and Ambrogio received their concluding payment from the confraternity.

TEAMWORK

The questions about what contributions Leonardo's colleagues made to the second *Virgin of the Rocks* highlight the role that collaboration played in his studio. We tend to think of artists as lone creators, holed in a garret, waiting for inspiration to strike. But as evident in his notebooks and in the process that led to his drawing of *Vitruvian Man*, much of Leonardo's thinking was collegial. Ever since his salad days in the art-production bottega run by Verrocchio, Leonardo knew the joys and advantages of having a team. According to Larry Keith, who led the restoration of the National Gallery's *Virgin of the Rocks*, "Leonardo's need to quickly create a studio capable of producing paintings, sculpture, courtly entertainments and other activities meant that he worked closely with established Milanese painters as well as training his own apprentices."[17]

In order to make money, Leonardo at times helped his apprentices produce pieces as if on an assembly line, as had been the practice in

Verrocchio's studio. "Designs circulated between master and pupil using a kind of cut and paste technique involving master drawings and cartoons," Syson explained.[18] Leonardo would create the compositions, cartoons, studies, and sketches. His students would copy them with pinpricks and work together on painting the finished version, often with Leonardo adding his own touches and making corrections. There were sometimes many variations, and different styles can be discerned in a single painting. One visitor to his studio described how "two of Leonardo's pupils were doing some portraits and he from time to time put a touch on them."[19]

Leonardo's apprentices and students did not merely copy his designs. A show at the Louvre in 2012 featured paintings that students and assistants in his workshop did of his masterpieces. Many were variations that were produced alongside his original, indicating that he and his colleagues were together exploring various alternative approaches to the planned painting. While Leonardo worked on the master version, other versions were being painted under his supervision.[20]

HEAD OF A YOUNG WOMAN

Depending on which religious stories you take as the text, the angel in *Virgin of the Rocks* is supposed to be either Gabriel or Uriel. (He's identified on the Louvre website as Gabriel, but the description next to the painting in the museum itself calls him Uriel, proving there is no consensus even within that museum.) Either way, Leonardo's drawing of him is so feminine that even some art critics have referred to him as a female.[21]

The angel, like the one he painted for Verrocchio's *Baptism of Christ*, is an example of Leonardo's proclivity for gender fluidity. Some nineteenth-century critics saw it as a mark of his homosexuality, especially since the positioning and outward gaze of the disturbingly alluring angel make him seem a proxy for the artist.[22]

The androgynous nature of the figure is heightened by comparing the angel to what is generally regarded as a preparatory study for it, a drawing by Leonardo, called *Head of a Young Woman* (fig. 66).[23] The

Fig. 66. Study for *Virgin of the Rocks*.

facial features of the young woman are virtually identical to those of Uriel/Gabriel.

The drawing is fascinating because it is one of the best displays of Leonardo's genius as a draftsman. With a few simple lines and brilliant strokes, concise and precise, he is able to create a sketch of unsurpassed beauty. At first glance it captivates you, then its deceptive simplicity draws you into a prolonged and profound engagement. The pioneering Renaissance art historian Bernard Berenson called it "one of the finest achievements of all draftsmanship," and his protégé Kenneth Clark proclaimed it "one of the most beautiful, I dare say, in the world."[24]

Leonardo sometimes used ink or chalk for his drawings, but in this case he used a silverpoint stylus to incise lines on paper that he had coated with a pale pigment. The grooves are still visible. For highlights, such as the luster on her left cheekbone, he used a white gouache, or watercolor.

The drawing is an exquisite example of Leonardo's use of hatching to create shadows and texture. These parallel strokes are delicate and tight in some places (the shadow on her left cheek) and bold and spacious in others (her back shoulder). The variations in the hatching allow, with just simple strokes, wondrous gradations of shadow and subtle blurring of contours. Look at the nose and marvel at how the hatching models the left nostril. Then look how slightly wider lines make the contour and shadow of her left cheek. The two strong lines creasing her neck and the three strokes delineating the front of her neck seem hasty, but they also convey motion. The free-form curves to the left and right of her head look modernist, yet what they reveal is Leonardo's brainstorming process as it flows through his pen. As the abstract lines cascade down the back of her neck, they hint at the signature curls that he will paint.

And then there are the eyes, which Leonardo made magically liquid. Her right eye has a rounded pupil with a full-on stare, but her left eyelid is heavy, pushing down over the pupil, as if she's dreamily disengaged. Like the angel in the Louvre's *Virgin of the Rocks*, she stares out at us even as her left eye drifts. As you walk back and forth, her eyes follow you. She drinks you in.

CHAPTER 16

The Milan Portraits

PORTRAIT OF A MUSICIAN

Among the many intriguing things about Leonardo are the mysteries that surround much of his work. Take, for example, *Portrait of a Musician* (fig. 67), painted in the mid-1480s. His only known portrait of a man, there are no surviving records or contemporary mentions of it. It is unclear who the subject is and whether the work was commissioned or if it was ever delivered. It is even not certain that Leonardo painted all of it. And like far too many of his pieces, it is unfinished, though it is not known why.

Painted on a walnut panel, which Leonardo had begun to favor, the portrait is of a young man with tightly coiled curls (no surprise there), seen in three-quarter profile, holding a folded sheet of music. His torso, brown vest, and hands are unfinished. Even parts of his face seem missing some of the final layers Leonardo usually applied. And unlike Leonardo's other works, his body faces in the same direction as his gaze, with no sense of movement.

The rigidity is one reason some have doubted that Leonardo painted it. But other elements—the curls, the expressive and liquid eyes, the use of light and shadow—have led most scholars to believe that he at least painted the face, and perhaps one of his students or

Fig. 67. *Portrait of a Musician.*

assistants, such as Giovanni Antonio Boltraffio, added the unfinished and unimpressive torso.[1] What most distinguishes the face as a Leonardo creation is the sense that this is an emotion-laden, real person, with inner thoughts and a whiff of melancholy, whose motions of the mind are about to trigger a movement of the lips.

There is no evidence that the painting was done as a paid commission, nor is it of a notable dignitary. It seems that Leonardo simply decided, on his own, to paint the young man. Perhaps Leonardo was moved by his delicate beauty and golden curls or had a personal connection to him. Some have suggested the subject was Leonardo's friend Franchino Gaffurio, who had become the conductor of the Cathedral choir in Milan in 1484, around the time the portrait was painted. But the portrait does not look like others known to be of Gaffurio, who would have been in his mid-thirties at the time, older than the man portrayed.

I prefer to believe that the portrait is of Atalante Migliorotti, the young musician who accompanied Leonardo a few years earlier from Florence to Milan, bearing the lyre.[2] He would go on to be a distinguished performer, but at the time he was in his early twenties and still working in the Sforza court along with Leonardo. If he was in fact the subject, it would make the *Musician* a personal work that Leonardo undertook for his own satisfaction. We know that Leonardo was taken by Atalante's looks. In his inventory from 1482, there is that item "a portrait of Atalante with his face raised." Perhaps that was a study for this portrait, or even the beginnings of the painting itself.

Although the *Musician* does not have "his face raised," he is gazing out into the light. Leonardo's treatment of the light on his face is the most striking feature of the painting. The spots of luster in the liquid eyeballs show how the light is falling. The illumination is stronger than in other paintings by Leonardo, who wrote that muted light is better for a portrait. But the strong light in this case allowed him to provide a brilliant demonstration of how light hits the contours of a face. The shadows beneath the cheekbone and chin and even the right eyelid make the portrait more lifelike than others of his era. In fact, one flaw in the painting is that the shadows are too harsh, especially under the nose. Leonardo would later warn about the crudeness produced by the use of sharp light:

> An object will display the greatest difference of light and shade when it is seen in the strongest light. . . . But this should not be much used in painting, because the works would be crude and ungraceful. An object seen in a moderate light displays little difference in its light and shade, and this is the case towards evening or when the day is cloudy; works painted then are tender, and every kind of face becomes graceful. Thus, in everything extremes are to be avoided: Too much light gives crudeness; too little prevents our seeing.[3]

The *Musician* illustrates the effects of light and the perils of too much of it. Perhaps the flaw can be explained by the fact that the painting is not fully finished. Parts of the face do not have as many thin layers of oil as Leonardo usually used. If he had continued to perfect the painting, a process that often took him years, there likely would have been a few more strokes, and a bit subtler texture, at least under the nose.

There is one other notable feature about the light. "The pupil of the eye dilates and contracts as it sees a less or greater light," Leonardo noted early on in his studies of the human eye and optics.[4] He also observed how the changes in pupil size take a few moments, as the eyes adjust to the light. Almost eerily, Leonardo has the two pupils of the musician dilated to different degrees: his left eye, which faces the light more directly, has a smaller pupil. Leonardo incorrectly believed that the pupils of the eye dilate separately, when in fact they dilate in unison, and I suspect that he is trying to convey a sense of the passing of a moment as our eyes sweep across the face of the musician, from his left eye to his right.

CECILIA GALLERANI, THE *LADY WITH AN ERMINE*

Cecilia Gallerani was a striking beauty who was born into Milan's educated middle class. Her father was a diplomat and financial agent for the duke, and her mother was the daughter of a noted law professor. They were not exceedingly wealthy; her father died when she was seven, and she had six brothers who divided up the inheritance. But they were cultured and educated. Cecilia composed poetry, delivered orations, wrote letters in Latin, and would later have two novels by Matteo Bandello dedicated to her.[5]

In 1483, when she was ten, her brothers were able to arrange a promising marriage contract for her to Giovanni Stefano Visconti, a member of the family that once ruled Milan. But four years later, before the wedding took place, the contract was dissolved. The brothers had not kept up with the dowry payments. The dissolution agreement noted that the marriage had not been consummated, protecting her virtue.

There may have been another reason the contract was dissolved and the stipulation made about her virtue. Around that time, she attracted the notice of Ludovico Sforza. The de facto Duke of Milan was a ruthless man, but he had good taste. He was attracted to Cecilia for both her mind and her beauty. By 1489, when she was fifteen, she was living not with her family but in rooms provided by Ludovico. The following year she was pregnant with his son.

There was one big problem with their relationship. Since 1480 Ludovico had been contracted to marry Beatrice d'Este, the daughter of Ercole d'Este, the Duke of Ferrara. The arrangement, which represented a major alliance for Ludovico with one of Italy's most ancient noble dynasties, had been made when Beatrice was five, and their wedding was scheduled to take place when she turned fifteen, in 1490. It was to be an occasion marked by great pomp and pageantry.

But Ludovico, enamored with Cecilia, was unenthusiastic. In late 1490 the Duke of Ferrara's ambassador to Milan sent back a candid report. Ludovico was besotted with an "inamorata," he told Beatrice's father. "He keeps her with him at the castle, and wherever he goes, and wants to give her everything. She is pregnant, and as beautiful as a flower, and often he brings me with him to visit her." As a result, the wedding between Ludovico and Beatrice was delayed. It finally took place the following year, with glorious celebrations in Pavia and then Milan.

Over time, Ludovico would come to respect Beatrice and, as we will see, be deeply bereaved when she died. But initially he continued his relationship with Cecilia, who stayed in a suite of rooms in the Sforza Castle. In those days before the pretense of sexual discretion was required of rulers, Ludovico continued to confide his feelings to the ever-informative Ferrara ambassador, who reported them back to Beatrice's father. Ludovico told the ambassador that "he wished he could go and make love to Cecilia, and be with her in peace, and this was what his wife wanted too, because she did not want to submit to him." Finally, after Cecilia gave birth to their son, who was fulsomely celebrated in sonnets by the court poets, Ludovico arranged for her to be married to a wealthy count, and she settled into the life of a respected literary patron.

Cecilia Gallerani's alluring beauty would be captured for the ages. At the height of their relationship, around 1489, when she was fifteen, Ludovico commissioned Leonardo to paint her portrait (fig. 68). It was his first painting assignment for Leonardo, who had been in Milan for seven years, had earned a role at court as an impresario, and had just begun work on the horse monument. The result is a stunning and innovative masterpiece, in many ways the most delightful and charming of Leonardo's paintings. Other than the *Mona Lisa*, it is my favorite of his works.

Painted in oil on a walnut panel, the portrait of Cecilia, now known as *Lady with an Ermine*, was so innovative, so emotionally charged and alive, that it helped to transform the art of portraiture. The twentieth-century art historian John Pope-Hennessy called it the "first modern portrait" and "the first painting in European art to introduce the idea that a portrait may express the sitter's thoughts through posture and gestures."[6] Instead of being shown in profile, as was traditional, she is in three-quarters view. Her body is turned to our left, but her head has seemingly snapped to our right to look at something, presumably Ludovico, coming from the direction of the light. The ermine she is holding also seems to have gone on alert, ears cocked. Exceedingly alive, neither have the vacant or undirected stare found in other portraits of the time, including Leonardo's only previous portrait of a woman, *Ginevra de' Benci*. Something is happening in the scene. Leonardo has captured a narrative contained in an instant,

Fig. 68. *Lady with an Ermine*, Cecilia Gallerani.

one involving outward lives and inner lives. In the medley of hands, paws, eyes, and a mysterious smile, we see both motions of the body and motions of the mind.

Leonardo loved puns, including visual ones, and just as the juniper plays on Ginevra de' Benci's name, so does the ermine (in Greek, *galée*) evoke the name of Gallerani. A white ermine also was a symbol of purity. "The ermine would die rather than soil itself," Leonardo wrote in one of his bestiary entries. And also: "The ermine out of moderation never eats but once a day, and it would rather let itself be captured by hunters than take refuge in a dirty lair, in order not to stain its purity." In addition, the ermine is a reference to Ludovico, who had been bestowed the Order of the Ermine by the king of Naples, prompting a court poet to lyricize him as "the Italian moor, the white ermine."[7]

The twisting head and body, a form of contrapposto, had become one of Leonardo's lively signatures, such as in the angel of *Virgin of the Rocks*. The writhing but poised ermine mimics Cecilia's movement, spiraling in synch with her. Both Cecilia's wrist and that of the ermine are gently cocked, protectively. Their shared vitality makes it seem that they are not merely characters in a picture but players in a real-life situation, part of a scene involving a third participant, the off-scene Ludovico who has caught their eye.

At the time, Leonardo was formulating his theories of how the mind works. There is clearly a lot going on in Cecilia's. We see it not only in her eyes but in her hint of a smile. Yet as would be the case with the *Mona Lisa*, the smile is mysterious. Look at Cecilia a hundred times, and you will sense a hundred different emotions. How happy is she to see Ludovico? Okay, now look again. The same is even true for her pet. Leonardo had such skill that he could make an ermine look intelligent.

Leonardo took exquisite care with each detail, from the knuckles and tendons of Cecilia's hand to her braided and gauze-veiled hair. The coiffure and its sheathing, known as a *coazzone*, and her Spanish-style dress, became fashionable in Milan in 1489, when Isabella of Aragon married the hapless Gian Galeazzo Sforza.

The light on Cecilia is softer than that Leonardo used for the *Mu-*

sician. The shadow under her nose is subtler. The greatest intensity of light, as Leonardo demonstrated in his optics studies, comes when a beam hits a surface head-on rather than at an oblique angle. This occurs on the top of Cecilia's left shoulder and right cheek. The illumination levels on the other contours of her face are done with delicate precision according to formulas he had developed for the proportional variations of light intensities at various angles of incidence. His scientific understanding of optics thus enhanced the three-dimensional illusion of the painting.[8]

Some of the shadows are softened by reflected or secondary radiance. For example, the lower edge of her right hand catches a glow from the ermine's white fur, and underneath her cheek the shadow is softened by light reflected from her chest. "When the arms cross in front of the breast," Leonardo wrote in his notebook, "you should show, between the shadow cast by the arms on the breast and the shadow on the arms themselves, a little light seeming to fall through a space between the breast and the arms; and the more you wish the arm to look detached from the breast the broader you must make the light."[9]

To truly appreciate Leonardo's genius, look at the spot in the painting where the ermine's furry head is set in front of the soft flesh of Cecilia's chest. The ermine's head is a marvel of modeling, rendered with three-dimensional clarity as the light strikes each strand of fur covering the subtly contoured skull. Cecilia's flesh is a soft blend of pale tones and reds, and its texture contrasts with that of the hard beads catching spots of lustrous light.[10]

The portrait was celebrated in a sonnet by the court poet Bernardo Bellincioni with his usual orotund exuberance, in this case justified:

Why are you angry? whom do you envy, Nature?
Vinci, who has portrayed one of your stars;
Cecilia, now so beautiful, is she
Whose lovely eyes cast the sun into dim shadow. . . .
He's made her seem to listen, but not to speak. . . .
Therefore you may now thank Ludovico,
And the genius and skill of Leonardo,
Who want her to belong to posterity.[11]

By noting that she seems to listen but not speak, Bellincioni conveyed what makes the portrait so momentous: it captures the sense of an inner mind at work. Her emotions seem to be revealed, or at least hinted at, by the look in her eyes, the enigma of her smile, and the erotic way she clutches and caresses the ermine. She is visibly thinking, and her face flickers with emotions. As Leonardo portrayed the motions of her mind and soul, he played with our own inner thoughts in a way that no portrait had done before.

LA BELLE FERRONNIÈRE

Leonardo's experimentation with light and shadow is seen in another portrait from this period of a woman in the Sforza court, known as *La Belle Ferronnière* (fig. 69). The subject is most likely Lucrezia Crivelli, who succeeded Cecilia as Ludovico's *maîtresse-en-titre* (official mistress), even though such duties would seem to conflict (or perhaps not) with her role as the lady-in-waiting to Ludovico's new wife, Beatrice d'Este.[12] Like Cecilia, Lucrezia bore Ludovico a son and apparently was similarly rewarded with a portrait of herself by Leonardo. Indeed, the walnut panel on which Leonardo painted it was likely from the same tree as the panel for Cecilia's portrait.

Leonardo's depiction of reflected light is most evident under Lucrezia's left cheek. Her chin and neck are in gentle muted shadows. But the light, which comes from the top left of the painting, falls directly on the smooth and flat plane of her shoulder, and then it bounces up and causes a streak of light—almost exaggerated and of a strange mottled hue—on her left jawbone. As Leonardo wrote in his notebook, "Reverberations are caused by bodies of bright nature with flat and semi-opaque surfaces; when struck by light they rebound it back like the bounce of a ball."[13]

Leonardo was then deeply immersed in his scientific study of how light varies according to the angle at which it strikes a curved surface, and his notebooks are filled with carefully measured and annotated diagrams (figs. 71 and 72). No painter captured so perfectly how shadows and highlights on a face can make it appear three-

Fig. 69. *La Belle Ferronnière.*

dimensional and perfectly modeled. The problem is that the streak of light on Lucrezia's cheekbone is so glaring that it seems unnatural, causing some to speculate that it was later painted by an overeager pupil or restorer. That seems unlikely. I think it's more probable that Leonardo was so intent on showing light reflected into a shadow that he overdid it slightly, daring to be unsubtle.

In this portrait, Leonardo also continued to experiment with his haunting method of creating a stare or gaze that seems to follow a viewer around a room. This "*Mona Lisa* effect" is not magical; it simply comes from drawing a realistic set of eyes staring directly at the viewer with proper perspective, shading, and modeling. But Leonardo discovered that the effect works best when the gaze is intense and the eyes slightly off-kilter, thus making it more noticeable. He was refining the technique he had used in *Ginevra de' Benci*. Ginevra's stare seems slightly averted and distant, until you look at each eye individually and directly; then you see that each in its own way is looking at you.

Likewise, in *La Belle Ferronnière*, Lucrezia seems to be staring so directly that it can make us uncomfortable. When you look at each eye individually, it seems to be looking right at you, and this seems true even as you walk back and forth in front of the painting. But when you try to engage both of her eyes at the same time, they seem slightly unaligned. Her left eye appears to be looking off into the distance, perhaps drifting a bit to the left, partly because the eyeball is shifted. It is hard to meet her gaze in both eyes.

La Belle Ferronnière is not in the same league as *Lady with an Ermine* or the *Mona Lisa*. There's a hint of a smile, but it's not truly alluring or mysterious. The reflected light on the left jawbone seems too studied. The hair is so flat and uninspired, especially compared to Leonardo's usual standards, that it seems to have been painted by others. The head is turned but the body is rigid rather than having even a hint of a Leonardesque twist. The headband and necklace display no mastery of modeling; in fact, they look somewhat unfinished. Only the ribbons on her shoulders flow and catch the light in a masterful way.

The great Bernard Berenson wrote in 1907, "One would regret to have to accept this as Leonardo's own work," though Berenson ultimately did. His protégé Kenneth Clark suggested that it was churned out to please the duke but not captivate the ages. "I am now inclined to think that the picture is by Leonardo, and shows how in these years he was willing to subdue his genius to the needs of the court." There is enough evidence, I think, to support an attribution, in whole or part, to Leonardo: the use of a walnut panel similar in grain to that of *Lady with an Ermine*, the existence of some court sonnets that seem to refer to his painting such a work, and the fact that some aspects of the painting have a beauty worthy of the master. Perhaps it was a collaborative work of his studio, produced to fulfill a ducal commission, with some involvement from Leonardo's brush but not his heart and soul.[14]

PORTRAIT OF A YOUNG FIANCÉE, ALSO KNOWN AS *LA BELLA PRINCIPESSA*

In early 1998 a profile of a young woman drawn with colored chalk on vellum was put up for auction at Christie's in Manhattan (fig. 70). The artist and subject were unknown, and it was described in the catalogue as the work of one of the early nineteenth-century Germans who imitated the style of the Italian Renaissance.[15] A collector named Peter Silverman, who had an eye for spotting hidden treasures, saw it in the catalogue and was so intrigued that he went to inspect it at the showroom. "This is really good," he later recalled thinking. "I don't understand why it's catalogued as nineteenth century." He sensed that it had actually been made during the Renaissance. So he submitted a bid of $18,000, double the minimum estimate set by the auction house. It was not quite enough. His bid was topped by one of $21,850, and Silverman assumed that he would never see the portrait again.[16]

But nine years later Silverman happened into a gallery on Manhattan's Upper East Side owned by Kate Ganz, a respected dealer who specialized in Italian Old Master drawings. On an easel in the middle of a table near the door sat the beguiling portrait. Once again he became convinced it was by a Renaissance master. "The young woman seemed alive and breathing, every feature perfect," he recalled. "Her mouth was serene, her lips gently parted with the subtlest hint of expression, but her eye in profile was radiant with emotion. The formality of the portrait could not mask her blushing youth.

Fig. 70. *Portrait of a Young Fiancée*, also known as *La Bella Principessa*.

She was exquisite."[17] Feigning nonchalance, he asked Ganz the price. She offered to sell it for about what it had sold for nine years earlier. Silverman's wife hastily arranged for a wire transfer of the money, and he walked out of the gallery with the picture wrapped in an envelope under his arm.

As a work of art, the picture is alluring but not extraordinary. The subject is portrayed in conventional profile, body rigid, with little of Leonardo's usual sense of coiled movements of the body and mind. Its primary artistic distinction is the subject's hint of a smile that changes slightly based on the viewer's angle and distance, thus prefiguring that of the *Mona Lisa*.

What is most interesting about the portrait is Silverman's quest to prove that it was by Leonardo. Like most artists of his time, Leonardo never signed his works nor kept a record of them. So the question of authentication—figuring out which truly deserve to be called autograph works by Leonardo—becomes yet another fascinating aspect of grappling with his genius. In the case of the portrait that Silverman bought, the saga involved a combination of detective work, technical wizardry, historical research, and connoisseurship. The interdisciplinary effort, which wove together art and science, was worthy of Leonardo, who would have appreciated the interplay between those who love the humanities and those who love technology.

The process began with connoisseurs, people with a deep intuition about works of art based on years of studied appreciation. Many of the attributions made during the nineteenth and twentieth century were driven by the connoisseurship of art authorities such as Walter Pater, Bernard Berenson, Roger Fry, and Kenneth Clark. But connoisseurship can be controversial. It was put on trial, for example, in a 1920s case involving the authenticity of another purported Leonardo work, a copy of *La Belle Ferronnière* that had turned up in Kansas City. "This is not for beginners," Berenson explained as an expert witness. "It takes a very long time before you get a sort of sixth sense that comes from accumulated experience." He declared that the picture in question was not by Leonardo, prompting the owner to dismiss him as "the majordomo of picture guessers." After fifteen hours, the jury declared it could not reach a verdict, and the case was later settled with a compromise. In this instance the connoisseurs were right. The picture in question was not by Leonardo. But the case became a rallying point for populists who felt the world of art connoisseurs was an elitist cabal.[18]

The connoisseurs who initially saw the drawing that Silverman purchased, including the experts at Christie's and those consulted by the dealer Kate Ganz, summarily dismissed the idea that it might be a true Renaissance work. But Silverman was convinced that it was. He brought it to Paris, where he had an apartment, and showed it to the art historian Mina Gregori. She told him, "This drawing shows dual influences: Florentine in its delicate beauty and Lombard in the costume and braid, or coazzone, which were typical of a court lady of the late fifteenth century. Of course, the most obvious artist to come to mind is Leonardo, one of the few artists who made the transition from Florentine to Milanese." She encouraged Silverman to investigate further.[19]

One day Silverman was at the Louvre admiring a portrait by Giovanni Antonio Boltraffio, who worked in Leonardo's studio. There he ran into Nicholas Turner, a former curator at the British Museum and the Getty in Los Angeles. Silverman pulled out his digital camera and showed him a photograph of the portrait. "I saw a transparency of this not long ago," Turner said, calling the work "remarkable." At that point Silverman still assumed the work was by one of Leonardo's pupils or disciples. Turner surprised him by disagreeing. Pointing out the left-handed slanted hatchings that were Leonardo's hallmark, he said that it was likely by the master himself. "All aspects of the shading of this portrait provide visual testimony of Leonardo's theories of illumination," Turner later pronounced.[20]

The problem with relying on connoisseurs is that in any difficult case there is usually an equal and opposite cadre of them. Among the most prominent naysayers were Thomas Hoving, director of New York's Metropolitan Museum, and Carmen Bambach, the curator of drawings there. Hoving, a charismatic showman, called the picture too "sweet," and Bambach, a respected and diligent scholar, invoked her intuition to declare, "It does not look like a Leonardo."[21]

Bambach also pointed out that there was no known case of Leonardo drawing on vellum. That is true for the four thousand known autograph drawings he made on his own, but the geometrical illustrations he made for two of the editions of Luca Pacioli's *On Divine Proportion* were on vellum. That would turn out to be a clue: it indicated that, if the portrait of the young woman was by Leonardo, then it may have been done for a book produced by someone else.

Ganz, the art dealer who had sold the picture to Silverman, not surprisingly agreed with the skeptical New York connoisseurs. "At the end of the day," she told the *New York Times*, "when you talk about connoisseurship, it comes down to whether something is beautiful enough to be a Leonardo, whether it resonates with all of the qualities that define his handwriting—sublime modeling, exquisite delicacy, an unparalleled understanding of anatomy—and to me this drawing has none of those things."[22]

With connoisseurs divided, the next step was to set up a Leonardesque interplay between intuition and scientific experimentation. Silverman began by having the vellum dated by a carbon-14 test, which measures the decay of carbon in organic material to determine how old it is. The results indicated that the vellum came from sometime between 1440 and 1650. That proved little, since a forger or copier could have found a piece of old vellum. But at least it didn't eliminate Leonardo.

Silverman then took the picture to Lumiere Technology, a Paris-based company that specializes in digital, infrared, and multispectral analysis of artworks. He rode there on the back of a friend's Vespa, clutching the portrait in his arms. Pascal Cotte, the firm's founder and chief technology officer, made a series of super-high-resolution digital photographs that could capture 1,600 pixels per square millimeter. That enabled the image to be magnified hundreds of times, showing each strand of hair.

The magnified images allowed a precise comparison of the picture's details with works known to be by Leonardo. The interlace ornamentation of the young woman's costume, for example, had loops and knotwork that were twined in the same way as the ornamentation in *Lady with an Ermine*, and they were even done with the shadows meticulously drawn and the proper perspective as the ornamentation receded.[23] As Vasari wrote of Leonardo, "He even went so far as to waste his time in drawing knots of cords." Another example was the iris of the eye. The comparison to *Lady with an Ermine*, Silverman said, "showed a thrillingly identical treatment of each detail, including the outer corner of the eyelid, the fold of the upper eyelid, the contour of the iris, the lower eyelashes, the upper eyelashes, and the juxtaposition of the edge of the lower eyelid with the bottom edge of the iris."[24]

Silverman and Cotte showed the high-resolution studies to other experts. The first was Cristina Geddo, a Leonardo scholar at the University of Geneva. She was struck by the use of three-color (black, white, red) pastel crayons, a technique that Leonardo pioneered and discussed in his notebooks. "Close examination of the portrait's surface reveals it is extensively drawn with fine, left-handed shading (slanting from top left to bottom right), which may be seen both with the naked eye and, far more effectively, in the digital scans made under infra-red light," she wrote in a scholarly journal.[25]

The dean of Leonardo scholars, Carlo Pedretti, also weighed in, writing, "The sitter's profile is sublime, and the eye is drawn exactly as it is in so many of Leonardo's drawings of this period."[26] For example, the proportions of the head and neck, along with the details of the way the eyes are delineated, correspond very closely to a drawing from around 1490, now in the Royal Collection at Windsor, called *Portrait of a Young Woman in Profile*,[27] and of a drawing he would do of Isabella d'Este in Mantua in 1500.[28]

At that point, Silverman and Cotte turned to Martin Kemp, an Oxford don of impeccable integrity whose career was focused on studying Leonardo. Kemp, who regularly received missives asking him to authenticate purported Leonardo works, was not optimistic when he opened, in March 2008, the email of a high-resolution of the portrait from Lumiere Technology. "Oh, dear, another bout of painful correspondence," he thought. But as he magnified the image on his computer and carefully studied the left-handed hatching and details, he felt a shiver of excitement. "If you look at the hair band, it pulls this little dip in the back of her hair," he said. "Leonardo always had that wonderful feeling for the stiffness of materials, for how they react under pressure."[29]

Kemp, who took no money or expenses for his expert opinions, agreed to travel to see the original, by then stored in a Zurich bank vault. He was cautious, but after studying the portrait for a few hours from every angle, he became more positive. "Her ear plays a subtle game of hide-and-seek below the gentle waves of her hair," he noticed. "The iris of her pensive eye retains the translucent radiance of a living, breathing person."[30]

Kemp became a believer. "After forty years in the Leonardo business, I thought I'd seen it all," he told Silverman. "But I had not. The delight I had when I first saw it has been reinforced enormously. I'm absolutely convinced." He partnered with Cotte to accumulate more evidence and publish it as a book, *La Bella Principessa: The Story of the New Masterpiece by Leonardo Da Vinci*.[31]

The subject's dress and her *coazzone* hairstyle indicate that she was connected to Ludovico Sforza's court in Milan in the 1490s. Leonardo had already painted two of Ludovico's mistresses, Cecilia Gallerani in *Lady with an Ermine* and Lucrezia Crivelli in *La Belle Ferronnière*. Who might this third woman be? Through a process of elimination, Kemp identified her as Bianca Sforza, the duke's illegitimate (but later legitimated) daughter. In 1496, when she was about thirteen, she was married to one of the most important members of the court: Galeazzo Sanseverino, the commander of Ludovico's military and a close friend of Leonardo, who spent time at his stables making drawings for his horse monument. A few months after she married, Bianca died of what may have been a problem pregnancy. Kemp decided to name the portrait *La Bella Principessa*, even though the duke's daughters weren't officially princesses.[32]

There was one other key piece of scientific evidence that sealed the authentication, or at least initially seemed to do so. Cotte had uncovered in his scans a fingerprint on the top of the portrait. If it could be matched to a fingerprint on another work by Leonardo, who often used his hands and fingers to smooth his colors, that would come close to being dispositive.

Cotte gave an image of the fingerprint to Christophe Champod, a professor at the Institute of Criminology and Criminal Law in Lausanne. Finding it almost impossible to read, he crowdsourced the task, posting it on a website and getting close to fifty people offering their annotations. Alas, the result was inconclusive. No patterns could be determined. "I consider this mark as being of no value," Champod declared.[33]

At this point a controversial character entered the tale. Peter Paul Biro, a forensic art examiner based in Montreal, specialized in finding and using fingerprints to authenticate art. He had done so, or claimed to have, with artists ranging from J. M. W. Turner to Jackson Pollock, shaking up the insular club of art connoisseurs in the process. Kemp, Cotte, and Silverman contacted him in early 2009 to render his verdict on *La Bella Principessa*.

Using a digital enlargement of the picture, Biro claimed that he was able to discern ridge-path details of the fingerprint, and he compared it to a fingerprint that Leonardo was known to have left on *Saint Jerome in the Wilderness*. He declared that there were at least eight points of similarity, and he also claimed that these were compatible with a fingerprint on Leonardo's *Ginevra de' Benci*.

Biro demonstrated his discoveries to David Grann, a respected best-selling author and staff writer at the *New Yorker*, who was writing a profile of him. Biro zoomed in on the blurry lines and then showed a series of images taken by multispectral cameras. That still did not make the prints clear enough. He told Grann that he had then applied a "proprietary" technique, which he didn't demonstrate, to produce a clearer image. This new image allowed him, he said, to pinpoint the eight points of similarity with the *Saint Jerome* print. "For a moment, Biro stared at the prints in silence, as if still awed by what he had found," Grann reported. "The discovery, he said, was a validation of his life's work."[34]

Biro detailed his claims in a chapter he wrote for the book by Kemp and Cotte, which was published in 2010. "The correspondence between the fingerprints on Leonardo's *Saint Jerome* and *La Bella Principessa* provides a highly valuable piece of evidence among the numerous other analyses presented in this book," Biro concluded.

Though he said that the evidence was not strong enough to decide a criminal legal case, "the coincidence of the eight marked characteristics is strongly supportive of Leonardo's authorship."[35]

The fingerprint evidence made headlines worldwide when it was released in October 2009. "The art world is abuzz with the recent discovery that a portrait thought to be the drawing of an unknown nineteenth century German artist is now being attributed to the Italian master Leonardo da Vinci," *Time* magazine reported. "And the way the revelation was made is straight out of a Sherlock Holmes novel: researchers traced the portrait to the artist using a 500-year-old fingerprint." The *Guardian* announced, "Art experts believe a new portrait by Leonardo da Vinci may have been discovered thanks to a 500-year-old fingerprint," and the BBC headline was "Finger Points to New da Vinci Art." Silverman gave the inside story to a friend at *Antiques Trade Gazette*, which reported, "*ATG* have had exclusive access to that scientific evidence and can reveal that it literally reveals the hand—and fingerprint—of the artist in the work." The picture that Silverman had bought for around $20,000 was now estimated to be worth close to $150 million.[36]

Then, as with any good detective tale, there was a twist. In July 2010, less than a year after the big headlines, David Grann's colorful and deeply reported profile of Biro appeared in the *New Yorker*. "Somewhere along the way," Grann wrote about the image Biro had been trying to project of himself, "I began to notice small, and then more glaring, imperfections in this picture."[37]

Grann's 16,000-word narrative painted a troubling portrait of Biro, his methods, and his motives. It pointed to discrepancies in his story about analyzing paint samples of Jackson Pollock, recounted the various lawsuits and allegations of fraud Biro had faced, and quoted people alleging that he had tried to milk them for money when authenticating a picture. It also raised questions about the reliability of his "enhanced" fingerprint images, and it quoted a renowned fingerprint examiner who said that the eight similarities Biro had identified didn't exist. Even more explosively, the article reported that the prints Biro claimed to be of Pollock seemed so uniform that an investigator thought it was possible that someone had fabricated them with a rubber stamp. The fingerprints "screamed forgery," the investigator told Grann.[38] Biro vigorously denied the charges and implications in the article. He sued Grann and the *New Yorker* for libel, but his suit was dismissed by a federal judge, whose ruling was later affirmed by an appeals court.[39]

The *New Yorker*'s attack on Biro's credibility undermined his assessment that Leonardo's fingerprints were on *La Bella Principessa*. Kemp and Cotte deleted the chapter of their book written by Biro when an Italian edition was published. Although they insisted that Biro's fingerprint evidence was just one element of the case, it had been a very public element. Opinion seemed to turn back in favor of the doubters.

Then, like a Leonardo spiral, the story took yet another twist. Cotte had noticed on the left side of the picture signs that someone had used a sharp knife to cut the tough vellum, making a couple of small slips, and that there were three tiny holes along the edge. Kemp began to explore the theory that the picture had once been bound in a book. That might also account for why the picture was on vellum, which was used for books at the time. "My hypothesis, at this stage, is that it was in a volume of poetry dedicated to Bianca," Kemp recalled, "and that it may have been a frontispiece."[40]

Kemp then received an email from David Wright, a retired professor of art history at the University of South Florida, telling him about a volume in Warsaw's National Library of Poland. It was a history of the Sforza family, richly illustrated on vellum, that was made to commemorate the wedding of Bianca Sforza. Each of the original versions had a different frontispiece illustration of whomever it was dedicated to. The edition in Warsaw, made in 1496, had been owned by the king of France, who gave it in 1518 to the king of Poland when he married Bona Sforza, a child of Ludovico's hapless nephew Gian Galeazzo Sforza.[41]

By this point there was enough public interest in the story that *National Geographic*, working with PBS, sent a camera crew to accompany Kemp and Cotte to the Polish National Library in 2011 to see what they would find. Using a high-resolution camera to trace how each folio was bound into the volume, they discovered that one sheet was apparently cut out. The vellum of that sheet matched the vellum of *La Bella Principessa.* The missing page would have been right after the introductory texts, just where an illustration was likely to have been located. In addition, the three holes in the picture aligned with three of the five stitching holes in the bound volume. The different number of holes, they surmised, could be explained by the untidy way the portrait was cut out or because two additional stitches were added when the book was rebound in the eighteenth century.[42]

Few things are ever completely certain in the misty realms surrounding Leonardo, and there are still skeptics who doubt that *La Bella Principessa* is by Leonardo.[43] The shapes in the drawing are too delineated, lacking Leonardo's sfumato, and the outlines of the eyeball and contours of the face are too sharp. The facial features are devoid of deep emotion, and the hair lacks luster or curls. "*La Bella Principessa* is not a Leonardo," the *Guardian* art critic Jonathan Jones wrote in 2015. "I honestly don't know how anyone who loves his art could make that mistake. There is a deadness to this woman's eye, a coldness to the way she is posed and drawn that has no resemblance to Leonardo da Vinci's energy or vitality." Referring jokingly to a very dubious claim by a noted art forger that he faked the piece in the 1970s using as a model a girl he knew from Bolton, England, Jones concluded, "She looks so miserable she may well be on a break from working at a Bolton supermarket in the 1970s."[44] The drawing was pointedly excluded when London's National Gallery held a major exhibition focused on Leonardo's work in Milan. "There was never a question that the so-called Principessa could be hung among Leonardo's masterworks," said one of the curators, Arturo Galansino.

On the other side, Kemp became increasingly convinced that it is "close to an open-and-shut case" that *La Bella Principessa* was drawn by Leonardo. "The dating of the portrait to 1496 and the identification of the sitter as Bianca are thus confirmed to a high level of probability," he and Cotte wrote after their examination of the Sforza book in Poland. "The authorship of the portrait by Leonardo is also powerfully supported. Assertions that it is a modern forgery, a

19th-century pastiche, or a copy of a lost Leonardo are all effectively eliminated."[45]

Whichever assessments are correct, the tale of *La Bella Principessa* provides us with some insights into what we do and do not know about Leonardo's art. The intense human and scientific drama surrounding attempts to authenticate the picture, and to debunk it, helps us better understand what makes something an autograph Leonardo.

CHAPTER 17

The Science of Art

THE *PARAGONE*

On February 9, 1498, Leonardo starred in an evening of debates at the Sforza Castle that involved the relative merits of geometry, sculpture, music, painting, and poetry. He gave a rigorous scientific and aesthetic defense of painting, which was then considered a mechanical art, arguing that it should instead be regarded as the highest of the liberal arts, transcending poetry and music and sculpture. The court mathematician Luca Pacioli, who was there to argue for the primacy of geometry, wrote that the audience included cardinals, generals, courtiers, and "eminent orators, expert in the noble arts of medicine and astrology." Most of Pacioli's praise was lavished on Leonardo. "One of the most illustrious participants," he wrote, was the "ingenious architect and engineer and inventor Leonardo, who with each accomplishment in sculpture, casting and painting proves true his name." Not only was this a pun on his name (Vinci, the victor), but it also showed that Leonardo was viewed by others, and not just himself, as an engineer and architect as well as a painter.[1]

This type of staged debate on the comparative value of various intellectual endeavors, ranging from math to philosophy to art, was a staple of evenings at the Sforza Castle. Known as a *paragone*, from the Italian word for "comparison," such a discourse was a way for artists and scholars to attract patrons and elevate their social status during the Italian Renaissance. This was another field in which Leonardo, with his love of both stagecraft and intellectual discussion, could excel as an ornament of the court.

The relative merit of painting in comparison to other forms of art and craft had been debated since the dawn of the Renaissance with a seriousness that transcended our current-day debates on such things as, say, the merit of television versus cinema. Cennino Cennini in his treatise *The Book of Art* wrote, in about 1400, about the skill and imagination required for painting and argued, "It justly deserves to be enthroned next to theory and crowned with poetry."[2] Alberti provided a similar panegyric on the primacy of painting in his 1435 treatise, *On Painting*. A counterargument was made in 1489 by Francesco Puteolano, who argued that poetry and historical writing were most important. The reputations and memories of the great rulers, including Caesar and Alexander the Great, came from historians rather than sculptors or painters, he said.[3]

Leonardo's *paragone*, which he seems to have written and revised multiple times, occasionally rambles, but it is important to remember that this polemic, like many of his prophecies and parables, was designed to be performed rather than published. Scholars sometimes analyze the *paragone* as an essay rather than another example of the importance that the staging of theatrical events played in Leonardo's life, art, and engineering. We should imagine him declaiming the words in front of an admiring ducal court audience.[4]

The goal of Leonardo's argument was to elevate the work of painters—and their social status—by linking their art to the science of optics and the mathematics of perspective. By exalting the interplay between art and science, Leonardo wove an argument that was integral to understanding his genius: that true creativity involves the ability to combine observation with imagination, thereby blurring the border between reality and fantasy. A great painter depicts both, he said.

One premise for his argument was the supremacy of sight over the other senses. "The eye, which is said to be the window of the soul, is the principal means by which the brain's sensory receptor may fully and magnificently contemplate the infinite works of nature." The sense of hearing was less useful, because sounds disappear after they are made. "Hearing is less noble than sight; as soon as it is born it dies, and its death is as swift as its birth. This does not apply to the sense of sight, because if you represent to the eye a beautiful human body composed of proportionately beautiful parts, this beauty . . . has great permanence and remains to be seen."[5]

As for poetry, it is less noble than painting, Leonardo argued, because it takes many words to convey what a single picture can:

> If you, O poet, tell a story with your pen, the painter with his brush can tell it more easily, with simpler completeness, and less tedious to follow. Take a poet who describes the charms of a woman to her lover, and a painter who represents her, and you will see where nature leads the enamored critic. You have classed painting among the mechanical arts, but, truly, if painters were as apt at praising their own works in writing as you are, it would not lie under the stigma of so unhonored a name.[6]

He admitted, yet again, that he was a man "without letters," and thus could not read all of the classic books, but as a painter he did something more glorious, which was to read nature.

Painting is also more elevated than sculpture, he argued. The painter has to depict "light, shade, and color," which the sculptor can generally ignore. "Therefore sculpture has fewer considerations and consequently requires less ingenuity than painting."[7] In addition, sculpting is a messier endeavor, one not suitable for a gentleman of the court. The sculptor is "pasted and smeared all over with marble powder . . . his dwelling is dirty and filled with dust and chips of stone," whereas the painter "sits before his work at the greatest of ease, well dressed and applying delicate colors with his light brush."

Creative endeavors had been divided since antiquity into two categories: the mechanical arts and the more exalted liberal arts. Painting had been classified as mechanical because it was a craft based on handiwork, like that of goldsmiths and tapestry weavers. Leonardo refuted this by arguing that painting is not only an art but also a science. In order to convey three-dimensional objects on a flat surface, the painter needs to understand perspective and optics. These are sciences that are grounded in mathematics. Therefore, painting is a creation of the intellect as well as the hands.

Leonardo then went one step further. Painting requires not only intellect, he said, but also imagination. This element of fantasia makes painting creative, thus more exalted. It allows not only the depiction of reality but also the conjuring up of imaginative inventions, such as dragons, monsters, angels with wondrous wings, and landscapes that are more magical than any that exist in reality. "Thus it was wrong, O writers, to have omitted painting from the category of the liberal arts, since she embraces not only the works of nature but also infinite things that nature never created."[8]

FANTASIA AND REALITY

That, in a nutshell, was Leonardo's signature talent: the ability to convey, by marrying observation with imagination, "not only the works of nature but also infinite things that nature never created."

Leonardo believed in basing knowledge on experience, but he also indulged his love of fantasy. He relished the wonders that can be seen by the eye but also those seen only by the imagination. As a result, his mind could dance magically, and sometimes frenetically, back and forth across the smudgy line that separates reality from fantasia.

Take, for example, his advice about looking at a wall that is "spotted with stains or has a mix of stones." Leonardo could stare at such a wall and observe with precision the striations of each stone and other factual details. But he also knew how to use the wall as a springboard for his imagination and as a "way to stimulate and arouse the mind to various inventions." He wrote in his advice for young artists:

> You may discover in the patterns on the wall a resemblance to various landscapes, adorned with mountains, rivers, rocks, trees, plains, wide valleys and hills in varied arrangement; or again you may see battles and figures in action; or strange faces and costumes, and an endless variety of objects, which you could turn

> into complete and well-drawn forms. The effect produced by these mottled walls is like that of the sound of bells, in which you may recognize any name or word you choose to imagine. . . . It should not be hard for you to look at stains on walls, or the ashes of a fire, or the clouds, or mud, and if you consider them well you will find marvelous new ideas, because the mind is stimulated to new inventions by obscure things.[9]

Leonardo was one of history's most disciplined observers of nature, but his observation skills colluded rather than conflicted with his imaginative skills. Like his love of art and science, his ability to both observe and imagine were interwoven to become the warp and woof of his genius. He had a combinatory creativity. Just as he could festoon a real lizard with various animal parts to turn it into a dragon-like monster, for either a parlor trick or a fanciful drawing, he was able to perceive the details and patterns of nature and then remix them in imaginative combinations.[10]

Not surprisingly, Leonardo tried to find a scientific explanation for this ability. When he mapped the human brain during his anatomy investigations, he located the talent for fantasia in a ventricle where it could interact closely with the capacity for rational thinking.

THE TREATISE

Leonardo's *paragone* presentation was so impressive that, according to his early biographer Lomazzo, the Duke of Milan suggested he write it as a treatise. Leonardo set out to do so, and apparently some of the drafts in his notebook were pulled together in a coherent enough fashion that Lomazzo referred to it as a book.[11] Likewise, Leonardo's friend Pacioli reported in 1498, "Leonardo with all diligence has finished his praiseworthy book on Painting and Human Motion." But as with many of his paintings and all of his treatises, Leonardo had a higher standard for using the word *finished*, and he never released his *paragone* nor any treatise on painting for publication. Pacioli was being overly kind when he ascribed to Leonardo the virtue of diligence.

Instead of publishing his notes on painting, Leonardo fiddled with them for the rest of his career, just as he did with many of his paintings. More than a decade later, he was still adding thoughts and making new outlines for a treatise. The result is a medley of notes in a variety of forms: entries he made in two notebooks during the early 1490s, known as Paris Manuscripts A and C; a set of ideas compiled around 1508, later repackaged in what is now called the Codex Atlanticus; and a lost compilation from the 1490s, Libro W. After Leonardo's death, his assistant and heir, Francesco Melzi, drew on these notebook pages to produce in the 1540s what is known, in various versions and lengths, as Leonardo's *Treatise on Painting.*[12] In most editions of that work, Leonardo's *paragone* was published as the opening section.

Most of the passages that Melzi collected were written by Leonardo between 1490 and 1492, around the time he was beginning the second (London) version of *Virgin of the Rocks* and had built up a studio that included young students and apprentices.[13] It is therefore useful to read Leonardo's words as if many of them had been intended to be studied in his workshop as he collaborated with his colleagues on that painting and tried to get the complex lighting challenges right.

In these writings, we can see how Leonardo treated art as a science. The title that Pacioli used for Leonardo's proposed treatise, "On Painting and Human Motion," indicates the connections his mind made. The topics he wove together include shadows, lighting, color, tone, perspective, optics, and the perception of movements. As with his study of anatomy, he began his work on these subjects to help perfect his painting techniques, but then proceeded to immerse himself in the complexities of science for the pure joy of understanding nature.

SHADOWS

Leonardo's power of observation was especially acute when it came to discerning the effects of light and shade. He studied how different types of shadows were caused by varying types of light, and he deployed these as his primary modeling tool to give his painted objects an impression of volume. He noticed how light bouncing off an object could subtly enliven a nearby shadow or cast a glow on the underside of a face. He could see how the color of an object was affected by a shadow cast over it. And he engaged in the interplay between observation and theory that characterized his science.

He had first tackled the complexities of shadows when drawing draperies as an exercise in Verrocchio's studio. He came to understand that the use of shadows, not lines, was the secret to modeling three-dimensional objects on a two-dimensional surface. The primary goal of a painter, Leonardo declared, "is to make a flat surface display a body as if modeled and separated from this plane." This crowning achievement of painting "arises from light and shade." He knew that the essence of good painting, and the key to making an object look three-dimensional, is getting the shadows right, and that's why he spent more time studying and writing about shadows than he did on any other artistic topic.

He felt that shadows were so important to art that, in the outline for his treatise, he planned that the longest section would be on that topic. "Shadows appear to me to be of supreme importance in perspective, because, without them opaque and solid bodies will be ill defined," he wrote. "Shadow is the means by which bodies display their form. The forms of bodies could not be understood in detail but for shadow."[14]

This emphasis on the use of shadows as the key to modeling three-dimensional objects in a painting was a break from common practice of the time. Following Alberti, most artists emphasized the primacy of contour lines. "Which is the most important, the Shadows or Outlines in Painting?" Leonardo asked in his notes for his treatise. The correct answer, he believed, was the former. "It requires much more observation and study to perfect the shadowing of a picture than in merely drawing the lines of it." Typically he used an experiment to show why shading is more subtle than line drawing. "The proof of this is that the lines may be traced upon a veil or a flat glass placed between the eye and the object to be imitated. But that cannot be of any use in shadowing, because of the infinite gradation of shades and the blending of them, which does not allow of any precise borders."[15]

Leonardo proceeded to write obsessively about shadows. A torrent of more than fifteen thousand words on the topic, which would fill thirty pages of a book, still survives, and that is probably less than half of what he originally wrote. His observations, charts, and diagrams became increasingly complex (figs. 71 and 72). Using his feel for proportional relations, he calculated the effects of light striking contoured objects at varying angles. "If the body is larger than the light, the shadow resembles a truncated and inverted pyramid, and its length has also no defined termination. But if the body is smaller than the light, the shadow will resemble a pyramid and come to an end, as is seen in eclipses of the moon."

The deft use of shadows became a unifying force in Leonardo's paintings, distinguishing them from those of other artists of the time. He was especially ingenious in the way he used gradations of color

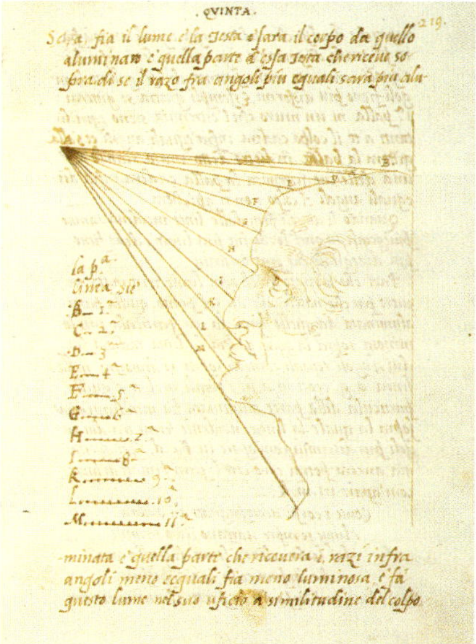

Fig. 71. Study of light hitting a head.

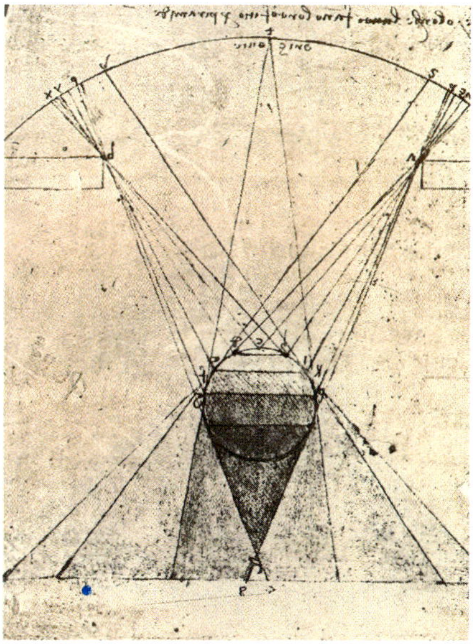

Fig. 72. Study of shadows.

tones to create shadows. The parts of a scene that get the most direct light have the greatest saturated color. This understanding of the relationship between shadows and color tones created a unified coherence to his art.

Having become, by now, a lover of received knowledge as well as a disciple of experience, Leonardo studied Aristotle's work on shadows and combined it with a variety of ingenious experiments involving different sizes of lamps and objects. He came up with multiple categories of shadows and plotted chapters on each: primary shadows that are caused by direct light hitting an object, derived shadows that result from ambient light diffused through the atmosphere, shadows that are subtly tinged with light reflected from nearby objects, compound shadows cast by multiple sources of light, shadows made by the subdued light at dawn or sunset, shadows made by light that has been filtered through linen or paper, and many other variations. With each category, he included striking observations, such as this: "There is always a space where the light falls and then is reflected back towards its cause; it meets the original shadow and mingles with it and modifies it somewhat."[16]

Reading his studies on reflected light provides us with a deeper appreciation for the subtleties of the light-dappled shadow on the edge of Cecilia's hand in *Lady with an Ermine* or the Madonna's hand in *Virgin of the Rocks*, and it reminds us why these are innovative masterpieces. Studying the paintings, in turn, leads to a more profound understanding of Leonardo's scientific inquiry into rebounding and reflected light. This iterative process was true for him as well: his analysis of nature informed his art, which informed his analysis of nature.[17]

SHAPES WITHOUT LINES

Leonardo's reliance on shadows, rather than contour lines, to define the shape of most objects stemmed from a radical insight, one that he derived from both observation and mathematics: there was no such thing in nature as a precisely visible outline or border to an object. It was not just our way of perceiving objects that made their borders look blurred. He realized that nature itself, independent of how our eyes perceive it, does not have precise lines.

In his mathematical studies, he made a distinction between numerical quantities, which involve discrete and indivisible units, and continuous quantities of the sort found in geometry, which involve measurements and gradations that are infinitely divisible. Shadows are in the latter category; they come in continuous, seamless gradations rather than in discrete units that can be delineated. "Between light and darkness there is infinite variation, because their quantity is continuous," he wrote.[18]

That was not a radical proposition. But Leonardo then took a further step. Nothing in nature, he realized, has precise mathematical lines or boundaries or borders. "Lines are not part of any quantity of an object's surface, nor are they part of the air which surrounds this surface," he wrote. He realized that points and lines are mathematical constructs. They do not have a physical presence. They are infinitely small. "The line has in itself neither matter nor substance and may rather be called an imaginary idea than a real object; and this being its nature it occupies no space."

This theory—based on a Leonardesque blend of observation, optics, and mathematics—reinforced his belief that artists should not use lines in their paintings. "Do not edge contours with a definite outline, because the contours are lines, and they are invisible, not only from a distance, but also close at hand," he wrote. "If the line and also the mathematical point are invisible, the outlines of things, also being lines, are invisible, even when they are near at hand." Instead an artist needs to represent the shape and volume of objects by relying on light and shadow. "The line forming the boundary of a surface is of invisible thickness. Therefore, O painter, do not surround your bodies with lines."[19] This was an upending of the Florentine tradition known as *disegno lineamentum*, praised by Vasari, which was founded on linear precision in drawing and the use of lines to create forms and designs.

Leonardo's insistence that all boundaries, both in nature and in art, are blurred led him to become the pioneer of sfumato, the technique of using hazy and smoky outlines such as those so notable in the *Mona Lisa*. Sfumato is not merely a technique for modeling reality more accurately in a painting. It is an analogy for the blurry distinction between the known and the mysterious, one of the core themes of Leonardo's life. Just as he blurred the boundaries between art and science, he did so to the boundaries between reality and fantasy, between experience and mystery, between objects and their surroundings.

OPTICS

Leonardo's realization that there are no precise boundary lines visible in nature was prompted by the observations he made as a painter and by his mathematical knowledge. There was one other cause: his study of optics. Like much of his science, his optics research was begun to help inform his art, but by the 1490s he was pursuing it with a relentless, seemingly insatiable and pure curiosity.

He had originally thought, along with others, that rays of light converged at a single point inside the eye. But he soon became uncomfortable with this idea. A point, like a line, is a mathematical concept that has no size or physical existence in the real world. "If all the images which come to the eye converged in a mathematical point, which is proved to be indivisible," he wrote, "then all the things in the universe would appear to be one and indivisible." Instead, he came to believe, correctly, that visual perception occurs along the entire area of the retina. It was an idea he developed from simple experiments as well as dissections of the eye. And it helped him explain why sharp lines are not visible in nature. "The true outlines of opaque bodies are never seen with sharp precision," he wrote. "This happens because the visual faculty does not occur in a point; it is diffused throughout the pupil [actually the retina] of the eye."[20]

One experiment he did, which was drawn from the work of the eleventh-century Arab mathematician Alhazen, was to move a needle closer and closer to one eye. As it gets near, it does not completely block the vision from the eye, as it would if sight were processed in only a single point on the retina. Instead the needle becomes blurry, a transparent fog. "If you place a sewing needle in front of the pupil as near to the eye as possible, you will see that the perception of any object placed behind this needle at however great a distance will not be impeded."[21] That is because the needle is narrower than the pupil (the hole in the center of the eye that allows light to come in) and the retina (the layer at the back of the eyeball that passes light impulses to the brain). The far left and right of the eye can still pick up light coming from objects behind the needle. Likewise, the eye cannot see a border of an object even if it is up close because different parts of the eye catch the light from the object and its surroundings slightly differently.

One question that stymied him was why images do not appear to be reversed and inverted in our brains. He had studied a device known as a camera obscura, and he knew that the image it produces is upside down and reversed because the lines from the object cross as they go through the aperture. Mistakenly, he assumed that somewhere deep in the eye or brain is another aperture that rights the image. He did not realize that the brain itself can make that adjustment, although his own ability to write and read in mirror script should have provided a clue.

The question of how images turn right-side up after passing through the eye prompted Leonardo to pursue dissections of human and cow eyes and then map the path of visual perceptions from the eyeball to the brain. In one astonishing page of drawings and notes (fig. 73), he shows a view looking down into a skull with its top sawed open. It has the eyeballs in front, and below them are the optic nerves and the x-shaped optic chiasma formed by the nerves on their way to the brain. On the sheet, he described his method:

> Ease away the brain substance from the borders of the dura mater [the hardest of the three membranes surrounding the brain]. . . . Then note all the places where the dura mater penetrates the basilar bone with nerves ensheathed in it, together with the pia mater [the innermost of the three membranes surrounding the brain]. And you will acquire such knowledge with certainty when

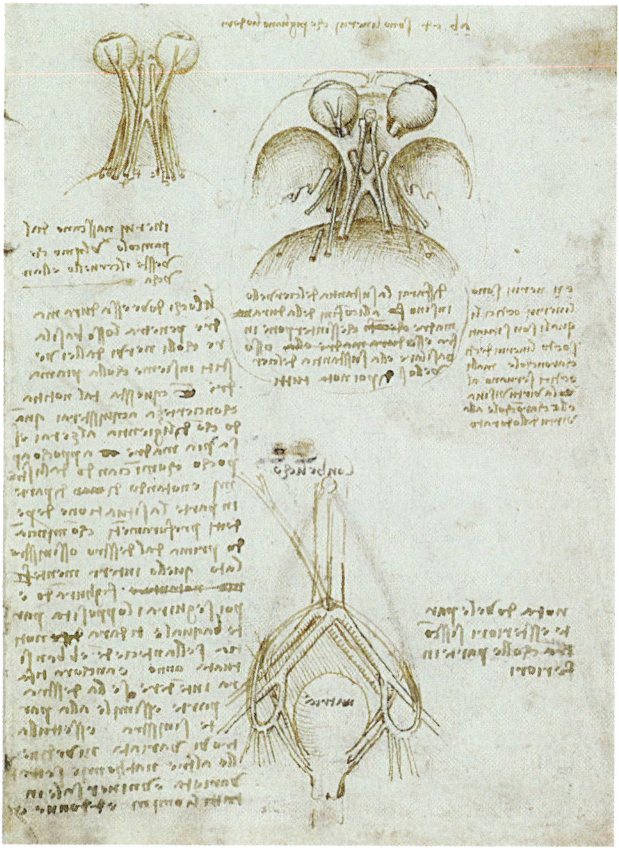

Fig. 73. A view into the skull.

you diligently raise the pia mater, little by little, commencing from the edges and noting bit by bit, the situation of the perforations, commencing first from the right or left side, and drawing this in its entirety.[22]

One problem he faced in dissecting an eyeball was that it tended to change shape when cut. So he came up with an inventive way to solve the problem: "One should place the whole eye in an egg white, boil it until it becomes solid, and cut the egg and the eye transversely in order that none of the middle portion of the eye be poured out."

Leonardo's optics experiments produced discoveries that would not be rediscovered for another century.[23] In addition, they were important in honing his ability to match theory with experiment, and they became an underpinning of his studies on perspective.

PERSPECTIVE

Leonardo realized that the art of painting and the science of optics were inseparable from the study of perspective. Along with the proper ability to deploy shadows, the mastery of various types of perspective allowed painters to convey a three-dimensional beauty on a flat surface. A true understanding of perspective involved more than merely a formulaic approach to sizing objects correctly; he knew it also required studying the science of optics. "Painting is based on perspective," he wrote, "and perspective is nothing else than a thorough knowledge of the function of the eye." So while he was composing his planned treatises on painting and optics, he also gathered ideas for one on perspective.[24]

The field had been well studied. Alhazen had written on the optical science of perspective, and the application of perspective theory to painting had been refined by Leonardo's artistic predecessors, including Giotto, Ghiberti, Masaccio, Uccello, and Donatello. The most important advances came from Brunelleschi, with his famous experiment using a mirror to compare his painting of Florence's Baptistery with the real view, and were codified by Alberti in his masterful *On Painting*.

In his early days in Florence, Leonardo had wrestled with the mathematics of perspective in his preparatory drawing for the *Adoration of the Magi*. The grid he sketched was such a rigorous application of Alberti's concepts that it looks labored, especially in contrast to the delightfully fanciful motions of the sketched horse and camel. Not surprisingly, when he began work on what was supposed to be the final painting, he adjusted the proportions to present a more imaginative picture in which the linear perspective does not constrain the sense of motion and fantasy.

As with many other subjects, Leonardo's serious work on perspective was stimulated in the early 1490s when he became a full participant in the intellectual hothouse surrounding the ducal court in Milan. On his visit to the university in nearby Pavia in 1490 (the same trip that resulted in *Vitruvian Man*), he discussed optics and perspective with Fazio Cardano, a professor who had edited the first printed edition of the study of perspective written by John Peckham in the thirteenth century.

Leonardo's notes on perspective are mixed in with his notes on optics and painting, but he seemed to be considering a separate treatise on the subject. The sixteenth-century artist Benvenuto Cellini said that he owned a manuscript on perspective by Leonardo, which he described as "the most beautiful a man ever made, showing how objects foreshorten not only in depth but also in breadth and height." Lomazzo called it "written very obscurely." Many of his precepts on perspective have survived, but alas, not this manuscript.[25]

Leonardo's most important contribution to the study of perspective was to broaden the concept to include not just linear perspective, which uses geometry to figure out the relative sizes of objects in the foreground and background of a painting, but also ways of conveying depth through changes in color and clarity. "There are three branches of perspective," he wrote. "The first deals with the apparent diminution of objects as they recede from the eye. . . . The second addresses the way colors vary as they recede from the eye. The third is concerned with how the objects in a picture ought to be less detailed as they become more remote."[26]

For linear perspective, he accepted the standard rule of proportion: an object that is twice as far from the eye as another object "will appear half the size of the first, though they be of the same size really, and as the space doubles the diminution will double." He realized that this rule applies to a painting of normal size, one in which the edges are not significantly farther away from the viewer than is the center. But what about a big fresco or mural? One edge might be twice as far from the viewer as the center of the picture is. "Complex perspective," as he called it, occurs when "no surface can be seen exactly as it is because the eye that sees it is not equally remote from all its edges." A wall-size painting, as he would soon show, requires a mix of natural perspective with "artificial perspective." He drew a diagram and explained, "In artificial perspective when objects of unequal size are placed at various distances, the smallest is nearer to the eye than the largest."[27]

His work on linear perspective was not groundbreaking; Alberti had explained much the same. But Leonardo was more innovative when he focused on acuity perspective, which describes how objects far away become less distinct. "You must diminish the sharpness of those objects in proportion to their increasing distance from the eye of the spectator," he instructed. "The parts that are near in the foreground should be finished in a bold determined manner; but those in the distance must be unfinished, and confused in their outlines." Because things appear smaller at a distance, he explained, the tiny details of an object vanish, and then even larger details begin to vanish. At a great distance, the outlines of the forms are indistinct.[28]

He used the examples of cities and towers behind walls, where the viewer does not see the base and may not know the size. By making their outlines blurrier, acuity perspective helps to indicate that these structures are in the distance. "How many, in the representation of towns and other objects remote from the eye, express every part of the buildings in the same manner as if they were very near," he wrote. "It is not so in nature, because it is not possible to perceive at any great distance the precise form of objects. The painter therefore who delineates the outlines and the tiny details of parts, as several have done, will not accurately depict distant objects, but by this error will make them appear exceedingly near."[29]

In a small notebook sketch done late in his life, which historian James Ackerman called "a token of one of the most consequential changes in the history of Western art," Leonardo shows a receding row of trees. Each one loses a little detail, until the ones near the horizon are just a simple shape devoid of individual branches. Even in his botanical drawings and the depiction of plants in some of his paintings, leaves in the foreground are more distinct than those in the background.[30]

Acuity perspective is related to what Leonardo called aerial perspective: things become blurrier in the distance not only because their details disappear as they become smaller but also because the air and mists soften distant objects. "When objects are distant, there is a great deal of air interposed, which weakens the appearance of forms, and prevents our seeing distinctly the minute parts of such objects," he wrote. "It behooves the painter therefore to touch those parts slightly, in an unfinished manner."[31]

We can see Leonardo experimenting with this concept in many of his drawings. A preliminary sketch of a stampede of horses done for the *Battle of Anghiari* shows those in the foreground drawn with great clarity and sharp focus, while those in the background are softer and less distinct. The effect, as often with Leonardo, is to convey a perception of movement in a still piece of art.

Just as details diminish as objects get more distant, so do colors. To render a scene correctly requires attending to both. "The eye can never arrive at a perfect knowledge of the interval between two objects by means of the linear perspective alone, if not assisted by the perspective of colors," he wrote. "Let the colors vanish in proportion as the objects diminish in size, according to the distance."[32]

Once again he blended theory and experiment. Using a pane of glass, he traced the outline of a nearby tree and then on paper colored it precisely. Then he did the same for a tree at a distance and then another one at double the distance. It will thus be possible, he wrote, to see how color diminishes in tandem with size.[33]

Leonardo's investigations of light and color were successful because he cared about the science of optics. Other perspective theorists, such as Brunelleschi and Alberti, wanted to know how objects could be projected onto a flat panel. Leonardo pursued that knowledge as well, but it led him to another level: he wanted to know how light from objects that enters the eye and is processed by the mind.

By pursuing science that went well beyond its utility for painting a picture, Leonardo could have fallen prey to academism. Some critics have suggested that his excess of diagrams showing light hitting contoured objects and his deluge of notes about shadows were at best a waste of time and at worst led him to be too studied in some later works. To disprove that, you only need to look at *Ginevra de' Benci* and then the *Mona Lisa* to see how a profound understanding of light and shadow, both intuitive and scientific, led to the latter being the historic masterpiece. And to be convinced that he could be flexible and clever in bending the rules of perspective given the needs of a complex situation, one only has to look at, and marvel at, *The Last Supper*.[34]

Fig. 74. *The Last Supper.*

CHAPTER 18

The Last Supper

THE COMMISSION

When Leonardo was painting *The Last Supper* (fig. 74), spectators would visit and sit quietly just so they could watch him work. The creation of art, like the discussion of science, had become at times a public event. According to the account of a priest, Leonardo would "come here in the early hours of the morning and mount the scaffolding," and then "remain there brush in hand from sunrise to sunset, forgetting to eat or drink, painting continually." On other days, however, nothing would be painted. "He would remain in front of it for one or two hours and contemplate it in solitude, examining and criticizing to himself the figures he had created." Then there were dramatic days that combined his obsessiveness and his penchant for procrastination. As if caught by whim or passion, he would arrive suddenly in the middle of the day, "climb the scaffolding, seize a brush, apply a brush stroke or two to one of the figures, and suddenly depart."[1]

Leonardo's quirky work habits may have fascinated the public, but they eventually began to worry Ludovico Sforza. Upon the death of his nephew, he had become the official Duke of Milan in early 1494, and he set about enhancing his stature in a time-honored way, through art patronage and public commissions. He also wanted to create a holy mausoleum for himself and his family, choosing a small but elegant church and monastery in the heart of Milan, Santa Maria delle Grazie, which he had Leonardo's friend Donato Bramante reconstruct. For the north wall of the new dining hall, or refectory, he had commissioned Leonardo to paint a Last Supper, one of the most popular scenes in religious art.

At first Leonardo's procrastination led to amusing tales, such as the time the church prior became frustrated and complained to Ludovico. "He wanted him never to lay down his brush, as if he were a laborer hoeing the Prior's garden," Vasari wrote. When Leonardo was summoned by the duke, they ended up having a discussion of how creativity occurs. Sometimes it requires going slowly, pausing, even procrastinating. That allows ideas to marinate, Leonardo explained. Intuition needs nurturing. "Men of lofty genius sometimes accomplish the most when they work least," he told the duke, "for their minds are occupied with their ideas and the perfection of their conceptions, to which they afterwards give form."

Leonardo added that there were two heads left to paint: that of Christ and of Judas. He was having trouble finding a model for Judas, he said, but he would use the image of the prior if he insisted on continuing to hound him. "The Duke was moved to wondrous laughter, saying that Leonardo had a thousand reasons on his side," Vasari wrote. "The poor prior was confounded and went back to worrying about his garden, leaving Leonardo in peace."

The duke, however, eventually began to get impatient, especially after his wife, Beatrice, died in early 1497, at age twenty-two. Even though he had a series of mistresses, he was bereft; he had come to admire Beatrice and depend on her counsel. She was buried in Santa Maria delle Grazie, and the duke started dining once a week in its refectory. In June of that year, he instructed his secretary "to urge Leonardo the Florentine to finish the work already begun in the Refectory of Santa Maria delle Grazie so that he can then attend to the other wall of the Refectory; and make him sign the contract with his own hand to oblige him to finish within the time to be agreed upon."[2]

It turned out to be worth the wait. The result is the most spellbinding narrative painting in history, displaying multiple elements of

Leonardo's brilliance. His ingenious composition shows his mastery of complex rules of natural and artificial perspective, but it also shows his flexibility at fudging those rules when necessary. His ability to convey motion is evident in the gestures of each of the apostles, and so is his famed ability to follow Alberti's injunction to make movements of the soul—emotions—known through movements of the body. In the same way that he used sfumato to blur hard lines delineating objects, Leonardo blurred the preciseness of perspective and of instants in time.

By conveying ripples of motions and emotions, Leonardo was able not merely to capture a moment but to stage a drama, as if he were choreographing a theatrical performance. *The Last Supper*'s artificial staging, exaggerated movements, tricks of perspective, and theatricality of hand gestures demonstrate the influence of Leonardo's work as a court impresario and producer.

A MOMENT IN MOTION

Leonardo's painting depicts the reactions just after Jesus tells his assembled apostles, "One of you will betray me."[3] At first it looks like a freeze-frame moment, as if Leonardo had used the quickness of his eye, which could make a stop-action image of dragonfly wings, to frame-grab a specific instant. Even Kenneth Clark, who called *The Last Supper* "the keystone of European art," was disconcerted by what he felt was a stationary snapshot of crafted gestures: "The movement is frozen . . . rather terrifying."[4]

I think not. Look longer at the picture. It vibrates with Leonardo's understanding that no moment is discrete, self-contained, frozen, delineated, just as no boundary in nature is sharply delineated. As with the river that Leonardo described, each moment is part of what just passed and what is about to come. This is one of the essences of Leonardo's art: from the *Adoration of the Magi* to *Lady with an Ermine* to *The Last Supper* and the *Mona Lisa*, each moment is not distinct but instead contains connections to a narrative.

The drama begins the second after Jesus' words have been spoken. His head is bowed in silence even as his hands are continuing their movement toward the bread. Like a stone thrown into a pond, his pronouncement causes ripples outward, spreading from him to the edges of the picture and creating a narrative reaction.

As Jesus' words reverberate, subsequent moments from the gospel become part of the drama. The next verses in Matthew are "And they were exceedingly sorrowful, and each of them began to say to him, 'Lord, is it I?'" And from John: "The disciples began to look at one another, perplexed as to which of them he meant."[5] Even as the three apostles on the far left are still reacting, the others are beginning to respond or ask each other questions.

In addition to portraying the motion contained in a moment, Leonardo was masterful at conveying *moti dell'anima*, motions of the soul. "A picture of human figures ought to be done in such a way as that the viewer may easily recognize, by means of their attitudes, the intentions of their minds," he wrote. *The Last Supper* is the grandest and most vibrant example of this in the history of art.[6]

Leonardo's primary method for showing the intentions of the mind was through gestures. Italy was then, as now, a nation of hand-gesture enthusiasts, and Leonardo in his notebooks recorded a variety of them. Here, for example, is his description of how to portray someone making an argument:

> Let the speaker, with the fingers of the right hand, hold one finger of the left hand, having the two smaller ones closed; and his face alert and turned towards the people with mouth a little open, to look as though he spoke. If he is sitting, let him appear as though about to rise, with his head forward. If you represent him standing, make him lean slightly forward with body and head towards the people. These you must represent as silent and attentive, all looking at the orator's face with gestures of admiration; and make some old men in astonishment at the things they hear, with the corners of their mouths pulled down and drawn in, their cheeks full of furrows, and their eyebrows raised, and wrinkling the forehead where they meet.[7]

He had learned how much could be communicated by gestures by watching Cristoforo de' Predis, the deaf brother of his painting partners in Milan. Gestures were also important to the monks who ate in the Santa Maria delle Grazie dining hall because they were obliged to observe silence many hours of the day, including at most meals. In one of his pocket notebooks he carried as he walked around town, Leonardo wrote a description of a group of people at a table making gestures as they talked:

> One who was drinking has left his glass in its position and turned his head towards the speaker. Another twists the fingers of his hands together and turns with a frown to his companion. Another with hands spread open showing the palm, shrugs his shoulders up to his ears and makes a grimace of astonishment. Another speaks into his neighbor's ear and the listener turns to him to lend an ear, while he holds a knife in one hand and in the other the loaf half cut through by the knife; and in turning round another, who holds a knife, upsets with his hand a glass on the table. Another lays his hand on the table and is looking. Another blows his mouthful. Another leans forward to see the speaker shading his eyes with his hand.[8]

These read like stage directions, and in *The Last Supper*, which includes many of these gestures, we can see Leonardo choreographing the action.

The twelve apostles are clustered into groups of three. Starting on our left, we can sense the flow of time, as if the narrative moves from left to right. On the far left is the cluster of Bartholomew, James the Minor, and Andrew, all still showing the immediate reaction of surprise at Jesus' announcement. Bartholomew, alert and tough, is in the process of leaping to his feet, "about to rise, his head forward," as Leonardo wrote.

The second trio from the left is Judas, Peter, and John. Dark and ugly and hook-nosed, Judas clutches in his right hand the bag of silver he has been given for promising to betray Jesus, whose words he knows are directed at him. He rears back, knocking over a salt cellar (which is clearly visible in early copies but not the current painting) in a gesture that becomes notorious. He leans away from Jesus and is painted in shadow. Even as his body recoils and twists, his left hand reaches for the incriminating bread that he and Jesus will share. "He that dippeth his hand with me in the dish shall betray me," Jesus says, according to Matthew. Or as in the gospel according to Mark, "Behold, the hand of him that betrayeth me is with me on the table."[9]

Peter is pugnacious and agitated, elbowing forward in indignation. "Who is it of whom he speaks?" he asks. He seems ready to take action. In his right hand is a long knife; he would, later that evening, slice off the ear of a servant of the high priest while trying to protect Jesus from the mob that came to arrest him.

By contrast, John is quiet, knowing that he is not suspect; he seems saddened by yet resigned to what he knows cannot be prevented. Traditionally, John is shown asleep or lying on Jesus' breast. Leonardo shows him a few seconds later, after Jesus' pronouncement, wilting sadly.

Dan Brown in his novel *The Da Vinci Code*, which draws on *The Templar Revelation* by Lynn Picknett and Clive Prince, wove a conspiracy theory that has as one piece of evidence the assertion that the effeminate-looking John is actually secretly meant to be Mary Magdalene, the faithful follower of Jesus. Although a wonderful plot twist for a rollicking novel, it is not supported by the facts. One character in the novel argues that the feminine look of the character was meant to be a clue because "Leonardo was skilled at painting the difference between the sexes." But Ross King points out in a book on *The Last Supper*, "On the contrary: Leonardo was skilled at blurring the differences between the sexes."[10] His alluring androgynous figures begin with his angel in Verrocchio's *Baptism of Christ* and continue through *Saint John the Baptist*, painted in his final years.

Jesus, sitting alone in the center of *The Last Supper*, his mouth still slightly open, has finished making his pronouncement. The expressions of the other figures are intense, almost exaggerated, as if they are players in a pageant. But Jesus' expression is serene and resigned. He looks calm, not agitated. He is slightly larger than the apostles, although Leonardo cleverly disguised the fact that he has used this trick. The open window with the bright landscape beyond forms a natural halo. His blue cloak is painted with ultramarine, the most expensive of pigments. In his studies of optics, Leonardo had discovered that objects against a light background look larger than when against a dark background.

The trio to the right of Jesus includes Thomas, James the Greater, and Philip. Thomas raises his index finger with his hand turned inward in a pointing gesture closely associated with Leonardo. (It appears in many of his paintings, such as *Saint John the Baptist*, and Raphael used it in his depiction of Plato that is believed to be based on Leonardo.) Later he will be known as doubting Thomas because he demanded proof of Jesus' resurrection, which Jesus provided by letting Thomas place a finger in his wounds. Preparatory drawings for Philip and James have survived; the former of them, very androgynous, appears to have also served as a model for the Virgin Mary in the London version of *Virgin of the Rocks*.

The final trio on the right comprises Matthew, Thaddeus, and Simon. They are already in a heated discussion about what Jesus may have meant. Look at the cupped right hand of Thaddeus. Leonardo was a master of gestures, but he also knew how to make them mysterious, so that the viewer could become engaged. Is he slapping his hand down as if to say, I knew it? Is he jerking his thumb toward Judas? Now look at Matthew. Are his two upturned palms gesturing toward Jesus or Judas? The viewer need not feel bad about being confused; in their own ways Matthew and Thaddeus are also confused about what has just occurred, and they are trying to sort it out and turning to Simon for answers.

Jesus' right hand is reaching out to a stemless glass one-third filled with red wine. In a dazzling detail, his little finger is seen through the glass itself. Just beyond the glass are a dish and a piece of bread. His left hand is palm up, gesturing at another piece of bread, which he gazes at with downcast eyes. The perspective and composition of the painting, especially as seen from the door that the monks would use to enter the hall, guide the viewer's eyes to follow those of Jesus, down his left arm to the piece of bread.

That gesture and glance create the second moment that shimmers in the narrative of the painting: that of the institution of the Eucharist. In the gospel of Matthew, it occurs in the moment after the announcement of the betrayal: "Jesus took bread, and blessed it, and broke it, and gave it to the disciples, and said, 'Take, eat; this is my body.' And he took the cup, and gave thanks, and gave it to them, saying, 'Drink ye all of it, for this is my blood of the new testament, which is shed for many for the remission of sins.'" This part of the narrative reverberates outward from Jesus, encompassing both the reaction to his revelation that Judas will betray him and the institution of the holy sacrament.[11]

PERSPECTIVE IN *THE LAST SUPPER*

The only thing straightforward about the perspective in *The Last Supper* is the vanishing point, where all the lines of sight "tend and converge," in Leonardo's words. These receding lines, or orthogonals, point to the forehead of Jesus (fig. 75). When he began his work, Leonardo hammered a small nail in the center of the wall. We can see that hole in Jesus' right temple. Then he cut thin incisions in the wall radiating

Fig. 75. Perspective lines of *The Last Supper.*

out. These would help to guide the lines that were parallel in the imaginary room, such as the beams in the ceiling and the tops of the tapestries, as they receded toward the vanishing point in the painting.[12]

To understand how Leonardo brilliantly manipulated the perspective, look at the tapestries hanging along the two walls. The tops of these tapestries form lines that recede to Jesus' forehead, just as all the perspective lines do. These tapestries were painted in a way that made them appear to be in line with the real tapestries in the actual dining hall, thus creating the illusion that the painting was an extension of the room. Yet it was not a perfect trompe l'oeil of an extended room, nor could it be. Because of the painting's size, the perspective is different depending on the viewer's vantage point (fig. 76). If you stand on the left side of the room, the wall next to you will appear

Fig. 76. The refectory with *The Last Supper.*

to flow seamlessly into the left wall of the painting, but if you look across the room at the right wall, you will notice it doesn't quite align with the painting.

This was just one of many clever manipulations Leonardo used to accommodate the fact that the painting would be seen from different parts of the room. When Alberti wrote about perspective in his treatise, he assumed that all viewers would look at a painting from the same vantage point. But with a painting as large as *The Last Supper*, the viewer might see it from the front or the side or while walking past. That required what Leonardo called "complex perspective," which is a mix of natural and artificial perspective. The artificial part was needed to adjust for the fact that a person looking at a very large painting would be closer to some parts of it than to other parts. "No surface can be seen exactly as it is," Leonardo wrote, "because the eye that sees it is not equally remote from all its edges."[13]

If you stand far enough away from a picture, even a large one, the problem of the edges being at a different distance from you diminishes. Leonardo determined that a proper vantage point for a large picture should be ten to twenty times its width or height. "Stand back until your eye is at least twenty times as far off as the greatest height and width of your work," he wrote at one point. "This will make so little difference when the eye of the spectator moves, that it will be hardly appreciable."[14]

In the case of *The Last Supper*, which is fifteen feet high and twenty-nine feet wide, that would mean the proper vantage would be three hundred to six hundred feet back—clearly not possible. So Leonardo created an artificial ideal vantage point that was about thirty feet from the wall. In addition, he made it fifteen feet off the ground, at eye level with Jesus. No friar would ever view it from such a location, of course. But after making that spot the ideal vantage point, Leonardo proceeded to use optical tricks to make it seem less distorted from a variety of other places in the room from which it would actually be viewed.

Most cleverly, he adjusted and fudged slightly so that the perspective looks natural when viewed from a door in the right wall from which the monks entered. This meant that their first striking perception was that of Jesus' left hand, palm up, directed right at them, as if welcoming them to the room. The angles of the ceiling are slightly higher on the right side. That makes the plane of the picture appear as if it is at eye level of the viewer coming in the door. Because the right wall of the painting is closer to the viewer entering from the door and is lit brighter, it looks bigger and feels a natural continuation of the refectory.[15]

Leonardo used a few tricks to disguise the fact that he had manipulated the perspective. The lines where the floor hits the back and side walls are completely hidden by the table. If you look at the picture carefully and try to imagine the floor lines, you can sense that they would have appeared distorted. In addition, a painted cornice disguises the fact that the ceiling does not extend all the way out to above the table. Otherwise viewers would have noticed that Leonardo slightly accelerated the perspective of the ceiling.

This use of accelerated perspective, in which the walls and ceiling recede toward the vanishing point more quickly than normal, was one of the many tricks that Leonardo learned from the theatrical events he produced. In Renaissance productions, the stage would contain not a rectangular room but one that rapidly became narrower and shorter, to give the illusion of greater depth. It sloped downward toward the audience, and the artificial nature of the scenery was disguised by a decorated cornice, just like the one Leonardo used atop *The Last Supper*. His use of such artifices is another example of why his work on plays and pageants was not time squandered.

In *The Last Supper*, the painted room diminishes in size so quickly that the back wall is just large enough to have three windows showing the landscape outside. The tapestries are not proportional. The table is too narrow for a comfortable supper, and the apostles are all on one side of it, where there are not enough places for them to sit. The floor is raked forward, like a stage, and the table is slanted a bit toward us as well. The characters are all at the forefront, as if in a play, and even their gestures are theatrical.

The tricks of perspective are accompanied by other clever contrivances, including little touches to make the scene appear as if it is connected to the monks eating in the refectory. The light in the painting appears to come from the actual window that is high on the left wall of the refectory, blending reality with imagination (fig. 76). Look at the right wall in the painting; it's bathed in afternoon light as if from the actual window. Also notice the legs of the table: their shadows are cast as if from this source.

The tablecloth shows alternating concave and convex folds, as if it had been pressed and stored in the monk's laundry room before being put on the table. Two little serving platters have eels garnished with fruit slices. They have no obvious religious or iconographic meaning; however, river eels were popular in Italy at the time, and we know that Leonardo, although usually a vegetarian, put "eels and apricots" on at least one of his shopping lists.[16]

All told, *The Last Supper* is a mix of scientific perspective and theatrical license, of intellect and fantasy, worthy of Leonardo. His study of perspective science had not made him rigid or academic as a painter. Instead, it was complemented by the cleverness and ingenuity he had picked up as a stage impresario. Once he knew the rules, he became a master at fudging and distorting them, as if creating perspectival sfumato.

DETERIORATION AND RESTORATION

When Leonardo used oil paint, he would apply a stroke or two, touch and retouch, meditate for a while, then add a few more layers until he had it perfect. This permitted him to show subtle gradations in shadows and blur the borders of objects. His strokes were so light and layered that individual brushstrokes are imperceptible, and he sometimes waited hours or days before gently adding more thin layers and retouchings.

Unfortunately, this leisurely process was not a luxury allowed the painter of a typical wall fresco, which required that the paint be applied onto wet plaster in order to remain fixed. Once a patch of plaster had been put on the wall, that area of the painting had to be completed in one day's session, before it dried, and could not easily be reworked later.

Verrocchio, who did not paint frescoes, never taught the technique to his pupils, and it was clearly unsuited to Leonardo's unhurried style. Instead, he decided to paint directly on the dry plaster wall, which he coated with a layer of ground white stone and then white lead primer. He used tempera paint, in which pigments were mixed into water and egg yolk, along with oil paint, in which pigments were mixed into walnut or linseed oil. Recent scientific analysis of *The Last Supper* shows that he experimented with varying oil-tempera proportions in different parts of the painting. Mixing water-based and oil-based pigments allowed him—or so he thought—to indulge in adding layer after layer of subtle strokes, building them up over weeks to create the shapes and tones he wanted.[17]

Leonardo finished the painting by early 1498, and the duke rewarded him with a bonus of a vineyard near the church, which he owned for the rest of his life. But after only twenty years, the paint began to flake, and it became evident that Leonardo's experimental technique was a failure. When Vasari published his biography of Leonardo in 1550, he reported that the painting was "ruined." By 1652 the painting was so faint and dissipated that the monks felt comfortable breaking a doorway through the wall at the bottom, cutting off the feet of Jesus, which were probably crossed in a manner prefiguring the crucifixion.

Over the years, there have been at least six major attempts to restore the painting, many of which only made the situation worse. The first recorded effort was in 1726 by a curator who used oil paint to fill in missing sections and then put a coat of varnish on top. Less than fifty years later, another restorer stripped away all that the first had done and started repainting the faces on his own; a public outcry forced him to stop with only three faces left to be done. During the French Revolution, anticlerical forces scratched out the eyes of the apostles, and then the refectory was used as a prison. A subsequent restorer tried to remove the painting from the wall, mistakenly thinking it was a fresco. In the early twentieth century, two cleanings were done that avoided further damaging the painting and slowed its deterioration. Allied bombs hit the refectory during World War II, but the painting was protected by sandbags.

The latest restoration, which began in 1978 and lasted twenty-one years, was the most extensive ever. Chief curator Pinin Brambilla Barcilon and her team began by using infrared reflectoscopy and microscopic samples to try to discover, as best as possible, the original elements of the painting. She also had her restorers study Leonardo's drawings and the copies of the painting made during his lifetime. The original intention was to have the wall display only what could be known to be done by Leonardo's hand, but that turned out to be unsatisfying because so little remained. So the restorers reconstructed the missing areas in a way that indicated what was and wasn't original; where it was not possible to discern the original artwork, the team used subtle watercolors with a lighter hue to give a sense of the original while indicating that these sections were speculative.[18]

Not everyone was pleased. Art critic Michael Daley wrote that the result was "a distinctly mongrel work showing alarmingly little original paint and very much alien 'compensatory' and 'reintegrating' new paint." But Brambilla Barcilon generally drew praise for creating and re-creating what is, in fact, a piece of art that seems to be as deeply faithful to the original as is possible. "Not only was the original color recovered, but also the clarity of the architectural structure, the perspective devices, and the physiognomies," she said. "The faces, burdened with grotesque features from so many restorations, again manifest a genuine expressiveness. Now the faces of the apostles seem to genuinely participate in the drama of the moment and evoke the gamut of emotional responses intended by Leonardo to Christ's revelation."[19]

As a result, *The Last Supper*, both in its creation and in its current state, becomes not just an example of Leonardo's genius but also a metaphor for it. It was innovative in its art and too innovative in its methods. The conception was brilliant but the execution flawed. The emotional narrative is profound but slightly mysterious, and the current state of the painting adds another thin veil of mystery to the ones that so often shroud Leonardo's life and work.

Chapter 19

Personal Turmoil

CATERINA'S DEATH

On the rare occasions when he recorded a family event in his notebooks, Leonardo sometimes displayed a notarial tic of repeating the date. Thus he recorded the arrival of his mother, Caterina, now widowed and in her sixties, to live with him in Milan:

On the 16th day of July.
Caterina came on the 16th day of July 1493.[1]

During her years with her husband, Accattabriga, Caterina had four daughters and a son. But sometime around 1490 her husband died and their son was killed by a shot from a crossbow. In his notebook shortly after that, Leonardo jotted, "Can you tell me what la Caterina wishes to do?" Apparently, she wanted to come live with him.

On a page adjoining the one in his notebook where he records Caterina's arrival, Leonardo writes a rudimentary family tree that she likely helped him make, listing the names of his father and grandparents. In June 1494 she is included in an accounting of his expenses: he gives 3 soldi to Salai and 20 soldi to her.[2]

She apparently died later that month. A record in the state archives of Milan reports, "On Thursday 26 June at the Parish of the

Saints Nabore and Felix at Porta Vercellina, Caterina from Florence, 60 years old, died of malaria." The evidence from the earlier archival records is that she was actually about fifty-eight, which is close enough to be in accord given the vagaries of records at the time.[3]

Leonardo sublimated whatever emotions he felt; he records nothing about her death, only an accounting of the cost of her funeral. On the listing of soldis he spent, he even crossed out the word "death" and wrote "burial."[4]

Expenses for Caterina's ~~death~~. burial:

For 3 pounds of candle wax	s. 27
For the bier	s. 8
A pall for the bier	s. 12
For bearing and placing a cross	s. 4
For the bearers	s. 8
For 4 priests and 4 clerks	s. 20
Bell, book, sponge,	s. 2
For the gravediggers	s. 16
For the dean	s. 8
For the license	s. 1
	s. 106
[Earlier expenses]	
Doctor	s. 5
Sugar and candles	s. 12
	s. 123

The detachment seems odd, and some have argued that the expenses seem low for a mother's funeral. He would spend four times as much in 1497 on the silver cloth, velvet trim, and tailoring for a cloak for Salai.[5] But a careful look shows that it was, in fact, a funeral suitable for his mother rather than a household servant. It was brightly lit, featured four priests, and was carefully planned and recorded for posterity.[6]

CAREER STRUGGLES

When he began painting *The Last Supper* around 1495, Leonardo was at a high point in his career. With his official appointment as artist and engineer of the Sforza court, he was comfortably ensconced at Milan's old palace, the Corte Vecchia, with his retinue of assistants and students. He was renowned as a painter, admired as the sculptor of the mammoth clay model for the horse monument, beloved as a pageant impresario, and respected as a student of optics, flight, hydraulics, and anatomy.

But his life became unsettled in the late 1490s, after Caterina's death and the completion of *The Last Supper*. The bronze for his horse monument had been redirected in 1494 to make cannon to defend against a possible French invasion, and it soon became clear that Ludovico was not going to replace it. Instead of major new commissions or portraits of ducal mistresses, he found himself doing interior design work and engaging in disputes over pay and performance. All the while, Duke Ludovico became increasingly preoccupied, and rightly so, by the French threats to his tenuous hold on power.

One of Leonardo's projects was doing the decorative painting for a set of small rooms in the Sforza Castle, known as the *camerini*, that the duke planned to use as his private retreat. One of the vaulted wood-paneled rooms, the Sala delle Asse, was designed by Leonardo as an enchanted painted forest with sixteen trees, figuratively serving as an architectural fantasia of columns. Their branches intertwined in complex patterns worthy of his mathematical mind, and woven through this caprice was a golden rope that twisted into beautifully complex knots, a lifelong love of his. "In the trees we find a beautiful invention by Leonardo, where all the branches transform themselves into bizarre knots," wrote Lomazzo.[7]

The execution did not go as well as the conception, as was often the case with Leonardo. There was a dispute, and one of the duke's secretaries wrote in June 1496, "The painter who is decorating the camerini caused something of a scandal today, and for this reason he has left."[8] The secretary asked if someone could be sent from Venice to finish the work.

That never happened, and Leonardo resumed the commission in early 1498, just as he was finishing work on *The Last Supper*. But there were other disputes that are revealed in letters drafted in his notebooks. One angry missive from 1497 has been ripped in half, so we have only fragments of sentences that express his frustration. "You remember the commission to paint the camerini" reads one phrase. "Of the horse I will say nothing because I know the times are bad," is another. Then comes a tumult of complaints, including "two years of my salary still not received."[9] In another letter drafted for the duke, Leonardo again complained about money and seems to imply that he had to put aside work on *The Last Supper* to make money by decorating the Sala delle Asse. "Perhaps your Excellency did not give further orders to [pay me], believing that I had money enough," he wrote. "It vexes me greatly that having to earn my living has forced me to interrupt the work and to attend to small matters, instead of following up the work which your Lordship entrusted to me."[10]

As with *The Last Supper*, Leonardo was too slow-paced in painting the Sala delle Asse to put up with using the traditional fresco method that required each section to be executed rapidly on wet plaster before it dried. Instead, he again used a tempera-oil mixture on a dry wall (the wood panels of the room had been removed, unfortunately). The dry plaster did not absorb the pigments, resulting in the same deterioration as suffered by *The Last Supper.* It was restored badly around 1901, salvaged in the 1950s, and in 2017 was in the midst of a more careful, laser-guided restoration.

After his temperamental disputes involving the Sala delle Asse, Leonardo hit a low point. He found himself drafting job applications, including a letter written in the third person to the council of the nearby town of Piacenza, which was commissioning brass doors for the cathedral there. He wrote the letter extolling himself as if he planned to have a supporter send it on his behalf. "Open your eyes and look carefully that your money is not spent as to purchase your own shame," the letter reads. "There is not a man who is capable—and you may believe me—except Leonardo the Florentine, who is making the bronze horse of the Duke Francesco."[11]

Larger forces intervened to rescue Leonardo from his employment concerns. In the summer of 1499, an invasion force sent by the new French king, Louis XII, was bearing down on Milan. Leonardo added up the money in his cash box, 1,280 lire, distributed some to Salai (20 lire) and others, and then proceeded to hide the rest in paper packets around his studio to keep it safe from invaders and looters. At the beginning of September, Duke Ludovico fled the city, which the French king entered a month later. As Leonardo feared, mobs destroyed the homes of many of his friends and looted their treasures. His studio was spared, but the French troops destroyed the clay model of his unbuilt horse monument by shooting arrows at it.

The French were, it turned out, protective of Leonardo. The day after his arrival, the king went to see *The Last Supper*, and he even asked whether it might be possible to cart it back to France. Fortunately, his engineers told him it was impossible. Instead of fleeing, Leonardo spent the next few months working with the French. He made a note to contact one of the painters who had arrived in Milan with King Louis and to get from him "the method of using dry colors and the white salt method and how to make coated paper." On the same page, he laid out a leisurely set of preparations for the long trip from Milan back to Florence and Vinci, which he would not begin until December. "Have two covered boxes made to be carried on mules. One of which leave at Vinci. Buy some tablecloths, napkins, cloaks, caps, and shoes, four pair of hose, a chamois jerkin and skins to make new ones. Sell what you cannot take with you." In other words, he was not scurrying to escape from the French.

In fact, he had forged a secret deal with the new French governor of Milan, the Count of Ligny, to meet him in Naples and act as a military engineer inspecting fortifications. In one of the most curious entries in his notebooks, on the same page as his list preparing for his trip, Leonardo writes not only in his mirror script but using a simplistic code in which he spells names and cities backward: "Go and find ingil [Ligny] and tell him you will wait for him at amor [Roma] and that you will go with him to ilopan [Napoli]."[12]

That plot never came to fruition. What made Leonardo finally leave Milan was the news that his former patron Ludovico was plotting a comeback. In late December, Leonardo made arrangements to transfer 600 florins from his Milanese bank to an account in Florence, then left with his retinue of assistants and his friend the mathematician Luca Pacioli. Eighteen years after he had arrived in Milan with a lute and a letter for Ludovico proclaiming his talents as an engineer and artist, Leonardo da Vinci was returning home to Florence.

CHAPTER 20

Florence Again

THE RETURN

Leonardo's first stop on his journey back to Florence in early 1500 was the town of Mantua. There he was hosted by Isabella d'Este, the sister of Ludovico's late wife, Beatrice. An avid and spoiled art collector from one of Italy's most venerable families, Isabella was eager to have a portrait of her done by Leonardo, and during his short stay he dutifully made a preparatory chalk drawing.

From there he went to Venice, where he offered military advice on defending against a threatened Turkish invasion. Always interested in the flow of water and its military uses, he devised a mobile wooden lock that he believed could allow the Isonzo River to flood a valley that would be used by any invaders.[1] Like many of his visionary schemes, it was never implemented.

He also dreamed up ideas for protecting a port such as Venice by equipping a corps of underwater defenders with diving suits, breathing gear, goggles, a mask, and wineskin airbags. The mask was attached to cane tubes that led up to a diving bell floating on the surface. After sketching some of these items in his notebook, he wrote that he was keeping a few of his plans secret: "Why is it that I do not describe my method for remaining underwater and how long I can remain there without coming up for air? I do not wish to publish this because of the evil nature of men, who might use it for murder on the sea bed."[2] As with many of his inventions, his scuba gear was, at least during his time, just over the edge of practicality. It would be centuries before his ideas came to fruition.

When Leonardo reached Florence in late March 1500, he found a city that had just lived through a reactionary spasm that threatened to destroy its role in the vanguard of Renaissance culture. In 1494 a radical friar named Girolamo Savonarola had led a religious rebellion against the ruling Medici and instituted a fundamentalist regime that imposed strict new laws against homosexuality, sodomy, and adultery. Some transgressions were punished by stoning and burning. A militia of young boys was organized to patrol the streets and enforce morals. On Mardi Gras of 1497 Savonarola led what became known as the "Bonfire of the Vanities," in which books, art, clothing, and cosmetics were set aflame. The following year, popular opinion turned on him, and he was hanged and burned in the central square of Florence. By Leonardo's return, the city had again become a republic that celebrated the classics and art, but its confidence was shaken, its exuberance dampened, and the finances of its government and guilds drained.

Leonardo would make Florence his base for most of 1500 to 1506, boarding comfortably with his entourage at the church of Santissima Annunziata. In many ways, it would be the most productive period of his life. There he began two of his greatest panel paintings, the *Mona Lisa* and *Virgin and Child with Saint Anne*, as well as an image of Leda and the swan that is now lost. As an engineer, he would find work consulting on buildings, such as a structurally challenging church, and serving the military aims of Cesare Borgia. And in his spare time, he would immerse himself again in mathematical and anatomical studies.

LIFE AT FIFTY

As Leonardo approached the age of fifty, living again in Florence, where he and his family were well-known, he was comfortable being a distinctive character. Rather than try to conform, he made a point of being different, dressing and carrying himself as a dandy. At one point he made an inventory in his notebook of clothing he had stored in a trunk. "One gown made of taffeta," he began. "One velvet lining that can be used as a gown. One Arab burnouse. One gown of dusty rose. One rose-colored Catalan gown. One cape of dark purple with wide collar and velvet hood. One coat of dark purple satin. One coat of crimson satin. One pair of dark purple stockings. One pair of dusty-rose stockings. One pink cap."[3] These might seem like costumes from one of his plays or masquerades, but we know from contemporary accounts that he actually dressed like this when walking about town. It is a delightful image: Leonardo in an Arab hooded cloak or strolling in purple and pink garb, heavy on the satin and velvet. He was tailor-made for a Florence that had rebelled against Savonarola's Bonfire of the Vanities and was again willing to embrace flamboyant, eccentric, and artistic free spirits.

Leonardo made sure that his companion Salai, then twenty-four, was dressed with similar brio, usually also in pink and rose. In one entry Leonardo noted, "On this day I paid Salai three gold ducats which he said he wanted for a pair of rose-colored hose with their trimming." The trimmings on the stocking must have been jewels. Four days later, he bought Salai a cloak of silver cloth with green velvet trim.[4]

In the list Leonardo made of the clothing he had stored in a trunk, it is telling that his own clothes and those of Salai are mixed together, unlike the possessions of anyone else in the household. The clothes included "a cape in the French mode, once owned by Cesare Borgia, belonging to Salai." Apparently Leonardo had cloaked his young companion in a cape given to him by the notoriously vicious warlord who was briefly his father figure. If Freud had only known. The trunk also contained "a tunic laced in the French fashion, belonging to Salai," and "a tunic of gray Flemish cloth, belonging to Salai."[5] These are not the types of garment that Leonardo, or anyone else of the time, bought for an ordinary house servant.

It's reassuring to discover that Leonardo spent as much on books as he did on clothes. In the inventories he made in 1504, he listed 116 volumes. These included Ptolemy's *Cosmography*, which he later cited in describing the human circulation and respiratory system as a microcosm of the earth's. He also acquired more books on math, including a three-volume translation of Euclid and a book he described as being about "the squaring of the circle," which was probably a text by Archimedes. There are many more texts on surgery, medicine, and architecture, but his tastes also ran to more popular fare. By then he owned three editions of Aesop's fables and multiple volumes of bawdy verse. He had also acquired the book on architecture written by his friend from Milan, Francesco di Giorgio, who had been a collaborator in conceiving *Vitruvian Man*. He made annotations throughout and copied some passages and drawings into his notebook.[6]

ISABELLA D'ESTE'S UNPAINTED PORTRAIT

We can get an impression of Leonardo's life in Florence at this time by looking at the amusing tale of a commission he did not take. Soon after he arrived, he was besieged by entreaties from Isabella d'Este to fulfill his promise to paint a picture for her, either a portrait based on the chalk drawing he had made of her when he passed through Mantua or, short of that, any other subject he chose. The saga of the two willful people, with a beleaguered friar caught in the middle, turned out to be so prolonged that it became, at least in retrospect, humorous as well as revealing of Leonardo's unwillingness to fulfill commissions that bored him. It also tells us about his interests in Florence, dilatory style, and aloof attitude toward wealthy patrons.

Isabella, a strong-willed first lady of Mantua and a stronger-willed patron of art, was twenty-six at the time. She was the daughter of the Duke of Ferrara and a scion of the Este family, the richest and oldest noble clan in Italy. She had received a rigorous classical education in Latin, Greek, history, and music. From the age of six, she had been betrothed to Francesco Gonzaga, the Marquess of Mantua. Isabella brought a dowry of 25,000 gold ducats (worth more than $3 million at 2017 gold prices), and her wedding in 1491 was lavish. After arriving in Mantua from Ferrara in a flotilla of more than fifty boats, she rode through the streets in a gold chariot cheered by seventeen thousand spectators and accompanied by ambassadors from a dozen realms.[7]

In an era of conspicuous consumption and competitive collecting, Isabella became the most conspicuous and competitive. She also triumphed in a tumultuous marriage. Her husband was a weak leader who was often away, at one point held hostage for three years in Venice, and she served as regent and took command of the city's military, holding off enemies. In return, her ungrateful husband conducted a long, passionate, and public affair with the notoriously beautiful and evil Lucrezia Borgia, who was married to Isabella's brother. (It was Lucrezia's third marriage. Her own brother, the brutal Cesare Borgia, had ordered her second husband to be strangled before her eyes.)

Isabella channeled her emotions into collecting art and, more specifically, seeking suitable portraits of herself. That proved difficult, because artists made the mistake of trying to produce passable likenesses, all of which she decried as making her look too fat. The respected Mantua court artist Andrea Mantegna tried in 1493, but Isabella pronounced, "The painter has done it so badly that it does not look like us in the least."

After a couple of other unsatisfactory portraits, she tried again with a painter who worked for her family in Ferrara, but when she sent it to Milan as a gift, she apologized to Ludovico Sforza. "I am afraid that I shall weary, not only Your Highness, but all Italy with the sight of my portraits," she wrote. "I send this one, which is not really very good and makes me look fatter than I am." Ludovico, who apparently did not know the proper response to a woman who said a portrait made her look fat, responded that he thought the picture was a good likeness. At one point Isabella lamented, "We only wish that we could be as well served by painters as we are by men of letters." Presumably, the many poets who dedicated poems to her could take more literary license with a subject than a painter could.[8]

In her continuing quest for the right artist to paint her, Isabella turned her sights on Leonardo. In 1498, soon after the death of her sister Beatrice, who had been married to Ludovico, Isabella wrote to Ludovico's mistress Cecilia Gallerani, the subject of Leonardo's *Lady with an Ermine*. She wanted to compare that portrait to ones done by the Venetian painter Giovanni Bellini to determine which of the two artists would be her next target. "Having seen today some fine portraits by the hand of Giovanni Bellini, we began to discuss the works of Leonardo, and wished we could compare them with these paintings," she wrote. "And since we remember that he painted your likeness, we beg you to be so good as to send us your portrait by this messenger whom we have dispatched on horseback, so that we may not only be able to compare the works of the two masters, but also have the pleasure of seeing your face again." She promised to return it. "I send it without delay," Cecilia replied, adding that it was no longer a good likeness. "But Your Highness must not think this proceeds from any defect in the master, for indeed I think there is no other painter to equal him in the world, but merely because the portrait was painted when I was much younger." Isabella liked the painting, but she kept her word and returned it to Cecilia.[9]

When Leonardo made his chalk drawing of Isabella on his way from Milan to Florence in early 1500, he also made a copy. He took it with him and showed it to a friend, who reported back to Isabella, "[The] portrait is exactly like you, and it could not be done better."[10] Leonardo had left the original drawing with Isabella, who in her flurry of subsequent correspondence asked him to send a replacement because her husband had given it away. "Will you also beg him to send us another drawing of our portrait," she wrote her agent, "since His Lordship our consort has given away the one which he left here?"[11]

The copy that Leonardo carried with him, which was large enough to be a preparatory cartoon for a painting, is likely the same drawing that is now in the Louvre (fig. 77). The portraits that Leonardo had painted in Milan show the sitters in Spanish-influenced dress, which had been the fashion. But Isabella was a trendsetter, and Leonardo drew her dressed in the very latest from France. That had an advantage: the loose sleeves and bodice hid her plumpness, though Leonardo gave her the hint of a double chin only slightly disguised by his chalky sfumato. There is a willfulness to her mouth and a dignified formality in the choice of a profile pose, which was the standard for portraits of royalty.

In most of his portraits, and all of those that were fully painted, Leonardo avoided the conventional approach of the period, which was to portray subjects in profile. Instead, he preferred to show his subjects facing the viewer or in three-quarters view, which allowed him to imbue them with a sense of motion and psychological engage-

Fig. 77. Drawing of Isabella d'Este.

ment. Ginevra de' Benci, Cecilia Gallerani, Lucrezia Crivelli, and Mona Lisa are posed this way.

But these women were not royalty; two were mistresses of Ludovico and two were upper-class wives. Isabella instead insisted on being portrayed in the classical profile that conveyed courtly decorum. As a result, Leonardo's drawing of her is lackluster. We cannot see into her eyes or mind or soul. She seems to be posing. No thoughts or emotions seem to be churning inside. The fact that she could have viewed Cecilia's *Lady with an Ermine* and then asked Leonardo for a conventional pose indicates that she had more money than taste. That may be one reason Leonardo had no desire to turn the drawing into a painting.[12]

Even though this drawing was pricked for transferring onto a panel, Leonardo showed no signs of fulfilling Isabella's request to produce a portrait painting. She was used to getting what she wanted, however, and after waiting a full year, she decided to launch a lobbying campaign. Caught in the middle was a well-connected friar named Pietro da Novellara, who had been Isabella's confessor.

"If Leonardo the Florentine, the painter, is to be found in Florence, we beg you will inform us what he is doing and whether he has begun any work," she wrote Pietro in late March 1501. "Your Reverence might find out, as you best know how, if he would undertake to paint a picture for our studio."[13]

The friar's reply, sent on April 3, gives a glimpse into what Leonardo was doing and his reluctance to make commitments. "From what I hear, Leonardo's life is very irregular and uncertain, and he seems to live for the day only," Pietro wrote. His only art, the friar reported, was a preparatory drawing for what would eventually become his great painting of the *Virgin and Child with Saint Anne*. "He has done nothing else, excepting that two of his apprentices are painting portraits to which he sometimes adds a few touches."

As usual, Leonardo was distracted by other pursuits. As the friar said at the end of his letter, "He devotes much of his time to geometry, and has no fondness at all for the paintbrush." He repeated that message after Salai arranged for him to meet with Leonardo. "I have succeeded in learning the intentions of the painter Leonardo by means of his pupil, Salai, and some of his other friends, who took me to see him on Wednesday," Pietro wrote on April 14. "In truth, his mathematical experiments have absorbed his thoughts so entirely that he cannot bear the sight of a paintbrush."

As always, Leonardo was charming, even when he was not being accommodating. One issue was that, when Louis XII of France took Milan, Leonardo had committed to do some paintings for him and his secretary, Florimond Robertet. "If he can get free from his engagement with the King of France without displeasing him, which he hopes to do by the end of a month at latest, he would rather serve Your Excellency than any other person in the world," Pietro wrote, stretching the truth. "But, in any case, as soon as he has finished a little picture which he is doing for a certain Robertet, a favorite of the King of France, he will do your portrait immediately." The friar described a painting Leonardo was working on that would become *Madonna of the Yarnwinder*. He ended with a note of resignation: "This is all that I could get from him."[14]

Had he wished to comply with Isabella, it would have been a lucrative commission, one that he could have mostly delegated to his assistants. But Leonardo, although not wealthy, was beyond that. He occasionally led his patrons on—perhaps he even thought he might eventually gratify their wishes—but he rarely allowed himself to be subservient to them. When Isabella wrote to him directly in July 1501, he didn't even deign to send back a formal answer. "I gave him to understand that if he wished to reply I could forward his letters on to Your Ladyship and thus save his costs," reported Isabella's agent. "He read your letter and said he would do so, but hearing nothing more from him I finally sent one of my men to him to learn what he wished to do. He sent back the answer that for now he was not in a position to send another reply to Your Ladyship, but that I should advise you that he has already begun work on that which Your Ladyship wanted from him." He ended his letter with the same resigned lament as Pietro had used. "In short, this is as much as I have been able to get from the said Leonardo."[15]

Three years later, despite all the entreaties, Leonardo had not sent a painting, nor is there any evidence that he had begun one. Finally, in May 1504, Isabella changed tactics and asked him to paint for her instead a picture of the young Jesus. "When you were in this city and drew our portrait in chalk, you promised us that you would some day paint it in colors," she wrote. "But because this would be almost impossible, since you are unable to come here, we beg you to keep your promise by converting our portrait into another figure, which would be still more acceptable to us, that is to say, a youthful Christ of about twelve years old."[16]

Although she implied she would pay whatever he wanted, Leonardo was unmoved. Salai, not surprisingly, was more mercenary, and in January 1505 he offered his own services to do such a painting. "A pupil of Leonardo Vinci, Salai by name, young in years but very talented . . . has a great wish to do some gallant thing for Your Excellency," her agent reported, "so if you desire a little picture from him, you have only to tell me the price you are ready to pay."[17] Isabella declined the offer.

The final chapter came in 1506, when Isabella personally went to Florence. She was not able to meet with Leonardo, who was staying in the countryside doing studies on the flight of birds, but she did meet with Alessandro Amadori, the brother of Leonardo's stepmother, Albiera. He promised to use his influence. "Here in Florence, I act at all hours as the representative of Your Excellency with Leonardo da Vinci, my nephew," he wrote in May, after she returned to Mantua, "and I do not cease to urge him by every argument in my power to satisfy your desire and paint the figure for which you asked him. This time he has really promised me that he will soon begin the work and satisfy your wish."[18]

Needless to say, Leonardo did not. He was pursuing more ambitious paintings as well as his endeavors in anatomy, engineering, math, and science. Painting a conventional portrait for a pushy patron did not interest him. Nor did money motivate him. He painted portraits if the subject struck his fancy, such as the *Musician*, or if a powerful ruler demanded it, as in the case of Ludovico with his mistresses. But he didn't dance to the music of patrons.

MADONNA OF THE YARNWINDER

Friar Pietro, in one of his letters to the persistent Isabella, described a painting that Leonardo was doing at the request of Louis XII's secretary, Florimond Robertet. "The little picture he is working on is of a Madonna who is seated as if she were about to spin yarn," he wrote, "and the child has placed his foot in the basket of yarns and has grasped the yarnwinder, and stares attentively at the four spokes, which are in the form of a cross, and he smiles and grips it tightly, as if he were longing for this cross, not wishing to yield it to his mother, who appears to want to take it away from him."[19]

Dozens of versions of this picture, either by Leonardo or his assistants and followers, still exist, and there has been much debate by experts, as well as some advocacy by owners and dealers, regarding which might be the one Leonardo himself painted and sent to Robertet. Two of the surviving versions, known as the Buccleuch Madonna and the Lansdowne Madonna (fig. 78), are considered most likely to reflect the most involvement of Leonardo's own hand. But the quest to designate the "real" or "original" Leonardo version actually misses the larger meaning of the tale of the *Yarnwinder*s. When he returned to Florence in 1500, Leonardo set up a collaborative workshop, and production of some pictures, especially small devotional ones, became a team effort, just as it had been in Verrocchio's studio.[20]

The emotional power of the *Yarnwinder* scene comes from the psychological complexity and intensity of the baby Jesus as he contemplates and grapples with the yarnwinder, which is in the shape of a cross. Other painters had shown Jesus looking at objects that foretold the Passion, as Leonardo had done in the devotional paintings of the Madonna and Child he had made Benois Madonna and other little paintings in his early years. But the *Yarnwinder* paintings are energized by what had become Leonardo's special ability to convey a psychological narrative.

There is a flow of physical motions as Jesus reaches toward the cross-like object, his finger pointed heavenward, the gesture that Leonardo loved. His moist eyes are shiny with a tiny sparkle of luster, and they have their own narrative: he is just the age when a baby can

Fig. 78. *Madonna of the Yarnwinder* (Lansdowne version).

discern objects and focus on them, and he is doing so with a concerted effort that combines his sight with his sense of touch. We sense that his ability to focus on the cross causes a premonition of his fate. He looks innocent and at first playful, but if you look at his mouth and eyes you sense a resigned and even loving comfort with what will be his destiny. By comparing *Madonna of the Yarnwinder* to the Benois Madonna (fig. 13), we can see the historic leap Leonardo made by turning static scenes into emotion-laden narratives.

Our eyes swirl counterclockwise as the narrative continues with Mary's motions and emotions. Her face and her hand indicate anxiety, a desire to intervene, but also an understanding and an acceptance of what shall be. In the *Virgin of the Rocks* paintings (figs. 64 and 65), Mary's hovering hand offers a serene benediction; in the *Yarnwinder*s, her gesture is more conflicted, as if coiled to grasp her child while also recoiling from the temptation to intervene. She reaches out nervously, as if trying to decide whether to restrain him from his fate.

The *Yarnwinder* paintings are only the size of a page of a tabloid newspaper, but they include, especially in the Lansdowne version, Leonardo's marks of genius. There are the tightly coiled and lustrous curls on both mother and child. There is the river winding down from the mystical and misty mountains as if it were an artery connecting the macrocosm of the earth to the veins of the two human bodies. He knew how to have the light play on her thin veil, making it look lighter than her skin but still letting the sunlight hit the top of her forehead and reflect back a shine. The sun highlights the leaves on the closest tree next to her knee, but as the trees recede so does their distinctness, as Leonardo prescribed in his writings on acuity perspective. Also reflecting his scientific exactitude are the sedimentary layers of rocks on which Jesus leans.

Leonardo's picture arrived at the French court in 1507, and Salai possessed a similar picture when he died, according to an accounting of his estate. But there is no clear historical documentation that connects either of these to the Lansdowne and Buccleuch versions, or to any of the at least forty existing versions of the picture that have some claim to have been produced by Leonardo's studio.

Given the lack of a historical record or documentary trail, people have used other methods to try to determine which of the *Yarnwinder* contenders is the "original." One approach is connoisseurship, the ability of a true art expert with a refined eye to discern paintings by the master. Unfortunately, connoisseurship over the years, both in this case and others, has created more disagreements than it has resolved, and it has sometimes been proven wrong when new evidence arises.

Another approach is scientific and technical analysis, which has been made more potent recently with infrared reflectography and other tools using multispectral imagery. Oxford professor Martin Kemp and his graduate student Thereza Crowe Wells began such a process of analysis in the early 1990s on the Buccleuch and then the Lansdowne Madonnas. One of their surprising discoveries is that both paintings have underdrawings that seem to have been made by Leonardo directly on the wood panel. In other words, they were not copied or transferred from a master preparatory drawing. The two underdrawings are similar. But interestingly, they were significantly modified in the course of creating the paintings.

For example, in both underdrawings there is a faint group of figures that includes Joseph making a baby walker for Jesus. It appears that Leonardo decided, as both paintings were being done, that the little scene was too much of a distraction, so it was left out. This and other bits of technical evidence point to the likelihood that the Lansdowne and Buccleuch versions were painted in the studio at the same time, with Leonardo overseeing and probably using his own hand on both. He probably had more of a hand in the Lansdowne, and saw it to completion, given that it has the more Leonardesque landscape and lustrous curls.

At least five of the surviving versions of the painting include the little scene of Joseph building the baby walker. This indicates that these versions were being painted in Leonardo's studio before he decided to eliminate that scene. In other words, the best way to make sense of the versions and variations of the painting is to imagine Leonardo in his studio creating and modifying the painting while his assistants are producing copies.

This aligns with the impression we get from Pietro da Novellara's letter to Isabella d'Este, in which he describes the scene in Leonardo's studio, where "two of his apprentices are painting portraits to which he sometimes adds a few touches." In other words, we should put aside our romantic image of the artist alone in his studio creating works of genius. Instead, Leonardo's studio was like a shop in which he devised a painting and his assistants worked with him to make multiple copies. This is similar to the way it had been in Verrocchio's bottega. "The process of production is more in keeping with the commissioning of a superbly made chair from a major designer-craftsman," Kemp wrote after the results of the technical analysis. "We do not ask if a certain glued joint in the chair was made by the head of the workshop or one of his assistants—providing the joint holds and looks good."

In the case of the *Madonna of the Yarnwinder*, as it was with the two versions of the *Virgin of the Rocks*, we should modify the traditional questions asked by art historians: Which version is the "authentic" or "autograph" or "original" one? Which are mere "copies"? Instead, the proper and more interesting questions to ask are: How did the collaboration occur? What was the nature of the team and the teamwork? As with so many examples in history where creativity was turned into products, Leonardo's Florence studio involved individual genius combined with teamwork. Both vision and execution were required.

Because it was delivered to the French court and extensively copied, *Madonna of the Yarnwinder* turned out to be one of Leonardo's most influential paintings. Leonardo's followers, such as Bernardino Luini and Raphael, and soon painters throughout Europe, upended the genre of staid Madonna-and-child devotional paintings, creating instead narratives of emotional drama. Raphael's 1507 painting *Madonna of the Pinks*, for example, is often compared to Leonardo's Benois Madonna, which it closely mimics, but in fact we can see that Raphael has also picked up on Leonardo's ability in the *Yarnwinder* to imbue a work with psychological movements. The same is true of

Luini's *Madonna of the Carnation* and *Madonna with Child and Young Saint John*.

In addition, the *Yarnwinder* set the stage for one of the most richly layered of Leonardo's masterpieces, another depiction of the emotional swirl that occurs when the baby Jesus apprehends his destiny, this one adding Mary's mother, Saint Anne, to the drama.

Chapter 21

Saint Anne

THE COMMISSION

When Friar Pietro da Novellara was floundering in his mission to convince Leonardo to paint a portrait for Isabella d'Este, he wrote to her in April 1501 to explain the situation: "Since he has been in Florence, he has only made one sketch—a cartoon of a child Christ, about a year old, almost jumping out of his mother's arms to seize hold of a lamb. The mother is in the act of rising from Saint Anne's lap and holds back the child from the lamb, which is a symbol of the Passion."[1]

The cartoon that the friar described was a full-size preparatory drawing for what would become one of Leonardo's greatest masterpieces, the *Virgin and Child with Saint Anne* (fig. 79), featuring Mary sitting on the lap of her mother. The final painting combines many elements of Leonardo's artistic genius: a moment transformed into a narrative, physical motions that match mental emotions, brilliant depictions of the dance of light, delicate sfumato, and a landscape informed by geology and color perspective. It was proclaimed to be "Leonardo da Vinci's ultimate masterpiece" (*l'ultime chef d'oeuvre*) in the title of the catalogue published by the Louvre for a 2012 exhibition celebrating its restoration—this from the museum that also owns the *Mona Lisa*.[2]

Fig. 79. *Virgin and Child with Saint Anne.*

The story of the commissioning of the painting probably began when Leonardo returned to Florence from Milan in 1500 and took up residence at the church of Santissima Annunziata. The monks there regularly provided accommodation to distinguished artists, and Leonardo was given five rooms for himself and his assistants. It was wonderfully convenient: the monastery had a library with five thousand volumes, and it was only three blocks from the Santa Maria Nuova hospital, where Leonardo performed his dissections.

The monks had commissioned an altarpiece by Filippino Lippi, the Florentine painter who had painted an *Adoration of the Magi* for a nearby church after Leonardo had abandoned that commission. Leonardo let it be known that he would gladly take on the job of painting the altarpiece himself, and, as Vasari wrote, "when Filippino heard this, like the good-hearted person he was, he decided to withdraw." Another factor working in Leonardo's favor: his father was the notary for the church.

DIFFERENT VERSIONS

Once he got the commission, Leonardo typically procrastinated. "He kept them waiting a long time without even starting anything," Vasari wrote, "then he finally did the cartoon showing Our Lady with Saint Anne and the Infant Christ." The cartoon was a sensation, evidence that Leonardo was now wildly famous in his hometown and that he was leading the way for artists to rise from being nameless artisans to being individual public stars. "Men and women, young and old, continued for two days to flock for a sight of it to the room where it was, as if to a grand festival, to gaze at the marvels of Leonardo," Vasari recorded.

Vasari was presumably referring to the cartoon that Friar Pietro had described to Isabella d'Este. Unfortunately, Vasari confused matters by reporting that the drawing also included "Saint John, depicted as a little boy playing with a lamb." The fact that Vasari's description does not comport exactly with that of the friar, who makes no mention of Saint John, is not surprising. It was probably just a mistake. Vasari, whose accuracy was invariably well below perfect, was writing fifty years later, and he never saw the cartoon in question. But his injection of Saint John into the picture reflects an interesting historical mystery that Leonardo scholars still wrestle with, because some of Leonardo's versions and variations on the drawing did indeed include Saint John in place of (not playing with) the lamb.

The cartoon that Friar Pietro wrote about—comprising Anne, Mary, Jesus, and a lamb—has the same four elements as the painting now in the Louvre. But here's the wrinkle: the only surviving cartoon by Leonardo related to this project is a drawing now in London known as the Burlington House cartoon (because of the Royal Academy headquarters where it was long displayed; fig. 80). Beautiful and haunting and large, it features Saint Anne, the Virgin Mary, and the baby Jesus, but with a young Saint John and no lamb. In other words, it is not the cartoon that Friar Pietro saw in 1501.

Scores of Leonardo scholars have puzzled over the sequencing of the various versions of the arrangement: there is the cartoon described by Friar Pietro that was publicly displayed and then apparently lost, the surviving Burlington House cartoon, and the Louvre painting. In which order did Leonardo create these?

For much of the late twentieth century, the consensus among scholars—including Arthur Popham, Philip Pouncey, Kenneth Clark, and Carlo Pedretti—was that Leonardo began with the cartoon described by Friar Pietro (with a lamb but no Saint John) in 1501, then changed his mind and drew the Burlington House cartoon a few years later (with Saint John but no lamb), and then changed his mind again and reverted to a final painted version that resembled the 1501 drawing (lamb and no Saint John). That theory was based on stylistic grounds and because some mechanical drawings on the reverse of a sketch for the Burlington House cartoon seem to have been done around 1508.[3]

This contorted sequencing began to be revised in 2005, when a note by Agostino Vespucci, who was Machiavelli's secretary and Leonardo's friend, was found in the margin of a book by Cicero he was reading. The ancient Roman philosopher had written that the painter Apelles "perfected the head and bust of his Venus with the

Fig. 80. Burlington House cartoon for *Saint Anne*.

most elaborate art but left the rest of her body in the rough." Vespucci wrote next to this passage, "So Leonardo da Vinci does in all his paintings, such as the head of Lisa del Giocondo, and Anne, Mother of the Virgin." His note is dated October 1503. Thus in one little discovery there is confirmation that in 1503 Leonardo had started painting the *Mona Lisa*, and that he had already begun work on the *Saint Anne* painting.[4]

If Leonardo was already working on his final painting in 1503, it makes little sense to think that the Burlington House cartoon was done after that. Instead, it may have been done shortly after his return to Florence or perhaps even as early as 1499, before he left Milan. He could have been planning the painting before he got the commission, and indeed might have volunteered for the commission because he had a composition that he had initially intended to do for some other patron. "It seems likely that Leonardo began the Burlington House cartoon while he was still in Milan," wrote Luke Syson in the catalogue for a 2011 London exhibition that included the cartoon. "His patron may well have been the French king Louis XII, whose wife was Anne of Brittany."[5]

That theory that the Burlington House cartoon was the first in the sequence was reinforced in a masterful 2012 exhibition at the Louvre celebrating the completion of a twelve-year restoration of the *Saint Anne* painting. The exhibition brought together the painting and the Burlington House cartoon for the first time since Leonardo's death, along with compositional sketches, preparatory drawings, and copies made by Leonardo's students and other painters. In addition, technical studies, including multispectral analysis, of the painting and cartoon were presented. The conclusion was unequivocal, according to the curator, Vincent Delieuvin: "After working through, then abandoning the solution shown in the Burlington House cartoon, Leonardo developed a different conception and drew a second cartoon in 1501 . . . in which Saint John the Baptist had been replaced by a lamb—the one that Fra Pietro de Novellera described in a letter to Isabella d'Este." The final painted version is based on the 1501 cartoon, but with one change: the figures are reversed. In the painting and in its underdrawing, discovered by an infrared reflectographic analysis, the lamb and the young Jesus are on the right side, not the left.[6]

By looking at some of the smaller sketches Leonardo made, we can see him working out options for showing how the young Jesus would squirm off his mother's lap and wrestle with the lamb. He thinks by sketching. It is a process he called "componimento inculto," an uncultivated composition that helps work out ideas through an intuitive process. It's also instructive to look at the copies of the painting made in his workshop. "It has always been thought that Leonardo's pupils and assistants created these works by copying Leonardo's painting or his cartoons or even his drawings," Francesca Fiorani noted, "but these 'copies' were actually produced while the original was in the making and they reflect alternative solutions Leonardo imagined for it."[7]

THE PAINTING

It is important, Leonardo wrote, to "have a movement of a person's limbs appropriate to that person's mental movements." His painting of the *Virgin and Child with Saint Anne* shows what he meant. Mary's right arm is stretched as she tries to restrain the Christ child, showing a protective but gentle love. But he is intent on wrestling with the lamb, his leg over its neck and his hands grappling with its head. The lamb, as Friar Pietro told us, represents the Passion, Jesus' fate, and he will not be restrained from it.

Both Mary and her mother look young, almost as if they were sisters, even though the apocryphal tale is that Saint Anne was past childbearing age when Mary was born through a miracle. In the cartoon that Friar Pietro described, Leonardo portrayed Saint Anne looking older. We know this because, even though that cartoon was lost, there was a good copy of it. The copy was itself lost in Budapest during World War II, but photographs and etchings of it exist. They show that Leonardo had conceived of Saint Anne as an older woman wearing a matronly cloth headdress.[8] By the time he got around to executing the final painting, he had changed his mind. He made Saint Anne look much younger. In the painting, her torso and that of her daughter seem fused as they dote on the young child.

The image of a squirming boy with what looks like two mothers conjures up Leonardo's own childhood being raised by both his birth mother, Caterina, and his slightly younger stepmother. Freud made much of this, writing, "Leonardo gave the boy two mothers, the one who stretched out her arms after him and another who is seen in the background, both are represented with the blissful smile of maternal happiness. Leonardo's childhood was precisely as remarkable as this picture. He had two mothers." Freud goes on to discern the shape of a vulture lying sideways in the picture composition, but since he got the name of the bird wrong it seems to reflect Freud's fantasy more than Leonardo's.[9]

Underneath the feet and elegant toes of Saint Anne we can see, as in the Louvre version of *Virgin of the Rocks*, how Leonardo's studies of geology informed his paintings. In one of his notebooks, he described what is now known as "graded bedding" in layers of sedimentary rock: "Each layer is composed of heavier and lighter parts, the lowest being the heaviest. And the reason for this is that these layers are formed by the sediments from the waters discharged into the sea by the current of the rivers that flow into it. The heaviest part of this sediment was the part that was discharged first in the sequence."[10] The stratified rock formations and perfectly variegated pebbles beneath Saint Anne's feet portray this phenomenon accurately.

Leonardo had also been wrestling with the question of why the sky appears blue, and around that time he had correctly concluded that it had to do with the water vapor in the air. In the *Saint Anne* painting, he portrays the sky's luminous and misty gradations of blue as no other painter had done. The recent cleaning of the painting fully reveals the magical realism, veiled in vapors, of his distant mountains and skyline.

Most significant, the painting conveys the paramount theme in Leonardo's art: the spiritual connection and analogy between the earth and humans. Echoing so many of his paintings—*Ginevra de' Benci*, *Virgin of the Rocks*, *Madonna of the Yarnwinder*, and of course the *Mona Lisa*—a river curls from the distant horizon of the macrocosm of the earth and seems to flow into the veins of the Holy Family, ending with the lamb that foreshadows the Passion. The curving flow of the river connects to the flowing composition of the characters.

As Vespucci's marginal note informs us, Leonardo had completed the central part of the painting by 1503. But he never delivered it to the church of Santissima Annunziata. Instead, he carried it with him for the rest of his life, making improvements on it for more than a decade. During those years, his assistants and students made copies based on the work in progress and on Leonardo's sketches. Some are actually more finished than the painting Leonardo left us, and they allow us to see various details, such as jeweled sandals on the feet of Saint Anne and ornate embroidery on her clothes, that Leonardo was considering or had sketched but never got around to painting.[11]

The *Saint Anne* is the most complex and layered of Leonardo's panel paintings, and many see it as a masterpiece on a par with the *Mona Lisa*, perhaps even surpassing it because it is more complex in its composition and motion. "We are always discovering new felicities of movement and harmony, growing more and more intricate, yet subordinate to the whole," wrote Kenneth Clark, "and, as with Bach, this is not only an intellectual performance; it is charged with human feeling."[12]

Perhaps. The painting's grandeur, brilliant color, and narrative movement are wondrous to behold. But a few elements of the masterpiece make it less than perfectly satisfying, at least to me. There is a slight artificiality in the poses. The bodies seem to swivel unnaturally, with the Virgin Mary awkwardly draped onto her mother's lap. Saint Anne's jutting left arm seems uncomfortably cocked, and Mary's sunlit right shoulder is too broad and prominent. As I stand before the brightly restored painting in the Louvre, I find myself respecting and admiring it, but not being mesmerized the way I am by the two nearby masterpieces, *Saint John the Baptist* and the *Mona Lisa*. There's a profound beauty to the picture, but Leonardo at his best also produces emotional connections tinged with mystery. In the *Saint Anne*, the eyes of the characters do not seem to be windows into their souls; their smiles do not linger with us, hinting at elusive emotions.

Then something interesting happens. I go back to London to see the Burlington House cartoon again in the soft-lit grotto where it is kept in the National Gallery. Even without the misty blue mountains and watery landscape, it has elements that, to me at least, are more interesting. In it, Saint Anne's left arm is not unnaturally cocked but instead her sketched hand points to heaven, Leonardo's quintessential and exhilarating gesture. After a few experimental lines, he has succeeded in rendering the Virgin's right shoulder masterfully. As Saint Anne glances lovingly yet quizzically at the Virgin, who is in turn glancing lovingly but warily at her child, there seems to be a greater depth of emotion than in the final painting.

So maybe there was another reason Leonardo decided not to finish some of his works. The unpainted renderings of the *Adoration of the Magi* and the Burlington House *Saint Anne* cartoon both have an unfinished perfection to them. For most people, "unfinished perfection" would seem to be a contradiction in terms, but sometimes it suits Leonardo. Among other things, he was the master of the unfinished. Vespucci was correct when he said that Leonardo was the new Apelles in that regard.

CHAPTER 22

Paintings Lost and Found

LEDA AND THE SWAN

One of the veils blurring our knowledge of Leonardo is the mystery surrounding the authenticity and dates of some of his paintings, including ones we think are lost and others we think are finds. Like most artist-craftsmen of his era, he did not sign his work. Although he copiously documented trivial items in his notebooks, including the amount he spent on food and on Salai's clothes, he did not record what he was painting, what he had completed, and where his works went. For some paintings we have detailed contracts and disputes to inform us; for others we have to rely on a snippet from the sometimes reliable Vasari or other early chroniclers.

That means we need to look at copies done by his followers to envision works now lost, such as the *Battle of Anghiari*, and to analyze what were thought to be works by his followers to see if they might actually be autograph Leonardos. These endeavors can be frustrating, but even when they do not produce certainty, they can lead to a better understanding of Leonardo, as we saw in the case of *La Bella Principessa*.

Leda and the Swan is the most tantalizing of Leonardo's lost paintings. The existence of multiple copies, including from students in his workshop, makes it seem likely that he actually finished his own version. Lomazzo says that a "nude Leda" was one of Leonardo's few finished paintings, and there seems to be a report of it in 1625 at the French royal chateau of Fontainebleau, where a visitor described "a standing figure of Leda almost totally naked [*quasi tutta ignuda*], with the swan at her side and two eggs, from whose broken shells come forth four babies." That sounds like Leonardo's purported painting, except that Leda, in both his own surviving preparatory drawing and in painted copies, was wholly naked.[1] One tale, which is so delicious that it's a shame it's probably untrue, is that it was destroyed by Madame de Maintenon, the mistress and secret second wife of Louis XIV, because she found it too salacious.

The myth of Leda and the swan tells how the Greek god Zeus assumed the form of a swan and seduced the beautiful mortal princess Leda. She produced two eggs, from which hatched two sets of twins Helen (later known as Helen of Troy) and Clytemnestra, and Castor and Pollux. Leonardo's depiction focuses more on fertility than sex; instead of painting the seduction scene, as others had done, he chose to portray the moment of the births, showing Leda caressing the swan as the four children squirm from their shells. One of the most vivid copies is by his pupil Francesco Melzi (fig. 81).

When Leonardo was working on this painting during his second period in Florence in the early 1500s, he was doing his most intense studies on the flight of birds and also planning a test flight of one of his flying machines, which he hoped to launch from the top of nearby Swan Mountain (Monte Ceceri). His note about his childhood memory of a bird flying into his crib and flapping its tail in his mouth is also from this period.

Leonardo produced a preparatory sketch of his planned painting sometime around 1505 (fig. 82). It shows Leda kneeling and her body twisting as if writhing with joy as the swan nuzzles her. Leonardo's signature left-handed hatch lines are curved, a technique he started using in his machinery drawings of the 1490s and now used to show volume and modeling of curved surfaces. The technique is especially pronounced in Leda's opulent belly and the swan's breast. As usual with Leonardo, the drawing conveys a narrative. As the swan seductively nuzzles Leda, she points to what they have wrought: the children hatching amid the dynamic spirals of the plants. The drawing swirls with motion and energy; no element seems static.

When Leonardo developed the drawing into a full painting, he changed the pose so that Leda was standing and her nude body appeared more lithe and gentle. She is turning her head slightly away from the swan and looking down demurely, yet at the same time she twists her upper body toward him. She caresses his neck; he wraps a

Fig. 81. Francesco Melzi copy of *Leda and the Swan*.

Fig. 82. Leonardo's preparatory drawing for *Leda and the Swan*.

wing firmly around her buttocks. Both exude a sensuous and sinuous beauty.

That earthly and earthy sexuality makes the picture atypical. A nonreligious narrative panel painting (assuming you do not consider the sexual exploits of Greek gods to be a religious subject), it was Leonardo's only overtly sexual or erotic scene.

And yet, at least in the copies available to us today, it is not actually very erotic. Leonardo is not Titian. He never painted romance or eros. Instead, two themes dominate. The painting conveys a domestic and familial harmony, a pleasant portrayal of a couple at home by their lake, cuddling as they admire their newborns. It also goes beyond the erotic to focus on the tale's procreative aspects. From the lushness of the seeding plants, to the fecundity of the soil and the hatching of the eggs, the painting is a celebration of the fertility of nature. Unlike the usual depictions of the Leda myth, Leonardo's is not about sex but birth.[2]

These themes of generational and natural renewal apparently resonated with him now that he was in his mid-fifties, with no heirs. Around the time he began to paint *Leda*, he adopted Francesco Melzi, who painted the *Leda* copy shown as figure 81, to be his surrogate son and heir.

SALVATOR MUNDI

In 2011 a newly rediscovered painting by Leonardo surprised the art world. Each decade, a dozen or so pieces are proposed or pushed as having a reasonable claim to be previously unknown Leonardos, but only twice before in modern times had such assertions ended up generally accepted: the Benois Madonna oil painting in St. Petersburg's Hermitage that was publicly revealed in 1909 and the chalk drawing *La Bella Principessa* that Kemp and others asserted as authentic a century later.

This 2011 addition to the list of autograph works is a painting known as *Salvator Mundi* (Savior of the World), with Jesus gesturing in blessing with his right hand while holding a solid crystal orb in his left (fig. 83). The Salvator Mundi motif, which features Christ with an orb topped by a cross, known as a *globus cruciger*, had become very popular by the early 1500s, especially among northern European painters. Leonardo's version contains some of his distinctive features: a figure that manages to be at once both reassuring and unsettling, a mysterious straight-on stare, an elusive smile, cascading curls, and sfumato softness.

Before the painting was authenticated, there was historic evidence that one like it existed. In the inventory of Salai's estate was a painting of "Christ in the Manner of God the Father." Such a piece was catalogued in the collections of the English king Charles I, who was beheaded in 1649, and also Charles II, who restored the monarchy

Fig. 83. *Salvator Mundi.*

in 1660. The historical trail of Leonardo's version was lost after the painting passed from Charles II to the Duke of Buckingham, whose son sold it in 1763. But a historic reference remained: the widow of Charles I had commissioned Wenceslaus Hollar to make an etching of the painting. There were also at least twenty copies painted by some of Leonardo's followers.

The trail of the painting reappeared in 1900, when it was acquired by a British collector who did not suspect that it was by Leonardo. It had been damaged, overpainted, and so heavily varnished that it was unrecognizable, and it was attributed to Leonardo's student Boltraffio. The work was later catalogued as a copy of Boltraffio's copy. When the collector's estate sold it at auction in 1958, it fetched less than one hundred dollars.

The painting was sold again in 2005, to a consortium of art dealers and collectors who believed that it might be more than just a copy of a copy of a Leonardo painting. As with the tale of *La Bella Principessa*, the subsequent authentication process reveals a lot about Leonardo's work. The consortium brought it to a Manhattan art historian and dealer named Robert Simon, who oversaw a five-year process of cleaning it carefully and quietly showing it to experts.

Among those consulted were Nicholas Penny, then director of London's National Gallery, and Carmen Bambach of New York's Metropolitan Museum. It was brought to London in 2008 so that it could be directly compared with the National Gallery's version of *Virgin of the Rocks* by other experts, including Luke Syson, who was then curator of Italian paintings at the gallery, David Alan Brown of Washington's National Gallery of Art, and Pietro Marani, professor of art history at the Politecnico di Milano. And, of course, a call went out to Martin Kemp, who was also then authenticating *La Bella Principessa*. "We've got something I think you would want to look at," Penny told Kemp. When Kemp saw it, he was struck by the orb and hair. "It had that kind of presence that Leonardos have," he recalled.[3]

But it was not merely gut, intuition, and connoisseurship that authenticated *Salvator Mundi*. The painting duplicated almost precisely the 1650 Wenceslaus Hollar engraving that had been made from the original; it had the same snaking and lustrous curls, the same Leonardesque knot pattern on the sashes, and the irregular pleats on Christ's blue cloak that are also in Leonardo's preparatory drawings.

These similarities, however, were not dispositive. There were many copies made by Leonardo's followers; was it possible that this newly rediscovered painting was also a copy? Technical analysis helped to answer that. After the picture was cleaned, high-resolution photos and X-rays helped reveal a pentimento showing that the thumb of Jesus' right hand had originally been placed differently. That is not something a copyist would need to do. In addition, shining an infrared light that reflected off the white priming of the panel showed that the painter had pressed his palm against the wet paint above Christ's left eye to achieve a sfumato blurring, which was a distinctive Leonardo technique. The work had been painted on walnut, just like other Leonardos of the period, in many very thin layers of almost translucent paint. By that point most of the experts agreed that it was an authentic Leonardo. As a result, the art consortium was able to sell it for close to $80 million in 2013 to a Swiss art dealer, who then resold it to a Russian fertilizer billionaire for $127 million.[4]

Unlike other *Salvator Mundi* paintings, Leonardo's offers the viewer shifting emotional interactions, similar to those found in the *Mona Lisa*. The misty aura and blurred sfumato lines, especially of the lips, produces a psychological mystery and an ambiguous smile that seems to change slightly with each new look. Is there a hint of a smile? Look again. Is Jesus staring at us or into the distance? Move from side to side and ask again.

The curling hair, coiled with energy, seems to spring into motion as it reaches the shoulders, as if Leonardo were painting the eddies of a flowing stream. They become more distinct and less soft as they reach the chest. This stems from his studies of acuity perspective: objects that are closer to a viewer are less blurred.

Around the time he was working on *Salvator Mundi*, Leonardo was doing his optics studies that explored how the eyes focus.[5] He knew that he could create the illusion of three-dimensional depth in a painting by making the objects in the foreground sharper. The two fingers on Christ's right hand that are closest to us are drawn with a crisper delineation. It makes the hand pop out toward us, as if it's in motion and giving us a blessing. Leonardo would reuse this technique a few years later with the pointing hands in two depictions of Saint John the Baptist.

There is, however, a puzzling anomaly in the painting, one that seems to be an unusual lapse or unwillingness by Leonardo to link art and science. It involves the clear crystal orb that Jesus is holding. In one respect, it is rendered with beautiful scientific precision. There are three jagged bubbles in it that have the irregular shape of the tiny gaps in crystal called inclusions. Around that time, Leonardo had evaluated rock crystals as a favor for Isabella d'Este, who was planning to purchase some, and he captured accurately the twinkle of inclusions. In addition, he included a deft and scientifically accurate touch, showing he had tried to get the image correct: the part of Jesus' palm pressing into the bottom of the orb is flattened and lighter, as it would indeed appear in reality.

But Leonardo failed to paint the distortion that would occur when looking through a solid clear orb at objects that are not touching the orb. Solid glass or crystal, whether shaped like an orb or a lens, produces magnified, inverted, and reversed images. Instead, Leonardo painted the orb as if it were a hollow glass bubble that does not refract or distort the light passing through it. At first glance it seems as if the heel of Christ's palm displays a hint of refraction, but a closer look shows the slight double image occurs even in the part of the hand not behind the orb; it is merely a pentimento that occurred when Leonardo decided to shift slightly the hand's position.

Christ's body and the folds of his robe are not inverted or distorted when seen through the orb. At issue is a complex optical phenomenon. Try it with a solid glass ball (fig. 84). A hand touching the orb will not appear to be distorted. But things viewed through the orb that are an inch or so away, such as Christ's robes, will be seen as inverted and reversed. The distortion varies depending on the distance of the objects from the orb. If Leonardo had accurately depicted the distortions, the palm touching the orb would have remained the way he painted it, but hovering inside the orb would be a reduced and inverted mirror image of Christ's robes and arm.[6]

Fig. 84. Image through a crystal orb.

Why did Leonardo not do this? It is possible that he had not noticed or surmised how light is refracted in a solid sphere. But I find that hard to believe. He was, at the time, deep into his optics studies, and how light reflects and refracts was an obsession. Scores of notebook pages are filled with diagrams of light bouncing around at different angles. I suspect that he knew full well how an object seen through a crystal orb would appear distorted, but he chose not to paint it that way, either because he thought it would be a distraction (it would indeed have looked very weird), or because he was subtly trying to impart a miraculous quality to Christ and his orb.

CHAPTER 23

Cesare Borgia

RUTHLESS WARRIOR

Ludovico Sforza, Leonardo's patron in Milan, had a reputation for ruthlessness that included, among other alleged acts, poisoning his nephew in order to seize the ducal crown. But Ludovico was a choir boy compared to Leonardo's next patron, Cesare Borgia. Name any odious activity and Borgia was the master of it: murder, treachery, incest, debauchery, wanton cruelty, betrayal, and corruption. He had a brutal tyrant's hunger for power combined with a sociopath's thirst for blood. Once, when he felt he had been libeled, he had the offender's tongue cut out, his right hand chopped off, and the hand with the tongue attached to its little finger hung from a church window. His only sliver of historical redemption, which is undeserved, came when Machiavelli used him as a model of cunning in *The Prince* and taught that his ruthlessness was a tool for power.[1]

Cesare Borgia was the son of the Spanish-Italian cardinal Rodrigo Borgia, soon to become Pope Alexander VI, who vies for the hotly contested title of most libertine Renaissance pope. "He had in the fullest measure all the vices of the flesh and of the spirit," the pope's contemporary Francesco Guicciardini wrote. He was the first pope to recognize openly his illegitimate children—ten in all, including Cesare and Lucrezia, by multiple mistresses—and he was able to get Cesare a dispensation from his illegitimacy so he could hold church offices. He made Cesare the bishop of Pamplona at fifteen and a cardinal three years later, even though the son showed less than zero predilection for piety. In fact, he had not even taken holy orders. Preferring to be a ruler rather than a religious figure, Cesare became the first person in history to fully resign from the cardinalate, and he likely had his brother stabbed to death and thrown into the Tiber so that he could replace him as the commander of the papal forces.

In that capacity, he forged an alliance with the French, and he was with King Louis XII marching into Milan in 1499. The day after their arrival, they went to see *The Last Supper*, and there Borgia first met Leonardo. Knowing Leonardo, it is likely that during the next few weeks he showed Borgia his military engineering designs.

Borgia subsequently launched a plan to carve out his own principality in the politically tumultuous Romagna region that stretched east of Florence to the Adriatic coast. These lands were supposed to be under his father, the pope, but the towns were controlled by their own independent princes, little tyrants, and vicars. Their violent rivalries regularly erupted into frenzied sieges and sackings accompanied by rampant rape and murder. By the spring of 1501, Borgia had conquered Imola, Forlì, Pesaro, Faenza, Rimini, and Cesena.[2]

Borgia next set his sights on Florence, which cowered in dread. Its treasury was depleted, and it had no military to defend it. In May 1501, as his forces neared Florence's walls, the ruling Signoria of the city capitulated by agreeing to pay Borgia 36,000 florins a year as protection money and permitting his army to cross Florentine territory at will as he conquered more towns.

NICCOLÒ MACHIAVELLI

The bribe bought Florence peace for a year, but in June 1502 Borgia was back. As his army sacked more surrounding towns, he commanded the leaders in Florence to send a delegation to hear his latest demands. Two people were selected to try to deal with him. The elder was Francesco Soderini, a wily Church leader who led one of the anti-Medici factions in Florence. Accompanying him was the son of a bankrupt lawyer, well-educated but poor, whose writing skills and savvy understanding of power games had established him as Florence's cleverest young diplomat: Niccolò Machiavelli.

Machiavelli had a smile right out of a Leonardo painting: enigmatic, at times laconic, always appearing to hide a secret. He shared with Leonardo the trait of being a sharp observer. He was not yet a famous author, but already he was known for his ability to produce lucid reports informed by insights into power balances, tactics, and personal motivations. He became a valued civil servant and secretary of Florence's chancery.

As soon as he left Florence, Machiavelli received word that Borgia was in Urbino, a town east of Florence between the Apennine Mountains and Adriatic coast. Borgia had captured Urbino through trickery, by feigning friendship and then striking unexpectedly. "He arrives in one place before anyone knows he has left the other," Machiavelli reported in a dispatch, and is able "to install himself in someone else's house before anyone else noticed it."

As soon as they arrived in Urbino, Soderini and Machiavelli were ushered into the ducal palace. Borgia knew how to put on a power show. He was seated in a dark room, his bearded and pockmarked face lit by a single candle. He insisted that Florence show him respect and support. Once again a vague accommodation seems to have been reached, and Borgia did not attack. A few days later, probably as part of his arrangement with Florence that Machiavelli had helped to negotiate, Borgia secured the services of the city's most famous artist and engineer, Leonardo da Vinci.[3]

LEONARDO AND BORGIA

Leonardo may have gone to work with Borgia at the behest of Machiavelli and Florence's leaders as a gesture of goodwill, similar to the way he had been dispatched twenty years earlier to Milan as a diplomatic gesture to Ludovico Sforza. Or he may have been sent as a way for Florence to have an agent embedded with Borgia's forces. Maybe it was both. But either way, Leonardo was no mere pawn or agent. He would not have gone to work for Borgia unless he wanted to.

On the first page of a pocket-size notebook he took on his journey in service of Borgia, Leonardo listed the equipment he packed: a pair of compasses, a sword belt, a light hat, a book of white paper for drawing, a leather vest, and a "swimming belt." The last item was something he had earlier described among his military inventions. "Have a coat made of leather, which must be double across the breast, that is having a hem on each side of about a finger breadth," he wrote. "When you want to leap into the sea, blow out the skirt of your coat through the double hems."[4]

Even though Borgia was in Urbino, Leonardo first headed southwest from Florence to Piombino, a coastal town that was occupied by Borgia's army. Apparently he had received orders from Borgia to make an inspection tour of the forts in Borgia's control. In addition to studying the fortifications, he looked at ways to drain the marshes and—easily gliding back and forth between practical engineering and pure scientific curiosity—made a study of the movement of the waves and tides.

From there, he headed eastward across the Apennine Mountains to the other side of the Italian peninsula, gathering topographical data for maps and observing landscapes and bridges that would later be reflected in the *Mona Lisa*. Finally, in midsummer 1502, he arrived in Urbino to join Borgia, almost three years after first meeting him in Milan.

Leonardo sketched the staircase of Urbino's palace and the dovecote, and he made a series of three red-chalk drawings that were likely of Borgia (fig. 85). The left-handed hatch lines of the drawing accentuate the shadows under Borgia's eyes; he looks pensive and subdued, his ringlets of curly beard covering a face that has become thickened with age and perhaps pockmarked by his syphilis. He no longer looks like "the handsomest man in Italy," as he was once called.[5]

Perhaps Borgia looked pensive because he was worried, rightly, that the king of France, Louis XII, was hedging his support for Borgia and promising protection to the Florentines. Swirling around the French court and the Vatican were intriguers who had been betrayed or divorced by various Borgias and were now seeking revenge. A week

Fig. 85. Leonardo's sketches probably of Cesare Borgia.

or so after his arrival in Urbino, Leonardo jotted in his notebook, "Where is Valentino?,"[6] using a nickname for Borgia, who had been made the Duke of Valentinois by the French king. Borgia, it turned out, had disguised himself as a Knight Hospitaller and snuck away with three trusted guards to ride north at a furious pace to reinstate himself in the good graces of Louis, which he did.

Borgia had not forgotten Leonardo. When he reached Pavia, where Louis was then holding court, he issued a floridly written "passport" for Leonardo, giving him special privileges and rights of passage, dated August 18, 1502:

> To all our lieutenants, castellans, captains, condottieri, soldiers, and subjects, who may be shown this document: You are hereby ordered and commanded on behalf of our most eminent and well-beloved familial friend [*dilectissimo familiare*], the architect and engineer general Leonardo Vinci, bearer of these documents, who has received our commission to inspect all the strongpoints and fortresses in our dominion, so that he may, according to their needs, provide for their maintenance. He shall be given free passage and be relieved of all public tax, both for himself and for his party, and shall be welcomed amicably, and may make measurements and examine whatever he pleases. For this purpose, provide

> him with as many men as he requisitions, and grant him all the help, succor and favor he may demand, for it is our will that every engineer in our dominions shall be bound to confer with him and follow his advice. And let no man dare to do the contrary, if he does not wish to incur our extreme displeasure.[7]

Borgia's passport described Leonardo as he had fancied himself ever since his letter to the Duke of Milan twenty years earlier: as a military engineer and innovator rather than a painter. He had been warmly embraced, in fulsome and familial terms, by the most vibrant warrior of the age. For the moment, the man who had been described as no longer able to bear the sight of a brush got to play the role of a man of action.

Borgia left Pavia to rejoin his army in September, and Leonardo traveled with him eastward as he captured Fossombrone, using a combination of trickery, betrayal, and surprise. That taught Leonardo a lesson about designs for the interiors of castles and fortresses: "Be sure that the escape tunnel does not lead to the inner fortress, lest the fortress be captured by treachery or betrayal of the lord."[8] He also suggested that fortress walls be curved because that would reduce the impact of cannonballs. "Percussion is less strong the more oblique it is," he wrote.[9] He then accompanied Borgia's army as it marched toward the Adriatic coast.

In the town of Rimini, he was enthralled by "the harmony of the different falls of water."[10] A few days later, in the port of Cesenatico, he sketched the harbor and drew up plans for defending the dykes "so that they are not vulnerable to artillery fire." He also directed that the harbor be dredged so that it would stay linked to the sea. Always enthralled by ambitious water projects, he looked at ways the harbor canal could be extended ten miles inland to Cesena.[11]

While in Cesena, which Borgia had made the capital of his Romagna region conquests, Leonardo made a drawing of the fortress. But by then his mind was wandering from military matters. He sketched a house window with a quarter-circle pane on top, which reflected his interest in curved and rectilinear geometric shapes, and a hook with two bunches of grapes. "This is how they carry grapes in

Cesena," he explained.[12] He also combined the compositional eye of a painter with that of an engineer to note how the workmen digging a ditch array themselves in a pyramid. He was not impressed with the engineering intelligence of the locals, at one point drawing a cart and saying of the Cesena region, "In Romagna, the chief realm of all stupidity [*capo d'ogni grossezza d'ingegno*], vehicles with four wheels are used, in which the two in front are small and the two high ones behind, an arrangement that is very unfavorable to motion, because on the front wheels more weight is laid than on those behind."[13] Ideas for building better wheelbarrows was a topic he had covered in one of his draft treatises on mechanics.

The mathematician Luca Pacioli later recounted a tale of Leonardo in action. "One day Cesare Borgia . . . found himself and his army at a river that was twenty-four paces wide, and could find no bridge, nor any material to make one except for a stack of wood all cut to a length of 16 paces," Pacioli wrote, probably based on hearing the story from Leonardo. "From this wood, using neither iron nor rope nor any other construction, his noble engineer made a bridge sufficiently strong for the army to pass over."[14] A sketch for such a self-supporting bridge in Leonardo's notebook (fig. 86, with a fainter

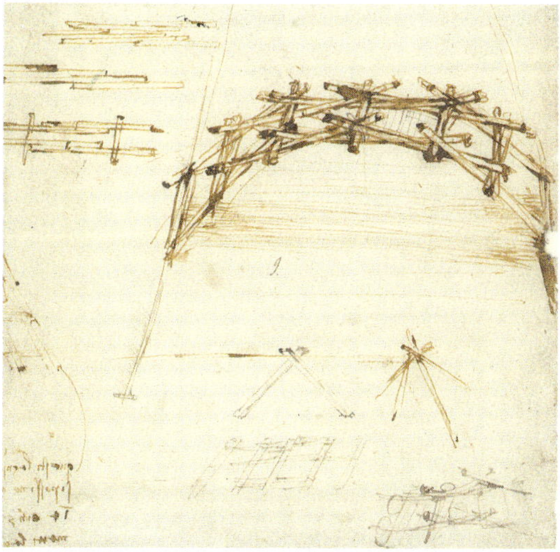

Fig. 86. Self-supporting bridge.

version in fig. 53) has seven short poles and ten longer, each notched so they can be fit together at the scene.[15]

As the fall of 1502 approached, Borgia moved his court to the highly fortified town of Imola, thirty miles inland from Cesena on the road to Bologna. Leonardo made drawings of the fortress compound, noting that its moat was forty feet deep and its walls fifteen feet thick. In front of the only entrance through the walls surrounding the town was a moat split by a man-made island; anyone trying to invade had to cross two bridges and be exposed to a defensive barrage. Borgia's plan was to turn the town into his permanent military headquarters by having Leonardo make it even more impregnable.[16]

Machiavelli arrived on October 7, sent by Florence to be an emissary and informant. In his daily dispatches back to Florence, which he knew were being read by Borgia's intelligence agents, Machiavelli apparently refers to Leonardo only as "another who is also acquainted with Cesare's secrets" and as a "friend" whose knowledge is "worthy of attention."[17] Imagine the scene. For three months during the winter of 1502–3, as if in a historical fantasy movie, three of the most fascinating figures of the Renaissance—a brutal and power-crazed son of a pope, a sly and amoral writer-diplomat, and a dazzling painter yearning to be an engineer—were holed up in a tiny fortified walled town that was approximately five blocks wide and eight blocks long.

While he was in Imola with Machiavelli and Borgia, Leonardo made what may be his greatest contribution to the art of war. It is a map of Imola, but not any ordinary map (fig. 87).[18] It is a work of beauty, innovative style, and military utility. It combines, in his inimitable manner, art and science.

Drawn in ink with colored washes and black chalk, the Imola map was an innovative step in cartography. The moat around the fortified town is tinted a subtle blue, the walls are silvery, and the roofs of the houses brick red. The aerial view is from directly overhead, unlike most maps of the time. On the edges he has specified the distances to nearby towns, useful information for military campaigns, but written in his elegant mirror script, indicating that the version that survives is a copy he made for himself rather than Borgia.

Leonardo used a magnetic compass, and the eight major direc-

Fig. 87. Leonardo's map of Imola.

tional lines (north, northwest, west, southwest, etc.) are shown with fine strokes. On a preliminary sketch, he marked the position and size of each house. The map is folded many times, indicating he tucked it in his pocket or pouch as he and his assistants paced off the distances.

Around this time, he perfected the odometer he had been developing to measure long distances (fig. 88).[19] On a cart he mounted a vertical cog wheel, which looks like the front wheel of a wheelbarrow, that intersects with a horizontal cog wheel. Every time the vertical wheel completed a revolution, it would move the horizontal wheel a notch, and that would cast a stone into a container. On his drawing of the device, Leonardo noted that it "makes the ear hear the sound of a little stone falling into a basin."[20]

The Imola map and others Leonardo made at the time would have been of great use to Borgia, whose victories came from conducting lightning strikes and, in the words of Machiavelli, being able "to install himself in someone else's house before anyone else noticed it." Acting as an artist-engineer, Leonardo had devised a new military weapon: accurate, detailed, and easily read maps. Over the years, visu-

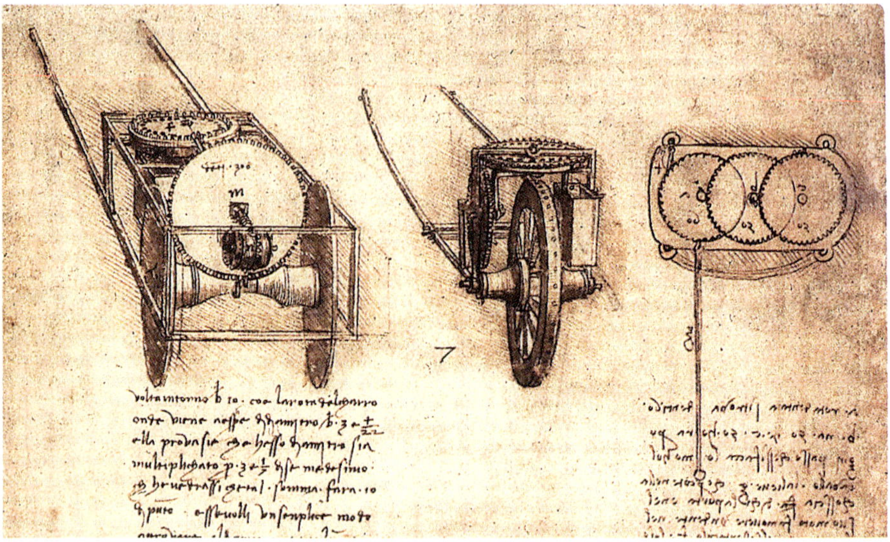

Fig. 88. An odometer.

ally clear maps would become a key component of warfare. For example, the U.S. National Geospatial-Intelligence Agency (originally known as the Defense Mapping Agency) had 14,500 employees and an annual budget exceeding $5 billion in 2017. Projected on the walls of its headquarters are maps combining accuracy with beauty, some of which bear a striking resemblance to Leonardo's map of Imola.

In a larger sense, Leonardo's maps are another example of one of his greatest, though underappreciated, innovations: devising new methods for the visual display of information. In his illustrations for Pacioli's book on geometry, Leonardo was able to show models of a variety of polyhedrons that were perfectly shaded to look three-dimensional. In his notebook entries on engineering and mechanics, he drew pieces of machinery with subtlety and precision, adding cutaway shots of various components. He was among the first to deconstruct complex mechanisms and make separate drawings of each element. Likewise, in his anatomy drawings, he drew muscles, nerves, bones, organs, and blood vessels from different angles, and he pioneered the method of depicting them in multiple layers, like the transparencies of body layers found in encyclopedias centuries later.

LEAVING BORGIA

In December 1502, Cesare Borgia committed a typical act of brutality. He had empowered a deputy, Ramiro de Lorca, to tyrannize Cesena and the surrounding territories with unremitting cruelty and gruesome slaughter to intimidate the populace. But once Ramiro had inspired enough fear, Borgia realized that it would be useful to sacrifice him. The day after Christmas, he had Ramiro brought to the central square in Cesena and sliced in two. The pieces of his body remained there on display. "Cesare Borgia decided that there was no more need for this excessive power," Machiavelli later explained in *The Prince*. "To purge the minds of the people and to win them over, Cesare determined to show the people that Ramiro's cruelties were inflicted by him and not Cesare. One morning, Ramiro's body was found cut in two pieces on the piazza at Cesena, with a block of wood and a bloody knife beside it. The brutality of this spectacle kept the people of the Romagna appeased and stupefied." The coldness of Borgia's brutality impressed Machiavelli, who called it "an example that deserves close study and imitation by others."[21]

Borgia then marched on the coastal town of Senigallia, where local leaders had rebelled against his occupation. He offered them a meeting to negotiate a reconciliation, and he promised that they could keep their leadership roles if they pledged to be loyal. They agreed. But when Borgia arrived, he had the men seized and strangled to death, then ordered that the town be pillaged. By this point even the cold-blooded and calculating Machiavelli was getting a bit squeamish. "The sack of the town continues although it is now the twenty-third hour," he scribbled in a dispatch. "I am much troubled."

One of the strangled men was a friend of Leonardo, Vitellozzo Vitelli, who had lent him a book by Archimedes. Leonardo traveled with Borgia's army for the conquest of Siena a few weeks later, but his notebooks suggest that he had mentally tuned out Borgia's horrors by focusing on other matters. He made a sketch of the church bell at Siena, twenty feet in diameter, and described "the manner of its movement and the position of the attachment of its clapper."[22]

A few days later, shortly after Machiavelli had been recalled to Florence, Leonardo left Borgia's service. By March 1503 he was settled back in Florence and withdrawing money from his bank account at the hospital of Santa Maria Nuova.

"Save me from strife and battle, a most beastly madness," Leonardo once wrote. Yet for eight months he had put himself at Borgia's service and traveled with his armies. Why would a person whose notebook aphorisms decry killing and whose personal morality led him to be a vegetarian go to work for the most brutal murderer of the era? Partly this choice reflects Leonardo's pragmatism. In a land where the Medici, Sforzas, and Borgias jostled for power, Leonardo was able to time his patronage affiliations well and know when to move on. But there is more. Even as he remained aloof from most current events, he seemed to be attracted to power.

It would take a Freudian analyst to explain Leonardo's affinity for attaching himself to strong men, and once again Freud himself tried to do so. He believed that Leonardo gravitated to them as substitutes for the manly but often absent father of his childhood. A simpler explanation is that Leonardo, who had just turned fifty, had dreamed for more than two decades of being a military engineer. As Isabella d'Este's agent reported, he was tired of painting. Borgia had just turned twenty-six. He combined bravado and elegance. "This lord is truly splendid and magnificent, and in war there is no enterprise so great that it does not seem small to him," Machiavelli wrote after meeting him.[23] Indifferent to the shifting political agendas of Italy yet attracted to military engineering and strongmen, Leonardo had a chance to live out his military fantasies, which he did until he realized they could become nightmares.

Chapter 24

Hydraulic Engineer

DIVERTING THE ARNO

In his job application to Ludovico Sforza, Leonardo had boasted of his talent for "guiding water from one place to another." That was, at best, an exaggeration. When he first arrived in Milan, in 1482, he had done no hydraulic engineering. But like many of his fantasy aspirations, he willed this one into reality. During his years in Milan, he diligently studied the city's system of canals, and he recorded in his notebooks details of the mechanisms of the locks and other feats of water engineering. In particular, he was fascinated by the city's artificial canals, including the Naviglio Grande, begun in the twelfth century, and the Naviglio Martesana, which was under construction while he lived there.[1]

Milan's waterworks had existed for centuries, even before the Romans built their famed aqueducts in the Po Valley around 200 BC. The flow of water each spring from the melting snow of the Alps was carefully managed in accordance with rules devised by ancient tribes to create controlled floods for the grain fields. Irrigation networks were created, and canals were built that both channeled water and facilitated barge shipping. By the time Leonardo moved to Milan, the system of large canals was three centuries old, and the duchy there raised much of its revenue from the sale of water allocations. Leonardo himself was at one point compensated with a water allocation, and his design for an ideal city near Milan was based on using man-made canals and waterways.[2]

In Florence, by contrast, there had been no major hydraulic works since ancient times. The city had few canals, drainage projects, irrigation systems, or river diversions. With the knowledge he had soaked up in Milan and his fascination with the flow of water, he set out to change that. In his notebooks, he began sketching ways that Florence could copy Milan.

Florence had controlled the town of Pisa, just over fifty miles down the Arno River toward the coast of the Mediterranean, for much of the fifteenth century. This was critical for Florence, which had no other outlet to the sea. But in 1494 Pisa managed to wriggle away and become a free republic. Florence's middling army was incapable of breaching Pisa's walls, and it could not successfully blockade the town because the Arno gave it access to supplies from the sea.

Just before Pisa broke away, a major world event made Florence even more eager to control a sea outlet. In March 1493 Christopher Columbus returned safely from his first voyage across the Atlantic Ocean, and the report of his discoveries quickly spread throughout Europe. This was soon followed by a flurry of other accounts of amazing explorations. Amerigo Vespucci, whose cousin Agostino worked with Machiavelli in the Florentine chancery, helped supply Columbus's third voyage in 1498, and the following year he made his own voyage across the Atlantic, landing in what is now Brazil. Unlike Columbus, who thought he was finding a route to India, Vespucci correctly reported to his Florentine patrons that he had "arrived at a new land which for many reasons . . . we observed to be a continent." His correct surmise led to its being named America, after him. The excitement over what portended to be a new age of exploration made Florence's desire to regain Pisa more urgent.[3]

In July 1503, a few months after he left Borgia's service, Leonardo was sent to join Florence's army at the fortress of Verruca, a square fortification atop a rocky outcropping (*verruca* means "wart") overlooking the Arno seven miles east of Pisa.[4] "Leonardo da Vinci himself came here with his companions, and we showed him everything, and we think that he likes La Verruca very much," a field commissary reported back to the Florentine authorities. "He said that he was thinking of making it impregnable."[5] An entry for an account book in Florence that month lists a set of expenses and then adds, "This money has been spent to provide six horse coaches and to pay the board expenses for the expedition with Leonardo in the territory of Pisa to divert the Arno from its course and take it away from Pisa."[6]

Diverting the Arno River from its course and taking it away from Pisa? It was an audacious way to reconquer the city without storming the wall or wielding any weapons. If the river could be channeled somewhere else, Pisa would be cut off from the sea and lose its source of supply. The primary advocates of the idea included the two clever friends who had been holed up together that past winter in Imola, Leonardo da Vinci and Niccolò Machiavelli.

"The river that is to be diverted from one course to another must be coaxed and not treated roughly or with violence," Leonardo wrote in his notebook. His plan was to dig a huge ditch, thirty-two feet deep, upriver from Pisa and use dams to divert the water from the river into the ditch. "To do this a sort of dam must be inserted into the river, then another one further downstream jutting out beyond it, and similarly third, fourth, and fifth dams, so that the river may discharge itself into the channel made for it."[7]

This would require moving a million tons of earth, and Leonardo calculated the man-hours necessary by doing a detailed time-and-motion study, one of the first in history. He figured out everything from the weight of one shovel-load of dirt (twenty-five pounds) to how many shovel-loads would fill a wheelbarrow (twenty). His answer: it would take approximately 1.3 million man-hours, or 540 men working 100 days, to dig the Arno diversion ditch.

At first he considered ways to use wheeled carts to carry the dirt away, showing why those with three wheels were more efficient than those with four. But he realized that it would be very difficult to push carts up the banks of a ditch. So he designed one of his ingenious machines (fig. 89), which features two crane-like arms that would move lines with twenty-four buckets. When a bucket deposited its dirt on top of the bank of the ditch, a worker would get in it and ride down to keep the weights counterbalanced. Leonardo also designed a treadmill system to harness human power to move the cranes.[8]

When digging began on the diversion ditch in August 1504, it was overseen by a new waterworks engineer, who revised Leonardo's plans and decided not to build the dirt-moving machine. Instead of one deep ditch, as Leonardo designed, the new engineer decided to dig two ditches and to make them shallower than the bed of the Arno, which Leonardo knew would not work. In fact, the ditches ended up being only fourteen feet deep rather than the thirty-two feet that Leonardo had specified. After consulting Leonardo in Florence, Machiavelli wrote a blunt warning to the engineer: "We fear that the bed of the ditch is shallower than the bed of the Arno; this would have negative effects and in our opinion it would not direct the project to the end we wish."

The warning was ignored, but it turned out to be well founded. When the ditch was opened to the Arno, Machiavelli's assistant on the scene reported, "the waters never went through the ditches except when the river was in flood, and as soon as it subsided the water flowed

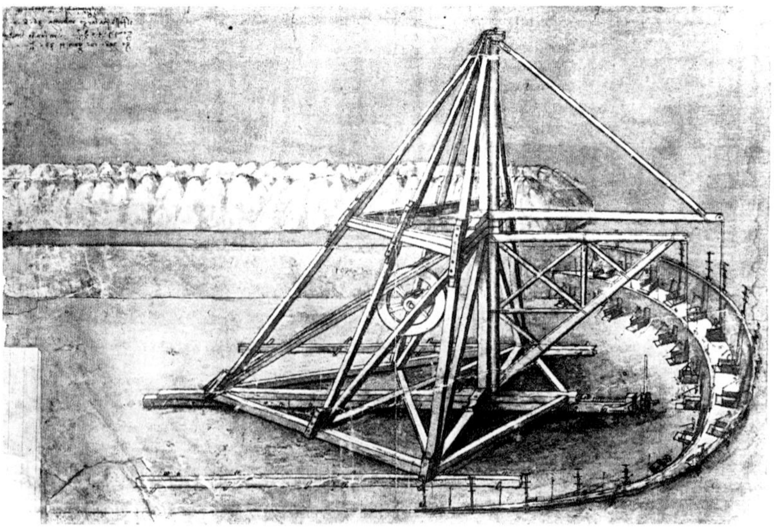

Fig. 89. Machine for digging canals.

back." A few weeks later, in early October, a violent storm caused the walls of the ditches to collapse, flooding the nearby farms but still not diverting the main course of the Arno. The project was abandoned.[9]

Even though it failed, the project to divert the Arno rekindled Leonardo's interest in a larger scheme: creating a navigable waterway between Florence and the Mediterranean Sea. Near Florence the Arno River often silted up, and it also had a series of waterfalls and rapids that kept boats from passing. Leonardo's solution was to bypass that part of the river with a canal. "Sluices should be made in the valley of la Chiana at Arezzo, so that when, in the summer, the Arno lacks water, the canal may not remain dry," he wrote. "Let this canal be twenty braccia [forty feet] wide." The plan would help mills and agriculture in the surrounding region, he suggested, so other towns would likely fund it.[10]

Leonardo drew a variety of maps in 1504 showing how the canal would work. One of them, done with brush and ink, was pricked with pins, evidence that he had made copies.[11] Another, done in delicate color with arresting details of tiny towns and fortifications, showed his plan to turn the swampy marshes of the Val di Chiana into a reservoir (fig. 90).[12] The fiasco of the Arno diversion project prob-

Fig. 90. Topographic view of the Chiana Valley.

ably persuaded the cash-strapped Florentine leaders not to attempt something even more ambitious, so Leonardo's canal proposals were shelved.

DRAINING THE PIOMBINO MARSHES

The failure of these projects did not immediately persuade Leonardo to give up hydraulic engineering, nor did his patrons want him to. At the end of October 1504, just weeks after the Arno diversion was abandoned, he was sent by the Florentine authorities, at Machiavelli's request, to provide technical assistance to the ruler of Piombino, a port city sixty miles south of Pisa that Florence was seeking to turn into an ally. Leonardo had been to Piombino two years earlier, while in the service of Cesare Borgia, and had studied the fortifications and looked at ways to drain the surrounding marshes. On this second visit, he spent two months designing a series of fortifications, moats, and secret passageways that could be used if the ruler was betrayed, "as happened at Fossombrone," a reference to Borgia's use of treachery in capturing that town.

The centerpiece of Leonardo's design was a circular fortress. Inside it had three rings of walls, with spaces between them that could be flooded and turned into moats during an attack. Leonardo had been studying the force exerted by objects hitting a wall at different angles, and he knew that the potency of a strike diminished as the angle became more oblique. Rounded walls, rather than straight ones, were thus more likely to deflect a cannonball. "It was Leonardo's most remarkable conception in the field of military engineering, and represented a total rethinking of the principles of fortification," Martin Kemp wrote. "Nowhere are Leonardo's theoretical principles, his sense of form, and his observational acumen more brilliantly combined than in the circular fortress designs."[13]

Leonardo's hydraulic challenge at Piombino was draining the marshlands surrounding the castle. His first idea was to divert some muddy water from the river into the marsh and allow the silt, dirt, and pebbles to settle to build up the land, similar to what is now being attempted with the marshes in southern Louisiana. Shallow channels would drain away the clear surface water, allowing more muddy water to enter.

Then he came up with another approach that was far more ambitious. At first glance, his plan may seem to skirt his blurred border with fantasy, but like many of his fantasies the basic idea is a good one ahead of its time. Drawing on his love of vortexes and eddies and swirling water, he sketched a way to create a "centrifugal pump" in the sea that was near the marsh. The idea was to stir the seawater in a circular way and thus create an artificial whirlpool. Tubes could then be used to siphon the water from the swamp and have it be sucked into the vortex of the whirlpool, which would be lower than the level of the marsh. In two separate notebooks, Leonardo described and drew a "method for drying up the swamps which border on the sea." The artificial whirlpool in the sea would be created by a "board that is turned by an axle," and "the siphon would expel its water at the back of the turning board." His drawings are extremely detailed and even include the width and speed that would be required of the artificial whirlpool.[14] Although it proved impractical, the theory was correct.

Typical of Leonardo, he also jotted down some observations on color and painting while in Piombino, observing closely the way sunlight and the reflected light from the sea colored the hull of a ship: "I saw the greenish shadows cast by the ropes, mast and spars on a white wall, as the sunlight struck it. The wall surface which was not lit by the sun took on the color of the sea."[15]

The Arno projects, the circular fortress, and the draining of the Piombino swamps had one thing in common with many of Leonardo's grandest projects, and even some of his less grand ones: they never came to fruition. They showed Leonardo at his most fantastical, dreaming up schemes that darted back and forth across the boundaries of practicality. Like the construction of his flying machines, they were too fanciful to execute.

This inability to ground his fantasies in reality has generally been regarded as one of Leonardo's major failings. Yet in order to be a true visionary, one has to be willing to overreach and to fail some of the time. Innovation requires a reality distortion field. The things he envisioned for the future often came to pass, even if it took a few centuries. Scuba gear, flying machines, and helicopters now exist. Suction pumps now drain swamps. Along the route of the canal that Leonardo drew there is now a major highway. Sometimes fantasies are paths to reality.

CHAPTER 25

Michelangelo and the Lost *Battles*

THE ASSIGNMENT

The commission that Leonardo received in October 1503 to paint a sprawling battle scene for Florence's Council Hall in the Palazzo della Signoria could have become one of the most important of his life. Had he completed the mural along the lines of the preparatory drawings he made, the result would have been a narrative masterpiece as captivating as *The Last Supper*, but one in which the motions of the bodies and the emotions of the minds would not have been constrained by the confined setting of a Passover Seder, as *The Last Supper* was. The finished work might have matched the emotional whirlwind that the *Adoration of the Magi* hinted at being, except wrought much larger.

But as with so many of his projects, Leonardo ended up not finishing the *Battle of Anghiari*, and what he painted is now lost. We can envision it mainly through copies. The best, which shows only the central part of what would have been a much larger mural, is by Peter Paul Rubens (fig. 91), which was made from other copies in 1603, after Leonardo's unfinished work was covered up.

Fig. 91. Peter Paul Rubens' copy of Leonardo's *Battle of Anghiari.*

Heightening the significance of the commission was the fact that Leonardo would end up pitted against his personal and professional young rival, Michelangelo, who was chosen in early 1504 to paint the other large mural in the hall. Even though neither painting was finished—like Leonardo's, Michelangelo's work is known to us only through copies and preparatory drawings—the saga provides a fascinating look at how the contrasting styles of Leonardo, then fifty-one, and Michelangelo, twenty-eight, each transformed the history of art.[1]

Florence's leaders wanted Leonardo's mural to be a celebration of a 1440 victory over Milan, one of the few examples of Florence's triumph on the battlefield. Their intent was to exalt the glory of their warriors. But Leonardo aimed to create something more profound. He had intense, conflicted feelings about war. After long fancying himself a military engineer, he had recently gained his first close-up experiences of war in the service of the brutal Cesare Borgia. At one point in his notebooks he called war "a most beastly madness," and some of his parables espouse pacifist sentiments. On the other hand, he had always been captivated and even beguiled by the martial arts. As we can see from his preparatory drawings, he planned to convey the enthralling passion that made war so gripping as well as the brutality that made it so abhorrent. The result would have been neither a commemoration of conquest like the *Bayeux Tapestry* nor an antiwar statement like Picasso's *Guernica*. In his own nature and in his art, Leonardo's attitude toward war was complex.

The location for the proposed painting was immense. It was to adorn almost one-third of the length of a 174-foot wall that was in the imposing meeting chamber for Florence's Signoria, or ruling council, on the second floor of what is now called the Palazzo Vecchio (fig. 92). The hall had been expanded in 1494 by Savonarola so that it would seat all five hundred members of the Grand Council. With Savonarola gone, the leader of the council was known as the *gonfaloniere*, or standard-bearer. That helped Leonardo determine what would be the central element of his *Battle of Anghiari* mural: the fight for the standard at the climax of the battle.

Leonardo was given workshop space for himself and his assistants in the "Popes' Room" in the cloisters of the Church of Santa Maria Novella, which was large enough to accommodate his full-size preparatory drawing. Machiavelli's secretary Agostino Vespucci provided Leonardo with a long narrative description of the original battle, including a blow-by-blow chronicle involving forty squadrons of cavalry and two thousand foot soldiers. Leonardo dutifully placed the account in his notebook (using a spare bit of the page to draw a new idea for hinged wings of a flying machine), and then proceeded to ignore it.[2] He decided instead to focus on an intimate struggle of a few horsemen flanked by scenes of two other tight skirmishes.

Fig. 92. Florence's Palazzo della Signoria, now the Palazzo Vecchio, in 1498 during the burning of Savonarola. The Duomo is on the left.

THE CONCEPTION

The idea of painting a battle scene that was both glorious and horrifying was not new for Leonardo. He had written a long description more than ten years earlier, when he was in Milan, of how it should be done. He paid particular attention to the colors of the dust and smoke. "First you must represent the smoke of artillery mingling in the air with the dust tossed up by the movement of horses and the combatants," he instructed. "The finest part of the dust rises highest; hence that part will be least visible and will look almost the same color as the air. . . . At the top, where the smoke is more separate from the dust, the smoke will assume a bluish tinge." He even specified how the dust clouds would be kicked up by the horses: "Make the little clouds of dust distant from each other in proportion to the strides made by the galloping horses; and the clouds which are furthest removed from the horses should be least visible; make them high and spreading and thin, and the nearer ones will be more conspicuous and smaller and denser."

He went on to describe, with his conflicted mix of fascination and repulsion, how to portray the brutality of battle: "If you show a man who has fallen to the ground, show the place where he has been dragged as bloody mud. A horse will drag the body of its dead rider, leaving traces of the corpse's blood in the dust and mud. Make the vanquished look pale and panic-stricken, their eyebrows raised high or knitted in grief, their faces stricken with painful lines." His account, more than a thousand words long, got more lurid as he warmed to his task. The brutality of war didn't repulse him as much as it seemed to mesmerize him, and the goriness he described would be reflected in the drawings he made for his battle mural:

> You must make the dead covered with dust, which is changed into crimson mire where it has mingled with the blood issuing in a stream from the corpse. The dying will be grinding their teeth, their eyeballs rolling heavenward as they beat their bodies with their fists and twist their limbs. Some might be shown disarmed and beaten down by the enemy, turning upon the foe to take an inhuman and bitter revenge with teeth and nails. . . . Some maimed warrior may be seen fallen to the earth, covering himself with his shield, while the enemy, bending over him, tries to deal him a deadly blow.

Just the thought of war brought out Leonardo's dark side and transformed the gentle artist. "There must not be a level spot that is not trampled and saturated with blood," he concluded.[3] His passion is visible in the frenzied sketches he drew in 1503 as he threw himself into his new commission.

THE DRAWINGS

Leonardo's initial drawings for the *Battle of Anghiari* show various moments of the battle, including one of cavalcades of infantry swarming to the scene, another of the Florentine troops arriving, and one showing them racing away with the battle standard that the Milanese carried. But gradually he tightened his focus on a single skirmish. The scene he finally chose for his central section was of three Florentine horsemen grappling the standard away from Milan's defeated but still-defiant general.[4]

In one preparatory drawing in the series (fig. 93), Leonardo used quick and sharp brown-ink strokes to show the fury of the four horses and riders struggling. On the lower half of the page he sketched nine versions of a nude soldier in frenzied twists as he swings a lance. Another drawing in the series shows soldiers being trampled, dragged, and lanced by the furious horsemen, just as he had described in his notebook. His depictions of the frantic clash of men and horses are messily tangled yet also gruesomely precise. One shows massive steeds rearing up and crashing down on naked soldiers squirming on the ground. The riders clinging atop the horses thrust lances into the bodies of the fallen. On another sheet he sketched a soldier beating a writhing enemy warrior who is also being lanced by a horseman. The brutality is frenzied, the savagery chaotic. Leonardo's astonishing ability to use simple pen strokes to capture movement has reached its peak. If you stare long enough at the pages, the horses and bodies seem as vibrant as a video.

He planned the expressions on the faces with great care. In one preparatory chalk drawing, he focused on the face of an old warrior, his bulging brows furrowed and nose wrinkled, as he stares down and shouts with rage (fig. 94). From the brows to the eyes to the mouth, Leonardo displayed his mastery of conveying emotions with every element of a face. His anatomy studies had taught him which of the facial muscles that move the lips also affect nostrils and brows. That allowed him to follow his own directions, written a decade earlier, on how to show an angry, anguished face: "The sides of the nose should have certain furrows, going in an arch from the nose and terminating

Fig. 93. Study for the *Battle of Anghiari*.

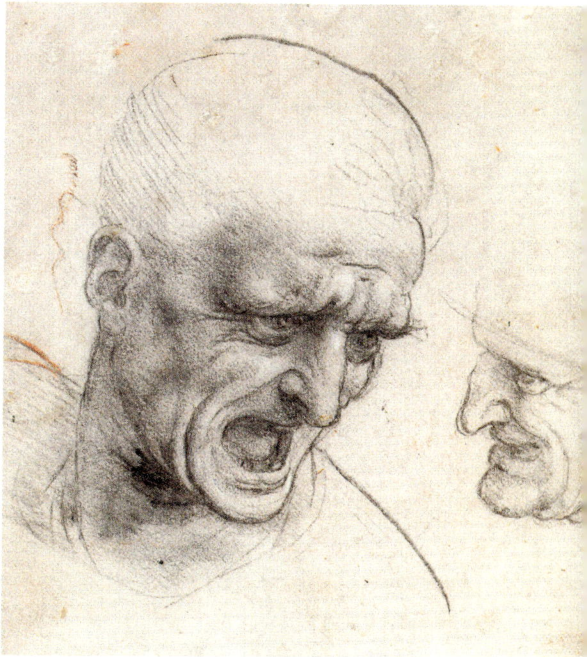

Fig. 94. A warrior for the *Battle of Anghiari*.

Fig. 95. Conveying the motion of horses.

at the edge of the eyes. Make the nostrils drawn up, causing these furrows, and the lips arched to disclose the upper teeth, with the teeth parted in order to shriek lamentations."[5] This sketch ended up being the model for the central warrior in his final full-size drawing for the painting.

Leonardo had long been fascinated by horses, which he obsessively drew and even dissected when he worked on the equestrian monument for Ludovico Sforza in Milan. In his preparatory drawings for the *Anghiari* mural, he reengaged in the subject. His possessions at the time included "a book of horses sketched for the cartoon,"[6] and they display the same intensity of motion and emotion as the human faces he drew. Vasari was among those impressed by how Leonardo was able to make the horses as much a part of the physical and emotional battle as the humans: "Rage, fury, and revenge are perceived as much in the men as in the horses, two of which have their forelegs interlocked and are fighting no less fiercely with their teeth than those who are riding them."

In one of these drawings (fig. 95), Leonardo used a frenzy of chalk strokes to combine two sequential instants, like a stop-action photographer or a precursor to Duchamp. The technique allowed him to convey the horse's wild lurching and lunging as it engaged in the battle with an intensity equal to that of its rider. In his best drawings, Leonardo amazes us by capturing the world precisely as an observant eye would see it; in the case of the wildly charging horses, he goes even further by capturing motion in a way that our eye cannot see. "They are among the greatest evocations of movement in the entire history of art," the British art critic Jonathan Jones wrote. "Movement, something that had obsessed Leonardo ever since he had tried to catch the blur of a cat's squirming limbs in an early drawing, is here clarified as a theme with blood-red intensity."[7]

On another page from his book of horses, he demonstrated how a horse could display emotion like a human (fig. 96). There are six horse heads, each showing a different degree of anger. Some bare their teeth and, like the old warrior, furrow their brow and flare their nostrils. In the midst of these boldly drawn horses, he lightly sketched, as if for comparison, the head of a man and of a lion with analogous expres-

Fig. 96. Horses showing fury, with an angry lion and man in the center.

sions of fury, their teeth bared and furrowed brow thrust forward. Here we have a cross between a piece of art and a study in comparative anatomy. What began as a preparatory drawing—and indeed had elements that found their way into the battle scene he began to paint—also became, in inimitable Leonardo fashion, an investigation into muscles and nerves.

For a final reminder of how varied his passions and curiosities were, we can turn over the page of horse sketches to see what else he was thinking about at the time. The reverse of the sheet also has an energetic sketch of a horse's head, but above it is a carefully rendered schematic of the solar system, showing the earth and sun and moon with projection lines explaining why we see the various phases of the moon. In a note, he analyzed the illusion of why the moon appears larger when it is on the horizon than when overhead. Look at an object through a lens and it will seem bigger, he wrote, and "by this means you will have produced an exact imitation of the atmosphere." On the bottom of the page are some geometrical illustrations of a square and slices of a circle, as Leonardo pursued his never-ending quest to transform geometric shapes into other shapes of the same area and to solve the challenge of squaring a circle. Even the horse seems a bit awed and reverential, as if it is marveling at how Leonardo has scattered around it the evidence of his amazing mind.[8]

THE PAINTING

Leonardo's immersion in his preparatory studies, which were driven by his passionate curiosity more than the mere utility of sketching out a painting, meant that he was not progressing as fast as the Signoria would have liked. At one point a pay dispute erupted. When he went to get his monthly fee, the cashier gave it to him in small coins. Leonardo refused the money. "I am no penny-painter," he objected. As the tension escalated, he raised money from some friends so he could pay back his fee and abandon the project, but the *gonfaloniere* of the Signoria, Piero Soderini (brother of the diplomat who had negotiated with Borgia), refused the repayment and convinced Leonardo to go back to work.

A revised contract was signed by Leonardo and witnessed by his friend Machiavelli in May 1504. By then the Florentines were beginning to worry about Leonardo's proclivity to procrastinate, so they wrote into the new contract that he would have to repay all his fees and forfeit all the work he had done if he did not finish by February 1505. The document declared:

> Several months ago Leonardo, son of Ser Piero da Vinci, and a Florentine citizen, undertook to do a painting for the Sala del Consiglio Grande, and seeing that this painting has already been begun as a cartoon by the said Leonardo, he moreover having received on such account 35 florins, and desiring that the work be concluded as soon as possible . . . the Signoria have resolved that Leonardo da Vinci is to have completely finished painting and brought it wholly to perfection by the end of next February without quibble or objection. . . . And in the event that Leonardo shall not have finished in the stipulated time, then the Signoria can compel him by whatever means appropriate to repay all the money received in connection with this work and Leonardo would be obliged to make over to the said Signoria as much as had been done.[9]

Soon after signing this new contract, Leonardo constructed a scissors-like platform that, Vasari reported, "was raised by contracting it and lowered by expanding." He requisitioned eighty-eight pounds of flour to make a paste with which to stick up his preparatory cartoon and the ingredients for whitewash to prepare the wall. After spending a few months at the end of the year on his swamp-draining and military mission to Piombino, he returned to the *Battle of Anghiari* in early 1505.

As with *The Last Supper*, Leonardo wanted to paint his mural using oil-based pigments and glazes, which enabled him to create luminous illusions. Oil permitted him to paint more slowly, with finer brushstrokes and greater nuance of color and shadow transitions, which would have been particularly suited for the hazy and dusty atmospheric effects he intended for the *Battle of Anghiari*.[10] Because there were already signs that his use of oil on dry plaster was causing *The Last Supper* to flake away, Leonardo experimented with new techniques. Unfortunately, painting on walls was one endeavor where his quest for innovation and scientific experimentation repeatedly failed him.

For the *Battle of Anghiari*, he treated the plaster wall with what he called Greek pitch ("pece grecha per la pictura"), probably a dark residue of distilled turpentine or a mix of resin and wax. His list of provisions also included almost twenty pounds of linseed oil. His small experiments with these materials seemed to work, so he became confident he could use them for the entire mural. But almost immediately he noticed that his mixtures were not sticking well. One early biographer said that Leonardo was cheated by his supplier and that the linseed oil was faulty. To dry the pigments and perhaps concentrate the oil, Leonardo lit a fire below his painting.

The February 1505 deadline came and went with the painting not close to completion. He was still making his delicate oil brushstrokes on the wall in June when all was almost ruined by a torrential rainstorm. "Friday the 6th of June, 1505, at the stroke of the thirteenth hour I began to paint in the palace," he recorded in a notebook. His brief description of the scene is unclear, but it seems to indicate that the storm caused great leaks that overwhelmed the vessels used to remove the water. "As I lowered the brush, the weather changed for the worse and the bell started to toll, calling the men to the court. The cartoon was torn, water poured down, and the vessel of water that was being carried broke. Suddenly the weather became even worse and it rained very heavily till nightfall."[11]

This entry is considered by some a notarial recording of the momentous day he first began painting the *Battle of Anghiari*, but I think not. He had signed his new contract and requisitioned materials a year earlier, and he had probably been working on and off since then. There is no other case when he recorded the moment of starting or finishing a painting, but he regularly wrote about storms, deluges, and other weather phenomena that stimulated his apocalyptic imagination. I suspect his notebook entry was prompted by the storm rather than some painting milestone.

Vasari, who saw Leonardo's unfinished painting, described it vividly:

> An old soldier in a red cap, crying out, grips the staff with one hand, and, raising a scimitar with the other, furiously aims a blow to cut off both the hands of those who, gnashing their teeth in the struggle, are striving in utmost fierceness to defend their banner. On the ground, between the legs of the horses, there are two figures that are fighting together, and the one on the ground has over him a soldier who has raised his arm as high as possible, that thus with greater force he may plunge a dagger into his throat, in order to end his life; while the other, struggling with his legs and arms, is doing what he can to escape death. It is not possible to describe the invention that Leonardo showed in the garments of the soldiers, all varied by him in different ways, and likewise in the helmet crests and other ornaments; not to mention the incredible mastery that he displayed in the forms and lineaments of the horses, which Leonardo, with their fiery spirit, muscles, and shapely beauty, drew better than any other master.

In trying to complete this painting and make it stick to the wall that summer of 1505, Leonardo could feel the presence of a younger man looking over his shoulder, both literally and figuratively. Preparing to paint a competing mural in the room was the rising star of Florence's art world, Michelangelo Buonarroti.

MICHELANGELO

When Leonardo left Florence for Milan in 1482, Michelangelo was only seven years old. His father was a member of Florence's minor nobility who subsisted on small public appointments, his mother had died, and he was living in the countryside with the family of a stone-cutter. During the seventeen years that Leonardo was away in Milan, Michelangelo became Florence's hot new artist. He was apprenticed to the thriving Florence workshop of the painter Domenico Ghirlandaio, won the patronage of the Medici, and traveled to Rome in 1496, where he carved his *Pietà*, showing Mary grieving over the body of Jesus.

By 1500 the two artists were back in Florence. Michelangelo, then twenty-five, was a celebrated but petulant sculptor, and Leonardo, forty-eight, was a genial and generous painter who had a following of friends and young students. It is enticing to think of what might have occurred if Michelangelo had treated him as a mentor. But that did not happen. As Vasari reported, he displayed instead "a very great disdain" toward Leonardo.

One day Leonardo was walking with a friend through one of the central piazzas of Florence wearing one of his distinctive rose-pink (*rosato*) tunics. There was a small group discussing a passage from Dante, and they asked Leonardo his opinion of its meaning. At that moment Michelangelo came by, and Leonardo suggested that he might be able to explain it. Michelangelo took offense, as if Leonardo were mocking him. "No, explain it yourself," he shot back. "You are the one who modelled a horse to be cast in bronze, was unable to do it, and was forced to give up the attempt in shame." He then turned and walked away. On another occasion when Michelangelo encountered Leonardo, he again referred to the fiasco of the Sforza horse monument, saying, "So those idiot [*caponi*] Milanese actually believed in you?"[12]

Unlike Leonardo, Michelangelo was often contentious. He had once insulted the young artist Pietro Torrigiano, who was drawing alongside him in a Florence chapel; Torrigiano recalled "clenching my fist and giving him such a blow on the nose that I felt bone and cartilage go down like biscuit beneath my knuckles." Michelangelo had a disfigured nose for the rest of his life. Combined with his slightly hunched back and unwashed appearance, that made him a contrast to the handsome, muscular, and stylish Leonardo. Michelangelo's rivalries extended to many other artists, including Pietro Perugino, whom he called a "clumsy [*goffo*] artist"; Perugino unsuccessfully sued him for defamation.

"Leonardo was handsome, urbane, eloquent and dandyishly well dressed," wrote Michelangelo's biographer Martin Gayford. "In contrast, Michelangelo was neurotically secretive." He was also "intense, disheveled, and irascible," according to another biographer, Miles Unger. He had powerful feelings of love and hate toward those around him but few close companions or protégés. "My delight is in melancholy," Michelangelo once confessed.[13]

Whereas Leonardo was disinterested in personal religious practice, Michelangelo was a pious Christian who found himself convulsed by the agony and the ecstasy of faith. They were both gay, but Michelangelo was tormented and apparently imposed celibacy on himself, whereas Leonardo was quite comfortable and open about having male companions. Leonardo took delight in clothes, sporting colorful short tunics and fur-lined cloaks. Michelangelo was ascetic in dress and demeanor; he slept in his dusty studio, rarely bathed or removed his dog-skin shoes, and dined on bread crusts. "How could he fail to envy and detest the easy charm, the elegance, refinement, amiable sweetness of manner, dilettantism, and above all the skepticism of Leonardo, a man of another generation, said to be without religious faith, around whom there constantly strutted a crowd of beautiful pupils, led by the insufferable Salai?" wrote Serge Bramly.[14]

Soon after his return to Florence, Michelangelo was commissioned to turn a hulking and imperfect piece of white marble into a statue of the biblical Goliath-slayer, David. Working with his usual secrecy, by early 1504 he had produced the most famous statue ever carved (fig. 97). Seventeen feet high and dazzlingly bright, it instantly eclipsed all previous statues of David, including the pretty-boy version by Verroc-

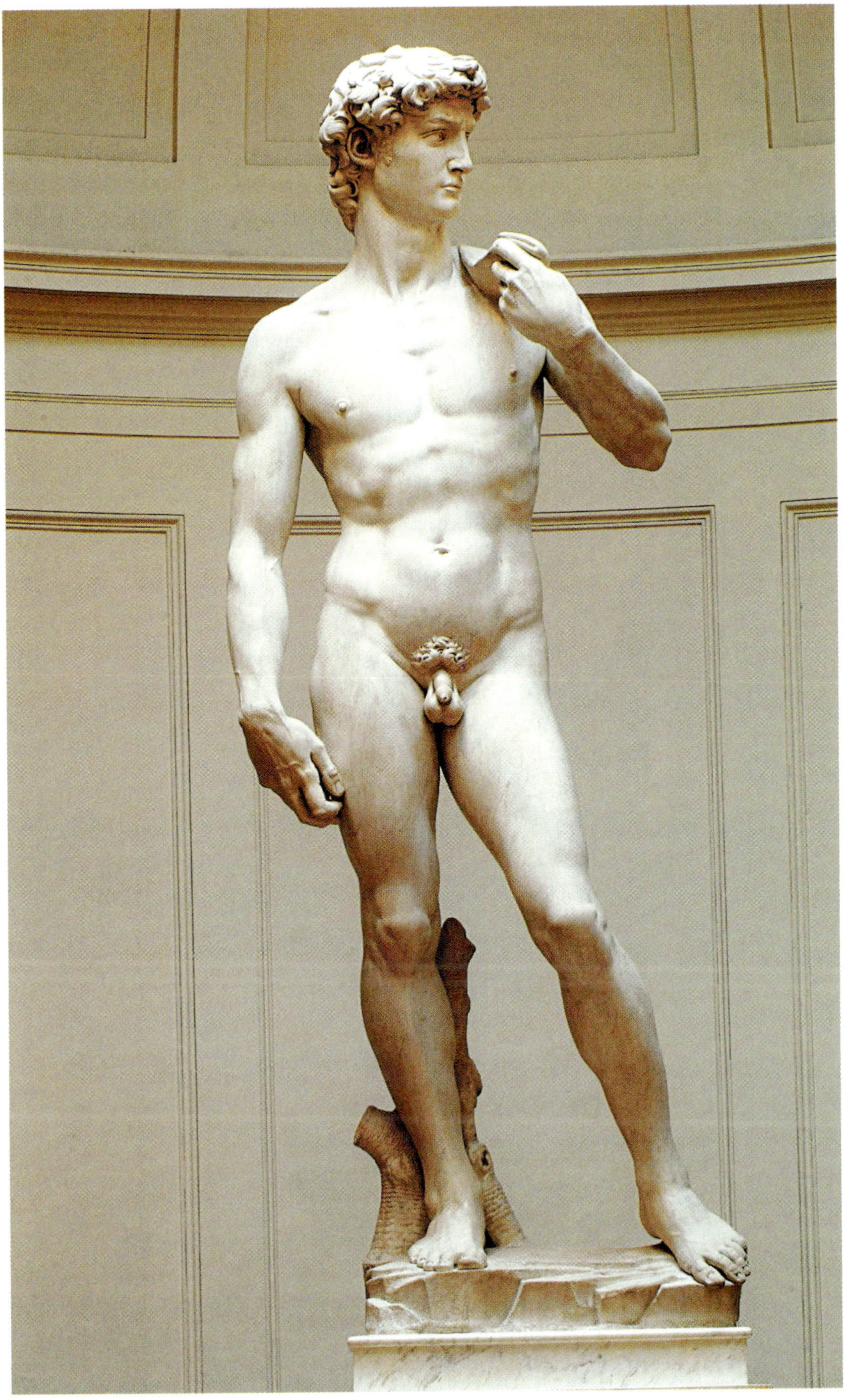

Fig. 97. Michelangelo's *David*.

chio for which the youthful Leonardo served as a model. Verrocchio and others had portrayed David as a young boy in triumph, often with Goliath's head at his feet. But Michelangelo showed him as a man, starkly nude, as he prepared to go into the fight. His stare is alert, his brow determined. He stands, with an air of affected casualness, in a *contrapposto* position, his weight on one leg, the other thrust forward. As Leonardo did in painting, Michelangelo showed the body in motion, torso twisting gently to the right, neck to the left. Though David seems relaxed, we can sense the tension in the muscles of his neck and see the veins bulging on the back of his right hand.

Florence's leaders were then faced with the question of where to place this astonishing colossus. The issue was so contentious that there was even an outbreak of stone-throwing by some protestors. Being a republic, Florence formed a committee. Thirty or so artists and civic leaders were convened to discuss the issue, including Filippino Lippi, Perugino, Botticelli, and of course Leonardo. They gathered on January 25, 1504, in a meeting room near the Duomo, in sight of the finished statue, and considered nine locations, two of which became finalists.

Michelangelo originally hoped that his statue would stand outside the entrance to the cathedral on the Piazza del Duomo, but he soon realized that it was better as a civic symbol of Florence and urged that it be placed in the piazza in front of the Palazzo della Signoria. Giuliano da Sangallo, who was one of Florence's best architects as well as a sculptor, favored a site underneath the wide-arched Loggia della Signoria, a building on the corner of the piazza. He and his supporters made the argument that tucking the *David* there would best protect it from the elements, but that choice also had the effect of making it less prominent, dominant, and visible. "We will go to see it, and not have the figure come to see us," said another supporter of the loggia location.

Not surprisingly, Leonardo came down on the side of stashing it inside the portico. When it was his turn to speak, he said, "I agree that it should be in the Loggia, as Giuliano has said, but on the parapet where they hang the tapestries." Clearly, he preferred that Michelangelo's statue be put in an inconspicuous space.[15]

Leonardo went on to add something surprising. He argued that the statue be installed "with decent ornament [*chon ornamento decente*]." It was clear what he meant. Michelangelo had sculpted David unabashedly naked, with prominent pubic hair and genitalia. Leonardo suggested that a decent ornament should be attached "in such a way that it does not spoil the ceremonies of the officials." In his notebook at the time, he drew a small sketch based on Michelangelo's *David* (fig. 98). Look carefully, and you can see what he is suggest-

Fig. 98. Leonardo's notebook sketch of Michelangelo's *David.*

ing; he has discreetly covered David's genitals with what looks like a bronze leaf.[16]

Leonardo was not generally prudish about nudity. From his *Vitruvian Man* to his portraits of Salai, he merrily drew naked men, and in his notebooks he once wrote that the penis should be displayed unashamedly. Indeed, a red-chalk and ink nude he drew in 1504, around the time of the statue placement discussions, seems to combine, in a psychologically interesting way, the fleshy face of Salai, then twenty-four, with the muscular physiognomy of Michelangelo's David (fig.31).[17] He also did sketches of a nude and muscular Hercules, front and back, that were probably for a statue he hoped someday to make as a counterpoint to *David*.[18] Yet there was something about Michelangelo's version of muscular, intrusive male nudity that Leonardo found disagreeable.

Michelangelo won the battle of placement. His *David* was carefully rolled from his workshop over a four-day period and installed at the entrance of the Palazzo della Signoria. It stayed there until 1873, when it was moved inside the Accademia Gallery, and in 1910 a replica was placed in front of what had by then been renamed the Palazzo Vecchio. But Leonardo won his argument that a "decent ornament" should be added. A gilded garland made of brass and twenty-eight copper leaves was strapped on, covering David's genitals. It stayed there for at least forty years.[19]

THE COMPETITION

As soon as his statue of David was placed in the most prominent spot in Florence's civic plaza, Michelangelo was commissioned to paint a battle scene that would be a companion to Leonardo's in the great hall. To the Signoria and its leader Soderini, the decision was a conscious effort to play off the rivalry between the era's two greatest artists. Accounts from the time all use the same word for it: *concorrenza*, or competition. At the funeral of Soderini years later, a eulogist praised him by saying, "To stage a competition with Leonardo, he assigned Michelangelo that other wall, where Michelangelo, to conquer him, began to paint." The near contemporary artist and writer Benvenuto Cellini, in praising Michelangelo's cartoon, stated, "He made it in competition with another artist, Leonardo da Vinci."[20] And Vasari used the same word: "While that rarest of painters Leonardo da Vinci was painting in the Great Council Hall, Piero Soderini, then Gonfalonier, because of the great ability he saw in Michelangelo, got part of that Hall allocated to him; which was how it came about that he did the other façade in competition with Leonardo."

The subject assigned to Michelangelo was another of Florence's rare battlefield victories, this one over Pisa in the Battle of Cascina in 1364. Like Leonardo, he failed to complete his painting, and once again we know it only through copies of the full-scale preparatory cartoon he drew, including one made by his pupil Bastiano da Sangallo (fig. 99).

Rather than focusing on a climactic event, as Leonardo did with his battle for the standard, Michelangelo chose to portray an oddly tangential scene, one that featured more than a dozen muscular and naked men. This is the moment when Florence's soldiers were bathing in the Arno River and received an alarm that the enemy was attack-

Fig. 99. A copy of Michelangelo's lost *Battle of Cascina*.

ing, causing them to scramble up the banks and grab their clothes. A rare event in military history that centered on nude wet men, it was a scene suited for Michelangelo, who had never been to war or seen a battle but was infatuated with the male body. "In all his works Michelangelo was drawn to the nude," Jonathan Jones wrote. "Here, he flaunted it as an obsession—drew attention to his habit, dramatized his penchant. . . . Anyone who hadn't registered before that young Michelangelo was utterly besotted with the bodies of men was certainly going to notice now."[21]

Leonardo rarely criticized other painters,[22] but after seeing Michelangelo's bathing nudes he repeatedly disparaged what he called the "anatomical painter." Clearly referring to his rival, he mocked those who "draw their nude figures looking like wood, devoid of grace, so that you would think you were looking at a sack of walnuts rather than the human form, or a bundle of radishes rather than the muscles of figures." The phrase *un sacco di noce* amused him; he used it more than once in his attacks on Michelangelo's muscular nudes. "You should not make all the muscles of the body too conspicuous . . . otherwise you will produce a sack of walnuts rather than a human figure."[23]

Therein lay another difference between the two artists. Michelangelo tended to specialize in muscular male nudes; even when he painted the ceiling of the Sistine Chapel a few years later he included twenty *ignudi*, athletic nude males, as corner figures. Leonardo, on the contrary, prided himself on the "universal" nature of his subjects. He believed "The painter should aim at universality, because there is a great want of self-respect in doing one thing well and another badly, as many do who study only the nude figure and do not seek after variety," Leonardo wrote. "This is a defect that demands stern reprehension."[24] He could certainly draw and paint male nudes, but his virtuosity came from his imagination and inventiveness, which required diversity and fantasy. "Let the painter composing narrative pictures take pleasure in variety," he directed.[25]

Leonardo's broader critique of Michelangelo was his argument that painting is a higher form of art than sculpture. In a passage written just after the showdown of battles in the Florentine hall, Leonardo argued:

> Painting embraces and contains within itself all things perceptible in nature, which the poverty of sculpture cannot do, such as show the colors of all things and their diminution. The painter will demonstrate various distances by the variation of color of the air interposed between objects and the eye. He will demonstrate how the species of objects penetrate mists with difficulty. He will demonstrate how mountains and valleys are seen through clouds in the rain. He will demonstrate dust itself, and how the combatants raise a commotion in it.[26]

Leonardo, of course, was referring to Michelangelo's sculptures, but judging from the extant copies his criticism also applied to Michelangelo's *Battle of Cascina* and even some of his finished paintings. In other words, he painted like a sculptor. Michelangelo was good at delineating forms with the use of sharp lines, but he showed little skill with the subtleties of sfumato, shadings, refracted lights, soft visuals, or changing color perspectives. He freely admitted that he preferred the chisel to the brush. "I am not in the right place, and I am not a painter," he confessed in a poem when he embarked on the ceiling of the Sistine Chapel a few years later.[27]

A look at Michelangelo's oil and tempera panel painting *Doni Tondo* (fig.100), done around the time of the Signoria competition, shows the difference between the styles of the two men. Michelangelo seems to have been influenced by the cartoon Leonardo had done for the *Virgin and Child with Saint Anne*, which had caused a sensation when displayed in Florence. Michelangelo's version has a similar narrative feel, with the characters twisting in a tight configuration. But there the similarities end. Michelangelo prominently includes Joseph; for reasons best left to Freud, Leonardo never conspicuously featured Joseph in any of his art. Though vividly colored, Michelangelo's three main figures seem sculpted rather than painted; they are lifeless, and their expressions lack charm or mystery. His background features not nature but his favorite motif: male nudes, lounging languorously and a bit pointlessly, even though there is no river for them to bathe in. They are in sharp focus, with no sign of Leonardo's understanding of atmospheric or distance perspective. "He had no use for Leonardo's

Fig. 100. Michelangelo's *Doni Tondo.*

famous sfumato," writes Unger. Gayford calls *Doni Tondo* "almost a rebuttal in paint of Leonardo's ideas."[28]

Michelangelo's painting has the sharp, delineated outlines that Leonardo, with his love of sfumato and blurred borders, scorned as a matter of philosophy, optics, mathematics, and aesthetics. To define objects, Michelangelo used lines rather than following Leonardo's practice of using shadows, which is why Michelangelo's look flat rather than three-dimensional. The sharply lined contours are also featured in his *Battle of Cascina*, as shown in some of his preparatory studies. It is as if he had looked at Leonardo's method of creating a dusty and hazy battle scene blurred by motion, as well as the *sfumatura* in Leonardo's other works, and decided to do just the opposite.

Their divergent approaches represent two schools in Florentine art: that of Leonardo, Andrea del Sarto, Raphael, Fra Bartolomeo, and others who emphasized the use of sfumato and chiaroscuro, and the more traditional approach taken by Michelangelo, Agnolo Bronzino, Alessandro Allori, and others who favored a *disegno* based on outlined contours.[29]

ABANDONED

In the spring of 1505, with his painting for Florence's council hall not yet begun, Michelangelo accepted a summons from Pope Julius II to Rome to sculpt a tomb. As if energized by Michelangelo's absence, Leonardo threw himself into painting his battle scene. But then the temperamental Michelangelo had a temporary falling out with the pope, who he felt was not being deferential enough. (Artists such as Leonardo and Michelangelo were reaching such a status that popes and marchesas had to defer to them on occasion.) "You can tell the pope that if he wants me from now on, he can seek me elsewhere," Michelangelo declared, and returned to Florence around April 1506.

His presence back in Florence unnerved Leonardo, who as usual was both procrastinating and having difficulty getting his oil-based paint mixtures to adhere to the wall. He would eventually move back to Milan, consigning the *Anghiari* mural to his long list of abandoned projects. Michelangelo too would leave again, kneeling to ask the pope's forgiveness and then returning to Rome. He would stay there for another decade and paint the ceiling of the Sistine Chapel.[30]

So neither painting was ever finished. The final loss of both men's work came at the hand, ironically, of Vasari, the painter-biographer who lionized them. He was commissioned in the 1560s to renovate the great hall, where he painted six battle scenes of his own. In recent years, a group of experts, including the high-technology art diagnostician Maurizio Seracini, discovered some evidence that Leonardo's partial painting may still exist under one of Vasari's. Tiny holes drilled into Vasari's work revealed pigments on the wall underneath that may be from Leonardo's painting. But authorities have resisted requests to allow further investigations that might harm Vasari's mural.[31]

Once again we have to wrestle with the reasons Leonardo decided to leave a work unfinished. The proximate cause was the problems he had with his materials. "Conceiving the wish to color on the wall in oils," Vasari reported, "he made a composition of so gross an admixture to act as a binder on the wall, that when he painted, it began to peel off in such a manner that in a short time he abandoned it, seeing it spoiling."[32] Added to that was the unnerving specter of Michelangelo hovering behind him; Leonardo did not have a competitive personality, so he likely did not relish the contest.

There was also a more artistic challenge, I think, that contributed to Leonardo's decision to abandon the commission. When painting *The Last Supper*, he became immersed in the difficulty of getting the proper visual perspective in a large mural that would be seen from multiple vantage points in a room. A conventional central-point perspective scheme would have made parts of the scene appear distorted. Other painters would not have noticed, or would have chosen to ignore, the way figures in a large painting could seem disproportionate when viewed from different parts of the room. But Leonardo was obsessed by the optics, mathematics, and art of perspective.

For *The Last Supper* he had come up with tricks and illusions and artifices to make his work appear realistic from different vantages. He was able to make a preferred vantage point that was far away from the painting; he calculated it would ideally be located ten to twenty times as far away as the painting was wide. But the area that he was supposed to paint in Florence's council hall was fifty-five feet long, twice that of *The Last Supper*, and his mural would be viewed from at most seventy feet away, far less than twice its width.

In addition, his painting was supposed to be an outdoor scene lit by broad daylight, unlike *The Last Supper*, which depicted an enclosed dining room on the wall of an enclosed dining room. The challenges of how to get all of the perspectives from each angle to look believable were combined with the difficulties of showing direct and reflected lighting and shadows in an open-air scene that was to be viewed inside a room. Leonardo had the authorities cut four more windows in the hall, but that did not eliminate the challenge.[33]

He was a perfectionist faced with challenges other artists would have disregarded but that he could not. So he put down his brushes. That behavior meant he would never again receive a public commission. But it is also what allowed him to go down in history as an obsessed genius rather than merely a reliable master painter.

"SCHOOL OF THE WORLD"

The unfinished battle scenes turned out to be two of the most influential lost paintings in history, and they helped to shape the High Renaissance. "These battle cartoons of Leonardo and Michelangelo are the turning point of the Renaissance," according to Kenneth Clark.[34] They were kept on display in Florence until 1512, and young artists flocked to see them. One of those was the sculptor Cellini, who described the competing display in his autobiography: "These cartoons stood one in the Medici Palace and the other in the Pope's Hall, and so long as they remained there, they served as the school of the world."[35]

Raphael traveled to Florence just to see the two cartoons that had caused such a sensation, Vasari reported, and he drew versions of them. The animated details of both unfinished works spurred the imaginations, and the mannerism, of subsequent generations. "Frenzied faces, monstrous armor, twisting bodies, convoluted poses, masks, and mad horses—between them the two great Council Hall images provided sixteenth-century artists with a banquet of oddities," Jonathan Jones wrote. "In these fantastical works, two geniuses tried to outdo one another in sheer quiddity."[36]

The showdown did more than any paragone could have to raise the status of artists. Leonardo and Michelangelo had become luminaries, paving the way for other artists—who until then had rarely even signed their work—to do the same. When the pope summoned Michelangelo, and when the Milanese vied with the Florentines over the services of Leonardo, it was recognition that super-artists had their own recognizable style, artistic personality, and individual genius. Instead of being treated as somewhat interchangeable members of the craftsman's class, the best artists were now treated as singular stars.

CHAPTER 26

Return to Milan

THE DEATH OF SER PIERO

In the midst of Leonardo's struggle to paint the *Battle of Anghiari*, his father died.

Their relationship had been complex. Piero da Vinci never legitimated Leonardo, but perhaps that was an act of intentional or unintentional kindness as well as coldness. Had he done so, Leonardo may have been expected to become a notary, despite guild rules that made that difficult, and Piero knew that vocation would not suit him. He helped his son get at least three major painting commissions, but he also drew up stringent contracts designed to force him to deliver. When Leonardo failed to do so, it likely caused strain between them.

After not marrying Leonardo's mother, Piero had four wives. The last two were much younger than Leonardo, and with them Piero had nine sons and two daughters, many of them sired when he was in his seventies. Leonardo's half-siblings were all young enough to be his children, and they didn't regard him as a potential family heir.

The difficult family dynamics became evident when Piero died. Leonardo, imperfectly displaying his notarial heritage, recorded the event in his notebook. He seemed agitated. On a page filled with lists of his expenditures in July 1504, including "one florin to Salai to spend on the house," he wrote the following: "On Wednesday at seven o'clock died Ser Piero da Vinci on the 9th of July 1504."[1] There was one little oddity: July 9 that year was a Tuesday.

Then Leonardo did something even more unusual. On the top right of another page, which contains some typical geometric drawings and a few columns of added numbers, he had the information repeated in a sloping script written in the conventional left-to-right manner. If you look at the manuscript carefully, you see that the note is in a different ink from the rest of the page; the fact that it is carefully scribed in a normal direction indicates that it may have been dictated to one of his assistants. It begins, "Wednesday at 7 o'clock." The next word would likely have been "died," but the line breaks off and is crossed out. On the next line the text begins anew: "On the 9th of July 1504 Wednesday at seven o'clock died Ser Piero da Vinci notary at the Palazzo del Popolo, my father, at seven o'clock, being eighty years old, leaving behind ten sons and two daughters." Again there is something wrong with the day, and this time he has stated the hour twice. He also got his father's age wrong by two years; Piero was only seventy-eight.[2]

In saying that Piero had ten sons, Leonardo was counting himself. Nevertheless, his father did not bequeath him any inheritance. Despite his advanced age and the fact that he was a notary, Piero had not made a will. Although he may not have made an active decision to disinherit Leonardo, he knew that dying intestate meant his property would be divided among only his legitimate sons. Perhaps he felt that leaving money to Leonardo wasn't necessary because he was already successful, though in fact he was never comfortably wealthy. Or maybe Piero thought an inheritance would make his son even more negligent about completing commissions. More likely is that Leonardo was not legally an heir and, with their relationship strained, Piero felt no reason to change that. He had brought Leonardo into this world as an *illegitimo*, had not legitimated him as a child, and on his death delegitimized him yet again.[3]

LEAVING FLORENCE

The first time he moved away from Florence to Milan, in 1482, Leonardo left the *Adoration of the Magi* as merely a cartoon. When he decided to move the second time, in 1506, he left with the *Battle of Anghiari* similarly promising but unpainted. He would end up making Milan his home base for seven years, with only temporary visits back to Florence.

His excuse for going to Milan this time was to resolve the dispute over the second version of *Virgin of the Rocks*. He and his partner on the work, Ambrogio de Predis, had not been paid, and they had taken the matter to court. An arbitrator in April 1506 ruled against them, saying that the painting was *imperfetto*, a word connoting "unfinished" as well as "imperfect." Specifically, the judgment was that there was not enough of Leonardo's hand in it, so he was required to come add his own finishing touches before payment would be made.

If he had wished, Leonardo could have deflected the demand that he return to Milan by forfeiting any more payments for the *Virgin of the Rocks*. Money had never dictated his actions, plus he would have earned just as much if he stayed in Florence and finished the *Battle of Anghiari*. He heeded the summons to Milan because he wanted to go there. He had no desire to continue to struggle with his battle scene, compete with a younger artist who painted like a sculptor, or live in a town with his half-siblings.

The Florentine authorities reluctantly let him leave at the end of May 1506 partly for diplomatic reasons. Florence had been protected from Borgia and then other potential invaders by the French king, Louis XII, who then controlled Milan and admired *The Last Supper* and its artist. Louis expressed his desire to have Leonardo return to Milan, at least temporarily, and Florence's leaders were afraid to refuse. However, they did want Leonardo's stay to be temporary, so they required him to sign a notarized document pledging to return in three months. His bank manager had to cosign and commit to pay a penalty of 150 florins if he failed to do so. (The final payment for *Virgin of the Rocks*, when he did collect it, was only 35 florins.)

When Leonardo's three months were almost up, it became clear that he would not be returning to Florence anytime soon. To stave off Florentine demands or a forfeiture of his florins, he had his French patrons launch a protracted and amusing barrage of diplomatic démarches. In August 1506 Charles d'Amboise, the French governor of Milan, sent two missives, one polite and the other more abrupt, saying that "in spite of all previous promises" Leonardo needed an extension of his leave from Florence because he had not finished all of the projects the king wanted. Florence's leaders acquiesced with the understanding that he would come back at the end of September.

Unsurprisingly, that did not occur, and in early October Florence's *gonfaloniere* Soderini lost patience. He sent a letter that attacked Leonardo's honor and threatened Florence's relations with Milan. "Leonardo has not behaved as he should have done towards the Republic, because he has taken a large sum of money and only made a small beginning on the great work he was commissioned to carry out," he wrote. "We do not wish any further requests to be made on this matter, for this great work is for the benefit of all our citizens, and for us to release him from his obligations would be a failure of our duty."[4]

But Leonardo stayed in Milan. Charles d'Amboise sent a flowery and polite rebuke to the Florentines, asserting, with some merit, that Leonardo was loved in Milan and, by implication, underappreciated in Florence, especially when it came to his engineering skills. "We were among those who loved him even before our eyes had rested upon him, and now, since we have known him and been much in his company, and have had personal experience of his various gifts, we truly see that his name, famous in painting, is relatively obscure so far as those other branches of knowledge in which he has reached so great a height." Although he agreed that Leonardo would be free to return to Florence if he wanted, he added a reproach couched as a mischievous recommendation that the Florentines should treat their native son better: "If it be fitting to give a man of such talent a recommendation to his fellow citizens, we recommend him to you as strongly as we can and assure you that everything you can do to increase either his fortune and well-being, or those honors to which he is entitled, would give us, as well as him, the greatest pleasure, and we should be much obliged to you."[5]

At that point King Louis, who had by then appointed Leonardo his "official painter and engineer" (*nostre peintre et ingeneur ordinaire*), intervened personally from the French court at Blois. Summoning Florence's ambassador, he firmly requested that Leonardo stay in Milan until his own arrival there. "Your Signoria must render me a service," he insisted. "He is an excellent master, and I desire to have several things from his hand, certain little Madonnas and other things, according to my fancy, and perhaps I shall ask him to do a portrait of me," he told the ambassador. Florence's leaders realized they had no choice but to please their military protector. The Signoria replied, "[Florence] cannot have any greater pleasure than to obey his wishes. . . . Not only the said Leonardo but all other citizens are at the service of his wishes and needs."[6]

Leonardo was therefore still in Milan in May 1507, when Louis made a triumphant visit, having quelled a rebellion in Genoa on the way. The procession was led by three hundred armored soldiers and "a triumphal chariot bearing the cardinal Virtues and the god Mars holding in one hand an arrow [and] in the other a palm."[7]

To celebrate the king's arrival, there were days of festivals and pageants, and Leonardo was, of course, involved in choreographing them. A tournament was held in the plaza, and Isabella d'Este, her desire for a Leonardo portrait still unfulfilled, was at the masked ball.[8] After Savonarola, the republic of Florence was restrained in its indulgence of such fetes, but Milan still relished them, which was another reason Leonardo loved Milan.

FRANCESCO MELZI

While in Milan in 1507, Leonardo met a fourteen-year-old named Francesco Melzi (fig. 101). He was the son of a distinguished nobleman who was a captain in the Milanese militia and later a civil engineer who worked to reinforce the city's fortifications, endeavors that fascinated Leonardo. The Melzis lived in the largest villa in the town of Vaprio, on a river overlooking Milan, and Leonardo often stayed there, making it a second home.[9]

Leonardo was then fifty-five, and he had no son or heir. Young Francesco was an aspiring artist, pretty in the slightly soft way of Salai, and possessing some talent. With his father's permission, he was effectively adopted by Leonardo, either through an informal agreement or a legal contract, one that would be honored in Leonardo's will a decade later. Leonardo became a mix of legal guardian, godfather,

Fig. 101. Francesco Melzi by Boltraffio.

adoptive father, teacher, and employer of the young Melzi. Although the decision may seem strange in our day, it was an opportunity for the Melzis to have their son become the pupil, heir, and amanuensis of a charming and beloved family intimate who also happened to be the most creative artist of the time. Afterward, Leonardo stayed close to the entire Melzi family, even helping to design improvements to the family's villa.

For the rest of Leonardo's life, Francesco Melzi would be by his side. He worked as Leonardo's personal assistant and scribe, drafted his letters, kept his papers, and preserved them after his death. He wrote in a graceful italic, and his notations are to be found throughout Leonardo's notebooks. He also was Leonardo's art student. Though never a master painter, he was a good artist and draftsman who made some respectable drawings, including a famous one of Leonardo, and copied many of Leonardo's works. With his talent, efficiency, and steady temperament, he was a devoted companion to Leonardo, and a less complicated and devilish one than Salai.

Years later, the biographer Vasari got to know Melzi and wrote that he "was a very beautiful boy [*bellissimo fanciullo*] and much loved by [*molto amato da*] Leonardo." Those are similar to the words Vasari wrote of Salai, but it is unclear whether in this case there was any romantic or sexual relationship. I doubt there was. It is unlikely that Melzi's father would have given him over to Leonardo for such an association, and we know that after Leonardo's death Melzi married a prominent noblewoman and had eight children. Like much of Leonardo's life, there is a cloak of mist over the truth about the full extent of their relationship.

What is clear is that their relationship was not only close but familial. Leonardo drafted a letter to him in early 1508 that displays both fondness and vulnerability:

> Good day, Master [*Messer*, a salutation that respects his noble rank] Francesco,
>
> Why in God's name have you not answered a single one of all the letters I sent you? You just wait till I get there, and by God I'll make you write so much you'll be sorry.[10]

There follows another draft of a letter to Melzi that is slightly more reserved. It describes a question that needed to be resolved about the water rights the king had granted Leonardo as a payment, and notes, "I wrote to the superintendent and to you, and then I repeated it, and never had an answer. So you will have the goodness to answer me as to what happened."

The letter mentioned that Leonardo was sending the messages by the hand of Salai, who was then twenty-seven. That raises the question of what Leonardo's longtime companion thought of this new, younger, aristocratic, and far more polished member of the household. We know that both stayed by Leonardo's side for the next decade of his life and that Melzi made a higher salary. There is a clue that Leonardo needed to work at keeping peace with Salai. It was around this time, in 1508, that the dictated note mentioned earlier appeared in one of his notebooks: "Salai, I want peace, not war. No more wars, I give in."[11]

Whether or not Melzi was ever a lover, he became something more significant. Leonardo loved him as a son, and he needed a son to love. It helped that Melzi was appealing and pretty, which was no doubt one reason Leonardo liked to have him in his retinue. But he was also a loyal and caring companion to whom Leonardo could pass along his papers, his estate, his knowledge, and his wisdom. He could help mold him as he would have a son.

By 1508 that was all the more important to Leonardo. As he passed through his fifties, his notebooks show intimations of his awareness of his mortality. His father had died. His mother had died. He was estranged from his half-brothers. He had no family, other than Francesco Melzi.

FLORENCE INTERLUDE: AN INHERITANCE BATTLE

It was an inheritance dispute with his half-brothers rather than the exhortations of the Signoria or any desire to resume painting the *Battle of Anghiari* that brought Leonardo back to Florence temporarily in August 1507.

After he failed to inherit anything from his father, his beloved uncle Francesco da Vinci, a gentle and unambitious country squire who had been like a doting brother or surrogate father, decided to make up for it. With no children of his own, Uncle Francesco changed his will and, when he died in early 1507, left his estate to Leonardo. This apparently contradicted an understanding that his property would go to Piero's legitimate children, and they sued Leonardo. The main issue was over a piece of farmland with two houses four miles east of Vinci.

For Leonardo, it was a matter of principle as well as property. He had lent his uncle money to improve the farmhouse, and he occasionally visited there to conduct experiments and make drawings of the surrounding landscape. The result was another of the angry draft letters to be found in his notebooks. It was addressed to his half-brothers but was written partly in the third person, perhaps because he had someone send it on his behalf. "You wished the utmost evil to Francesco," he wrote. "You do not wish to repay his heir the money he lent for the property." You have treated Leonardo "not as a brother but as a complete alien."[12]

The king of France came to Leonardo's aid, hoping to speed his return to Milan. He wrote to the Signoria of Florence, "We have been informed that our dear and much-beloved Leonardo da Vinci, official painter and engineer, has some dispute and litigation pending in Florence against his brothers over certain inheritances." Emphasizing that it was important for Leonardo to be "in our entourage and in our presence," the king urged the Florentines to "bring the said dispute and litigation to an end and see that true justice is done with as little delay as possible; and you will give us very agreeable pleasure by doing so."[13] The letter was countersigned and probably arranged and written by the king's secretary Robertet, for whom Leonardo had painted *Madonna of the Yarnwinder*.

The king's letter did not have much effect. By September, Leonardo's inheritance case was still pending, so he tried pulling another string. He composed a letter, which was then scribed for him by Machiavelli's secretary Agostino Vespucci, to Cardinal Ippolito d'Este, the brother of Isabella and Beatrice. The cardinal was a friend of the judge. "I entreat you, as urgently as I know how," Leonardo pleaded, "to write a letter to Ser Raphaello [the judge] in that skillful and affectionate manner which you know so well, recommending to him Leonardo Vincio, Your Lordship's most abject servant, requesting him and urging him not only to do me justice but to do so with propitious urgency."[14]

Leonardo eventually won a partial victory based on a settlement he had proposed in his angry letter to his half-brothers: "Oh why don't you let him [Leonardo] enjoy the property and its proceeds during his life, as long as they would return to your children?" That is probably what happened. Leonardo was given possession of the property and the money it made, but when he died he left it not to Melzi but to his half-brothers.[15]

The litigation settled, Leonardo was ready to return to Milan. He had not, during his eight months back in Florence, set brush to his unfinished *Battle of Anghiari*, nor did he have any desire to do so. He had not figured out how to make the painting work to his satisfaction, I think, and he was eager to abandon it and move back to a city more suited to his wide variety of interests.

But he was worried that he may have lost the favor of Milan's French rulers. He had been away longer than expected, his requests to secure some water rights the king had given him had proven problematic, and some of his letters to Charles d'Amboise, the king's governor in Milan, had gone unanswered. So he sent Salai to Milan to assess the situation and deliver another letter to Charles. "I suspect that my feeble recognition of the great benefits I have received from your Excellency may have made you annoyed with me, and for this reason you have not answered the many letters I have addressed to you," he wrote. "I am now sending Salai to you to inform Your Excellency that I am almost at an end of my litigation with my brothers and I hope to be in Milan this Easter." He would come bearing gifts. "I shall bring with me two pictures of the Madonna, different in size, intended for the Most Christian King or for anyone else that your lordship may choose."

Then he turned somewhat plaintive. He had previously stayed in the palace of the governor, but now he wanted an apartment of his own. "I would like to know where I am to have my living quarters when I return, as I wish no longer to incommode your Excellency." He also inquired whether his salary from the king would continue and if the governor could straighten out the matter of the water rights he had been granted. As he had done in his famous letter to Milan's previous ruler when he first went there in 1482, Leonardo made a point of noting that he was not merely a painter. "I hope when I come to make machines and other things which will give great pleasure to our Most Christian King."[16]

All worked out, and by the end of April 1508 Leonardo was back in Milan, with a home in a parish church; regular payments began arriving from the king, and a final payment for *Virgin of the Rocks* came in October. Both Salai and Melzi were with him, and all was again right with his world. Over the next decade, he would return to Florence only for brief personal visits, but he would never work there again. His heart and his home were once again in Milan.

MILAN'S DELIGHTFUL DIVERSIONS

To understand Leonardo, it is necessary to understand why he moved away from Florence, this time for good. One reason is simple: he liked Milan better. It had no Michelangelo, no cadre of half-brothers suing him, no ghost of his father hovering. It had royalty rather than republicans, with jubilant pageants rather than the after-stench of bonfires of the vanities. It had doting patrons rather than oversight committees. And the foremost patron there was the one who loved Leonardo the most, Charles d'Amboise, the French royal governor who had written a flowery letter reminding the Florentines how brilliant their native son was.

But there was more to Leonardo's move than merely a preference for life in Milan. The first time he went there, he did so to recast himself as an engineer, scientist, and inventor. Now, more than twenty-five years later, he was fleeing not only Florence but also life as a public artist, a man defined mainly by his painting. As Isabella d'Este's agent had reported, "He cannot bear the sight of a paintbrush."

Florence was the artistic center of the Italian Renaissance, but Milan and its nearby university town of Pavia had become more intellectually diverse. Charles d'Amboise was dedicated to creating a court like that of the Sforzas, which included painters, entertainers, scientists, mathematicians, and engineers. Leonardo was the most valued jewel because he embodied all of those vocations.

During his sojourn back in Florence for his inheritance battle, he had focused mainly on scientific endeavors rather than painting commissions. He dissected the corpse of a man who claimed to be a hundred, planned a test of one of his flying machines, began a treatise on geology and water, devised a glass tank to examine the way flowing water deposits sediment, and swam underwater to compare the propulsion of a fish tail to a bird's wing, jotting his conclusions on the same notebook page where he drafted his angry letter to his half-brothers. These interests, he believed, could be better pursued amid the intellectual ferment of Milan.

"Begun in Milan on the day of September 12, 1508," he wrote on the opening page of a new notebook shortly after his return.[17] It is filled with studies of geology, water, birds, optics, astronomy, and architecture. He also busied himself drawing a bird's-eye schematic map of the city, suggesting the proper choir stalls to build in the Duomo, and devising military machinery that could be used against Venice.

In addition to its intellectual ferment, Milan had dazzling pageants and festivities that far surpassed those now to be found in republican Florence. When King Louis came for another visit, in July 1509, the procession included five chariots representing the towns recently conquered by France, followed by a triumphal chariot with three costumed allegorical figures, of the type Leonardo loved to design, representing Victory, Fame, and Happiness. To herald the king's arrival, Leonardo built a mechanical lion. One observer wrote, "Leonardo da Vinci, the famous painter and our Florentine, devised the following intervention: he created a lion above the gate, which was lying down, and then got onto its feet when the King entered the city, and with its paw it opened up its chest and pulled out blue balls full of golden lilies, which he threw and scattered on the ground." The lion, also described by Vasari, became a standard feature at future extravaganzas choreographed or inspired by Leonardo, including the entry of Francis I into Lyons in 1515 and into Argentan in 1517.[18]

Leonardo even had the joy of combining pageantry and architecture. For the palace of his patron Charles d'Amboise, he drew up plans for expanding a great hall so that it could better accommodate masquerades and performances. "The hall for the festival should be situated so that you come first into the presence of the lord, and then of the guests," he wrote. "On the other side should be the entrance of the hall and a convenient staircase, which should be wide, so that the people in passing along them do not push against the masqueraders and damage their costumes."[19]

In imagining a "garden of delights" for the estate, Leonardo indulged his love of water, proposing it as both an aesthetic feature and a method for cooling. "In the summer I shall make the water spring up fresh and bubbling and flow along in the space between the tables," he wrote, drawing how the tables would be arranged. The water would power a mill, which would be used to force breezes. "By means of the mill I shall be able at any time to produce a current of air," he promised, and "many water-conduits through the house, and springs in various places, and a certain passage where, when anyone passes, the water will leap up from all sides below, and so it will be there ready in case anyone should wish to give a shower-bath from below to the women or others who pass there." The flowing water would power a large clock, copper mesh netting would cover the garden to make it an aviary, and "with the help of the mill I will make unending sounds from all sorts of instruments, which will sound for so long as the mill shall continue to move."[20]

Neither the villa additions nor the garden of delights was ever built, which could reinforce the perception that the time Leonardo spent on engineering was to some extent wasted. Kenneth Clark was dismissive after rattling off a list of these nonpainterly passions: "One day he could be deciding on the form of the choir stalls in the Duomo; another, acting as military engineer in the war against

Venice; another, arranging pageants for the entry of Louis XII into Milan." Clark added sorrowfully, "It was a variety of employment which Leonardo enjoyed, but which has left posterity the poorer."[21]

Perhaps Clark is right, in that our store of art does not include a *Battle of Anghiari* or other potential masterpieces. But if posterity is poorer because of the time Leonardo spent immersed in passions from pageantry to architecture, it is also true that his life was richer.

CHAPTER 27

Anatomy, Round Two

THE CENTENARIAN

Shortly before he left Florence in 1508, Leonardo was at the hospital of Santa Maria Nuova, where he struck up a conversation with a man who said he was more than a hundred years old and had never been ill. A few hours later, the old man quietly passed away "without any movement or sign of distress."[1] Leonardo proceeded to dissect his body, launching what would be, from 1508 to 1513, his second round of anatomical studies.

We should pause to imagine the dandy-dressing Leonardo, now in his mid-fifties and at the height of his fame as a painter, spending his night hours at an old hospital in his neighborhood talking to patients and dissecting bodies. It is another example of his relentless curiosity that would astonish us if we had not become so used to it.

Twenty years earlier, while living in Milan, he had filled notebooks with his first round of anatomy drawings, including beautiful renderings of the human skull. Now he picked up the work again, and on one of the pages, above a set of drawings of muscles and veins in a partially skinned cadaver, he drew a respectful little drawing of his centenarian's peaceful face, eyes closed, moments after his death (fig. 102).[2] Then, on thirty more pages, he proceeded to record his dissection.

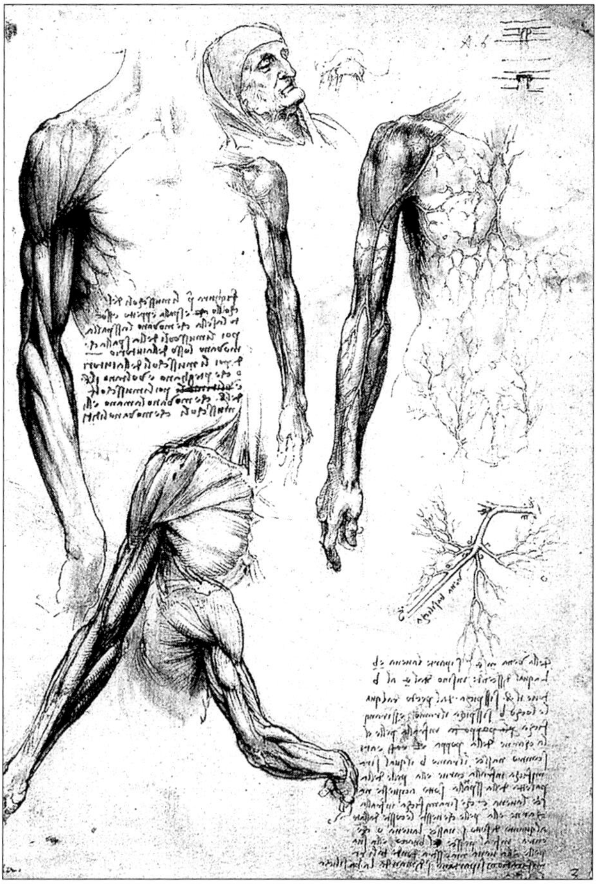

Fig. 102. The centenarian and his muscles.

Leonardo's hand was deft with both pen and scalpel. His close observation plus the strength of his visual memory made his drawings strikingly better than those in any anatomy texts before him. Mustering all of his draftsman's techniques, he made detailed underdrawings in black chalk, then finished them with different colors of ink and washes. With his left-handed curved hatching lines, he gave shape and volume to the form of bones and muscles and with light lines added the tendons and fibers. Each bone and muscle was shown from three or four angles, sometimes in layers or in an exploded view, as if it were a piece of machinery he was deconstructing and delineating. The results are triumphs of both science and art.

His rudimentary dissecting tools took him down layer by layer even as the body, untreated, decomposed. First he showed the surface muscles of the old man, then the inside muscles and veins as he pulled off the skin. He started with the right arm and neck, then the torso. He noted how the spine was curved, then he got to the abdominal wall, the intestines, the stomach, and the membranes connecting them all. Finally he exposed the liver, which he said "resembled frozen bran both in color and substance." He never reached the legs, perhaps because by then the body had decomposed too badly to make it bearable to handle. But there would be other dissections, probably twenty more, and by the time he finished his anatomy studies he would have beautifully illustrated every body part and limb.

In his quest to figure out how the centenarian died, Leonardo made a significant scientific discovery: he documented the process that leads to arteriosclerosis, in which the walls of arteries are thickened and stiffened by the accumulation of plaque-like substances. "I made an autopsy in order to ascertain the cause of so peaceful a death, and found that it proceeded from weakness through the failure of blood and of the artery that feeds the heart and the other lower members, which I found to be very dry, shrunken and withered," he wrote. Next to a drawing of the veins in the right arm, he compared the centenarian's blood vessels to those of a two-year-old boy who also died at the hospital. He found those of the boy to be supple and unconstricted, "contrary to what I found in the old man." Using his skill of thinking and describing through analogies, he concluded, "The network of vessels behaves in man as in oranges, in which the peel becomes tougher and the pulp diminishes the older they become."[3]

The constriction of blood flow had caused, among other things, the centenarian's liver to become so dry that "when it is subjected to even the slightest friction its substance falls away in tiny flakes like sawdust and leaves behind the veins and arteries." It also led to his flesh becoming "the color of wood or dried chestnut, because the skin is almost completely deprived of sustenance." The noted medical historian and cardiologist Kenneth Keele called Leonardo's analysis "the first description of arteriosclerosis as a function of time."[4]

DISSECTIONS

By Leonardo's day, the Church no longer completely prohibited dissections, although its attitude was murky and depended on local authorities. In Florence and Milan, though not in Rome, the practice had become common as Renaissance science progressed. The Florentine physician Antonio Benivieni, born nine years before Leonardo, was a pioneer of autopsies, performing more than 150 of them. Leonardo, who was not strongly religious, pushed back on the fundamentalists who considered dissection heretical. He believed it was a way to appreciate God's handiwork. "You should not be distressed that your discoveries come through another's death; rather you should rejoice that our Creator has provided an instrument of such excellence," he wrote on a tinted blue notebook page on which he drew the muscles and bones of the neck.[5]

Traditional anatomy instructors would stand at a lectern and read aloud from their texts while an assistant dissected a corpse and held up its components for students to view. Leonardo insisted that his drawings were even better than watching a live dissection: "You who say it is better to watch an anatomist at work than to see these drawings would be right, if it were possible to see all those things which are shown in these drawings." The reason it was possible to see more in the drawings, he said, was because they had been based on multiple dissections and also showed views from multiple angles. "I have dissected more than ten human bodies," he wrote, and after making that statement he would dissect even more, working on each as long as possible, until they decomposed so badly he was forced to move on. "As one body did not last so long, it was necessary to proceed by stages with as many bodies as would render my knowledge complete." He then performed even more dissections so that he could ascertain the variances between humans.[6]

When Leonardo began this second round of anatomy studies in 1508, he made a to-do list that surely must rank as one of the quirkiest and most enchanting such lists in the history of intellectual inquiry.[7] On one side of the page are a few sketches of dissecting instruments and, on the other side, some small drawings of veins and nerves found in the brain of the centenarian, with writing crammed all around them. "Have Avicenna's book on useful inventions translated," he wrote, referring to a book by the eleventh-century Persian polymath. Having drawn various surgical tools, he jotted down some of the equipment he needed: "Spectacles with case, firestick, fork, curved knife, charcoal, boards, sheets of paper, white chalk, wax, forceps, pane of glass, fine-tooth bone saw, scalpel, inkhorn, pen-knife, and get hold of a skull."

Then comes my favorite item on any Leonardo list: "Describe the tongue of the woodpecker." This is not just a random entry. He mentioned the woodpecker's tongue again on a later page, where he described and drew the human tongue. "Make the motions of the woodpecker," he wrote. When I first saw his entry about the woodpecker, I regarded it, as most scholars have, as an entertaining oddity—an *amuse-bouche*, so to speak—evidence of the eccentric nature of Leonardo's relentless curiosity. That it indeed is. But there is more, as I discovered after pushing myself to be more like Leonardo and drill down into random curiosities. Leonardo, I realized, had become fascinated by the muscles of the tongue. All of the other muscles he studied acted by pulling rather than pushing a body part, but the tongue seemed to be an exception. This was true in humans and in other animals. The most notable example is the tongue of the woodpecker. Nobody had drawn or fully written about it before, but Leonardo with his acute ability to observe objects in motion knew that there was something to be learned from it.[8]

On the same list, Leonardo instructed himself to describe "the jaw of the crocodile." Once again, if we follow his curiosity, rather than merely be amused by it, we can see that he was on to an important topic. A crocodile, unlike any mammal, has a second jaw joint, which spreads out the force when it snaps shut its mouth. That gives the crocodile the most forceful bite of any animal. It can exert 3,700 pounds per square inch of force, which is more than thirty times that of a human bite.

Leonardo engaged in dissections before proper fixatives and preservatives had been invented, so alongside his to-do list he issued a warning directed at those who would undertake such a task. It doubles as a subtle boast about the talents—a strong stomach, good drawing skills, knowledge of perspective, an understanding of the math underlying mechanics, along with an obsessive curiosity—that he uniquely brought to his work as an anatomist:

> You will perhaps be deterred by your stomach; and if this does not deter you, you may be deterred by the fear of living through the night hours in the company of quartered and flayed corpses, fearful to behold. And if this does not deter you, perhaps you will lack the good draftsmanship that such a depiction requires; and even if you have skill in drawing, it may not be accompanied by a knowledge of perspective; and if it were so accompanied, you may lack the methods of geometrical demonstration and of calculating the forces and strengths of the muscles; or perhaps you will lack patience so that you will not be diligent.[9]

There is an echo in this passage of Leonardo's memory of coming across the mouth of a cave as a young man. As in that tale, he had to overcome his fear to go into a dark and fearful space. Although at times he was irresolute and willing to abandon tasks, his powerful curiosity tended to overcome any hesitations when it came to exploring nature's wonders.

Leonardo's anatomy studies were another example of the influence of the printing press, which was spawning publishing houses throughout Italy. By then Leonardo owned 116 books, including Johannes de Ketham's *Fasciculus Medicinae*, published in Venice in 1498; Bartolomeo Montagnana's *Tractatus de Urinarum*, published in Padua in 1487; and *Anatomice*, by Leonardo's contemporary Alessandro Benedetti, printed in Venice in 1502. He had an edition of the standard dissection guide by the Bologna physician Mondino de Luzzi, which had been written in about 1316 and was printed in Italian in 1493. He used Mondino's book as a manual for his early dissections, and he even replicated one of Mondino's mistakes in identifying some of the muscles of the abdomen.[10]

But, true to form, Leonardo preferred learning from experiment rather than from established authority. His most important hands-on inquiries came during the winter of 1510–11, when he collaborated with Marcantonio della Torre, a twenty-nine-year-old anatomy professor at the University of Pavia. "Each helped and was helped by the other," Vasari wrote of their relationship. The young professor provided the human cadavers—probably twenty of them were dissected that winter—and lectured while his students did the actual cutting and Leonardo made notes and drawings.[11]

During this period of intense anatomical study, Leonardo made 240 drawings and wrote at least thirteen thousand words of text, illustrating and describing every bone, muscle group, and major organ in the human body for what would have been, if it had been published, his most historic scientific triumph. On an elegant drawing showing a man's muscular calf and the tendons of his foot, modeled and shaded with his signature curved cross-hatchings, Leonardo wrote, "This winter of 1510 I believe I will finish all this anatomy."[12]

It was not to be. Marcantonio died in 1511 of the plague that was devastating Italy that year. It is enticing to imagine what he and Leonardo could have accomplished. One of the things that could have most benefited Leonardo in his career was a partner who would help him follow through and publish his brilliant work. Together he and Marcantonio could have produced a groundbreaking illustrated treatise on anatomy that would have transformed a field still dominated by scholars who mainly regurgitated the notions of the second-century Greek physician Galen. Instead, Leonardo's anatomy studies became another example of how he was disadvantaged by having few rigorous and disciplined collaborators along the lines of Luca Pacioli, whose text on geometric proportions Leonardo had illustrated. With Marcantonio dead, Leonardo retreated to the country villa of Francesco Melzi's family to ride out the plague.

ANALOGIES

In most of his studies of nature, Leonardo theorized by making analogies. His quest for knowledge across all the disciplines of arts and sciences helped him see patterns. Occasionally this mode of thinking misled him, and it sometimes substituted for reaching more profound scientific theories. But this cross-disciplinary thinking and pattern-seeking was his hallmark as the quintessential Renaissance Man, and it made him a pioneer of scientific humanism.

For example, when he looked at the veins and arteries he was dissecting, he compared their flow and branching to that of the human digestive, urinary, and respiratory systems. He made analogies with the flows of rivers, the movements of air, and the branching of plants. On one of his detailed depictions of the human blood circulation system, based on his dissection of the centenarian in 1508, he made a large drawing of the great vessels of the heart, with the aorta and vena cava connecting to increasingly smaller offshoots of veins and arteries and capillaries (fig. 103). Then he moved to his left to make a smaller drawing of a seed, which he labeled "nut," with its roots stretching into the ground and its branches stretching upward. "The heart is the nut which generates the tree of the veins," he wrote on the page.[13]

Another analogy Leonardo made was between the human body and machines. He compared the movement of muscles and the body to the mechanical rules he had learned from his engineering stud-

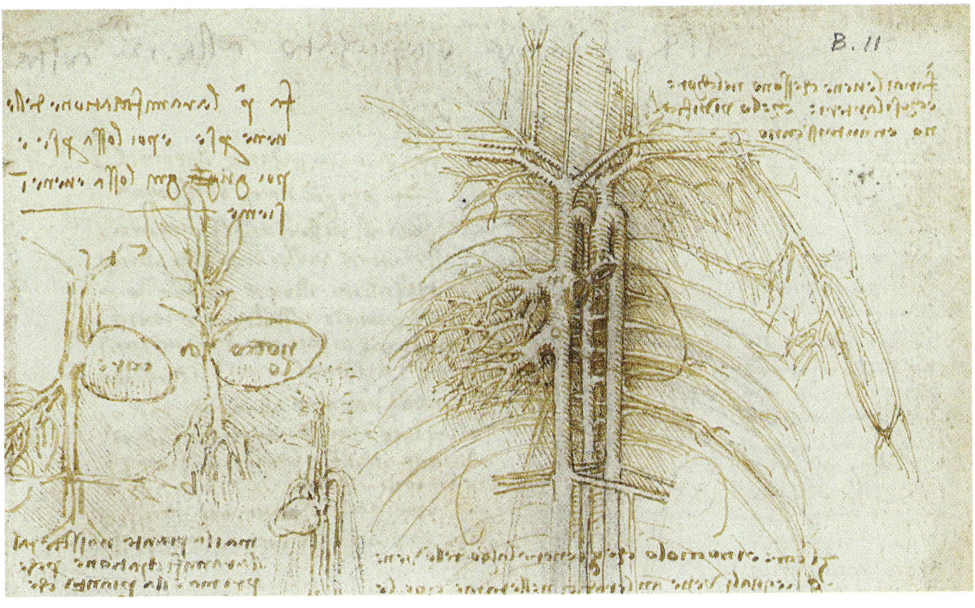

Fig. 103. The heart and arteries juxtaposed with a sprouting seed.

ies. As he had done with machines, he illustrated body parts using exploded views, multiple angles, and stacked-up layers (fig. 104). He studied the movements of various muscles and bones, as if they operated like strings and levers, and layered the muscles on top of the bones to show the mechanics of each joint. "Muscles always arise and end in bones adjoining one another," he explained. "They never arise and end on one and the same bone because nothing would be able to move." It all added up to an ingenious mechanism of moving parts: "The joints between bones obey the tendon, and the tendon obeys the muscle, and the muscle the nerve."[14]

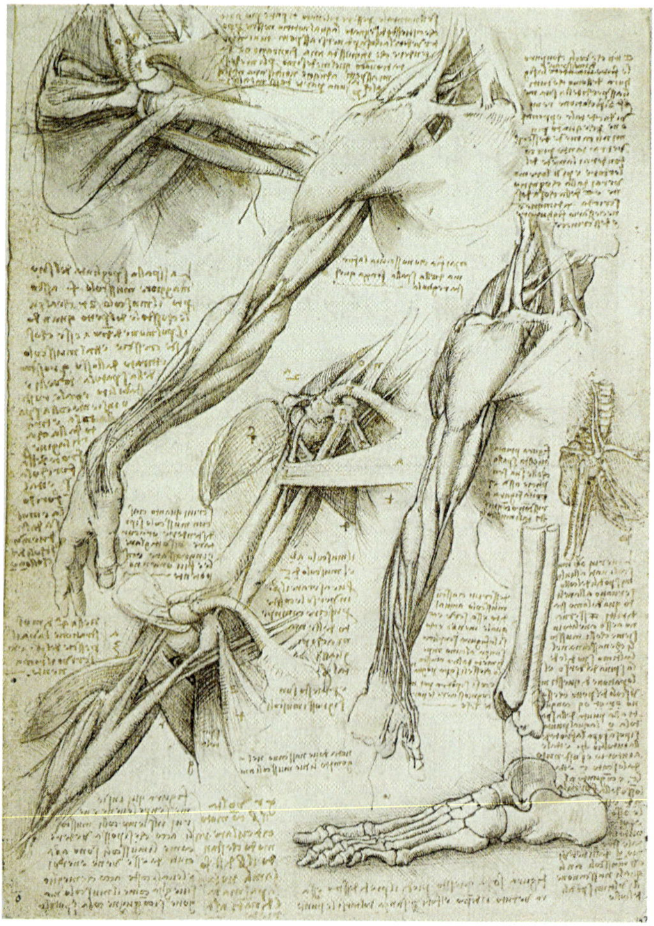

Fig. 104. Multiple layers of bone and muscle.

His comparisons between man-made machinery and the handiwork of nature produced in him a deep reverence for the latter. "Though human ingenuity may make various inventions," he wrote, "it will never devise an invention more beautiful, more simple, more direct than does Nature; because in her inventions nothing is lacking and nothing is superfluous."[15]

Just as Leonardo's anatomy informed his art, so was the reverse true: his artistic, sculpting, drawing, and engineering skills crossed disciplines and aided his anatomical studies. In a groundbreaking experiment, he used sculpture and casting techniques to map the hollow cavities, known as cerebral ventricles, in the human brain (fig. 105). From his studies of ways to cast the great horse monument in Milan, Leonardo knew how to inject molten wax into the brain and provide ventilation holes for the air and fluids in the cavities to escape. "Make two vent-holes in the horns of the greater ventricles, and insert

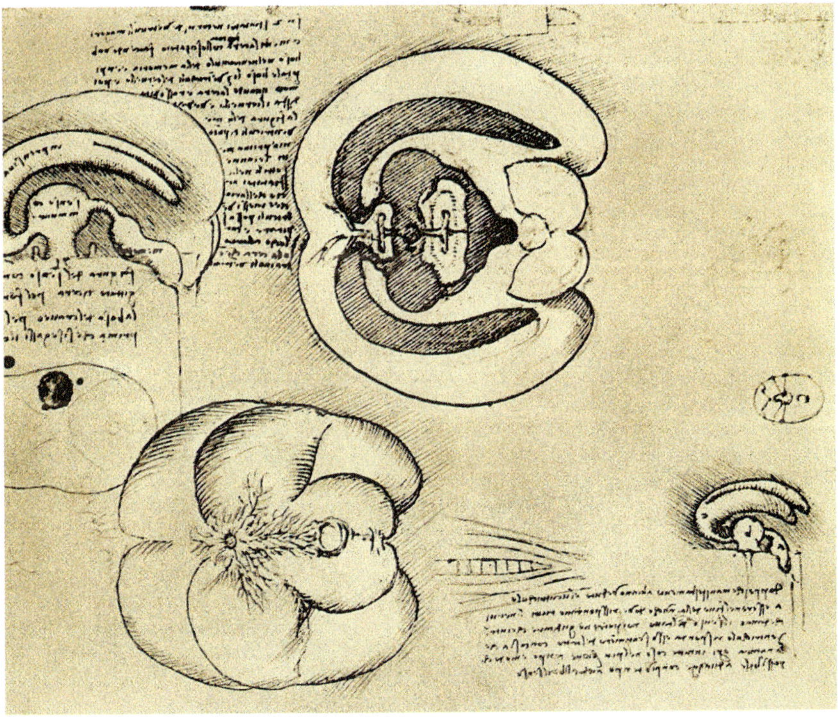

Fig. 105. Method for making a wax cast of the brain.

melted wax with a syringe, making a hole in the ventricle of memory; and through such a hole fill the three ventricles of the brain. Then when the wax has set, take apart the brain, and you will see the shape of the ventricles exactly." A small sketch on the bottom-right of the page illustrates the technique.[16]

Leonardo did the experiment using the brain of a cow, since it was easier to get than a human brain. But from his readings and earlier human dissections, he knew how to modify his findings and apply them to a human brain, which he did with impressive accuracy on

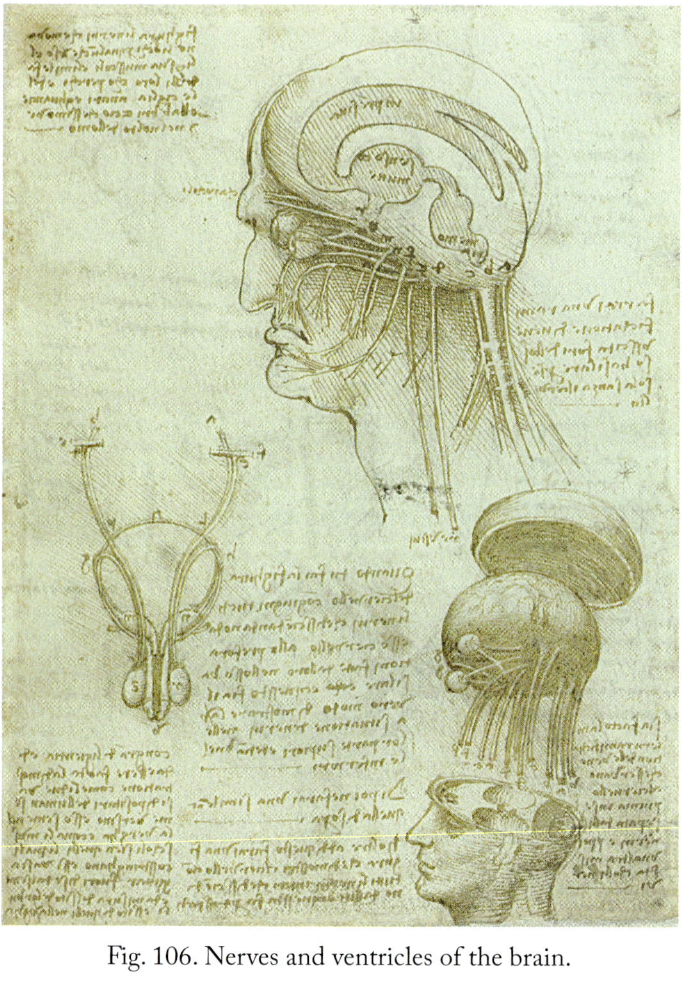

Fig. 106. Nerves and ventricles of the brain.

a set of drawings that display it in an exploded view (fig. 106).[17] His only mistakes were that the middle ventricle is slightly enlarged because of the pressure of the wax, and the ends of the lateral ventricles were not completely filled by the wax. Otherwise, the results were extraordinary. Leonardo had for the first time in history injected a molding material into a human cavity. It was a technique that would not be replicated until the studies by the Dutch anatomist Frederik Ruysch more than two centuries later. Along with his discoveries about heart valves, it was Leonardo's most important anatomical breakthrough, and it happened because he was a sculptor as well as a scientist.

MUSCLES AND BONES

Leonardo's methods as well as his art are displayed on a page on which he depicted the muscles of the shoulder (fig. 107). "Before you form the muscles," he wrote, "make in their place threads that should demonstrate their positions." He did just that in the schematic sketch of threads in the shoulder on the top right of the page (which is the first drawing he made on the page since in his left-handed fashion he starts on the right). Directly to the left and below his sketch of threads we can see the centenarian in two different poses, his skin peeled off to show the muscles of his right shoulder. Leonardo then moved to the top left of the page, where he correctly drew and labeled with letters the pectoralis major, latissimus dorsi, rhomboid, and other muscles.[18]

Leonardo began his studies of human muscles, as with most of his scientific work, to serve his art, but he was soon pursuing them out of pure curiosity. In the former category is a drawing he made that shows the muscles of a right arm in four different views. Understanding how they change shape as they move, he wrote, "will be an advantage for artists who have to exaggerate the muscles that cause the movements of limbs more than the ones that are not employed in such movement."[19] Another anatomy drawing that appears to be related to his *Battle of Anghiari* cartoon is a forceful-looking frontal

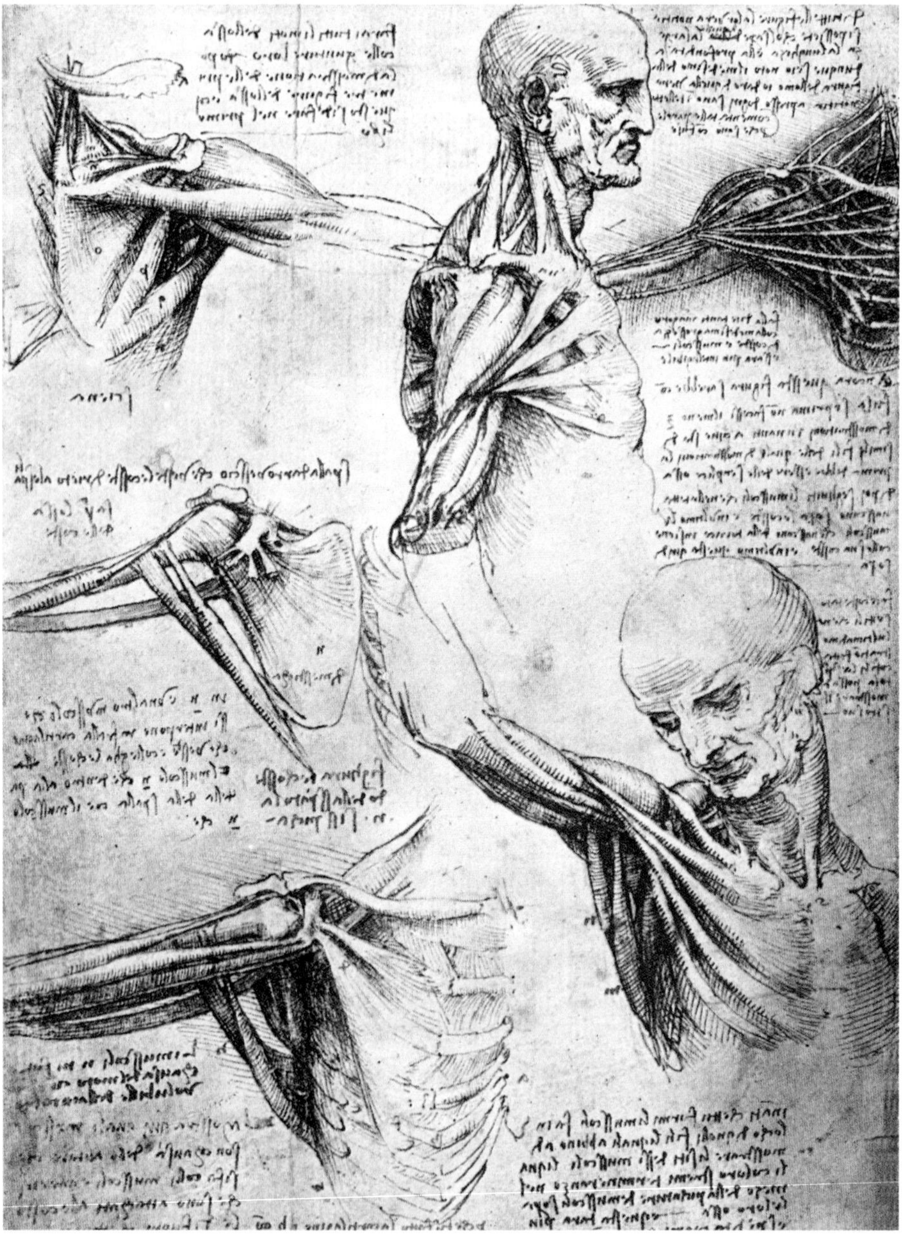

Fig. 107. Muscles of the shoulder.

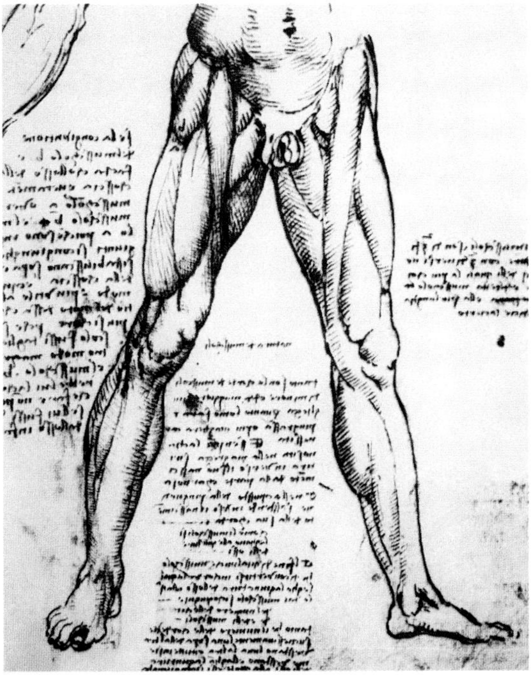

Fig. 108. Muscles of the leg.

view of a man's leg muscles, artistically modeled and shaded with fine cross-hatch strokes (fig. 108). In a note titled "Nature of Muscles," he described the way body fat is distributed in muscular men: "A man will be fatter or leaner in proportion to the greater or lesser lengths of the tendons of muscles."[20]

By the time Leonardo got around to studying and drawing the human spine, he had been captivated by curiosity and the joy of research rather than merely the pursuit of practical painting knowledge. His page showing the spine accurately rendered and notated from a variety of angles is a masterpiece of both anatomy and draftsmanship (fig. 109). Through the use of light and shadows, he was able to make each of the vertebrae seem three-dimensional, and he conveyed a sense of twisting motion in the curved spine at the top middle of the page. Complexity is magically transformed into an elegance that is unrivaled by any anatomical drawings of his time—or ours.

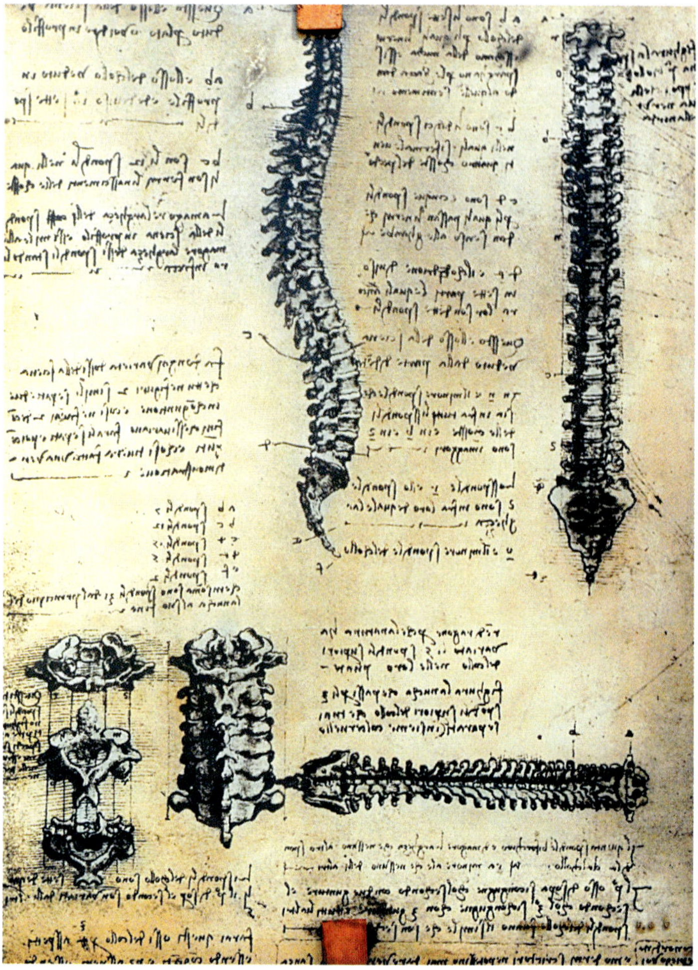

Fig. 109. The spine, with exploded view.

His precise renderings of the five sets of vertebrae are marked with letters, listed in a table, and explained in his notes. This led him to ask questions about details that most people would not have noticed. "Explain why nature has varied the five superior vertebrae of the neck at their extremities," he instructed himself.

The last drawing he made on this sheet, at the bottom left of the page, is one of his exploded views, of the kind he made of machines, showing the first three cervical vertebrae, with their interlocking mechanisms rendered masterfully. It was important, he said, to depict the spine "separate and then joined together," with views from the front, back, side, above, and below. At the bottom of the page, when he had finished, he could not refrain from a bit of boasting about his method, which he declared would produce "knowledge that neither ancient writers nor the moderns would ever have been able to give without an immense, tiresome, and confused amount of writing and time."[21]

LIPS AND SMILE

Leonardo was especially interested in how the human brain and nervous system translate emotions into movements of the body. On one drawing, he showed the spinal cord sawed in half and he delineated all the nerves that ran down to it from the brain. "The spinal cord is the source of the nerves that gives voluntary movement to the limbs," he explained.[22]

Of all these nerves and related muscles, the ones controlling the lips were the most important to Leonardo. Dissecting them was exceedingly difficult, because lip muscles are small and plentiful and originate deep in the skin. "The muscles which move the lips are more numerous in man than in any other animal," he wrote. "One will always find as many muscles as there are positions of the lips and many more that serve to undo these positions." Despite these difficulties, he depicted the facial muscles and nerves with remarkable accuracy.

On one delightfully crammed anatomical sheet (fig. 110), Leonardo drew the muscles of two dissected arms and hands, and he placed between them two partially dissected faces in profile. The faces show the muscles and nerves that control the lips and other elements of expression. In the one on the left, Leonardo has removed part of the jawbone to expose the buccinator muscle, which pulls back the angle of the mouth and flattens the cheek as a smile begins to form. Here we can see, exposed with scalpel cuts and then pen strokes, the actual mechanisms that transmit emotions into facial expressions. He wrote next to one of the faces, "Represent all the causes of motion possessed by the skin, flesh and muscles of the face and see if these

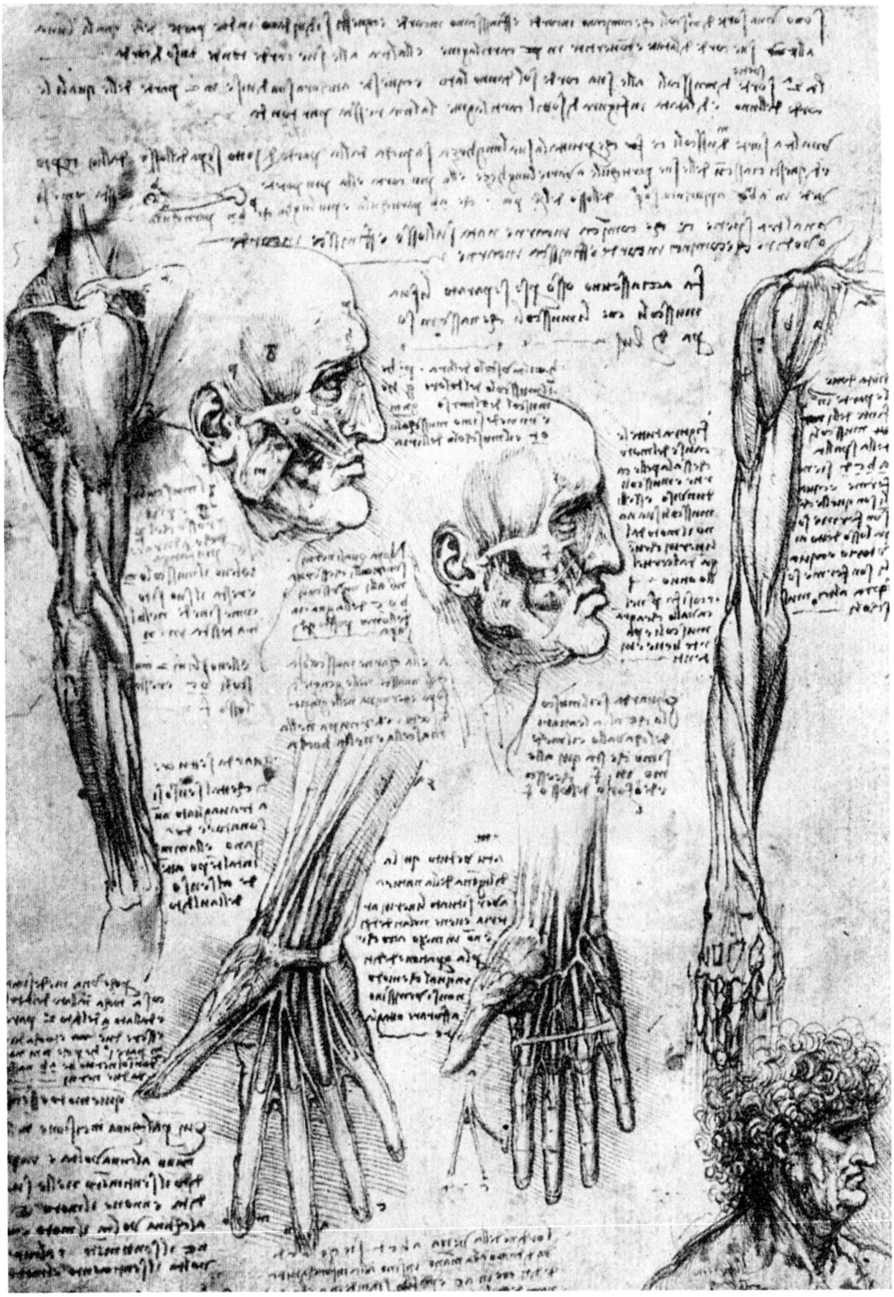

Fig. 110. Dissections of arms and face.

muscles receive their motion from nerves which come from the brain or not."

He labeled one of the muscles in the left-hand drawing "H" and called it "the muscle of anger." Another is labeled "P" and designated as the muscle of sadness or pain. He showed how these muscles not only move the lips but also serve to move the eyebrows downward and together, causing wrinkles.

On this page of dissected faces and lips, we can also see Leonardo pursuing the comparative anatomy he needed for his *Battle of Anghiari* drawings, in which the anger on the faces of the humans is matched by that on the faces of the horses. After his note about representing the causes of motion of the human face, he added, "And do this first for the horse that has large muscles. Notice whether the muscle that raises the nostrils of the horse is the same as that which lies here in man."[23] So here is another secret to Leonardo's unique ability to paint a facial expression: he is probably the only artist in history ever to dissect with his own hands the face of a human and that of a horse to see if the muscles that move human lips are the same ones that can raise the nostrils of the nose.

Finally, as he got to the bottom of the crammed page, Leonardo's mind began to wander, to our delight. He paused to draw his favorite doodle: that of a curly haired man with nutcracker nose and chin. This one seems to hover between being a portrait of a younger version of himself and an older version of Salai. The man's lips are set in a way that displays resolve but also a touch of melancholy.

After his excursion into comparative anatomy, Leonardo proceeded to delve deeper into the mechanisms of humans as they smile or grimace (fig. 111). He focused on the role of various nerves in sending signals to the muscles, and he asked a question that was central to his art: Which of these are cranial nerves originating in the brain, and which are spinal nerves?

His notes begin as if he were focused on a battle scene filled with angry expressions: "Make the nostrils drawn up, causing furrows in the side of the nose, and the lips arched to disclose the upper teeth, with the teeth parted in order to shriek lamentations." But he then

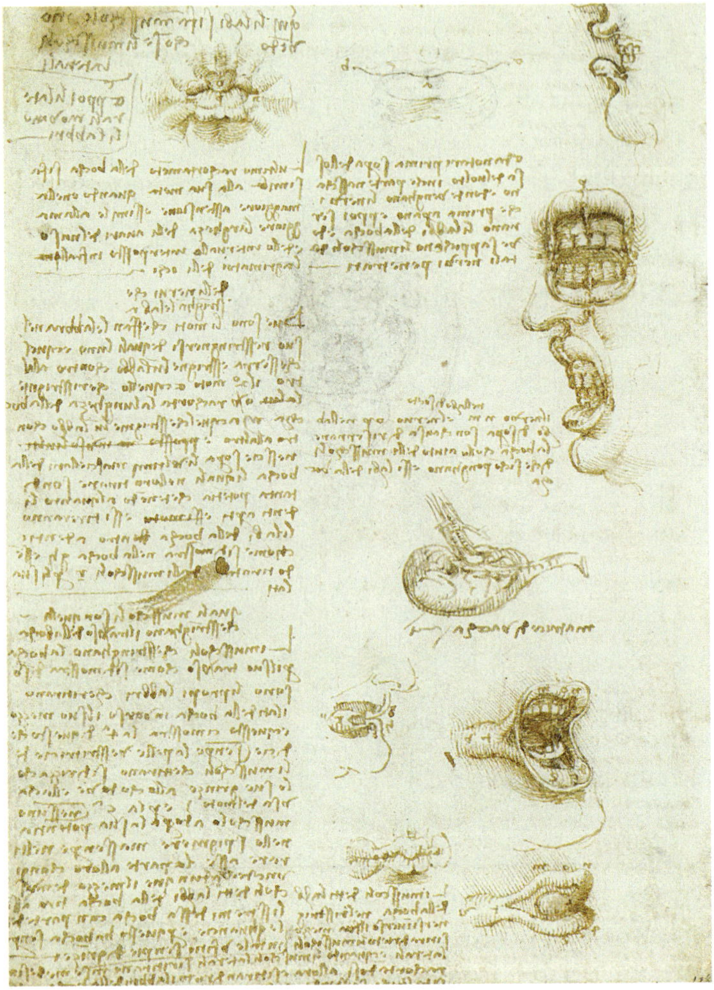

Fig. 111. Nerves and muscles of the mouth.

began to explore other expressions. On the top left are lips tightly pursed, underneath which he wrote, "The maximum shortening of the mouth is equal to half its maximum extension, and it is equal to the greatest width of the nostrils of the nose and to the interval between the ducts of the eye." He tested on himself and on the cadaver how each muscle of the cheek could move the lips, and how the muscle of the lips can also pull the lateral muscles of the wall of the cheek. "The muscle shortening the lips is the same muscle forming the lower lip itself. Other muscles are those which bring the lips to a point, others which spread them, others which curl them back, others which straighten them out, others which twist them transversely, and others which return them to their first position." On the top right of the page are front and profile drawings of retracted lips with the skin still on; at the bottom of the page, he made the drawings after removing the facial skin, showing the muscles that pull the lips. These are the first known examples of the scientific anatomy of the human smile.[24]

Floating above the grotesque grimaces on the top of the page is a faint sketch of a simple set of lips drawn in a way that is artistic rather than anatomical. The lips peek out of the page directly at us with just a hint—flickering and haunting and alluring—of a mysterious smile. At the time, Leonardo was working on the *Mona Lisa*.

THE HEART

On one of Leonardo's pages of drawings of the human heart (fig. 112), done in ink on blue paper, is a reminder of the humanity, and even humanness, that suffuse his anatomical studies.[25] At the top is a drawing of the heart's papillary muscle and a description of how it shortens and elongates when the heart beats. Then, as if he were being too clinical, he let his mind wander and pen begin to doodle. And there, in loving profile, is a drawing of Salai, his beautiful curls flowing down his long neck, his signature receding chin and fleshy throat softly modeled with Leonardo's left-handed hatching. In his chest is a section of a heart, with its muscles sketched in. An analysis of the drawing shows that the heart was sketched first. It seems as if Leonardo drew it, then sketched Salai around it.

Leonardo's studies of the human heart, conducted as part of his overall anatomical and dissection work, were the most sustained and successful of his scientific endeavors.[26] Informed by his love of hydraulic engineering and his fascination with the flow of liquids, he made discoveries that were not fully appreciated for centuries.

In the early 1500s the European understanding of the heart was

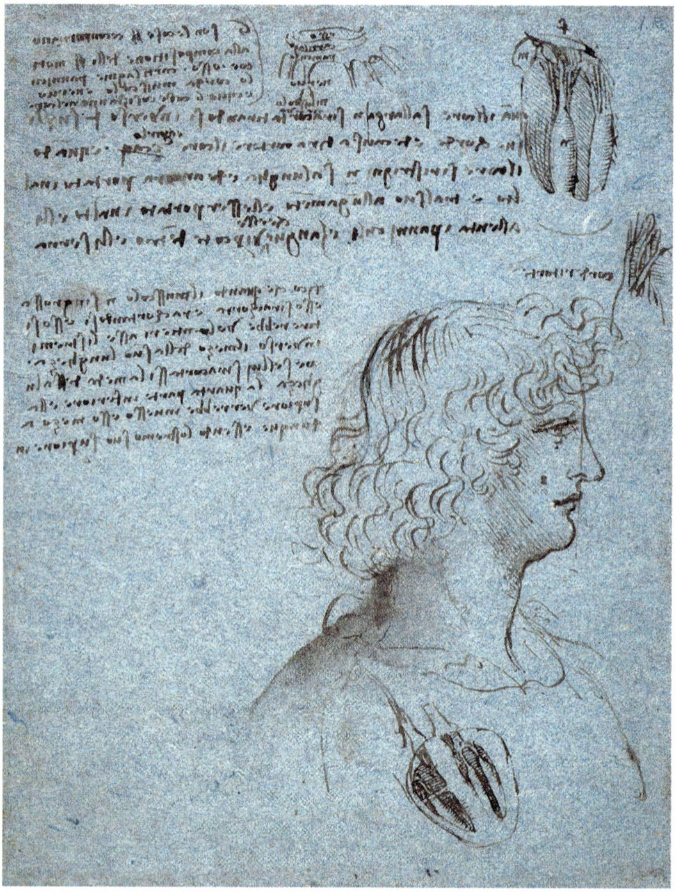

Fig. 112. The heart with Salai.

not all that different from that described in the second century AD by Galen, whose work was revived during the Renaissance. Galen believed that the heart was not merely a muscle but was made of a special substance that gave it a vital force. Blood was made in the liver, he taught, and distributed through the veins. Vital spirits were produced by the heart and distributed through arteries, which Galen and his successors considered a separate system. Neither the blood nor vital spirits circulated, he thought; instead, they pulsed back and forth in the veins and arteries.

Leonardo was among the first to fully appreciate that the heart, not the liver, was the center of the blood system. "All the veins and arteries arise from the heart," he wrote on the page that includes the drawings comparing the branches and roots of a seed with the veins and arteries emanating from the heart. He proved this by showing, in both words and a detailed drawing, "that the largest veins and arteries are found where they join with the heart, and the further they are removed from the heart, the finer they become, dividing into very small branches." He became the first to analyze how the size of the branches diminish with each split, and he traced them down to tiny capillaries that were almost invisible. To those who would respond that the veins are rooted in the liver the way a plant is rooted in the soil, he pointed out that a plant's roots and branches emanate from a central seed, which is analogous to the heart.[27]

Leonardo was also able to show, contrary to Galen, that the heart is simply a muscle rather than some form of special vital tissue. Like all muscles, the heart has its own blood supply and nerves. "It is nourished by an artery and veins, as are other muscles," he found.[28]

He also corrected the Galenic belief that the heart has only two ventricles. His dissections showed that there are two upper and two lower ventricles. These must have distinct functions, he argued, because they were separated by valves and membranes. "If they were one and the same, there would be no need for the valves that separate them." In order to figure out how the ventricles work, Leonardo opened up a pig whose heart was still beating. The upper and lower ventricles open at different times, he discovered. "The upper ventricles of the heart are different in their functions and nature from those below, and they are separated by gristle and various substances."[29]

Leonardo did accept Galen's incorrect theory that blood is warm because it is heated by the heart, and he wrestled with many theories of how this happened. He finally settled on the supposition that the heat is generated by the friction of the moving heart and the blood rubbing against the heart walls. "The whirling round of the blood in different eddies, and the friction it makes with the walls, and the percussions in the recesses, are the cause of the heating of the blood," he concluded. In order to test his theory by analogy, as he often did, he considered whether milk became heated when it was churned. "Observe whether the revolution of milk when butter is made heats it" he put on his to-do list.[30]

THE AORTIC VALVE

Leonardo's greatest achievement in his heart studies, and indeed in all of his anatomical work, was his discovery of the way the aortic valve works, a triumph that was confirmed only in modern times. It was birthed by his understanding, indeed love, of spiral flows. For his entire career, Leonardo was fascinated by the swirls of water eddies, wind currents, and hair curls cascading down a neck. He applied this knowledge to determining how the spiral flow of blood through a part of the aorta known as the sinus of Valsalva creates eddies and swirls that serve to close the valve of a beating heart. His analysis filled six pages, crammed with twenty drawings and hundreds of words of notations.[31]

On top of one of the first of these pages he wrote a dictum, derived from the maxim Plato inscribed over the door of his Academy: "Let no one who is not a mathematician read my work."[32] This did not mean that his study of the heart's blood flow would involve rigorous equations; his study of the math describing swirls and curls had not gone beyond a bit of dabbling with the Fibonacci sequence of numbers. Instead, the injunction was an expression of his belief that nature's actions obey physical laws and math-like certainties.

His discoveries about the heart valve derived from the intense inquiries into fluid dynamics he was doing around 1510, including an analysis of how water flowing from pipes into a tank creates eddies. One phenomenon that interested him was fluid drag. When a current flows through a pipe or a channel or a river, he discovered, the water that is closest to the sides flows slower than the water in the middle. This is because the water on the sides rubs up against the wall of the pipe or the banks of the river, and the friction slows it down. The layer of water right next to this will also slow down a little bit; the water flowing at the center of the pipe or river will be slowed the least. When the water flows out of the pipe into a tank, or out of the river into a pool, the difference in speed between the fast central flow and the slower side flow causes whirlpools and eddies. "Of the water that pours out of a horizontal pipe, the part that originates nearer the center of the mouth will go further away from the mouth of the pipe," he wrote. He also described how vortexes and eddies are formed by fluids that flow past curved surfaces or in a channel that gets wider. He applied this to his study of the erosion of riverbanks, his depiction in his art of flowing water, and his inquiries into how blood is pumped out of the heart.[33]

Specifically, Leonardo focused on the blood that was pumped upward from the heart through a triangle-shaped opening into the root of the aorta, which is the large vessel that carries blood from the heart to the body. "The middle of the blood that spouts up through the triangle acquires much more height than that which rises up along the sides," he declared. He went on to describe how that causes it to form spiraling eddies as it pours into the blood that is already in the widened sections of the aorta. These sections are now known as the sinuses of Valsalva, after the Italian anatomist Antonio Valsalva, who wrote about them in the early 1700s. By right they should be called the sinuses of Leonardo, and they probably would have been if Leonardo had published the discoveries he had made about them two centuries before Valsalva.[34]

This swirling action of the blood after it is pumped into the aorta causes the leaflets of the triangular valves between the heart and the aorta to spread out and then cover the opening. "The revolving blood beats against the sides of the three valves and closes them so that the blood cannot descend." It was like wind swirls spreading out the corners of a triangular sail, an analogy Leonardo employed in explaining his discovery. On a drawing that shows how the eddies of blood pull open the cusps of the valve, he wrote, "Give names to the cords that open and shut the two sails."

The common view, which was held by most heart specialists until the 1960s, was that the valve is pushed shut from above once enough blood has rushed into the aorta and begun to back up. Most other kinds of valve work that way, swinging shut when the flow begins to reverse. For more than four centuries, heart researchers paid little attention to Leonardo's argument that the valve would not be properly closed by pressure from above: "The blood which turns back when the heart reopens is not that which closes the valves of the heart. This would be impossible, because if the blood beats against the valves of the heart while they are wrinkled and folded, the blood that presses from above would press down and crumple the membrane." On the top of the last of the six pages, he sketched how the crumpled valve would scrunch up if a backflow of blood pressured it from above (fig. 113).[35]

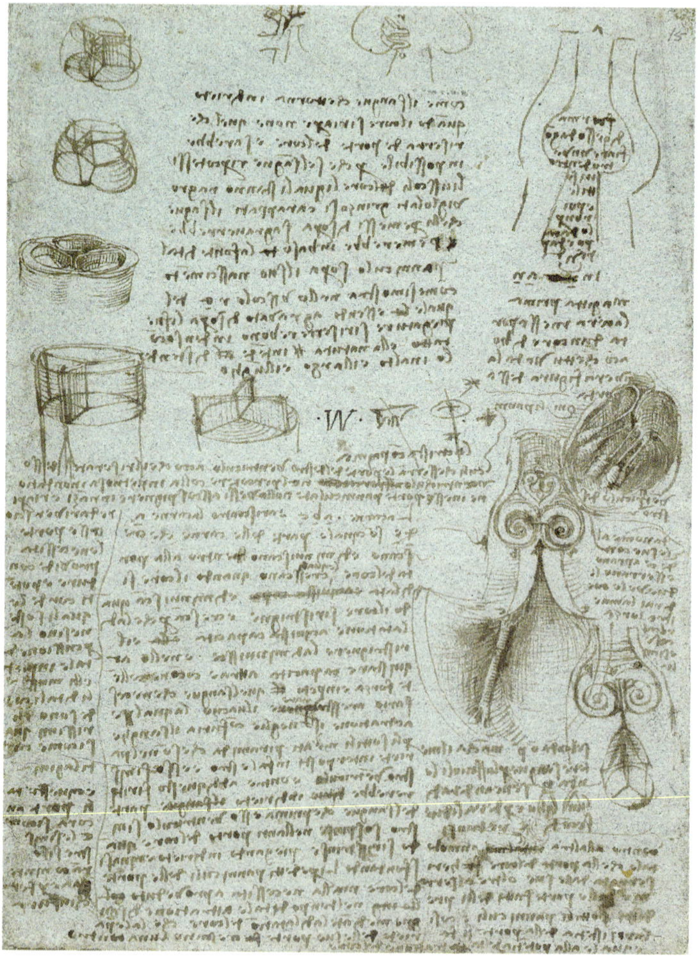

Fig. 113. The aortic valve.

Leonardo had developed his hypothesis through analogy: using what he knew about eddies of water and air, he surmised how the blood would spiral into the aorta. But then he devised an ingenious way to test his idea. On the top of this crammed notebook page, he described and drew a way to make a glass model of the heart. When filled with water, it would allow him to observe the way blood would swirl as it passed into the aorta. He used a bull's heart as a model, filling it with wax using the sculptor's technique he had used in creating a model of the brain. When the wax hardened, he made a mold to build a glass model of the heart chamber, valve, and aorta. By sprinkling in grass seeds, he made the flow of water more visible. "Make this test in the glass and put water and panic-grass seed inside it," he directed.[36]

It took 450 years for anatomists to realize that Leonardo was correct. In the 1960s a team of medical researchers led by Brian Bellhouse at Oxford used dyes and radiography methods to observe blood flows. As Leonardo had done, they used a transparent model of the aorta filled with water to observe the swirls and flow. The experiments showed that the valve required "a fluid dynamic control mechanism which positions the cusps away from the wall of the aorta, so that the slightest reversed flow will close the valve." That mechanism, they realized, was the vortex or swirling flow of blood that Leonardo had discovered in the aorta root. "The vortices produce a thrust on both the cusp and the sinus wall, and the closure of the cusps is thus steady and synchronized," they wrote. "Leonardo da Vinci correctly predicted the formation of vortices between the cusp and its sinus and appreciated that these would help close the valve." The surgeon Sherwin Nuland declared, "Of all the amazements that Leonardo left for the ages, this one would seem to be the most extraordinary."

In 1991 Francis Robicsek of the Carolina Heart Institute showed how closely the Bellhouse experiments resembled the ones that Leonardo described in his notebooks. And in 2014 another Oxford team was able to study blood flow in a living human to prove conclusively that Leonardo was right. To do so they used magnetic resonance techniques to view in real time the complex blood flow patterns in the aortic root of a living person. "We confirm in a human *in vivo* that Leonardo's prediction of systolic flow vortices was accurate and that he provided a strikingly precise depiction of these vortices in proportion to the aortic root," they concluded.[37]

Leonardo's breakthroughs on heart valves were followed, however, by a failure: not discovering that the blood in the body circulates. His understanding of one-way valves should have made him realize the flaw in the Galenic theory, universally accepted during his time, that the blood is pulsed back and forth by the heart, moving to-and-fro. But Leonardo, somewhat unusually, was blinded by book learning. The "unlettered" man who disdained those who relied on received wisdom and vowed to make experiment his mistress failed to do so in this case. His genius and creativity had always come from proceeding without preconceptions. His study of blood flow, however, was one of the rare cases where he had acquired enough textbooks and expert tutors that he failed to think differently. A full explanation of blood circulation in the human body would have to wait for William Harvey a century later.

THE FETUS

Leonardo's anatomical studies culminated with his depiction of the beginning of life. On a cluttered notebook page (fig. 114), he carefully rendered in ink over subtle red chalk his iconic image of a fetus in the womb.[38] The drawing rivals *Vitruvian Man* as an emblem of Leonardo's combination of art and science. It is good as an anatomical study, but purely divine, almost literally so, as a work of art. Drawn with meticulous curved hatchings that are designed to dazzle our eyes as much as inform our minds, it captures the human condition with a spiritual beauty that is at once unnerving and ennobling. We can see ourselves embodied in the wonder of creation: innocent, miraculous, mysterious. Though the drawing is usually parsed and analyzed as a work of anatomy, the *Guardian* art critic Jonathan Jones got closer to its essence when he wrote, "It is for me the most beautiful work of art in the world."[39]

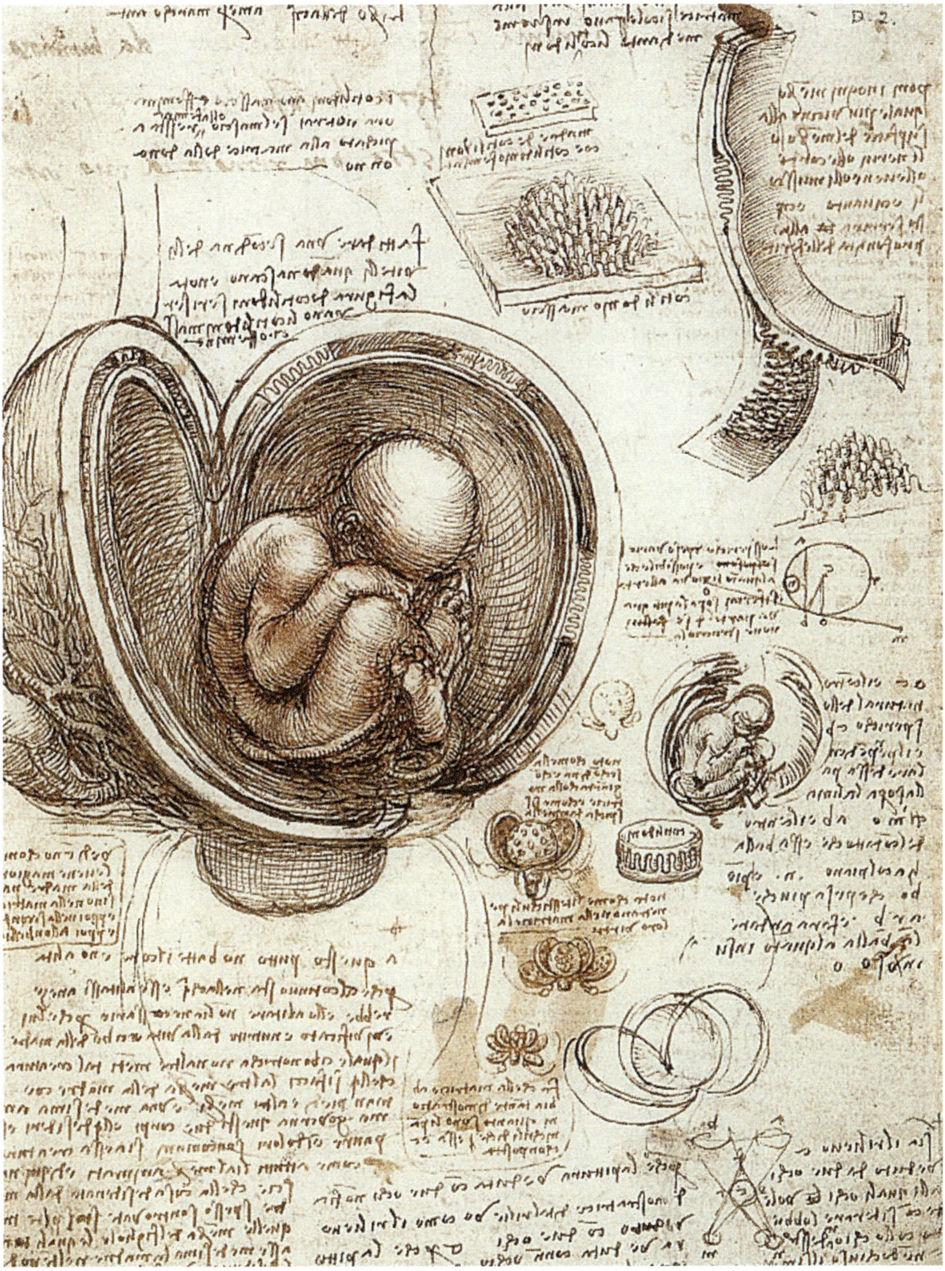

Fig. 114. Fetus in the womb.

Leonardo did not have a female cadaver to dissect, so some of the elements are drawn from a cow dissection. The womb is therefore spherical, unlike in a human. But he did improve on the conventional wisdom of his era. He correctly drew the uterus with one chamber, in contrast to contemporary belief that it had multiple chambers. His depictions of the uterine artery, vascular system of the vagina, and blood vessels in the umbilical cord are also groundbreaking.

As usual, Leonardo saw patterns across disciplines and used analogies as a method of inquiry. At the time of his fetus drawing, he had reengaged in his study of plants. Just as he had made an analogy between the branching of plants and rivers and blood vessels, so he noticed the similarities between the way plant seeds and human embryos develop. Plants have a stalk, known as a funiculus, that connects the seed to the wall of its ovule until the seed becomes ripe, and Leonardo realized that it served the same purpose as an umbilical cord. "All seeds have an umbilical cord, which is broken when the seed is ripe," he wrote on one of his anatomical drawings of a human fetus.[40]

Leonardo was aware that his fetus drawing had a spiritual quality that transcended his other anatomical studies. A few years later, he returned to the sketch to write a paragraph at the bottom of the page. It is more essay than dissection notes. He began scientifically by arguing that the embryo does not breathe in the womb because it is surrounded by fluids. "If it breathed it would drown," he explained, "and breathing is not necessary because it is nourished by the life and food of the mother." Then he added some thoughts that the Church, which believed that individual human life begins at conception, would have considered heretical. The embryo is still as much a part of the mother as her hands and feet are. "One and the same soul governs these two bodies," he added, "and one and the same soul nourishes both."

Leonardo's rejection of Church teachings on the soul was done without drama or angst. He was naturally comfortable with scientific humanism and tended to look at facts. He believed in the glorious and awe-inspiring nature of creation, but for him these were things to be studied and appreciated through science and art, not through the dogmas handed down by the Church.

LOST IMPACT

Leonardo dedicated himself to his anatomy studies with a persistence and diligence that were often lacking in his other endeavors. During his frenzied years of work from 1508 to 1513, he seemed never to tire of it and kept digging deeper, even though it meant nights spent amid cadavers and the stench of decaying organs.

He was mainly motivated by his own curiosity. He may have considered, as well, that he was making a contribution to public knowledge, but here it gets murky. He wrote that he intended his findings to be published, but when it came to editing and organizing his notes he was once again dilatory rather than diligent. He was more interested in pursuing knowledge than in publishing it. And even though he was collegial in his life and work, he made little effort to share his findings.

This is true for all of his studies, not just his work on anatomy. The trove of treatises that he left unpublished testifies to the unusual nature of what motivated him. He wanted to accumulate knowledge for its own sake, and for his own personal joy, rather than out of a desire to make a public name for himself as a scholar or to be part of the progress of history. Some have even said that he wrote in mirror script partly to guard his discoveries from prying eyes; I do not think that is true, but it is indisputable that his passion for gathering knowledge was not matched by one for sharing it widely. As the Leonardo scholar Charles Hope has pointed out, "He had no real understanding of the way in which the growth of knowledge was a cumulative and collaborative process."[41] Although he would occasionally let visitors glimpse his work, he did not seem to realize or care that the importance of research comes from its dissemination.

Years later, when he was living in France in 1517, a visitor reported that Leonardo had dissected more than thirty bodies and "written a treatise on anatomy, showing the limbs, muscles, nerves, veins, joints, intestines, and everything that can be explained in the body of men and women, in a way that has never been done by anyone before." He added that Leonardo had "also written on the nature of water, and has filled an infinite number of volumes with treatises on machines and other subjects, all written in the vulgar tongue, which, when published, will be of the greatest profit and delight."[42] But when he died, Leonardo would leave to Melzi only piles of unedited notebook pages and drawings.

Modern anatomy instead began twenty-five years after Leonardo's death, when Andreas Vesalius published his epochal and beautifully produced *On the Fabric of the Human Body*. That was the book that Leonardo—perhaps in conjunction with Marcantonio della Torre, had he not died young from the plague—could have preceded and surpassed. Instead, Leonardo's anatomical work had minimal influence. Over the years, and even centuries, his discoveries had to be rediscovered by others. The fact that he didn't publish served to diminish his impact on the history of science. But it did not diminish his genius.

CHAPTER 28

The World and Its Waters

THE MICROCOSM AND THE MACROCOSM

During the period when he was probing the human body, Leonardo was also studying the body of the earth. True to form, he made analogies between the two. He was skillful at discerning how patterns resonate in nature, and the grandest and most encompassing of these analogies, in both his art and his science, was the comparison between the body of man and the body of the earth. "Man is the image of the world," he wrote.[1]

Known as the microcosm-macrocosm relationship, it harkened back to the ancients. Leonardo first discussed this analogy in a notebook entry from the early 1490s:

> The ancients called man a lesser world, and certainly the use of this name is well bestowed, because his body is an analog for the world. As man has in him bones that support his flesh, the world has its rocks that support the earth. As man has a pool of blood in which the lungs rise and fall in breathing, so the body of the earth has its ocean tide which likewise rises and falls every six hours, as if the world breathed. As the blood veins originate in that pool

> and spread all over the human body, so likewise the ocean sea fills the body of the earth with infinite springs of water.[2]

This echoed what Plato had written in the *Timaeus*, where he argued that just as the body is nourished by blood, so the earth draws water to replenish itself. Leonardo also drew on theorists of the Middle Ages, in particular a compendium by the thirteenth-century Italian monk and geologist Restoro d'Arezzo.

As a painter who marveled at nature's patterns, Leonardo embraced the microcosm-macrocosm connection as more than merely an analogy. He viewed it as having a spiritual component, which he expressed in his drawing of *Vitruvian Man*. As we have seen, this mystical connection between humans and the earth is reflected in many of his masterpieces, from *Ginevra de' Benci* to *Saint Anne* to *Madonna of the Yarnwinder* and eventually the *Mona Lisa.* It also became an organizing principle for his scientific inquiries. When he was immersed in his anatomical research on the human digestive system, he instructed himself, "First give the comparison with the water of the rivers; then with that of the bile which goes to the stomach against the course of the food."[3]

Around 1508, while simultaneously pursuing his anatomy and earth studies in Milan, Leonardo returned to the analogy in a fascinating notebook, the Codex Leicester.* More focused than most of his other notebooks, it contains seventy-two pages jammed with long written passages and 360 drawings on geology, astronomy, and the dynamics of flowing water. His goal was the one that Renaissance thinkers, himself foremost among them, bequeathed to the subsequent ages of science and enlightenment: understanding the causes and effects that rule our cosmos, ranging from the mechanics of our muscles to the movement of the planets, from the flow in our arteries to that in the earth's rivers.[4] Among the questions it addresses:

---

* It was named after the Earl of Leicester, who purchased it in 1717. In 1980 it was purchased by the industrialist Armand Hammer, who renamed it the Codex Hammer. When Bill Gates bought it in 1994, his ego was not that intrusive, and he let the name revert to the Codex Leicester.

What causes springs of water to emerge from mountains? Why do valleys exist? What makes the moon shine? How did fossils get on mountains? What causes water and air to swirl in a vortex? And, most emblematically, why is the sky blue?

As he embarked on the Codex Leicester, Leonardo reached back to the microcosm-macrocosm analogy as his framework. "The body of the earth, like the bodies of animals, is interwoven with ramifications of veins, which are all joined together and are formed for the nutrition and vivification of this earth and of its creatures," he wrote, echoing his words from almost two decades earlier.[5] And on the following page he added, "Its flesh is the soil, its bones are the arrangements of the connections of the rocks of which the mountains are composed, its cartilage is the porous rock, its blood is the veins of waters; the lake of the blood, which is throughout the heart, is the ocean; its breathing and the increase and decrease of the blood through the pulses in the earth is thus: it is the flow and ebb of the sea."[6]

The analogy helped him look at the earth in a pioneering way. Rather than assuming that it had been static since its creation, Leonardo realized that the earth had a dynamic history in which powerful forces caused it to change and mature over the centuries. "We might say that the earth has a vegetative soul," he declared.[7] By regarding the earth as a living organism, he was inspired to explore the way it aged and evolved: how mountains laced with fossils arose from the sea, how rocks became layers, how rivers cut valleys, and how rugged outcroppings eroded.[8]

But even though Leonardo embraced the microcosm-macrocosm analogy, he did not do so blindly. He tested it against experience and experiments, engaging in the great dialogue that shaped his understanding of the world. By the time he finished the Codex Leicester, he would discover that the comparison between the earth and the human body was not always useful. Instead, he came to fathom how nature had two traits that sometimes appeared to be in conflict: there was a unity to nature that resonated in its patterns and analogies, but there was also a wondrously infinite variety.

WATER

The primary focus of the Codex Leicester is the topic that Leonardo regarded as the most fundamental force in the life of the planet and in our bodies: the role and movements of fluids and, in particular, water. More than any other subject except the human body, hydrodynamics engaged his artistic and scientific and engineering interests, and he addressed it on various levels: detailed observations, practical inventions, grand projects, beautiful paintings, and cosmic analogies.[9] One of his earliest drawings was of the landscape carved by the cascading Arno River. In Verrocchio's *Baptism of Christ*, Leonardo painted flowing water as it passed over the feet of Jesus with a combination of beauty and sharply observed realism that had never been seen. In an early notebook, he drew an array of mechanical devices—including pumps, hydraulic tubes, water screws, and bucket wheels—designed to move water to different levels. In his job-seeking letter to Ludovico Sforza, he boasted of his abilities "to take the water out of the trenches" and "in guiding water from one place to another." While in Milan, he studied that city's large network of canals, including the grand canal dug in 1460 to Lake Como, as well as its well-tended waterways, dams, locks, fountains, and irrigation systems.[10] He drilled holes in a barrel to study the trajectory and pressure of the water jets at differing heights.[11] He devised grandiose schemes and practical devices for diverting the Arno River and draining swamps. And by using his knowledge of how water pouring from a pipe causes water eddies, he was able to envision the vortexes inside the human heart and how they would close a valve.

Leonardo's studies of water began with practical and artistic purposes in mind, but as with his studies of anatomy and flight, he became enthralled by the beauty of the science. Water provided the perfect manifestation of Leonardo's fascination with how shapes are transformed when in motion. How can something change its shape—a square becoming a circle, a torso narrowing as it twists—and keep the exact same area or volume? Water provides an answer. Leonardo learned early on that it cannot be compressed; a given quantity always has the exact same volume, whatever the shape of the river or container. So flowing water is constantly going through perfect geometric transformations. No wonder he loved it.

In the 1490s Leonardo began a treatise on hydraulics, which included notes on the speed of river currents at various depths, studies of whirlpools formed by the friction of the banks, and the turbulence caused when different currents collide. Not surprisingly, he never finished it, but in 1508 he tackled the topic again. In the Codex Leicester, he made an outline, as he often did, for the proposed tract. It was to have fifteen chapters, starting with "Of the Waters in Themselves," followed by "Of the Sea" and "Of Underground Rivers," and concluding with "Of Making Water to Rise" and "Of Things Consumed by the Waters." One of the topics he planned to explore arose from his scheme to redirect the Arno River: "How with a few stones a river can be diverted, if one understands the line of its current."[12]

His studies at times became such a deluge of details that they reveal more about his passion than about water's dynamics. He spent hours fixated on flowing water, sometimes observing it and at other times manipulating it to test out his theories. In one part of the Codex Leicester he crammed 730 conclusions about water onto eight pages, causing Martin Kemp to comment, "We may feel that the boundary between dedication and obsession has been overstepped."[13] In another notebook, he made a list of different words that can be used to describe concepts involving the flow of water: "risaltazione, circolazione, revoluzione, ravvoltamento, raggiramento, sommergimento, surgimento, declinazione, elevazione, cavamento." By the end, he had listed sixty-seven of them.[14]

He was able to avoid pedantry by regularly bringing his theories down to earth, so to speak, and tying them to practical applications. As he instructed himself in a typical notebook jotting, "When you put together the science of the motions of water, remember to include under each proposition its application, in order that this science may not be useless."[15]

As usual, he combined experience and experiment; in fact he used the same word, *esperienza*, for both. While in Florence, he devised a pair of goggles for his dives in the Arno so he could study the water as it flowed past a weir. He threw oak apples or corks into a river and counted "beats of time" to study how long it took those in the center and those nearer the banks to move two hundred feet. He made floats that could hover at different depths to see how the currents changed from the surface to the bottom, and he crafted instruments that could measure a river's downhill course so he could determine the "rate of fall of a river per mile."

He also devised studio experiments so that he could test in a controlled environment the concepts he had observed in nature. These included making vessels of varying shapes and sizes so that he could see how water reacted when he disturbed it. He was especially interested in re-creating the eddies that he found in nature, so he built himself a glass tank, which he also used to test his theories of erosion. Make this experiment "in a square glass vessel like a box," he wrote, "and you will see the revolution of this water."[16]

To observe the movements of water, he used millet seeds, leaves, wooden rods, dyes, and colored inks.[17] "Drop a few grains of panic-grass because the movement of these grains can quickly let you know the movement of the water that carries them. From this experiment you will be able to proceed to investigate many beautiful movements which result from one element penetrating into another."[18] Pause for a moment on that word *beautiful*. You have to love Leonardo for realizing that there is beauty in the way different water currents mingle. In another example, he instructed, "Let the water that strikes there have millet or fragments of papyrus mixed in it, so that you can better see its course." In each case, he varied the conditions, such as using a gravel bed, then a bed of sand, then a smooth bed.

Some of the tests he proposed were merely thought experiments, to be conducted in his imagination or on paper. In one of his friction studies, for example, he wrote of doing an experiment "to increase or decrease in my imagination and to find out what is willed by the laws of nature." He did the same type of thought experiments regarding the world and its water. What would happen to nearby underground streams, he asked, if the air were sucked out of a cave?

The primary tool he used, however, was simple observation, though his acute visual focus meant that he saw things the rest of us would miss. When we watch water flowing into a glass or coursing by in a river, we tend not to marvel the way he did at the many types of swirls and movements it makes. But he saw that "running water has within itself an infinite number of movements."[19]

An "infinite number"? For Leonardo, that was not just a figure of speech. When he spoke of the infinite variety in nature, and especially of phenomena such as flowing water, he was making a distinction based on his preference for analog over digital systems. In an analog system, there are infinite gradations. That applies to most of the things that fascinated him: sfumato shadows, colors, movement, waves, the passage of time, the flow of fluids. That is why he believed that geometry was better than arithmetic at describing nature, and even though calculus had not yet been invented, he seemed to sense the need for such a mathematics of continuous quantities.

DIVERSIONS, EDDIES, WHIRLPOOLS, AND VORTEXES

From his care at depicting how the River Jordan would ripple past the ankles of Christ to his schemes for changing the course of the Arno, Leonardo had a keen interest in what happens when a flow of water is obstructed. The dynamics of water, he realized, are connected to the two proto-Newtonian ideas about motion that he embraced: impetus and percussion.

Impetus, a concept developed in the Middle Ages and adopted by Leonardo, describes how a body set in motion tends to keep moving in the same direction. It is a rudimentary precursor to the concepts of inertia, momentum, and Newton's first law. Percussion involves what happens when a body in motion hits another object; it will be reflected or deflected at an angle and with a force that can be calculated. Leonardo's understanding of fluid dynamics was also informed by his studies of transformations; when water is deflected, it changes path and shape, but it always remains the exact same volume.

In the margins of one crammed page of the Codex Leicester, Leonardo drew fourteen exquisite examples of what different obstacles do to the flow of water.[20] Combining the pictures with text, he explored ways that a diversion could influence the erosion of riverbanks and how obstacles affect river flows below the surface. His studies informed his artistic renderings of water flow as well as his engineering aspirations to alter the course of rivers. But as he became more immersed, he began indulging his curiosity about water flow for its own sake.

A display of this can be seen on a stunning page, now at Windsor Castle, that starts with ink and red-chalk drawings of diversions of rivers and then proceeds to a sketch of water falling into a pond (fig. 115). This combination of scientific curiosity and artistic virtuosity begins with drawings of boards placed on an angle to obstruct the flow of a current, one of many such drawings he made after he studied ways to divert the Arno. The interlacing curves of the water

Fig. 115. Water passing obstacles and falling into a pool.

as it rushes past the obstacles are drawn with the gusto Leonardo displayed whenever he drew spirals and curls. The currents look like pennants twisting together at a windy pageant, or the mane of a galloping horse, or the angelic curls of hair Leonardo loved to draw in his paintings of women and sketches of Salai.

As usual, he made an analogy, comparing the forces that create water eddies to those that create a hair curl: "The curling motion of the surface of water resembles the behavior of hair, which has two motions, one of which depends on the weight of the strands, the other on the direction of its revolving; thus water makes eddies, one part of which is due to the impetus of the principal current, and the other is due to the incidental motion and return flow."[21] This brief notation captures the essence of what motivated Leonardo: a joy in seeing the patterns that connect two things that delighted him, in this case ringlets of hair and eddies of water.

After drawing the two obstacles in a river, Leonardo drew a stream of water gushing out of an opening and forming complex patterns as it falls into a pond. These patterns resemble not only his renderings of human curls but also many of his drawings of plants, such as his beautiful rendering of a Star of Bethlehem (fig. 116).[22] His depiction of water falling into a pond does not merely try to capture a moment; like his greatest paintings, it conveys movement.

As always, Leonardo observed details that most of us overlook. He drew and described the effect of the column of water hitting the surface, the waves that emanate from the impact, the percussions of the water in the pool, the movement of the air bubbles that are submerged by the falling water, and the way the bubbles pop into floral-like rosettes when they reach the surface. He noticed that eddies containing bubbles are short-lived because they dissipate as the bubbles rise, but he drew the eddies that have no bubbles with longer lines. "The eddies that begin on the surface are filled with air," he saw. "Those that have their origin within the water are filled with water and these are more lasting because water within water has no weight."[23] Try noticing all that when you next fill a sink.

Leonardo was especially interested in eddies that form when flowing water is deflected from its path. As his drawings show, the water

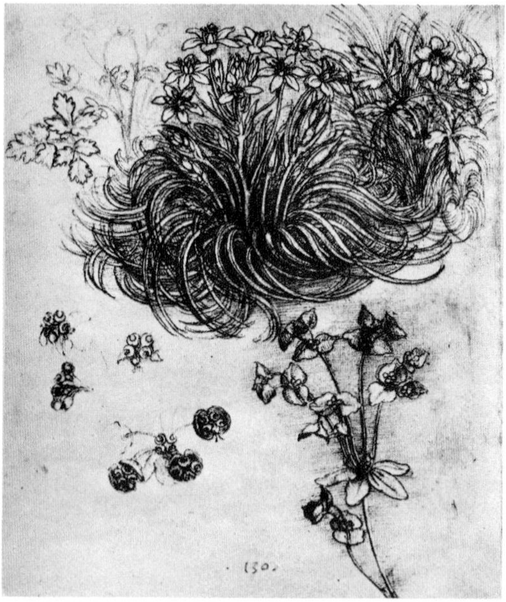

Fig. 116. Star of Bethlehem flower.

flowing past an obstacle curves toward the area directly behind the obstacle, where there is less water, forming a vortex. To this he applied his understanding of impetus and percussion; the water would attempt to continue moving in the same direction, but it would do so in a curved and spiraling manner because of the percussive force of hitting the obstacle.[24]

He realized that vortexes likewise occur in air when it blows past an object or when a beating wing causes an area of low air pressure. Like curls of hair, these swirls of water or air form geometric patterns—a spiral—that follow mathematical laws. It is another example of willfully noticing something in nature, discovering its pattern, and applying it to other aspects of nature. The result was so powerful and beautiful that spiraling vortexes would become an obsession, one that would reach its ultimate expression in a final set of drawings he did near the end of his life.

Leonardo's studies of water movements also led him to understand the concept of waves. He realized that waves do not actually involve water moving forward. Waves in the sea and ripples emanating from a pebble falling into a pond progress in a certain direction, but these "tremors," as he called them, merely cause the water to move up for a moment before returning to where it had been. He compared them to waves caused by a breeze in a field of grain. By the time he wrote the Codex Leicester and other, concurrent notebook pages on the movement of water, Leonardo had a deep feel for how waves propagate in a medium, and he correctly assumed that sound and light travel in waves. With his gift for analogy and ability to notice movement, he even viewed emotions as traveling in waves. At the core of the narrative in *The Last Supper* are the waves of emotion that emanate from the disturbance caused by the utterance of Jesus.

REVISING THE ANALOGY

One mark of a great mind is the willingness to change it. We can see that in Leonardo. As he wrestled with his earth and water studies during the early 1500s, he ran into evidence that caused him to revise his belief in the microcosm-macrocosm analogy. It was Leonardo at his best, and we have the great fortune of being able to watch that evolution as he wrote the Codex Leicester. There he engaged in a dialogue between theories and experience, and when they conflicted he was receptive to trying a new theory. That willingness to surrender preconceptions was key to his creativity.

The evolution of Leonardo's thinking about the microcosm-macrocosm analogy began with his curiosity about why water, which should in theory tend to settle on the earth's surface, emerges from springs and flows into rivers at the top of mountains. The veins of the earth, he wrote, carry "the blood that keeps the mountains alive."[25] He noticed a similar pattern involving plants as well as humans. Just as the blood in the human body goes up to the head and can flow out from cuts and nosebleeds, the sap of plants rises to the top leaves and branches. This pattern is found in both the microcosm and the macrocosm. "The waters circulate with continuous motion from the lowest depths of the seas to the highest summits of the mountains, not obeying the nature of heavy things," he wrote. "And in this case they act like the blood in animals; which always moves from the sea of the heart and flows to the summit of their heads; and if a vein breaks here, as one sees a vein ruptured in the nose, all of the blood rises from below to the height of the broken vein."[26]

Assuming that similar effects have similar causes, he began his quest to figure out what force impels liquids to move upward to become mountain springs. "The same cause which moves the fluids in all kinds of living bodies against the natural course of gravity also propels the water through the veins of the Earth," he surmised. "As the blood rises from below and pours out through the broken veins of the forehead, and as the water rises from the lower part of the vine to the branches that are cut, so from the lowest depth of the sea the water rises to the summits of the mountains where, finding the veins broken, it pours down."[27]

What was the force that did this? Over the years Leonardo considered several explanations. He initially thought the heat of the sun causes the water to rise inside the mountains, either as vapor that is then condensed or through some other method. "Where there is heat there is movement of vapor," he noted, then made this analogy:

> Just as the natural heat of the blood in the veins keeps it in the head of man—for when the man is dead the cold blood sinks to the lower parts—when the sun is hot on the head of a man the blood increases and rises so much that by pressuring the veins often causes headaches; in the same way that veins ramify through the body of the earth, and by the natural heat which is distributed throughout the containing body, the water is raised through the veins to the tops of mountains.[28]

He also considered whether the water may be sucked up, as in a siphon. His interest in water management and swamp drainage had led him over the years to experiment with different kinds of siphons and distillation equipment. On one large sheet of the Codex Leicester folded into folios (fig. 117), each possibility is sketched out in drawings and explained in words.[29] He used drawings as tools to help him think. For example, on this page he made twelve pen-and-ink sketches of siphons to imagine how they could be connected to lift

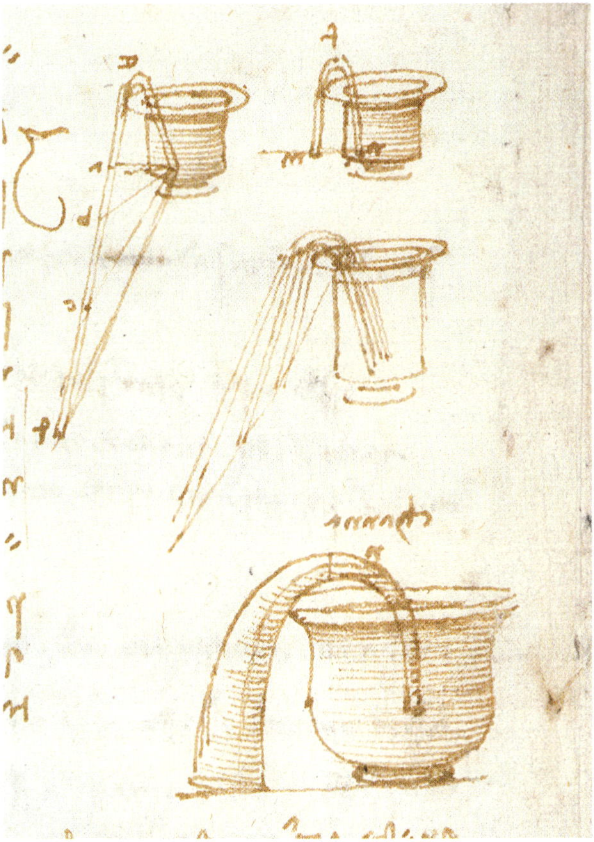

Fig. 117. Thought experiment using siphons.

water to the top of mountains, but none of his configurations worked. It cannot be done, he concluded.

Leonardo proceeded to dismiss all of the explanations for why the earth's water circulates to the top of mountains, including theories he had once accepted. Most notably, he cast away his long-standing belief that heat draws water up inside mountains just like (he thought) it draws blood up to the human head, because he realized that mountain streams are just as prevalent in cold climes and months as they are in warm. "If you said that the heat of the sun draws it up high from the caverns of the mountains as far as the summit of the mountains, thereby drawing it up from the uncovered lakes and seas in the form of vapor for the composition of clouds," he wrote in the Codex

Leicester, "then there would be greater and more abundant veins of waters where the heat is greater than in colder countries, but we see the contrary." He also noted that the veins of humans narrow with age, but the springs and rivers of the earth continually enlarge their channels.[30]

In other words, experience and experiment taught him that the received wisdom from the analogy between the macrocosm of the earth and the microcosm of man was flawed. The analogy had misled him about geology. So, like a good scientist, he revised his thinking. "The ocean does not penetrate under the earth," he wrote in one of his other notebooks, "and cannot penetrate from the roots to the summits of mountains."[31]

Only after pitting various theories against experience did Leonardo eventually get to the correct answer: the existence of springs and mountain rivers, indeed the entire circulation of water on the earth, results from the evaporation of surface water, the formation of clouds, and the subsequent rains. On one of his anatomical drawings from around 1510, written at the same time as he was revising his geological thoughts in his Codex Leicester, Leonardo jotted down a note "on the nature of veins" that declared, "The origin of the sea is contrary to the origin of the blood . . . [because] all the rivers are caused solely by the water vapors raised up into the air." The amount of water on the earth is constant, he concluded, and it is "constantly circulating and returning."[32]

Leonardo's willingness to question and then abandon the enticing analogy between the circulation of water on the earth and the circulation of blood in the human body shows his curiosity and ability to be open-minded. Throughout his life, he was brilliant at discerning patterns and abstracting from them a framework that could be applied across disciplines. His geology studies show an even greater talent: not letting these patterns blind him. He came to appreciate not only nature's similarities but also its infinite variety. Yet even as he abandoned the simplistic version of the microcosm-macrocosm analogy, he retained the aesthetic and spiritual concept underlying it: the harmonies of the cosmos are reflected in the beauty of living creatures.

FLOODS AND FOSSILS

Leonardo's experience as an engineer and enthusiast of flowing water helped him understand erosion, which he realized is caused when water currents carve away dirt from riverbanks. He applied that knowledge to determining how valleys are created: "Rivulets will originate in the lowest parts of a surface, and these will begin to hollow out and form receptacles for other surrounding waters. In this way, every part of their course will become wider and deeper."[33] The rivers thus eventually wear away the earth and create valleys.

Part of his evidence came from sharp observations. The rock strata on one side of a valley, he noticed, has the same sequence of sedimentation as that on the other side. "One sees the strata on one side of the river corresponding with those on the other," he wrote in the Codex Leicester. "With this argument, Leonardo was two hundred years ahead of his time," the science historian Fritjof Capra asserted. "The superposition of rock strata would not be recognized and studied in similar detail until the second half of the seventeenth century."[34]

These observations led Leonardo to consider how fossils—especially those of sea animals—ended up in these high stratified layers of rock. "Why are the bones of great fishes and oysters and corals and other various shells and sea-snails found on the tops of mountains?" he asked. Writing more than 3,500 words on the topic in the Codex Leicester, he described his detailed observations of fossils and argued that the biblical story of the Flood was incorrect. Showing no fear of combining heresy with blasphemy, he wrote "of the foolishness and simple-mindedness of those who require that these animals should be carried by the Deluge to these places, far from the sea."[35]

Because fossils appear in several sediment layers that were deposited at different times, he argued, their location cannot be explained by a single flood. He also provided evidence from his close studies that the fossils did not come from a great swelling of the seas. "If the Deluge had carried the shells three hundred and four hundred miles far from the sea, it would have carried them there mixed up with different species, amassed together. But we see, at such distances, the oysters, and the shells, and the squids and all the other shells which stay congregated together."[36]

His conclusion, which is correct, was that there had been enormous shifts and fluctuations in the crust of the earth that had given rise to mountains. "From time to time the bottom of the sea was raised, depositing these shells in layers," he declared. He had seen it for himself as he hiked on Collegonzi Road near the Arno River south of Vinci, where the river had eroded the mountains and layers of shells were plainly visible in the bluish clay.[37] As he later noted, "The ancient bottoms of the sea have become mountain ridges."[38]

Among the evidence he cited was his discovery of what are now called "trace fossils." These are formed not by the remains of animals but by the tracks and traces that animals left in the sediment when they were still alive. "In rock layers are still found the tracks of the worms, which proceeded through them when they were not yet dried out," he wrote in the Codex Leicester.[39] That proved, Leonardo said, that the sea animals had not been washed up by a deluge to the mountain but instead had been alive, at what was then the bottom of the sea, when the strata were formed. Leonardo thus became a pioneer of ichnology, the study of fossil traces, a field that did not come into full existence for another three hundred years.

When he examined the fossils of shellfish, he noticed a pattern that would help determine how long they had lived: "We can count in the crusts of cockles and snails the years and months of their life, as we do in the horns of oxen and sheep, and in the branches of trees."[40] It was a leap that was far ahead of its time. "That he was able to associate the annual rings in the branches of trees with the growth rings in the horns of sheep is remarkable enough," Capra wrote. "To use the same analysis to infer the lifespan of a fossilized shell is extraordinary."[41]

ASTRONOMY

Il sole nó si muóve. The sun does not move.

These words of Leonardo are written in unusually large letters on the top left of one of his notebook pages that is filled with geometric sketches, mathematical transformations, a cross section of the brain, a drawing of the male urinary tract, and doodles of his old warrior.[42] Is this statement a brilliant leap decades ahead of Copernicus, Galileo, and the realization that the sun does not revolve around the earth? Or is it merely a random thought, perhaps a note for a pageant or play?

Leonardo leaves us in the dark, providing no elaboration. But when he wrote the sentence, around 1510, his geological studies had led him to pursue questions about the earth's place in the cosmos and other wonders of astronomy. He does not seem to have discovered that the movements of the sun and stars are caused by the earth's rotation (a young Copernicus was just formulating this theory at the time),[43] but he did come to the realization that the earth is only one of many cosmic bodies, and not necessarily the central one. "The earth is not in the center of the sun's orbit nor at the center of the universe, but in the center of its companion elements, and united with them,"[44] he wrote. And he understood that gravity kept the seas from falling off the earth. "Let the earth turn on whichever side it may, the surface of the waters will never move from its spherical form, but will always remain equidistant from the center of the globe."[45]

More impressive was his realization that the moon does not emit light but reflects the light of the sun, and that a person standing on the moon would see that the earth reflects light in the same way. "Anyone standing on the moon would see our earth just as we see the moon, and the earth would light it, just as the moon lights us." That earthshine is what gives a new moon its faint glow, he realized. Drawing on the fastidious attention he paid to reflected secondhand light in the shadowed parts of his paintings, he wrote that when we can dimly see the dark part of the moon, it is because the parts not lit by the sun can catch the reflected light from the earth. He erred, however, in applying this theory to stars, which he also thought emitted no light of their own but instead merely reflected light from the sun. "The sun gives light to all celestial bodies," he wrote.[46]

As with so many topics, he said that he was planning to write a treatise on astronomy, but he never did so. "In my book, I propose to show how the oceans and seas must, by means of the sun, make our world shine with the appearance of a moon, and to the remoter worlds it looks like a star."[47] It would have been an ambitious project.

In a memo to himself he wrote, "I have first to demonstrate the distance of the sun from the earth, then to find its true size with one of its rays passed through a small hole into a dark place, and besides this, to find the size of the earth."[48]

BLUE SKY

In pursuing his studies on the perspective of color and later on geology and astronomy, Leonardo pondered a question that seems so ordinary and mundane that most of us forget to marvel about it after age eight or so. But the greatest geniuses, from Aristotle to Leonardo, Newton, Rayleigh, and Einstein, have studied it: Why is the sky blue?

Leonardo worked on many explanations but finally settled on one, basically correct, that he recorded amid the geology and astronomy notes in his Codex Leicester: "I say that the azure in which the air shows itself is not its own color, but it is caused by warm humidity, evaporated in very minute and insensible atoms, which catches behind itself the percussion of the solar rays and makes itself luminous under the vast shades." Or, as he put it more succinctly, "The air takes the azure through the corpuscles of humidity, which catch the luminous rays of the sun."[49]

A similar theory had been handed down from Aristotle, but Leonardo refined it based on personal observations. After climbing to the top of Monte Rosa in the Italian Alps, he noticed how much bluer the sky looked. "If you go to the top of a high mountain the sky will look proportionately darker above you as the atmosphere becomes rarer between you and the outer darkness; and this will be more visible at each degree of increasing height till at last we should find darkness."

He also conducted experiments to test this explanation. First, he re-created the blue by painting a misty white wash over a dark background. "Anyone who wants to see the ultimate proofs, let him tint a board with various colors, among which a most beautiful black should be included, and over all let a thin and transparent white lead be applied; then it will be seen that the brightness of this white lead will nowhere show itself as a more beautiful azure than over the black."[50] Another experiment involved smoke. "Let smoke be made out of a small quantity of dry wood, and let the solar rays percuss this smoke; and behind this smoke place a piece of black velvet, which is not exposed to the sun, and you will see that all the smoke between the eye and the darkness of the velvet shows itself to be of a very fine blue color."[51] He reproduced the phenomenon with "water violently ejected in a fine spray and in a dark chamber." Showing his diligence as an experimenter, he used regular water filled with impurities and then water that had been purified. He discovered that the process "makes the sunbeam blue, and particularly if it is distilled water."[52]

Leonardo found himself stymied by a related question: What causes a rainbow? That would have to wait for Newton, who showed how white light can be scattered by a water mist into its component colors based on wavelengths. Nor did Leonardo figure out that light of shorter wavelengths, at the blue end of the spectrum, scatters more than light of longer wavelengths; that would have to wait for Lord Rayleigh in the late nineteenth century and then for Einstein to calculate the exact formula for the scattering.

Chapter 29

Rome

VILLA MELZI

The ongoing hostilities involving the French and their shifting alliances with Italian city-states often resembled pageantry and processionals more than war. "A march through Italy was an occasion for feasts, spectacles, firework displays, jousts, the expropriation of estates, and occasional massacres," wrote Robert Payne. "The French aristocracy acquired new titles, new experiences, new mistresses, new diseases."[1]

In the latest episode, the French in 1512 were losing their grip on Milan, which they had held since expelling Duke Ludovico Sforza thirteen years earlier. By the end of the year, his son Maximilian (Massimiliano) Sforza would retake the city, holding it for three years.

Leonardo had the ability to float above such political disruptions, usually by leaving town, though he also tried to catch the currents that would bring him to powerful patrons of whatever stripe. As a young man in Florence, he had been a second-tier recipient of Medici patronage before moving to Milan and aligning himself with the Sforzas. When they were ousted by the French, Leonardo switched allegiances, then enlisted with Cesare Borgia, and finally found a reliable patron in Charles d'Amboise, the French governor of Milan. But after Charles died in 1511 and the Sforzas were poised to retake the dukedom, Leonardo decided to leave Milan. With no desire to move back to Florence, where both the *Adoration of the Magi* and the *Battle of Anghiari* loomed unfinished, he began a four-year period during which he wandered in search of new patronage, carrying with him some paintings that he had been slowly perfecting.

For most of 1512, he resided comfortably in the family home of his student and surrogate son, Francesco Melzi, who turned twenty-one that year. It was an odd familial menagerie: Francesco had been adopted as a ward by Leonardo, and they were staying with his biological father, Girolamo Melzi. Also there was the still-beloved Salai, now thirty-two. The home was a stately square villa on a bluff overlooking the Adda River nineteen miles from Milan, just far enough away that Leonardo could avoid being swirled into the vortex of the geopolitics there.

Leonardo got to pursue, in a leisurely and broad fashion, all of his curiosities and passions at the Melzi villa. Though he no longer had access to human corpses, he dissected animals, including the rib cages of oxen and still-beating hearts of pigs. He completed his geology writings in the Codex Leicester, analyzing the nearby rock formations and eddies of the Adda. "Flux and reflux of water as demonstrated at the mill of Vaprio," he captioned one sheet. He also offered the Melzi family some architectural suggestions. In his notebooks he drew ground plans of the estate and possible cupolas to be built, and on a page containing anatomical sketches, he added a sketch of the villa and a note about a tower room that likely was his study. He did not, however, use the time to collate his geography, anatomy, flight, or hydraulics studies into publishable treatises. He was still Leonardo, always pursuing a curiosity, less passionate about tying up loose ends.[2]

PORTRAITS OF LEONARDO

While at Villa Melzi, surrounded by the closest thing he had to a family, Leonardo turned sixty. What did he look like? How had his handsome face and flowing curls responded to age? A few portraits and possible portraits of Leonardo exist from this period. What they have in common is that they tend to make him look old, perhaps prematurely old, and they treat him as an iconic venerable sage, beard flowing and brows furrowed.

There is one tantalizing sketch that was drawn by Leonardo himself (fig. 118).[3] The hatchings are left-handed, the notes are in mirror script, and the architectural studies on the verso side are of Villa Melzi, so we know he drew it around 1512. It shows an old man with a walking stick sitting on a rock, his left hand held up to his head as if in contemplation or perhaps feeling melancholy. His balding hair

Fig. 118. Old man and studies of moving water.

is wispy on top, though still curly. His beard flows down almost to his chest. His eye stares alertly, though with signs of fatigue. His lips are turned down—as is the case with most other possible Leonardo portraits—and his nose is distinguished and hooked, like those of his oft-doodled nutcracker man.

The melancholy man seems to be staring across the page at one of Leonardo's many drawings of swirling water forming turbulent eddies that look like curls. Indeed, it is in the note at the bottom of this sheet where Leonardo makes his comparison between water eddies and curls of hair. But this image of the aging artist contemplating the vortexes of water may be more figurative than real; the folio page is folded, and the drawing of the man may have been done separately from that of the turbulent water. As always there is a bit of mystery with Leonardo. Is he imagining himself ruefully contemplating flowing water? Is the connection across the folded sheet subconscious, or is it mere coincidence?

And is Leonardo, consciously or not, sketching himself? The man in the drawing looks older than sixty, but maybe that is how Leonardo actually looked at sixty. Many of the possible portraits make him look older than his age at the time, so it's likely that he had prematurely aged into a bearded sage. Or maybe that is how he imagined he looked. As Kenneth Clark wrote, "Even if this is not strictly a self-portrait, we may call it a self-caricature, using the word to mean a simplified expression of essential character."[4]

Leonardo's contemplative sketch bears some resemblance to a profile portrait we can be pretty confident depicts him: a red-chalk drawing usually attributed to Melzi, probably done sometime between 1512 and 1518, and labeled "Leonardo Vinci" in capital letters (fig. 119).[5] The similarities are tantalizing: Melzi's portrait shows a still-handsome Leonardo with wavy hair tumbling to his shoulders, a bushy beard almost to his chest, and a distinguished nose that is pointed though not quite as hooked as a nutcracker caricature. The forehead looks similar, as does the eye. Most comparable is the overall iconography of the distinguished aging sage with flowing hair and beard.

Fig. 119. Melzi's drawing of Leonardo.

If indeed both Melzi's red-chalk drawing and Leonardo's notebook sketch of an old man are portraits of Leonardo, then master and pupil have portrayed him in different ways. Leonardo made his subject look older, as perhaps he envisioned himself becoming. Melzi, on the other hand, made his subject look younger, still vibrant and barely wrinkled, his face and gaze strong, as he no doubt liked to remember him.

Over the years, Leonardo was often depicted as an iconic bearded philosopher, which was probably based both on reality and on some mythmaking. A prime example of this is a Vatican fresco by Raphael, the Italian artist who was Leonardo's young follower. His *School of Athens*, painted around the time that Leonardo was turning sixty, depicts two dozen ancient philosophers standing in discourse. At the center is Plato, striding alongside Aristotle (fig. 120). Raphael used his contemporaries as models for most of the philosophers, and Plato looks to be a depiction of Leonardo. He wears a rose-colored toga, matching the colorful tunics that Leonardo famously sported. As in the Melzi portrait and others of Leonardo, Plato is balding, with wisps of curly hair on top and curls flowing in waves from the side of his head to his shoulder. There is also the curly beard, coming down to the top of his chest. And he is making a gesture characteristic of Leonardo: his right index finger is pointing up to the heavens.[6]

Another probable portrait of Leonardo, likely by one of his students, is sketched faintly on a page of horse drawings that Leonardo had done in his notebook (fig. 121).[7] We can tell from the left-

Fig. 120. Raphael's pointing Plato, possibly based on Leonardo.

handed hatching and beautiful modeling that Leonardo did the horse legs on the other side of the sheet, but the faint sketch of a man is done with right-hand hatching in a different style. His beard is wavy, and he seems to be wearing a cap. Sweetly, there is a fainter portrait just below of a very young man with a similar cap and curly hair, perhaps the student himself.

A cap is a feature found in many sixteenth-century portraits of Leonardo done after his death, such as the woodcut used to illustrate Vasari's lives in the 1560s (fig. 122). Another disputed example, discovered in 2008 and known as the Lucan portrait (fig. 123), shows the subject in three-quarter profile with a cloth hat that has long been associated with him. It seems to be the model for, or based on, many similar paintings and engravings of a man with a hat and flowing beard, usually identified as Leonardo, such as a famous one in Florence's Uffizi Museum (fig. 124), which appears on the cover of this book.

Fig. 121. A student sketch possibly of Leonardo.

Fig. 122. Portrait of Leonardo in Vasari's book.

Fig. 123. The Lucan portrait.

Fig. 124. Portrait in the Uffizi.

The most glorious and famous of all the possible portraits is a haunting red-chalk drawing done by Leonardo himself with his left-handed hatching. The Turin portrait (fig. 125), so called because of where it resides, has been reproduced so often that it defines our image of Leonardo, whether or not it is truly a self-portrait. It shows an old man with flowing beard, waves of curly hair, and bushy eyebrows. Crisp lines of hair are juxtaposed with the sfumato softness of the cheeks. The nose, subtly shaded and modeled with curved and

Fig. 125. The Turin portrait.

straight hatch lines, is distinctively hooked, though not as pronounced as in Leonardo's nutcracker-man sketches. Like many Leonardo works, the face displays different mingled emotions each time you look at it: strength and vulnerability, resignation and impatience, fatalism and resolve. The tired eyes are contemplative, the down-turned lips are melancholy.

Oddly, the eyes do not look at us but downward and to the left. Leonardo was experimenting with mirrors at the time, and he built some that connected at angles, resembling the three flapped mirrors that can be found on a modern medicine cabinet; he even devised an octagonal enclosure of mirrors that a person could stand in. So perhaps he made the drawing while in his studio using hinged mirrors to view himself obliquely. With its averted gaze, the Turin portrait echoes a recently discovered faint sketch by Leonardo, another possible self-portrait, that was largely obscured and covered by notes in his Codex on the Flight of Birds (fig. 126).[8]

But is the Turin drawing really a self-portrait? Like Leonardo's notebook drawing of an old man seeming to gaze at torrents of water, the man in the Turin portrait looks older than sixty. The hair has receded more, the eyebrows are bushier, and the mustache is sparser than in the portrait drawn by Melzi. Did Leonardo by then actually

Fig. 126. Possible self-portrait in notebook.

look older than his age? There is evidence that he did; a traveler who later visited him in France reported his age as ten years older than he really was at the time. Or did Leonardo, when being self-reflective, tend to portray himself as he envisioned he might become? Perhaps it is an extension of his nutcracker-man doodles and drawings of grotesques. Then again, maybe Leonardo is portraying in the Turin drawing someone else, such as his father or uncle, who both lived to around eighty.[9]

If we consider the Turin portrait in conjunction with the various other possible portraits and self-portraits, including the likely ones by Raphael and Melzi, we can see a pattern that probably approximates reality. Taken together, these drawings and paintings circumscribe the image of Leonardo as an iconic bearded genius and noble Renaissance seeker: intense yet also distracted, passionate yet also melancholy. In this he fits the description offered by his near contemporary, the sixteenth-century Italian painter and art writer Gian Paolo Lomazzo: "He had long hair and such long eyelashes and beard that he seemed to embody the true nobility of learning, like the druid Hermes and ancient Prometheus did in the past."[10]

TO ROME

Leonardo was always on the lookout for powerful patrons, and in 1513, with Milan still controlled by his former patrons the Sforzas, a new one appeared in Rome. In March of that year, Giovanni de' Medici was elected to become Pope Leo X. The son of Lorenzo "the Magnificent" de' Medici, the Florentine ruler who was a halfhearted patron to Leonardo and sent him off to Milan as a young man, Giovanni was the last non-priest to maneuver himself into the papacy. Much of his time was spent tending to the Vatican's uncertain alliance with France, which was again aiming to retake Milan and was making pacts with various other Italian cities. The new pope would also later face the threat of Martin Luther and his Reformation. But in 1513 he had time to be a profligate arts patron and indulge his love of theater, music, verse, and art. "Let us enjoy the papacy since God has given it to us," he said, and he did so with gusto.

In his free-spending support of the arts, Pope Leo was aided by his brother Giuliano, who moved from Florence to Rome and established an intellectual court. A lover of both art and science, he was an ideal patron for Leonardo, whom he courted and offered a stipend; Leonardo, tired of having to support himself by completing commissions, accepted. For a few years, the two sons of Lorenzo "the Magnificent" would make up for their father's relative indifference toward him.[11]

"I left Milan for Rome on 24 September 1513, in the company of Giovan, Francesco de Melzi, Salai, Lorenzo and Il Fanfoia," Leonardo recorded on the opening page of a new notebook. Melzi was then twenty-two; Salai was thirty-three. He also recorded that he had paid to ship five hundred pounds of personal belongings from Milan to Rome. The trove included more than a hundred books, his growing but unsorted assortment of notebooks, anatomical drawings, scientific instruments, art equipment, clothes, and furniture. Most important, it included five or six paintings that he was still obsessing over, trying to perfect.[12]

As he traveled across the mountains, Leonardo looked for fossils. "I found some shells in the rocks of the high Apennines and mostly at the rock of La Verna," he recorded.[13] Once on the other side, he made a brief stop in Florence and checked on some relatives. He made a note to inquire "whether Alessandro Amadori, the priest, is alive or not," referring to the brother of his stepmother, Albiera.[14] He was. But the city of his early years held little allure for Leonardo, even though it was back under Medici control. It had too many ghosts.

Rome was a new city for him, a place he had never lived. It was teeming with great architects, including his friend Donato Bramante, who was modernizing vast swatches of roads and buildings. Among his other projects, Bramante was building a formal, terraced courtyard, flanked by arched corridors, that would connect the Vatican to the elegant papal summer palace, the Villa Belvedere. The villa, built less than thirty years earlier, caught the summer breezes on high ground overlooking Rome. It had been designed by Antonio del Pollaiuolo, whom Leonardo knew well from Florence.

In this villa, which housed favorites of Pope Leo and Giuliano,

Leonardo was given his living quarters. It was the perfect place for him. Slightly aloof and secluded, but containing a court of artists and scientists, the Belvedere and its grounds encompassed a mix of great architecture and natural wonders, including a menagerie, a botanical garden, orchards, a fish pond, and classical sculptures collected by the recent popes, such as *Laocoön and His Sons* and the *Apollo Belvedere*.

To make matters even better, the pope ordered one of his architects to modernize quarters in the Villa Belvedere "for the rooms of Master Leonardo da Vinci." The work included the widening of a window and the addition of wooden partitions, a chest for grinding colors, and four dining tables—an indication that Leonardo supported a large household of assistants and students.[15]

In the Belvedere gardens was a sanctuary containing rare plants from different parts of the world. Leonardo studied how a wide variety of leaves grew in spiral arrangements, known as phyllotactic spirals, as they sought to maximize exposure to the sun and rain. The gardens were also a stage for the pranks that he loved. One day a vine keeper in the garden showed him a strange lizard. "Leonardo made some wings of the scales of other lizards and fastened them on its back with a mixture of quicksilver, so that they trembled when it walked," Vasari wrote. "Having made for it eyes, horns, and a beard, he tamed it and kept it in a box, but all his friends to whom he showed it used to run away from fear." Another trick was making animals out of wax and blowing air into them so they would fly, a parlor trick that amused the pope.

Leonardo's relationships with his half-brothers had improved since the resolution of the family's inheritance disputes, and when he got to Rome he sought out his father's oldest legitimate son, Giuliano da Vinci, who, not surprisingly, was a notary. Giuliano had been promised a benefice—a Church appointment that came with a stipend—but there had been a glitch, and Leonardo offered to intercede on his behalf. He personally went to check the registry, and finding that the appointment was not yet in the works he asked for help from the datary, the officer in charge of papal benefices. There ensued a discussion about costs and difficulties, apparently a solicitation for a bribe. However the case got settled, Giuliano's wife seemed pleased. In a letter she wrote to her husband, she appended a postscript: "I forgot to ask you to remember me to your brother Lionardo, a most excellent and singular man [*vuomo eccellentissimo e singhularissimo*]."[16] Giuliano gave the letter to Leonardo, who kept it among his papers for the rest of his life.

Leonardo's conflicted feelings about fathers, sons, and family ties were expressed with a dash of wry humor when another of his half-brothers, Domenico, celebrated the birth of a son. The letter Leonardo sent him is suffused with irony and feigned condolences that may have been only half-joking. "My beloved brother," he wrote. "A short time ago I received a letter from you saying that you have an heir, which I understand has afforded you a great deal of pleasure. Insofar as I had judged you to be prudent, I am now entirely convinced that I am as far removed from having accurate judgment as you are from prudence; seeing that you have been congratulating yourself on having created a watchful enemy, who will strive with all his energies seeking liberty, which can only come into being at your death."[17]

Even though the pope and his brother were liberally commissioning works of art, including from Raphael and Michelangelo, Leonardo had not regained his desire to be a painter. It must have been a test of his impressive stubbornness not to be prodded into painting while being pampered by patrons who were so hungry for art. Baldassare Castiglione, an author and courtier who knew Leonardo in Rome, described him as one "of the world's finest painters, who despises the art for which he has so rare a talent and has set himself to learn philosophy [meaning the sciences]."[18] He received one commission from the pope but apparently did not finish it. As Leonardo lingered over the process of distilling the varnish he planned to use to coat the painting when it was complete, the pope complained, "Alas, this man will never get anything done, for he is thinking about the end before he begins."[19]

Other than that, Leonardo seems to have received no new commission or started any new artwork. His only encounters with the brush involved perfecting, in a slow and studied manner, paintings he had long been working on and resisted relinquishing.

Leonardo instead was still more interested in science and engineering. He accepted the job of devising a way to drain the Pontine Marshes, fifty miles southeast of Rome, for Giuliano de' Medici, who had been assigned the task of reclaiming the land by his brother. Leonardo visited the area and drew one of his subtly colored aerial maps, the lettering done by Melzi, which shows plans for the creation of two new canals that would drain the mountain streams into the sea before they reached the marshes.[20] He also devised for Giuliano a mill for minting coins with good edges.

Leonardo's most intense technology interest while in Rome involved mirrors. Ever since he was nineteen and part of Verrocchio's team that soldered a copper ball and placed it on top of the dome of Florence's cathedral, Leonardo had been fascinated by ways to make concave mirrors that would concentrate light from the sun to produce heat. During his career, he made close to two hundred drawings of ways to focus light and construct such mirrors, calculated the math of how light rays reflect from a curved surface, and studied the technology of using grinding stones to shape and polish metal.[21] One of his drawings from the late 1470s in Florence (fig. 127) shows designs for a furnace, a mechanism to grind a mold, a press using the mold to shape a piece of metal, and a geometric drawing of curved shapes inside a cone.[22] Another shows a machine that turns a large metal bowl and raises it to press up against a curved grindstone, with accompanying text on how "to make a concave sphere to throw fire."[23]

Over the years, Leonardo became increasingly interested in the mathematics involved in focusing a mirror, drawing scores of diagrams of light rays from different directions hitting a curved surface and showing the angles at which they would be reflected. He tackled the problem identified by Ptolemy in AD 150 and studied by the eleventh-century Arab mathematician Alhazen of finding the point on a concave mirror where light coming from a certain source will be reflected to a designated spot (akin to finding the spot on the edge of a circular billiard table where you have to hit a cue ball so that it will bounce

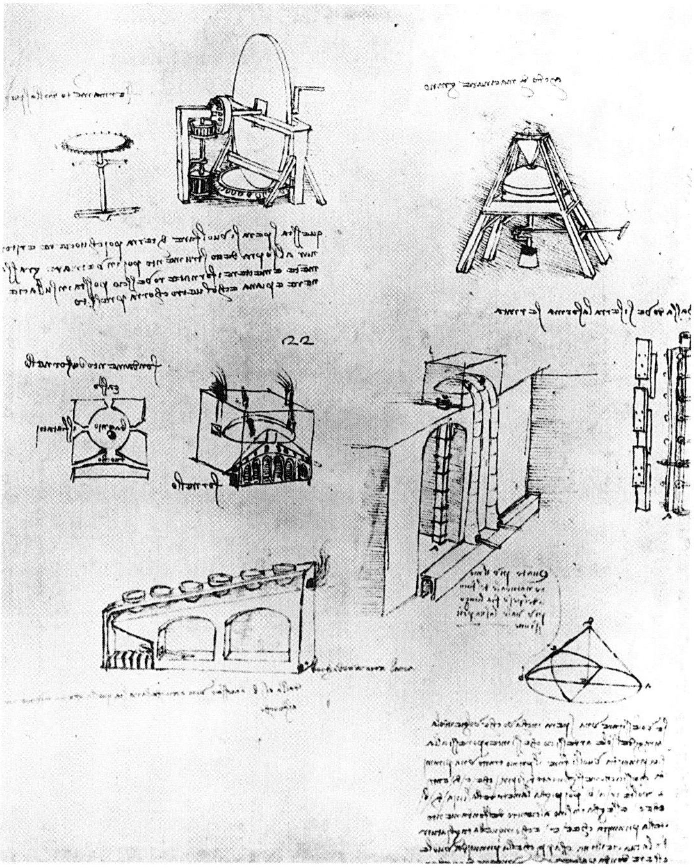

Fig. 127. Machine for making mirrors.

and hit your target). Leonardo failed to solve this using pure math. So in a series of drawings, he made a device that could solve the problem mechanically. He was better at using visualizations than equations.

During his time in Rome, he filled at least twenty more pages with ideas about the mathematics and construction techniques of concave mirrors, especially very large ones.[24] Part of his interest by then was related to his astronomy studies; he was seeking ways to better observe the moon. But primarily he was still interested in using mirrors to focus sunlight into heat. He continued to think of himself as a military engineer, and the mirrors could serve as a weapon, as Archimedes had reportedly done against the Roman ships besieging

Syracuse. They could also be useful for soldering metals and for powering large boilers. "With this one can supply heat for any boiler in a dyeing factory," he wrote. "And with this a pool can be warmed up, because there will be always boiling water."[25]

Living with Leonardo at the Belvedere was a German assistant who was supposed to be helping him construct his mirrors and produce some for the wardrobe rooms of the pope and Giuliano. But he was disloyal, lazy, and erratic, causing Leonardo to go into a tailspin of rage. He became physically ill as well as petulant, and his psychological unhinging was splayed out in three long drafts of complaining letters intended for Giuliano.

This was not the first time that Leonardo's bouts of torment seemed to spiral out of control. Back when he was in Milan, he had walked off the job of decorating rooms for the duke, drafted a fiery letter of complaint, and then torn it in half. But the letters he drafted for Giuliano were of a different order of megatonnage. He told the stories of his clashes with the German in lengthy and disjointed diatribes that verged on the paranoid and were cluttered with details and digressions that would likely have baffled Giuliano. He wrote of "the wickedness of that German deceiver" and of how the boy betrayed him by building his own workshop so he could do jobs for other people. Leonardo also denounced him for wasting his days bird-hunting with the Swiss guards. This is not the sweet Leonardo we usually see, tending to young acolytes and twinkling fondly at the transgressions of the rascally Salai.

Leonardo's other nemesis was another German staying at the Belvedere, a rival mirror-maker named Giovanni. Leonardo wrote in a draft letter, "That German, Giovanni the mirror-maker, was in the workshop every day, wanting to see everything that I was doing and then broadcasting it around, and criticizing whatever he could not understand." He accused Giovanni of being jealous, then rambled on semicoherently about how Giovanni had turned the young assistant against him.[26]

During this time, Leonardo continued his anatomical studies, dissecting at least three corpses in Rome, probably at the Hospital of the Holy Spirit (Santo Spirito), and refining his drawings of the human heart. Dissections were not illegal, but Leonardo was stopped from continuing with them. "The pope has found out that I have skinned three corpses," he wrote, and he blamed it on the jealous Giovanni. "This person has hindered me in anatomy, denouncing it before the Pope and also at the hospital."[27]

Leonardo's foul mood and his lack of artistic productivity, in stark contrast to Michelangelo and Raphael at the time, served to alienate him from the Medici orbit. The situation worsened when Giuliano's influence declined; he was sent off in early 1515 to marry the daughter of a French duke and then died a year later after a long bout with tuberculosis. It was time for Leonardo to move on once again.

He found a new opportunity when he was invited to be part of Pope Leo's entourage to Florence and Bologna. The Medici pope triumphantly entered his native Florence in November 1515. One observer reported, "All the chief citizens went in procession to meet him and among others about fifty youths, only the richest and foremost, dressed in a livery of clothing of purple cloth with fur collars, going on foot, and each with a type of small, silvered lance in his hands—a most beautiful thing." Leonardo drew in his notebook the temporary arch that had been built for the procession. When the pope arrived at the Council Hall for a gathering of cardinals, the remnants of Leonardo's unfinished *Battle of Anghiari* was still visible on the wall.

In Florence the pope also convened a gaggle of top artists and architects to discuss renewing Florence the way Bramante was Rome. Leonardo made drawings of his ideas for completely reworking and expanding the plaza in the Medici quarters and demolishing the houses in front of the church of San Lorenzo, which would have destroyed many of the streets and alleys of his younger days, and drew the Medici Palace with a new façade that faced the new grand plaza.[28]

But Leonardo did not stay in Florence. Instead, he followed the papal procession to Bologna, where the pope had scheduled a secret parley with the new king of France, Francis I, who had just turned twenty-one. Francis had wrested control of Milan from the Sforzas in September 1515, which convinced the pope he had to make peace with him.

The parley did not settle the French-Italian wars, but it would eventually result in finding Leonardo a new patron. He was at the meetings between the pope and the king, and at one session he made a black-pencil sketch of Artus Gouffier, the king's tutor and chamber master. It is likely that, in Bologna, the king first tried to entice Leonardo to come to France.

CHAPTER 30

Pointing the Way

THE WORD BECOMES FLESH

During the decade of 1506–16, as he wandered between Milan and Rome pursuing his passions and seeking patronage, Leonardo worked on three paintings that have an elegiac and spiritual quality, as if he realized that his days were numbered and was contemplating what lay on the road ahead. These include two sensuous paintings of Saint John the Baptist, one of them converted into a rendering of Bacchus by someone many years later, and a painting of an angel of the Annunciation that has been lost. They feature, as do their related drawings, a sweetly androgynous young man with an enigmatic aura, looking (or perhaps even leering) directly at the viewer and pointing a finger. Despite his immersion into science, or perhaps because of it, Leonardo had developed an ever-deepening appreciation for the profound spiritual mystery of our place in the cosmos. And as Kenneth Clark noted, "Mystery to Leonardo was a shadow, a smile and a finger pointing into darkness."[1]

What distinguishes these paintings is not that they have a religious theme; like the work of every other Renaissance master, most of Leonardo's paintings did. Nor are they the only times that Leonardo used a pointing gesture; Saint Anne in the Burlington House cartoon and Saint Thomas in *The Last Supper* both point upward. What makes this late trio of paintings distinctive is that the spiritual pointing gesture is directed personally to us, the viewer. When this late-career version of the angel of the Annunciation delivers his divine message, he is speaking and gesturing not to the Virgin Mary but to us. Likewise, in both pictures of Saint John, he is looking intimately at us, pointing the way to our own salvation.

Some critics over the centuries have asserted that Leonardo marred the spiritual nature of these pieces—perhaps heretically and intentionally so—by giving them an erotic allure. A cataloguer of the French royal collection complained in 1625 that the Saint John painting "does not please because it does not arouse feelings of devotion." In a similar vein, Kenneth Clark wrote, "Our whole sense of propriety is outraged," adding that the depiction of Saint John is "almost blasphemously unlike the fiery ascetic of the Gospels."[2]

I doubt Leonardo thought he was being blasphemous or heretical, nor should we. The seductive and sensuous elements of these works enhance rather than lessen the powerful spiritual intimacy that Leonardo intended them to convey. Saint John comes across as less the Baptist than the Seducer, but in portraying him this way Leonardo connected the spiritual to the sensual. By highlighting the ambiguity between spirit and flesh, Leonardo gave his own charged meaning to "the Word became flesh and dwelt among us."[3]

SAINT JOHN THE BAPTIST

From sketches in his notebook, we know that Leonardo had already begun working on his portrait of Saint John the Baptist (fig. 128) while in Milan in 1509.[4] But as with many of his late paintings, most of which he ended up working on out of personal passion rather than to fulfill a commission, he carried it around with him and intermittently enhanced it until the end of his life. His focus was on the saint's eyes, mouth, and gesture. The close-up of him emerging from the darkness confronts us starkly. There are no distracting landscapes or lights, and only the Leonardesque ringlets of hair provide any ornamentation.

As he gestures heavenward in a recognition of divine providence,

Fig. 128. *Saint John the Baptist.*

John is also pointing toward the source of the light that radiates on him, thus fulfilling his biblical role "to bear witness of the Light."[5] Leonardo's use of chiaroscuro, contrasting deep shadows with striking illumination, not only enhances the sense of mystery of the scene; it also conveys a powerful feeling of John's role as witness to the true Light.[6]

John wears one of the enigmatic smiles that became a Leonardo signature, but it has a come-hither naughtiness to it that is missing in the smiles of Saint Anne and the *Mona Lisa*. His smile beckons in ways that are sultry and seductive as well as spiritual. That gives the picture its erotic frisson, as does John's androgynous appearance. His shoulders and chest are broad yet feminine. The model seems to be Salai, with his soft face and cascade of curls.

Leonardo's oil-painting technique, which involved applying multiple thin layers of translucent glazes, was by now even more painstaking and slow. He rushed no painting, to a fault. In *Saint John the Baptist*, this pace enhanced the delicacy of his sfumato. The contours are soft, the lines are blurred, and the transitions between light and dark are exceedingly subtle.

There is, however, one exception. Leonardo has painted John's hand with a greater sharpness and clarity, just as he had done with the blessing hand of Christ in *Salvator Mundi*. The line separating John's pointing index finger from his second finger is as distinct as any line in any of Leonardo's paintings, almost like one of Michelangelo's. It is possible this is due to a misguided restoration at some point. But I suspect it was intentional on Leonardo's part, especially since he uses a similar sharp delineation for the pointing hand in what became the Bacchus version of the painting. With his theory of acuity perspective, Leonardo knew that such sharpness would make the hand appear nearer, as if in a different plane. There is a visual disjuncture: the hand is positioned at the same distance as the softly delineated arm, but because it is sharper it seems to pop out toward us and be more in focus.[7]

SAINT JOHN WITH THE ATTRIBUTES OF BACCHUS

The other variation of this theme to emerge from Leonardo's studio—probably based on a drawing by Leonardo and partly painted by him, but also the product of others in his workshop—shows a full-length Saint John sitting on a dark rock formation with a sunny landscape of a mountain and a river to his right (fig. 129). In an inventory of Salai's estate in 1525, it is referred to as a large-scale painting of Saint John,

Fig. 129. Saint John converted to a Bacchus.

and it is identified this way in an inventory of the French royal art collection at Fontainebleau in 1625. But in a subsequent inventory of that collection done in 1695, the designation of Saint John is crossed out and replaced by "Bacchus in a landscape." From this we can surmise that, sometime in the late 1600s, the painting was altered, perhaps for reasons of religious and sexual propriety, to turn Saint John into Bacchus, the Roman god of wine and revelry.[8]

There was once a beautiful red-chalk preparatory drawing by Leonardo for this painting housed in a small museum at a mountaintop religious sanctuary above the town of Varese, north of Milan. It showed Saint John sitting on a rocky ledge, his left leg crossed atop his right, his body muscular but a bit fleshy, like Salai's, his eyes set deep in shadow and staring at us intensely. "I have seldom seen an original Leonardo of more revealing character," Carlo Pedretti wrote in the early 1970s after making a pilgrimage to view it.[9] Sadly, the drawing was stolen from the little museum in 1973, and it has not been publicly seen since. In this drawing, Leonardo had depicted Saint John completely nude, and there is evidence that is the way he was originally rendered in the painting. But when he was converted from a Baptist to a Bacchus, a leopard-skin cloth was placed over his crotch, a wreath of ivy was put on his head, and his staff or cross was turned into a thyrsus. Leonardo's discomforting ambiguity between spirit and flesh was thus replaced by a less jarring depiction of a pagan god whose lustiness is not heretical.[10]

In both Leonardo's drawing and in the painting, the most striking element is the pointing gesture. Instead of pointing heavenward, as in Leonardo's starker rendition of the saint, this time he is pointing off into the darkness to his left, out of the scene of the picture. As with *The Last Supper*, the viewer can almost hear the words that accompany the gesture, in this case John heralding the arrival of "he who cometh after me, whose sandals I am not worthy to carry."[11]

The smile is not as seductive and the body is more muscular and masculine than in Leonardo's other treatment of Saint John, but the face is just as androgynous and the curls just as Salaicious. Once again, the pointing hand as well as the left leg are more sharply delineated than is typical of Leonardo, whose signature sfumato is evident in other parts of the picture. It is unclear whether this is because the leg and hand were retouched or were the work of a student, or because Leonardo made their lines sharper so they would feel closer to the viewer. I suspect it was the latter.

ANGEL OF THE ANNUNCIATION AND *ANGEL INCARNATE*

Around this time, Leonardo painted another pointing figure, an angel of the Annunciation making a gesture that was similar to that in *Saint John the Baptist.* The painting is now lost, but we know what it looked like from copies made by some of Leonardo's followers, including one by Bernardino Luini (fig. 130). There is also a charcoal

Fig. 130. Copy of the lost *Angel of the Annunciation.*

drawing of it (fig. 131) by a student on one of Leonardo's notebook pages, which is surrounded by Leonardo's own drawings of horses and men and geometrical figures. On the student's sketch, Leonardo used his left-handed hatches to correct the pointing arm to put it in the proper foreshortened perspective.

The scene of the Annunciation, in which the angel Gabriel announces to the Virgin Mary that she will become the mother of Christ, was the subject of the first painting that Leonardo did mainly on his own during the early 1470s, while working in Verrocchio's studio (fig. 11). This time, however, there is no Virgin Mary in the picture for the angel to address. Instead, he looks directly at us, and his upward-pointing gesture seems addressed to us. Like Saint John, he is heralding the impending arrival of Christ the savior in human form, a miraculous union of spirit and flesh.

Fig. 131. Student sketch of *Angel of the Annunciation*, corrected by Leonardo.

The angel and Saint John are depicted in the exact same pose, with the same come-hither stare, enigmatic smile, seductive cocking of the head and twisting of the neck, and glorious curls lustrously lit. Only the arm of the hand pointing to heaven has changed. Saint John is turning to the left, so the upraised arm is seen going across the body. Then as now, Leonardo's boy angels are feminine to the point of being androgynous; it is true of the angel in his early *Annunciation* and also of the one in *Virgin of the Rocks*. In this new *Annunciation*, the androgyny is more pronounced than ever. The angel has budding breasts, and his face is even more girlish.

There is another drawing of the angel, one that is astonishing and still controversial. Made around 1513, while Leonardo was in Rome, it

Fig. 132. *Angel Incarnate*, with breasts and erection.

shows a lewdly leering transgender version of the *Angel of the Annunciation* with female breasts and a large erect penis (fig. 132). Known as the *Angel Incarnate* or *Angel in the Flesh*, it is the extreme example of Leonardo's dance around what he viewed as the ambiguous border between flesh and spirit as well as the one between feminine and masculine.

Although it is on one of Leonardo's sheets of blue-tinted paper, which he used for many of his anatomical studies and drawings of mirrors, it is unlikely that he was the primary draftsman of this *Angel Incarnate*. It is not rendered beautifully, and it is delineated and shaded clumsily, without Leonardo's distinctive left-handed hatching. It seems to have been drawn by the same student—probably Salai—who drew the notebook sketch of the *Angel of the Annunciation* that Leonardo corrected; the smile, the gesture, the hollow eyes, the pose, and even the flawed foreshortening of the raised arm are similar. Since it was done on Leonardo's paper, it was likely done for his amusement and perhaps with a few corrections by him, just as he had corrected the *Angel of the Annunciation* drawing.

The result looks like a catamite, eager to please, signaling a willingness for an assignation. The juxtaposition of the angel's female-nippled breasts and girlish face with its prominent erection and dangling balls makes the drawing a cross between playful caricature and hermaphroditic pornography. The drawing echoes the theme from Leonardo's Saint John drawings: it combines the angelic and the devilish, and it links spiritual aspiration with sexual arousal. At one point someone apparently tried to erase the penis but succeeded mainly in rubbing away the blue tint of the paper and leaving some erasure marks.[12]

The history of the drawing is a bit mysterious, perhaps because the British royal family, in whose collection it once resided, was embarrassed by it. One story is that a German scholar came to view it at the Royal Library and whisked it away under his cape; whether or not that is true, it was rediscovered in 1990 in the private collection of an aristocratic German family.[13]

A counterpoint to the gesturing androgynous angels and saints is a poetic and sweet drawing known as the *Pointing Lady* (fig. 133), which the renowned scholar Carlo Pedretti called "perhaps the most beautiful drawing by Leonardo."[14] The subject has the same mysterious and enticing smile as her male counterparts, and she likewise is looking directly at us, directing our attention to a mystery unseen. But unlike Leonardo's various angels of the period, there is nothing devilish about her.

The black-chalk drawing is simple, but it encompasses many facets of Leonardo's life and work: his love of plays and pageants, his feel for fantasy, his mastery of enigmatic smiles, his ability to make women come alive, and the twisting movement. It is filled with the curls and

Fig. 133. *Pointing Lady.*

spirals that Leonardo loved: there is a hint of a stream and waterfall creating eddies, and there are flowers and reeds whose curves echo those of the lady's diaphanous dress and blowing hair.

Most notably, the lady is pointing. In his last decade, Leonardo is mesmerized by that gesture, the signal of tidings borne by a mysterious guide who has come to show us the way. The drawing may have been meant as an illustration for Dante's *Purgatorio*, showing the beautiful Matelda, who guides the poet through ritual bathings in a forest, or it could have been a drawing for a costume pageant. But whatever was the original intent, it became more. It is a profoundly expressive and poetic drawing by a man entering the twilight and still searching for guidance about the eternal mysteries that his science and his art have not, and cannot, explain.

CHAPTER 31

The *Mona Lisa*

THE CULMINATION

And now, the *Mona Lisa* (fig. 134). The discussion of Leonardo's pièce de résistance could have come earlier in this book. He began working on it in 1503, when he returned to Florence after serving Cesare Borgia. But he had not finished it when he moved back to Milan in 1506. In fact, he carried it with him, and continued to work on it, throughout his second period in Milan and then during his three years in Rome. He would even take it to France on the final leg of his life journey, adding tiny strokes and light layers through 1517. It would be in his studio there when he died.

So it makes sense to consider the *Mona Lisa* near the end of his career, exploring it as the culmination of a life spent perfecting an ability to stand at the intersection of art and nature. The poplar panel with multiple layers of light oil glazes, applied over the course of many years, exemplifies the multiple layers of Leonardo's genius. What began as a portrait of a silk merchant's young wife became a quest to portray the complexities of human emotion, made memorable through the mysteries of a hinted smile, and to connect our nature to that of our universe. The landscape of her soul and of nature's soul are intertwined.

Fig. 134. The *Mona Lisa.*

Forty years before he put his last touches on the *Mona Lisa*, while still working in Verrocchio's shop in Florence, a young Leonardo had painted another commissioned portrait of a woman, *Ginevra de' Benci* (fig. 14). On the surface, the two pictures have similarities. Both are of new wives of Florentine cloth merchants portrayed against a river landscape, their bodies in a three-quarters pose. But more striking are the differences between the two paintings. They show the development of Leonardo's painterly skills and, more important, his maturation as a scientist, philosopher, and humanist. *Ginevra de' Benci* was made by a young artist with astonishing skills of observation. The *Mona Lisa* is the work of a man who had used those skills to immerse himself in a lifetime of intellectual passions. The inquiries chronicled on his thousands of notebook pages—of light rays striking curved objects, dissections of human faces, geometrical volumes being transformed into new shapes, flows of turbulent water, the analogies between the earth and human bodies—had helped him fathom the subtleties of depicting motion and emotion. "His insatiable curiosity, his restless leaps from one subject to another, have been harmonized in a single work," Kenneth Clark wrote of the *Mona Lisa*. "The science, the pictorial skill, the obsession with nature, the psychological insight are all there, and so perfectly balanced that at first we are hardly aware of them."[1]

THE COMMISSION

Vasari provided a vivid description of the *Mona Lisa* in his life of Leonardo, first published in 1550. Facts were not Vasari's forte, and it is unlikely that he ever saw the painting (though it is conceivable that he could have if Salai had brought it back to Milan after Leonardo's death, as the confusing inventory of his estate made in 1525 possibly suggests, before it was sold to the king of France). It is more probable that Vasari had seen, at best, a copy or was writing from secondhand descriptions and allowing himself some literary license. Whatever the case, subsequent discoveries have tended to confirm much of his account, so it provides a good starting point for chronicling the masterpiece:

> Leonardo undertook to paint, for Francesco del Giocondo, the portrait of Mona Lisa, his wife. . . . Whoever wished to see how nearly art could imitate nature was able to comprehend it when he saw this portrait. . . . The eyes had that luster and watery sheen which are seen in life, and around them were rosy and pearly tints, together with the eyelashes, that cannot be represented without the greatest subtlety. . . . The nose, with its beautiful nostrils, rosy and tender, appeared to be alive. The mouth, with its opening, and with the ends united by the red of the lips to the flesh tints of the face, seemed in truth to be not colors but flesh. In the pit of the throat, if one gazed upon it most intensely, could be seen the beating of the pulse.

Vasari was referring to Lisa del Giocondo, who was born in 1479 into a minor branch of the distinguished Gherardini family, whose roots as landowners stretched from feudal times but whose money had not survived quite so long. At fifteen, she married into the wealthy but not quite so prominent Giocondo family, which had made its riches in the silk trade. Her father had to cede one of their farms as a dowry since they had little cash, but the marriage between frayed landed gentry and rising merchant class turned out to be beneficial to all concerned.

Her new husband, Francesco del Giocondo, had lost his first wife eight months earlier and had a two-year-old son to raise. Having become the purveyor of silks to the Medici, he was increasingly prosperous, with clients throughout Europe, and he bought a few women Moors from North Africa to serve as his household slaves. From all indications he was in love with Lisa, which was not usually a factor in the arrangement of such marriages. He helped support her family, and by 1503 she had borne him two sons. Until then they had been living at his parents' house, but with a growing family and financial prospects he bought a home of their own and around that time commissioned Leonardo to paint a portrait of his wife, who was turning twenty-four.[2]

Why did Leonardo accept the assignment? He was at the time fending off the incessant pleadings of the far wealthier and more prominent art patron Isabella d'Este, and he was so engrossed in his scientific explorations that he was known to pick up a brush only reluctantly.

Perhaps one reason Leonardo accepted was out of family friendship. His father had long served as a notary for Francesco del Giocondo and had represented him in legal disputes several times. Their families shared a close connection to the church of Santissima Annunziata. Leonardo had moved into the church's cloistered complex with his entourage three years earlier, when he returned to Florence from Milan. His father was the notary for the church, and Francesco del Giocondo worshipped there, lent it money, and would eventually endow a family chapel. Given his nature as a sharp and sometimes contentious merchant, Giocondo occasionally got into disputes with the church, and it fell to Piero da Vinci to work them out. One of them in 1497 involved a bill from Giocondo that the friars of Santissima Annunziata disputed; Piero drew up a settlement in the Giocondo silk workshop.[3]

So the aging Piero, then seventy-six, likely had his hand in helping to arrange for his famous son to accept the commission. In addition to doing a favor for a family friend and client, Piero was probably also looking after his son. Although Leonardo was now widely celebrated as an artist and engineer, he had begun to withdraw regularly from his bank account the savings he had brought with him from Milan.

But I suspect the main reason that Leonardo decided to paint Lisa del Giocondo is that he wanted to paint her. Because she was somewhat obscure, not a famed noble or even the mistress of one, he could portray her as he wished. There was no need to cater to or take directions from a powerful patron. Most important, she was beautiful and enticing—and she had an alluring smile.

BUT IS IT REALLY LISA?

The assertion by Vasari and others, including the sixteenth-century Florentine writer Raffaello Borghini, that the *Mona Lisa* is a portrait of Lisa del Giocondo seems straightforward. Vasari knew Francesco and Lisa, who were still alive when he made numerous visits to Florence between 1527 and 1536, and he became friends with their children, who likely were the source for some of his information. When the first edition of his book was printed in 1550, the children were still alive, and Vasari lived diagonally across from the church complex of Santissima Annunziata. If he was incorrect about Lisa being the subject of the painting, there were a lot of her family members and friends who could have corrected him for his second edition in 1568. Yet even though he made a lot of other corrections, the *Mona Lisa* story remained the same.[4]

But this being Leonardo, there have been some mysteries and disputes. Questions arose even before Leonardo finished the painting. In 1517 he was visited at his studio in France by Antonio de Beatis, secretary to Cardinal Luigi of Aragon, who recorded in his diary that he saw three paintings: *Saint John the Baptist*, the *Virgin and Child with Saint Anne*, and a portrait of "a certain Florentine lady." So far, so good. De Beatis apparently was told this by Leonardo, which would comport with the portrait's not being of some rich marchesa or notable mistress, whom de Beatis might know, but of a person such as Lisa del Giocondo, who was not famous enough to mention by name.

There follows, however, a confusing sentence. The painting, de Beatis reported, was "done from life at the instigation [*instantia*] of the late Giuliano de' Medici." This is baffling. When Leonardo started the painting, Giuliano had not yet moved to Rome or become Leonardo's patron. In 1503 he had been exiled by the republican leaders of Florence and was living in Urbino and Venice. If Giuliano "instigated" the portrait, might it have been of one of his mistresses, as some have suggested? But none of his known mistresses was a "Florentine lady," and the ones he had were famous enough that de Beatis would have recognized them if any were the model for the painting.

There is, however, a plausible and delightful possibility that Giuliano was somehow involved in urging Leonardo to paint or keep working on a portrait of Lisa del Giocondo. Giuliano and Lisa were born the same year, 1479, and knew each other through their interrelated families in the small world of the Florentine elite. Among other connections, Lisa's stepmother was Giuliano's cousin. Lisa and Giuliano were both fifteen when he was forced to leave Florence, and a few months later she married the older widower Francesco. Perhaps, as in a Shakespeare play, they were star-crossed lovers. Giuliano may have been Lisa's pining teenage lover or, as Bernardo Bembo was to Ginevra de' Benci, a wistfully Platonic one. Perhaps when Leonardo passed through Venice in 1500, Giuliano asked him to report back, when he got to Florence, on how the beautiful Lisa was faring and what she now looked like. He may have even expressed the desire for a portrait of her. Or, when Leonardo arrived in Rome with the painting unfinished, his new patron Giuliano may have recognized its potential universal beauty and urged him to complete it. These explanations need not replace the narrative that Francesco del Giocondo commissioned the painting. Instead they could supplement it, perhaps add a reason Leonardo accepted the assignment, and even help explain why he never actually delivered the painting to Francesco.[5]

Another wrinkle in the narrative is that the name *Mona Lisa*, a contraction of "Madonna (Madam) Lisa," which was widely adopted based on Vasari's account, is not the only name used for the painting. It is also called *La Gioconda* (in French, *La Joconde*). That is how it, or a copy of it, was listed in the settlement of Salai's estate in 1525,[6] which seems to strengthen the case that the *Mona Lisa* and *La Gioconda* are one and the same. It would be a pun on her last name, which would appeal to Leonardo; the word means "jocund" or "jocular." But some have argued that there might be two different paintings, citing the fact that Lomazzo, writing in the 1580s, mentioned "the portrait of La Gioconda and Mona Lisa," as if they were separate works. Various theorists have scurried down rabbit holes trying to figure out who the jocund lady might be if she is not the *Mona Lisa*. It's more likely, however, either that Lomazzo was mistaken or that an early transcription of his text substituted "and" for "or" in his sentence.[7]

What should put an end to any mystery or confusion is the evidence discovered in 2005, mentioned earlier in my discussion of the *Saint Anne* chronology, of the note scribbled by Agostino Vespucci in 1503 in the margin of an edition of Cicero, which mentions "the head of Lisa del Giocondo" as one of the paintings Leonardo was working on at the time.[8] Sometimes, even with Leonardo, what seems like a mystery isn't. Instead, a straightforward explanation suffices. I am confident that is true in this case. The *Mona Lisa* is Mona Lisa. It is Lisa del Giocondo.

That said, the painting became more than a portrait of a silk-merchant's wife and certainly more than a mere commission. After a few years, and perhaps from the outset, Leonardo was painting it as a universal work for himself and for eternity rather than for Francesco del Giocondo.[9] He never delivered the painting and, judging from his bank records, never collected any money for it. Instead, he kept it with him in Florence, Milan, Rome, and France until he died, sixteen years after he began. Over that period, he added thin layer after layer of little glaze strokes as he perfected it, retouched it, and imbued it with new depths of understanding about humans and nature. Some new insight, new appreciation, new inspiration would strike him, and the brush would alight gently on the poplar panel yet again. As it was with Leonardo, who became more profoundly layered with each step of his journey, so it was with the *Mona Lisa*.

THE PAINTING

The mysterious allure of the *Mona Lisa* begins with Leonardo's preparation of its wood panel. On a thin-grained plank cut from the center of a trunk of poplar, larger than usual for a household portrait, he applied a thick primer coat of lead white rather than a more typical mix of gesso, chalk, and white pigment. That undercoat, he knew, would be better at reflecting back the light that made it through his fine layers of translucent glazes and thereby enhance the impression of depth, luminosity, and volume.[10]

As a result, light penetrates the layers, and some of it reaches the white undercoat to be reflected back through the layers. Our eyes see an interplay between light rays that bounce from the colors on the surface and those that dance back from the depths. This creates shifting and elusive subtleties of modeling. The contours of her cheeks and smile are created by soft transitions of tone that seem veiled by the glaze layers, and they vary as the light in the room and the angle of our gaze changes. The painting comes alive.

Like the fifteenth-century Netherlandish painters such as Jan van Eyck, Leonardo used glazes that had a very small proportion of pigment mixed into the oil. For the shadows on Lisa's face, he pioneered the use of an iron and manganese mix to create a pigment that was burnt umber in color and absorbed oil well. He applied it with brushstrokes so delicate that they are imperceptible, brushing on, over time, up to thirty fine layers. "The thickness of a brown glaze placed over the pink base of the Mona Lisa's cheek grades smoothly from just two to five micrometers to around thirty micrometers in the deepest shadow," according to an X-ray fluorescence spectroscopy study published in 2010. That analysis showed that the strokes were applied in an intentionally irregular way that serves to make the grain of the skin look more lifelike.[11]

Leonardo shows Lisa sitting on a loggia, the base of its columns barely visible at the edges, with her hands folded in the foreground, resting on the arm of her chair. Her body and especially her hands feel unusually close to us, while the jagged mountain landscape recedes into a faraway and misty distance. An analysis of the underpainting shows that he initially drew her left hand grasping the chair arm as if she were about to rise, but then thought better of it. Nevertheless, she still appears to be in motion. We have caught her in the act of turning, as if we had just walked onto the loggia and captured her attention. Her torso twists slightly as her head rotates to look and smile directly at us.

Throughout his career, Leonardo had immersed himself in the study of light, shade, and optics. In a passage in his notebooks, he wrote an analysis that comports closely to the way he let light strike Lisa's face: "When you want to make a portrait, do it in dull weather, or as evening falls. Note in the streets, as evening falls, the faces of the men and women, and when the weather is dull, what softness and delicacy you may perceive in them."[12]

In the *Mona Lisa*, he made the light shine from on high and slightly from the left. To do this, he had to resort to a little sleight of hand, but he did it so subtly that it takes some scrutiny to notice. Judging from the columns, the loggia on which she is sitting is covered; therefore, the light should be coming from the landscape behind her. Instead, it shines on her from the front. Perhaps we are meant to think that the loggia is open on its side, but even that would not explain the full effect. It's an artificial arrangement employed by Leonardo to allow him to use his mastery of shading to create the contours and modeling he needs. His understanding of optics and how light strikes curved surfaces is so brilliant, so convincing, that his trick in the *Mona Lisa* is not conspicuous.[13]

There is another small anomaly about the way light strikes Lisa's face. In his optics writings, Leonardo was studying how long it takes the pupils of an eye to become smaller when exposed to more light. In the *Musician*, the eyes are dilated differently in a way that gives the painting a sense of movement and accords with Leonardo's use of bright light in that painting. In the *Mona Lisa*, the pupil of her right eye is slightly larger. Leonardo incorrectly believed that our eyes dilate separately when exposed to light, but in this case he shows the pupil of the eye facing the light as being smaller. This seems confusing. Was he observant enough to notice a case of anisocoria, in which one eye is more dilated than the other, which occurs in 20 percent of humans? Or was it that he knew that pleasure also causes eyes to widen and was indicating, by showing one of her eyes dilating faster than the other, that Lisa was pleased to see us?

Then again, maybe this is being too obsessive about a tiny, perhaps irrelevant, observation. Call it the Leonardo Effect. His skill of observation was so acute that even an obscure anomaly in his paintings, such as an uneven dilation of pupils, causes us to wrestle, perhaps too much, with what he might have noticed and thought. If so, it is a good thing. By being around him, viewers are stimulated to observe the little details of nature, like the cause of a dilated pupil, and to regain our sense of wonder about them. Inspired by his desire to notice every detail, we try to do the same.

Also a bit puzzling is the issue of Lisa's eyebrows, or lack thereof. In Vasari's fulsome description, he makes a point of lavishing praise on them: "The eyebrows, because he has shown the manner in which the hairs spring from the flesh, growing thickly in one place and lightly in another and curving according to the pores of the skin, could not be more natural." That seems to be another example of Vasari's effusiveness and of Leonardo's brilliant combination of art, observation, and anatomy—until we notice that *Mona Lisa* has no eyebrows. Indeed, a description of the painting from 1625 notes that "this lady, in other respects beautiful, is almost without eyebrows." This has fueled some of the farfetched theories that the painting now in the Louvre is a different work than the one Vasari saw.

One explanation is that Vasari never saw the painting and embellished parts of his account, as he was wont to do. But his description is so precise that this seems improbable. A more plausible explanation is based on what seems to be two faint and blurry oblong patches where the eyebrows should have been, which suggest that they were painted as Vasari described, each hair meticulous, but Leonardo took so long to do them that he painted them over a layer of oil that had completely dried. This would mean that the first time the painting was cleaned, they could have been wiped away. This explanation was supported in 2007 by high-resolution scans made by the French art technician Pascal Cotte. Using light filters, he found tiny indications of eyebrows that originally existed.[14]

Although Lisa is sparsely adorned, without the jewels or fancy costuming that would indicate aristocratic status, her clothing is rendered with dazzling care and scientific astuteness. Ever since he was an apprentice drawing drapery studies in Verrocchio's studio, Leonardo had been observant of the folds and flows of fabric. Her dress billows gently, the light catching the vertical waves and pleats. Most noticeable are the mustard-copper sleeves, rippling and shining with a silky luster that would have dazzled Verrocchio.

Because he was painting a portrait that, at least in theory, was for a merchant of the finest silk, it's not surprising that he included delightful details in Lisa's layers of clothing. To appreciate the exquisite care that Leonardo took, look at an enlarged high-resolution reproduction, many of which can be found in books and online,[15] and study the neckline of her dress. It begins with two rows of braided spirals, the pattern in nature most beloved by Leonardo, between which are interlocked golden rings that catch the light as if in three-dimensional relief. The next row is a series of knots, like those Leonardo loved to draw in his notebooks. They form the shape of crosses, each separated by two hexagonal coils. But there is one place, in the center of the neckline of the dress, where the pattern is slightly broken and there seem to be three hexagonals in a row. Only on very close examination of high-resolution and infrared images does it become clear that Leonardo did not make a mistake; instead, he was very subtly depicting a fold in the bodice right below her cleavage. The infrared images reveal something that is likewise amazing but also, because we are dealing with Leonardo, not surprising: he painted the embroidered patterns on the bodice even in the places where he would later cover it by painting another layer of garment, so that we can faintly sense its presence even where we cannot see it.[16]

Covering Lisa's hair is a gossamer veil, worn as a mark of virtue (not mourning), which is so transparent that it would be almost unnoticeable were it not for the line it makes across the top of her forehead. Look carefully at how it drapes loosely over her hair near her right ear; it is evident that Leonardo was meticulous enough to paint the background landscape first and then used almost-transparent glazes to paint the veil over it. Also look at where her hair comes out from under her veil at her right forehead. Although the veil is almost transparent, the hair underneath is painted to look a tiny bit gauzier and lighter than the hair flowing from underneath it and covering her right ear. When the unveiled hair cascades over her chest on both sides, Leonardo is back to creating the swirling curls he adored.

Depicting veils came naturally to Leonardo. He had a fingertip feel for the elusive nature of reality and the uncertainties of perception. Understanding that light hits multiple points on the retina, he wrote that humans perceive reality as lacking razor-sharp edges and lines; instead, we see everything with a sfumato-like softness of the edges. This is true not only of the misty landscape stretching out to infinity; it applies even to the outlines of Lisa's fingers that seem so close we think we can touch them. We see everything, Leonardo knew, through a veil.

The portrayal of the landscape behind Lisa contains other tricks of the eye. We see it from high above, as if from a bird's-eye view. The geological formations and misty mountains incorporate a mix, as did much of what Leonardo produced, of science and fantasy. The barren jaggedness evokes prehistoric eons, but it is connected to the present by a faint arched bridge (perhaps a depiction of the thirteenth-century Ponte Buriano over the Arno River near Arezzo)[17] spanning the river just above Lisa's left shoulder.

The horizon on the right side seems higher and more distant than the one on the left, a disjuncture that gives the painting a sense of dynamism. The earth seems to twist like Lisa's torso does, and her head seems to cock slightly when you shift from focusing on the left horizon to the right horizon.

The flow of the landscape into the image of Lisa is the ultimate expression of Leonardo's embrace of the analogy between the macrocosm of the world and the microcosm of the human body. The landscape shows the living and breathing and pulsing body of the earth: its veins as rivers, its roads as tendons, its rocks as bones. More than being merely the backdrop for Lisa, the earth flows into her and becomes a part of her.

Follow with your eye the winding path of the river on the right as it passes under the bridge; it seems to flow into the silky scarf draped over her left shoulder. The scarf's folds are straight until they reach her breast, where they start gently twisting and twirling in a way that looks almost exactly like Leonardo's drawings of water flows. On the left side of the picture, the winding road coils as if it will connect to her heart. Her dress just below the neckline ripples and flows down her torso like a waterfall. The background and her garments have the same streaked highlights, reinforcing what has progressed from being an analogy into a union. This is the heart of Leonardo's philosophy: the replication and relationships of the patterns of nature, from the cosmic to the human.

More than that, the painting conveys this unity not only across nature but across time. The landscape shows how the earth and its offspring have been shaped and carved and replenished by flows, from the distant mountains and valleys created eons ago, through the bridges and roads created during human history, to the pulsing throat and inner currents of a young Florentine mother. And thus she is transported into an icon that is eternal. As Walter Pater wrote in his famous effusion of praise of the *Mona Lisa* in 1893, "Hers is the head upon which all the ends of the world are come . . . a perpetual life, sweeping together ten thousand experiences."[18]

THE EYES AND THE SMILE

There are many portraits, including Leonardo's earlier *La Belle Ferronnière*, in which the subject's eyes appear to move as the viewer moves. It works even with a good reproduction of that painting or of the *Mona Lisa*. Stand in front, and the subject is staring at you; move from side to side, and the stare still seems direct. Even though Leonardo was not the first to create the appearance that the eyes of a portrait are following you around the room, the effect is so closely associated with him that it is sometimes called "the *Mona Lisa* effect."

Dozens of experts have studied the *Mona Lisa* to determine the scientific reasons for this effect. One is that in the three-dimensional real world, shadows and light on a face shift as our vantage changes, but in a two-dimensional portrait this is not the case. Consequently, we have the perception that eyes staring straight out are looking at us, even if we are not directly in front of the painting. Leonardo's mastery of shadows and lighting helps make the phenomenon more pronounced in the *Mona Lisa*.[19]

And finally, there is the *Mona Lisa*'s most mystical and engaging element of all: her smile. "In this work of Leonardo," wrote Vasari, "there was a smile so pleasing that it was more divine than human." He even told a tale of how Leonardo kept the real Lisa smiling during the portrait sessions: "While painting her portrait, he employed people to play and sing for her, and jesters to keep her merry, to put an end to the melancholy that painters often succeed in giving to their portraits."

There is a mystery to the smile. As we stare, it flickers. What is she thinking? Our eyes move a bit, and her smile seems to change.

The mystery compounds. We look away, and the smile lingers in our minds, as it does in the collective mind of humanity. Never in a painting have motion and emotion, the paired touchstones of Leonardo's art, been so intertwined.

At the time when he was perfecting Lisa's smile, Leonardo was spending his nights in the depths of the morgue under the hospital of Santa Maria Nuova, peeling the flesh off cadavers and exposing the muscles and nerves underneath. He became fascinated about how a smile begins to form and instructed himself to analyze every possible movement of each part of the face and determine the origin of every nerve that controls each facial muscle. Tracing which of those nerves are cranial and which are spinal may not have been necessary for painting a smile, but Leonardo needed to know.

The *Mona Lisa*'s smile makes it worth revisiting the remarkable page of anatomical drawings from around 1508, discussed in chapter 27, that shows a pair of lips in an open-mouth grimace and then drawn pursed (fig. 111). The muscle that purses the lips is the same muscle that forms the lower lip, he discovered. Pucker your lower lip and you can see that this is true; it can pucker on its own, with or without the upper lip, but it is impossible to pucker the upper lip alone. It was a tiny discovery, but for an anatomist who was also an artist, especially one who was in the midst of painting the *Mona Lisa*, it was worth noting. Other movements of the lips involve different muscles, including "those which bring the lips to a point, others which spread them, and others which curl them back, others which straighten them out, others which twist them transversely, and others which return them to their first position." Then he drew a row of lips with the skin layer peeled off.[20] At the top of this page is something delightful: a simpler drawing of a gentle smile, sketched lightly in black chalk. Even though the fine lines at the ends of the mouth turn down almost imperceptibly, the impression is that the lips are smiling. Here amid the anatomy drawings we find the makings of *Mona Lisa*'s smile.

There is other science involved in the smile. From his optics studies, Leonardo realized that light rays do not come to a single point in the eye but instead hit the whole area of the retina. The central area of the retina, known as the fovea, is best at seeing color and small details; the area surrounding the fovea is best at picking up shadows and shadings of black and white. When we look at an object straight on, it appears sharper. When we look at it peripherally, glimpsing it out of the corner of our eye, it is a bit blurred, as if it were farther away.

With this knowledge, Leonardo was able to create an uncatchable smile, one that is elusive if we are too intent on seeing it. The very fine lines at the corner of Lisa's mouth show a small downturn, just like the mouth floating atop the anatomy sheet. If you stare directly at the mouth, your retina catches these tiny details and delineations, making her appear not to be smiling. But if you move your gaze slightly away from the mouth, to look at her eyes or cheeks or some other part of the painting, you will catch sight of her mouth only peripherally. It will be a bit blurrier. The tiny delineations at the corners of the mouth become indistinct, but you still will see the shadows there. These shadows and the soft sfumato at the edge of her mouth make her lips seem to turn upward into a subtle smile. The result is a smile that flickers brighter the less you search for it.

Scientists recently found a technical way to describe all of this. "A clear smile is much more apparent in the low spatial frequency [blurrier] images than in the high spatial frequency image," according to Harvard Medical School neuroscientist Margaret Livingstone. "Thus, if you look at the painting so that your gaze falls on the background or on Mona Lisa's hands, your perception of her mouth would be dominated by low spatial frequencies, so it would appear much more cheerful than when you look directly at her mouth." A study at Sheffield Hallam University showed that Leonardo used the same technique not only on *La Belle Ferronnière* but also on the recently discovered drawing *La Bella Principessa*.[21]

So the world's most famous smile is inherently and fundamentally elusive, and therein lies Leonardo's ultimate realization about human nature. His expertise was in depicting the outer manifestation of inner emotions. But here in the *Mona Lisa* he shows something more important: that we can never fully know true emotion from outer manifestations. There is always a sfumato quality to other people's emotions, always a veil.

OTHER VERSIONS

Even as Leonardo was perfecting the *Mona Lisa*, his followers and some of his students were making copies, perhaps with an occasional helping hand from the master. Some are very good, including those known as the Vernon *Mona Lisa* and the Isleworth *Mona Lisa*, prompting claims that they may have been painted wholly or mostly by Leonardo, though most academic experts are skeptical.

The most beautiful copy is one in Madrid's Prado Museum, which was cleaned and restored in 2012 (fig. 135). It provides a glimpse of

Fig. 135. The Prado copy.

what the original looked like before its varnish became yellowed and cracked.[22] In addition to showing a wispy line of eyebrows, the copy displays the vibrant copper tones of Lisa's sleeves, the vividness of the blue-misty landscape, the gold embroidered into her neckline, the transparency of the thin shawl over her left shoulder, and the luster highlighting her ringlets of curls.

That raises the question, considered heretical by some, of whether the original *Mona Lisa* should be cleaned and restored, as the Louvre did its *Virgin and Child with Saint Anne* and *Saint John the Baptist.* Vincent Delieuvin, *Mona Lisa*'s insightful curator at the Louvre, has described the sensation he feels on the one day a year when the painting is removed from behind its glass and taken out of its frame for careful inspection. The impressions of movement are even more vibrant. He knows that just by removing most of the varnish, and not touching the paint itself, the *Mona Lisa*, which has gotten noticeably darker even in modern times, could be seen in more of its original glory. But the painting is such an icon, and so beloved in its varnished darkness, that even the lightest amount of cleaning would spark huge controversy. French governments have fallen over less.

Perhaps the most interesting derivatives of the *Mona Lisa* made by Leonardo's followers are the seminude variations often called *Monna Vanna*, of which there remain at least eight, one of them attributed to Salai (fig. 136). Given that there were so many of these seminude versions done at the time, Leonardo probably approved of them, found them amusing, and may even have provided a preparatory drawing or a now-lost original. One cartoon in the Chateau of Chantilly, which is pricked as if used as the basis for a painting, is of high quality and has some left-handed hatching, indicating that Leonardo may have contributed to it and even conceived it.[23]

FOR THE AGES

When the British needed to contact their allies in the French Resistance during World War II, they used a code phrase: *La Joconde garde un sourire.* The *Mona Lisa* keeps her smile. Even though it may seem to flicker, her smile contains the immutable wisdom of the ages. Her

Fig. 136. The *Monna Vanna*.

portrait is a profound expression of our human connections, both to our inner selves and to our universe.

The *Mona Lisa* became the most famous painting in the world not just due to hype and happenstance but because viewers were able to feel an emotional engagement with her. She provokes a complex series of psychological reactions, which she herself seems to exhibit as well. Most miraculously, she seems aware—conscious—both of us and of herself. That is what makes her seem alive, the most alive of any portrait ever painted. It is also what makes her unique, one of humankind's unsurpassed creations. As Vasari said, "It was painted in a way to make every brave artist tremble and lose heart."

Stand before the *Mona Lisa*, and the historical discussions about how it was commissioned fade into oblivion. As Leonardo worked on it for most of the last sixteen years of his life, it became more than a portrait of an individual. It became universal, a distillation of his accumulated wisdom about the outward manifestations of our inner lives and about the connections between ourselves and our world. Like *Vitruvian Man* standing in the square of the earth and the circle of the heavens, Lisa sitting on her balcony against the backdrop of geological eons is Leonardo's profound meditation on what it means to be human.

And what about all of the scholars and critics over the years who despaired that Leonardo squandered too much time immersed in studying optics and anatomy and the patterns of the cosmos? The *Mona Lisa* answers them with a smile.

CHAPTER 32

France

FINAL JOURNEY

Much of Leonardo's career was consumed by his quest for patrons who would be unconditionally paternalistic, supportive, and indulgent in ways that his own father had only occasionally been. Although Piero da Vinci got his son a good apprenticeship and helped him get commissions, his behavior was variable from beginning to end: he declined to legitimate his son and excluded him from his will. His primary bequest to his son was to give him an insatiable drive for an unconditional patron.

So far all of Leonardo's benefactors had fallen short. When he was a young painter in Florence, the city was ruled by one of history's super-patrons, but Lorenzo de' Medici gave him few if any commissions and sent him away carrying a lyre as a diplomatic gift. As for Ludovico Sforza, it was many years after Leonardo's arrival in Milan before he was invited to become part of the ducal court, and his most important commission, the horse monument, was scuttled by the duke. After France captured Milan in 1499, Leonardo tried to curry favor with a variety of powerful men, including the French governor of Milan Charles d'Amboise, the brutal Italian warrior Cesare Borgia, and the hapless papal brother Giuliano de' Medici. But in each case the fit was not perfect.

Then, on his trip to Bologna with Pope Leo X in December 1515, Leonardo met the new king of France, Francis I, who had just turned twenty-one (fig. 137). At the beginning of that year, he had succeeded his father-in-law, Louis XII, who admired Leonardo, collected his works, and was among the few who could entice him to paint. Right before he met Leonardo in Bologna, Francis had wrested control of Milan from the Sforzas, just as Louis had done in 1499.

When they were in Bologna together, Francis probably invited Leonardo to come to France. Leonardo instead returned to Rome, but only briefly, perhaps to get his affairs in order. During that period, Francis and his court kept up efforts to recruit him, encouraged in that task by Francis's mother, Louise de Savoie. "I beg you to urge Master Leonardo that he should come to the King's presence," a

Fig. 137. King Francis I of France, Leonardo's final patron.

member of Francis's court wrote to their ambassador in Rome in March 1516, adding that Leonardo should be "wholeheartedly assured that he will be most welcome both by the King and by Madame his mother."[1]

That month, Giuliano de' Medici died. Beginning during his early career in Florence, Leonardo's relationship to the Medici family had been uncomfortable. "The Medici made me and destroyed me," he wrote cryptically in his notebook at the time of Giuliano's death.[2] He then accepted the French invitation, and in the summer of 1516, before the snows made the Alps impassable, he left Rome to join the court of the king who would be his final and most devoted patron.

Leonardo had never been out of Italy before. He was sixty-four but looked older and knew this was likely to be his last journey. His entourage was accompanied by several mules that carried his household furniture, trunks of clothing and manuscripts, and at least three paintings he was still obsessively perfecting: the *Virgin and Child with Saint Anne*, *Saint John the Baptist*, and the *Mona Lisa*.

Along the way, he and his traveling party stopped in Milan. Salai decided to stay there, at least temporarily. He was then thirty-six, solidly middle-aged and no longer playing the role of Leonardo's pretty-boy companion or competing for attention with the aristocratic Melzi, who was still only twenty-five and remained at Leonardo's side. Salai would settle down at the vineyard and house on the edge of Milan that had been given to Leonardo by Ludovico Sforza. Over the next three years, until Leonardo's death, he would visit Leonardo in France but spend little time there: he received only one stipend payment, which was one-eighth the total of the regular ones that Melzi received.

Perhaps another reason Salai stayed behind was that Leonardo had a new manservant, Battista de Vilanis, who traveled with him from Rome to France. He would soon replace Salai in Leonardo's affections. Salai would end up inheriting only half of the Milan vineyard and its rights; Battista would get the other half.[3]

FRANCIS I

King Francis I was six feet tall, had broad shoulders, and displayed the charisma and courage that appealed to Leonardo. He loved leading his troops into battle. With his standard flying high, he would ride directly to the front lines. He was also, unlike Borgia and some of Leonardo's previous patrons, a civilized and decent man. When Francis captured Milan, instead of killing or even imprisoning its duke, Maximilian Sforza, he let him live at the French court.

Through his cultured mother, Louise de Savoie, and his bevy of dedicated and accomplished tutors, Francis was inculcated with a love of the Italian Renaissance. Unlike the Italian dukes and princes, French kings had collected very few paintings and almost no sculpture, and French art was greatly overshadowed by that of the Italians and Flemish. Francis set out to change that. He had the ambition, which he largely fulfilled, of launching in France the Renaissance that had been sweeping Italy.

He was also a voracious seeker of knowledge, with interests as universal as Leonardo's. He loved science and math, geography and history, poetry and music and literature. He learned Italian, Latin, Spanish, and Hebrew. Personally gregarious and with women lascivious, he cut a dashing figure as a graceful dancer, expert hunter, and powerful wrestler. After spending a few hours each morning on affairs of state, he would have someone read to him the great writers of ancient Rome and Greece. He also put on plays and pageants in the evening. Leonardo was the perfect recruit for his court.[4]

Likewise, Francis proved to be the perfect patron for Leonardo. He would admire Leonardo unconditionally, never pester him about finishing paintings, indulge his love of engineering and architecture, encourage him to stage pageants and fantasias, give him a comfortable home, and pay him a regular stipend. Leonardo was given the title "First Painter, Engineer, and Architect to the King," but his value to Francis was his intellect and not his output. Francis had an unquenchable thirst for learning, and Leonardo was the world's best source of experiential knowledge. He could teach the king about almost any subject there was to know, from how the eye works to why the moon shines. In turn, Leonardo could learn from the erudite and graceful young king. As Leonardo once wrote in his notebooks, referring to Alexander the Great and his tutor, "Alexander and Aristotle were teachers of one another."[5]

Francis became "completely enamored" with Leonardo, according to the sculptor Cellini. "He took such pleasure in hearing him discourse that there were few days in the year when he was parted from him, which was one of the reasons why Leonardo did not manage to pursue to the end his miraculous studies." Cellini later quoted Francis declaring that he "could never believe there was another man born in this world who knew as much as Leonardo, and not only of sculpture, painting and architecture, and that he was truly a great philosopher."[6]

Francis gave Leonardo something he had continually sought: a comfortable stipend that was not dependent on producing any paintings. In addition, he was given the use of a small red-brick manor house, with sandstone trimming and playful spires, next to Francis's castle in the Loire Valley village of Amboise. Known as the Château de Cloux, and now called Clos Lucé, Leonardo's house (fig. 138) was

Fig. 138. Château de Cloux, now called Clos Lucé.

set amid almost three acres of gardens and vineyards and connected by an underground tunnel to the king's Château d'Amboise, about five hundred yards away.

The large hall on the ground floor was spacious without being cold and formal. There Leonardo ate with his retinue and visitors. Above it was Leonardo's large bedroom (fig. 139), which had thick oak beams, a stone fireplace, and a view over a grassy slope to the king's château. Melzi probably had the other room on the second floor; he drew a sketch of the view from one of its windows. He kept a list of books that Leonardo, ever curious, wanted him to procure, among them a study of the formation of the fetus in the womb, which had just been published in Paris, and a printed volume by Roger Bacon, the thirteenth-century friar from Oxford who was a forerunner of Leonardo as a scientific experimenter.

As he had for his previous patrons, Leonardo designed and staged pageants for King Francis. In May 1518, for example, there were celebrations at Amboise to mark the baptism of the king's son and the marriage of his niece. The preparations included the construction of an arch topped by a salamander and an ermine, symbolizing the rap-

Fig. 139. Leonardo's last bedroom.

prochement between France and Italy. The piazza was transformed into a theatrical fortress with fake artillery "firing air-inflated balls with great blasting and smoking effects," according to a dispatch from one diplomat. "These balls, falling on the piazza, bounced all over to everyone's delight and without any damage." (A Leonardo drawing from 1518 showing a mechanical device to hurl balls is usually regarded as an example of his military engineering, but it was, I think, for this pageant.)[7]

At an open-air banquet and dance for the king in the gardens of the Château de Cloux the following month, Leonardo helped to re-create scenes from the performance he had staged almost thirty years earlier in Milan for the wedding of Gian Galeazzo Sforza to Isabella of Aragon: the play *Paradiso* by the poet Bernardo Bellincioni, with players costumed as each of the seven known planets and the mechanical marvel of an egg-shaped orb opening up to reveal paradise. "The courtyard was entirely covered with sky-blue sheets with golden-hued stars to look like the sky," one ambassador reported. "There must have been four hundred two-branched candelabras,

Fig. 140. Drawing for a masquerade.

which gave so much light that it was as if the night had been chased away."[8] The plays and masquerades were fleeting, but some of Leonardo's drawings for them remain. One beautiful sheet (fig. 140) shows a young man on horseback holding a lance and wearing an elaborate costume with helmet, feathers, and multiple layers of garment.

THE DE BEATIS VISIT

In October 1517, after Leonardo had been in Amboise for a year, he received a distinguished visitor, Cardinal Luigi of Aragon, who was taking a prolonged trip through Europe accompanied by more than forty members of his entourage. They had known each other in Rome, where the cardinal entertained grandly and was renowned for his gorgeous mistress, with whom he had a daughter. Accompanying him was his chaplain and secretary, Antonio de Beatis, whose diary provides us with our final close-up scene of Leonardo as a lion in winter.[9]

De Beatis referred to Leonardo as "the most eminent painter of our time," which was certainly true but provides evidence that he was regarded as such by his contemporaries, even though the *Mona Lisa*, the *Saint Anne*, and the *Saint John* had not been widely seen, and many of his public commissions, from the *Adoration of the Magi* to the *Battle of Anghiari*, had been left unfinished.

De Beatis described Leonardo, then sixty-five, as "a greybeard of more than seventy years." This is interesting, because many of the possible portraits of Leonardo, including the one in red chalk in Turin widely considered a self-portrait, are sometimes dismissed because they show a subject who seems to be older than Leonardo was. Perhaps, however, Leonardo did in fact look older than he was. By the time he reached his sixties, his despairs and demons may have wizened him.

We can imagine the scene. The visitors are welcomed into the large oak-beamed hall of the manor house, are served drinks by Leonardo's cook, Mathurine, and Leonardo then proceeds to play the role of the venerable icon of art and science, hosting the guests in his upstairs studio chamber. He begins by showing the cardinal and his retinue three easel paintings that he had carried with him on his travels: "One of a certain Florentine lady, done from life at the instigation of the late Giuliano de' Medici, the second is of the youthful Saint John the Baptist, and a third of the Madonna with the Child placed on the lap of Saint Anne, all of the highest perfection." Other than launching a subcult of scholars who have come up with alternative theories about the *Mona Lisa* based on de Beatis's account, the scene is sweetly reassuring. Here is Leonardo, in a comfortable room with a large fireplace, nurturing the paintings he loves and showing them off as his private treasures.

De Beatis also reported that Leonardo's ailments now included an apparent stroke: "Because of a paralysis in his right hand, one can no longer expect any masterpieces from him. He has trained a Milanese disciple [Melzi] who works very well, for if Master Leonardo is no longer capable of painting with the gentleness of touch which was his, he nevertheless continues to draw and teach." There is a typical Leonardo mystery here: he is left-handed, so perhaps the paralysis did not affect him much; we know that he was still drawing in Amboise, and while there he reworked the face and the blue drapery clothing on the left side of his *Saint Anne*.[10]

Leonardo's carefully staged tour also included some glimpses of his notebooks and treatises. "This gentleman has written a great deal about anatomy," de Beatis reported, "with many illustrations of the parts of the body, such as the muscles, nerves, veins and the coilings of intestines, and this makes it possible to understand the bodies of both men and women in a way that has never been done before. All this we saw with our own eyes, and he told us he had already dissected more than thirty bodies, both men and women, of all ages."

Leonardo also described, but apparently did not put on display, the work he had done on science and engineering. "He has also written, as he himself put it, an infinity of volumes on the nature of waters, on various machines, and on other things, all in the vernacular, and if these were to be brought to light they would be both useful and delightful." De Beatis recorded that the books were in Italian ("the vernacular"), but he does not mention the very notable fact that they were written in mirror script; he probably was shown the anatomy drawings but not the actual notebook pages. He is right about one thing: if they were to be published, they would be "both useful and delightful." Alas, Leonardo was not spending his final years at Amboise preparing them for publication.

ROMORANTIN

Rather than commissioning a big piece of public art, the king offered Leonardo an ideal assignment for the culmination of his career: designing a new town and palace complex for the royal court at the village of Romorantin, on the Sauldre River in the center of France, some fifty miles from Amboise. It would, if it came to pass, allow the expression of many of Leonardo's passions: architecture, urban planning, waterworks, engineering, even pageantry and spectacle.

In late 1517 he accompanied the king to Romorantin, where they stayed until January 1518. Drawing on the ideas and fantasies he had developed for an ideal city while living in Milan thirty years earlier, Leonardo began sketching in his notebook his radical and utopian aspirations for inventing a town from scratch.

The plan was for an idyllic palace rather than a fortress-like castle; his interest in military engineering and fortifications had waned. Melzi took charge of pacing the measurements of the existing streets and recording them. Then Leonardo sketched several designs. One is centered on a three-story palace with arched walkways facing the river. Another imagines two castles, one of which would be for the king's mother, with part of the river between them. Featured in all the designs are a profusion of different types of staircases: double doglegs, triple spirals, and various other curves and twists. For Leonardo, staircases were locations for complex flows and twisting motions, which he always loved.[11]

All of the plans were conceived with great outdoor spectacles and water pageants in mind. The galleries facing the river could serve as tiered viewing areas accommodating the entire French court, and there are broad steps that gently lead down to the water level. His drawings show small boats parading on the river and on man-made lakes for aquatic spectacles. "The jousters are to be on the boats," he writes next to one.

Leonardo's lifelong fascination with water suffuses all aspects of his plans for Romorantin, which feature a variety of aquatic engineering both practical and decorative. As with the earth, the waterways serve, both metaphorically and in reality, as the veins of the palace complex. Leonardo envisioned their use for irrigation, street cleaning, flushing out horse stables, carrying away rubbish, and as wonderful displays and decorations. "There should be fountains in every plaza," he declared. There should be "four mills where the water enters the town and four at the outlet, and this may be done by damming the water above Romorantin."[12]

Leonardo had soon expanded his watery dreams to include the entire region. He envisioned a system of canals that would connect the Sauldre to the Loire and Saône rivers, irrigate the region, and drain its marshes. Ever since he had marveled at the locks and canals that tamed the waters of Milan, he had tried to conquer the flow of water. He failed to do it with his plan for diverting the Arno near Florence or draining the Pontine Marshes near Rome. Now he hoped to succeed at Romorantin. "If the tributary of the Loire River were turned with its muddy waters into the river of Romorantin, it would fatten the land it waters, make the land fertile, supply food to the inhabitants, and serve as a navigable canal for commerce," he wrote.[13]

It was not to be. The project was abandoned in 1519, the year Leonardo died. Instead, the king decided to build his new château at Chambord, in the Loire Valley between Amboise and Romorantin. There the ground was less marshy and fewer canals were required.

THE DELUGE DRAWINGS

Leonardo's interest in the art and science of movement, and in particular the flow and swirl of water and wind, climaxed in a series of turbulent drawings that he made during his final years in France.[14] Sixteen of them are known to still exist, eleven of which were done together as a series using black chalk sometimes finished with ink; they are now part of the Windsor collection (for example, figs. 141 and 142).[15] Deeply personal yet coolly analytic in parts, they provide a powerful and dark expression of many of the themes of his life: the

Fig. 141.

Fig. 142.

Deluge drawings.

melding of art and science, the blurred line between experience and fantasy, and the frightful power of nature.

The drawings also convey, I believe, his own emotional turmoil as he faced his final days, partly hobbled by a stroke. They became an outlet for his feelings and fears. "They are an outpouring of something really personal," according to Windsor curator Martin Clayton, "a kind of crescendo at a time when his concerns are more strongly expressed."[16]

Throughout his life he had been obsessed with water and its movements. One of his first drawings, the landscape of the Arno done when he was twenty-one, shows a placid river, calm and life-giving as it meanders gently past fertile land and tranquil villages. It displays no signs of turbulence, just a few gentle ripples. Like a vein, it nourishes life. In his notebooks, there are dozens of references to water as the life-giving fluid that forms the vein that nourishes the earth. "Water is the vital humor [*vitale umore*] of the arid earth," he wrote. "Flowing with unceasing vehemence through the ramifying veins, it replenishes all the parts."[17] In the Codex Leicester he described, by his own count, "657 cases of water and its depths."[18] His mechanical engineering work included close to a hundred devices for moving and diverting water. Year after year he devised plans involving hydrodynamics, which included improving Milan's canal system, flooding the plains around Venice to defend against a Turkish invasion, channeling a direct link from Florence to the sea, diverting the Arno River around Pisa, draining the Pontine Marshes for Pope Leo X, and creating a canal system at Romorantin for King Francis I. But now, near the end of his life, he depicted water and its swirls not as calm or tamed but as filled with fury.

The deluge drawings are powerful works of art. The pages contain framing lines, and the back side of each is blank, signaling that they were drawn for display, or perhaps as artistic accompaniments to a reading of an apocalyptic tale, not just as scientific illustrations in a notebook. Some of the most vivid are done in chalk, then lined with ink and tinted with a color wash. Especially for those who love curls and swirls, as Leonardo did, the drawings are an artistic expression of great aesthetic power. They remind us of the curls cascading down the back of the angel in his *Annunciation*, the painting he made some forty years earlier. Indeed, the underdrawing of the angel's curls, as revealed by a spectrographic analysis, is strikingly similar to the spirals of the deluge drawings.[19]

The careful and detailed observation of motion was one of Leonardo's specialties, and so too was extending his observations into the realm of fantasy. His deluge drawings are based on storms he had witnessed and described in his notebooks, but they are also the product of a fevered and frenzied imagination. He was a master at blurring lines, and in his deluge drawings he did so between reality and fantasia.

Leonardo liked to use both words and drawings to depict his ideas, and this was especially true of the deluge. In three very long passages totaling more than two thousand words, he wrote "of the deluge and how to represent it in a picture." Much of this was intended for his planned treatise on painting. He wrote as if he were instructing both himself and students:

> Let the dark and gloomy air be seen buffeted by the rush of contrary winds and dense from the continued rain mingled with hail and bearing hither and thither an infinite number of branches torn from the trees and mixed with numberless leaves. All round may be seen venerable trees, uprooted by the fury of the winds; and fragments of mountains, already scoured bare by the torrents, falling into those torrents and choking their valleys till the swollen rivers overflow and submerge the wide lowlands and their inhabitants. You might see on many of the hill-tops terrified animals of different kinds, collected together and subdued to tameness, in company with men and women who had fled there with their children.

Leonardo's description continues for two closely written pages of his notebook, and by halfway through he is no longer instructing how to paint a scene. Instead, he has whipped himself into a frenzy describing the apocalyptic deluge and the emotions of the humans as they are thrashed. Perhaps parts were intended to be performed for the king, accompanied by the pictures. Whatever its purpose, the description descends into the darkest of all Leonardo's fantasia scenes:

> Others, with desperate act, took their own lives, hopeless of being able to endure such suffering; and of these, some flung themselves from lofty rocks, others strangled themselves with their own hands, other seized their own children and violently slew them at a blow; some wounded and killed themselves with their own weapons; others, falling on their knees recommended themselves to God. Ah! how many mothers wept over their drowned sons, holding them upon their knees, with arms raised spread out towards heaven and with words and various threatening gestures, upbraiding the wrath of the gods. Others with clasped hands and fingers clenched gnawed them and devoured them till they bled, crouching with their breast down on their knees in their intense and unbearable anguish.[20]

Mixed in with the gloomy fantasy are careful observations about how flowing water when diverted forms swirls and eddies: "The swollen waters will sweep around the pool that contains them, striking in eddying whirlpools against the different obstacles." Even amid the darkest passages there are specific scientific injunctions. "If the heavy masses of large mountains or grand buildings fall into the vast pools of water, a great quantity will be flung into the air and its movement will be in a contrary direction to that of the object which struck the water; the angle of reflection will be equal to the angle of incidence."[21]

The deluge drawings conjure up the story of the Flood in Genesis, a topic treated by Michelangelo and many other artists over the years, but Leonardo makes no mention of Noah. He was conveying more than a biblical tale. At one point he adds Greek and Roman classical gods to the fray: "Neptune will be seen in the midst of the water with his trident, and let Aeolus with his winds be shown entangling the trees floating uprooted and whirling in the huge waves."[22] He drew on Virgil's *Aeneid*, Ovid's *Metamorphoses*, and the thunderous natural phenomena in book 6 of Lucretius's *On the Nature of Things*. The drawings and text also conjure up the tale he wrote in Milan in the 1490s, ostensibly addressed to "the Devatdar of Syria." In that story, performed at Ludovico Sforza's court, Leonardo vividly described "a sudden rain, or rather a ruinous storm full of water, sand, mud, and stones all mingled together with roots, stems, and branches of various trees; and every kind of thing came hurtling through the air and descended upon us."[23]

Leonardo did not focus on, or for that matter even hint at, the wrath of God in his deluge writings and drawings. He conveyed instead his belief that chaos and destruction are inherent in the raw power of nature. The psychological effect is more harrowing than if he were merely depicting a tale of punishment from an angry God. He was imparting his own emotions and thereby tapping into ours. Hallucinatory and hypnotic, the deluge drawings are the unnerving bookend to a life of nature drawing that began with a sketch of the placid Arno flowing near his native village.

THE END

On what may be the last page he wrote in his notebooks, Leonardo drew four right triangles with bases of differing lengths (fig. 143). Inside of each he fit a rectangle, and then he shaded the remaining areas of the triangle. In the center of the page he made a chart with boxes labeled with the letter of each rectangle, and below it he described what he was trying to accomplish. As he had done obsessively over the years, he was using the visualization of geometry to help him understand the transformation of shapes. Specifically, he was trying to understand the formula for keeping the area of a right triangle the same while varying the lengths of its two legs. He had fussed with this problem, explored by Euclid, repeatedly over the years. It was a puzzle that, by this point in his life, as he turned sixty-seven and his health faded, might seem unnecessary to solve. To anyone other than Leonardo, it may have been.

Then abruptly, almost at the end of the page, he breaks off his writing with an "et cetera." That is followed by a line, written in the same meticulous mirror script as the previous lines of his analysis,

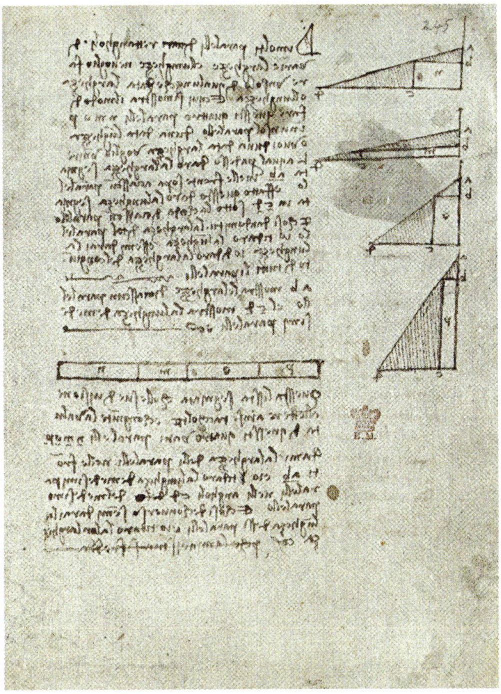

Fig. 143. Studies of right triangle areas, ending with "the soup is getting cold."

explaining why he is putting down his pen. "Perché la minestra si fredda," he writes. Because the soup is getting cold.[24]

It is the final piece of writing we have by Leonardo's hand, our last scene of him working. Picture him in the upstairs study of his manor house, with its beamed ceiling and fireplace and the view of his royal patron's Château d'Amboise. Mathurine, his cook, is down in the kitchen. Perhaps Melzi and others of the household are already at the table. After all these years, he is still stabbing away at geometry problems that have not yielded the world very much but have given him a profound appreciation of the patterns of nature. Now, however, the soup is getting cold.

There is one final document. On April 23, 1518, eight days after his sixty-seventh birthday, Leonardo had his last will and testament drawn up by a notary in Amboise, witnessed, and signed. He had been ill, and like a good son of a notary he began getting his affairs in order. It begins, "Be it known to all persons, present and to come, that at the court of our Lord the King at Amboise before ourselves in person, Messer Leonardo da Vinci, painter to the King, at present staying at the place known as Cloux near Amboise, duly considering the certainty of death and the uncertainty of its time . . ."

In his will, Leonardo commended his "soul to our Lord, Almighty God, and to the glorious Virgin Mary," but that seems to have been merely a literary flourish. His science led him to adopt many heretical beliefs, including that the fetus in the womb does not have a soul of its own and that the biblical Flood did not happen. Unlike Michelangelo, a man consumed at times with religious fervor, Leonardo made a point of not expounding much on religion during his lifetime. He said that he would not endeavor "to write or give information of those things of which the human mind is incapable and which cannot be proved by an instance of nature," and he left such matters "to the minds of friars, fathers of the people, who by inspiration possess the secrets."[25]

The first items in his will prescribe what shall be his funeral services. His body will be carried to the church at Amboise by its chaplains. "In the said church of Saint Florentin," he specified, "three high masses shall be celebrated by the deacon and sub-deacon and on the same day thirty low masses shall also be performed at Saint Gregory." This will be followed by three masses at the nearby church of Saint Denis. He wanted "sixty candles carried by sixty poor men, to whom shall be given money for carrying them."

To Mathurine, the serving woman who made the soup, he bequeathed "a cloak of good black woolen cloth lined with fur" and 2 ducats. To his half-brothers, he fulfilled what had probably been the legal settlement of their earlier dispute by giving them a sizable cash payment and the property he had inherited from his uncle Francesco.

As Leonardo's de facto and perhaps legally adopted son and heir, Francesco Melzi was named the executor and bequeathed most of the estate. This included Leonardo's pension, all sums of money owed to him, his clothes, books, writings, and "all the instruments and portraits pertaining to his art and calling as a painter." To his most recently hired house servant and companion, Battista de Vilanis, Leonardo left the water rights that had been granted him in Milan as well as half of the vineyard given to him by Ludovico Sforza. He also gave Battista "each and all of the articles of furniture and utensils in his house at Cloux."

And then there was Salai. He was designated to get the other half of the vineyard. Since he was already living there and had built a house on a portion of the land, it would be hard for Leonardo to have done otherwise with the property. But that was all Salai was bequeathed in the will. There had apparently been an estrangement, one that had grown with the ascent of Melzi and the arrival of Battista. Salai was no longer at Leonardo's side when he made the will. Nevertheless, he lived up to his reputation as a sticky-fingered little devil, one who was somehow able to get his hands on things. When he was killed five years later by a crossbow, the inventory of his estate showed that, perhaps during a visit to France, he had been given or had taken many copies of Leonardo's paintings and possibly some of the originals, perhaps including the *Mona Lisa* and *Leda and the Swan*. Always the con artist, it is unclear whether the prices listed in his estate are true values, thus making it hard to know which were copies. Except for the *Leda*, which was lost, whatever original paintings Salai had were returned to France, perhaps having previously been sold by him to the king, and eventually ended up in the Louvre.[26]

"As a well-spent day brings a happy sleep," Leonardo had written thirty years earlier, "so a well-employed life brings a happy death."[27] His came on May 2, 1519, less than three weeks after he turned sixty-seven.

In his biographical essay on Leonardo, Vasari describes a final scene that, as with many of his passages, is likely a mix of truth and his own wishful imagination. Leonardo, he wrote, "feeling himself near to death, asked to have himself diligently informed of the teaching of the Catholic faith, and of the good way and holy Christian religion; and then, with many moans, he confessed and was penitent;

and although he could not raise himself well on his feet, supporting himself on the arms of his friends and servants, he was pleased to take devoutly the most holy Sacrament."

This trope of a deathbed confession feels like something Vasari, who was not there, would invent, or at least embellish. He was more eager to have Leonardo embrace faith than Leonardo himself probably was. As Vasari knew, Leonardo was not conventionally religious. In the first edition of his biography, he wrote that Leonardo "formed in his mind a doctrine so heretical that he depended no more on any religion, perhaps placing scientific knowledge higher than Christian faith." He eliminated that passage in the second edition of the book, presumably to protect Leonardo's reputation.

Vasari goes on to recount that King Francis, "who was in the habit of making frequent affectionate visits to him," arrived in Leonardo's chambers just as the priest who had performed the last rites was leaving. Leonardo then summoned the strength to sit up and give a description of his illness and its symptoms. Of all parts of Vasari's deathbed account, that is the most believable. It is easy to imagine Leonardo explaining to the smart and curious young king the intricacies of a failing heart and blood vessels.

"Thereupon he was seized by a paroxysm, the messenger of death," Vasari reports, "the King having risen and having taken his head, in order to assist him and show him favor to the end, in the hope of alleviating his sufferings, the spirit of Leonardo, which was most divine, conscious that it could attain to no greater honor, breathed its last in the arms of the King."

It was a moment so perfect that it was later portrayed by many admiring painters, most notably Jean-Auguste-Dominique Ingres (fig. 144). And thus we have a fitting and beautiful final scene: Leonardo cradled on his deathbed by a powerful and doting patron in a comfortable house surrounded by his favorite paintings.

But with Leonardo, nothing is quite so simple. The image of him dying in the arms of the king may, or may not, be another sentimental myth. We know that King Francis issued a proclamation on May 3 at Saint-Germain-en-Laye, which was a two-day ride from Amboise. So it seems that he could not have actually been with Leonardo the

Fig. 144. Jean-Auguste-Dominique Ingres, *The Death of Leonardo*.

day before. Or then again, perhaps he could have been. The proclamation in question was issued by the king but was not signed by him. Instead it was signed by his chancellor, and the records coming out of the council do not mention the king's presence. So there remains the possibility that the king stayed in Amboise to cradle the head of his dying genius.[28]

Leonardo was buried in the church of the Château d'Amboise, but the current location of his remains is another mystery. That church was demolished in the early nineteenth century, and sixty years later the site was excavated and a collection of bones found that may have been those of Leonardo. The bones were reburied at the chapel of Saint-Hubert adjoining the château, and a tomb slab was installed saying it was the site of his "presumed remains" (*restes présumés*).

As always with Leonardo, in his art and in his life, in his birthplace and now even in his death, there is a veil of mystery. We cannot portray him with crisp sharp lines, nor should we want to, just as he would not have wanted to portray Mona Lisa that way. There is something nice about leaving a little to our imagination. As he knew, the outlines of reality are inherently blurry, leaving a hint of uncertainty that we should embrace. The best way to approach his life is the way he approached the world: filled with a sense of curiosity and an appreciation for its infinite wonders.

Chapter 33

Conclusion

GENIUS

In the introduction to this book, I suggested that it was unhelpful to toss around the word *genius* as if it were a superhuman trait, bestowed by heaven and not within the ken of mere mortals. As I hope you will by now agree, Leonardo was a genius, one of the few people in history who indisputably deserved—or, to be more precise, *earned*—that appellation. Yet it is also true that he was a mere mortal.

The most obvious evidence that he was human rather than superhuman is the trail of projects he left unfinished. Among them were a horse model that archers reduced to rubble, an Adoration scene and battle mural that were abandoned, flying machines that never flew, tanks that never rolled, a river that was never diverted, and pages of brilliant treatises that piled up unpublished. "Tell me if anything was ever done," he repeatedly scribbled in notebook after notebook. "Tell me. Tell me. Tell me if ever I did a thing. . . . Tell me if anything was ever made."[1]

Of course, the things he did finish were enough to prove his genius. The *Mona Lisa* alone does that, as do all of his art masterpieces as well as his anatomical drawings. But by the end of writing this book, I even began to appreciate the genius inherent in his designs left unexecuted and masterpieces left unfinished. By skirting the edge of fantasy with his flying machines and water projects and military devices, he envisioned what innovators would invent centuries later. And by refusing to churn out works that he had not perfected, he sealed his reputation as a genius rather than a master craftsman. He enjoyed the challenge of conception more than the chore of completion.

One reason that he was reluctant to relinquish some of his works and declare them completed was that he relished a world in flux. He had an uncanny ability to convey movements—of the body and the mind, of machines and horses, and of rivers and everything else that flows. No instant, he wrote, is self-contained, just as no action in a theatrical pageant nor any drop in a flowing river is self-contained. Each moment incorporates what came right before and what is coming right after. Similarly, he looked upon his art and engineering and his treatises as a part of a dynamic process, always receptive to a refinement by the application of a new insight. He updated *Saint Jerome in the Wilderness* after thirty years, when his anatomy experiments taught him something new about neck muscles. If he had lived another decade, he likely would have continued to refine the *Mona Lisa* for that much longer. Relinquishing a work, declaring it finished, froze its evolution. Leonardo did not like to do that. There was always something more to be learned, another stroke to be gleaned from nature that would make a picture closer to perfect.

What made Leonardo a genius, what set him apart from people who are merely extraordinarily smart, was creativity, the ability to apply imagination to intellect. His facility for combining observation with fantasy allowed him, like other creative geniuses, to make unexpected leaps that related things seen to things unseen. "Talent hits a target that no one else can hit," wrote the German philosopher Arthur Schopenhauer. "Genius hits a target no one else can see."[2] Because they "think different," creative masterminds are sometimes considered misfits, but in the words that Steve Jobs helped craft for an Apple advertisement, "While some may see them as the crazy ones, we see genius. Because the people who are crazy enough to think they can change the world are the ones who do."[3]

What also distinguished Leonardo's genius was its universal nature. The world has produced other thinkers who were more profound or logical, and many who were more practical, but none who was as creative in so many different fields. Some people are geniuses in a particular arena, such as Mozart in music and Euler in math. But Leonardo's brilliance spanned multiple disciplines, which gave him a profound feel for nature's patterns and crosscurrents. His curiosity impelled him to become among the handful of people in history who tried to know all there was to know about everything that could be known.

There have been, of course, many other insatiable polymaths, and even the Renaissance produced other Renaissance Men. But none painted the *Mona Lisa*, much less did so at the same time as producing unsurpassed anatomy drawings based on multiple dissections, coming up with schemes to divert rivers, explaining the reflection of light from the earth to the moon, opening the still-beating heart of a butchered pig to show how ventricles work, designing musical instruments, choreographing pageants, using fossils to dispute the biblical account of the deluge, and then drawing the deluge. Leonardo was a genius, but more: he was the epitome of the universal mind, one who sought to understand all of creation, including how we fit into it.

LEARNING FROM LEONARDO

The fact that Leonardo was not only a genius but also very human—quirky and obsessive and playful and easily distracted—makes him more accessible. He was not graced with the type of brilliance that is completely unfathomable to us. Instead, he was self-taught and willed his way to his genius. So even though we may never be able to match his talents, we can learn from him and try to be more like him. His life offers a wealth of lessons.

Be curious, relentlessly curious. "I have no special talents," Einstein once wrote to a friend. "I am just passionately curious."[4] Leonardo actually did have special talents, as did Einstein, but his distinguishing and most inspiring trait was his intense curiosity. He wanted to know what causes people to yawn, how they walk on ice in Flanders, methods for squaring a circle, what makes the aortic valve close, how light is processed in the eye and what that means for the perspective in a painting. He instructed himself to learn about the placenta of a calf, the jaw of a crocodile, the tongue of a woodpecker, the muscles of a face, the light of the moon, and the edges of shadows. Being relentlessly and randomly curious about everything around us is something that each of us can push ourselves to do, every waking hour, just as he did.

Seek knowledge for its own sake. Not all knowledge needs to be useful. Sometimes it should be pursued for pure pleasure. Leonardo did not need to know how heart valves work to paint the *Mona Lisa*, nor did he need to figure out how fossils got to the top of mountains to produce *Virgin of the Rocks*. By allowing himself to be driven by pure curiosity, he got to explore more horizons and see more connections than anyone else of his era.

Retain a childlike sense of wonder. At a certain point in life, most of us quit puzzling over everyday phenomena. We might savor the beauty of a blue sky, but we no longer bother to wonder why it is that color. Leonardo did. So did Einstein, who wrote to another friend, "You and I never cease to stand like curious children before the great mystery into which we were born."[5] We should be careful to never outgrow our wonder years, or to let our children do so.

Observe. Leonardo's greatest skill was his acute ability to observe things. It was the talent that empowered his curiosity, and vice versa. It was not some magical gift but a product of his own effort. When he visited the moats surrounding Sforza Castle, he looked at the four-wing dragonflies and noticed how the wing pairs alternate in motion. When he walked around town, he observed how the facial expressions of people relate to their emotions, and he discerned how light bounces off differing surfaces. He saw which birds move their wings faster on the upswing than on the downswing, and which do the opposite. This, too, we can emulate. Water flowing into a bowl? Look, as he did, at exactly how the eddies swirl. Then wonder why.

Start with the details. In his notebook, Leonardo shared a trick for observing something carefully: Do it in steps, starting with each detail. A page of a book, he noted, cannot be absorbed in one stare; you need to go word by word. "If you wish to have a sound knowledge of the forms of objects, begin with the details of them, and do not go on to the second step until you have the first well fixed in memory."[6]

See things unseen. Leonardo's primary activity in many of his formative years was conjuring up pageants, performances, and plays. He mixed theatrical ingenuity with fantasy. This gave him a combinatory creativity. He could see birds in flight and also angels, lions roaring and also dragons.

Go down rabbit holes. He filled the opening pages of one of his notebooks with 169 attempts to square a circle. In eight pages of his Codex Leicester, he recorded 730 findings about the flow of water; in another notebook, he listed sixty-seven words that describe different types of moving water. He measured every segment of the human body, calculated their proportional relationships, and then did the same for a horse. He drilled down for the pure joy of geeking out.

Get distracted. The greatest rap on Leonardo was that these passionate pursuits caused him to wander off on tangents, literally in the case of his math inquiries. It "has left posterity the poorer," Kenneth Clark lamented. But in fact, Leonardo's willingness to pursue whatever shiny subject caught his eye made his mind richer and filled with more connections.

Respect facts. Leonardo was a forerunner of the age of observational experiments and critical thinking. When he came up with an idea, he devised an experiment to test it. And when his experience showed that a theory was flawed—such as his belief that the springs within the earth are replenished the same way as blood vessels in humans—he abandoned his theory and sought a new one. This practice became common a century later, during the age of Galileo and Bacon. It has, however, become a bit less prevalent these days. If we want to be more like Leonardo, we have to be fearless about changing our minds based on new information.

Procrastinate. While painting *The Last Supper*, Leonardo would sometimes stare at the work for an hour, finally make one small stroke, and then leave. He told Duke Ludovico that creativity requires time for ideas to marinate and intuitions to gel. "Men of lofty genius sometimes accomplish the most when they work least," he explained, "for their minds are occupied with their ideas and the perfection of their conceptions, to which they afterwards give form." Most of us don't need advice to procrastinate; we do it naturally. But procrastinating like Leonardo requires work: it involves gathering all the possible facts and ideas, and only after that allowing the collection to simmer.

Let the perfect be the enemy of the good. When Leonardo could not make the perspective in the *Battle of Anghiari* or the interaction in the *Adoration of the Magi* work perfectly, he abandoned them rather than produce a work that was merely good enough. He carried around masterpieces such as his *Saint Anne* and the *Mona Lisa* to the end, knowing there would always be a new stroke he could add. Likewise, Steve Jobs was such a perfectionist that he held up shipping the original Macintosh until his team could make the circuit boards inside look beautiful, even though no one would ever see them. Both he and Leonardo knew that real artists care about the beauty even of the parts unseen. Eventually, Jobs embraced a countermaxim, "Real artists ship," which means that sometimes you ought to deliver a product even when there are still improvements that could be made. That is a good rule for daily life. But there are times when it's nice to be like Leonardo and not let go of something until it's perfect.

Think visually. Leonardo was not blessed with the ability to formulate math equations or abstractions. So he had to visualize them, which he did with his studies of proportions, his rules of perspective, his method for calculating reflections from concave mirrors, and his ways of changing one shape into another of the same size. Too often, when we learn a formula or a rule—even one so simple as the method for multiplying numbers or mixing a paint color—we no longer visualize how it works. As a result, we lose our appreciation for the underlying beauty of nature's laws.

Avoid silos. At the end of many of his product presentations, Jobs displayed a slide of a sign that showed the intersection of "Liberal Arts" and "Technology" streets. He knew that at such crossroads lay creativity. Leonardo had a free-range mind that merrily wandered across all the disciplines of the arts, sciences, engineering, and humanities. His knowledge of how light strikes the retina helped inform the perspective in *The Last Supper*, and on a page of anatomical drawings depicting the dissection of lips he drew the smile that would reappear in the *Mona Lisa*. He knew that art was a science and that science was an art. Whether he was drawing a fetus in the womb or the swirls of a deluge, he blurred the distinction between the two.

Let your reach exceed your grasp. Imagine, as he did, how you would build a human-powered flying machine or divert a river. Even try to devise a perpetual-motion machine or square a circle using only a ruler and a compass. There are some problems we will never solve. Learn why.

Indulge fantasy. His giant crossbow? The turtle-like tanks? His plan for an ideal city? The man-powered mechanisms to flap a flying machine? Just as Leonardo blurred the lines between science and art, he did so between reality and fantasy. It may not have produced flying machines, but it allowed his imagination to soar.

Create for yourself, not just for patrons. No matter how hard the rich and powerful marchesa Isabella d'Este begged, Leonardo would not paint her portrait. But he did begin one of a silk-merchant's wife named Lisa. He did it because he wanted to, and he kept working on it for the rest of his life, never delivering it to the silk merchant.

Collaborate. Genius is often considered the purview of loners who retreat to their garrets and are struck by creative lightning. Like many myths, that of the lone genius has some truth to it. But there's usually more to the story. The Madonnas and drapery studies produced in Verrocchio's studio, and the versions of *Virgin of the Rocks* and *Madonna of the Yarnwinder* and other paintings from Leonardo's studio, were created in such a collaborative manner that it is hard to tell whose hand made which strokes. *Vitruvian Man* was produced after sharing ideas and sketches with friends. Leonardo's best anatomy studies came when he was working in partnership with Marcantonio della Torre. And his most fun work came from collaborations on theatrical productions and evening entertainments at the Sforza court. Genius starts with individual brilliance. It requires singular vision. But executing it often entails working with others. Innovation is a team sport. Creativity is a collaborative endeavor.

Make lists. And be sure to put odd things on them. Leonardo's to-do lists may have been the greatest testaments to pure curiosity the world has ever seen.

Take notes, on paper. Five hundred years later, Leonardo's notebooks are around to astonish and inspire us. Fifty years from now, our own notebooks, if we work up the initiative to start writing them, will be around to astonish and inspire our grandchildren, unlike our tweets and Facebook posts.

Be open to mystery. Not everything needs sharp lines.

CODA

Describe the tongue of the woodpecker

The tongue of a woodpecker can extend more than three times the length of its bill. When not in use, it retracts into the skull and its cartilage-like structure continues past the jaw to wrap around the bird's head and then curve down to its nostril. In addition to digging out grubs from a tree, the long tongue protects the woodpecker's brain. When the bird smashes its beak repeatedly into tree bark, the force exerted on its head is ten times what would kill a human. But its bizarre tongue and supporting structure act as a cushion, shielding the brain from shock.[1]

There is no reason you actually need to know any of this. It is information that has no real utility for your life, just as it had none for Leonardo. But I thought maybe, after reading this book, that you, like Leonardo, who one day put "Describe the tongue of the woodpecker" on one of his eclectic and oddly inspiring to-do lists, would want to know. Just out of curiosity. Pure curiosity.

ABBREVIATIONS OF FREQUENTLY CITED SOURCES

Leonardo's Notebooks

Codex Arundel = Codex Arundel (c. 1492–c. 1518), British Library, London. Contains 238 pages taken from different original Leonardo notebooks, mainly on architecture and machinery.

Codex Ash. = Codex Ashburnham, vols. 1 (1486–90) and 2 (1490–92), l'Institut de France, Paris, formerly (and now once again) parts of Paris Mss. A and B. In the 1840s, folios 81–114 of Paris Ms. A and folios 91–100 of Paris Ms. B were stolen by Count Guglielmo Libri. He sold them to Lord Ashburnham in 1875, who returned them to Paris in 1890. J. P. Richter, in his notebook compilation, cites the Codices Ashburnham, but later literature tends to cite the folio numbers from the restored Paris Ms. A and Ms. B. (See below on the Paris manuscripts.)

Codex Atl. = Codex Atlanticus (1478–1518), Biblioteca Ambrosiana, Milan. The largest compilation of Leonardo's papers, now arranged in twelve volumes. The folios were given new numbers in a restoration in the late 1970s. Folios are usually cited in the old style/new style.

Codex Atl./Pedretti = Carlo Pedretti, *Leonardo da Vinci Codex Atlanticus: A Catalogue of Its Newly Restored Sheets* (Giunti, 1978).

Codex Forster = Codex Forster, vols. 1–3 (1487–1505), Victoria and Albert Museum, London. The three volumes comprise five pocket notebooks, mainly on machinery, geometry, and the transformation of volumes.

Codex Leic. = Codex Leicester (1508–12), Bill Gates's home near Seattle, Washington. Contains seventy-two pages mainly on the earth and its waters.

Codex Madrid = Codex Madrid, vols. 1 (1493–99) and 2 (1493–1505), Biblioteca Nacional de España, Madrid. Rediscovered in 1966.

Codex on Flight = Codex on the Flight of Birds (c. 1505), Biblioteca Reale, Turin. Originally part of Paris Ms. B. A facsimile with translation is on the website of the Smithsonian Air and Space Museum at https://airandspace.si.edu/exhibitions/codex.

Codex Triv. = Codex Trivulzianus (c. 1487–90), Castle Sforza, Milan. One of Leonardo's earliest manuscripts, now contains fifty-five sheets.

Codex Urb. = Codex Urbinas Latinus, Vatican Library. Contains selections from various manuscripts copied and compiled by Francesco Melzi around 1530. An abbreviated version was published in Paris in 1651 as *Trattato della Pittura* or *Treatise on Painting*.

Leonardo on Painting = *Leonardo on Painting*, selected and translated by Martin Kemp and Margaret Walker (Yale, 2001). An anthology, based partly on the Codex Urbinas, of the writings that Leonardo intended to be in his *Treatise on Painting*.

Leonardo Treatise/Pedretti = Leonardo da Vinci, *Libro di Pittura*, edited by Carlo Pedretti, critical transcription by Carlo Vecce (Giunti, 1995). A two-volume facsimile, transcription, and anotation of the Codex Urbinas. Numbers refer to sections assigned by Pedretti.

Leonardo Treatise/Rigaud = Leonardo da Vinci, *A Treatise on Painting*, translated by John Francis Rigaud (Dover, 2005; originally published 1651). Based on the Codex Urbinas. Numbers refer to the numbered entries in the book.

Notebooks/Irma Richter = *Leonardo da Vinci Notebooks*, selected by Irma A. Richter, new edition edited by Thereza Wells with a preface by Martin Kemp (Oxford, 2008; first published 1939). Irma Richter was the daughter of J. P. Richter (see below). This edition includes her refinement and selection from her father's work, further updated with commentary by Wells and Kemp.

Notebooks/J. P. Richter = *The Notebooks of Leonardo da Vinci*, compiled and edited by Jean Paul Richter, 2 vols. (Dover, 1970; first published in 1883). These volumes contain Italian transcriptions and English translations side by side, with many of Leonardo's illustrations plus notes and commentary. I cite the passage numbers used by Richter, 1–1566, which remain consistent in the many editions of his seminal compilation. The two-volume dual-language Dover edition also gives the name and folio number of the original Leonardo notebook.

Notebooks/MacCurdy = Edward MacCurdy, *The Notebooks of Leonardo da Vinci* (Cape, 1938). Numerous editions are available online. Numbers refer to the passage number given by MacCurdy.

Paris Ms. = Manuscripts in l'Institut de France, which include A (written 1490–92), B (1486–90), C (1490–91), D (1508–9), E (1513–14), F (1508–13), G (1510–15), H (1493–94), I (1497–1505), K1, K2, K3 (1503–8), L (1497–1502), M (1495–1500).

Windsor = Royal Collection, Windsor Castle. The Royal Collection Inventory Number (RCIN) entries for Leonardo have a 9 before the catalogue number.

Other Frequently Cited Sources

Anonimo Gaddiano = The Anonimo Gaddiano or Anonimo Magliabecchiano, in "Life of Leonardo," translated by Kate Steinitz and Ebria Feinblatt (Los Angeles County Museum, 1949), 37, and in Ludwig Goldscheider, *Leonardo da Vinci: Life and Work* (Phaidon, 1959), 28.

Arasse = Daniel Arasse, *Leonardo da Vinci* (Konecky, 1998).

Bambach *Master Draftsman* = Carmen C. Bambach, ed., *Leonardo da Vinci Master Draftsman* (Metropolitan Museum of New York, 2003).

Bramly = Serge Bramly, *Leonardo: The Artist and the Man* (HarperCollins, 1991).

Brown = David Alan Brown, *Leonardo da Vinci: Origins of a Genius* (Yale, 1998).

Capra *Learning* = Fritjof Capra, *Learning from Leonardo* (Berrett-Koehler, 2013).

Capra *Science* = Fritjof Capra, *The Science of Leonardo* (Doubleday, 2007).

Clark = Kenneth Clark, *Leonardo da Vinci* (Penguin, 1939; revised edition edited by Martin Kemp, 1988).

Clayton = Martin Clayton, *Leonardo da Vinci: The Divine and the Grotesque* (Royal Collection, 2002).

Clayton and Philo = Martin Clayton and Ron Philo, *Leonardo da Vinci: Anatomist* (Royal Collection, 2012).

Delieuvin = Vincent Delieuvin, ed., *Saint Anne: Leonardo da Vinci's Ultimate Masterpiece* (Louvre, 2012). Catalogue of the exhibition at the Louvre, 2012.

Fiorani and Kim = Francesca Fiorani and Anna Marazeula Kim, "Leonardo da Vinci: Between Art and Science," University of Virginia, March 2014, http://faculty.virginia.edu/Fiorani/NEH-Institute/essays/.

Keele and Roberts = Kenneth Keele and Jane Roberts, *Leonardo da Vinci: Anatomical Drawings from the Royal Library, Windsor Castle* (Metropolitan Museum of New York, 2013).

Keele *Elements* = Kenneth Keele, *Leonardo da Vinci's Elements of the Science of Man* (Academic, 1983).

Kemp *Leonardo* = Martin Kemp, *Leonardo* (Oxford, 2004; revised 2011).

Kemp *Marvellous* = Martin Kemp, *Leonardo da Vinci: The Marvellous Works of Nature and Man* (Harvard, 1981; revised edition Oxford, 2006).

King = Ross King, *Leonardo and the Last Supper* (Bloomsbury, 2013).

Laurenza = Domenico Laurenza, *Leonardo's Machines* (David and Charles, 2006).

Lester = Toby Lester, *Da Vinci's Ghost* (Simon and Schuster, 2012).

Marani = Pietro C. Marani, *Leonardo da Vinci: The Complete Paintings* (Abrams, 2000).

Marani and Fiorio = Pietro C. Marani and Maria Teresa Fiorio, *Leonardo da Vinci: The Design of the World* (Skira, 2015). Catalogue of the Palazzo Reale exhibition, Milan, 2015.

Moffatt and Taglialagamba = Constance Moffatt and Sara Taglialagamba, *Illuminating Leonardo: A Festschrift for Carlo Pedretti Celebrating His 70 Years of Scholarship* (Brill, 2016).

Nicholl = Charles Nicholl, *Leonardo da Vinci: Flights of the Mind* (Viking, 2004).

O'Malley = Charles D. O'Malley, ed., *Leonardo's Legacy* (University of California, 1969).

Payne = Robert Payne, *Leonardo* (Doubleday, 1978).

Pedretti *Chronology* = Carlo Pedretti, *Leonardo: A Study in Chronology and Style* (University of California, 1973).

Pedretti *Commentary* = Carlo Pedretti, *The Literary Works of Leonardo da Vinci: Commentary* (Phaidon, 1977). A two-volume set of notes and comments on Leonardo's notebooks and J. P. Richter's compilation.

Reti *Unknown* = Ladislao Reti, ed., *The Unknown Leonardo* (McGraw-Hill, 1974).

Syson = Luke Syson, *Leonardo da Vinci, Painter at the Court of Milan* (National Gallery of London, 2011).

Vasari = Giorgio Vasari, *Lives of the Most Eminent Painters, Sculptors, and Architects* (first published in 1550, revised in 1568). Available in multiple print and online editions. Margot Pritzker provided me with an original copy of the corrected edition and some scholarship surrounding it.

Wells = Francis Wells, *The Heart of Leonardo* (Springer, 2013).

Zöllner = Frank Zöllner, *Leonardo da Vinci: The Complete Paintings and Drawings*, 2 vols. (Taschen, 2015). Vol. 1 for paintings, vol. 2 for drawings.

NOTES

INTRODUCTION

1 Codex Atl., 391r-a/1082r; Notebooks/J. P. Richter, 1340. The issue of the date of this letter is addressed in chapter 4. Only a draft that he made in his notebook still survives, not the final version he sent.

2 Kemp *Leonardo*, vii, 4; Kemp's theme in this and other works is the unifying patterns that lie below Leonardo's diverse endeavors.

3 Codex Urb., 133r-v; Leonardo Treatise/Rigaud, ch. 178; *Leonardo on Painting*, 15.

4 Author's interview with Steve Jobs, 2010.

5 Vasari, vol. 4.

6 Clark, 258; Kenneth Clark, *Civilization* (Harper & Row, 1969), 135.

7 Codex Atl., 222a/664a; Notebooks/J. P. Richter, 1448; Robert Krulwich, "Leonardo's To-Do List," *Krulwich Wonders*, NPR, November 18, 2011. Portinari was a Milanese merchant who had been to Flanders.

8 Notebooks/Irma Richter, 91.

9 Windsor, RCIN 919070; Notebooks/J. P. Richter, 819.

10 Paris Ms. F, 0; Notebooks/J. P. Richter, 1421.

11 Adam Gopnik, "Renaissance Man," *New Yorker*, January 17, 2005.

12 Codex Atl., 196b/586b; Notebooks/J. P. Richter, 490.

13 I would like to thank Margot Pritzker for an original of the second edition and some scholarship surrounding it. Vasari's book is available in many places online.

14 Vasari declared that his theme was "the rise of the arts to perfection [during the era of ancient Rome], their decline, and their restoration or rather renaissance."

15 Anonimo Gaddiano.

16 Depending on definitions and standards, different scholars put this number as low as twelve and as high as eighteen. According to Luke Syson, curator at the National Gallery of London and then the Metropolitan Museum of New York: "He started probably no more than 20 pictures in a career that lasted nearly half a century and only 15 surviving pictures are currently agreed to be entirely his, of which at least four are to some degree incomplete." A running discussion of the changing expert attributions and disputes over Leonardo autograph paintings can be found at "List of Works by Leonardo da Vinci," *Wikipedia*, https://en.wikipedia.org/wiki/List_of_works_by_Leonardo_da_Vinci.

17 Paris Ms. K, 2:1b; Notebooks/J. P. Richter, 1308.

1. CHILDHOOD

1 Alessandro Cecchi, "New Light on Leonardo's Florentine Patrons," in Bambach *Master Draftsman*, 123.
2 Nicholl, 20; Bramly, 37. The sun set in Florence on that date at 6:40 p.m. The "hour of the night" was usually counted from the bell ringing after vespers.
3 Francesco Cianchi, *La Madre di Leonardo era una Schiava?* (Museo Ideale Leonardo da Vinci, 2008); Angelo Paratico, *Leonardo Da Vinci: A Chinese Scholar Lost in Renaissance Italy* (Lascar, 2015); Anna Zamejc, "Was Leonardo Da Vinci's Mother Azeri?," Radio Free Europe, November 25, 2009.
4 Martin Kemp and Giuseppe Pallanti, *Mona Lisa* (Oxford, 2017), 87. I am grateful to Prof. Kemp for sharing their findings and to Pallanti for discussing them with me.
5 Anonimo Gaddiano.
6 Author's communications with archival researcher Giuseppe Pallanti, 2017; Alberto Malvolti, "In Search of Malvolto Piero: Notes on the Witnesses of the Baptism of Leonardo da Vinci," *Erba d'Arno*, no. 141 (2015), 37. Kemp and Pallanti, *Mona Lisa*, do not believe that Leonardo was born in this cottage because it is listed on a tax document as being uninhabitable. However, that description may have been to minimize taxes on a dilapidated cottage that was, most of the time, left vacant.
7 Kemp and Pallanti, *Mona Lisa*, 85.
8 Leonardo, "Weimar Sheet," recto, Schloss-Museum, Weimar; Pedretti, *Commentary*, 2:110.
9 James Beck, "Ser Piero da Vinci and His Son Leonardo," *Notes in the History of Art* 5.1 (Fall 1985), 29.
10 Jacob Burckhardt, *The Civilization of the Renaissance in Italy* (Dover, 2010; originally published in English in 1878 and German in 1860), 51, 310.
11 Jane Fair Bestor, "Bastardy and Legitimacy in the Formation of a Regional State in Italy: The Estense Succession," *Comparative Studies in Society and History* 38.3 (July 1996), 549–85.
12 Thomas Kuehn, *Illegitimacy in Renaissance Florence* (University of Michigan, 2002), 80. See also Thomas Kuehn, "Reading between the Patrilines: Leon Battista Alberti's 'Della Famiglia' in Light of His Illegitimacy," *I Tatti Studies in the Italian Renaissance* 1 (1985), 161–87.
13 Kuehn, *Illegitimacy*, 7, ix.
14 Kuehn, *Illegitimacy*, 80. See Brown; Beck, "Ser Piero da Vinci and His Son Leonardo," 32.
15 Charles Nauert, *Humanism and the Culture of Renaissance Europe* (Cambridge, 2006), 5.
16 Codex Atl., 520r/191r-a; Notebooks/MacCurdy, 2:989.
17 Notebooks/J. P. Richter, 10–11; Notebooks/Irma Richter, 4; Codex Atl., 119v, 327v.
18 Paris Ms. E, 55r; Notebooks/Irma Richter, 8; Capra, *Science*, 161, 169.
19 Paris Ms. L, 58v; Notebooks/Irma Richter, 95.
20 Codex Atl., 66v/199b; Notebooks/J. P. Richter, 1363; Notebooks/Irma Richter, 269.
21 Original German title: *Eine Kindheitserinnerung des Leonardo da Vinci*. Translated by Abraham Brill in 1916 and available in multiple online editions.
22 *Sigmund Freud–Lou Andreas-Salomé Correspondence*, ed. Ernst Pfeiffer (Frankfurt: S. Fischer, 1966), 100.
23 Meyer Schapiro, "Leonardo and Freud," *Journal of the History of Ideas* 17.2 (April 1956), 147. For defenses of Freud and a discussion of the *Envy* drawing's connection to the kite, see Kurt Eissler, *Leonardo da Vinci: Psychoanalytic Notes on the Enigma* (In-

ternational Universities, 1961) and Alessandro Nova, "The Kite, Envy and a Memory of Leonardo da Vinci's Childhood," in Lars Jones, ed., *Coming About* (Harvard, 2001), 381.

24 Codex Atl., 358v; Notebooks/MacCurdy, 1:66; Sherwin Nuland, *Leonardo da Vinci* (Viking, 2000), 18.

25 Codex Arundel, 155r; Notebooks/J. P. Richter, 1339; Notebooks/Irma Richter, 247.

26 Codex Arundel, 156r; Notebooks/J. P. Richter, 1217; Notebooks/Irma Richter, 246.

27 Kay Etheridge, "Leonardo and the Whale," in Fiorani and Kim.

28 Codex Arundel, 155b; Notebooks/J. P. Richter, 1218, 1339n.

2. APPRENTICE

1 Nicholl, 161. Among those arguing that Leonardo began his apprenticeship around 1466 are Beck, "Ser Piero da Vinci and His Son Leonardo," 29; Brown, 76. Piero da Vinci's 1469 tax return lists Leonardo as one of his dependents in Vinci, but this was not a specific claim of residence; Piero himself did not live there, and it was not accepted by the tax authorities, who crossed out Leonardo's name.

2 Notebooks/Irma Richter, 227.

3 Nicholl, 47; Codex Urb., 12r; Notebooks/J. P. Richter, 494.

4 Codex Ash., 1:9a; Notebooks/Richter, 495. (Richter claims that the two quotes are not contradictory, for the latter refers to students, but I think they do express conflicting sentiments and that the latter is closer to Leonardo's reality.)

5 Kuehn, *Illegitimacy*, 52; Robert Genestal, *Histoire de la legitimation des enfants naturels en droit canonique* (Paris: Leroux, 1905), 100.

6 Stefano Ugo Baldassarri and Arielle Saiber, *Images of Quattrocento Florence* (Yale, 2000), 84.

7 John M. Najemym, *A History of Florence 1200–1575* (Wiley, 2008), 315; Eric Weiner, *Geography of Genius* (Simon and Schuster, 2016), 97.

8 Lester, 71; Gene Brucker, *Living on the Edge in Leonardo's Florence* (University of California, 2005), 115; Nicholl, 65.

9 Francesco Guicciardini, *Opere Inedite: The Position of Florence at the Death of Lorenzo*, (Bianchi, 1857), 3:82.

10 Paul Robert Walker, *The Feud That Sparked the Renaissance: How Brunelleschi and Ghiberti Changed the Art World* (William Morrow, 2002); Ross King, *Brunelleschi's Dome: The Story of the Great Cathedral of Florence* (Penguin, 2001).

11 Antonio Manetti, *The Life of Brunelleschi*, trans. Catherine Enggass (Pennsylvania State, 1970; originally published in the 1480s), 115; Martin Kemp, "Science, Non-science and Nonsense: The Interpretation of Brunelleschi's Perspective," *Art History* 1:2, June 1978, 134.

12 Anthony Grafton, *Leon Battista Alberti: Master Builder of the Italian Renaissance* (Harvard, 2002), 27, 21, 139. See also Franco Borsi, *Leon Battista Alberti* (Harper & Row, 1975), 7–11.

13 Samuel Y. Edgerton, *The Mirror, the Window, and the Telescope: How Renaissance Linear Perspective Changed Our Vision of the Universe* (Cornell, 2009); Richard McLanathan, *Images of the Universe* (Doubleday, 1966), 72; Leon Rocco Sinisgalli, *Battista Alberti: On Painting. A New Translation and Critical Edition* (Cambridge, 2011), 3; Grafton, *Leon Battista Alberti*, 124. Sinisgalli argues that Alberti's Italian (Tuscan) vulgate version was written first and his Latin version came a year later.

14 Arasse, 38, 43. Arasse notes, "As the codex Trivulziano and the Manuscript B show, Leonardo transcribed almost half of Luigi Pulci's 'All Latin Words in order.' . . . The

list in codex Trivulziano follows almost to the letter pages 7–10 of *De Re Militari* by Valturio." The Codex Trivulziano dates from around 1487–90.

15 Carmen Bambach, "Leonardo: Left-Handed Draftsman and Writer," in Bambach *Master Draftsman*, 50.

16 Bambach, "Leonardo: Left-Handed Draftsman and Writer," 48; Thomas Micchelli, "The Most Beautiful Drawing in the World," *Hyperallergic*, November 2, 2013.

17 Geoffrey Schott, "Some Neurological Observations on Leonardo da Vinci's Handwriting," *Journal of Neurological Science* 42.3 (August 1979), 321.

18 Cecchi, "New Light on Leonardo's Florentine Patrons," 121; Bramly, 62.

19 Evelyn Welch, *Art and Society in Italy 1300–1500* (Oxford, 1997), 86; Richard David Serros, "The Verrocchio Workshop: Techniques, Production, and Influences," PhD dissertation, University of California, Santa Barbara, 1999.

20 J. K. Cadogan, "Verrocchio's Drawings Reconsidered," *Zeitschrift fikr Kunstgeschichte* 46.1 (1983), 367; Kemp *Marvellous*, 18.

21 There is a record of the Lords of Florence paying Lorenzo de' Medici 150 florins for the statue in 1476, but most experts now date its actual creation to between 1466 and 1468. See Nicholl, 74; Brown, 8; Andrew Butterfield, *The Sculptures of Andrea del Verrocchio* (Yale, 1997), 18.

22 Many scholars believe that Leonardo was the model for David. Martin Kemp is among those more skeptical. "Seems to be a romantic fantasy to me," he told me, "but I am austere about evidence! They exploit statements of naturalism, but their statues would not have been 'portraits' of their models."

23 John 20:27; Clark, 44.

24 Kim Williams, "Verrocchio's Tombslab for Cosimo de' Medici: Designing with a Mathematical Vocabulary," in *Nexus I* (Florence: Edizioni dell'Erba, 1996), 193.

25 Carlo Pedretti, *Leonardo: The Machines* (Giunti, 2000), 16; Bramly, 72.

26 Pedretti *Commentary*, 1:20; Pedretti, *The Machines*, 18; Paris Ms. G, 84v; Codex Atl., fols. 17v, 879r, 1103v; Sven Dupré, "Optic, Picture and Evidence: Leonardo's Drawings of Mirrors and Machinery," *Early Science and Medicine* 10.2 (2005), 211.

27 Bernard Berenson, *The Florentine Painters of the Renaissance* (Putnam, 1909), section 8.

28 Leonardo Treatise/Rigaud, 353; Codex Ash. 1:6b; Notebooks/J. P. Richter, 585.

29 Brown, 82; Carmen Bambach, "Leonardo and Drapery Studies on 'Tela sottilissima di lino,'" *Apollo*, January 1, 2004; Jean K. Cadogan, "Linen Drapery Studies by Verrocchio, Leonardo and Ghirlandaio," *Zeitschrift für Kunstgeschichte* 46 (1983), 27–62; Francesca Fiorani, "The Genealogy of Leonardo's Shadows in a Drapery Study," Harvard Center for Italian Renaissance Studies at Villa I Tatti, Series no. 29 (Harvard, 2013), 267–73, 840–41; Françoise Viatte, "The Early Drapery Studies," in Bambach *Master Draftsman*, 111; Keith Christiansen, "Leonardo's Drapery Studies," *Burlington Magazine* 132.1049 (1990), 572–73; Martin Clayton, review of Bambach *Master Draftsman* catalogue, *Master Drawings* 43.3 (Fall 2005), 376.

30 Codex Urb., 133r-v; Leonardo Treatise/Rigaud, ch. 178; *Leonardo on Painting*, 15.

31 Ernst Gombrich, *The Story of Art* (Phaidon, 1950), 187.

32 Alexander Nagel, "Leonardo and Sfumato," *Anthropology and Aesthetics* 24 (Autumn 1993), 7; Leonardo Treatise/Rigaud, ch. 181.

33 "Visit of Galeazzo Maria Sforza and Bona of Savoy," *Mediateca Medicea*, http://www.palazzo-medici.it/mediateca/en/Scheda_1471_-_Visita_di_Galeazzo_Maria_Sforza_e_di_Bona_di_Savoia; Nicholl, 92.

34 Niccolò Machiavelli, *History of Florence* (Dunne, 1901; originally written 1525), bk. 7, ch. 5.

35 Many scholars date the drawing to circa 1472, which I think is correct, but the British Museum, where it is located, dates it to 1475–80.

36 Martin Kemp and Juliana Barone, *I disegni di Leonardo da Vinci e della sua cerchia: Collezioni in Gran Bretagna* (Giunti, 2010), item 6. There are various versions and copies of reliefs done by Verrocchio's workshop. The *Alexander the Great* in the National Gallery of Washington, DC, can be seen at http://www.nga.gov/content/ngaweb/Collection/art-object-page.43513.html. For a discussion of these works, see Brown, 72–74, 194nn103 and 104. See also Butterfield, *The Sculptures of Andrea Del Verrocchio*, 231.

37 Gary Radke makes the argument that Leonardo was involved in sculpting the *Beheading of Saint John*. See Gary Radke, ed., *Leonardo da Vinci and the Art of Sculpture* (Yale, 2009); Carol Vogel, "Indications of a Hidden Leonardo," *New York Times*, April 23, 2009; Ann Landi, "Looking for Leonardo," *Smithsonian*, October 2009. For the dating of Leonardo's drawing and Verrocchio's sculptures, and who was influencing whom by the late 1470s, see Brown, 68–72.

38 Javier Berzal de Dios, "Perspective in the Public Sphere," Renaissance Society of America conference, Montreal, 2011; George Kernodle, *From Art to Theatre: Form and Convention in the Renaissance* (University of Chicago, 1944), 177; Thomas Pallen, *Vasari on Theatre* (Southern Illinois University, 1999), 21.

39 Codex Atl., 75r-v.

40 Paris Ms. B, 83r; Laurenza, 42; Pedretti, *The Machines*, 9; Kemp *Marvellous*, 104.

41 Nicholl, 98.

42 "Io morando dant sono chontento," he wrote. Serge Bramly is among those who assumes that "dant" is a contraction for "d'Antonio" (84). Carlo Pedretti, in his commentary on Richter's translations of Leonardo's notebooks, has a totally different interpretation, interpreting the words as "Jo Morando dant sono contento" ("I, Morando d'Antonio, agree as to") and suggesting that it was a draft for some agreement (*Commentary*, 314).

43 Uffizi, Cabinet of Prints and Drawings, no. 8P. His drawing of a helmeted warrior may have been earlier, circa 1472; see note 35 above.

44 Codex Urb., 5r; *Leonardo on Painting*, 32.

45 Ernst Gombrich, "Tobias and the Angel," in *Symbolic Images: Studies in the Art of the Renaissance* (Phaidon, 1972), 27; Trevor Hart, "Tobit in the Art of the Florentine Renaissance," in Mark Bredin, ed., *Studies in the Book of Tobit* (Bloomsbury, 2006), 72–89.

46 Brown, 47–52; Nicholl, 88.

47 The argument is made most forcefully by David Alan Brown (51). For a pushback, see Jill Dunkerton, "Leonardo in Verrocchio's Workshop: Re-examining the Technical Evidence," *National Gallery Technical Bulletin* 32 (2011), 4–31: "That he was capable of making observant studies of nature in his paintings as well as his sculpture is confirmed by the bright-eyed raptor that swoops down over the head of the Baptist. . . . It is important never to underestimate the painting skills of Verrocchio." Luke Syson, who once had *Tobias* in his care as a curator, told me he thought that Verrocchio was in fact very good with nature and may have painted the dog and fish.

48 Nicholl, 89.

49 Vasari, 1486. Verrocchio subsequently was commissioned to paint the altar in the Pistoia Cathedral, but he delegated most of the work to Lorenzo di Credi. Jill Dunkerton and Luke Syson, "In Search of Verrocchio the Painter," *National Gallery Technical Bulletin* 31 (2010), 4; Zöllner, 1:18; Brown, 151.

50 The evidence shows that Verrocchio started the painting in the 1460s, then put it aside. Work on it was resumed in the mid-1470s, with Leonardo reworking the landscape,

finishing the body of Christ (though the loincloth had already been done by Verrocchio), as well as painting his angel. Dunkerton, "Leonardo in Verrocchio's Workshop," 21; Brown, 138, 92; Marani, 65.

51 Codex Ash., 1:5b; Notebooks/J. P. Richter, 595.

52 Clark, 51.

53 Codex Ash., 1:21a; Notebooks/J. P. Richter 236; Janis Bell, "Sfumato and Acuity Perspective," in Claire Farago, ed., *Leonardo da Vinci and the Ethics of Style* (Manchester Univ., 2008), ch. 6.

54 Codex Arundel, 169a; Notebooks/J. P. Richter, 305.

55 See, for example, Cecil Gould, *Leonardo* (Weidenfeld & Nicolson, 1975), 24. For a listing of differing opinions, see Brown, 195nn6, 7, and 8.

56 Zöllner, 1:34; Brown, 64; Marani, 61.

57 Brown, 88. See also Leonardo's "Study of a Lily" drawing, Windsor, RCIN 912418.

58 Matt Ancell, "Leonardo's *Annunciation* in Perspective," in Fiorani and Kim; Lyle Massey, *Picturing Space, Displacing Bodies* (Pennsylvania State, 2007), 42–44.

59 Francesca Fiorani, "The Shadows of Leonardo's *Annunciation* and Their Lost Legacy," in Roy Eriksen and Magne Malmanger, eds., *Imitation, Representation and Printing in the Italian Renaissance* (Pisa: Fabrizio Serra, 2009), 119; Francesca Fiorani, "The Colors of Leonardo's Shadows," *Leonardo* 41.3 (2008), 271.

60 Leonardo Treatise/Rigaud, section 262.

61 Jane Long, "Leonardo's Virgin of the Annunciation," in Fiorani and Kim.

62 Brown, 122.

63 Codex Ash., 1:7a; Notebooks/J. P. Richter, 367; Leonardo Treatise/Rigaud, 34.

64 Brown, 150.

65 Jennifer Fletcher, "Bernardo Bembo and Leonardo's Portrait of Ginevra de' Benci," *Burlington Magazine*, no. 1041 (1989), 811; Mary Garrard, "Who Was Ginevra de' Benci? Leonardo's Portrait and Its Sitter Recontextualized," *Artibus et Historiae* 27.53 (2006), 23; John Walker, "Ginevra de' Benci," in *Report and Studies in the History of Art* (Washington National Gallery, 1967), 1:32; David Alan Brown, ed., *Virtue and Beauty* (Princeton, 2003); Brown, 101–21; Marani, 38–48.

66 Leonardo, "A Study of a Woman's Hands," Windsor, RCIN 912558; Butterfield, *The Sculptures of Andrea Del Verrocchio*, 90.

67 Andrea Kirsh and Rustin Levenson, *Seeing through Paintings: Physical Examination in Art Historical Studies* (Yale, 2002), 135; Leonardo da Vinci, *Ginevra de' Benci*, oil on panel, National Gallery, Washington, DC, https://www.nga.gov/kids/ginevra.htm.

68 Notebooks/J. P. Richter, 132, 135; Paris Ms. A, 113v; Codex Ash., 1:3a.

69 Brown, 104.

3. ON HIS OWN

1 Louis Crompton, *Homosexuality and Civilization* (Harvard, 2006), 265; Payne, 747.

2 Notebooks/Irma Richter, 271.

3 Notebooks/J. P. Richter, 1383. Jean Paul Richter surmises in brackets that Leonardo was going to write "brother," but Richter is being polite. There is no word at the end of the sentence.

4 Nicholl, 131.

5 Anonimo Gaddiano; Notebooks/Irma Richter, 258; Leonardo, "Sketches and Figures for a Last Supper and a Hydrometer," Louvre Inv. 2258r.; Zöllner, item 130, 2:335; Bambach *Master Draftsman*, 325.

6 Anthony Cummings, *The Maecenas and the Madrigalist* (American Philosophical So-

ciety, 2004), 86; Donald Sanders, *Music at the Gonzaga Court in Mantua* (Lexington, 2012), 25.

7 Pedretti *Commentary*, 112; Windsor, RCIN 919009r; Keele *Elements*, 350.

8 Michael Rocke, *Forbidden Friendships: Homosexuality and Male Culture in Renaissance Florence* (Oxford, 1998), 4.

9 Paris Ms. H, 1:12a; Notebooks/J. P. Richter, 1192.

10 Clark, 107.

11 Windsor, RCIN 919030r; Kenneth Keele and Carlo Pedretti, *Corpus of the Anatomical Studies by Leonardo da Vinci: The Queen's Collection at Windsor Castle* (Johnson, 1978), 71v–72r; Keele *Elements*, 350; Notebooks/MacCurdy, section 120.

12 Patricia Simons, "Women in Frames: The Gaze, the Eye, the Profile in Renaissance Portraiture," *History Workshop* 25 (Spring, 1988), 4.

13 Robert Kiely, *Blessed and Beautiful: Picturing the Saints* (Yale, 2010), 11; James Saslow, *Pictures and Passions: A History of Homosexuality in the Visual Arts* (Viking, 1999), 99.

14 *Saint Sebastian Tied to a Tree*, Hamburger Kunsthalle, inv. 21489; Bambach *Master Draftsman*, 342.

15 Scott Reyburn, "An Artistic Discovery Makes a Curator's Heart Pound," *New York Times*, December 11, 2016.

16 Syson, 16. For a more tentative opinion about the subject, see Bambach *Master Draftsman*, 323.

17 Clark, 80.

18 Beck, "Ser Piero da Vinci and His Son Leonardo," 29.

19 Nicholl, 169.

20 Zöllner, 1:60.

21 Leonardo Treatise/Rigaud, 35; Codex Urb., 32v; *Leonardo on Painting*, 200.

22 Leonardo Treatise/Rigaud, 93; Codex Urb., 33v; *Leonardo on Painting*, 36.

23 Michael Kwakkelstein, "Did Leonardo Always Practice What He Preached?," in S. U. Baldassarri, ed., *Proxima Studia* (Fabrizio Serra Editore, 2011), 107; Michael Kwakkelstein, "Leonardo da Vinci's Recurrent Use of Patterns of Individual Limbs, Stock Poses and Facial Stereotypes," in Ingrid Ciulisova, ed., *Artistic Innovations and Cultural Zones* (Peter Lang, 2014), 45.

24 Carmen Bambach, "Figure Studies for the *Adoration of the Magi*," in Bambach *Master Draftsman*, 320; Bulent Atalay and Keith Wamsley, *Leonardo's Universe* (National Geographic, 2009), 85.

25 Clark, 74; Richard Turner, *Inventing Leonardo* (University of California, 1992), 27; Clark, 124.

26 Francesca Fiorani, "Why Did Leonardo Not Finish the *Adoration of the Magi*?," in Moffatt and Taglialagamba, 137; Zöllner, 1:22–35.

27 Melinda Henneberger, "The Leonardo Cover-Up," *New York Times*, April 21, 2002; "Scientific Analysis of the *Adoration of the Magi*," Museo Galileo, http://brunelleschi.imss.fi.it/menteleonardo/emdl.asp?c=13419&k=1470&rif=14071&xsl=1.

28 Alexandra Korey interview with Cecilia Frosinini, art historian on the Uffizi project, Art Trav, http://www.arttrav.com/art-history-tools/leonardo-da-vinci-adoration/.

29 *Leonardo on Painting*, 222; Fiorani, "Why Did Leonardo Not Finish the *Adoration of the Magi*?"

30 Larry Feinberg, *The Young Leonardo* (Santa Barbara Museum, 2011), 177, and Zöllner, 1:58, agree that the figure behind Mary is Joseph. Kemp *Marvellous*, 46, and Nicholl, 171, are among those who say Joseph is hard to identify in the final version. Nicholl wrote, "The father is unidentified, submerged into the periphery. One might resist

a psychoanalytical interpretation of this, but it is a motif too recurrent to ignore—Leonardo always excises Joseph from the Holy Family."

31 *Leonardo on Painting*, 220.

32 Bambach *Master Draftsman*, 54.

33 Codex Atl., 847r.

34 Fiorani, "Why Did Leonardo Not Finish the *Adoration of the Magi*?," 22. See also Francesca Fiorani and Alessandro Nova, eds., *Leonardo da Vinci and Optics: Theory and Pictorial Practice* (Marsilio Editore, 2013), 265.

35 Carlo Pedretti, "The Pointing Lady," *Burlington Magazine*, no. 795 (June 1969), 338.

36 Some scholars have suggested a later date, including the late 1480s, based on the similarity of the pose to the *Virgin of the Rocks*, the use of walnut panel, and the resemblance of the church to sketches he made while in Milan. I think (following Juliana Barone, Martin Clayton, Frank Zöllner, and others) that he made the drawing around 1480 and then modified it over the years, including while in Milan and then after he did his anatomy studies of 1510. See Syson (with essay by Scott Nethersole), 139; Juliana Barone, "Review of *Leonardo da Vinci, Painter at the Court of Milan*," *Renaissance Studies* 27.5 (2013), 28; Luke Syson and Rachel Billinge, "Leonardo da Vinci's Use of Underdrawing in the 'Virgin of the Rocks' in the National Gallery and 'St Jerome' in the Vatican," *Burlington Magazine*, no. 147 (2005), 450.

37 Paris Ms. L, 79r; Notebooks/J. P. Richter, 488; Notebooks/MacCurdy, 184.

38 Windsor, RCIN 919003.

39 Keele and Roberts, 28.

40 Martin Clayton, "Leonardo's Anatomical Drawings and His Artistic Practice," lecture, September 18, 2015, https://www.youtube.com/watch?v=KLwnN2g2Mqg.

41 Leonardo da Vinci, *Libro di Pittura*, ed. Carlo Vecce and Carlo Pedretti (Giunti, 1995), 285b, 286a; Bambach *Master Draftsman*, 328.

42 Frank Zöllner, "The Motions of the Mind in Renaissance Portraits: The Spiritual Dimension of Portraiture," *Zeitschrift für Kunstgeschichte* 68 (2005), 23–40; Pliny the Elder, *Historia Naturalis*, section 35.

43 Leon Battista Alberti, *On Painting*, trans. John Spencer (Yale, 1966; originally written 1435), 77; Paul Barolsky, "Leonardo's Epiphany," *Notes in the History of Art* 11.1 (Fall 1991), 18.

44 Codex Urb., 60v; Pietro Marani, "Movements of the Soul," in Marani and Fiorio, 223; Pedretti *Commentary*, 2:263, 1:219; Paris Ms. A, 100; *Leonardo on Painting*, 144.

45 Codex Urb., 110r; *Leonardo on Painting*, 144.

46 Codex Atl., 42v; Kemp *Marvellous*, 66.

47 Kemp *Marvellous*, 67.

48 Codex Atl., 252r; Notebooks/MacCurdy, 65.

49 Nicholl, 154. The friend is Antonio Cammelli, known as "Il Pistoiese," a popular poet of the day.

50 Windsor, RCIN 912349; Notebooks/J. P. Richter, 1547; Notebooks/MacCurdy, 86.

51 Windsor, RCIN 912349; Dante, *Inferno* XXIV, trans. Dorothy L. Sayers (Penguin Classics, 1949), 46–51.

52 Vasari, "Pietro Perugino," in *Lives of the Most Eminent Painters*.

4. MILAN

1 Anonimo Gaddiano; Notebooks/Irma Richter, 258.

2 Felix Gilbert, "Bernardo Rucellai and the Orti Oricellari," *Journal of the Warburg and Courtauld Institutes* 12 (1949), 101.

3 Codex Atl., 888r; Kemp *Marvellous*, 22. Because the list includes what seems to be a drawing of the head of the Duke of Milan, I think he wrote the list in his notebook after he arrived in Milan.

4 David Mateer, *Courts, Patrons, and Poets* (Yale, 2000), 26.

5 For the letter and discussions of its probable date, see Notebooks/J. P. Richter, 1340; Kemp *Marvellous*, 57; Nicholl, 180; Kemp *Leonardo*, 442; Bramly, 174; Payne, 1349; Matt Landrus, *Leonardo da Vinci's Giant Crossbow* (Springer, 2010), 21; Richard Schofield, "Leonardo's Milanese Architecture," *Journal of Leonardo Studies* 4 (1991); Hannah Brooks-Motl, "Inventing Leonardo, Again," *New Republic*, May 2, 2012.

6 Codex Atl., 382a/1182a; Notebooks/J. P. Richter, 1340.

7 Ladislao Reti and Bern Dibner, *Leonardo da Vinci, Technologist* (Burndy, 1969); Bertrand Gille, *The Renaissance Engineers* (MIT, 1966).

8 Codex Atl., 139r/49v-b; Zöllner, 2:622.

9 Codex Atl., 89r/32v-a, 1084r/391v-a; Zöllner, 2:622.

10 Roger Bacon, *Letter on the Secret Workings of Art and Nature and on the Vanity of Magic*, ch. 4; Domenico Laurenza, *Leonardo on Flight* (Giunti, 2004), 24.

11 Roberto Valturio, *On the Military Arts*, fol. 146v–147r, Bodleian Library, Oxford University, http://bodley30.bodley.ox.ac.uk:8180/luna/servlet/detail/ODLodl~1~1~36082~121456?printerFriendly=1.

12 Zöllner, 2:636.

13 Biblioteca Reale, Turin, inv. 15583r; Zöllner, 2:638.

14 Codex Atl., 149b-r/53v-b; Zöllner, 2:632.

15 Landrus, *Leonardo da Vinci's Giant Crossbow*, 5 and passim; Matthew Landrus, "The Proportional Consistency and Geometry of Leonardo's Giant Crossbow," *Leonardo* 41.1 (2008), 56; Kemp *Leonardo*, 48.

16 Dennis Simms, "Archimedes' Weapons of War and Leonardo," *British Journal for the History of Science* 21.2 (June 1988), 195.

17 Codex Atl., 157r/56v-a.

18 Vernard Foley, "Leonardo da Vinci and the Invention of the Wheellock," *Scientific American*, January 1998; Vernard Foley et al., "Leonardo, the Wheel Lock, and the Milling Process," *Technology and Culture* 24.3 (July 1983), 399. Giulio Tedesco came to live with Leonardo in March 1493, and he fixed two locks in Leonardo's studio in September 1494. Codex Forster 2:88v; Paris Ms. H, 106v; Notebooks/J. P. Richter, 1459, 1460, 1462; *Leonardo on Painting*, 266–67.

19 Pascal Brioist, *Leonard de Vinci, l'homme de Guerre* (Alma, 2013).

20 Paris Ms. I, 32a, 34a; Codex Atl., 22r; Notebooks/J. P. Richter, 1017–18; Notebooks/MacCurdy, 1042.

21 Codex Atl., 64b/197b; Notebooks/J. P. Richter, 1203; Paris Ms. B, 15v, 16r, 36r.

22 Paris Ms. B, 15v, 37v; Notebooks/J. P. Richter, 741, 746, 742; Richard Schofield, "Reality and Utopia in Leonardo's Thinking about Architecture," in Marani and Fiorio, 325; Paolo Galluzzi, ed., *Leonardo Da Vinci: Engineer and Architect* (Montreal Museum, 1987), 258.

5. LEONARDO'S NOTEBOOKS

1 Codex Ash., 1:8a, 2:27; Notebooks/J. P. Richter, 571; Notebooks/Irma Richter, 208.

2 Notebooks/Irma Richter, 301.

3 Lester, 120. See also Clark, 258; Charles Nicholl, *Traces Remain* (Penguin, 2012), 135.

4 The collection of writings on art compiled by his pupil Francesco Melzi has one thousand passages; only one-quarter of these are in Leonardo notebook pages known to

exist today, so we can roughly estimate that at least three-quarters of his manuscripts have been lost. Martin Kemp, *Leonardo da Vinci: Experience, Experiment, and Design*, catalogue for Victoria and Albert Collection (2006), 2.

5 Pedretti *Commentary*.

6 Clark, 110.

7 Windsor, RCIN 912283; Carlo Pedretti, *Studi di Natura* (Giunti Barbera, 1982), 24; Kenneth Clark and Carlo Pedretti, *The Drawings of Leonardo da Vinci in the Collection of Her Majesty the Queen at Windsor Castle* (Phaidon, 1968), introduction; Kemp *Marvellous*, 3–19.

8 Francis Ames-Lewis, "Leonardo's Botanical Drawings," *Achademia Leonardo da Vinci* 10 (1997), 117.

6. COURT ENTERTAINER

1 The primary description of *The Feast of Paradise* comes from a report by Jacopo Trotti, the ambassador of Ferrara to Milan: "The Party of Leonardo da Vinci's *Paradise* and Bernardo Bellincore (January 13, 1490)," *Journal of the Historical Society of Lombard*, quarta series, 1 (1904), 75–89; Bernardo Bellincioni, "Chiamata Paradiso che fece Il Signor Ludovico," ACNR, http://www.nuovaricerca.org/leonardo_inf_e_par/BELLINCIONI.pdf; Kate Steinitz, "Leonardo Architetto Teatrale e Organizzatore di Feste," *Lettura Vinciana* 9 (April 15, 1969); Arasse, 227; Bramly, 221; Kemp *Marvellous*, 137, 152; Nicholl, 259.

2 Codex Arundel, 250a; Arasse, 235; Notebooks/J. P. Richter, 674.

3 Codex Atl., 996v; Leonardo da Vinci, "Design for a Stage Setting," Metropolitan Museum of New York, Accession #17.142.2v, with notes by Carmen Bambach; Pedretti *Commentary*, 1:402; Carlo Vecce, "The Sculptor Says," in Moffatt and Taglialagamba, 229; Marie Herzfeld, *La Rappresentazione della "Danai" Organizzata da Leonardo* (Raccolta Vinciana XI, 1920), 226–28.

4 Codex Arundel, 231v, 224r; Notebooks/J. P. Richter, 678; Kemp *Marvellous*, 154. There is no consensus on the dating of the Pluto's Paradise drawings.

5 Codex Atl., 228b/687b; Notebooks/J. P. Richter, 703.

6 Vasari; Anonimo Gaddiano; Emanuel Winternitz, *Leonardo da Vinci as a Musician* (Yale, 1982), 39; Emanuel Winternitz, "Musical Instruments in the Madrid Notebooks of Leonardo da Vinci," *Metropolitan Museum Journal* 2 (1969), 115; Emanuel Winternitz, "Leonardo and Music," in Reti *Unknown*, 110.

7 Codex Ash., 1:Cr; Winternitz, *Leonardo da Vinci as a Musician*, 40; Nicholl, 158, 178.

8 Codex Madrid, 2:folio 75; Winternitz, "Musical Instruments in the Madrid Notebooks of Leonardo da Vinci," 115; Winternitz, "Leonardo and Music," 110; Michael Eisenberg, "Sonic Mapping in Leonardo's *Disegni*," in Fiorani and Kim.

9 Codex Arundel, 175r.

10 Codex Atl., 118r.

11 Codex Atl., 355r.

12 Codex Atl., 34r-b, 213v-a, 218r-c; Paris Ms. H, 28r, 28v, 45v, 46r, 104v; Paris Ms. B, 50v; Codex Madrid, 2:76r.

13 Stawomir Zubrzycki, *Viola Organista* website, 2002, http://www.violaorganista.com.

14 Winternitz, "Leonardo and Music," 112.

15 Notebooks/J. P. Richter, ch. 10 introduction; Zöllner, 2:94, 2:492; Christ Church, Oxford, inv. JBS 18r.

16 Christ Church, Oxford; Notebooks/J. P. Richter, 677.

17 Leonardo, "Two Allegories of Envy," 1490–94, Christ Church, Oxford, inv. JBS 17r; Zöllner, catalogue #394, 2:494.

18 Leonardo, "The Unmasking of Envy," c. 1494, Musee Bonnat, Bayonne; *Leonardo on Painting*, 241.

19 Windsor, RCIN 912490, 912491, 912492, 912493, and others at Windsor; Carmen Bambach, "Laughing Man with Busy Hair," "Old Woman with Beetling Brow," Snub-Nosed Old Man," "Old Woman with Horned Dress," "Four Fragments with Grotesque Heads," "Old Man Standing to the Right," "Head of an Old Man or Woman in Profile," all in Bambach *Master Draftsman*, 451–65, and for copies, 678–722; Johannes Nathan, "Profile Studies, Character Heads, and Grotesques," in Zöllner, 2:366. See also Clark and Pedretti, *The Drawings of Leonardo da Vinci in the Collection of Her Majesty the Queen at Windsor Castle*, 84; Katherine Roosevelt Reeve Losee, "Satire and Medicine in Renaissance Florence: Leonardo da Vinci's Grotesque Drawings," Master's thesis, American University, 2015; Ernst Gombrich, "Leonardo da Vinci's Method of Analysis and Permutation: The Grotesque Heads," in *The Heritage of Apelles* (Cornell, 1976), 57–75; Michael Kwakkelstein, *Leonardo as a Physiognomist: Theory and Drawing Practice* (Primavera, 1994), 55; Michael Kwakkelstein, "Leonardo da Vinci's Grotesque Heads and the Breaking of the Physiognomic Mould," *Journal of the Warburg and Courtauld Institutes* 54 (1991), 135; Varena Forcione, "Leonardo's Grotesques: Originals and Copies," in Bambach *Master Draftsman*, 203.

20 Codex Urb., 13; Notebooks/Irma Richter, 184; Jonathan Jones, "The Marvellous Ugly Mugs," *The Guardian*, December 4, 2002; Clayton, 11; Turner, *Inventing Leonardo*, 158.

21 Notebooks/Irma Richter, 286.

22 Codex Ash., 1:8a; Notebooks/J. P. Richter, 571.

23 Carmen Bambach, introduction to Bambach *Master Draftsman*, 12; King.

24 Aristotle, *Prior Analytics*, 2:27.

25 Codex Urb., 109v; *Leonardo on Painting*, 147.

26 Codex Urb., 108v–109r; Notebooks/J. P. Richter, 571–72; Notebooks/Irma Richter, 208.

27 These interpretations reflect those in Kemp *Marvellous*, 146; Nicholl, 263; Clayton, 96; Windsor, RCIN 912495.

28 Codex Atl., 1033r/370r-a.

29 Filomena Calabrese, "Leonardo's Literary Writings: History, Genre, Philosophy," PhD dissertation, University of Toronto, 2011.

30 Notebooks/J. P. Richter, 1265, 1229.

31 Notebooks/J. P. Richter, 1237, 1239, 1234, 1241.

32 Notebooks/J. P. Richter, 1297–312.

33 Notebooks/J. P. Richter, 649.

34 Capra *Science*, 26.

35 Nicholl, 219.

36 Codex Atl., 265r, 852r; Notebooks/Irma Richter, 253; Kemp *Marvellous*, 145.

37 Some commentators, including Edward MacCurdy (Notebooks/MacCurdy, 388), speculate that Leonardo may have actually gone to Syria in the 1480s, but there is no evidence of this, and it seems highly unlikely.

38 Codex Atl., 393v/145v-b; Notebooks/Irma Richter, 252; Notebooks/J. P. Richter, 1336.

39 Codex Atl., 96v/311r; Notebooks/MacCurdy, 265; Notebooks/J. P. Richter, 1354; Nicholl, 217.

7. PERSONAL LIFE

1 Paolo Giovio, "A Life of Leonardo," c. 1527, in Notebooks/J. P. Richter, revised edition of 1939, 1:2.
2 Codex Atl., 119v-a/327v; Notebooks/J. P. Richter, 10.
3 Lester, 2014; Nicholl, 43.
4 Notebooks/J. P. Richter, 844; Notebooks/MacCurdy, 84.
5 Paris Ms. H, 60r; Notebooks/MacCurdy, 130.
6 Paris Ms. C, 15b; Notebooks/J. P. Richter, 1458.
7 Leonardo first refers to him as Salai in 1494; Paris Ms. H, 2:16v. The term is usually translated as "little devil," but it has the connotation of someone a bit unclean as well as devilish, like a little rascal or scamp. It derives from a Tuscan word meaning "limb of the devil." His name is sometimes written Salaì, with an accent creating a third syllable, thus making the pronunciation sah-lie-yee. The name comes from a demon in Luigi Pulci's epic poem *Il Morgante*, a work that Leonardo owned; in the poem, the name is given as Salai, without an accent on the *i*.
8 Pedretti, *Chronology*, 141.
9 Paris Ms. C, 15b; Notebooks/J. P. Richter, 1458; Notebooks/Irma Richter, 291.
10 Codex Atl., 663v/244r; Pedretti *Chronology*, 64; Notebooks/Irma Richter, 290, 291; Bramly, 223, 228; Nicholl, 276.
11 John Garton, "Leonardo's Early Grotesque Head of 1478," in Fiorani and Kim; Notebooks/Irma Richter, 289; *Leonardo on Painting*, 220; Codex Urb., 61r-v; Jens Thus, *The Florentine Years of Leonardo and Verrocchio* (Jenkins, 1913).
12 Clark, 121.
13 Uffizi, Florence, inv. 446E; Notebooks/J. P. Richter, 1383.
14 Pedretti *Chronology*, 140.
15 Windsor, RCIN 912557, 912554, 912594, 912596.
16 Leonardo, "Allegorical Drawing of Pleasure and Pain," c. 1480, Christ Church Picture Gallery, Oxford; Notebooks/J. P. Richter, 676; Nicholl, 204.

8. *VITRUVIAN MAN*

1 Frances Ferguson, "Leonardo da Vinci and the Tiburio of the Milan Cathedral," in Claire Farago, ed., *An Overview of Leonardo's Career and Projects until c. 1500* (Taylor & Francis, 1999), 389; Richard Schofield, "Amadeo, Bramante, and Leonardo and the Tiburio of Milan Cathedral," *Journal of Leonardo Studies* 2 (1989), 68.
2 Ludwig Heydenreich, "Leonardo and Bramante: Genius in Architecture," in O'Malley, 125; King, 129; Notebooks/J. P. Richter, 1427; Carlo Pedretti, "Newly Discovered Evidence of Leonardo's Association with Bramante," *Journal of the Society of Architectural Historians* 32 (1973), 224. Nicholl, 309, discusses alternate attributions for the poems.
3 Bramante's piece has been given many dates, but the authoritative Milan exhibit of 2015 dated it to 1486–87 (Milan catalogue, 423).
4 Codex Atl., 270r/730r; Notebooks/Irma Richter, 282; Nicholl, 223.
5 Codex Arundel, 158a; Notebooks/J. P. Richter, 773.
6 Paris Ms. B, 27r; Notebooks/J. P. Richter, 788; Nicholl, 222.
7 Codex Atl., 310r-b/850r; Heydenreich, "Leonardo and Bramante," 139; Schofield, "Amadeo, Bramante, and Leonardo and the Tiburio of Milan Cathedral," 68; Schofield, "Leonardo's Milanese Architecture," 111; Jean Guillaume, "Léonard et Bramante L'emploi des ordres à Milan à la fin du XV e siècle," *Arte Lombarda* 86–87 (1988), 101; Carlo Pedretti, *Leonardo Architect* (Rizzoli, 1985), 42; Francesco P. Di Teodoro,

"Leonardo da Vinci: The Proportions of the Drawings of Sacred Buildings in Ms. B," *Architectural Histories* 3.1 (2015), 1.

8 Allen Weller, *Francesco di Giorgio* (University of Chicago, 1943), 366; Pietro Marani, "Leonardo, Francesco di Giorgio e il tiburio del Duomo di Milano," *Arte Lombarda* 62.2 (1982), 81; Pari Rahi, *Ars et Ingenium: The Embodiment of Imagination in Francesco di Giorgio Martini's Drawings* (Routledge, 2015), 45.

9 Teodoro, "Leonardo da Vinci: The Proportions of the Drawings of Sacred Buildings in Ms. B," 9.

10 Lester, 2, 207; Heydenreich, "Leonardo and Bramante," 135.

11 Ludwig Heydenreich and Paul Davies, *Architecture in Italy, 1400–1500* (Yale, 1974), 110.

12 Lester, 11.

13 Indra Kagis McEwen, *Vitruvius: Writing the Body of Architecture* (MIT Press, 2004); Vitruvius, *The Ten Books on Architecture*, trans. Morris Hicky Morgan (Harvard, 1914).

14 Paris Ms. F, 0; Notebooks/J. P. Richter, 1471.

15 Elizabeth Mays Merrill, "The Trattato as Textbook," *Architectural Histories* 1 (2013); Lester, 290; Keele *Elements*, 22; Kemp *Leonardo*, 115; Feinberg, *The Young Leonardo*, 696; Walter Kruft, *History of Architectural Theory* (Princeton, 1994), 57.

16 Paris Ms. A, 55v; Notebooks/J. P. Richter, 929.

17 Vitruvius, *Ten Books on Architecture*, bk. 3, para. 1; Morgan translation, 96.

18 Vitruvius, *Ten Books on Architecture*, bk. 3, para. 3; Morgan translation, 97.

19 Lester, 201.

20 Paris Ms. C, 15b; Notebooks/J. P. Richter, 1458.

21 Paris Ms. K, 3:29b; Notebooks/J. P. Richter, 1501.

22 Claudio Sgarbi, "A Newly Discovered Corpus of Vitruvian Images," *Anthropology and Aesthetics*, no. 23 (Spring 1993), 31–51; Claudio Sgarbi, "Il Vitruvio Ferrarese, alcuni dettagli quasi invisibili e un autore—Giacomo Andrea da Ferrara," in Pierre Gros, ed., *Giovanni Giocondo* (Marsilio, 2014), 121; Claudio Sgarbi, "All'origine dell'Uomo Ideale di Leonardo," *Disegnarecon*, no. 9 (June 2012), 177; Richard Schofield, "Notes on Leonardo and Vitruvius," in Moffatt and Taglialagamba, 129; Toby Lester, "The Other Vitruvian Man?," *Smithsonian*, February 2012.

23 Lester, 208.

24 Codex Urb., 157r; *Leonardo da Vinci on Painting*, ed. Carlo Pedretti (University of California, 1964), 35.

25 Toby Lester interview, *Talk of the Nation*, NPR, March 8, 2012; Lester, xii, 214.

26 Edward MacCurdy, *The Mind of Leonardo da Vinci* (Dodd, Mead, 1928), 35.

9. THE HORSE MONUMENT

1 Notebooks/Irma Richter, 286; Kemp *Marvellous*, 191.

2 Codex Atl., 328b/983b; Notebooks/J. P. Richter, 1345.

3 Codex Ash, 1:29a; Notebooks/J. P. Richter, 512.

4 Leonardo da Vinci, "The Leg Muscles and Bones of Man and Horse," Windsor, RCIN 912625.

5 Codex Atl., 96v; Codex Triv., 21; Paris Ms. B, 38v.

6 Windsor, RCIN 912285 to RCIN 91327.

7 Evelyn Welch, *Art and Authority in Renaissance Milan* (Yale, 1995), 201; Andrea Gamberini, ed., *Companion to Late Medieval and Early Modern Milan* (Brill, 2014), 186.

8 Paris Ms. C, 15v; Notebooks/J. P. Richter, 720.

9 Codex Atl., 399r; Kemp *Marvellous*, 194.

10 Bramly, 232.
11 Kemp *Marvellous*, 194.
12 Codex Madrid, 2:157v.
13 Windsor, RCIN 912349.
14 Notebooks/J. P. Richter, 711.
15 Codex Madrid, 2:143, 149, 157; Notebooks/J. P. Richter, 710–11; Windsor, RCIN 912349; Bramly, 234; Kemp *Marvellous*, 194.
16 Codex Atl., 914ar/335v; Notebooks/J. P. Richter, 723.
17 Ercole d'Este to Giovanni Valla, September 19, 1501.

10. SCIENTIST

1 Codex Atl., 119v/327v; Notebooks/J. P. Richter, 10–11; Notebooks/Irma Richter, 4. In his commentaries, Carlo Pedretti (1:110) dates this page to circa 1490.
2 Codex Atl., 196b/596b; Notebooks/J. P. Richter, 490.
3 Brian Richardson, *Printing, Writers and Readers in Renaissance Italy* (Cambridge, 1999), 3; Lotte Hellinga, "The Introduction of Printing in Italy," unpublished ms., University of Manchester Library, undated.
4 A fuller description can be found in Nicholl, 209, and Kemp *Marvellous*, 240.
5 Notebooks/J. P. Richter, 1488, 1501, 1452, 1496, 1448. Vitolone is a text on optics by a Polish scientist.
6 Paris Ms. E, 55r; Notebooks/Irma Richter, 8; James Ackerman, "Science and Art in the Work of Leonardo," in O'Malley, 205.
7 Paris Ms. A, 47r; Capra *Science*, 156, 162.
8 For more, see Leopold Infeld, "Leonardo Da Vinci and the Fundamental Laws of Science," *Science & Society* 17.1 (Winter 1953), 26–41.
9 Codex Atl., 730r; *Leonardo on Painting*, 256.
10 Codex Atl., 200a/594a; Notebooks/J. P. Richter, 13.
11 Paris Ms. G, 8a; Codex Urb., 39v; Notebooks/J. P. Richter, 19; Pedretti *Commentary*, 114.
12 Capra *Learning*, 5.
13 James S. Ackerman, "Leonardo Da Vinci: Art in Science," *Daedalus* 127.1 (Winter 1998), 207.
14 Gopnik, "Renaissance Man."
15 Paris Ms. I, 12b; Notebooks/J. P. Richter, 394.
16 Ryoko Minamino and Masakai Tateno, "Tree Branching: Leonardo da Vinci's Rule versus Biomechanical Models," *PLoS One* 9.4 (April, 2014).
17 Codex Atl., 126r-a; Winternitz, "Leonardo and Music," 116.
18 Paris Ms. E, 54r; Capra *Learning*, 277.
19 Windsor, RCIN 919059; Notebooks/J. P. Richter, 805.
20 Windsor, RCIN 919070; Notebooks/J. P. Richter, 818–19.
21 Codex Atl., 124a; Notebooks/J. P. Richter, 246.
22 Paris Ms. H, 1a; Notebooks/J. P. Richter, 232.
23 Codex Ash., 1:7b; Notebooks/J. P. Richter, 491.
24 Codex Ash., 1:9a; Notebooks/J. P. Richter, 507.
25 Codex Atl., 377v/1051v; Notebooks/Irma Richter, 98; Stefan Klein, *Leonardo's Legacy* (Da Capo, 2010), 26.
26 Codex Arundel, 176r.
27 Paris Ms. B, 1:176r, 131r; Codex Triv., 34v, 49v, Codex Arundel, 190v; Notebooks/Irma Richter, 62–63; Nuland, *Leonardo da Vinci*, 47; Keele *Elements*, 106.

11. BIRDS AND FLIGHT

1 Codex Atl. 45r/124r, 178a/536a; Notebooks/J. P. Richter, 374.
2 Laurenza, 10.
3 Laurenza, 8–10; Pallen, *Vasari on Theater*, 15; Paul Kuritz, *The Making of Theater History* (Prentice Hall, 1988), 145; Alessandra Buccheri, *The Spectacle of Clouds, 1439–1650: Italian Art and Theatre* (Ashgate, 2014), 31.
4 Codex Atl., 858r, 860r.
5 Uffizi Museum, inv. 447Ev.
6 Paris Ms. L, 58; Notebooks/Irma Richter, 95.
7 Windsor, RCIN 912657; Notebooks/Irma Richter, 84.
8 Codex on Flight, fol. 17v.
9 Paris Ms. E, 53r; Paris Ms. L, 58v; Notebooks/Irma Richter, 95, 89.
10 Biblioteca Reale, Turin, Italy. A facsimile with translation is available on the website of the Smithsonian National Air and Space Museum, https://airandspace.si.edu/exhibitions/codex/. For a discussion of the structure of the codex, see Martin Kemp and Juliana Barone, "What Is Leonardo's Codex on the Flight of Birds About?," in Jeannine O'Grody, ed., *Leonardo da Vinci: Drawings from the Biblioteca Reale in Turin* (Birmingham [Ala.] Museum of Fine Arts, 2008), 97.
11 Paris Ms. E, 54r; Notebooks/Irma Richter, 84.
12 Aristotle, *Movement of Animals*, ch. 2.
13 Codex on Flight, fol. 1r-2r.
14 Codex Atl., 20r/64r; Notebooks/Irma Richter, 25.
15 Paris Ms. F, 87v; Notebooks/Irma Richter, 87.
16 Codex Atl., 381v/1051v; Notebooks/Irma Richter, 99.
17 Notebooks/Irma Richter, 86.
18 Codex Atl., 79r/215r.
19 Paris Ms. E, 45v; Richard Prum, "Leonardo and the Science of Bird Flight," in O'Grody, *Leonardo da Vinci: Drawings from the Biblioteca Reale in Turin*; Capra *Learning*, 266.
20 Codex Atl., 161/434r, 381v/1058v; Notebooks/Irma Richter, 99.
21 Paris Ms. B, 80r; Laurenza, 45.
22 Paris Ms. B, 88v; Laurenza, 41; Pedretti, *The Machines*, 8.
23 Martin Kemp, "Leonardo Lifts Off," *Nature* 421.792 (February 20, 2003).
24 Codex Atl., 1006v; Laurenza, 32.
25 Paris Ms. B, 74v.
26 Codex on Flight, fol. 18v and inside back cover; Notebooks/J. P. Richter, 1428.
27 Codex Atl., 231av.

12. THE MECHANICAL ARTS

1 Codex Atl., 8v/30v; Ladislao Reti, "Elements of Machines," in Reti *Unknown*, 264; Marco Cianchi, *Leonardo da Vinci's Machines* (Becocci, 1988), 69; Arasse, 11.
2 Codex Madrid, 1:45r.
3 Paris Ms. H, 43v, 44r; Lynn White Jr., *Medieval Technology and Social Change* (Oxford, 1962); Ladislao Reti, "Leonardo da Vinci the Technologist," in O'Malley, 67.
4 Paris Ms. A, 30v.
5 Codex Atl., 289r.
6 Paris Ms. H, 80v; Codex Leic., 28v; Reti, "Leonardo da Vinci the Technologist," 75.
7 Paris Ms. B, 33v–34r; Codex Atl., 207v-b, 209v-b; Codex Forster, 1:50v.
8 Codex Atl., 318v; Bern Dibner, "Leonardo: Prophet of Automation,' in O'Malley, 104.

9 Codex on Flight, 12r.
10 Infeld, "Leonardo da Vinci and the Fundamental Laws of Science," 26.
11 Codex Forster, vol. 1; Allan Mills, "Leonardo da Vinci and Perpetual Motion," *Leonardo* 41.1 (February 2008), 39; Benjamin Olshin, "Leonardo da Vinci's Investigations of Perpetual Motion," *Icon* 15 (2009), 1. Leonardo's most interesting wheels with pinballs are in Codex Forster, 2:91r; Codex Atl., 1062r. Wheels with crescent-shaped pieces are in Codex Arundel, 263; Codex Forster, 2:91v, 34v; Madrid, 1:176r. Those of wheels with weights on arms are in Codex Atl., 778r; Madrid, 1:147r, 148r. Archimedean water screws are in Codex Atl., 541v; Codex Forster, 1:42v.
12 Codex Atl., 7v-a/147v-a; Reti, "Leonardo da Vinci the Technologist," 87.
13 Codex Madrid, 1:flysheet; Ladislao Reti, "Leonardo on Bearings and Gears," *Scientific American*, February 1971, 101.
14 Valentin Popov, *Contact Mechanics and Friction* (Springer, 2010), 3.
15 Codex Madrid, 1:122r, 176a; Codex Forster, 2:85v; Codex Forster, 3:72r; Codex Atl., 72r; Keele *Elements*, 123; Ian Hutchings, "Leonardo da Vinci's Studies of Friction," *Wear*, August 15, 2016, 51; Angela Pitenis, Duncan Dowson, and W. Gregory Sawyer, "Leonardo da Vinci's Friction Experiments," *Tribology Letters* 56.3 (December 2014), 509.
16 Codex Madrid, 1:20v, 26r.
17 Ladislao Reti, "The Leonardo da Vinci Codices in the Biblioteca Nacional of Madrid," *Technology and Culture* 84 (October 1967), 437.
18 Cianchi, *Leonardo da Vinci's Machines*, 16.

13. MATH

1 Paris Ms. G, 95b; Notebooks/J. P. Richter, 1158, 3; James McCabe, "Leonardo da Vinci's De Ludo Geometrico," PhD dissertation, UCLA, 1972.
2 Codex Madrid, 1:75r.
3 Codex Madrid, 2:62r; Keele *Elements*, 158.
4 Codex Atl., 183v-a.
5 Kemp *Leonardo*, 969.
6 Paris Ms. K, 49r.
7 Codex Atl., 228r/104r.
8 King, 164; Lucy McDonald, "And That's Renaissance Magic," *The Guardian*, April 10, 2007; Tiago Wolfram Nunes dos Santos Hirth, "Luca Pacioli and His 1500 Book De Viribus Quantitatis," PhD dissertation, University of Lisbon, 2015.
9 Codex Atl., 118a/366a; Notebooks/J. P. Richter, 1444.
10 McCabe, "Leonardo da Vinci's De Ludo Geometrico"; Nicholl, 304.
11 Dan Brown, *The Da Vinci Code* (Doubleday, 2003), 120–24; Gary Meisner, "Da Vinci and the Divine Proportion in Art Composition," *Golden Number*, July 7, 2014, online.
12 Paris Ms. M, 66v; Codex Atl., 152v; Capra *Science*, 267; Keele *Elements*, 100.
13 Codex Arundel, 182v, Codex Atl., 252r, 264r, 471r, among many examples.
14 McCabe, "Leonardo da Vinci's De Ludo Geometrico."
15 Codex Forster, 1:3r.
16 Windsor, RCIN 919145; Kemp *Marvellous*, 290.
17 Codex Atl., 471.
18 Codex Atl., 124v.
19 McCabe, "Leonardo da Vinci's De Ludo Geometrico," 45.
20 Squaring a circle in this manner is even more mathematically complex than doubling a cube. It was not until 1882 that it was proven impossible. That is because π is a tran-

scendental number, rather than merely being an algebraic irrational number. It is not the root of any polynomial with rational coefficients, and it is impossible to construct its square root with a compass and ruler.

21 Kemp *Leonardo,* 247; Codex Madrid, 2:12r.

22 Kenneth Clark, "Leonardo's Notebooks," *New York Review of Books*, December 12, 1974.

14. THE NATURE OF MAN

1 Alberti, *On Painting*, bk. 2.

2 Codex Urb., 118v; Notebooks/J. P. Richter, 488; *Leonardo on Painting*, 130.

3 Domenica Laurenza, *Art and Anatomy in Renaissance Italy* (Metropolitan Museum of New York, 2012), 8.

4 Laurenza, *Art and Anatomy in Renaissance Italy*, 9.

5 Windsor, RCIN 919059v; Notebooks/J. P. Richter, 805.

6 Windsor, RCIN 919037v; Notebooks/J. P. Richter, 797.

7 Notebooks/J. P. Richter, 798.

8 Windsor, RCIN 919058v; Clayton and Philo, 58; Keele and Roberts, 47; Wells, 27.

9 Peter Gerrits and Jan Veening, "Leonardo da Vinci's 'A Skull Sectioned': Skull and Dental Formula Revisited," *Clinical Anatomy* 26 (2013), 430.

10 Windsor, RCIN 919057r; Frank Fehrenbach, "The Pathos of Function: Leonardo's Technical Drawings," in Helmar Schramm, ed., *Instruments in Arts and Science* (Theatrum Scientarum, 2008), 81; Carmen Bambach, "Studies of the Human Skull," in Bambach *Master Draftsman*; Clark, 129.

11 Notebooks/J. P. Richter, 838.

12 Martin Clayton, "Anatomy and the Soul," in Marani and Fiorio, 215; Jonathan Pevsner, "Leonardo da Vinci's Studies of the Brain and Soul," *Scientific American Mind* 16: (2005), 84.

13 Windsor, RCIN 912613; Clayton and Philo, 37; Kenneth Keele, "Leonardo da Vinci's 'Anatomia Naturale,'" *Yale Journal of Biology and Medicine* 52 (1979), 369. Leonardo's experiment was not described and illustrated again until the Scottish physician Alexander Stuart did it in 1739.

14 Martin Kemp, "'Il Concetto dell'Anima' in Leonardo's Early Skull Studies," *Journal of the Warburg and Courtauld Institutes* 34 (1971), 115.

15 Notebooks/J. P. Richter, 308–59; Zöllner, 2:108.

16 Notebooks/J. P. Richter, 348–59.

17 Notebooks/J. P. Richter, preface to ch. 7.

15. *VIRGIN OF THE ROCKS*

1 Leonardo Treatise/Rigaud, ch. 165.

2 My narrative comports with these sources: Martin Kemp, "Beyond Compare," *Artforum International* 50.5 (January 2012), 68; Zöllner, 1:223; W. S. Cannell, "The *Virgin of the Rocks*: A Reconsideration of the Documents and a New Interpretation," *Gazette des Beaux-Arts* 47 (1984), 99; Syson, 63, 161, 170; Larry Keith, Ashok Roy, et al., "Leonardo da Vinci's *Virgin of the Rocks*: Treatment, Technique and Display," *National Galler (London) Technical Bulletin* 32 (2011); Marani, 137; the web page materials of the Louvre and National Gallery (London); personal interview with Vincent Delieuvin. For a contrary view, holding that the London version was painted first, see Tamsyn Taylor, "A Different Opinion," *Leonardo da Vinci and "the Virgin of the Rocks,"* November 8, 2011, http://leonardovirginoftherocks.blogspot.com/. For another take

on when each picture was painted, see Charles Hope, "The Wrong Leonardo?," *New York Review of Books*, February 9, 2012. After going through what we know of the commission and legal disputes, Hope argues, "This suggests that the real problem was something different, namely that when the patrons said that the picture had not been finished, they meant that it had not been completed according to the terms of the contract. Instead of showing the Virgin and Child with angels, as was required, it showed the Virgin and Child with an angel and Saint John." He contends, "It has been argued therefore that the Paris picture was removed from the church, probably in the 1490s, and that the London picture was a substitute. But the documents exclude this possibility. They make it clear beyond reasonable doubt that the picture commissioned in 1483 was still in the church in 1508. Had the patrons disposed of it before that time, the painters would have had no contractual obligation to provide a new version, and no payment was made to them for one. Equally, the documents indicate that the patrons did not return the picture to Leonardo. In order to make a second version, he needed access to the original, and this was not provided before 1508. Accordingly, one picture, evidently the one in the Louvre, was supplied between 1483 and 1490, and the London version cannot have been painted before 1508."

3 Regina Stefaniak, "On Looking into the Abyss: Leonardo's *Virgin of the Rocks*," *Journal of Art History* 66.1 (1997), 1.

4 Larry Keith, "In Pursuit of Perfection," in Syson, 64; Syson, 162n; Claire Farago, "A Conference on Leonardo da Vinci's Technical Practice," *Leonardo da Vinci Society Newsletter*, no. 38 (May 2012); Vincent Delieuvin et al., "The Paris *Virgin of the Rocks*: A New Approach Based on Scientific Analysis," in Michel Menu, ed., *Leonardo da Vinci's Technical Practice* (Hermann, 2014), ch. 9.

5 Michael Thomas Jahosky, "Some Marvelous Thing: Leonardo, Caterina, and the *Madonna of the Rocks*," Master's thesis, University of South Florida, 2010; Julian Bell, "Leonardo in London," *Times Literary Supplement*, November 23, 2011.

6 Bramly, 106; Capra *Science*, 46.

7 Kemp *Marvellous*, 75; Codex Urb., 67v; Edward J. Olszewski, "How Leonardo Invented Sfumato," *Notes in the History of Art* 31.1 (Fall 2011), 4–9.

8 Ann Pizzorusso, "Leonardo's Geology: The Authenticity of the *Virgin of the Rocks*," *Leonardo* 29.3 (Fall 1996). See also Ann Pizzorusso, *Tweeting Da Vinci* (Da Vinci Press, 2014); Bas den Hond, "Science Offers New Clues about Paintings by Munch and da Vinci," *Eos* 98 (April 2017).

9 William Emboden, *Leonardo da Vinci on Plants and Gardens* (Timber Press, 1987), 1, 125.

10 Luke Syson and Rachel Billinge, "Leonardo da Vinci's Use of Underdrawing in the 'Virgin of the Rocks' in the National Gallery and 'St. Jerome' in the Vatican," *Burlington Magazine* 147 (July 2005), 450; Keith et al., "Leonardo da Vinci's *Virgin of the Rocks*"; Francesca Fiorani, "Reflections on Leonardo da Vinci Exhibitions in London and Paris," in *Studiolo revue d'histoire de l'art de l'Académie de France à Rome* (Somogy, 2013); Larry Keith, "In Pursuit of Perfection," in Syson, 64; Kemp, "Beyond Compare," 68; "The Hidden Leonardo," National Gallery (London) website, https://www.nationalgallery.org.uk/paintings/learn-about-art/paintings-in-depth/the-hidden-leonardo.

11 John Shearman, "Leonardo's Colour and Chiaroscuro," *Zeitschrift für Kunstgeschichte* 25 (1962), 13.

12 Dalya Alberge, "The Daffodil Code: Doubts Revived over Leonardo's *Virgin of the Rocks* in London," *The Guardian*, December 9, 2014.

13 Pizzorusso, "Leonardo's Geology," 197. For a compilation of the attacks on the Na-

tional Gallery's pronouncement, see Michael Daley, "Could the Louvre's 'Virgin and St. Anne' Provide the Proof That the (London) National Gallery's 'Virgin of the Rocks' Is Not by Leonardo da Vinci?," *ArtWatch UK*, June 12, 2012.

14 Syson, 36.

15 Clark, 204.

16 Kemp *Marvellous*, 274.

17 Keith, "In Pursuit of Perfection," in Syson, 64

18 Christine Lin, "Inside Leonardo Da Vinci's Collaborative Workshop," *Epoch Times*, March 31, 2015; Luke Syson, "Leonardo da Vinci: Singular and Plural," lecture, Metropolitan Museum, New York, March 6, 2013; author's interview with Syson.

19 Clark, 171; Fra Pietro da Novellara to Isabella d'Este, April 3, 1501.

20 Fiorani, "Reflections on Leonardo da Vinci Exhibitions in London and Paris"; Delieuvin.

21 Jonathan Jones, "The *Virgin of the Rocks*: Da Vinci decoded," *The Guardian*, July 13, 2010.

22 Andrew Graham-Dixon, "The Mystery of Leonardo's Two Madonnas," *The Telegraph* (London), October 23, 2011.

23 The drawing is almost identical in most traits to the painted angel, and it is considered by most critics to be a study. But in Bambach *Master Draftsman* there is one essay (Carlo Pedretti, 96) that calls it a study and another essay (Pietro Marani, 160) that argues it is not.

24 Clark, 94.

16. THE MILAN PORTRAITS

1 Zöllner, 2:225; Marani, 160; Syson, 86, 95.

2 Syson, 86.

3 Codex Ash., 1:2a; Notebooks/J. P. Richter, 516.

4 Codex Arundel, 64b; Notebooks/J. P. Richter, 830; Codex Forster, 3:158v.

5 Janice Shell and Grazioso Sironi, "Cecilia Gallerani: Leonardo's *Lady with an Ermine*," *Artibus et Historiae* 13.25 (1992), 47–66; David Alan Brown, "Leonardo and the Ladies with the Ermine and the Book," *Artibus et Historiae* 11.22 (1990), 47–61; Syson, 11; Nicholl, 229; Gregory Lubkin, *A Renaissance Court: Milan under Galleazzo Maria Sforza* (University of California, 1994), 50.

6 John Pope-Hennessy, *The Portrait in the Renaissance* (Pantheon, 1963), 103; Brown, "Leonardo and the Ladies with the Ermine and the Book," 47.

7 Paris Ms. H, 1:48b, 12a; Notebooks/J. P. Richter, 1263, 1234; Syson, 111.

8 Kemp *Marvellous*, 188; Codex Atl., 87r, 88r.

9 Codex Ash., 1:14a; Notebooks/J. P. Richter, 552; Bell, "Sfumato and Acuity Perspective"; Marani, "Movements of the Soul," 230; Clayton, "Anatomy and the Soul," 216; Jackie Wullschlager, "Leonardo As You'll Never See Him Again," *Financial Times*, November 11, 2011.

10 Bull, "Two Portraits by Leonardo," 67.

11 Shell and Sironi, "Cecilia Gallerani," 47

12 Most scholars now agree that it is Lucrezia Crivelli, and that seems to comport with three court poet sonnets in praise of such a painting. However, Luke Syson, who organized the London 2011 show of Leonardo's Milan paintings, suggests in the catalogue (105) that "it is not impossible" that the subject may actually be Beatrice d'Este, even though there is scant resemblance to other portrayals of her and no poems of praise that almost surely would have accompanied such a painting.

13 Leonardo Treatise/Rigaud, ch. 213; Codex Ash., 2:14v.
14 Bernard Berenson, *North Italian Painters* (Putnam, 1907), 260; Clark, 101.
15 "Head of a Young Girl in Profile to the Left in Renaissance Dress, German School, Early 19th Century," Christie's sale 8812, lot 402, January 30, 1998, http://www.christies.com/LotFinder/lot_details.aspx?intObjectID=473187.
16 Peter Silverman interview, in "Mystery of a Masterpiece," NOVA/National Geographic/PBS, January 25, 2012; Peter Silverman, *Leonardo's Lost Princess: One Man's Quest to Authenticate an Unknown Portrait by Leonardo Da Vinci* (Wiley, 2012), 6. The owner who consigned the picture for auction sued Christie's for breaches of fiduciary duty and negligence. The suit was dismissed because the statute of limitations had expired.
17 Silverman, *Leonardo's Lost Princess*, 8.
18 John Brewer, "Art and Science: A Da Vinci Detective Story," *Engineering & Science* 1.2 (2005); John Brewer, *The American Leonardo* (Oxford, 2009); Carol Vogel, "Not by Leonardo, but Sotheby's Sells a Work for $1.5 Million," *New York Times*, January 28, 2010; Silverman, *Leonardo's Lost Princess*, 44.
19 Silverman, *Leonardo's Lost Princess*, 16.
20 Nicholas Turner, introduction to Martin Kemp and Pascal Cotte, *La Bella Principessa* (Hodder & Stoughton, 2010), 16; Nicholas Turner, "Statement concerning the Portrait on Vellum," Lumiere Technology, September 2008, http://www.lumiere-technology.com/images/Download/Nicholas_Turner_Statement.pdf; Silverman, *Leonardo's Lost Princess*, 19.
21 David Grann, "The Mark of a Masterpiece," *New Yorker*, July 12, 2010.
22 Elisabetta Povoledo, "Dealer Who Sold Portrait Joins Leonardo Debate," *New York Times*, August 29, 2008.
23 Pascal Cotte, "Further Comparisons with Cecilia Gallerani," in Kemp and Cotte, *La Bella Principessa*, 176.
24 Silverman, *Leonardo's Lost Princess*, 64; "Mystery of a Masterpiece"; Lumiere Technology studies on *La Bella Principessa*, http://www.lumiere-technology.com.
25 Christina Geddo, "The 'Pastel' Found: A New Portrait by Leonardo da Vinci?," in *Artes*, no. 14 (2009), 63; Christina Geddo, "Leonardo da Vinci: The Extraordinary Discovery of the Last Portrait," lecture, Société genevoise d'études italiennes Geneva, October 2, 2012.
26 Carlo Pedretti, abstract of the introduction to *Leonardo Infinito: La vita, l'opera completa, la modernità* by Alessandro Vezzosi, Lumiere Technology, 2008, http://www.lumiere-technology.com/images/Download/Abstract_Pr_Pedretti.pdf.
27 Windsor, RCIN 912505. The Royal Collection dates the drawing to c. 1490.
28 See chapter 21.
29 Grann, "The Mark of a Masterpiece"; "Mystery of a Masterpiece"; author's interview with Martin Kemp; Silverman, *Leonardo's Lost Princess*, 73.
30 Kemp and Cotte, *La Bella Principessa*, 24; Silverman, *Leonardo's Lost Princess*, 74; Grann, "The Mark of a Masterpiece."
31 Silverman, *Leonardo's Lost Princess*, 103.
32 Kemp and Cotte, *La Bella Principessa*, 72; Pascal Cotte and Martin Kemp, "*La Bella Principessa* and the Warsaw Sforziad, 2011," Lumiere Technology, http://www.lumiere-technology.com//news/Study_Bella_Principessa_and_Warsaw_Sforziad.pdf; Martin Kemp, *La Bella Principessa*, exhibition catalogue, Palazzo Ducale, Urbino, 2014; Silverman, *Leonardo's Lost Princess*, 75; Grann, "The Mark of a Masterpiece"; author's interview with Kemp.

33 "Mystery of a Masterpiece."
34 Grann, "The Mark of a Masterpiece."
35 Peter Paul Biro, "Fingerprint Examination," in Kemp and Cotte, *La Bella Principessa*, 148.
36 Jeff Israely, "How a 'New' da Vinci Was Discovered, *Time*, October 15, 2009; Helen Pidd, "New Leonardo da Vinci Painting 'Discovered,'" *The Guardian*, October 13, 2009; "Fingerprint Unmasks Original da Vinci Painting," CNN, October 13, 2009; "Finger Points to New da Vinci Art," BBC, October 13, 2009; Simon Hewitt, "Fingerprint Points to $19,000 Portrait Being Revalued as £100m Work by Leonardo da Vinci," *Antiques Trade Gazette*, October 12, 2009.
37 Grann, "The Mark of a Masterpiece."
38 The article is worth reading in its entirety: Grann, "The Mark of a Masterpiece," www.newyorker.com/magazine/2010/07/12/the-mark-of-a-masterpiece.
39 Barbara Leonard, "Art Critic Loses Libel Suit against the *New Yorker*," *Courthouse News Service*, December 8, 2015.
40 "Mystery of a Masterpiece."
41 "New Leonardo da Vinci *Bella Principessa* Confirmed," Lumiere Technology website, September 28, 2011; Cotte and Kemp, "*La Bella Principessa* and the Warsaw Sforziad"; "Mystery of a Masterpiece."
42 Cotte and Kemp, "*La Bella Principessa* and the Warsaw Sforziad"; Simon Hewitt, "New Evidence Strengthens Leonardo Claim for Portrait," *Antiques Trade Gazette*, October 3, 2011.
43 Scott Reyburn, "An Art World Mystery Worthy of Leonardo," *New York Times*, December 4, 2015; Katarzyna Krzyzagórska-Pisarek, "*La Bella Principessa*: Arguments against the Attribution to Leonardo," *Artibus et Historiae* 36 (June 2015), 61; Martin Kemp, "Errors, Misconceptions, and Allegations of Forgery," Lumiere Technology, 2015, http://www.lumiere-technology.com/A&HresponseMK.pdf; "Problems with La Bella Principessa, Part III: Dr. Pisarek Responds to Prof. Kemp," *ArtWatch UK*, 2016, artwatch.org.uk/problems-with-la-bella-principessa-part-iii-dr-pisarek-responds-to-prof-kemp/; Martin Kemp, "Attribution and Other Issues," *Martin Kemp's This and That*, May 16, 2015, martinkempsthisandthat.blogspot.com/; Josh Boswell and Tim Rayment, "It's Not a da Vinci, It's Sally from the Co-op," *Sunday Times* (London), November 29, 2015; Lorena Muñoz-Alonso, "Forger Claims Leonardo da Vinci's *La Bella Principessa* Is Actually His Painting of a Supermarket Cashier," *Artnet News*, November 30, 2015; "Some of the Many Inconsistencies and Dubious Assertions in Greenhalgh's 'A Forger's Tale,'" Lumiere Technology, http://www.lumiere-technology.com/Some%20of%20the%20Many%20Inconsistencies.pdf; Vincent Noce, "*La Bella Principessa*: Still an Enigma," *Art Newspaper*, May 2016, from The Authentication in Art Congress, Louwman Museum, The Hague, May 11, 2016.
44 Jonathan Jones, "This Is a Leonardo da Vinci?," *The Guardian*, November 30, 2015.
45 Cotte and Kemp, "*La Bella Principessa* and the Warsaw Sforziad"; author's interview with Martin Kemp.

17. THE SCIENCE OF ART

1 Zöllner, 2:108; Monica Azzolini, "Anatomy of a Dispute: Leonardo, Pacioli and Scientific Courtly Entertainment in Renaissance Milan," *Early Science and Medicine* 9.2 (2004), 115.
2 Cennino d'Andrea Cennini, *Il Libro dell' Arte*, trans. Daniel V. Thompson Jr. (Dover, 1933).

3 Carlo Dionisotti, "Leonardo uomo di lettere," *Italia Medioevale e Umanistica* 5 (1962), 209.

4 Claire Farago, *Leonardo da Vinci's Paragone: A Critical Interpretation* (Leiden: Brill Studies, 1992). Most of the quotations I use come from her new translation. The primary source of Leonardo's *paragone* and his proposed treatise on painting is a manuscript, probably compiled by Melzi, that is known as the Codex Urbinas 1270 and is in the Vatican. The *paragone* forms the opening section of the treatise; it originated in Paris Ms. A and what is known as the lost Libro A, which has been reconstructed by Carlo Pedretti from passages in the Codex Urbinas. See note 12 below.

5 Codex Ash., 2:19r-v.

6 Codex Ash., 2:20r; Notebooks/Irma Richter, 189; Notebooks/J. P. Richter, 654.

7 Codex Urb., 21v.

8 Codex Urb., 15v.

9 Codex Ash., 1:13a, 2:22v; Codex Urb., 66; Notebooks/J. P. Richter, 508; Notebooks/Irma Richter, 172. See also Kenneth Clark, "A Note on the Relationship of His Science and Art," *History Today*, May 1, 1952, 303; Kemp *Marvellous*, 145; Martin Kemp, "Analogy and Observation in the Codex Hammer," in Mario Pedini, ed., *Studi Vinciani in Memoria di Nando di Toni* (Brescia, 1986), 103.

10 For an example, see Windsor, RCIN 912371.

11 The early biographer Gian Paolo Lomazzo is the source for the assertion that the treatise was written at Ludovico Sforza's request. Pedretti *Commentary*, 1:76; Farago, *Leonardo da Vinci's Paragone*, 162.

12 For a full chronology of manuscripts and a history of *Treatise* versions, see Carlo Pedretti, *Leonardo da Vinci on Painting* (University of California, 1964), which reassembles a version of the *Treatise* from the Melzi manuscript known as the Codex Urbinas 1270 and other codices (see p. 9 for the Pacioli quote). Melzi listed eighteen manuscripts of Leonardo that he drew upon, but only seven are still known to exist. For a comparison of the manuscripts, see the website *Leonardo da Vinci and His "Treatise on Painting,"* www.treatiseonpainting.org. See also Claire Farago, *Re-reading Leonardo: The Treatise on Painting across Europe, 1550–1900* (Ashgate, 2009), and essays in that book by Martin Kemp and Juliana Barone, "What Might Leonardo's Own Trattato Have Looked Like?" and Claire Farago, "Who Abridged Leonardo da Vinci's Treatise on Painting?"; Monica Azzolini, "In Praise of Art: Text and Context of Leonardo's 'Paragone' and Its Critique of the Arts and Sciences," *Renaissance Studies* 19.4 (September 2005), 487; Fiorani, "The Shadows of Leonardo's *Annunciation* and Their Lost Legacy," 119; Fiorani, "The Colors of Leonardo's Shadows," 271. Claire Farago has raised questions about whether Melzi was the editor.

13 Claire Farago, "A Short Note on Artisanal Epistemology in Leonardo's Treatise on Painting," in Moffatt and Taglialagamba, 51.

14 Codex Urb., 133r-v; Codex Atl., 246a/733a; Leonardo Treatise/Rigaud, ch. 178; *Leonardo on Painting*, 15; Notebooks/J. P. Richter, 111, 121.

15 Leonardo Treatise/Rigaud, ch. 177.

16 Notebooks/J. P. Richter 160, 111–18; Nagel, "Leonardo and Sfumato," 7; Janis Bell, "Aristotle as a Source for Leonardo's Theory of Colour Perspective after 1500," *Journal of the Warburg and Courtauld Institutes* 56 (1993), 100; Codex Atl., 676r; Codex Ash., 2:13v.

17 Jürgen Renn, ed., *Galileo in Context* (Cambridge, 2001), 202.

18 Notebooks/J. P. Richter, 121; Nagel, "Leonardo and Sfumato."

19 Leonardo Treatise/Pedretti, ch. 443, p. 694; Notebooks/J. P. Richter, 49, 47; Bell, "Sfu-

mato and Acuity Perspective"; Carlo Vecce, "The Fading Evidence of Reality: Leonardo and the End," lecture, University of Durham, November 4, 2015.

20 Leonardo da Vinci, *A Treatise on Painting*, trans. A. Philip McMahon (Princeton, 1956), 1:806 (based on the Codex Urbinas); Martin Kemp, "Leonardo and the Visual Pyramid," *Journal of the Warburg and Courtauld Institutes* 40 (1977); James Ackerman, "Leonardo's Eye," *Journal of the Warburg and Courtauld Institutes* 41 (1978).

21 Notebooks/MacCurdy, 224.

22 Leonardo da Vinci, "The Cranial Nerves," Windsor, RCIN 919052; Keele and Roberts, 54.

23 Notebooks/MacCurdy, 253; Rumy Hilloowalla, "Leonardo da Vinci, Visual Perspective and the Crystalline Sphere (Lens): If Only Leonardo Had Had a Freezer," *Vesalius* 10.5 (2004); Ackerman, "Leonardo's Eye," 108. For less laudatory assessments of his optical studies, see David C. Lindberg, *Theories of Vision from Al-kindi to Kepler* (University of Chicago, 1981), ch. 8; Dominique Raynaud, "Leonardo, Optics, and Ophthalmology," in Fiorani and Nova, *Leonardo da Vinci and Optics*, 293.

24 Codex Atl., 200a/594a; Paris Ms. A, 3a; Notebooks/J. P. Richter, 50, 13.

25 Ackerman, "Leonardo's Eye"; Anthony Grafton, *Cardano's Cosmos* (Harvard, 1999), 57.

26 Codex Urb., 154v; Notebooks/J. P. Richter, 14–16.

27 Notebooks/J. P. Richter, 100, 91, 109.

28 Paris Ms. E., 79b; Notebooks/J. P. Richter, 225; Leonardo Treatise/Rigaud, chs. 309, 315; Janis Bell, "Leonardo's prospettiva delle ombre," in Fiorani and Nova, *Leonardo da Vinci and Optics*, 79.

29 Leonardo Treatise/Rigaud, ch. 305.

30 Bell, "Sfumato and Acuity Perspective"; Ackerman, "Leonardo Da Vinci: Art in Science," 207; Paris Ms. G, 26v,

31 Leonardo Treatise/Rigaud, 306.

32 Leonardo Treatise/Rigaud, 283, 286; Notebooks/J. P. Richter, 296.

33 Codex Ash., 1:13a; Notebooks/J. P. Richter, 294.

34 Ackerman, "Leonardo's Eye"; Kemp, "Leonardo and the Visual Pyramid," 128.

18. *THE LAST SUPPER*

1 Matteo Bandello, *Tutte le Opere*, ed. Francesco Flora (Mondadori, 1934; originally published 1554), 1:646; Norman Land, "Leonardo da Vinci in a Tale by Matteo Bandello," *Discoveries* 2006, 1; King, 145; Kemp *Marvellous*, 166.

2 Pinin Brambilla Barcilon and Pietro Marani, *Leonardo's* Last Supper (University of Chicago, 1999), 2.

3 Matthew 26:21.

4 Clark, 149, 153.

5 Matthew 26:22–23; John 13:22.

6 Codex Atl., 137a/415a; Notebooks/J. P. Richter, 593; Marani, "Movements of the Soul," 233.

7 Codex Atl., 383r; Notebooks/J. P. Richter, 593–94.

8 Codex Forster, 2:62v/1v-2r; Notebooks/J. P. Richter, 665–66.

9 Matthew 26:23, 26:25; Luke 22:21; Matthew Landrus, "The Proportions of Leonardo's *Last Supper*," *Raccolta Vinciana* 32 (December 2007), 43.

10 Brown, *The Da Vinci Code*, 263; King, 189.

11 Matthew 26:26–28; Leonardo Steinberg, *Leonardo's Incessant* Last Supper (Zone, 2001), 38; Jack Wasserman, "Rethinking Leonardo da Vinci's *Last Supper*," *Artibus et Historiae* 28.55 (2007), 23; King, 216. Charles Hope, "The Last 'Last Supper,'" *New*

York Review of Books, August 9, 2001, argues against Steinberg and others who believe that Leonardo means to portray the Eucharist: "Leonardo omitted the one indispensable element of the Eucharist, namely the chalice, which was regularly included in depictions of the Institution. The table is full of fruit, rolls, and wine glasses, so Christ's hands had to be in proximity to them; but it is difficult to believe that Renaissance Christians would have associated the Eucharist with a half-drunk wine tumbler. In any case, the eucharistic theme, though regularly shown in altarpieces for obvious reasons, was not regarded as appropriate for refectories."

12 Notebooks/J. P. Richter, 55; King, 142.

13 Notebooks/J. P. Richter, 100, 91, 109.

14 Notebooks/J. P. Richter, 545.

15 Lillian F. Schwartz, "The Staging of Leonardo's *Last Supper*: A Computer-Based Exploration of Its Perspective," *Leonardo*, supplemental issue, 1988, 89–96; Kemp *Leonardo*, 1761; Kemp *Marvellous*, 182.

16 Ernst Gombrich, "Paper Given on the Occasion of the Dedication of *The Last Supper* (after Leonardo)," Magdalen College, Oxford, March 10, 1993 (includes his translation of Goethe); Kemp, *Marvellous*, 186; John Varriano, "At Supper with Leonardo," *Gastronomica* 8.1 (2014).

17 Barcilon and Marani, *Leonardo's* Last Supper, 327; Claire J. Farago, "Leonardo's *Battle of Anghiari*: A Study in the Exchange between Theory and Practice," *Art Bulletin* 76.2 (June 1994), 311; Pietro Marani, *The Genius and the Passions: Leonardo's Last Supper* (Skira, 2001).

18 Alessandra Stanley, "After a 20-Year Cleanup, a Brighter, Clearer 'Last Supper' Emerges," *New York Times*, May 27, 1999; Hope, "The Last 'Last Supper.'"

19 Michael Daley, "The Perpetual Restoration of Leonardo's *Last Supper*," part 2, *ArtWatch UK*, March 14, 2012; Barcilon and Marani, *Leonardo's* Last Supper, 341.

19. PERSONAL TURMOIL

1 Codex Forster, 3:88r; Notebooks/J. P. Richter, 1384. Some scholars, including Richter, assume that Caterina was a servant; more recent research, including the discovery of a hospital death notice for "Caterina of Florence," provides evidence that she was his mother. See Angelo Paratico, *Beyond Thirty-Nine* blog, May 18, 2015; Vanna Arrighi, Anna Bellinazzi, and Edoardo Villata, *Leonardo da Vinci: La vera immagine. Documenti E Testimonianze Sulla Vita E Sull'opera* (Giunti, 2005), 79.

2 Codex Forster, 3:74v, 88v; Notebooks/J. P. Richter, 1517; Bramly, 242; Nicholl, 536.

3 Arrighi et al., *Leonardo da Vinci: La vera immagine.*

4 Codex Forster, 2:95a; Notebooks/J. P. Richter, 1522.

5 Notebooks/J. P. Richter, 1523.

6 Bramly, 243.

7 Patrizia Costa, "The Sala Delle Asse in the Sforza Castle," Master's thesis, University of Pittsburgh, 2006. The rooms are currently being renovated and are open to visitors and researchers.

8 MacCurdy, *The Mind of Leonardo da Vinci*, 35.

9 Codex Atl., 335v; MacCurdy, *The Mind of Leonardo da Vinci*, 25; Notebooks/J. P. Richter, 1345.

10 Codex Atl., 866r/315v; Notebooks/J. P. Richter, 1345.

11 Codex Atl., 323v; Notebooks/Irma Richter, 302; Notebooks/J. P. Richter, 1346; Pedretti *Commentary*, 2:332.

12 Codex Atl., 243a/669r; *Leonardo on Painting*, 265; Notebooks/J. P. Richter, 1379.

20. FLORENCE AGAIN

1 Codex Atl., 638bv; Bramly, 313.
2 Codex Leic., 22b.
3 Codex Madrid, 2:4b; Pedretti *Commentary*, 2:332.
4 Codex Arundel, 229b; Notebooks/J. P. Richter, 1425, 1423; Notebooks/Irma Richter, 325.
5 Codex Madrid, 2:4b; Codex Atl., 312b/949b.
6 It is in the Biblioteca Medicea Laurenziana, Florence.
7 Julia Cartwright, *Isabella d'Este* (Dutton, 1905), 15.
8 Cartwright, *Isabella d'Este*, 92, 150; Brown, "Leonardo and the Ladies with the Ermine and the Book," 47.
9 Brown, "Leonardo and the Ladies with the Ermine and the Book," 49; Shell and Sironi, "Cecilia Gallerani," 48.
10 Brown, "Leonardo and the Ladies with the Ermine and the Book," 50.
11 All of the letters, in Italian with English translations, are in Francis Ames-Lewis, *Isabella and Leonardo* (Yale, 2012), 223–40, and discussed in chapters 4 and 6 of that book. The letters and story are also in Cartwright, *Isabella d'Este*, 92; Nicholl, 326–36. Nicholl retranslated all of the letters and provides a full account of the saga.
12 Ames-Lewis, *Isabella and Leonardo*, 109. Titian painted two portraits of Isabella in a more frontal view, but those were not done until 1529 and 1534.
13 Isabella d'Este to Pietro da Novellara, March 1501.
14 Pietro da Novellara to Isabella d'Este, April 14, 1501.
15 Manfredo de' Manfredi to Isabella d'Este, July 31, 1501.
16 Isabella d'Este to Leonardo and to Angelo del Tovaglia, May 14, 1504.
17 Aloisius Ciocca to Isabella d'Este, January 22, 1505.
18 Alessandro Amadori to Isabella d'Este, May 3, 1506.
19 Pietro da Novellara to Isabella d'Este, April 14, 1501; Nicholl, 337; Cristina Acidini, Roberto Bellucci, and Cecilia Frosinini, "New Hypotheses on the *Madonna of the Yarnwinders* Series," in Michel Menu, ed., *Leonardo da Vinci's Technical Practice: Paintings, Drawings and Influence, Proceedings of the Charisma Conference* (Paris: Hermann), 114–25. None of the primary versions or known copies actually shows the basket of yarn at Christ's feet.
20 Martin Kemp and Thereza Wells, *Leonardo da Vinci's* Madonna of the Yarnwinder (National Gallery of Scotland, 1992); Martin Kemp, "The *Madonna of the Yarn Winder* in the Buccleuch Collection Reconsidered in the Context of Leonardo's Studio Practice," in Pietro Marani and Maria Teresa Fiorio, eds., *I Leonardeschi a Milano: Fortuna e collezionismo* (Milan, 1991), 35–48; Acidini et al., "New Hypotheses on the *Madonna of the Yarnwinders* Series," 114.

21. SAINT ANNE

1 Pietro da Novellara to Isabella d'Este, April 3, 1501; Ames-Lewis, *Isabella and Leonardo*, 224; Nicholl, 333.
2 Delieuvin. The French edition calls it "l'ultime chef d'oeuvre," which could also connote "last masterpiece." The catalogue is a good guide for exploring the sequence of Leonardo's drawings and paintings as well as the copies made of them.
3 Those who thought it likely that the Burlington House cartoon was done after the 1501 drawing include Arthur Popham, *The Drawings of Leonardo da Vinci* (Harcourt, 1945), 102; Arthur Popham and Philip Pouncey, *Italian Drawings in the British Mu-*

seum (British Museum, 1950); Clark, 164; Pedretti *Chronology*, 120; Nicholl, 334, 424; Eric Harding, Allan Braham, Martin Wyld, and Aviva Burnstock, "The Restoration of the Leonardo Cartoon," *National Gallery Technical Bulletin* 13 (1989), 4. See also Virginia Budny, "The Sequence of Leonardo's Sketches for *The Virgin and Child with Saint Anne and Saint John the Baptist*," *Art Bulletin* 65.1 (March 1983), 34; Johannes Nathan, "Some Drawing Practices of Leonardo da Vinci: New Light on the St. Anne," *Mitteilungen des Kunsthistorischen Institutes in Florenz* 36.1 (1992), 85.

4 The marginal note was first published by Armin Schlecter in a 2005 catalogue of an exhibition of books in Heidelberg University Library. See Jill Burke, "The Bureaucrat, the *Mona Lisa*, and Leaving Things Rough," *Leonardo da Vinci Society Newsletter*, May 2008.

5 Jack Wasserman, "The Dating and Patronage of Leonardo's Burlington House Cartoon," *Art Bulletin* 53.3 (September 1971), 312; Luke Syson, "The Rewards of Service," in Syson, 44.

6 Delieuvin, 49, 56; Louvre press release, December 1, 2011; author's interview with Delieuvin, 2016.

7 Fiorani, "Reflections on Leonardo da Vinci Exhibitions in London and Paris."

8 The copy was called the Resta-Esterházy Cartoon. It disappeared in Budapest in World War II. Photographs and copies of it still exist. Delieuvin, 108.

9 Sigmund Freud, *Leonardo da Vinci, and a Memory of His Childhood* (Norton, 1990), 72.

10 Codex Arundel, 138r.

11 Author's interview with Delieuvin.

12 Clark, 217.

22. PAINTINGS LOST AND FOUND

1 Barbara Hochstetler Meyer, "Leonardo's Hypothetical Painting of Leda and the Swan," *Mitteilungen des Kunsthistorischen Institutes in Florenz* 34.3 (1990), 279.

2 Kemp *Marvellous*, 265; Zöllner, 1:188, 1:246; Nicholl, 397.

3 Martin Kemp, "Sight and Sound," *Nature* 479 (November 2011), 174; Andrew Goldstein, "The Male *Mona Lisa*?," *Blouin Artinfo*, November 17, 2011; Kemp *Leonardo*, 208; Milton Esterow, "A Long Lost Leonardo," *Art News*, August 15, 2011; Syson, 300; Scott Reyburn and Robert Simon, "Leonardo da Vinci Painting Discovered," PR Newswire, July 7, 2011.

4 Graham Bowley and William Rashbaum, "Sotheby's Tries to Block Suit over a Leonardo Sold and Resold at a Big Markup," *New York Times*, November 8, 2016; Sam Knight, "The Bouvier Affair," *New Yorker*, February 8, 2016.

5 Paris Ms. D, written around 1507.

6 André J. Noest, "No Refraction in Leonardo's Orb," and Martin Kemp's reply, *Nature* 480 (December 22, 2011), 457. Noest correctly points out the lack of distortion or inversion of the robes and body, but I think he is incorrect in saying that the palm that is touching the glass would be subject to a similar distortion.

23. CESARE BORGIA

1 Rafael Sabatini, *The Life of Cesare Borgia* (Stanley Paul, 1912), 311; Machiavelli, *The Prince*, ch. 7.

2 Paul Strathern, *The Artist, the Philosopher, and the Warrior: The Intersecting Lives of Da Vinci, Machiavelli, and Borgia and the World They Shaped* (Random House, 2009), 83–90. (Cardinal Ardicino Della Porta the Younger tried to resign a few years earlier, but returned.)

3 Ladislao Reti, "Leonardo da Vinci and Cesare Borgia," *Viator*, January 1973, 333; Strathern, *The Artist, the Philosopher, and the Warrior*, 1, 59; Nicholl, 343; Roger Masters, *Fortune Is a River* (Free Press, 1998), 79.
4 Paris Ms. L, 1b; Paris Ms. B, 81b; Notebooks/J. P. Richter, 1416, 1117.
5 Strathern, *The Artist, the Philosopher, and the Warrior*, 112.
6 Codex Arundel, 202b; Notebooks/J. P. Richter, 1420. Oddly, tantalizingly, perhaps even tellingly, Cesare Borgia is not mentioned any other time in Leonardo's notebooks.
7 Bramly, 324.
8 Codex Atl., 121v/43v-b; Kemp *Marvellous*, 225; Strathern, *The Artist, the Philosopher, and the Warrior*, 138.
9 Strathern, *The Artist, the Philosopher, and the Warrior*, 138; Codex Atl., 43v, 48r.
10 Paris Ms. L, 78a; Notebooks/J. P. Richter, 1048.
11 Paris Ms. L, 66b; Notebooks/J. P. Richter, 1044, 1047; Codex Atl., 3, 4.
12 Paris Ms. L, 47a, 77a; Notebooks/J. P. Richter, 1043, 1047.
13 Paris Ms. L, 72r; Notebooks/J. P. Richter, 1046.
14 Nicholl, 348.
15 Codex Atl., 22a/69r; see also 71v.
16 Klein, *Leonardo's Legacy*, 91; Nicholl, 349; Codex Atl., 133r/48r-b; Paris Ms. L, 29r.
17 Strathern, *The Artist, the Philosopher, and the Warrior*, 163.
18 Windsor, RCIN 912284.
19 Codex Atl., f.1.r.
20 Codex Atl., 1.1r; Laurenza, 231; Schofield, "Notes on Leonardo and Vitruvius," 129; Klein, *Leonardo's Legacy*, 91; Keele *Elements*, 134.
21 Machiavelli, *The Prince*, ch. 7.
22 Paris Ms. L, 33v; Notebooks/J. P. Richter, 1039; Notebooks/Irma Richter, 320.
23 Strathern, *The Artist, the Philosopher, and the Warrior*, 105.

24. HYDRAULIC ENGINEER

1 Claudio Giorgione, "Leonardo da Vinci and Waterways in Lombardy," lecture at UCLA, May 20, 2016.
2 Carlo Zammattio, *Leonardo the Scientist* (London, 1961), 10.
3 Masters, *Fortune Is a River*, 102.
4 Now called Rocca della Verruca, it is not to be confused with Castello della Verrucola, north of Pisa. See Carlo Pedretti, "La Verruca," *Renaissance Quarterly* 25.4 (Winter 1972), 417.
5 Pier Francesco Tosinghi to the Florentine Republic, June 21, 1503, in Pedretti, "La Verruca," 418; Masters, *Fortune Is a River*, 95; Nicholl, 358.
6 Signoria of Florence account book, July 26, 1503, in Masters, *Fortune Is a River*, 96.
7 Codex Leic., 13a; Notebooks/J. P. Richter, 1008.
8 Codex Atl., 4r/1v-b (machine drawing) and 562r/210r-b; Nicholl, 358; Strathern, *The Artist, the Philosopher, and the Warrior*, 318; Kemp *Marvellous*, 224; Masters, *Fortune Is a River*, 123; Codex Madrid, 2:22v.
9 Machiavelli to Colombino, September 21, 1504; Strathern, *The Artist, the Philosopher, and the Warrior*, 320; Nicholl, 359; Masters, *Fortune Is a River*, 132.
10 Codex Atl., 127r/46r-b; Notebooks/J. P. Richter, 774, 1001.
11 Windsor, RCIN 912279. See also other maps: RCIN 912678, 912680, 912683.
12 Leonardo, "A Map of the Valdichiana," Windsor, RCIN 912278; Notebooks/J. P. Richter, 1001; Pedretti *Commentary*, 2:174.

13 Kemp *Marvellous*, 225; Codex Atl., 121v, 133r; Codex Madrid, 2:125r.
14 Paris Ms. F, 13 r-v, 15r–16r; Codex Arundel, 63v; Reti, "Leonardo da Vinci the Technologist," 90.
15 Codex Madrid, 2:125r.

25. MICHELANGELO AND THE LOST *BATTLES*

1 Jonathan Jones, *The Lost Battles: Leonardo, Michelangelo, and the Artistic Duel That Defines the Renaissance* (Knopf, 2010); Michael Cole, *Leonardo, Michelangelo, and the Art of the Figure* (Yale, 2104); Paula Rae Duncan, "Michelangelo and Leonardo: The Frescoes for the Palazzo Vecchio," Master's thesis, University of Montana, 2004; Clark, 198.
2 Codex Atl., 74rb-vc/202r; Notebooks/J. P. Richter, 669.
3 Codex Ash., 30v–31r; Notebooks/J. P. Richter, 601.
4 Günther Neufeld, "Leonardo da Vinci's *Battle of Anghiari*: A Genetic Reconstruction," *Art Bulletin* 31.3 (September 1949), 170–183; Farago, "Leonardo's *Battle of Anghiari*"; Claire J. Farago, "The *Battle of Anghiari*: A Speculative Reconstruction of Leonardo's Design Process," *Achademia Leonardi Vinci* 9 (1996), 73–86; Barbara Hochstetler Meyer, "Leonardo's *Battle of Anghiari*: Proposals for Some Sources and a Reflection," *Art Bulletin* 66.3 (September 1984), 367–82; Cecil Gould, "Leonardo's Great Battle-piece: A Conjectural Reconstruction," *Art Bulletin* 36.2 (June 1954), 117–29; Paul Joannides, "Leonardo da Vinci, Peter Paul Rubens, Pierre-Nolasque Bergeret and the Fight for the Standard," *Achademia Leonardo da Vinci* 1 (1988), 76–86; Kemp *Marvellous*, 225; Jones, *The Lost Battles*, 227.
5 Codex Ash., 2:30v; Kemp *Marvellous*, 235.
6 Codex Madrid, 2:2.
7 Jones, *The Lost Battles*, 138.
8 Windsor, RCIN 912326.
9 Contract of "The Magnificent and Sublime Signoria, the priors of Liberty and the Standardbearer of Justice of the Florentine People," May 4, 1504.
10 Cole, *Leonardo, Michelangelo, and the Art of the Figure*, 31.
11 Codex Madrid, 2:1r; Anna Maria Brizio, "The Madrid Notebooks," *The UNESCO Courier*, October 1974, 36.
12 The tale is in the Anonimo Gaddiano. See also Notebooks/Irma Richter, 356; Nicholl, 376, 380.
13 Martin Gayford, "Was Michelangelo a Better Artist Than Leonardo da Vinci?," *The Telegraph*, November 16, 2013; Martin Gayford, *Michelangelo: His Epic Life* (Penguin, 2015), 252; Miles Unger, *Michelangelo: A Life in Six Masterpieces* (Simon & Schuster, 2014), 112.
14 Bramly, 343.
15 The notes of the meeting were taken by Luca Landucci, a spice dealer and diarist. Saul Levine, "The Location of Michelangelo's *David*: The Meeting of January 25, 1504," *Art Bulletin* 56.1 (March 1974), 31–49; Rona Goffen, *Renaissance Rivals: Michelangelo, Leonardo, Raphael, Titian* (Yale, 2002), 124; N. Randolph Parks, "The Placement of Michelangelo's *David*: A Review of the Documents," *Art Bulletin* 57.4 (December 1975), 560–70; John Paoletti, *Michelangelo's* David (Cambridge, 2015), 345; Nicholl, 378; Bramly, 343.
16 Windsor, RCIN 912591; Jones, *The Lost Battles*, 82; Jonathan Jones, "Leonardo and the Battle of Michelangelo's Penis," *The Guardian*, November 16, 2010; David M. Gunn, "Covering David," Monash University, Melbourne, Australia, July 2001, www.gunnzone.org/KingDavid/CoveringDavid.html. Leonardo's sketch on the Windsor

sheet (and a similar one he did on the reverse of that sheet) very closely resembles the pose of Michelangelo's *David*. Leonardo has very lightly drawn what seems to be a seahorse on a leash, thus suggesting that he was thinking of transforming the figure into a Neptune.

17 Windsor, RCIN 912594.

18 Bambach *Master Draftsman*, catalogue entries 101v-r and 102, pp. 538–48; "Studies for Hercules Holding a Club Seen in Frontal and Rear View," Metropolitan Museum (New York), Accession #2000.328a,b.

19 Anton Gill, *Il Gigante: Michelangelo, Florence, and the* David (St. Martin's, 2004), 295; Victor Coonin, *From Marble to Flesh: The Biography of Michelangelo's* David (Florentine Press, 2014), 90–93; Jones, *The Lost Battles*, 82.

20 Goffen, *Renaissance Rivals*, 143.

21 Jones, *The Lost Battles*, 186.

22 Botticelli being another notable exception.

23 Codex Madrid, 2:128r; Paris Ms. L, 79r; Notebooks/J. P. Richter, 488.

24 Paris Ms. G, 5b; Notebooks/J. P. Richter, 503; Clark, 200.

25 Codex Urbina, 61r.

26 Leonardo Treatise/Rigaud, ch. 40; Claire Farago, *Leonardo's Treatise on Painting: A Critical Interpretation with a New Edition of the Text in the Codex Urbinas* (Brill, 1992), 273. Farago provides a new translation and critical interpretation, and she discusses the dating of this passage on p. 403. Similar descriptions by Leonardo are in chapters 20 and 41 of the *paragone*.

27 Michelangelo, "To Giovanni Da Pistoia When the Author Was Painting the Vault of the Sistine Chapel" (1509), in Andrew Graham-Dixon, *Michelangelo and the Sistine Chapel* (Skyhorse, 2009), ii, 65; modified translation in Joel Agee, *New York Review of Books*, June 19, 2014; modified translation in Gail Mazur, Poetry Foundation, http://www.poetryfoundation.org/poems-and-poets/poems/detail/57328.

28 Gayford, *Michelangelo*, 251; Unger, *Michelangelo*, 117.

29 Cole, *Leonardo, Michelangelo, and the Art of the Figure*, 17, 34, 77, and passim.

30 John Addington Symonds, *The Life of Michelangelo Buonarroti* (Nimmo, 1893), 129, 156.

31 Rab Hatfield, *Finding Leonardo* (Florentine Press, 2007); "Finding the Lost da Vinci," *National Geographic*, March 2012, nationalgeographic.com/explorers/projects/lost-da-vinci/.

32 Farago, "Leonardo's *Battle of Anghiari*," 312; Kemp *Marvellous*, 224; Bramly, 348.

33 Farago, "Leonardo's *Battle of Anghiari*," 329.

34 Clark, 198.

35 *The Life of Benvenuto Cellini, Written by Himself*, many versions on the Internet.

36 Jones, *The Lost Battles*, 256.

26. RETURN TO MILAN

1 Codex Atl., 70b/208b; Notebooks/J. P. Richter, 1526, 1373.

2 Codex Arundel, 272r; Notebooks/J. P. Richter, 1372. See Richter's footnote for documentation of Piero's age.

3 Beck, "Ser Piero da Vinci and His Son Leonardo," 29; Bramly, 356.

4 Soderini letter, October 9, 1506, in Farago, "Leonardo's *Battle of Anghiari*," 329; Nicholl, 407.

5 Charles d'Amboise letter, December 16, 1506; Eugène Müntz, *Leonardo da Vinci* (Parkstone, 2012; original French edition 1898), 2:197; Nicholl, 408.

6 Florentine envoy Francesco Pandolfino, January 7, 1507; Müntz, *Leonardo da Vinci*, 2:200; Kemp *Marvellous*, 209.
7 The king arrived on May 24, 1507, not in April, as some accounts say. Nicholl, 409; Ella Noyes, *The Story of Milan* (Dent, 1908), 380; Arthur Tilley, *The Dawn of the French Renaissance* (Cambridge, 1918), 122.
8 Julia Cartright, "The Castello of Milan," *Monthly Review*, August 1901, 117.
9 This section draws from Nicholl, 412ff.; Bramly, 368ff.; Payne, Kindle loc. 4500ff.; Marrion Wilcox, "Francesco Melzi, Disciple of Leonardo," *Art & Life* 11.6 (December 1919).
10 Notebooks/J. P. Richter, 1350; Codex Atl., 1037v/372v-a.
11 Paris Ms. C; Notebooks/Irma Richter, 290, 291; Bramly, 223, 228; Codex Atl., 663v; Nicholl, 276.
12 Codex Atl., 571a-v/214r-a; Pedretti *Commentary*, 1:298. Carlo Pedretti transcribed the property in question as "Il botro," but others see the meaning of the phrase as "your property."
13 Louis, by the grace of God King of France, to the Perpetual Gonfalonier and the Signoria of Florence, July 26, 1507; Müntz, 186; Payne, Kindle loc. 4280.
14 Leonardo letter, September 18, 1507, in Notebooks/Irma Richter, 336.
15 Melzi's letter to Leonardo's half brothers on June 1, 1519, informing them of Leonardo's death, refers to property in Fiesole, which would not seem to be the same property. However, it seems most probable that Francesco da Vinci's property in question was used by Leonardo, then went to his half brothers.
16 Codex Atl., 317r; Notebooks/J. P. Richter, 1349.
17 Paris Ms. F.
18 Jill Burke, "Meaning and Crisis in the Early Sixteenth Century: Interpreting Leonardo's Lion," *Oxford Art Journal* 29.1 (2006), 79–91.
19 Codex Atl., 214r-b; Notebooks/MacCurdy, 1036; Carlo Pedretti, *Chronology of Leonardo Da Vinci's Architectural Studies after 1500* (Droz, 1962), 41; Sabine Frommel, "Leonardo and the Villa of Charles d'Amboise," in Carlo Pedretti, ed., *Leonardo da Vinci and France* (Amboise, 2019), 117.
20 Windsor, RCIN 912688, 912716; Sara Taglialagamba, "Leonardo da Vinci's Hydraulic Systems and Fountains for His French Patrons Louis XII, Charles d'Amboise, and Francis I," in Moffatt and Taglialagamba, 301.
21 Clark, 211.

27. ANATOMY, ROUND TWO

1 Windsor, RCIN 919027v; Notebooks/Irma Richter, 325; Keele and Roberts, 69; Keele *Elements*, 37.
2 Windsor, RCIN 919005r.
3 Windsor, RCIN 919027v.
4 Windsor, RCIN 919027v; Bauth Boon, "Leonardo da Vinci on Atherosclerosis and the Function of the Sinuses of Valsalva," *Netherland Heart Journal*, December 2009, 496; Keele, "Leonardo da Vinci's 'Anatomia Naturale,'" 369. Atherosclerosis is the thickening of the artery wall caused by the buildup of plaque, fats, cholesterol, and other substances. It is a specific form of arteriosclerosis, but the terms are sometimes used interchangeably.
5 Windsor, RCIN 919075; Leonardo Treatise/Rigaud, 199; Keele and Roberts, 91.
6 Notebooks/J. P. Richter, 796; Clayton and Philo, 18.
7 Windsor, RCIN 919070; "Previously unexhibited page from Leonardo's notebooks includes artist's 'to do' list," Royal Collection press release, April 5, 2012.

8 Windsor, RCIN 919070v, RCIN 919115r; Charles O'Malley and J. B. Saunders, *Leonardo on the Human Body* (Dover, 1983; first published 1952), 122; Notebooks/J. P. Richter, 819.
9 Windsor, RCIN 919070v; Notebooks/J. P. Richter, 796.
10 Keele *Elements*, 200; Windsor, RCIN 919031v.
11 Martin Clayton, "Leonardo's Anatomy Years," *Nature* 484 (April 2012), 314; Nicholl, 443.
12 Windsor, RCIN 919016.
13 Windsor, RCIN 919028r; Wells, 191.
14 Keele *Elements*, 268; Windsor, RCIN 919035v, 919019r.
15 Windsor, RCIN 919115r.
16 Jonathan Pevsner, "Leonardo da Vinci's Contributions to Neuroscience," *Scientific American Mind* 16.1 (2005), 217; Clayton and Philo, 144; Keele and Roberts, 54; Windsor, RCIN 919127.
17 Leonardo, "Weimar Sheet."
18 Windsor, RCIN 919003v; Keele and Roberts, 101.
19 Windsor, RCIN 919005v.
20 Windsor, RCIN 919014r; Keele *Elements*, 344; O'Malley and Saunders, *Leonardo on the Human Body*, 164; Clayton and Philo, 188.
21 Windsor, RCIN 919007v; Keele and Roberts, 82; O'Malley and Saunders, *Leonardo on the Human Body*, 44.
22 Windsor, RCIN 919040r.
23 Windsor, RCIN 919012v; Keele and Roberts, 110; O'Malley and Saunders, *Leonardo on the Human Body*, 156.
24 Windsor, RCIN 919055v; Keele and Roberts, 66; Clayton and Philo, 188. Grace Glueck, "Anatomy Lessons by Leonardo," *New York Times*, January 20, 1984; O'Malley and Saunders, *Leonardo on the Human Body*, 186, 414.
25 Windsor, RCIN 919093.
26 Windsor, RCIN 919093. This section draws on Mohammadali Shoja, Paul Agutter, et al., "Leonardo da Vinci's Studies of the Heart," *International Journal of Cardiology* 167 (2013), 1126; Morteza Gharib, David Kremers, Martin Kemp, et al., "Leonardo's Vision of Flow Visualization," *Experiments in Fluids* 33 (July 2002), 219; Larry Zaroff, "Leonardo's Heart," *Hektoen International Journal*, Spring 2013; Wells, Capra *Learning*, 288; Kenneth Keele, "Leonardo da Vinci and the Movement of the Heart," *Proceedings of the Royal Society of Medicine* 44 (1951), 209. I am grateful to David Linley and Martin Clayton for showing me some of the drawings at Windsor.
27 Windsor, RCIN 919028r.
28 Windsor, RCIN 919050v; Paris Ms. G, 1v; Keele, "Leonardo da Vinci's 'Anatomia Naturale,'" 376; Nuland, *Leonardo da Vinci*, 142.
29 Windsor, RCIN 919062r; Keele, "Leonardo da Vinci's 'Anatomia Naturale,'" 376; Wells, 202.
30 Windsor, RCIN 919063v, RCIN 919118; Wells, 83, 195; Nuland, *Leonardo da Vinci*, 143; Capra *Learning*, Kindle loc. 4574.
31 Windsor, RCIN 919082r, and also 919116r&v, 919117v, 919118r, 919083v. This section draws on Wells, 229–36; Keele and Roberts, 124, 131; Keele *Elements*, 316; Capra *Learning*, 290.
32 Windsor, RCIN 919118r.
33 Windsor, RCIN 912666; Keele *Elements*, 315.
34 Windsor, RCIN 919116r.

35 Windsor, RCIN 919082r; Capra *Learning*, 290; O'Malley and Saunders, *Leonardo on the Human Body*, 269.
36 Windsor, RCIN 919082r, 919116v; Clayton and Philo, 242.
37 Brian Bellhouse et al., "Mechanism of the Closure of the Aortic Valve," *Nature*, 217 (January 6, 1968), 86; Francis Robicsek, "Leonardo da Vinci and the Sinuses of Valsalva," *Annals of Thoracic Surgery* 52.2 (August 1991), 328; Malenka Bissell, Erica Dall'Armellina, and Robin Choudhury, "Flow Vortices in the Aortic Root," *European Heart Journal*, February 3, 2014, 1344; Nuland, *Leonardo da Vinci*, 147. The paper by Bellhouse and his team is interesting because it is a rare scholarly piece with only one reference note, and that reference is to a paper written almost five hundred years before. See also Brian Bellhouse and L. Talbott, "The Fluid Mechanics of the Aortic Valve," *Journal of Fluid Mechanics* 35.4 (1969), 721; Wells, xxii.
38 Windsor, RCIN 919102.
39 Windsor, RCIN 919102r; Jonathan Jones, "The Ten Greatest Works of Art Ever," *The Guardian*, March 21, 2014.
40 Windsor, RCIN 919103; Notebooks/Irma Richter, 166.
41 Hope, "The Last 'Last Supper.'"
42 Antonio de Beatis, *The Travel Journal* (Hakluyt/Routledge, 1979, originally written c. 1518), 132–34.

28. THE WORLD AND ITS WATERS

1 Codex Arundel, 156v; Notebooks/J. P. Richter, 1162.
2 Paris Ms. A, 55v; Notebooks/J. P. Richter, 929.
3 Windsor, RCIN 919102v.
4 Kemp, "Analogy and Observation in the Codex Hammer," 103; T. J. Fairbrother, C. Ishikawa, et al., *Leonardo Lives: The Codex Leicester and Leonardo da Vinci's Legacy of Art and Science* (Seattle Art Museum, 1997); Claire Farago, ed., *Leonardo da Vinci: The Codex Leicester* (American Museum of Natural History, 1996); Claire Farago, "The Codex Leicester," in Bambach *Master Draftsman*, 191. I am grateful to Bill Gates's curator, Frederick Schroeder, for displaying and discussing the Codex Leicester with me and for arranging for me to use a new and unpublished translation by Martin Kemp and Domenico Laurenza, as noted below.
5 Codex Leic., 33v; Notebooks/MacCurdy, 350. The quotations from the Codex Leicester in this chapter, unless otherwise noted, are based on a new translation, edited by Martin Kemp and Domenico Laurenza, to be published by Oxford University Press in 2018.
6 Codex Leic., 34r; Notebooks/J. P. Richter, 1000.
7 Codex Leic., 34r.
8 Domenico Laurenza, "Leonardo's Theory of the Earth," in Fabio Frosini and Alessandro Nova, eds., *Leonardo on Nature* (Marsilio, 2015), 257.
9 Irving Lavin, "Leonardo's Watery Chaos," paper, Institute for Advanced Study, April 21, 1993; Leslie Geddes, "Infinite Slowness and Infinite Velocity: The Representation of Time and Motion in Leonardo's Studies of Geology and Water," in Frosini and Nova, *Leonardo on Nature*, 269.
10 Bramly, 335.
11 Codex Madrid, 1:134v.
12 Codex Leic., 15v, 27v; Kemp *Marvellous*, 302; Nicholl, 431.
13 Codex Leic., 26v; Kemp *Marvellous*, 305.
14 Paris Ms. I, 72r–71u.

15 Paris Ms. F, 2b; Notebooks/J. P. Richter, 2.
16 Codex Leic., 29v.
17 Codex Triv., 32r; Windsor, RCIN 919108v; Keele *Elements*, 135.
18 Paris Ms. F, 34v; Notebooks/MacCurdy, 2:681, 724.
19 Paris Ms. G, 93r; Kemp *Marvellous*, 304.
20 Codex Leic., 14r; Bambach *Master Draftsman*, 624.
21 Windsor, RCIN 912579; Notebooks/J. P. Richter, 389.
22 Windsor, RCIN 912424.
23 Codex Atl., 118a-r; Kemp *Marvellous*, 305.
24 E. H. Gombrich, "The Form of Movement in Water and Air," in O'Malley, 171.
25 Paris Ms. H, 77r; Kemp *Leonardo*, 155.
26 Codex Leic., 21v; Notebooks/J. P. Richter 963.
27 Codex Atl., fol. 468.
28 Paris Ms. A, folio 56r; Notebooks/J. P. Richter, 941, 968.
29 Codex Leicester's sheet 3 is folded into folios, the most important of which is 34v, showing siphons and other ways to move water. See also Bambach *Master Draftsman*, 619.
30 Codex Leic., 28r, 3v; Keele *Elements*, 81, 102; Kemp *Marvellous*, 313.
31 Paris Ms. G, 38r, 70r.
32 Windsor, RCIN 919003r.
33 Paris Ms. F, 11v.
34 Capra *Learning*, Kindle loc. 1201; Codex Leic., 10r. Capra attributes the rediscovery of this type of rock stratification to the seventeenth-century Danish geologist Nicolas Steno.
35 Codex Leic., 10r; Notebooks/J. P. Richter, 990.
36 Codex Leic., 9v; Notebooks/Irma Richter, 28.
37 Codex Leic., 8b; Notebooks/J. P. Richter, 987.
38 Paris Ms. E, 4r; Notebooks/Irma Richter, 349.
39 Codex Leic., 10r; Notebooks/J. P. Richter, 990.
40 Codex Leic., 10r; Notebooks/J. P. Richter, 990. In this case, I have used the Richter translation rather than the one prepared by Domenico Laurenza and the Bill Gates team.
41 Paris Ms. E, 4r; Codex Leic., 10r; Notebooks/J. P. Richter, 990; Capra *Learning*, 70, 83; Stephen Jay Gould, *Leonardo's Mountain of Clams and the Diet of Worms* (Harmony, 1998), 17; Andrea Baucon, "Leonardo da Vinci, the Founding Father of Ichnology," *Palaios* 25 (2010), 361.
42 Windsor, RCIN 912669v; Notebooks/J. P. Richter, 886.
43 Copernicus in his *Commentariolus*, written c. 1510–14, first proposed his heliocentric theory that the apparent movements of heavenly bodies came from the Earth's rotation and movements.
44 Paris Ms. F, 41b; Notebooks/J. P. Richter, 858.
45 Paris Ms. F, 22b; Notebooks/J. P. Richter, 861.
46 Paris Ms. F, 41b; 4b; Notebooks/J. P. Richter, 858, 880.
47 Paris Ms. F, 94b; Notebooks/J. P. Richter, 874.
48 Codex Leic., 1a; Notebooks/J. P. Richter, 864.
49 Codex Leic., 4r; Notebooks/J. P. Richter, 300; Notebooks/MacCurdy, 128.
50 Codex Leic., 4r; Notebooks/J. P. Richter, 300; Notebooks/MacCurdy, 128.
51 Codex Leic., 36r.
52 Codex Leic., 36r; Notebooks/J. P. Richter, 300–301; Bell, "Aristotle as a Source for Leonardo's Theory of Colour Perspective after 1500," 100.

29. ROME

1 Payne, Kindle loc. 3204.
2 Nicholl, 110; Clayton and Philo, 23.
3 Windsor, RCIN 912579.
4 Clark, 237.
5 Windsor, RCIN 912726. Although most scholars attribute the drawing to Melzi, it is possible that it was by another student.
6 Bramly, 6, n7.
7 Windsor, RCIN 912300v.
8 Nick Squires, "Leonardo da Vinci Self Portrait Discovered Hidden in Manuscript," *The Telegraph* (London), February 28, 2009.
9 Scholars are divided. "I continue to believe in it as a potent and unflinching portrait of himself at the end of his life," Charles Nicholl wrote (Nicholl, 493). On the other hand, Martin Kemp says it "is generally but incorrectly taken to be a self-portrait." Some skeptics say the style more resembles Leonardo's work from just after 1500, which would make it less likely as a self-portrait given that the drawing is of an older man.
10 Gian Paolo Lomazzo, *Idea of the Temple of Painting* (Pennsylvania State, 2013; originally published 1590), 92.
11 Clark, 235; Carmen Bambach, "Leonardo and Raphael in Rome," in Miguel Falomir, ed., *Late Raphael* (Museo del Prado, 2013), 26.
12 Carmen Bambach, "Leonardo and Raphael, circa 1513–16," Museo Nacional del Prado lecture, June 2011; Nicholl, 450–65.
13 Windsor, RCIN 919084r; Notebooks/Irma Richter, 349; Notebooks/J. P. Richter, 1064.
14 Codex Atl., 225r.
15 Nicholl, 459.
16 Alessandro da Vinci to Giuliano da Vinci, December 14, 1514.
17 Notebooks/MacCurdy, 2:438.
18 Syson, "The Rewards of Service," 48.
19 Vasari, *Lives*; Notebooks/Irma Richter, 349.
20 Windsor, RCIN 912684.
21 Pedretti *Commentary*, 1:20; Pedretti, *The Machines*, 18; Paris Ms. G, 84v; Codex Atl., f. 17v; Dupré, "Optic, Picture and Evidence," 211.
22 Codex Atl., f. 87r.
23 Codex Atl., f. 17v.
24 Codex Atl., folios 96r, 257r, 672r, 672v, 750r, 751a-v, 751b-r, 751b-v, 1017r, 1017v, 1036a-r, 1036a-v, 1036b-r, 1036b-v; Dupré, "Optic, Picture and Evidence," 221.
25 Codex Atl., 1036a-v; Pedretti *Commentary*, 1:19; Dupré, "Optic, Picture and Evidence," 223.
26 Codex Atl., 247r/671r; Notebooks/J. P. Richter, 1351; Notebooks/Irma Richter, 380.
27 Codex Atl., 182v-c/500; Keele *Elements*, 38.
28 Nicholl, 484.

30. POINTING THE WAY

1 Clark, 248.
2 Clark, 250.
3 John 1:14.

4 Codex Atl., 179r-a, from May 1509, shows a pupil's sketch of the pointing hand. Carlo Pedretti, who dated the Codex Atlanticus sheet, also believes that the *Saint John* was begun about 1509 and provided the inspiration for some copies in Italy beginning then (*Chronology*, 166). Martin Kemp agrees (*Marvellous*, 336). Luke Syson suggests it may have been begun in Milan in 1499 and viewed in 1506 in Florence, where it may have provided the inspiration for an altarpiece there ("The Rewards of Service," 44). Kenneth Clark dated the picture to 1514–15 (248). Frank Zöllner suggests it was 1513–16 (2:248).

5 John 1:7.

6 Paul Barolsky, "The Mysterious Meaning of Leonardo's *Saint John the Baptist*," *Notes in the History of Art* 8.3 (Spring 1989), 14.

7 See Kemp *Marvellous*, 336, for the argument that this is the result of an overzealous restoration.

8 Syson, 249; Janice Shell and Grazioso Sironi, "Salai and Leonardo's Legacy," *Burlington Magazine*, February 1991, no. 104; Zöllner, 2:9.

9 Pedretti *Chronology*, 165. It was in the Baroffio Museum of the Sanctuary of Sacro Monte.

10 Clark, 251; Zöllner, 2:91.

11 Matthew 3:11.

12 Andre Green, *Revelations de l'inachevement* (Flammarion, 1992), 111; Carlo Pedretti, ed., *Angel in the Flesh* (Cartei & Bianchi, 2009).

13 Brian Sewell, *Sunday Telegraph*, April 5, 1992, quoted in Nicholl, 562n26. Sewell once worked in the Royal Library.

14 Pedretti, "The Pointing Lady," 339.

31. THE *MONA LISA*

1 Kenneth Clark, "Mona Lisa," *Burlington Magazine* 115.840 (March 1973), 144.

2 Kemp and Pallanti, *Mona Lisa*, 10; Giuseppe Pallanti, Mona Lisa *Revealed* (Skira, 2006); Dianne Hales, Mona Lisa: *A Life Discovered* (Simon & Schuster, 2014). Some writers have asserted that Francesco had been married twice before, but there is no evidence for this.

3 Pallanti, Mona Lisa *Revealed*, 89–92.

4 Jack Greenstein, "Leonardo, *Mona Lisa*, and *La Gioconda*," *Artibus et Historiae* 25.50 (2004), 17; Pallanti, Mona Lisa *Revealed*, 75, 96; Kemp and Pallanti, *Mona Lisa*, 50; Zöllner, 1:241, 1:251.

5 Nicholl, 366; Kemp and Pallanti, *Mona Lisa*, 110; Kemp *Marvellous*, 261.

6 Shell and Sironi, "Salai and Leonardo's Legacy," 95.

7 Kemp and Pallanti, *Mona Lisa*, 118.

8 Jill Burke, "Agostino Vespucci's Marginal Note about Leonardo da Vinci in Heidelberg," *Leonardo da Vinci Society Newsletter* 30 (May 2008), 3; Martin Kemp, *Christ to Coke* (Oxford, 2011), 146.

9 For an argument that the portrait from the very outset was a project initiated by Leonardo rather than by Francesco del Giocondo, and that Lisa's plain clothing and grooming make it unlikely that it was a commissioned portrait, see Joanna Woods-Marsden, "Leonardo da Vinci's *Mona Lisa*: A Portrait without a Commissioner?," in Moffatt and Taglialagamba, 169.

10 Laurence de Viguerie, Philippe Walter, et al., "Revealing the Sfumato Technique of Leonardo da Vinci by X-Ray Fluorescence Spectroscopy," *Angewandte Chemie* 49.35 (August 16, 2010), 6125; Sandra Šustić, "Paint Handling in Leonardo's *Mona Lisa*,"

CeROArt, January 13, 2014; Philip Ball, "Behind the *Mona Lisa*'s smile," *Nature*, August 5, 2010; Hales, Mona Lisa: *A Life Discovered*, 158; Alasdair Palmer, "How Leonardo Did It," *Spectator*, September 16, 2006, describing the work of Jacques Franck, a French artist and art historian who studied how to replicate Leonardo's technique.

11 Elisabeth Martin, "The Painter's Palette," in Jean-Pierre Mohen et al., eds., *The* Mona Lisa: *Inside the Painting* (Abrams, 2006), 62. This volume has twenty-five essays along with high-resolution pictures that detail the findings of multispectral imaging techniques.

12 Codex Ash., 1:15a; Notebooks/J. P. Richter, 520.

13 Z. Zaremba Filipczak, "New Light on *Mona Lisa*: Leonardo's Optical Knowledge and His Choice of Lighting," *Art Bulletin* 59.4 (December 1977), 518; Zöllner, 1:160; Klein, *Leonardo's Legacy*, 32.

14 Clark, "Mona Lisa," 144; Pascal Cotte, *Lumiere on the* Mona Lisa (Vinci Editions, 2015); "New Technology Sheds Light On Centuries-Old Debate about *Mona Lisa*," PR Newswire, October 17, 2007; "High Resolution Image Hints at 'Mona Lisa's' Eyebrows," CNN, October 18, 2007.

15 Good books include Mohen et al., *The* Mona Lisa; Cotte, *Lumiere on the* Mona Lisa; Zöllner. The best online versions are from the Paris research firm C2RMF, available on its website, http://en.c2rmf.fr/, and also at *Wikimedia Commons*, https://commons.wikimedia.org/wiki/File:Mona_Lisa,_by_Leonardo_da_Vinci,_from_C2RMF_natural_color.jpg.

16 Bruno Mottin, "Reading the Image," in Mohen et al., *The* Mona Lisa, 68.

17 Carlo Starnazzi, *Leonardo Cartografo* (Istituto geografico militare, 2003), 76.

18 Walter Pater, *The Renaissance* (University of California, 1980; originally published 1893), 79.

19 Takao Sato and Kenchi Hosokawa, "*Mona Lisa* Effect of Eyes and Face," *i-Perception* 3.9 (October 2012), 707; Sheena Rogers, Melanie Lunsford, et al., "The *Mona Lisa* Effect: Perception of Gaze Direction in Real and Pictured Faces," in Sheena Rogers and Judith Effken, eds., *Studies in Perception and Action VII* (Lawrence Erlbaum, 2003), 19; Evgenia Boyarskaya, Alexandra Sebastian, et al., "The *Mona Lisa* Effect: Neural Correlates of Centered and Off-centered Gaze," *Human Brain Mapping* 36.2 (February 2015), 415.

20 Windsor, RCIN 919055v.

21 Margaret Livingstone, "Is It Warm? Is It Real? Or Just Low Spatial Frequency?," *Science* 290.5495 (November 17, 2000), 1299; Alessandro Soranzo and Michelle Newberry, "The Uncatchable Smile in Leonardo da Vinci's *La Bella Principessa* Portrait," *Vision Research*, June 4, 2015, 78; Isabel Bohrn, Claus-Christian Carbon, and Florian Hutzler, "*Mona Lisa*'s Smile: Perception or Deception?," *Psychological Science*, March 2010, 378.

22 Mark Brown, "The Real *Mona Lisa*? Prado Museum Finds Leonardo da Vinci Pupil's Take," *The Guardian*, February 1, 2012.

23 Kemp and Pallanti, *Mona Lisa*, 171.

32. FRANCE

1 Jan Sammer, "The Royal Invitation," in Carlo Pedretti, ed., *Leonardo da Vinci in France* (CB Edizioni, 2010), 32.

2 Codex Atl., 471r/172v-a; Notebooks/J. P. Richter, 1368A.

3 Nicholl, 486–93; Bramly, 397–99; Notebooks/J. P. Richter, 1566.

4 Robert Knecht, *Renaissance Warrior and Patron: The Reign of Francis I* (Cambridge, 1994), 427 and passim; Robert Knecht, *The French Renaissance Court* (Yale, 2008).

5 Bramly, 401; Codex Madrid, 2:24a.

6 Notebooks/Irma Richter, 383.

7 Codex Atl., 106r-a/294v; Luca Garai, "The Staging of *The Besieged Fortress*," in Pedretti, *Leonardo da Vinci in France*, 141.

8 Pedretti, *Leonardo da Vinci in France*, 24, 154.

9 De Beatis, *The Travel Journal*, 132–34.

10 Author's interview with Delieuvin.

11 Taglialagamba, "Leonardo da Vinci's Hydraulic Systems and Fountains for His French Patrons," 300; Carlo Pedretti, *Leonardo da Vincí: The Royal Palace at Romorantin* (Harvard, 1972); Pascal Brioist, "The Royal Palace in Romorantin," and Pascal Brioist and Romano Nanni, "Leonardo's French Canal Projects," in Pedretti, *Leonardo da Vinci in France*, 83, 95; Pedretti, *A Chronology of Leonardo's Architectural Studies after 1500*, 140; Matthew Landrus, "Evidence of Leonardo's Systematic Design Process for Palaces and Canals in Romorantin," in Moffatt and Taglialagamba, 100; Ludwig Heydenreich, "Leonardo da Vinci, Architect of Francis I," *Burlington Magazine* 595.94 (October 1952), 27; Jean Guillaume, "Leonardo and Architecture," in *Leonardo da Vinci: Engineer and Architect* (Montreal Museum, 1987), 278; Hidemichi Tanaka, "Leonardo da Vinci, Architect of Chambord?," *Artibus et Historiae* 13.25 (1992), 85.

12 Notebooks/J. P. Richter, 747.

13 Codex Atl., f. 76v-b/209r., 336v-b/920r; Codex Arundel, 270v.

14 Most of the drawings are in Windsor, which officially dates them to 1517–18, during his period in France. That date was accepted by the Milan exhibition of 2015. Others, including Carmen Bambach (in *Master Draftsman*, 630), have suggested a slightly earlier date of 1515–17. Whenever he started them, Leonardo had them with him when he died in France in 1519, and they were part of the bequest to Francesco Melzi.

15 Windsor, RCIN 912377, 912378, 912380, 912382, 912383, 912384, 912385, 912386.

16 Margaret Mathews-Berenson, *Leonardo da Vinci and the "Deluge Drawings": Interviews with Carmen C. Bambach and Martin Clayton* (Drawing Society, 1998), 7.

17 Codex Atl., 171r-a; Notebooks/J. P. Richter, 965 (the translation of *vitale umore* as "vital human" is a mistake).

18 Codex Leic., sheets 12r and 26v.

19 Brown, 86.

20 Windsor, RCIN 912665; Notebooks/J. P. Richter, 608; Gombrich, "The Form of Movement in Water and Air," 171.

21 Notebooks/J. P. Richter, 609.

22 Paris Ms. G, 6b; Notebooks/J. P. Richter, 607.

23 Codex Atl., 393v/145v-b; Notebooks/Irma Richter, 252; Notebooks/J. P. Richter, 1336; Beth Stewart, "Interesting Weather Ahead: Thoughts on Leonardo's 'Deluge' Drawings," UCLA lecture, May 21, 2016.

24 Codex Arundel, 245v; Pedretti *Commentary*, 2:325 and plate 44; Carlo Pedretti, introduction to *Leonardo's Codex Arundel* (British Library/Giunti, 1998); Nicholl, 1.

25 Windsor, RCIN 919084r, 919115r.

26 Shell and Sironi, "Salai and Leonardo's Legacy," 95; Laure Fagnart, "The French History of Leonardo da Vinci's Paintings," in Pedretti, *Leonardo da Vinci in France*, 113; Bertrand Jestaz, "François I, Salai et les tableaux de Léonard," *Revue de l'art* 4 (1999), 68.

27 Notebooks/J. P. Richter, 1173.

28 Pedretti *Chronology*, 171; Arsène Houssaye, "The Death-Bed of Leonardo," in Mrs. Charles Heaton, *Leonardo da Vinci and His Works* (Macmillan, 1874), 192.

33. CONCLUSION

1 Notebooks/J. P. Richter, 1360, 1365, 1366.
2 Arthur Schopenhauer, *The World as Representation* (1818), vol. 1, ch. 3, para. 31.
3 Steve Jobs, Rob Siltanen, Lee Clow, and others, Apple print and television advertisement, 1998.
4 Albert Einstein to Carl Seelig, March 11, 1952, Einstein Archives 39-013, online.
5 Albert Einstein to Otto Juliusburger, September 29, 1942, Einstein Archives 38-238, online.
6 Codex Ash., 1:7b; Notebooks/J. P. Richter, 491.

CODA

1 Sang-Hee Yoon and Sungmin Park, "A Mechanical Analysis of Woodpecker Drumming," *Bioinspiration & Biomimetics* 6.1 (March 2011). The first good illustrations of the tongue of the woodpecker were done by Dutch anatomist Volcher Coiter in 1575.

ILLUSTRATION CREDITS

Endpapers: Getty Images

Timeline design by Katie Kissane Viola in conjunction with Elizabth Foley, Peter Kaplan, Jonathan Melgaard, Jamie Miller, Deborah Murphy, and Chloe Tabah of the Aspen Institute

Royal Collection Trust/© Her Majesty Queen Elizabeth II 2017: Intro opener, 73, 96, 103, 111, 112, 113, 121
James L. Amos/Corbis Documentary/Getty Images: Ch 1 opener
DEA PICTURE LIBRARY/De Agostini Picture Library/Getty Images: Ch 2 opener, 10, 11, 82
DEA/G. NIMATALLAH/De Agostini Picture Library/Getty Images: 1, 7
DEA/A. DAGLI ORTI/De Agostini Picture Library/Getty Images: 2, 15
Musée du Louvre/©RMN-Grand Palais/Art Resource, NY: 3
Print Collector/Contributor/Hulton Archive/Getty Images: 5, 28, 47, 85, 95
Claudio Divizia/Hemera/Getty Images Plus: 6
Leemage/Contributor/Hulton Fine Art Collection/Getty Images: 8, 30
Leemage/Contributor/Corbis Historical/Getty Images: 9, 17, 79, 92
PHAS/Contributor/Universal Images Group/Getty Images: 12, 69, 108, 109
Heritage Images/Contributor/Hulton Fine Art Collection/Getty Images: 13, 90, 100, 132, 144
National Gallery of Art, Washington DC, USA/Getty Images: 14
DEA/R. BARDAZZI/De Agostini Picture Library/Getty Images: 16
Print Collector/Contributor/Hulton Fine Art Collection/Getty Images: 18, 19, 26, 33, 35, 38, 45, 68, 72, 93, 107, 110, 116
Fratelli Alinari IDEA S.p.A./Contributor/Corbis Historical/Getty Images: 20, 22, 24, 27, 31, 32, 62, 87, 118, 131, 140
Science & Society Picture Library/Contributor/SSPL/Getty Images: 21, 54, 89, 127
Time Life Pictures/Contributor/The LIFE Picture Collection/Getty Images: 23
Biblioteca Nacional de España/Códices Madrid de la BNE: 25, 56
Alinari Archives/Contributor/Hulton Archive/Getty Images: 29
Universal Images Group/Contributor/Universal Images Group/Getty Images: 34, 48

Massimo Merlini/Getty Images: 36
DEA PICTURE LIBRARY/Contributor/DeAgostini/Getty Images: 37, 46, 49, 65, 66, 77, 125
De Agostini/W. Buss/De Agostini Picture Library/Getty Images: 39
Trattati di architettura ingegneria e arte militare/Beinecke MS 491/Beinecke Rare Book & Manuscript Library/Yale University Library: 40, 42
Biblioteca Ariostea, Ferrara: 43
Universal History Archive/Contributor/Universal Images Group/Getty Images: 44, 50, 64, 91
DEA/VENERANDA BIBLIOTECA AMBROSIANA/Da Vinci Codex Atlanticus/Getty Images: 52, 55, 59, 86
Dennis Hallinan/Alamy Stock Photo: 53, 88
DEA/A. DAGLI ORTI/Contributor/De Agostini/Getty Images: 57
DEA/VENERANDA BIBLIOTECA AMBROSIANA/Contributor/De Agostini/Getty Images: 58
GraphicaArtis/Contributor/Hulton Archive/Getty Images: 60, 61
Mondadori Portfolio/Getty Images: 63, 71, 74
Buyenlarge/Contributor/Archive Photos/Getty Images: 67
Private Collection/Getty Images: 70
Ted Spiegel/Contributor/Corbis Historical/Getty Images: 76
Heritage Images/Contributor/Hulton Archive/Getty Images: 80, 122
Thekla Clark/Contributor/Corbis Historical/Getty Images: 81
Fine Art/Contributor/Corbis Historical/Getty Images: 83, 94, 141
Sachit Chainani/EyeEm/Getty Images: 84
Apic/Contributor/Hulton Archive/Getty Images: 102, 114
GraphicaArtis/Contributor/Archive Photos/Getty Images: 104, 115
De Agostini Picture Library/Contributor/De Agostini/Getty Images: 105
Seth Joel/Contributor/Corbis Historical/Getty Images: 117
DEA/G. CIGOLINI/VENERANDA BIBLIOTECA AMBROSIANA/Contributor/De Agostini/Getty Images: 119
Godong/Contributor/Universal Images Group/Getty Images: 120
DEA/A. DAGLI ORTI/Contributor/De Agostini/Getty Images: 124
DEA/J. E. BULLOZ/Contributor/De Agostini/Getty Images: 128
Christophel Fine Art/Contributor/Universal Images Group/Getty Images: 129
Print Collector/Contributor/Hulton Archive/Getty Images: 133
Universal Images Group/Contributor/Getty Images: 134, 142
AFP/Stringer/Getty Images: 135
DEA/C. SAPPA/Contributor/De Agostini/Getty Images: 138
Xavier ROSSI/Contributor/Gamma-Rapho/Getty Images: 139
Alinari Archives/Contributor/Getty Images: 143

INDEX

Page numbers in *italics* refer to illustrations.

About the Author

Walter Isaacson, University Professor of History at Tulane, has been CEO of the Aspen Institute, chairman of CNN, and editor of *Time* magazine. He is the author of *The Innovators*; *Steve Jobs*; *Einstein: His Life and Universe*; *Benjamin Franklin: An American Life*; and *Kissinger: A Biography* and the coauthor, with Evan Thomas, of *The Wise Men: Six Friends and the World They Made*.

Facebook: Walter Isaacson

Twitter: @WalterIsaacson